P9-DDG-442

JOHN F. TANNER, JR.

Dr. Tanner is the research director of Baylor University's Center for Professional Selling and professor of marketing. He earned his PhD from the University of Georgia. Prior to entering academia, Dr. Tanner spent eight years in industry with Rockwell International and Xerox Corporation, as both salesperson and marketing manager.

Dr. Tanner has received several awards for teaching effectiveness and research. His sales teaching efforts have been recognized by *Sales & Marketing Management* and the *Dallas Morning News*. Dr. Tanner has authored or co-authored 10 books, including *Business Marketing: Connecting Strategy, Relationships, and Learning* with Bob Dwyer.

Research grants from the Center for Exhibition Industry Research, the Institute for the Study of Business Markets, the University Research Council, the Texas Department of Health, and others have supported his research efforts. Dr. Tanner has published over 45 articles in the *Journal of Marketing, Journal of Business Research, Journal of Personal Selling and Sales Management,* international journals, and others. He serves on the review boards of several journals, including *Marketing Education Review, Journal of Personal Selling and Sales Management,* and *Journal of Marketing Theory and Practice.*

Dr. Tanner writes a bimonthly column on sales and sales management topics for *Sales and Marketing Strategies & News.* His other trade publications include *Advertising Age's Business Marketing, Decisions, Sales Managers' Bulletin, American Salesman,* and *Potentials in Marketing.* A nationally recognized speaker and author on issues regarding customer relationships, Dr. Tanner has presented seminars at international conventions of several trade organizations, including the International Exhibitor's Association and the Canadian Association of Exposition Managers. More recently, he has taught executive and graduate programs in India, France, and Mexico.

Jeff Tanner

Jeff_Tanner@BAYLOR.EDU
http://hsb.baylor.edu/html/tanner

PREFACE

The demand for highly educated, capable salespeople is growing. At our universities, and at the universities of many of our colleagues, recruiters are flocking as companies recognize the value of well-educated businesspeople fulfilling the sales role. And although this is our sixth edition, we are excited about the way we've adapted this book to fit the realities of the sales profession. To our faithful adopters, you'll find that we've remained true to the philosophy of partnering relationships while at the same time revitalizing the entire book. To potential adopters, we hope you'll agree that our theory-based, application-oriented approach is what your students need to meet the increasing demand for well-educated salespeople.

OUR PHILOSOPHY

The skills of partnering go well beyond the arena of selling a product. Strategic alliances are important to virtually all businesses and all aspects of business. That is why we are excited to see professional selling continue to grow in numbers of schools teaching the course, to grow as a required course for marketing majors at many schools, and to become part of the core curriculum for all business majors at a few institutions.

Our assumption, though, is not that all students of sales will become salespeople. Students in this course will learn principles of selling so well that they will have enough confidence to begin making calls if provided no additional training by their employers, even if those calls occur in a nonselling field (for example, an accountant soliciting new business). At the same time, more students than ever before are being exposed to selling even though they have no plans to enter the sales profession. One of our objectives in this book is to provide sound partnering and communication skills that will be useful in any occupation.

Another objective is to integrate material from other "theory-driven" courses. Although good theory can be quite practical, students sometimes say that this is the only class in which they learned something they could use. That is unfortunate. We continue to work on integrating

material from other courses and disciplines to illustrate the application of theories in the practice of selling. Several of you have told us that you have had the same experience and found this book to be useful in integrating material. We're glad that we have been successful, and we hope you find this edition does an even better job.

PARTNERING AND SALES EDUCATION

The importance of partnering to business and partnering skills to students has changed how selling is taught. Several unique features place this book at the cutting edge of sales technology and partnering research:

1. Continued emphasis on the partnering process, with recognition that multiple sales models may be appropriate in a company's total go-to-market strategy. We focus on the partnering process as the highest level of selling because the other models of transaction focus, problem solver, and relational partner still need to be learned as a foundation to partnering.

2. A thorough description of the partnering and buying processes used by business firms and the changes occurring in these processes. Methods of internal and external partnering are covered so that the supply chain delivers the right value, in recognition of the salesperson's role in relationship management.

3. An emphasis throughout the text on the need for salespeople to be flexible—to adapt their strategies to customer needs, buyer social styles, and relationship needs and strategies.

4. A complete discussion of how effective selling and career growth are achieved through planning and continual learning.

5. The growing role of salespeople in organizations to carry the voice of the customer to all parts of the organization—and beyond to suppliers and facilitators. This role is reflected in new product development, supply chain management, and many other functions in a customer-centric organization.

To Edward Weitz, a great father and salesperson.

—Bart Weitz

To Susie, my lovely wife of over 25 years. You're still my best friend, my trusted confidant, and my partner in all things. I love you. And to my Creator and Redeemer, without whom I would be nothing.

—Steve Castleberry

To those most precious: My God, my wife Karen, my children, my parents.

—Jeff Tanner

The McGraw·Hill Companies

SELLING: BUILDING PARTNERSHIPS
Published by McGraw-Hill/Irwin, a business unit of The McGraw-Hill Companies, Inc., 1221 Avenue of the Americas, New York, NY, 10020. Copyright © 2007 by The McGraw-Hill Companies, Inc. All rights reserved. No part of this publication may be reproduced or distributed in any form or by any means, or stored in a database or retrieval system, without the prior written consent of The McGraw-Hill Companies, Inc., including, but not limited to, in any network or other electronic storage or transmission, or broadcast for distance learning.

Some ancillaries, including electronic and print components, may not be available to customers outside the United States.

This book is printed on acid-free paper.

1 2 3 4 5 6 7 8 9 0 WCK/WCK 0 9 8 7 6 5

ISBN-13:   978-0-07-313690-5
ISBN-10:   0-07-313690-5

Publisher: *Andy Winston*
Developmental editor: *Sarah Crago*
Executive marketing manager: *Dan Silverburg*
Media producer: *Benjamin Curless*
Project manager: *Kristin Bradley*
Senior production supervisor: *Sesha Bolisetty*
Senior designer: *Adam Rooke*
Photo research coordinator: *Lori Kramer*
Photo researcher: *Teri Stratford*
Lead media project manager: *Cathy L. Tepper*
Typeface: *10/12 Sabon*
Compositor: *Precision Graphics*
Printer: *Quebecor World Versailles Inc.*

Library of Congress Cataloging in Publication Data
Weitz, Barton A.
    Selling : building partnerships / Barton A. Weitz, Stephen B. Castleberry, John F. Tanner, Jr.—6th ed.
        p. cm.
    Includes index.
    ISBN-13 978-0-07-313690-5 (alk. paper)
    ISBN-10: 0-07-313690-5 (alk. paper)
    1. Selling.   I. Castleberry, Stephen Bryon. II. Tanner, John F. III. Title.
HF5438.25.W2933 2007
658.85--dc22

                                                                    2005044526

www.mhhe.com

SELLING

Building Partnerships

Barton A. Weitz
University of Florida

Stephen B. Castleberry
University of Minnesota, Duluth

John F. Tanner, Jr.
Baylor University

6

**McGraw-Hill
Irwin**

Boston   Burr Ridge, IL   Dubuque, IA   Madison, WI   New York
San Francisco   St. Louis   Bangkok   Bogotá   Caracas   Kuala Lumpur
Lisbon   London   Madrid   Mexico City   Milan   Montreal   New Delhi
Santiago   Seoul   Singapore   Sydney   Taipei   Toronto

These unique content features are presented in a highly readable format, supported with examples from current sales programs and salespeople, many of whom took the class and used this book. For that reason, these examples were written specifically for this book. Further, you'll find many examples illustrated with four-color exhibits and photographs. If you've used this book before, you'll recognize that many Selling Scenario and Building Partnership field examples are new to this edition, and all profiles of salespeople (that open each chapter) are new. You'll also see that they involve students who studied under many of our adopters. We encourage you to provide us with great examples and the contact information of your best students so they can be profiled in the future. With so many changes in selling over the past few years, a new edition must, necessarily, be *new*. Yet you will find the same practicality and theory of the previous editions.

PARTNERING: FROM THE FIELD TO THE CLASSROOM

Textbooks are generally developed, reviewed, and edited by academicians. In that respect, this book is no different. We have improved the text based on feedback from users and reviewers. What is different is that sales executives and field salespeople who are immersed in the daily struggle of adapting to the new realities of selling also reviewed *Selling: Building Partnerships*. They have told us what the field is like now, where it is going, and what students must do to prepare for the challenges that will face them.

Students have also reviewed chapters. They are, after all, the ones who must learn from the book. We asked for their input before and during the revision process. And judging by their comments and suggestions, this book is effectively delivering its content. There are, however, several places where their comments have enabled us to clarify material and improve on its presentation.

As you can see in "About the Authors," we have spent considerable time in the field in a variety of sales positions. We continue to spend time in the field engaging in personal selling ourselves, as well as observing and serving professional salespeople. We believe the book has benefited greatly because of such a never-ending development process.

Users of the earlier editions will find several improvements in this edition:

A strengthened focus on ethics. Professional sales ethics have always been a hallmark of *Selling: Building Partnerships*, but in addition to the ethical issues discussed in every chapter, there are now separate discussion questions devoted to ethical issues at the end of each chapter. Many of these ethics discussions are identified by a special icon in the margin.

More role-playing experiences. We've developed a new end-of-chapter feature, ACT! role plays. These are short role play exercises designed to be completed in class as methods of practicing concepts introduced in the chapter. Students should also learn more about ACT! that will help them understand how salespeople operate.

An expanded emphasis on technology. We've added a new feature, Sales Technology discussions. This feature addresses how technology impacts issues and activities discussed in the chapter. Students not only learn more about the use of technology in selling, but they also can understand concepts in the chapters more clearly because they are already technologically savvy. They can now transfer that knowledge to the sales field.

Continued emphasis on Canadian and Mexican examples, and more global sales examples. We reflect both the reality of NAFTA and the global nature of selling. This means including not only Canadian and Mexican examples but also examples of global account management, particularly in relation to technology and how that enhances global account management.

An updated CD-Rom supplement. Transparencies are available in PowerPoint; but given feedback from users (and our own experience), we've simplified their presentation. This will enable you to adapt them to your own needs more easily, adding material as you need. Video clips are also available from our Web site so you can either download them or simply access the Web site during class if your classroom is Web-enabled. This means you can illustrate individual techniques of selling quickly and easily.

Chapter 15, "Selling to Resellers," has been integrated into other chapters. For example, how resellers buy is now part of Chapter 4, "Buying Behavior and the Buying Process." This move was due to adopter feedback—let us know if you like the result! We also reordered some chapters, moving the negotiations chapter to follow closing. These two topics are so closely related it made more sense to put them together, and again, we responded to adopter feedback.

TEXT FEATURES AND SUPPLEMENT

An Integrated Teaching and Testing System Everything in this edition of *Selling: Building Partnerships* is designed to help teachers be more effective and to help students develop skills they can use every day and in the field. Several features help both students and teachers achieve their objectives.

Profiles of field salespeople set the stage for each chapter in the text. In each profile, the salesperson discusses his or her experiences and how they relate to the material that follows. All profiles are new for this edition. Each chapter also begins with a series of questions to guide the student's reading experience.

In each chapter, Selling Scenario features present the real-life experiences of professional salespeople and issues such as the impact of technology. Most selling scenarios are new to this edition; many were written specifically for the text either with or by former students who took the class using this text. They understand the philosophy and the chapter material, tying selling scenarios to the material within each chapter, reinforcing the concepts, and presenting applications of selling principles.

Building Partnerships field examples focus on the partnership aspects of selling. These scenarios examine case studies of how salespeople were able to build relationships by applying the concepts presented in the chapter. Again, many were written either by or with former students, so they are particular to this book.

Sales Technology boxes integrate the chapter concepts into the world of technology. Students today are intimately familiar with many technologies—wi-fi, Internet, cellular, and so on. While many professors may find the technologies new, students are able to understand many sales concepts because of their familiarity with the associated technology. Technology has had such an impact on selling that the only way to integrate it fully was to not only continue to develop technology-based examples but to also add this unique feature.

A feature called Thinking It Through helps students internalize key concepts. Thinking It Through is an involving exercise that could be the start of wonderful classroom dialogue or a short essay exam question. But most important for students, reading and using Thinking It Through is a method of experiencing the concepts as they read, which increases their comprehension and retention.

Key terms are listed at the end of each chapter. The list of key terms will help students prepare for exams; the chapter references will improve their retention because they will be more likely to read supporting material, and not just a definition. You'll find many new terms, such as lifetime customer value and more, discussed in detail in this new edition.

The questions and problems at the end of each chapter are also designed to involve the student, but in a slightly different manner. There are now two or three ethics questions and issues presented first (except in Chapter 3, where all questions are about ethics). These are followed by at least 10 questions and problems that focus on other concepts in the chapter. The questions are designed to (a) integrate concepts and definitions, (b) require the student to apply a concept to a selling situation, or (c) start discussion during class. Therefore, students will want to review the questions to study for exams, while the teacher can use the questions to stimulate classroom discussion. These questions are more than just a look-up list in the chapter—they will require thought and help develop critical thinking skills. And because many are new to this edition, students cannot rely on libraries of answers.

Cases are also available at the end of each chapter. We have found that these cases work well as daily assignments and as frameworks for lectures, discussion, or small group practice. Many of them have been tested in our classes and have been refined based on student feedback. A few user favorites have been revised and updated, but you'll find new cases in every chapter.

New role play scenarios are also provided in the text, with various buyer roles in the Instructor's Manual. One set of role plays makes use of ACT! software, increasing students' knowledge of what contact management software is and how it helps salespeople manage their time and territory. These role plays serve two functions. First, students practice their skills in a friendly environment. They can try out their partnering skills in an environment that will encourage personal growth. Second, and this is unique, the role plays are written to serve as minicases. Student observers will see situations that call for application of many of the concepts and principles from the book. Both vicarious and experiential learning is enhanced for the observers. These role play scenarios are all completely new for the sixth edition, and we've included in the text an essay for students on how to prepare for role plays.

Instructor's manuals are available with any text, but the quality often varies. Because we teach the course every semester, as well as presenting and participating in sales seminars in industry, we feel that we have created an Instructor's Manual (on CD-ROM) that can significantly assist the teacher. We've also asked instructors what they would like to see in a manual. In addition to suggested course outlines, chapter outlines, lecture suggestions, answers to questions, and cases, we include helpful suggestions on how to use the videotapes. On that CD you'll also find the slides, which are integrated into our teaching notes. You can also find information on how to use the book with "The Sales Connection" telecourse, for which Steve Castleberry was the content adviser and appears in eight segments. We also include many of the in-class exercises we have developed over the years.

These have been subjected to student critique, and we are confident you will find them useful. You will also find a number of additional role play scenarios.

Students need to practice their selling skills in a selling environment, and they must do it in a way that is helpful. Small group practice exercises, complete with instructions for student evaluations, are provided in the Instructor's Manual. These sessions can be held as part of class but are also designed for out-of-class time for teachers who want to save class time for full-length role plays.

The Test Bank has been carefully and completely rewritten. Questions are directly tied to the learning goals presented at the beginning of each chapter and the material covered in the questions and problems. In addition, key terms are covered in the test questions. Application questions are available so students can demonstrate their understanding of the key concepts by applying those selling principles.

Teachers and students alike have been thrilled with the videotapes that have been created especially for this package. Corporate training videos and a new series from Achieve Global's Professional Selling Skills seminar have been carefully integrated with material from the text. Each segment is short, generally under 10 minutes, with opportunities to stop and discuss what has been viewed. Or students can watch the videos outside class and still learn. Video information, including in-class and homework exercises, is incorporated for the teacher in the Instructor's Manual so that all can make the most of the video.

ACKNOWLEDGMENTS

Staying current with the rapidly changing field of professional selling is a challenge. Our work has been blessed with the excellent support of reviewers, users, editors, salespeople, and students. Reviewers also added important insights:

Larry Butts, Southwest Tennessee Community College

Anthony Carter, William Paterson University

Jim Castagna, DeSales University

Patricia Clarke, Boston University

Lucette Comer, Purdue University

Mike Drafke, College of DuPage

Ashley Geisewite, Southwest Tennessee Community College

Susan Geringer, California State-Fresno

Jon Hawes, University of Akron

Roscoe Hightower, Florida A&M

Anthony Kerr, Louisiana State University

Anthony Lucas, Community College of Allegheny City

Don McBane, Central Michigan University

Stephen Moff, Pennsylvania College of Technology

David Nemi, Niagara Community College

Peggy Osbourne, Morehead University

Rick Ridnour, Northern Illinois University

Leroy Robinson, University of Houston Clear Lake

Dr. Doris Shaw, Northern Kentucky University

Professor Karl Sooder, University of Central Florida

Roland Sparks, Johnson S. Smith University

Bob Tangsrud, University of North Dakota

Dr. Vicki West, Texas State University

Readers will become familiar with many of the salespeople who contributed to the development of the sixth edition through various selling scenarios or profiles. But other salespeople, sales executives, and sales professors contributed in less obvious, but no less important, ways. For providing video material, reviewing chapters, updating cases, providing material for selling scenarios, or other support, we'd like to thank these people:

Jim Allgood, Cingular Wireless

Joaquin Azanza, Andina Food LLC

Stan Banks, DeWalt

Dr. Thomas Barley, Palm Beach Community College

Brad Bischoff, Carlson Marketing

Katherine Bowe, IGN Entertainment

Amy Boynton, Cardinal Health

Tracey Brill, Abbott Labs

Becky Cole, Southwest Foods

Amanda Dietz, Pfizer

Dr. Greg DiNovis, College of St. Catherine

Professor Susan Emens, Kent State University

Brad Englin, BarDan Supply

Chris Evers, Swisher International

Rachel Fisher, Pfizer

Susan Flaviano, Milliken

David Gauthreaux, Freeman Companies

Sarah Gottry, Restaurant Supply Company

Matt Haberle, Maximum Impact

Dr. David Henard, North Carolina State University

Shirley Hunter, NCR–Teradata

Anna-Catherine Johnson, TAC–Tour Andover Controls

Barbara Kellgren, Lutron Electronics

Richard Langlotz, Konica–Minolta

Jonathan Lawrence, Lawrence Media Group

Jane Linenfelser, Paychex

Danielle Lord, US Foodservice

Jeff Lynn, Hartford Insurance Group

Bryan Macakanja, Pulte Homes

Angie Main, Midwest Communications

Amy Mancini, Paychex

Alex Marquette, PartStock Computer Solutions

Wes McDaniel, TAC–Tour Andover Controls

Craig Murchison, ABCO

Paul Nelson, IBM

Carrie Parsons, Freeman Companies

Eddy Patterson, Stubbs Barbecue

Eric Pollack, Global Crown Capital

Dr. Louis Preysz III, Flagler College

Dr. Jim Prost, University of San Francisco

Mark Prude, CrossMark

Neil Rackham, Huthwaite Inc.

Steve Reel, Martin Marietta Materials

Dr. Rick Ridnour, Northern Illinois University

Dr. Glenn Rosenthal, University of the Sciences

Dr. Doris Shaw, Northern Kentucky University

Juan Silvera, Cable & Wireless Panama

Professor Karl Sooder, University of Central Florida

Chad Stinchfield, Hospira Worldwide

Dr. Jeff Strieter, State University of New York College at Brockport

Tasha Stulz, Parker Marketing Research

Ron Swift, NCR–Teradata

Dr. Brian Tietje, California Polytechnic State University

Peter Troup, Jaffe Insurance Concepts

Marvin Wagner, John Deere

Dr. Vicki West, Texas State University

Kevin Westbrock, ADP

Virginia Wichern, 3M

Dean Yeck, Qwest

In addition to the support of these individuals, many companies also provided us with material. We'd like to express our sincere gratitude for their support.

The editorial and staff support from McGraw-Hill was again exceptional. Andy Winston took over as sponsoring editor and has really carried the vision of this book forward. Working with Sarah Crago has been a joy, and having her for two editions has tremendously strengthened this package. For some reason, becoming absent-minded is an occupational hazard for us, but with Sarah, the details, crises, and creative needs get handled with equal flair. Project Manager Kristin Bradley did a great job for us, and it has been a real pleasure to work with Teri Stratford, the photo researcher. Dan Silverburg, our marketing guy, has also been a great help in getting this book to you! If you like the design of this book, and we do, then thank Adam Rooke, our designer. Cathy Tepper once again made sure all the pieces of the package fit properly as our media project manager, not an easy job with as many supplements as this text has. You can see that it takes quite a team to produce a product with this kind of quality, and we think they deserve a great many kudos for their work.

Several people assisted in manuscript preparation, and we gratefully appreciate their help: Hongchao Zeng and Ted and John R. Tanner. Students who made helpful comments and reviewed for us include Tyler Crowder, Lindsey St. Philip, Lauren Pierce, and James Schuler. Many other students and teachers have made comments that have helped us strengthen the overall package. They deserve our thanks, as do others who prefer to remain anonymous.

Steve Castleberry

Jeff Tanner

Selling: Building Partnerships was the first text to bring a partnership/relationship approach into the selling course, offering a solid framework on which to hang plenty of practice and real-world application. The Sixth Edition of this popular text builds on that foundation with updated content, improved hands-on exercises, and powerful technology that's sure to make the material more engaging for professors and students alike.

The **Chapter Opening** profiles in this edition are the product of strong selling partnerships. Faculty from around the country introduced Steve Castleberry and Jeff Tanner to their former students who had gone on to careers in sales. The results are exciting new profiles from sales professionals who were students with an earlier edition and understand the philosophy of this book. Students can easily relate to these young professionals who have benefited from wonderful faculty and Selling: Building Partnerships.

PROFILE

As a graduate of Texas State University with a Bachelor in Business Administration where I took my personal selling class from Dr. Vicki West, I transitioned from college to a career in business-to-business insurance sales. My college experiences included the presidency of the Students in Free Enterprise team and representing the university at the National Collegiate Sales Competition. Through these experiences, I began to build sales techniques and learn fundamental strategies for how to become a successful salesperson. I was hired by the Hartford Insurance Group in January 2004 to be a commercial property/casualty business underwriter. After an intense training program, I served as a middle market renewal underwriter in the Southern California region, responsible for accounts under $100,000. Recently, I have been promoted to middle market sales underwriter for the Northern California region, handling renewal accounts and new business over $100,000. I sell to and work with agents who have sold policies to individuals.

Business has changed dramatically over the last 20 years. Now firms compete in global markets, using sophisticated communication, transportation, and management information systems. More customers are demanding 24/7 service (which means they expect a selling firm to be available for them 24 hours a day, seven days a week). These changes in the business environment have expanded the responsibilities of salespeople and increased their importance to the success of their firms.

This chapter discusses the importance of personal selling to business firms and how the nature of selling is changing from persuading prospects to buy products to managing the firm's relationships with its customers. The chapter concludes by describing the activities salespeople perform, the skills needed by a successful salesperson, and the rewards of a sales career.

Insurance is a field that most people don't plan to get into; they just fall into it. When I first applied for this job, I did not have the faintest idea of the immensity of the profession. Once I was hired, and after training, I realized how much opportunity there is for success. Talking with my agents, I have found that they are naturally interested in the product, but are more interested in building a relationship with me. Today's market for insurance has created heavy competition and, like many other sales jobs, you have to find a competency to separate yourself from the rest of your industry. Agents want someone who will go an extra step and not just sell the product, but sell a relationship. Their desire is to find someone who is easy to work with and who will work hard to help them achieve their goals.

My everyday work activities include answering e-mails and phone calls and, every other month, traveling to agencies in my territory to close deals on upcoming accounts. When I first get an application from the agent, I underwrite the account to see if it is desirable for Hartford's book of business. Then I begin to underwrite the file. Going back and forth obtaining information from the agent, I document the account's exposures and controls, price the account, and send a quote to the agent. This part of the job is rewarding and why I love coming to work every day. A sale is like a game of poker; it's all about being able to read the person on the other side of the table. Relationship building is definitely the key to business-to-business selling.

Get to know your client; they are looking for something that separates you from the competition.

"Relationship building is definitely the key to business-to-business selling."

Jeffrey P. Lynn

ETHICS PROBLEMS

1. Some buyers are now demanding 24/7 response (24 hours a day, seven days a week) from their suppliers. What impact do you think that would have on a salesperson's personal life?
2. One important trait of successful salespeople is product knowledge. Let's say you've just started in a new sales job right out of college and haven't been fully trained yet. A prospect asks you a question that has to do with a technical

Professional sales **ethics** have always been the hallmark of this text and the new edition integrates ethics throughout each chapter, as well as in devoted discussion questions to this topic. Each chapter now has separate ethics discussion questions, some of which were suggested by former students' experiences or current events.

Current and continued emphasis on selling examples from Canada, Mexico, and all around the globe serve to reflect the reality of the global nature of selling.

If you want to sell a part such as a belt to go on a John Deere harvester made in Ottumwa, Iowa, then you have to also be able to sell and service this plant in Arc-les-Gray, France, too.

plants. A harv
same belt as th
France. Thus a
with the corp
employees at e
There's no dou
increasing the
sourcing is also
tive advantage.

DERIVED V
Salespeople se

SALES Technology

HOW CAN YOU BUILD YOUR EMOTIC BY USING TECHNOLOGY, OF COURSE

Identifying strengths and weaknesses is a critical first step in improving emotional intelligence. TalentSmart offers an online Emotional Intelligence Appraisal™ to do just that. The company also encourages your peers to evaluate you because chances are they are better judges than you are.

Many technologies, including PDAs, cell phones, the internet, and CRM software, have changed how salespeople operate. The Sixth Edition introduces a new feature, **Sales Technology,** which discusses how selling and technology interact within the context of the chapter.

How do you think the greater use of te
ing over the Internet—will affect the di
sales jobs decline in importance? Why

Thinking It Through boxes (2 per
chapter) are engaging exercises that can
inspire classroom dialogue or serve as a
short-essay exam question to help students
experience concepts as they read.

THE SALES JOBS CONTINU

Exhibit 1.5 uses the factors just discu
in terms of creativity. Sales jobs descr
require salespeople to go into the f
important buying decisions. These s
c___mers rather than b___ding relati

Featured in each chapter, **Selling
Scenarios** reinforce the concepts
and present applications of selling
principles through realistic examples. **Building Partnerships**
boxes examines how successful
salespeople build relationships.
Many are original to the book,
using examples provided by
former students and other sales
professionals.

SELLING Scenario

SELLING IS MUCH MORE THAN PUS

Matt Haberle is owner of and salesperson for Maximum
Impact, a promotional services company that focuses on
client appreciation, employee recognition, and brand
awareness. Matt is in the business for the long run, desiring
to develop long-term relationships with customers. As Matt
puts it, "There are several ways in which I differentiate
myself from the myriad of so-called promotional agencies.

BUILDING Partnerships

INTEGRITY: IS THERE ANY OTHER WAY

This story starts back when I was interviewing for my   pi
sales job with Hospira, a specialty pharmaceutical and   the
medication delivery company. During the interview the   ov
sales manager told me this company is built on integrity. I   co
hate to admit it, but before Hospira, I couldn't even   ple
define the word *integrity*.   qu
                                                                 life
Now it means the d___ ce between landing ___ sale

CASE PROBLEMS

case **1.1**

S & T Cleaners

S & T Cleaners is a well-establish
been in business since 1976. The
annual sales of $750,000.

The company provides same-da
vate clubs in the area. Additiona
cleaning business (offered to indep
office complexes and individual r
cleaning. S & T also does a small a
at its dry cleaning plant.

S & T has a well-established cus
reputation in the community is
decline in its primary market (tr:
three years due to national econon
rently seeing indications of an imp
sue new business. Its workforce is
In the past S & T has had only

Class-tested **mini-cases** at the end
of each chapter work well as daily
assignments and as frameworks
for lectures, discussion, or small-
group practices. Each chapter
includes at least one new mini-
case. The cases encourage the student to apply theories and skills
learned in the text to solve sales
situations.

ROLE PLAY

At the end of each chapter, beginning just below this
paragraph, you'll find a short role play exercise that
focuses on the product ACT!. ACT! is the leading contact
management software. Contact management software is
a form of software designed to help salespeople increase
their productivity by helping them keep track of the customers they call. In addition to a calendar that tells them
when to call on an account, the software can track
account information concerning what has been bought,
when it was bought, the decision-making process, and
even personal information about each person in the
account. In addition, sales managers can generate reports
automatically when reps download information to the

pape
their
C
Unfo
you l
home
vices
Appa
You'
you'
view
help
may

Students can practice their
partnering skills in **role-play
exercises** that encourage personal
growth and experiential learning.
Each chapter features a role play
for three students using ACT!
software, which enables students
to also learn more about sales
technology. Also, comprehensive
role plays are available at the end
of the book, with additional role-
plays included in the Instructor's
Manual.

ACT! ROLE PLAY

In this class, you may role play selling situations to practice concepts discussed in the chapter. In this role play, you are a salesperson for ACT! software. For additional information concerning ACT!, you may want to review the information in the ACT! role play at the end of Chapter 1; additional information can also be found at the end of the text.

Bell Audio is a manufacturer of hearing aids. They have 24 salespeople who call on audiologists, independent Bell retailers, who then sell hearing aids to consumers. There are two sales managers and one national sales vice president.

minut
will h
appro
what
thoug
were
Bu
relati
about
devel
would
the li

Included with the textbook is **ACT! Express,** a real-world business tool. Based on the best-selling ACT! contact management system, ACT! Express shows students how to become more productive—resulting in better business relationships and greater business opportunities.

The **Instructor's Resource CD** contains the Instructor's Manual, the Test Bank (and computerized test bank) and the PowerPoint Lecture slides. The IM includes a course outline, chapter outlines, lecture suggestions, answers to discussion and case questions, video case suggestions, in-class exercises including information for each chapter's ACT! role play, and additional role-plays. The completely new PowerPoint slides feature exhibits from the text and additional lecture support, and are in a new friendlier format that makes it easier to adapt or change to fit any instructor's needs.

Supplements

The **Video Library** features new video segments customized for the text in addition to new material from Achieve Global's Professional Selling Skills Seminar (PSS).

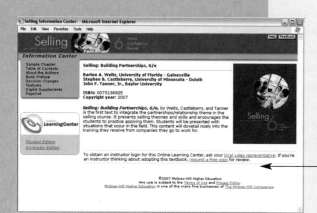

The **Online Learning Center** houses the Instructor's Manual, PowerPoint slides and a link out to McGraw-Hill's course management system, PageOut for the Instructor and study outlines, quizzes, key terms, career information, video clips, and online resources for the student.

CONTENTS IN BRIEF

CONTENTS

part 3

THE PARTNERSHIP PROCESS   168

Chapter 10
Strengthening the Presentation   248

Chapter 11
Responding to Objections   276

Chapter 12
Obtaining Commitment   304

SELLING AND SALESPEOPLE

chapter **1**

part 1

SOME QUESTIONS ANSWERED IN THIS CHAPTER . . .

- What is selling?
- Why should you learn about selling even if you do not plan to be a salesperson?
- What is the role of personal selling in a firm?
- What are the different types of salespeople?
- What are the rewards of a selling career?

PROFILE

As a graduate of Texas State University with a Bachelor in Business Administration where I took my personal selling class from Dr. Vicki West, I transitioned from college to a career in business-to-business insurance sales. My college experiences included the presidency of the Students in Free Enterprise team and representing the university at the National Collegiate Sales Competition. Through these experiences, I began to build sales techniques and learn fundamental strategies for how to become a successful salesperson. I was hired by the Hartford Insurance Group in January 2004 to be a commercial property/casualty business underwriter. After an intense training program, I served as a middle market renewal underwriter in the Southern California region, responsible for accounts under $100,000. Recently, I have been promoted to middle market sales underwriter for the Northern California region, handling renewal accounts and new business over $100,000. I sell to and work with agents who have sold policies to individuals.

Insurance is a field that most people don't plan to get into; they just fall into it. When I first applied for this job, I did not have the faintest idea of the immensity of the profession. Once I was hired, and after training, I realized how much opportunity there is for success. Talking with my agents, I have found that they are naturally interested in the product, but are more interested in building a relationship with me. Today's market for insurance has created heavy competition and, like many other sales jobs, you have to find a competency to separate yourself from the rest of your industry. Agents want someone who will go an extra step and not just sell the product, but sell a relationship. Their desire is to find someone who is easy to work with and who will work hard to help them achieve their goals.

My everyday work activities include answering e-mails and phone calls and, every other month, traveling to agencies in my territory to close deals on upcoming accounts. When I first get an application from the agent, I underwrite the account to see if it is desirable for Hartford's book of business. Then I begin to underwrite the file. Going back and forth obtaining information from the agent, I document the account's exposures and controls, price the account, and send a quote to the agent. This part of the job is rewarding and why I love coming to work every day. A sale is like a game of poker; it's all about being able to read the person on the other side of the table. Relationship building is definitely the key to business-to-business selling.

Get to know your client; they are looking for something that separates you from the competition. In a lot of competitive industries, your ability to sell yourself is what closes the deal. The smallest details of an event sometimes can matter a great deal to your customer. Whether it is bringing coffee and donuts into their office, or just simply making a random phone call to say hello, agents remember if you go beyond what you are required to do. The more an agent knows that you are there not only to service an account, but also to build a strong relationship, the better your chances are of securing repeat business from them.

I have found that setting goals for yourself is key not only in your personal life, but in the business world as well. Once these goals have been established, the next step is planning how to accomplish these goals. For example, my short-term goals for this past year included 100 percent retention on my renewal accounts, quoting at least 30 days before my accounts' effective dates, strengthening my rela-

"Relationship building is definitely the key to business-to-business selling."

Jeffrey P. Lynn

tionships with my agents, and on a personal level, taking the appropriate exams to further my career. As my career continues to evolve, I will undoubtedly have many obstacles to overcome and many challenges to face. With my basic philosophy of "building relationships," hopefully I will continue to produce results and be successful.

See our Web site at http://www.thehartford.com.

Business has changed dramatically over the last 20 years. Now firms compete in global markets, using sophisticated communication, transportation, and management information systems. More customers are demanding **24/7 service** (which means they expect a selling firm to be available for them 24 hours a day, seven days a week). These changes in the business environment have expanded the responsibilities of salespeople and increased their importance to the success of their firms.

This chapter discusses the importance of personal selling to business firms and how the nature of selling is changing from persuading prospects to buy products to managing the firm's relationships with its customers. The chapter concludes by describing the activities salespeople perform, the skills needed by a successful salesperson, and the rewards of a sales career.

WHY LEARN ABOUT PERSONAL SELLING?

What's the first thing that pops into your mind when you hear the phrase: "personal selling"? Do you conjure up images of fast-talking, nonlistening, pushy guys who won't take "no" for an answer? Does the cartoon in Exhibit 1.1 resonate with your idea of a seller? Maybe your definition would be something like this: "Personal selling is the craft of persuading people to buy what they do not want and do not need for more than it is worth."[1]

If that's what you think selling is, then please read and study this book carefully. You're going to learn things about selling that you never knew before. Let's start with a more accurate definition of a professional salesperson, which is quite different from the one just mentioned. **Personal selling** is a person-to-person business activity in which a salesperson uncovers and satisfies the needs of a buyer to the mutual, long-term benefit of both parties. This definition stresses that selling is more than making a sale and getting an order. Selling involves helping customers identify problems, offering information about potential solutions, and providing after-the-sale service to ensure long-term satisfaction. The phrase often used to describe this is **customer-centric**, which means making the customer the very center of everything that the selling firm does.[2] Quite a bit different from the image of the seller in the cartoon, isn't it?

The days of salespeople carrying briefcases overstuffed with brochures and knocking on every door they can find to drum up interest in their companies' products are waning. Now firms compete in global markets, using sophisticated communication, transportation, and management information systems. More customers are demanding **24/7 service** (which means they expect a selling firm to be available for them 24 hours a day, seven days a week). Today's professional salespeople coordinate the resources of their companies to help customers solve problems. They use e-mail, faxes, and videoconferencing to communicate with customers and support staff around the world; download information from their firms' data warehouses into laptop computers so they can know more about their prospects and customers; and develop client-specific multimedia presentations to illustrate the benefits of their firms' products and services. In all of this, the seller's

Exhibit 1.1

THE FAR SIDE® BY GARY LARSON

Ralph Harrison, king of salespersons

goal is to add **value,** which is the total benefit that the seller's products and services provide to the buyer. When describing this to prospects, the seller often refers to this collection of benefits as the **value proposition.** A recent study found that 70 percent of *Fortune* 1,000 firms are "distinguishing customers by value and allocating marketing budgets based on that unique value."[3]

This text discusses personal selling as a business activity undertaken by salespeople. But keep in mind that the principles of selling are useful to everyone, not just people with the title of salesperson. Developing mutually beneficial, long-term relationships is vital to all of us. Thus the principles discussed in this book will be useful even if you never plan to work as a salesperson. Let's look at some examples.

As a college student, you might use selling techniques when asking another student to go out on a date or to ask a professor to let you enroll in a course that is closed out. When you near graduation, you will certainly confront a very important sales job: selling yourself to an employer.

To get a job after graduation, you will go through the same steps used in the sales process (discussed in Part 3, Chapters 7 through 14). First you will identify some potential employers (customers). On the basis of an analysis of each employer's needs, you will develop a presentation to demonstrate your ability to satisfy their needs. During the interview you will listen to what the recruiter says, ask and answer questions, and perhaps alter your presentation based on the new information you receive during the interview. At some point you might negotiate with the employer over starting salary. Eventually you will try to secure a commitment from the employer to hire you. This process is selling at a very personal level. Chapter 17 reviews the steps you need to undertake to get a sales job.

People in business use selling principles all the time. Engineers convince managers to support their R&D projects; industrial relations executives use selling approaches when negotiating with unions; and aspiring management trainees sell themselves to associates, superiors, and subordinates to get raises and promotions.

But it's not just businesspeople who practice the art of selling. Presidents encourage politicians in Congress to support certain programs; charities solicit contributions and volunteers to run organizations; scientists try to convince foundations and government agencies to fund research; and doctors try to get their patients to adopt more healthful lifestyles. People skilled at influencing others and developing long-term relationships are usually leaders in our society.[4]

THE ROLE OF SALESPEOPLE IN BUSINESS

Firms exist only when their products and services are sold. The various options that firms have to sell their products are called **go-to-market strategies.** Strategies include selling through the Internet, field sales representatives, business partners, value added resellers, manufacturer agents, franchises, telemarketers, and others.[5] Selling firms determine which strategy to use based on such factors as the estimated value of the customer over the lifetime of the relationship, often called **lifetime customer value.**[6] (Because this concept is so important, it will be more fully discussed in Chapter 2.) Sometimes firms use several of these strategies at the same time. For example, Motorola uses the Internet for very small customers, telemarketers for midsized customers, and a field sales force for large, important customers. Using various strategies at the same time is called a **multichannel strategy.**

Even with changes in technology, salespeople are still one of the most important elements in many go-to-market strategies.[7] Organizations whose go-to-market strategies rely heavily on salespeople are called **sales-force intensive organizations.**

Another way to view the role of salespeople in business is to realize that they are one element in the firms' marketing communications program, as Exhibit 1.2 indicates. Advertising uses impersonal mass media such as newspapers and TV to

Exhibit 1.2
Communication
Methods

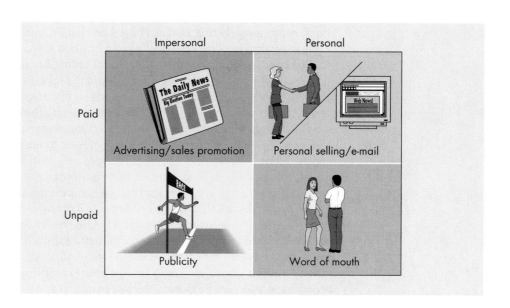

give information to customers. Sales promotions offer incentives to customers to purchase products during a specific period. For example, Burger King offered special prices and gifts when the movie *A Series of Unfortunate Events* was first shown in theaters. Salespeople provide paid personal communication to customers, whereas *publicity* is communication through significant unpaid presentations about the firm (usually a news story). Finally, communication also occurs at no cost through word of mouth (communication among buyers about the selling firm).

Each of the communication methods in Exhibit 1.2 has strengths and weaknesses. For example, firms have more control when using paid versus unpaid methods. However, because publicity and word of mouth are communicated by independent sources, their information is usually perceived as more credible than information in paid communication sources. When using advertising, Internet sites, and sales promotions, companies can determine the message's exact content and the time of its delivery. They have less control over the communication delivered by salespeople and have very little control over the content or timing of publicity and word-of-mouth communication. But personal selling offers the most flexibility because salespeople can talk with each customer, discover the customer's specific needs, and develop unique presentations for that customer. Personal selling is the most costly method of communication. An average sales call costs around $400, which can be 10,000 times more expensive than exposing a customer to a newspaper, radio, or TV ad.[8]

Because each communication vehicle in Exhibit 1.2 has strengths and weaknesses, firms often use **integrated marketing communications,** which are communication programs that coordinate the use of various vehicles to maximize the total impact of the program on customers.[9]

For example, when Stouffer's introduced their new Spa Cuisine Classics, dinners that were inspired by chefs from wellness spas across the country, they used integrated marketing communications. Salespeople called on supermarkets and wholesale clubs. Advertising was created to generate awareness in consumers' minds. Coupons were offered to consumers to create interest and spur more rapid sales. Taste testings in stores were offered to build excitement and word of mouth. Publicity was generated that focused on the dinners' balance of great taste combined with the nutrition of whole grains.

Many students think—incorrectly—that advertising is the most important part of a firm's promotion program. However, industrial companies place far more emphasis on personal selling than on advertising. Even in consumer products firms such as Lever Brothers, which spends more than $1 billion annually on advertising, personal selling plays a critical role.

Students sometimes also have the mistaken notion that the growing world of e-commerce is causing the demise of salespeople. Studies have shown, however, that customers still want to interact with a salesperson and value their interactions with salespeople.[10] As you will learn as you read this book, salespeople add value that the buyer can't get by simply relying on e-commerce.

WHAT DO SALESPEOPLE DO?

The activities of salespeople depend on the type of selling job they choose. The responsibilities of salespeople selling financial services for General Electric differ greatly from those of salespeople selling pharmaceuticals for Merck or paper products for James River. Salespeople often have multiple roles, including client relationship manager, account team manager, vendor and channel manager, and information provider for their firms.

SELLING IS MUCH MORE THAN PUSHING A PRODUCT OR SERVICE

Matt Haberle is owner of and salesperson for Maximum Impact, a promotional services company that focuses on client appreciation, employee recognition, and brand awareness. Matt is in the business for the long run, desiring to develop long-term relationships with customers. As Matt puts it, "There are several ways in which I differentiate myself from the myriad of so-called promotional agencies. The primary way is the process of needs discovery and presentation of options. My industry, sometimes referred to as 'the trash-n-trinkets industry,' is very heavily laden with catalogs and literature. Most companies simply send out thousands of catalogs, wait for the phone to ring, be the cheapest they can be, and try to handle the order as cost-effectively as possible." That's not Matt's method, though.

"When a client has a project coming up, I do not arm myself with catalogs for that first meeting. I arm myself with questions: Who is the target audience? What is the message? How do you want them to feel? What do you want them to do? How important are they to your overall success? What is the scope, time frame, and estimated budget?"

For example, Target, a major national retailer, wanted to appropriately show thanks to employees (from part-timers to executives all over the country) for the time they volunteered on various Habitat for Humanity projects. By discovering their needs, Matt determined that Target's original idea would not convey the message thoroughly. He returned with several options and presented them to Target from the viewpoint of the intended recipients. The ensuing promotion was declared a success on all levels. In fact, the promotion was received so well that it is still evident today.

Selling is an important blend of finding out what the customer really needs and then providing a solution to that need. In the long run, it's the only way to do business.

Source: Matt Haberle, personal correspondence; used with permission.

CLIENT RELATIONSHIP MANAGER

Sales jobs involve prospecting for new customers, making sales presentations, demonstrating products, negotiating price and delivery terms, writing orders, and increasing sales to existing customers. Selling Scenario 1.1 provides an example of some of these activities. But these sales-generating activities (discussed in Chapters 7 through 14) are only part of the job. As Exhibit 1.3 indicates, salespeople spend less than 35 percent of their time on-site in a face-to-face meeting with customers

Exhibit 1.3

How Salespeople Spend Their Time Each Week

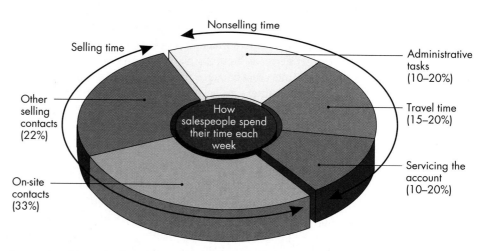

Source: adapted from The Alexander Group, Inc. Sales Time Maker, Software Services, February 8, 2002 <http://tools.saleslobby.com/perfMgmt/2001_STM_Presentation.pdf>

Sales reps help with installations to ensure proper use.

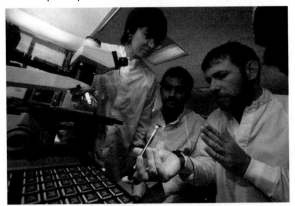

Romily Lockyer/The Image Bank/Getty Images

and prospects. It is interesting to note that for world-class firms, that percentage rises to 40 percent, while for poorly performing firms, the percentage drops to just 20 percent.[11] The rest of salespeople's time is spent in meetings, working with support people in their companies (internal selling), traveling, waiting for a sales interview, doing paperwork, and servicing customers.

Rather than buying from the lowest-cost suppliers, many buyers now are building competitive advantages by developing and maintaining close, cooperative relationships with a select set of suppliers. Salespeople play a key role in the development, growth, and maintenance of these long-term buyer–seller relationships. As relationship managers, salespeople are responsible for identifying opportunities that create value for customers.

The salesperson's job does not end when the customer places an order. Sales representatives must make sure customers get the benefits they expect from the product. Thus salespeople work with other company employees to ensure that deliveries are made on time, equipment is properly installed, operators are trained to use the equipment, and questions or complaints are resolved quickly. Chapter 14 will provide more insights on developing relationships through customer services.

Making sales and servicing customers can be very challenging in less developed countries where many customers are difficult to reach. For example, some food companies have an extensive distribution system to reach customers in isolated mountain and jungle villages. Salespeople drive specially equipped vans to make weekly calls on these remote villages and often sleep in their vans or in customers' stores. Salespeople reach villages in some lake regions by canoe and ride donkeys into some mountain villages.

ACCOUNT TEAM MANAGER

Salespeople also coordinate the activities within their firms to solve customer problems. In fact, many sales situations call for team selling. For example, Dick Holder, president of Reynolds Metal Company, spent five years "selling" Campbell Soup Company on using aluminum cans for its tomato juice products. He coordinated a team of graphic designers, marketing people, and engineers to educate Campbell about a packaging material it had not used before.

To provide solutions and build relationships, salespeople need to thoroughly understand the operations of all areas in their firm. Tom Wolven, regional president for Ailing & Cory, a paper supplier, says that his salespeople are effective because they really understand all aspects of their firm—from shipping systems to finances to credit. Because of this knowledge, their salespeople know where to go to get things done. Approaches for improving efficiency in performing these nonselling activities are discussed in Chapter 16.

VENDOR AND CHANNEL MANAGER

Sometimes it is necessary to interact with other partners and vendors to meet a customer's needs. Salespeople are often the key managers of these many relationships to ensure that the customers' needs are fully met. For example, if a customer buys a new jet from Boeing Business Jets, with features that will be added by a third party vendor, the salesperson will need to coordinate the efforts of the vendor with Boeing. As another example, pharmaceutical salespeople must coordinate the activities of the channel with regard to prescription drugs. Such a salesperson would make calls not only on a doctor, hoping that the doctor will prescribe the drug, but also on pharmacists to make sure the drug will be available when the patient walks in with a prescription.

Glenn Price, who sells life and disability insurance with Northwestern Mutual, realizes the importance of working with channel partners. "Today, the financial services industry is very complex, as are the needs of my clients. With hundreds of insurance and equity products I must have an excellent understanding of my clients' needs so I can make the right recommendation with the right product. I realize that in this complex world I live in I can't be all things to all people. I can, however, become a guru or a specialist in a couple of things and surround myself with specialists in all the other areas to create a team of specialists. For areas outside of my expertise all I have to do is identify which specialists are needed and bring them in. This approach allows me to operate at maximum efficiency while providing the highest level of expertise and service to my clients. It's also good from a business perspective because each specialist is like a profit center with no overhead. Whatever the specialist does for my clients I share in 50 percent of the revenue. Successful salespeople are good at time management, and being a specialist has helped me improve this skill by leveraging my time so I can focus my energy on what I do best."[12]

INFORMATION PROVIDER TO THEIR FIRM

Salespeople are the eyes and ears of the company in the marketplace. For example, when Bob Meyer, a salesperson at Ballard Medical Products, was demonstrating a medical device, a surgeon commented that he could not tell whether the device was working properly because the tube was opaque. Meyer relayed this information to the vice president of engineering, and the product was redesigned, substituting a clear tube for the opaque tube. Meyer also learns a lot about customer needs when he conducts training sessions for the nurses in hospitals that use Ballard devices. This information provides valuable input to distribution, pricing, and advertising decisions for Ballard's present product lines.

As another example, at Flexatard, a manufacturer of fitness bodywear, salespeople relay customer reactions to changing fashions, new styles introduced by competitors, and approaches the company is considering to satisfy activewear users' needs. Salespeople know what the trends are and what new ideas will capture the imaginations of their customers.

To truly have effective impact on their organization, salespeople need to be skillful at disseminating the knowledge they have acquired from customers to other people in their companies. In their reporting activities, salespeople provide information to their firms about expenses, calls made, future calls scheduled, sales forecasts, competitor activities, business conditions, and unsatisfied customer needs. Much of this information is now transmitted electronically to the company, its salespeople, and its customers. For example, each night salespeople at Curtin Matheson Scientific, a distributor of clinical and laboratory supplies in Baton Rouge, Louisiana, enter call report information and download all the ordering and shipping information for their customers from the company mainframe to

Salespeople share important market information with their boss and others in the firm.

Mark Richards/Photoedit

their laptop computers. Chapter 16 discusses the relationship between salespeople and their companies in great detail.

TYPES OF SALESPEOPLE

Almost everyone is familiar with people who sell products and services to consumers in retail outlets. Behind these retail salespeople is an army of salespeople working for commercial firms. Consider a DVD player you might purchase in a store. To make the DVD player, the manufacturer bought processed material, such as plastic and electronic components, from various salespeople. In addition, it purchased capital equipment from other salespeople to mold the plastic, assemble the components, and test the player. Finally, the DVD player manufacturer bought services such as an employment agency to hire people and an accounting firm to audit the company's financial statements. The manufacturer's salespeople then sold the players to a wholesaler. The wholesaler purchased transportation services and warehouse space from other salespeople. Then the wholesaler's salespeople sold the players to a retailer.

SELLING AND DISTRIBUTION CHANNELS

As the DVD player example shows, salespeople work for different types of firms and call on different types of customers. These differences in sales positions come from the many roles salespeople play in a firm's distribution channel. A **distribution channel** is a set of people and organizations responsible for the flow of products and services from the producer to the ultimate user. Exhibit 1.4 shows the principal types of distribution channels used for business-to-business and consumer products and the varied roles salespeople play.

Business-to-Business Channels

The two main channels for producers and providers of business-to-business, or industrial, products and services are (1) direct sales to a business customer and (2) sales through distributors. In the direct channel, salespeople working for the manufacturer call directly on other manufacturers. For example, Nucor salespeople sell steel directly to automobile manufacturers, Dow Chemical salespeople sell plastics directly to toy manufacturers, and Nielsen salespeople sell marketing research services directly to business customers.

In the distributor channel the manufacturer employs salespeople to sell to distributors. These salespeople are referred to as **trade salespeople** because they sell to firms that resell the products rather than using them within the firm. Distributor salespeople sell products made by a number of manufacturers to businesses. For example, some Intel salespeople sell microprocessors to distributors such as Arrow Electronics, and Arrow salespeople then resell the microprocessors and other electronic components to customers such as HP.

Many firms use more than one channel of distribution and thus employ several types of salespeople. For example, Motorola and Dow Chemical have trade salespeople who call on distributors as well as direct salespeople who call on large companies.

In the second business-to-business channel (see Exhibit 1.4), a missionary salesperson is employed. **Missionary salespeople** work for a manufacturer and promote the manufacturer's products to other firms. However, those firms buy the products from distributors or other manufacturers, not directly from the salesperson's firm. For example, sales representatives at Driltech, a manufacturer of mining equipment, call on mine owners to promote their products. The mines,

Exhibit 1.4

Sales Jobs and the Distribution Channel

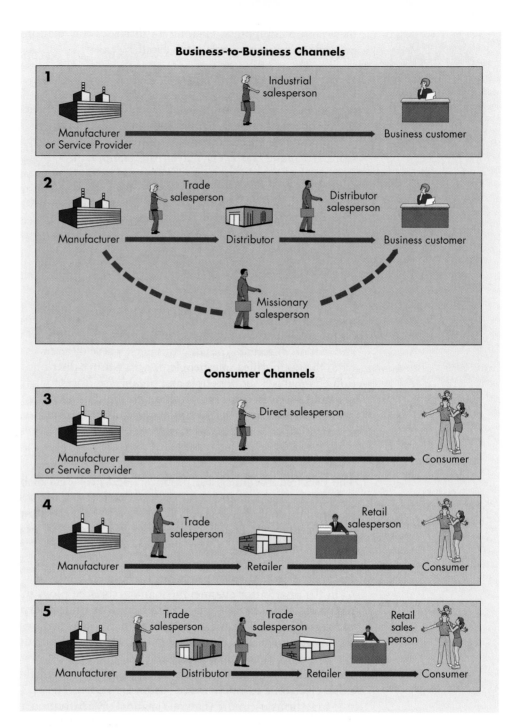

Business-to-Business Channels

1 Manufacturer or Service Provider → Industrial salesperson → Business customer

2 Manufacturer → Trade salesperson → Distributor → Distributor salesperson → Business customer / Missionary salesperson

Consumer Channels

3 Manufacturer or Service Provider → Direct salesperson → Consumer

4 Manufacturer → Trade salesperson → Retailer → Retail salesperson → Consumer

5 Manufacturer → Trade salesperson → Distributor → Trade salesperson → Retailer → Retail salesperson → Consumer

however, place orders for drills with the local Driltech distributor rather than with Driltech directly. Normally missionary and local distributor salespeople work together to build relationships with customers.

Frequently missionary salespeople call on people who influence a buying decision but do not actually place the order. For example, Du Pont sales representatives call on Liz Claiborne and other clothing designers to encourage them to design garments made with Teflon, and Merck sales representatives call on physicians to encourage them to prescribe Merck pharmaceutical products.

Consumer Channels

The remaining channels shown in Exhibit 1.4 are used by producers and providers of consumer products and services. The third channel shows a firm, such as State Farm Insurance, whose salespeople sell insurance directly to consumers. The fourth and fifth channels show manufacturers that employ trade salespeople to sell to either retailers or distributors. For example, Revlon uses the fourth channel when its salespeople sell directly to Wal-Mart. However, Revlon uses the fifth channel to sell to small, owner-operated stores through distributors.

Some of the salespeople shown in Exhibit 1.4 may be manufacturers' agents. **Manufacturers' agents** are independent businesspeople who are paid a commission by a manufacturer for all products or services sold. Unlike distributors and retailers, agents never own the products. They simply perform the selling activities and then transmit the orders to the manufacturers.

DESCRIBING SALES JOBS

Descriptions of sales jobs focus on six factors:

1. The stage of the buyer–seller relationship.
2. The salesperson's role.
3. Importance of the customer's purchase decision.
4. Location of salesperson–customer contact.
5. The nature of the offering sold by the salesperson.
6. The salesperson's role in securing customer commitment.

Stage of Buyer–Seller Relationship: New or Continuing

Some sales jobs emphasize finding and selling to new customers. Selling to prospects requires different skills than selling to existing customers. To convince prospects to purchase a product they have never used before, salespeople need to be especially self-confident and be able to deal with the inevitable rejections that occur when making initial contacts. On the other hand, salespeople responsible for existing customers place more emphasis on building relationships and servicing customers. For example, Lou Pritchett of Procter & Gamble, in a continuing relationship with Wal-Mart, increased sales to Wal-Mart from $400 million a year to over $6 billion a year by being creative and building partnerships.[13] And the more important the buyer, the larger the group of sellers engaged in selling to that buyer. Hormel has a team of 50 who sell to Wal-Mart in Bentonville, Arkansas.

Salesperson's Role: Taking Orders or Creating New Solutions

Some sales jobs focus primarily on taking orders. For example, most Frito-Lay salespeople go to grocery stores, check the stock, and prepare an order for the store manager to sign. However, some Frito-Lay salespeople sell only to buyers in the headquarters of supermarket chains. Headquarters selling requires a much higher level of skill and creativity to do the job effectively. These salespeople work with buyers to develop new systems and methods to increase the retailer's sales and profits.

Importance of the Purchase to the Customer

Consumers and businesses make many purchase decisions each year. Some decisions are important to them, such as purchasing a building or a business telephone system. Others are less crucial, such as buying candy or cleaning supplies.

Sales jobs involving important decisions for customers differ greatly from sales jobs involving minor decisions. Consider the company that needs a computer-

Field salespeople go directly to the customer's place of business.

Digital Vision/Getty Images

controlled drill press. Buying the drill press is a big decision. The drill press sales representative needs to be knowledgeable about the customer's needs and the features of drill presses. The salesperson will have to interact with a number of people involved in the purchase decision.

Location of Salesperson–Customer Contact: Field or Inside Sales

Field salespeople spend considerable time in the customer's place of business, communicating with the customer face-to-face. **Inside salespeople** work at their employer's location and typically communicate with customers by telephone or letter.

Field selling typically is more demanding than inside selling because the former entails more intense interactions with customers. Field salespeople are more involved in problem solving with customers, whereas inside salespeople often respond to customer-initiated requests.

The Nature of the Offering Sold by the Salesperson: Products or Services

The type of benefits provided by products and services affects the nature of the sales job. Products such as chemicals and trucks typically have tangible benefits: Customers can objectively measure a chemical's purity and a truck's payload. The benefits of services, such as business insurance or investment opportunities, are more intangible: Customers cannot easily see how the insurance company handles claims or objectively measure the riskiness of an investment.

Intangible benefits are harder to sell than tangible benefits because it is difficult to demonstrate intangible benefits to customers. It is much easier to show a customer the payload of a truck than the benefits of carrying insurance.

Salesperson's Role in Securing Customer Commitment: Information or Placing an Order

Sales jobs differ by the types of commitments sought and the manner in which they are obtained. For example, the Du Pont missionary salesperson might encourage a clothing designer to use Du Pont Teflon fibers. The salesperson might ask the designer to consider using the fiber but does not undertake the more difficult task of asking the designer to place an order. If the designer decides to use Teflon fabric in a dress, the order for nylon will be secured by the salesperson calling on a company that makes the fabric.

thinking **it** through   How do you think the greater use of technology—laptop computers and communicating over the Internet—will affect the different types of sales jobs? Will some types of sales jobs decline in importance? Why?

THE SALES JOBS CONTINUUM

Exhibit 1.5 uses the factors just discussed to illustrate the continuum of sales jobs in terms of creativity. Sales jobs described by the responses in the far right column require salespeople to go into the field and call on new customers who make important buying decisions. These selling assignments emphasize selling to new customers rather than building relations with old customers, promoting products

Exhibit 1.5
Creativity Level of Sales
Jobs

Factors in Sales Jobs	Lower Creativity	Higher Creativity
1. Stage of the customer–firm relationship	Existing customer	New customer
2. The salesperson's role	Order taking	Creating new solutions
3. Importance of the customer's purchase decision	Low	High
4. Location of salesperson–customer contact	Inside company	Field customer
5. Nature of the offering sold by the salesperson	Products	Services
6. Salesperson's role in securing customer commitment	Limited role	Significant role

or services with intangible benefits, and/or gaining commitments from customers. These types of sales jobs require the most creativity and skill and, consequently, offer the highest pay.

The next section examines the responsibilities of specific types of salespeople in more detail.

EXAMPLES OF SALES JOBS

Best Buy Retail Salesperson

Best Buy salespeople sell to customers who come into their stores. In many cases the customers know what they want; the salesperson just rings up the sale. However, Best Buy, like most progressive retailers, is upgrading its salespeople from order takers to relationship builders. The company is training salespeople to understand and meet the specific needs of five types of customers: affluent professionals; active, young males; family men; busy suburban mothers, and small business customers.[14]

Hershey Foods Salesperson

Hershey salespeople increase the sales of their firm's chocolate and candy products by influencing retailers and distributors to stock Hershey brands and then servicing them. Most Hershey salespeople typically make regularly scheduled calls on existing customers in an assigned territory and generally are not expected to find new customers. Some of the responsibilities of a Hershey trade salesperson are

- Convincing retailers to buy and display all Hershey products in their stores.
- Making sure that retailers have enough stock displayed on shelves and stored in the back room so that an out-of-stock condition will not arise.
- Counting stock and preparing orders for store managers if inventories are low.
- Checking to see that Hershey products are priced competitively.
- Trying to get Hershey products displayed on shelves where consumers can see them easily.
- Encouraging managers to develop special displays for Hershey and helping to build the displays.
- Convincing store managers to feature Hershey products in advertising and place in-store ads and signs to promote the sale of Hershey products.

Abbott Labs Pharmaceutical Salesperson

Traditionally, salespeople working for pharmaceutical companies such as Abbott have been classic examples of missionary salespeople. They provide information on their products to physicians, surgeons, and other people licensed to provide medical services in their territories. Typically, they make about eight calls on doctors each day, usually without an appointment. The salespeople spend 2 to 15 minutes with doctors on each call. The presentations include accurate information about the symptoms for which a pharmaceutical is effective, how effective it is, and the side effects that might occur. Doctors consider these presentations an important source of information about new products.

However, the world of pharmaceutical selling is changing. With the growing importance of cost reduction, many Abbott salespeople are calling on hospitals and health maintenance organizations (HMOs). These Abbott salespeople are working with customers to develop creative solutions for halting the rising cost of health care.

IBM Computer Servers Salesperson

Some of the most challenging sales jobs involve selling capital goods. IBM sells world-class server technology that helps businesses adapt to new conditions quickly and easily. IBM salespeople outline the benefits of a customized computer server configuration for each department in the buyer's company.

Because these capital equipment sales are made infrequently, IBM salespeople often approach new customers. The selling task requires working with customers who are making a major investment and are involved in an important buying decision. Many people are involved in this sort of purchase decision. IBM salespeople need to demonstrate both immediate, tangible benefits and future, intangible benefits to executives ranging from the chief information officer (CIO) to the chief financial officer (CFO).

The next section reviews the skills required to be effective in the sales positions just discussed.

CHARACTERISTICS OF SUCCESSFUL SALESPEOPLE

For the last 100 years, books and articles discussing why some people are successful in selling and others are not have flooded the market. After all of this research, no one has identified the profile of the "perfect" salesperson because sales jobs are so different. As the job descriptions in the preceding section show, the characteristics and skills needed for success when selling for Hershey Foods differ from those needed for success when selling for IBM.

In addition, each customer is unique. Some like to interact with aggressive salespeople, whereas others are turned off by aggressive behavior. Some are all business and want formal relationships with salespeople, whereas others look forward to chatting with salespeople in an informal way. No magic selling formula works in all sales jobs or with all customers.

Although no one personality profile exists for the ideal salesperson, successful salespeople are hard workers and smart workers. They are highly motivated, dependable, ethical, knowledgeable, good communicators, flexible, creative, confident, and emotionally intelligent.

MOTIVATION

Most salespeople work in the field without direct supervision. Under these conditions they may be tempted to get up late, take long lunch breaks, and stop work early. But successful salespeople do not succumb to these temptations. They are self-starters who do not need the fear inspired by a glaring supervisor to get them going in the morning or to keep them working hard all day.[15]

Spending long hours on the job is not enough. Salespeople must use their time efficiently. They need to maximize the time spent in contacting customers and

INTEGRITY: IS THERE ANY OTHER WAY?

This story starts back when I was interviewing for my sales job with Hospira, a specialty pharmaceutical and medication delivery company. During the interview the sales manager told me this company is built on integrity. I hate to admit it, but before Hospira, I couldn't even define the word *integrity*.

Now it means the difference between landing a big sale and being content with the small ones. When I started my sales calls, one of my accounts opened up a perfect opportunity for me to trash the competition. As I sat there in the buyer's office, I thought about many things I could say to really cut the competition. But then I thought back to my interview with Hospira and also what I had been taught after getting hired. Integrity is the only way.

I decided to take the high road and not trash the competition. Instead, I brought the conversation back to what Hos-

pira could offer the buyer. I kept the concept of integrity at the front of my mind as I continued to deal with this buyer over the next several weeks. I made sure to follow through completely with everything I had promised. I was completely honest, like the time when I made a mistake by misquoting a price. The result? I landed the biggest sale of my life with this customer. I owe it all to integrity.

Integrity means to me following through on promises, taking personal responsibility for mistakes, being totally honest, and being modest. It also means treating everyone at the buyer's firm with respect and courtesy, through such actions as sending thank-you cards to everyone involved, even the smallest person on the totem pole. Integrity is the key to success.

Source: Chad R. Stinchfield, salesperson at Hospira Worldwide; used by permission.

minimize the time spent in traveling and waiting for customers. To do their job effectively, salespeople must organize and plan their work (a subject discussed in more detail in Chapter 15).

Finally, successful salespeople are motivated to learn. They must continually work at improving their skills by analyzing their past performance and using their mistakes as learning opportunities.

DEPENDABILITY AND TRUSTWORTHINESS

In some types of selling, such as used-car sales, the salesperson rarely deals with the same customer twice. However, this book focuses on business-to-business selling situations in which the customer and salesperson often have a continuing relationship. Such salespeople are interested not just in what the customers will buy this time but also in getting orders in the years to come.

Customers develop long-term relationships only with salespeople who are dependable and trustworthy. When salespeople say the equipment will perform in a certain way, they had better make sure the equipment performs that way! If it doesn't, the customer will not rely on them again. Chapter 2 discusses the various types of relationships that buyers desire, and describes how salespeople can develop long-term relationships with customers.

ETHICAL SALES BEHAVIOR

Honesty and integrity are important components of dependability. Over the long run, customers will find out who can be trusted and who cannot. Good ethics are good business. Ethical sales behavior is such an important topic that Chapter 3 is devoted to it. Building Partnerships 1.1 discusses the importance of integrity in the life of one successful salesperson.

CUSTOMER AND PRODUCT KNOWLEDGE

Effective salespeople need to know how businesses make purchase decisions and how individuals evaluate product alternatives. In addition, effective salespeople need product knowledge—how their products work and how the products' features are related to the benefits customers are seeking. Chapter 4 reviews the buying process, and Chapter 6 discusses product knowledge.

COMMUNICATION SKILLS

The key to building strong long-term relationships is to be responsive to a customer's needs. To do that, the salesperson needs to be a good communicator. But talking is not enough; the salesperson must also listen to what the customer says, ask questions that uncover problems and needs, and pay attention to the responses.

To compete in world markets, salespeople need to learn how to communicate in international markets. For example, business is conducted differently in Europe than in the United States. In the United States business transactions generally proceed at a rapid pace, whereas Europeans take more time reaching decisions. European customers place more emphasis on the rapport developed with a salesperson, whereas U.S. firms look more at the size and reputation of the salesperson's company. Because Europeans want to do business with salespeople they like and trust, the latter devote a lot of time to building close personal relationships with customers. Chapter 5 is devoted to developing communication skills, with considerable emphasis on communicating in other cultures.

FLEXIBILITY

The successful salesperson realizes that the same sales approach does not work with all customers; it must be adapted to each selling situation. The salesperson must be sensitive to what is happening and flexible enough to make those adaptations during the sales presentation.

As mentioned earlier in this chapter, personal selling is the most costly marketing communication vehicle. Why do companies spend money on personal selling when it is so expensive? The higher cost is justified by its greater effectiveness. Personal selling works better than any other communication vehicle because salespeople are able to develop a unique message for each customer. Salespeople can do "market research" on each customer by asking questions and listening carefully. They then use this information to develop and deliver a sales presentation tailored to the needs and beliefs of each customer. In addition, salespeople can observe verbal and nonverbal behaviors (body language) in their customers and, in response, adjust their presentation. If the customer is uninterested in the contents of the presentation or turned off by the salesperson's style, the salesperson can make changes quickly.

In contrast, advertising messages are tailored to the typical customer in a segment and thus are not ideally suited to many of the customers who may see the ad. Advertisers are also limited in how fast they can make adjustments. Salespeople can adjust on the spot, but it may take months to determine that an advertisement is not working and then to develop a new one. Only personal selling provides the opportunity to be truly real-time adaptive in making presentations. Consequently, selling effectiveness hinges on the salesperson's ability to practice adaptive selling and exploit this unique opportunity. Adaptive selling is treated in detail in Chapter 6.

CREATIVITY

Successful salespeople use their creative juices to build bridges to their customers, gain long-term commitments, and effectively manage relationships.[16] **Creativity** is the trait of having imagination and inventiveness and using it to come up with new solutions and ideas. Sometimes it takes creativity to get an appointment with a prospect. It may take creativity to develop a long-remembered presentation in the buyer's mind. It may take creativity to solve a sticky installation problem after the product is sold.

Some people don't see themselves as creative because they've been told by family, friends, or teachers that they're not creative. Others refuse to allow their natural creativity to flow, due to fears of being laughed at or fears of having the idea fail. Still other salespeople come up with creative ideas, but fail to act on them.[17] We can probably all improve our creative genius.

CONFIDENCE

Successful salespeople tend to be confident about themselves, their company, and their products. They believe that their efforts will lead to success. Don't confuse confidence, however, with wishful thinking. According to research, truly confident people are willing to work hard to achieve their goals. They are open to criticism, seek advice from others, and learn from their mistakes. They expect good things to happen, but they take personal responsibility for their fate. People who lack confidence, according to these same studies, are not honest about their own limits, react defensively when criticized, and set unrealistic goals.[18]

EMOTIONAL INTELLIGENCE

Salespeople span the boundary between their companies and the companies' customers. At times the objectives of the company can differ from those of the customers. The company wants the salesperson to make profits, and the customer wants to buy a product that meets his or her needs at the lowest price. Dealing with these conflicting objectives can be stressful for salespeople.

Salespeople need emotional intelligence to be able to recognize customers' emotions.

C. Borland/PhotoLink/Getty Images/MGH-DIL

To cope with conflicting company and customer objectives, rude customers, and indifferent support staff members, effective selling requires a high degree of emotional intelligence.[19] **Emotional intelligence** is the ability to effectively understand and use one's own emotions and the emotions of people with whom one interacts. Emotional intelligence has four aspects: (1) knowing one's own feelings and emotions as they are experienced, (2) controlling one's emotions to avoid acting impulsively, (3) recognizing customers' emotions (called *empathy*), and (4) using one's emotions to interact effectively with customers.[20] We discuss aspects of emotional intelligence as they relate to adaptive selling and effective verbal and nonverbal intelligence in Chapters 5 and 6. Sales Technology 1.1 tells how you can improve your emotional intelligence by using technology.[21]

thinking **it** through
Which of the characteristics listed in this section are needed to be an effective teacher, engineer, banker, or actor?

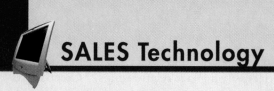

SALES Technology

HOW CAN YOU BUILD YOUR EMOTIONAL INTELLIGENCE? BY USING TECHNOLOGY, OF COURSE

Identifying strengths and weaknesses is a critical first step in improving emotional intelligence. TalentSmart offers an online Emotional Intelligence Appraisal™ to do just that. The company also encourages your peers to evaluate you because chances are they are better judges than you are.

Okay, now you know where you stand. What's next? A number of tools are available. TalentSmart offers interesting videos that include Hollywood movies, TV show clips, and historical events to teach the topic. Of course, interactive training is usually called for, including videotaped role playing.

Salespeople can also engage in interactive Web-based training. SkillSoft, a Web-based software company in New Hampshire, and TalentSmart are two major vendors of such services. For example, TalentSmart's Emotional Intelligence Appraisal—Team Edition™ allows an entire group to be appraised and then delivers a customized six-month e-learning course that the entire team works through.

Sources: www.skillsoft.com, www.talentsmart.com.

ARE SALESPEOPLE BORN OR MADE?

On the basis of the preceding discussion, you can see that the skills required to be a successful salesperson can be learned. People can learn to work hard, plan their time, and adapt their sales approach to their customers' needs. Research has shown that innate characteristics such as personality traits, gender, and height are largely unrelated to sales performance. In fact, companies show their faith in their ability to teach sales skills by spending billions of dollars each year on training programs. The next section discusses the rewards you can realize if you develop the skills required for sales success.

REWARDS IN SELLING

Personal selling offers interesting and rewarding career opportunities. More than 7 million people in the United States currently work in sales positions, and the number of sales positions is growing.[22] Exhibit 1.6 provides a breakdown of employment by the type of sales job. Sales positions are challenging, exciting, and

Exhibit 1.6

Employment in Sales Positions

Type of Sales Job	Number Employed
Retail salespeople	4,100,000
Manufacturers' and wholesale sales representatives	1,900,000
Insurance sales agents	381,000
Securities, commodities, and financial sales agents	300,000
Real estate agents	308,000
Real estate brokers	99,000
Sales engineers	82,000
Total number of salespeople	7,170,000

Source: *Occupational Outlook Handbook*, 2004–2005 edition, U.S. Department of Labor, Bureau of Labor Statistics.

financially rewarding. They can provide the base for promotion to management positions in a firm or for launching a new business.

INDEPENDENCE AND RESPONSIBILITY

Many people do not want to spend long hours behind a desk, doing the same thing every day. They prefer to be outside, moving around, meeting people, and working on various problems. Selling ideally suits people with these interests. The typical salesperson interacts with dozens of people daily. Most of these contacts involve challenging new experiences.

Selling also offers unusual freedom and flexibility. It is not a nine-to-five job. Most salespeople decide how to spend their time; they do not have to report in. They have the freedom to determine what they do during a day, to decide which customers to call on and when to do paperwork. Long hours may be required on some days, and other days may bring fewer demands.

Because of this freedom, salespeople are like independent entrepreneurs. They have a territory to manage and few restrictions on how to do it. They are responsible for the sales and profits the territory generates. Thus their success or failure rests largely on their own skills and efforts.

FINANCIAL REWARDS

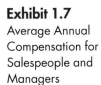

Exhibit 1.7 shows the annual compensation for average and top sales performers. As you can see, successful salespeople often earn more than $150,000 a year; some earn more than $1 million. Occasionally the top salespeople in a firm will even earn more than the sales executives, as the exhibit indicates.

Exhibit 1.7
Average Annual Compensation for Salespeople and Managers

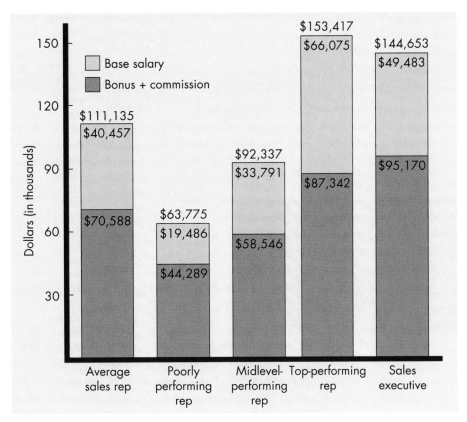

Source: 2004 Salary Survey, *Sales & Marketing Management*, May 2004, p. 29.

Exhibit 1.8

Average Compensation for Salespeople in Various Positions

Sales Occupation	Average Annual Compensation
Retail salespeople (clothing stores)	$7.77 per hour
Retail salespeople (new and used car dealers)	$18.25 per hour
Real estate agents	$30,930
Real estate brokers	$50,330
Insurance sales agents	$40,750
Grocery and related products wholesale salespeople	$41,840
Wholesale electronic markets salespeople	$55,740
Machinery, equipment, and supplies salespeople (technical products)	$53,140
Drug merchant wholesale salespeople	$57,890
Professional and commercial equipment wholesale salespeople (nontechnical products)	$43,880
Sales engineers	$63,660
Security brokers and dealers	$78,140

Note: These are just the averages. Some salespeople in these positions make much more than these averages indicate.
Sources: *Occupational Outlook Handbook,* 2004–2005 edition, U.S. Department of Labor, Bureau of Labor Statistics.

The financial rewards of selling depend on the level of skill and sophistication needed to do the job. For example, salespeople who sell to businesses typically are paid more than retail salespeople because the buying process in businesses is more complex and difficult to manage.

Exhibit 1.8 shows the average compensation for salespeople in various jobs.

MANAGEMENT OPPORTUNITIES

Selling jobs provide a firm base for launching a business career. For example, Mark Alvarez started his sales career in the Medical Systems Division at General Electric (GE) selling diagnostic imaging equipment to hospitals in central Illinois. Over the years he held positions in the firm that included district and regional sales manager and product manager; at one point he had responsibility for all Medical Systems Division business in Latin America. Sixteen years later, he was in corporate marketing and was responsible for managing the relationships between GE's 39 divisions and key customers in the southeastern United States. These include such accounts as Federal Express, Disney, and Home Depot. Some of his businesses do more than $500 million worth of business with GE annually. His entry-level job in selling provided great experience for his current assignment.

This young manager learned the ropes as a salesperson before moving into product management at his firm.

David P. Hall/Masterfile

THE BUILDING PARTNERSHIPS MODEL

This book is divided into four parts, as illustrated in Exhibit 1.9. Part 1 discusses the partnering landscape—the field of selling. Topics include the nature, role, and rewards of selling and what partnering really means.

The knowledge and skills needed for successful partnerships are covered in Part 2. You will learn about the legal and ethical responsibilities of salespeople, the buying process, the principles for communicating effectively, and methods for adapting to the unique styles and needs of each customer.

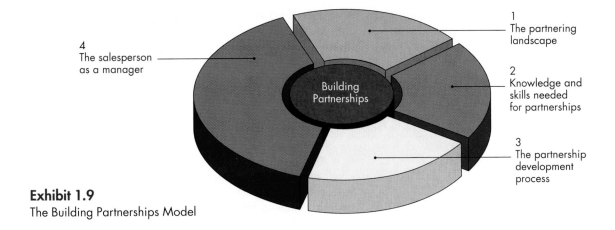

Exhibit 1.9
The Building Partnerships Model

In Part 3 you will explore the partnership development process and the activities needed for this to occur. After completing this section, you should have enhanced skills and understanding about prospecting, planning, discovering needs, using visual aids and conducting demonstrations effectively, responding to objections, obtaining commitment, formally negotiating, and providing excellent after-sale service.

Finally, Part 4 discusses the role of the salesperson as a manager. You'll learn how you can improve your effectiveness as a salesperson by managing your time and territory and by managing the relationships within your own company. This section also discusses ways to manage your career.

SUMMARY

You should study personal selling because we all use selling techniques. If you want to work in business, you need to know about selling because salespeople play a vital role in business activities. Finally, you might become a salesperson. Selling jobs are inherently interesting because of the variety of people encountered and activities undertaken. In addition, selling offers opportunities for financial rewards and promotions.

Salespeople engage in a wide range of activities, including providing information on products and services to customers and employees within their firms. Most of us are not aware of many of these activities because the salespeople we meet most frequently work in retail stores. However, the most exciting, rewarding, and challenging sales positions involve building partnerships: long-term, win–win relationships with customers.

The specific duties and responsibilities of salespeople depend on the type of selling position. However, most salespeople engage in various tasks in addition to influencing customers. These tasks include managing customer relations, serving as the account team manager for their firm, managing the relationships with vendor and channel members, and providing information to their firm.

Sales jobs can be classified by the roles salespeople and their firms play in the channel of distribution. The nature of the selling job is affected by whom salespeople work for and whether they sell to manufacturers, distributors, or retailers. Other factors affecting the nature of selling jobs are the customer's relationship to the salesperson's firm, the salesperson's duties, the importance of the buying decision to the customer, where the selling occurs, the tangibility of the benefits considered by the customer, and the degree to which the salesperson seeks a commitment from customers.

Research on the characteristics of effective salespeople indicates that many different personality types can be successful in sales. However, successful salespeople do share some common characteristics. They are highly motivated, dependable, ethical, knowledgeable, good communicators, flexible, creative, confident, and emotionally intelligent.

KEY TERMS

creativity
customer-centric
distribution channel
emotional intelligence
field salespeople
go-to-market strategies
inside salespeople
integrated marketing communications
lifetime customer value
manufacturers' agents

missionary salespeople
multichannel strategy
personal selling
relationship marketing
sales-force intensive organization
trade salespeople
value
value proposition
24/7 service

ETHICS PROBLEMS

1. Some buyers are now demanding 24/7 response (24 hours a day, seven days a week) from their suppliers. What impact do you think that would have on a salesperson's personal life?
2. One important trait of successful salespeople is product knowledge. Let's say you've just started in a new sales job right out of college and haven't been fully trained yet. A prospect asks you a question that has to do with a technical aspect of your product. You're pretty sure you know the answer, but can't guarantee it is totally correct. However, you don't want to look or sound young or inexperienced, so you answer, "Sure, our printer can be networked with a Linux operating system." What are the implications of answering when you are not certain of the answer? Is there a better answer you could have given this prospect?

QUESTIONS AND PROBLEMS

1. There are many different go-to-market strategies. For which of the following products/services do you think a sales-force intensive strategy would probably not be used? Why? Make any assumptions needed and list your assumptions in your answer.
   a. Promotional ink pens with the business name and company logo on the side.
   b. Copiers and fax machines.
   c. Printer cartridges for desk-top printers.
   d. Heating system for a commercial building.
2. Think of three people you know whom you would identify as very confident. Make a grid of the following traits and indicate whether each of these people exhibits the trait:
   a. Open to criticism.
   b. Seeks advice from others.
   c. Seems to learn from mistakes.
   d. Honest about his or her own limits.
   e. Sets realistic goals.
3. Discuss the following myths about selling:
   a. Salespeople do not serve a useful role in society.
   b. Salespeople are born, not made.
   c. Selling is just a bag of tricks.
   d. A salesperson should never take no for an answer.
   e. A good salesperson can sell anything to anybody.
4. Betsy Tolan has been working as a bookkeeper at her father's business for two years since graduating from college. She is considering taking a selling job with a pharmaceutical company. The job involves calling on doctors

and explaining the benefits of the firm's products. What are the similarities and differences between her bookkeeper job and the selling job she is considering?

5. Chad Feroz worked his way through college by selling in a local department store. He has done well on the job and is one of the top salespeople in the appliances department. Last week Makita offered him a job selling industrial tools to retailers. Explain the differences between selling in a department store and the Makita sales job.

6. Poll at least five students who are not taking your selling course (and who, better yet, are outside the business school or program). What are their opinions about salespeople? How accurate are their opinions based on what you've read in this chapter?

7. Think about what you want in your first job out of college. Based on what you know so far from this chapter, how well does selling match your desires in a job?

8. According to the text, some sales jobs involve taking orders instead of creating new solutions. Why would anyone want a job that involves only taking orders?

9. Would society benefit if new car companies eliminated salespeople and sold new cars at a lower price to the customer over the Internet?

10. Assume you are a sales manager and you need to recruit someone for the following sales positions. For each position, list the qualities you would want in the recruit:
   a. Salesperson selling Internet access to small businesses.
   b. College textbook salesperson.
   c. Used-car salesperson.
   d. Salesperson selling janitorial services to a county courthouse.

11. Assume you are selling office supplies. Rank the following in terms of potential lifetime customer value. Explain the reasons for your ranking. Make any assumptions needed, and list your assumptions in your answer.
   a. A five-year old company, employing two people, that performs veterinary services on-site at farms in the area. Farming is mostly being replaced in the area by light industry.
   b. A new company that will employ approximately 50 people to administer insurance programs for companies across the state. The company handles all the claims forms and writes checks to health care providers and insured people.
   c. A 10-year-old entertainment service company that employs 15 people. The company provides music for local weddings, birthdays, corporate events, and school dances.

CASE PROBLEMS

case **1.1**

S & T Cleaners

S & T Cleaners is a well-established commercial dry cleaning company that has been in business since 1976. The company is located in Atlanta, Georgia, with annual sales of $750,000.

The company provides same-day full services to over 50 major hotels and private clubs in the area. Additionally, the company has a successful wholesale cleaning business (offered to independent retail outlets); valet/delivery services to office complexes and individual residences; and commercial drapery and linen cleaning. S & T also does a small amount of retail dry cleaning for local residents at its dry cleaning plant.

S & T has a well-established customer base that has recurring service needs. Its reputation in the community is excellent. However, there has been a severe decline in its primary market (travel and lodging establishment) over the last three years due to national economic conditions beyond its control. S & T is currently seeing indications of an improving marketplace and wants to actively pursue new business. Its workforce is relatively stable and very productive.

In the past S & T has had only one salesperson. However, they would like to add a new position to seek new business in the area.

Questions

1. This chapter described sales jobs in terms of six factors (the stage of the buyer–seller relationship, the salesperson's role, the importance of the customer's purchase decision, the location of salesperson–customer contact, the nature of the offering sold by the salesperson, and the salesperson's role in securing customer commitment). Based on what you know about the new selling position at S & T, describe the position in terms of the six factors.
2. To what extent do you think this new selling position would require the salesperson to be a client relationship manager? A vendor and channel manager?

case 1.2

Julie Artim

Julie Artim is a junior at Del Ray Beach College. Yesterday she was talking to two friends, Aaron Wick and Gary Johnson, at the cafeteria. Let's pick up at one point in their conversation . . .

AARON: My class in Modern Middle East is going to be so cool!

JULIE: Really? What kind of stuff would you cover in a class like that?

AARON: We're going to be looking at the Ottoman Empire and how things have progressed to the present. I've heard that the prof usually does this really big debate in the middle of the semester. I hear that it gets pretty hairy. Shouting and that kind of stuff!

AARON: That does sound slick. So what's your favorite course this semester, Julie?

JULIE: I think it's going to be selling. [Aaron laughs under his breath.] Well, that's what I want to do when I graduate, you know.

AARON: Why!? I mean, I've got friends who are selling right now without a college education or anything.

GARY: Yeah, and who wants to be a pushy salesman, anyway? I can't stand the guys who are always calling on the phone. No offense, of course, Julie.

AARON: [Laughing] Besides Julie, I'm not sure you've got enough of a poker face to pull off a selling job. You're too honest. I'll never forget your telling the cashier at the bookstore that she gave you back $5 too much in change!

GARY: I've got to agree with Aaron, Julie. You're just too honest to be a seller. And you're too sharp. Let's face it. You've got a lot of creativity. Just think about that poster competition you won last year for the Health Services. That was awesome! You need a job that can use your creativity, not stifle it. Something like graphic design, like I'm in. That's what I think you should consider. You'd be a natural.

AARON: No, I'm not so sure about the graphic design idea, Julie. You don't seem like a computer jockey to me. But didn't you say you wanted to have a family someday? How are you going to pull that off when you're on the road all the time?

Questions

1. How would you reply to each statement by Gary and Aaron?
2. Why do Gary and Aaron have the perceptions they have? Are they at all accurate?

ROLE PLAY

At the end of each chapter, beginning just below this paragraph, you'll find a short role play exercise that focuses on the product ACT!. ACT! is the leading contact management software. Contact management software is a form of software designed to help salespeople increase their productivity by helping them keep track of the customers they call. In addition to a calendar that tells them when to call on an account, the software can track account information concerning what has been bought, when it was bought, the decision-making process, and even personal information about each person in the account. In addition, sales managers can generate reports automatically when reps download information to the company network. Reps don't have to type up as many reports as they would otherwise, such as sales forecasts and call reports. Further, the system can tie into the company's ordering system, which helps save the salesperson

paperwork time. You can learn more about ACT! from their Web page: www.act.com.

Congratulations, you've just graduated from college! Unfortunately, you focused so much on your studies that you have not interviewed for any jobs. You moved back home, but you keep in touch with the school's Career Services Center, where you saw a job posting for ACT! Apparently it is some sort of software for salespeople. You've not had any serious interviews, so you thought you'd sign up. Today is your interview. Be yourself; interview honestly as if you were truly talking with ACT! To help you prepare for this role play of a job interview, you may want to take some time to find out about ACT! by visiting www.act.com for more information.

To the instructor: Additional information needed to complete the role play is available in the Instructor's Manual.

ADDITIONAL REFERENCES

Avery, Susan. "Advanced Partnering." *Purchasing* 133 (March 2004), pp. 25–33.

Bauer, Hans H.; Mark Grether; and Mark Leach. "Building Customer Relations over the Internet." *Industrial Marketing Management* 31 (2002), pp. 155–63.

Bowman, Douglas, and Das Narayandas "Linking Customer Management Effort to Customer Profitability in Business Markets." *Journal of Marketing Research* 61 (November 2004), pp. 433–47.

DelVecchio, Susan, and Earl D. Honeycutt, Jr. "Explaining the Appeal of Sales Careers." *Journal of Marketing Education* 24 (April 2002), pp. 56–63.

Dixon, Andrea L.; Jule B. Gassenheimer; and Terri Feldman Barr. "Identifying the Lone Wolf: A Team Perspective." *Journal of Personal Selling and Sales Management* 23 (Summer 2003), pp. 205–220.

Ehret, Michael. "Managing the Trade-off between Relationships and Value Networks." *Industrial Marketing Management* 33, 2004, pp. 465–73.

Hawes, Jon M.; Anne K. Rich; and Scott M. Widmeir. "Assessing the Development of the Sales Profession." *Journal of Personal Selling and Sales Management* 24 (Winter 2004), pp. 27–38.

Ingram, Thomas N.; Raymond W. LaForge; and Thomas W. Leigh. "Selling in the New Millennium: A Joint Agenda." *Industrial Marketing Management* 31 (2002), pp. 559–67.

Manasco, Britton. "Future Force: The Next Era of Sales Effectiveness." *1to1 Magazine,* May/June 2004, pp. 31–34.

Moncrief, William C., and Greg W. Marshall. "The Evolution of the Seven Steps of Selling." *Industrial Marketing Management* 34 (2005), pp. 13–22.

Pass, Michael W.; Kenneth R. Evans; and John L. Schlacter. "Sales Force Involvement in CRM Information Systems: Participation, Support and Focus." *Journal of Personal Selling and Sales Management* 24, no. 3 (Summer 2004), pp. 229–34.

Pitt, Leland F.; Michael T. Ewing; and Pierre R. Berthon. "Proactive Behavior and Industrial Salesforce Performance." *Industrial Marketing Management* 31 (2002), pp. 639–44.

Ross, W. T.; F. Dalsace; and G. T. M. Hult. "Should You Set Up Your Own Sales Force or Should You Outsource It? Pitfalls in the Standard Analysis." *Business Horizons* 48, no. 1 (2005), pp. 23–36.

Rozell, Elizabeth; Charles E. Pettijohn; and Stephen R. Parker. "Customer-Oriented Selling: Exploring the Roles of Emotional Intelligence and Organizational Commitment." *Psychology and Marketing* 21 (June 2004), pp. 405–25.

Schultz, Don E. "Summit Explores Where IMC, CRM Meet." *Marketing News,* March 4, 2002, pp. 11–12.

Schwepeker, Charles H. Jr. Customer-Oriented Selling: A Review, Extension, and Directions for Future Research." *Journal of Personal Selling and Sales Management* 23 (Spring 2003), pp. 151–72.

Schwepeker, Charles H. Jr., and David J. Good. "Marketing Control and Sales Force Customer Orientation." *Journal of Personal Selling and Sales Management* 24, no. 3 (Summer 2004), pp. 167–79.

Sojka, Jane Z., and Dawn R. Deeter-Schmeiz. "Enhancing the Emotional Intelligence of Salespeople." *Mid-American Journal of Business* 17 (Spring 2002), pp. 43–53.

Stalh, Heinz K.; Kurt Matzler; and Hans H. Hinterhuber. "Linking Customer Lifetime Value with Shareholder Value." *Industrial Marketing Management* 32 (2003), pp. 267–79.

Stevens, Charles D., and Gerrard Macintosh. "Personality and Attractiveness of Activities within Sales Jobs." *Journal of Personal Selling and Sales Management* 23 (Winter 2002–3), pp. 23–38.

Tanner, John F. Jr., "Comments on 'Selling in the New Millennium: A Joint Agenda'" *Industrial Marketing Management* 31 (2002), pp. 569–72.

Widmier, Scott M.; Donald W. Jackson, Jr.; and Deborah Brown McCabe. "Infusing Technology into Personal Selling." *Journal of Personal Selling and Sales Management* 22 (Summer 2002), pp. 189–98.

Verhoef, Peter C. "Understanding the Effect of Customer Relationship Management Efforts on Customer Retention and Customer Share Development." *Journal of Marketing* 67 (October 2003), pp. 30–45.

BUILDING PARTNERING RELATIONSHIPS

SOME QUESTIONS ANSWERED IN THIS CHAPTER . . .

- What different types of relationships exist between buyers and sellers?

- When is each type of relationship appropriate?

- What are the characteristics of successful partnerships?

- What are the benefits and risks in partnering relationships?

- How do relationships develop over time?

- What are the responsibilities of salespeople in partnerships?

PROFILE

I graduated from North Carolina State University in 2003 after studying sales with Dr. Henard, and was hired by Martin Marietta Materials. I spent six months in sales training. My training consisted of hands-on work within the production environment, understanding the forces in the aggregates market, and working directly with sales representatives and managers within our company.

Martin Marietta Materials is the second largest aggregate producer in the United States. Aggregate is a natural resource such as crushed rock, sand, and stone that is used in construction. Without this material, asphalt or concrete would not exist. To build anything, you must use aggregate or stone in some way, shape, or form. For example, your house, your church, and the local shopping mall are made with aggregate materials. This stone exists under the parking lot, in the concrete masonry blocks that make up the walls, and in asphalt. In short, aggregate is vital to our community and its growth.

After I completed training, I was given the responsibility of handling sales for two of our quarries that produce stone for construction use. I am responsible for providing price quotes to general contractors and supplying material to concrete and asphalt plants. A plant that I supply on an annual basis is called a fixed-base customer. This means that I am committed to keeping up with their need for material so that they can produce asphalt or concrete to supply to their customers. I spend a lot of my time working on building relationships with these customers.

A very important key to building relationships with customers is to remember that you have to start from the beginning. Even though other sales reps and managers will know and have relationships with these customers, you must not be naive in thinking that you can start at that point. These experienced employees have spent years establishing trust, honesty, and working relationships with their customers. It is your job to spend time building and creating a trusting relationship of your own.

In the first year of being a sales representative for Martin Marietta Materials, I attended many customer meetings in order to get to know my customers and their wants and needs. It is important to be involved in the community where you work so you can relate with your customers' surroundings and marketing needs. In building relationships, keep in mind that sincerity is a must. No matter how good a sales representative you may be, customers will be able to read you. If you are trying to build a relationship with a customer and you are not sincere, you will negate all of the good things you may want to accomplish. In my job, I am not just developing one relationship with one customer. I am working on various relationships with large and small accounts that are all equally important.

Relationships are unique in the sense that each one is very different from the next. So how can you sit down and explain the dynamics of a relationship? Your challenge as a professional will be to understand the different types of relationships and how those relationships can impact you and your company, whether positive or negative.

As you develop a business relationship, it is important to remember the fine balance of working with the customers to create an alliance so it becomes a win–win situation. My challenge is to continue to build these relationships to benefit Martin Marietta Materials as well as help my customers grow and succeed in their own respective markets.

Visit Martin Marietta Materials on the Web at www.martinmarietta.com.

"Your challenge as a professional will be to understand the different types of relationships and how those relationships can impact you and your company, whether positive or negative."

Steve Reel, Martin Marietta Materials

THE EVOLUTION OF PERSONAL SELLING

Have you purchased anything from the Internet? Probably every student has—travel, music, clothing, books, and more. Have you noticed that, other than Internet services, everything you purchased on the Internet existed in some form before the Internet? Why, then, has the Internet become such a ubiquitous place for commerce?

Simple: The Internet makes products and services available the way the consumer wants to buy them. Those who sell via the Web gain competitive advantage by selling the way the buyers (or at least, some buyers in some situations) want to buy. The reality for salespeople is that if they want to sell effectively, they have to recognize that not only does the buyer have needs that are met by the product, there are also needs met by the selling process. These needs include time, shopping costs such as gas if they drive around, and others. Part of the salesperson's responsibility is to sell the way the buyer wants to buy.

In general, sellers sell to make a profit. Why do buyers buy? Typically a student will say "to satisfy a need or a want," and that is a good basic answer. More helpful is to recognize that buyers buy to also make a profit; it is just that they calculate profit differently. A seller's profit is selling price minus cost of goods sold and selling costs. A buyer's profit is the benefit received minus the selling price and costs and hassles of buying. When someone buys a product off the Internet, the buyer's profit is increased due to lower costs of shopping, even if the net cost (including shipping) is the same as found in a store. (For some buyers, there are benefits in buying from the store that can increase buyer profit when they use that channel.)

Even though the Internet has been a place to do business for only about a decade, the selling function has been a part of humankind since the beginning when one person traded meat for a club. With the arrival of the Industrial Revolution in the 1800s, companies began to make more goods more cheaply. Even so, demand outstripped supply, and for many companies, the key issue in selling was to make people aware of the product and what it could do. Forward-thinking companies such as NCR and Singer Sewing Machines hired salespeople, called *drummers* or *peddlers*, and sent them across the country to sell. Then they brought the most effective salespeople back into the company office and wrote down their sales pitch. These **canned sales pitches** were distributed to all salespeople, who were expected to follow the script every time, without deviation.

Since that time, things have changed greatly. The nature of business evolved, necessarily changing how people sell. Exhibit 2.1 illustrates how the role of the salesperson has evolved from taking orders through persuading customers to building partnerships.[1]

As Exhibit 2.1 shows, the orientations of salespeople emerged in different time periods. However, all these selling orientations still exist in business today. For example, inbound telephone salespeople working for direct mail catalog retailers like Lands' End and Spiegel are providers with a production orientation. They answer a toll-free telephone number and simply take orders. Many outbound telephone, real

Singer was one of the first companies to use a canned sales pitch and train its sales force.

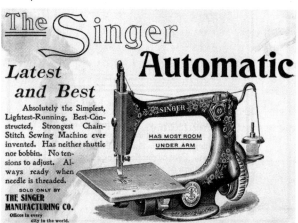

Bettmann/Corbis

Exhibit 2.1

The Evolution of
Personal Selling

	Production	Sales	Marketing	Partnering
Time Period	Before 1930	1930 to 1960	1960 to 1990	After 1990
Objective	Making sales	Making sales	Satisfying customer needs	Building relationships
Orientation	Short-term seller needs	Short-term seller needs	Short-term customer needs	Long-term customer and seller needs
Role of Salesperson	Provider	Persuader	Problem solver	Value creator
Activities of Salespeople	Taking orders, delivering goods	Aggressively convincing buyers to buy products	Matching available offerings to buyer needs	Creating new alternatives, matching buyer needs with seller capabilities

estate, and insurance salespeople are persuaders with a sales orientation. Partnering-oriented selling is becoming more common as companies make strategic choices about the type of selling best suited to their situation, but recent research indicates that even within partnerships, there are times when the buyer needs to hear persuasive messages that might be scripted.[2]

Even though many sales jobs do not involve building long-term partnerships, we stress the concept of developing partnering relationships throughout this textbook because the roles of salespeople in many companies are evolving toward a partnering orientation. As you'll see in Chapter 16, partnering orientations are important within one's own organization as well as with customers. Further, salespeople are called upon to build partnerships with some accounts and other types of relationships with other accounts. The partnering orientation does not prevent salespeople from developing other types of relationships; rather, people who are good partners are more likely to also be good at other types of relationships. Understanding partnerships is critical to understanding the professional selling process, as will become apparent as the book unfolds.

RELATIONSHIPS AND SELLING

Many students may have heard of relationship marketing or customer relationship management (CRM) and wonder what the difference is when compared with building partnerships. *Relationship marketing* is a term with several meanings, but all reflect companies' attempts to develop stronger relationships with their customers. The premise is that loyal customers buy more, are willing to pay more, and are more valuable customers.[3] Building a stronger relationship is accomplished through building loyalty. For example, American Airlines may think of its AAdvantage frequent flyer program as the heart of relationship marketing; loyalty is rewarded with air miles that can be redeemed for free flights. But in professional selling, **relationship marketing** refers to creating the type of relationship that best suits the customer's need, which may or may not require a partnership.

Fans who stayed with the Red Sox through the 80+ years of the curse of the Bambino are very attitudinally loyal.

Rick Friedman/Corbis

There are two types of loyalty: behavioral and attitudinal.[4] **Behavioral loyalty** refers to the purchase of the same product from the same vendor over time. When someone purchases out of habit, for example, that pattern is behavioral loyalty. Recall that earlier we pointed out that buyers calculate profit by subtracting both price and shopping costs from the benefits received. Buying out of habit can reduce shopping costs, increasing profit. **Attitudinal loyalty** is an emotional attachment to a brand, company, or salesperson. At the personal level, it is a friendship, but you might also think of fans of a sports team as attitudinally loyal. They may also be behaviorally loyal, buying season tickets, authentic jerseys, and other accessories.

For the most part, all companies would like to increase loyalty, preferably both attitudinal and behavioral. You may love Jaguar cars, for example, but cannot afford one on a student's income. Your attitudinal loyalty, by itself, has not translated into actually buying a Jag. Companies want their customers to both like and buy their products.

Moreover, companies want loyal customers who stay customers forever. Companies recognize that customers have a total **lifetime customer value (LCV)**, or the sum of their purchases over their entire life. Ford, which owns the Jaguar brand, would like for you to start out as a Ford customer, perhaps with a Ford Focus. Then, after graduation, maybe you move up to a Ford Explorer. Along come a spouse and kids, and you buy a Ford Expedition. When the kids leave home, you buy that Jag you always wanted. In addition to the revenue from buying cars, Ford's dealer also benefits from the service work you have done over the years. When viewed in terms of LCV, you are a much more important customer than the customer who buys only a Ford Focus and never buys another car. Exhibit 2.2 illustrates how value grows over a customer's lifetime.

As you can see, in just one decade the buyer in Exhibit 2.2 is worth over $120,000 to that Ford dealership, if treated as a customer for life instead of a transaction. How much more might this customer be worth in terms of referrals, sales to the children when they get older, and additional repeat business if the Ford dealership really kept this customer for life? There are entire books written just on loyalty; the important element to recognize here is that the emphasis in this book is on building long-term relationships, in part to capture as much LCV as possible. Salespeople who recognize the power of LCV and consider both behavioral and attitudinal loyalty as an objective sell in a different way than if focused only on making the next sale. There are, however, different types of relationships, as we discuss next.

Exhibit 2.2

An Example of Lifetime Customer Value

Age 23	Purchase of a Ford Focus	$14,995
	Maintenance of the Focus	$1,000
Age 27	Replace Focus with a Ford Explorer	$32,595
	Maintenance of the Explorer	$2,000
Age 28	Purchase of a Windstar, a second vehicle	$33,400
	Maintenance	$2,000
Age 33	Replace the Explorer with another	$39,899
	Maintenance of the Explorer	$2,500
Total: First 10 years		$128,389

TYPES OF RELATIONSHIPS

Each time a transaction occurs between a buyer and a seller, the buyer and the seller have a relationship. Some relationships may involve many transactions and last for years; others may exist only for the few minutes during which the exchange of goods for money is made.

This section describes two basic relationship types: market exchanges and partnerships.[5] There are two types of each, summarized in Exhibit 2.3.

MARKET EXCHANGES

A **market exchange** is a transaction between a buyer and a seller in which each party is concerned only about that party's benefit. The seller is concerned only with making the sale; the buyer with getting the product at the lowest possible price. Most business transactions are market exchanges, and there are two types: solo exchanges and functional relationships.

Solo Exchanges

For example, suppose you are driving to the beach for spring break. A warning light on your car's dashboard comes on. You stop at the next gas station, and the service attendant says your car needs a new generator. The generator will cost $650, including installation. At this point you might pay the quoted price, bargain with the service attendant for a lower price, or drive to another service station a block away and get a second opinion. After you select a service station, agree on a price, have the generator replaced, and pay for the service, you have completed a one-shot market exchange. Neither you nor the service station attendant expects to engage in future transactions.

Because the parties in the transaction do not plan on doing business together again, both the buyer and the seller in a **solo exchange** pursue their own self-interests. In this example, you try to pay the lowest price for the generator, and the service station tries to charge the highest price for it. The service station is not concerned about your welfare, just as you are not concerned about the service station's welfare. Or perhaps more accurately, the service station calculates profit from the relationship immediately after the transaction. The issue is not an ethical one; there is no intent to maliciously hurt the other party. At the same time, however, there is no future consideration to worry about in terms of whether the transaction was worthwhile.

Exhibit 2.3
Types of Relationships between Buyers and Sellers

Factors Involved in the Relationship	Type of Relationship			
	Solo Exchange	Functional Relationship	Relational Partnership	Strategic Partnership
Time horizon	Short term	Long term	Long term	Long term
Concern for other party	Low	Low	Medium	High
Trust	Low	Low	High	High
Investment in the relationship	Low	Low	Low	High
Nature of the relationship	Conflict, bargaining	Cooperation	Accommodation	Coordination
Risk in relationship	Low	Medium	High	High
Potential benefits	Low	Medium	High	High

Functional Relationships

Functional relationships are long-term market exchanges characterized by behavioral loyalty; the buyer purchases the same product out of habit or routine. Buyers in this type of relationship tend to have the same orientation as they do in solo exchanges, but the previous purchase does influence the next purchase. As long as the buyer is satisfied and the product is available at a reasonable price and does what it is supposed to do, the buyer will continue to buy.

Sometimes firms buy from the same supplier for a long time because the buyers find it easier to buy repeatedly from the same supplier rather than search for a new supplier every time they need an item. Less hassle means more buyer profit, in that instance. For example, a buyer for your school purchases janitorial supplies—paper towels, soap, cleanser, and mops—for the cleaning crew. However, the buyer and the janitorial supply distributor have little interest in working closely together. The relationship between the buyer and the distributor's salesperson is not critical to the school's success as an educational institution. The purchase and sale of janitorial supplies is routine. The buyer can decide to deal with another distributor if service is poor, if the product fails to perform, or if another distributor works harder to get the business.

Even in these long-term market exchanges, both parties are interested primarily in their own profits and are unconcerned about the welfare of the other party. In market exchanges price may be the critical decision factor. It serves as a rapid means of communicating the bases for the exchange. Basically, the buyer and the salesperson in a market exchange are always negotiating over how to "split up the pie" or how to make more in the transaction. Each calculates profit at the end of each transaction or at least on a frequent basis, usually reflective of the billing cycle. If the janitorial supply company invoices the university monthly, for example, then each side will calculate profit on a monthly basis. If the school's buyer gets an invoice that seems too large, for example, it may cause the buyer to shop around next time because there was insufficient "profit" or value for the buyer.

On the positive side, market exchanges offer buyers and sellers a lot of flexibility. Buyers and sellers are not locked into a continuing relationship, and thus buyers can switch from one supplier to another to make the best possible deal. However, these minimal relationships do not work well when buyers and sellers have an opportunity to increase the size of the pie by developing products and services tailored to their needs. These more complex transactions cannot be conducted solely on the basis of price. A high level of trust and commitment is needed to manage these types of relationships because buyers and sellers need to share sensitive information.

PARTNERSHIPS

There are two types of partnerships: relational and strategic. In partnerships both parties are concerned about each other's welfare and in developing **win–win relationships.** By working together, both parties benefit because the size of the pie increases.

Relational Partnerships

Many times the buyer and the salesperson have a close personal relationship that allows them to communicate effectively. These friendships create a cooperative climate between the salesperson and the customer. When both partners feel safe and stable in the relationship, open and honest communication takes place. Salesperson and buyer work together to solve important problems. The partners are not concerned about little details because they trust each other enough to know these will be worked out. These types of partnerships are not necessarily strategic to either organization, although they may be to the individuals involved, and are called **relational partnerships.**

The benefits of a relational partnership go beyond simple increased short-term profits. Although both partners are striving to make money in the relationship, they are also trying to build a working relationship that will last a long time. For example, Todd Greenwald, director of operations for Heartland Computers, a seller of barcode scanners, says this about his relationship with Ron Kelly, sales rep for CDW: "He's my sales rep but he's also my friend. Most of the time we don't even talk about price. I trust Ron."[6]

Relational partnerships can occur between a buyer and seller not only because of personal ties but also because each is important to the other professionally. For example, a trade show program may not be important enough to the organization to demand a strategic partner but is very important to the trade show manager. That manager may seek a relational partnership with a supplier, complete with personal investment of time and departmental resources, rather than a strategic organizational investment and commitment.

In Asian countries, the personal relationship is an important precursor to strategic partnerships. Several studies have found that social bonding and interpersonal commitment are necessary ingredients to any long-term partnership between Asian organizations.[7] In one study examining relationships between Australians and Chinese, interpersonal commitment was a precursor to organizational relationships, so without friendship, there was no partnership.[8]

In this chapter we talk about relationships between buyers and sellers, but these concepts also apply to personal relationships. A relational partnership is like a close friendship. In a close friendship you are not concerned with how the pie is split up each day because you are confident that, over the long run, each of you will get a fair share; further, the pie will be bigger because of your friendship. You trust your friend to care about you, and she or he trusts you in return. The founder of the country's largest department store chain, James Cash Penney, once said, "All great businesses are built on friendship."

Strategic Partnerships

Strategic partnerships are long-term business relationships in which the partner organizations make significant investments to improve the profitability of both parties. In these relationships the partners have gone beyond trusting each other to "putting their money where their mouths are." They take risks to expand the pie, to give the partnership a strategic advantage over other companies.

Strategic partnerships are created for the purpose of uncovering and exploiting joint opportunities. Members of strategic partnerships have a high level of dependence on and trust in each other; share goals and agree on how to accomplish those goals; and show a willingness to take risks, share confidential information, and make significant investments for the sake of the relationship. An example is the partnership between Simmons Mattress and Westin Hotels. Simmons manufacturers a special mattress for Westin, called the Heavenly Bed. This special product can be purchased through Westin Hotels or through other channels, but Westin is the only hotel to which Simmons will sell the Heavenly Bed mattress.

Similarly, Levi Strauss teams worked with JCPenney to create a specially designed area in its stores to display Dockers merchandise. Then teams from each company developed sophisticated inventory control systems to make sure that the stores were always stocked with the styles and sizes that were selling well. As a result, JCPenney is now Levi Strauss's largest customer worldwide. JCPenney also

Westin Hotels' partnership with Simmons created the Heavenly Bed, a mattress and bedlinens product line that is very popular with business travelers. You can even buy the mattress and linens through Westin's Web site.

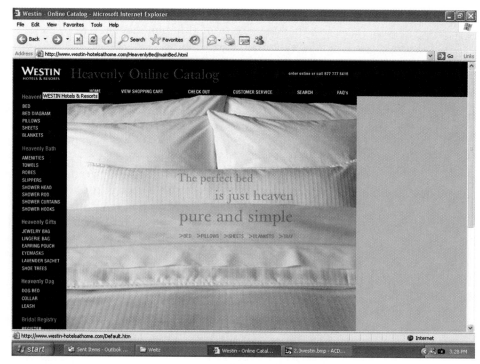

Reprinted with permission of Starwood Hotels & Resorts Worldwide, Inc.

increased its own profits because it was able to offer merchandise to its customers that was not available from its competitors.

Many students wonder about the exclusivity of strategic partnerships. Does a strategic partnership mean, for example, that JCPenney cannot carry Wranglers or that Westin can't use Sealy? In the Westin situation the agreement was for an exclusive arrangement that tied the two companies together. But Penney also sells Wrangler jeans as well as a private-label brand. Strategic partnerships do not necessarily mean exclusivity for either buyer or seller—Levi can still sell to customers that compete with Penney.

In cultures outside the United States, long-term relationships are very important. In Japan, for example, several organizations may join together to form a **keiretsu,** or family of companies. These families of companies may include a bank, a transportation company, a manufacturing company, and distribution companies that share risks and rewards and jointly develop plans to exploit market opportunities. Keiretsus are thus exclusive strategic partnerships among several companies rather than between only two.

Most salespeople are involved in both solo exchanges and functional relationships. Some customers buy once and are never heard from again. Others become loyal as long as everything goes smoothly. A few become friends, but strategic partnerships are rare. Exhibit 2.4 illustrates the differences in the nature of selling in market exchanges and long-term relationships.

Each type of relationship has its pluses and minuses. Companies cannot develop a strategic advantage from a market exchange, but they do get the flexibility to buy products from the supplier with the lowest cost when the order is placed. On the other hand, strategic partnerships create a win–win situation, but the companies are committed to each other and flexibility can be reduced. In the next section we talk about the characteristics of successful relationships, relationships that have the potential to develop into strategic partnerships.

Exhibit 2.4
Selling in Market
Exchanges and Long-
Term Relationships

Market Exchange Selling Goal: Making a Sale	Long-Term Relationship Selling Goal: Building Trust
Making Contact	**Initiating the Relationship**
• Find someone to listen.	• Engage in strategic prospecting and qualifying.
• Make small talk.	• Gather and study precall information.
• Ingratiate and build rapport.	• Identify buying influences.
	• Plan the initial sales call.
Closing the Sale	• Demonstrate an understanding of the customer's needs.
• Deliver a sales pitch to:	• Identify opportunities to build a relationship.
• Get the prospect's attention.	• Illustrate the value of a relationship with the customer.
• Create interest.	
• Build desire.	**Developing the Relationship**
• Get the prospect to take action.	• Select an appropriate offering.
• Stay alert for closing signals.	• Customize the relationship.
• Use trial closes.	• Link the solution to the customer's needs.
• Overcome objections.	• Discuss customer concerns.
• Close early and often.	• Summarize the solution to confirm benefits.
	• Secure commitment.
Following Through	
• Reestablish contact.	**Enhancing the Relationship**
• Resell self, company, and products.	• Assess customer satisfaction.
	• Take actions to ensure satisfaction.
	• Maintain open, two-way communications.
	• Expand collaborative involvement.
	• Work to add value and enhance mutual opportunities.

Source: Adapted from Thomas Ingram, "Relationship Selling: Moving from Rhetoric to Reality," *Mid-American Journal of Business* 11 (1996), p. 6.

thinking **it** through

Think about how you are treated when you walk into a clothing store. How much do you spend on average per month for clothing? How much would that be during your time in school? Does the store treat you on the basis of your value as a solo exchange? How would this change if the store considered your lifetime value as a customer? What form of relationship would be needed for the store to capture your LCV?

CHARACTERISTICS OF SUCCESSFUL PARTNERSHIPS

Successful relationships involve cultivating mutual benefits as the partners learn to trust and depend on each other more and more. As trust develops, buyer and salesperson are able to resolve conflicts as they arise, settle differences, and compromise when necessary. Without trust, there is no loyalty and unhappy customers leave. While trust is important, there are other elements that characterize successful, long-term relationships; the five foundational elements of strategic partnerships are (1) mutual trust, (2) open communication, (3) common

Exhibit 2.5
Foundations of
Successful Relationships

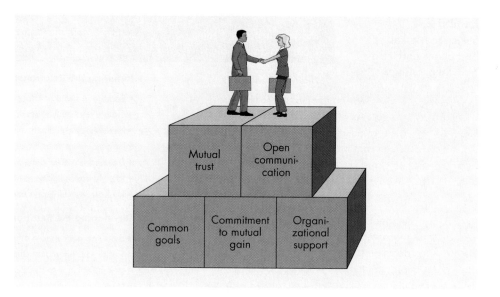

goals, (4) commitment to mutual gain, and (5) organizational support (see Exhibit 2.5).

MUTUAL TRUST

The most important element in the development of successful, long-term customer relationships is trust. **Trust** is a belief by one party that the other party will fulfill its obligations in a relationship. Daniel Fries, account executive for Relizon, states, "A little trust and confidence go a long way in motivating the supplier to go beyond the single requirements of a contract."[9] That trust has to be mutual, however. When salespeople and buyers trust each other, they are more willing to share relevant ideas, clarify goals and problems, and communicate more efficiently. Information shared between the parties becomes increasingly comprehensive, accurate, and timely. There is less need for salesperson and buyer to constantly monitor and check up on each other's actions because both believe the other party would not take advantage of them if given the opportunity. Building Partnerships 2.1 illustrates how Craig Murchison responded to a customer's trust.

Trust is an important building block for long-term relationships. A study of partnerships in Europe found trust to be the most important variable that contributes to the success of the relationship, as measured by the value created.[10] Trust is a combination of five factors: dependability, competence, customer orientation, honesty, and likability. In this section we discuss these factors and how salespeople demonstrate their own trustworthiness.

Dependability

Dependability, the buyer's perception that the salesperson, and the product and company he or she represents, will live up to promises made, is not something a salesperson can demonstrate immediately. Promises must be made and then kept. Early in the selling process, a salesperson can demonstrate dependability by calling at times agreed to, showing up a few minutes early for appointments, and providing information as promised.

Third-party references can be useful in proving dependability, especially if the salesperson has not yet had an opportunity to prove it personally. If the seller can point to a similar situation and illustrate, through the words of another customer,

BUILDING Partnerships

2.1

TRUST WORKS BOTH WAYS

Craig Murchison knows how important trust is, and how quickly it can be lost. As a sales representative for a commercial printer, Craig called for six months on Matt Kooistra, graphic design manager for Wyndham International Hotels & Resorts, and had built up a great relationship but no sales. Finally, Kooistra offered Murchison a good-sized first sale.

"I felt very confident in my people and our product, so I was able to guarantee Matt he would be completely satisfied with his decision to work with me and my company," says Murchison, smiling ruefully. He notes that Kooistra even went out of town, trusting Murchison completely. "Unfortunately, this is where things began to get a bit more difficult." When Kooistra got back, he noticed a flaw in the printing that made the product unacceptable.

Even though the problem was caused by the original sent over from Wyndham and was not Murchison's fault, "I took full responsibility for the unusable product as long as Mr. Kooistra and Wyndham verbally committed to working with my corporation over the next few years in order for us to make up our losses for this misfortune." Because he knew Kooistra well, they were able to reach an agreement that Murchison believes will result in a long relational partnership. "Kooistra trusted me to do the job right; I trust him to honor our agreement over time, even though there is no contract. People buy from people they like."

Source: Craig Murchison, personal correspondence; used with permission.

how the situation was resolved, the buyer can verify the seller's dependability. Some companies also prepare case studies of how they solved a particular customer's problem to aid salespeople in proving the company's dependability.

Product demonstrations, plant tours, and other special types of presentations can also illustrate dependability. A product demonstration can show how the product will work, even under difficult conditions. A buyer for component parts for appliances was concerned about one company's ability to produce the large volumes required. The salesperson offered a plant tour to prove that the company could live up to its promises of on-time delivery. When the buyer saw the size of the plant and the employees' dedication to making quality products, she was convinced.

The salesperson's prior experience and training can also be used to prove dependability. For a company (and a salesperson) to remain in business there must be some level of dependability. Length of experience, however, is a weak substitute for proving dependability with action.

As time goes on and the relationship grows, the buyer assumes dependability. For example, a buyer may say, "Well, let's call Sue at Mega. We know we can depend on her." At this point the salesperson has developed a reputation within the account as dependable. But reputations can spread beyond that account through the buyer's community. A reputation for dependability, however, can be quickly lost if the salesperson fails to continue to deliver as promised.

Competence

Salespeople demonstrate **competence** when they can show that they know what they are talking about. Knowledge of the customer, the product, the industry, and the competition are all necessary to the success of the salesperson; in fact, recent research suggests that competence is a key component in developing loyalty.[11] Through the use of this knowledge, a salesperson demonstrates competence. For example, when a pharmaceutical representative can discuss the treatment of a

Chapter 2   Building Partnering Relationships   **41**

disease in medical terms, the physician is more likely to believe that the rep is medically competent.

Salespeople recognize the need to appear competent. Unfortunately, their recognition of the importance of competence may lead them to try to fake knowledge. Because buyers test the trustworthiness of a seller early in the relationship, they may ask questions just to see the salesperson's response. Salespeople should never make up a response to a tough question; if you don't know, say so but promise to get the answer quickly and then do it. At the same time, salespeople should try to present information objectively. Buyers can tell when salespeople are exaggerating the performance of their products.

Product knowledge is the minimum; customers expect salespeople to know everything about their own products and their company. That's why company training is so important. Arrow Electronics, a global distributor of electronics parts, creates competence through intensive training. Each salesperson undergoes 90 days of training before going into the field. Once in the field, salespeople undergo an additional six months of training, including two weeks at the company's headquarters in Melville, New York (see Exhibit 2.6). The result is a

Exhibit 2.6
Arrow Electronics' Pathways Training Program Builds Competence

Phase 1		Phase 2		Phase 3
Classroom Training Corporate HQ Melville, NY (Three Weeks)	Field Training Branches throughout United States (Two Months)	Classroom Training Corporate HQ Melville, NY (Two Weeks)	Field Training Branches throughout United States (Three Months)	Field Training Assigned to Business Group (Three Months)
• Introduction to the electronics distribution industry. • Customer and supplier dynamics. • Technical product training. • Introduction to Arrow Electronics, Inc. • Exceeding customer and supplier expectations. • Field visit: touring a customer's facility. • Professional development. • Business savvy—having impact on day 1. • Customer service, team building, communication skills.	• Work with active accounts under supervision of field sales managers. • Participate in sales calls with customers and suppliers. • Work in Arrow facilities at customer's manufacturing facility.	• Arrow sales system. • Roles and responsibilities. • Intergroup selling strategies. • Inventory management. • Professional selling skills. • Collaborative selling. • Account management. • Financial management—creating profitable businesses. • Professional development. • Career development and personal learning. • Presentation skills.	• Work with active accounts under supervision of field sales managers. • Research account potential and formulate account strategies. • Collaborate with suppliers on strategies for assigned accounts.	• Based on demonstrated expertise and company staffing needs, associates are assigned a sales territory. • Associates continue with training specific to their assigned business group. • Associates are eligible for rewards and incentives for meeting or exceeding sales goals.

Source: Jeffrey Uschok, "Pathways: Putting Your Career on the Fast Track," *Careers in Professional Selling*, Spring 2001, pp. 16–17.

highly competent sales force that works in partnership with customers, helping them to run their businesses more successfully.[12]

Customer Orientation

Customer orientation is the degree to which the salesperson puts the customer's needs first. Salespeople who think only of making sales are sales oriented rather than customer oriented. Buyers perceive salespeople as customer oriented when sellers stress benefits and solutions to problems over features. Buyers who perceive that the product is tailored to their unique requirements are likely to infer a customer orientation. Stating pros and cons can also be perceived as being customer oriented because understanding the cons also indicates that the salesperson understands the buyer's needs.

Emphasizing the salesperson's availability and desire to provide service also indicates a customer orientation. For example, the statement "Call me anytime for anything that you need" indicates availability. Offering the numbers for toll-free hot lines, voice mail, and similar concrete information indicates a desire to respond promptly to the buyer and can serve as proof of a customer orientation.

Honesty

Honesty is both truthfulness and sincerity. While honesty is highly related to dependability ("We can count on you and your word because you are honest"), it is also related to how candid a salesperson is. For example, giving pros and cons can increase perceptions of honesty as well as customer orientation.

Honesty is also related to competence. As we said earlier, salespeople must be willing to admit that they do not know something rather than trying to fake it; buyers consider salespeople who bluff to be dishonest.

The opposite, of course, is lying. Buyers figure out pretty quickly when they've been lied to. One salesperson lied to his customer about the response the marketing program would get that he sold; when it failed, not only did the customer refuse to purchase again, he threatened to blow up the salesperson's house![13] Although not every customer who has been lied to will threaten physical harm, without honesty, a customer cannot trust a salesperson. Chapter 3 will discuss other issues about ethics in greater detail.

Likability

According to research, likability may be the least important component of trust because most people can be nice.[14] **Likability** refers to behaving in a friendly manner and finding common ground between buyer and seller. Although likability is not as important as other dimensions, salespeople should still attempt to find common ground or interests with all buyers. Buyers resent any attempts, though, at insincere rapport building. Do not feign interest if you truly aren't interested.

Likability can also be influenced with personal communications such as birthday cards, handwritten notes, and so forth. Many businesses send holiday cards and gifts to all customers, but personal touches make these gestures meaningful.

As you have probably noticed, the five dimensions of trust are tightly interrelated. Honesty affects customer orientation, which also influences dependability, for example. Salespeople should recognize the interdependence among these factors rather than simply focusing on one or two. For example, at one time many salespeople emphasized only likability. In today's market, professional salespeople must also be competent, dependable, honest, and customer oriented.

OPEN COMMUNICATION

Open and honest communication is a key building block for developing successful relationships. Buyers and salespeople in a relationship need to understand what is driving each other's business, their roles in the relationship, each firm's strategies, and any problems that arise over the course of the relationship. (Chapter 5 focuses on approaches for improving communication.)

Open communication should lead to stronger relationships, though Suzanne Morgan, president of Print Buyers Online (a buying group for commercial printers) worries that concern for the other party may make customers reluctant to share their opinions when something goes wrong. Buyers, perhaps more so than sellers, may worry about hurting the salesperson's feelings, and thus not be as open as the situation requires. She recommends that salespeople make it as easy as possible for the buyer to speak up.[15]

Conflict can occur even in the strongest of partnerships, and how it is handled says more about the relationship than if or when it happens. Joint problem solving and cooperation when there is conflict are much more likely to strengthen a partnership; whereas blaming, demanding, and the like are likely to lead to a breakup.[16] We'll talk more about breakups later, but it is important to recognize the importance of open communication, especially when there is conflict.

One difference between a relational partnership and a strategic partnership is the lines of communication. In a relational partnership, most communication between the buyer and the selling organization goes through the salesperson. In a strategic partnership, there will be more direct communication ties between the buying organization and the selling organization. For example, the selling company's shipping department may talk directly with the buying organization's receiving department when a problem arises with a shipment.

Cultural differences in communication style can be easily misunderstood and thus hinder open and honest communication. For example, all cultures have ways to avoid saying no when they really mean no. In Japan maintaining long-lasting, stable relationships is very important. To avoid damaging a relationship, customers rarely say no directly. Some phrases used in Japan to say no indirectly are *It's very difficult, We'll think about it,* and *I'm not sure;* alternatively, customers may leave the room with an apology. In general, when Japanese customers do not say yes or no directly, it means they want to say no.

COMMON GOALS

Salespeople and customers must have common goals for a successful relationship to develop. Shared goals give both members of the relationship a strong incentive to pool their strengths and abilities. When goals are shared, the partners can focus on exploiting opportunities rather than arguing about who will benefit the most from the relationship.

Shirley Hunter is an account executive for Teradata (a division of NCR) and has only one account, EDS. Her primary job is to help EDS sell Teradata as a part of the solutions EDS offers its clients. Hunter spends most of her time coordinating the efforts of Teradata and EDS salespeople selling to end users, but it is important that she understands EDS's goals and that she makes sure that everyone in Teradata understands and shares those goals.

Shared goals also help to sustain the partnership when the expected benefit flows are not realized. If one Teradata shipment fails to reach an EDS customer on time because of an uncontrollable event, such as misrouting by a trucking firm, EDS will not suddenly call off the whole arrangement. Instead, EDS is likely to view the incident as a simple mistake and will remain in the relationship. EDS knows that it and Teradata are committed to the same goals in the long run.

Clearly defined, measurable goals are also very important. Hunter has a sales budget that she has to meet; but more important, the two organizations set joint goals such as sales revenue, on-time delivery, service response time, and others. Performance is assessed monthly to determine if these goals are being met, so that the two organizations can work together to rectify any problems quickly.

Effective measuring of performance is particularly critical in the early stages of the partnership. The achievement of explicitly stated goals lays the groundwork for a history of shared success, which serves as powerful motivation for continuing the relationship and working closely together into the future.

COMMITMENT TO MUTUAL GAIN

Members of successful partnerships actively work to create win–win relationships by making commitments to the relationship. For example, Bama Pies and McDonalds have shared a long-term relationship for over three decades. Bama Pies makes apple pies, biscuits, and other baked goods sold exclusively through McDonalds. When McDonalds was growing rapidly, it was outstripping Bama's ability to add manufacturing capacity. McDonalds stepped in and helped Bama secure the financing that it needed to add new plants.

McDonalds is clearly the more powerful of the two companies; but in a partnership, commitment to mutual gain means that McDonalds does not take advantage of Bama. One party is always more powerful than the other party; but in a partnership, it does not exercise that power over the other. Mutual dependence creates a cooperative spirit. Both parties search for ways to expand the pie and minimize time spent on resolving conflicts over how to split it.

Mutual investment

As a successful relationship develops, both parties make investments in the relationship. **Mutual investments** are tangible investments in the relationship by both parties. They go beyond merely making the hollow statement "I want to be a partner." Mutual investment may involve spending money to improve the products and services sold to the other party, though research says that sellers tend to invest more in relationships than buyers.[17] For example, a firm may hire or train employees, invest in equipment, and develop computer and communication systems to meet the needs of a specific customer. These investments signal the partner's commitment to the relationship in the long run.

McDonalds lent its financial support to Bama Pie so Bama could expand. That is an investment to the relationship. Thus it is not enough to say that you are committed to the relationship; actions of commitment must follow that signal that the commitment is real. These actions make the commitment believable. Mutual investments are also called *relationship-specific assets;* in other words, these are resources specific to the relationship and cannot be easily transferred to another relationship.

ORGANIZATIONAL SUPPORT

Another critical element in fostering good relationships is giving **boundary-spanning employees**—those employees who cross the organizational boundary and interact with customers or vendors—the necessary support. Some areas of support are training, rewards that support partnering behavior, and structure and culture. We'll start with structure and culture because these elements foster the others.

Structure and Culture

The organizational structure and management provide the necessary support for the salespeople and buyers in a partnering relationship. All employees in the firm need to "buy in"—in other words, accept the salesperson's and buyer's roles in developing the partnership. Partnerships created at headquarters should be recognized and treated as such by local offices, and vice versa. Without the support of the respective companies, the partnership is destined to fail.

The issue isn't just creating a culture among salespeople, however. The entire firm must have an orientation to building partnerships. Recall that strategic partnerships are characterized by direct, open communication between multiple members of both firms. If nonselling members of the selling firm do not have a customer orientation, then the partnership may be doomed.

Training

Special training is required to sell effectively in a relationship-building environment. Salespeople need to be taught how to identify customer needs and work with the customer to achieve better performance.

Steve Trerotola, of Alfa Color Imaging Inc., constantly trains his salespeople in relationship skills, needs identification skills, and other sales skills. In fact, he regularly puts salespeople in situations where he knows customers might need services the company can't offer, then waits to see if a rep overpromises or exaggerates company capabilities. These opportunities are used to train the rep on how to respond in ways that improve, not damage, the relationship.[18]

Training is critical in helping salespeople identify ways to make it easier for the customer to do business with them. At Alcoa Aluminum sales representatives are trained to look at what their customers do to a product that Alcoa could make for them. For example, one salesperson noticed that customers stack materials in skids in various-size stacks, sometimes 10 feet tall. When an order is pulled from inventory, a forklift driver must go into the stacks and pull a particular skid. Sometimes the skids are not stacked with a packing ticket on the outside, so the driver has a hard time identifying the right skid. Alcoa began to put a packing ticket on both ends of the skid so that the driver can always see the package number, no matter how the skid is stacked.

Training can also support the customer-oriented culture for all boundary-spanning employees. Many companies now offer service-oriented training to all customer-facing employees. For example, ING US Financial Services, a financial services company (formerly Aetna), continues to train all of its customer-facing employees, which has led to a continuing increase in customer satisfaction scores.[19] Selling Scenario 2.1 illustrates the importance of satisfaction with how well the salesperson takes care of the buyer.

Rewards

Reward systems on both sides of the relationship should be coordinated to encourage supportive behaviors. In market exchanges buyers are rewarded for wringing out concessions from the salespeople, and salespeople are rewarded on the basis of sales volume. In a partnering relationship, rewarding short-term behaviors can be detrimental. Thus companies like Nortel, AT&T, Seibel and others are beginning to reward salespeople and buyers based on the quality of the relationships they develop.[20]

Research indicates that compensation strategies can influence salespeople's customer orientation.[21] For example, Bob Smith, vice president of sales and marketing at Pass & Seymour/Legrand, Syracuse, New York, described how his company developed a sales compensation plan: "In developing the plan we involved our rep council and communicated with individual reps," Smith explained. He added that as the plan developed, it became clear that how the plan was structured would impact how customers were treated.[22]

WHAT IS SATISFACTION?

Most people think of satisfaction as an outcome of a product satisfying a buyer's needs. Satisfaction is an important factor in the creation of any relationship, and it has been shown to influence repurchase. But business buyers think of satisfaction a little differently.

One study showed that satisfaction with the product isn't enough. In fact, the most important factor found to drive repurchase intentions was interpersonal satisfaction, or gratification that buyers receive from their relationships with salespeople. After all, products are easily copied, and most products are not that different. Often the most important point of difference is who represents the product. Similarly, another important component of satisfaction is satisfaction with the company.

Such was the case with Bobby Whitson, vice president of SmartDM, provider of marketing software and support to sports teams and leagues such as the National Basketball Association (NBA). When it was time to renew their contract, one of his accounts had to go out for bids. "My decision maker had to have three bids because her boss told her to." Whitson made sure his pricing was competitive, and made his pitch. At the presentation, one of the department heads complained, "This is a waste of time. We've never gotten service that approaches the quality Bobby gives us." The decision maker agreed, but ruefully noted that she had to follow company procedure.

"We do offer a somewhat unique product, but that's because our individual expertise makes it possible to deliver exactly what the customer wants," notes Whitson. The result is not just a high customer retention rate; accounts like the NBA are also quick to recommend SmartDM to others. Such recommendations began with teams like the Nashville Predators (hockey) and now include the Texas Rangers (baseball) and even venues such as Madison Square Garden.

Sources: Michael W. Preis, "The Impact of Interpersonal Satisfaction on Repurchase Decisions," *Journal of Supply Chain Management* 39 (Summer 2003), pp. 30–47; Bobby Whitson, personal correspondence, used with permission.

One challenge is how to reward nonselling employees. If their reward systems do not favor a customer orientation, then customer relationships can be damaged. The employees are doing what they are being rewarded for, so the problem isn't necessarily theirs. Creating appropriate reward structures, though, can be difficult. That's why some companies call in consultants such as SatMetrix Systems, the company that helps Nortel, AT&T, Seibel, and others measure customer relationship quality. "We can dice and slice the numbers so that each sales rep and sales manager knows which customers were unhappy and why," says Rod Lehman, vice president of marketing for SatMetrix. "We can say to them, 'You got dinged by these three customers and here are the issues that are bothering them.' Often the sales rep can turn it around with that information," Lehman says.[23]

PHASES OF RELATIONSHIP DEVELOPMENT

Although not all relationships should become partnerships, strategic partnerships tend to go through several phases. These phases are (1) awareness, (2) exploration, (3) expansion, (4) commitment, and sometimes (5) dissolution.[24] Recent research indicates that the middle three stages are most important.[25] Cultural differences may alter the way buyers and sellers move through these phases, but strategic partnerships go through these stages in most situations.

Awareness

In the **awareness** stage, it is likely that no transaction has taken place. During the awareness phase salespeople locate and qualify prospects, while buyers identify various sources of supply. Buyers may see a booth at a trade show, an ad in a magazine, or some other form of marketing communication and seek additional information. Reputation and image in the marketplace can be very important for sellers at this point. One important trend is toward supplier relationship management. **Supplier relationship management** (SRM) is the use of technology and statistics to identify important suppliers and opportunities for cost reduction, greater efficiency, and other benefits. Thus awareness may result from analyzing current suppliers to identify those with whom a partnership may be possible.

Recognize, though, that relationships do not necessarily move from solo exchange to functional relationship to relational partnership to strategic partnership. Customers may actively seek partnerships for key areas of the firm's purchases, which may mean working to develop a strategic partnership with a new vendor. Or the relationship may develop over time, and may involve one or more of the other forms of relationship. There is no requirement, however, that a partnership must start out as a solo exchange.

Exploration

The **exploration** stage is a search and trial phase for both buyer and seller. Both parties may explore the potential benefits and costs of a partnership. At this point the buyer may make purchases, but these are likely in the form of market exchanges because neither side has committed to the relationship. Each purchase, though, can be thought of as a test of the supplier's capability.

Expansion

At this point the supplier has passed enough tests to be considered for additional business. The **expansion** stage involves efforts by both parties to investigate the benefits of a long-term relationship. The relationship can still devolve into a functional relationship rather than a strategic partnership, but the intention of both parties is to develop the appropriate type of relationship. The buyer's dependence on the seller as a primary source of supply grows and may lead to the purchase of additional products. Further, both sides begin to probe regarding interest in a partnership; such probing is both internal and external. The decision for a strategic partnership requires credible commitments, so many in the selling organization may need to review the opportunity.

Commitment

In the **commitment** stage the customer and seller have implicitly or explicitly pledged to continue the relationship for a period of time. Commitment represents the most advanced stage of the relationship. Investments are made in the relationship, especially in the form of sharing proprietary information, plans, goals, and the like.

In later chapters we discuss obtaining commitment as a stage in the sales process. In that sense we are talking about asking the buyer to make a decision: either to buy the product or to take the next step in the decision process. The commitment stage in a relationship involves a promise by both buyer and seller to work together over many transactions, not just the one decision.

Dissolution

Dissolution can occur at any time in the relationship process, though it doesn't necessarily have to occur at all. Dissolution is the process of terminating the relationship and can occur because of poor performance, clash in culture, change in needs, and other factors. When dissolution occurs in latter stages of the relationship, the loss of investments made in the relationship can be significant and have an impact throughout both organizations.

In the next section we explore the factors used in selecting partners. Not every customer should become a strategic partner, but the general principles of creating value by satisfying needs do apply to all customer types. Thus understanding some of the issues involved in evaluating potential partners is important to salespeople.

MANAGING RELATIONSHIPS AND PARTNERING

Salespeople are usually responsible for determining the appropriate form of relationship and for making sure that their companies develop the appropriate types of relationships with each customer. In other words, some customers want, and need, a market exchange; others need a functional relationship; and still others need a strategic partnership. As salespeople identify customer needs for product benefits, they also identify needs for relationship benefits and select the appropriate strategy as a result. Salespeople are likely to manage a portfolio of relationships.[26] With some accounts, a strategic partnership may be called for. With others, it may be a relational partnership or functional relationship. The salesperson must determine which relationship type is appropriate for optimizing the customer's lifetime value.

CHOOSING THE RIGHT RELATIONSHIP

As you can see from the discussion about what makes for a strategic relationship, at least one factor that influences a salesperson's choice of relationship is the type of relationship the customer desires. Becoming a strategic partner requires investment by both parties, and if the customer isn't willing to make that investment, then another type of relationship is called for. But even then, not every customer who wants a strategic partnership should become your strategic partner. Some of the factors to consider are size of the account, access and image in the market, and access to technology.

Size

JCPenney has a strategic partnership with Levi Strauss. Would Levi Strauss have a similar partnership with Kestner's Department Store, a three-store chain in central Texas? Probably not. The return could not be great enough to justify the investment. The thought is that by partnering with large accounts, the accounts invest in the supplier and become locked in. Economies of scale can often justify lower prices and higher investments. Size of the account, then, is one aspect to consider. But that doesn't mean that one should partner only with the largest accounts. In some cases larger accounts are not necessarily the most profitable, particularly

Size matters! Most strategic partnerships involve larger customers like JCPenney rather than Jordans because their size makes the investments into the partnerships worthwhile.

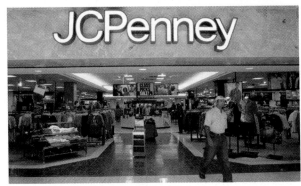

Lm Otero/AP Wide World

Dennis MacDonald/Photoedit

when the seller's investments are factored in.[27] In other cases smaller accounts provide important benefits that larger accounts cannot, as we will discuss.

Access and Image

A strategic partnership may be called for if an account can provide access to a specific, desired market or can enhance the image of the seller. For example, Heineken was shocked to discover that Albert Heijn, the largest supermarket chain in the Netherlands, placed Heineken beer on the store's "mega-losers" list. Heineken could not afford the damage to its image that such a list would cause with all retailers in Europe, so it quickly made major commitments to meet Albert Heijn's needs and to rebuild the relationship it had taken for granted.[28] Thus Heineken believed it was important to partner with Albert Heijn because working with the leader in the market was critical to Heineken's image.

Access to Innovation

Some companies are called **lead users** because they face and resolve needs months or years ahead of the rest of the marketplace. These companies often develop innovations, either in the way they use a product or by altering a product, that the supplier can copy. Diamond Shamrock, for example, has a vice president of future systems who works closely with technology suppliers. Diamond Shamrock actively codevelops software with its suppliers to meet its own needs, while the suppliers can then market the products to other potential users. Other companies seek to jointly develop products with their customers. For example, Oki Data Americas, a printer manufacturer in Mt. Laurel, New Jersey, asked retailers who use Oki Data printers to print in-store promotional materials to suggest design elements for printers. Then it designed printers exactly to retailers' specifications. Sue Kirvan, Oki Data's marketing manager for vertical markets, believes more product customization is in their future. "Exclusivity makes customers feel special, and that leads to loyalty."[29]

Note that one important function salespeople provide is the ability to listen to customers and deliver that knowledge back to the company so that better products can be developed.[30] That function is important in new product development, but does not necessarily require deep relationships. What lead users provide is more than information; they provide the opportunity to co-create innovations that can then be converted into products.

Other lead users may develop innovations in other areas of the business, such as logistics, that suppliers can copy. For example, Wal-Mart has a long-established reputation as an innovator in logistics. On September 11, 2001, Wal-Mart's inventory control system enabled the company to place orders every five minutes for products such as bottled water, batteries, flashlights, and American flags. On September 12, Wal-Mart had trucks rolling into stores with new inventory. Target and other competitors were unable to order as quickly and suffered stock-outs as a result. It is this type of innovation that Procter & Gamble and other suppliers learn of and work to incorporate into their own business that represents a benefit of partnering with Wal-Mart. Astute salespeople can identify such companies and develop strategic partnerships that lead to joint development of new products or technologies, important outcomes regardless of the size of the account.

USING TECHNOLOGY TO INCREASE EFFICIENCY

Partnering relationships are built on effective communications. To improve communications with customers, salespeople are using technology more efficiently. Companies are also creating direct links with customers via technology.

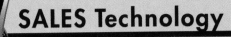
USING TECHNOLOGY TO BUILD RELATIONSHIPS

Richard Langlotz, branch manager for Konica-Minolta, says his average salesperson's territory includes 1,500 potential customers. How can a salesperson keep track of all of those accounts? "They can't," laughs Langlotz.

Konica-Minolta uses GoldMine, a contact management software program. At the end of each day, salespeople input information on the calls they made, including personal information and notes about each customer. Langlotz and other managers can immediately see how each salesperson is doing, where each prospect is in the sales cycle, or summaries of sales performance by activity. During the day, the system then reminds salespeople when their next sales call is to be made, and managers can e-mail the reps with suggestions for the sales call.

Langlotz says that the system has done a lot for new salespeople. "When they walk into a territory, they have all the notes and knowledge of the previous rep. Not only are they more knowledgeable about their customers when they call, they are more confident and a lot happier with their job." With such support, Langlotz's division has enjoyed double-digit sales growth.

Source: Richard Langlotz, personal correspondence; used with permission.

Computer use ranges from providing information during a sales call to analyzing a customer's problems. Ryder Truck developed a computer model that salespeople use to help customers compare the costs of leasing and purchasing trucks. The salesperson questions the customer about estimated mileage and the type of trucks needed, enters the answers into a laptop computer, presses a single key, and reviews the printout with the customer.

Companies are developing video presentations to demonstrate complex product benefits. According to Thomas Bird, president of Gould Inc.'s test and measurements division, "One of the problems in technical sales is that some salespeople do not exactly convey what the inventor or manufacturer had in mind when the product was designed." DVDs played on portable computers can provide the company some control over how key product information is presented.

Companies are also creating direct links with their customers and suppliers. Xerox and Baxter have developed electronic ordering mechanisms with their customers, and IBM uses private Web sites and Lotus Notes software to enable suppliers to communicate with each other and with IBM buyers. Sales Technology 2.1 describes how Konica-Minolta uses GoldMine software to manage relationships.

SUMMARY

As we discussed in Chapter 1, many businesses are moving toward partnering strategies. A key premise is that long-term relationships can enable sellers to capture much, if not all, of a customer's lifetime value. Loyal buyers buy more and are willing to work more closely with sellers in mutually beneficial ways. However, most transactions between buyers and sellers will not be strategic partnerships. Many exchanges will continue to be market transactions and functional relationships.

Functional relationships and strategic partnerships are characterized by a mutual concern of each party for the long-run welfare of the other party. Both types of long-term relationships are based on mutual trust. However, strategic partnerships involve the greatest commitment because the parties are willing to make significant investments in the relationship.

Mutual trust, open communication, common goals, a commitment to mutual gain, and organizational support are key ingredients in successful relationships. These five factors form the foundation for win–win relationships between customers and salespeople.

Customers trust salespeople who are dependable, capable, and concerned about the customers' welfare. To build trust, salespeople need to be consistent in meeting the commitments they make to customers. Salespeople also need to demonstrate their concern for the well-being of customers.

KEY TERMS

attitudinal loyalty
awareness
bartering
behavioral loyalty
boundary-spanning employees
canned sales pitch
commitment
competence
customer orientation
customer relationship management (CRM)
dependability
dissolution
expansion
exploration
functional relationship

honesty
keiretsu
lead user
lifetime customer value (LCV)
likability
market exchange
mutual investment
relational partnership
relationship marketing
solo exchange
strategic partnership
supplier relationship management (SRM)
trust
win–win relationship

ETHICS PROBLEMS

1. If partnerships are win–win, does that mean that market exchanges are win–lose? Is there an ethical difference between win–win and win–lose?
2. A customer is very loyal to one of your competitors but the contract is expiring soon. An RFP (request for proposals) has been written and issued; but as it is written, only that competitor can win the contract renewal. You know that your product and service could satisfy the needs of the company better. Is there an ethics problem here? If so, what is it and why? If not, why not?

QUESTIONS AND PROBLEMS

1. Why are relational partnerships potentially dangerous for selling companies to encourage?
2. Is either form of loyalty more important to the seller than the other? What can a salesperson do to increase loyalty in buyers? How does loyalty relate to lifetime customer value?
3. What are the responsibilities that a customer has in making the relationship work? Should the customer have a relationship manager? If so, what would that person's responsibilities be?
4. How could culture influence the nature of buyer–seller relationships? What are some cultural barriers to developing partnerships in your culture?
5. Which factors should a salesperson consider when deciding whether to develop a close relationship with a customer? How would these factors change when considering functional relationships versus strategic partnerships? What factors should the customer consider?

6. How do buyers calculate profit? What is the role of the relationship type in increasing buyer profit?

7. When a salesperson negotiates price with a buyer, somebody wins and somebody loses. If the seller makes a price concession, the salesperson's company makes less money and the buyer makes more. How is it possible for a buyer and a salesperson to have a win–win relationship and still arrive at a price?

8. Assume you have a functional relationship with a buyer. You have been informed that the next order placed by the buyer is going to be shipped late. The buyer has already told you that the order must be delivered on time. You contact the factory and cannot do anything to speed up delivery. What should you do next?

9. There are five foundational elements to strategic partnerships. How do these differ for relational partnerships? Functional relationships? What if four of the five are strong—what type of relationship is that?

10. What can salespeople do to increase the level of trust a buyer has in them?

CASE PROBLEMS

case **2.1**

How to Lose an Account

Robert Lawrence was aghast. In spite of practicing the sales call four times, in spite of being told before the sales call exactly what to say when the question arose, and in spite of being directed by the account manager how to respond while in the sales call, the regional director of service still blew it. And away walked a $5.5 million customer.

Robert, branch manager for Mobile Connections, knew that the customer, Health Resources of Texas (HRT), was having problems with two of the copiers provided by Mobile. Further, these were recurring problems that should be resolved by replacing the equipment. To make matters worse, one of the problem copiers was used by Sharon Collins, one of the decision makers. He knew that Sharon was going to raise the issue of how Mobile would handle "lemons" and whether Mobile would honor its replacement promise. The service director was also aware of the problems but had not processed the request to replace them yet, so he didn't know with certainty whether the copiers would be approved. But Robert had rehearsed with Tony Lagera, the service director, to say that the company was reviewing the request and the copiers would either be replaced in the week or shifted to areas with less volume.

Sharon raised the question, just as Robert expected. And Tony flubbed it. He hemmed. He hawed. He did everything but answer the question directly. Unfortunately, Robert couldn't just answer for Tony—the service area was Tony's responsibility, not Robert's.

After the call, Robert asked, "So, Tony, how do you think it went?"

"Fine, Robert!" he replied with a smile. "You were right on target about Sharon's question."

"And you think you handled it?"

"Oh yes—I think she really liked my response!"

Robert didn't respond, though he thought about asking Tony why she repeated the question four times. Two weeks later, Robert got a copy of the letter that went to his salesperson, thanking Mobile for the presentation but informing them that Mobile would not be allowed to bid on the job. After serving HRT for three years without any hitch other than those two machines (and there were over 100 machines), Mobile wasn't even going to get a chance to bid. Robert and the account manager sat in stunned silence.

Source: This really happened, but the names have been changed at the request of the innocent. Used with permission.

Questions

1. How could this have been avoided?

2. Was there anything the sales rep or his boss, Robert Lawrence, could have done after the sales call to save the business?

3. Not only were there no other problems during the previous three-year contract, Mobile had originally won the business away from a competitor and significantly improved HRT's situation. Why didn't that enter into the picture?

case **2.2**

American
Advertising

Trent Williams owns and operates a production shirt printing and embroidery company that also sells promotional products manufactured by other companies. For example, he and his team of five salespeople will sell T-shirts on which his company will print the customer's logo, but they may also sell cups and pens with the same logo on them manufactured by other people.

University Books is one of his biggest accounts. Each year University Books has a sales meeting, and Trent usually provides them with a mix of products, including some kind of shirts. The meeting is held in late July. Trent offered University 500 embroidered sleeveless sweaters at a great price as part of an overall package. When University made the decision, they decided to go with a screen-printed polo instead.

No problem, thought Trent. But a problem did arise. One week before the meeting, University wanted to change to the embroidered sweaters. The only problem was that Trent and his salespeople had already sold all of that capacity. The only way he could make the delivery was to bump another order. Of course, none of the salespeople had an order that could be bumped. One order was the first from a new customer with potential to be another University. Another order was from a loyal but small customer at a price with a margin much superior to the University sale. The only other order was for a sorority event that was to be held on Friday, so there was no possible way to bump that one.

What should Trent do?

ACT! ROLE PLAY

In this class, you may role play selling situations to practice concepts discussed in the chapter. In this role play, you are a salesperson for ACT! software. For additional information concerning ACT!, you may want to review the information in the ACT! role play at the end of Chapter 1; additional information can also be found at the end of the text.

Bell Audio is a manufacturer of hearing aids. They have 24 salespeople who call on audiologists, independent Bell retailers, who then sell hearing aids to consumers. There are two sales managers and one national sales vice president.

Seller: You are calling on the national sales vice president, and you would like to understand that person's interest in relationship type. Take a few minutes to prepare some questions that you think will help you determine what relationship will be appropriate. After you are finished, tell the buyer what relationship type (choose only one) you thought you were dealing with and why. See if you were right!

Buyer: As you role play the buyer, pick one of the relationship types. Before the role play starts, think about how you would answer the questions you developed. Also consider what your expectations would be in terms of after-sale service, pricing, and the like based on the relationship type you select.

Note: There is no additional information provided in the Instructor's Manual needed to complete this assignment. However, teaching notes are provided.

ADDITIONAL REFERENCES

Andersen, Paul H., and Paul Chao. "Country-of-Origin Effects in Global Industrial Sourcing: Toward an Integrated Framework." *Management International Review* 43, no. 4 (2003), pp. 339–61.

Anderson, Eugene W.; Claes Fornell; and Sanal K. Mazvancheryl. "Customer Satisfaction and Shareholder Value." *Journal of Marketing* 68, no. 3 (2004), 172–85.

Bantham, John H.; Keven G. Celuch; and Chickery J. Kasouf. "A Perspective of Partnerships Based on Interdependence and Dialectical Theory." *Journal of Business Research* 56 (2003), pp. 265–74.

Bendapudi, Neeli, and Robert P. Leone. "Psychological Implications of Customer Participation in Co-Production." *Journal of Marketing* 67, no.1 (2003), pp. 14–28.

Buschken, Joachim. *Higher Profits Through Customer Lock-In.* Mason OH: Texere, 2004.

Dalhstrom, Robert, and Rhea Ingram. "Social Networks and the Adverse Selection Problem in Agency Relationships." *Journal of Business Research* 56 (2003), pp. 767–73.

De Jong, Ad; Ko de Ruyter; and Jos Lemmink. "Antecedents and Consequences of the Service Climate in Boundary-Spanning Self-Managing Service Teams." *Journal of Marketing* 68, no. 2 (2004), pp. 18–35.

Frels, Judy K.; Tasaddug Shervani; and Rajendra K. Srivastava. "The Integrated Networks Model: Explaining Resource Allocations in Network Markets." *Journal of Marketing* 67, no. 1 (2003), pp. 29–45.

Jones, Michael A.; David L. Mothersbaugh; and Sharon E. Beatty. "Why Customers Stay: Measuring the Underlying Dimensions of Services Switching Costs and Their Differential Strategic Outcomes." *Journal of Business Research* 55 (2002), 441–50.

Kumar, V.; Timothy R. Bohling; and Rajendra N. Ladda. "Antecedents and Consequences of Relationship Intention: Implications for Transaction and Relationship Marketing." *Industrial Marketing Management* 32 (2003), pp. 667–76.

Lemon, Katherine N.; Tiffany Barnett White; and Russell S. Winer. "Dynamic Customer Relationship Management: Incorporating Future Consideration into the Service Retention Decision." *Journal of Marketing* 66, no. 1 (2002), pp. 1–14.

McIntyre, Faye S.; James L. Thomas; K. J. Tullis; and Joyce A. Young. "Assessing Effective Exchange Relationships: An Exploratory Examination." *Journal of Marketing Theory and Practice* 12 (Winter), pp. 36–48.

Preis, Michael W. "The Impact of Interpersonal Satisfaction on Repurchase Decisions." *Journal of Supply Chain Management* 39 (Summer 2003), pp. 30–47.

Reinartz, Werner, and V. Kumar. "The Impact of Customer Relationship Characteristics on Profitable Lifetime Duration." *Journal of Marketing* 67, no. 1 (2003), pp. 77–99.

Ritter, Thomas, and Hans Georg Gemunden. "Interorganizational Relationships and Networks: An Overview." *Journal of Business Research* 56 (2003), pp. 691–97.

Selnes, Fred, and James Sallis. "Promoting Relationship Learning." *Journal of Marketing* 67 (July), pp. 80–95.

Sirdeshmuckh, Deepak; Jagdip Singh; and Barry Sabol. "Consumer Trust, Value, and Loyalty in Relational Exchanges." *Journal of Marketing* 66, no. 1 (2002), pp. 15–37.

Von Wangenheim, Florian. "Situational Characteristics as Moderators of the Satisfaction–Loyalty Link: An Investigation in a Business-to-Business Context." *Journal of Consumer Satisfaction, Dissatisfaction and Complaining Behavior* 16 (2003), pp. 145–68.

Wagner, Judy A.; Noreen M. Klein; and Janet E. Keith. "Buyer–Seller Relationships and Selling Effectiveness: The Moderating Influence of Buyer Expertise and Product Competitive Position." *Journal of Business Research* 56 (2003), pp. 295–302.

Wagner, Stephan M., and Roman Boutellier. "Capabilities for Managing a Portfolio of Supplier Relationships." *Business Horizons* (Nov/Dec 2002), pp. 79–88.

Williams, Michael, and Jill S. Attaway. "At the Interface: The Nature of Buyer–Seller Interactions and Relationships." *Journal of Business Research* 56 (2002), pp. 243–46.

ETHICAL AND LEGAL ISSUES IN SELLING

chapter 3

SOME QUESTIONS ANSWERED
IN THIS CHAPTER . . .

- Why do salespeople need to develop their own codes of ethics?

- What ethical responsibilities do salespeople have toward themselves, their firms, and their customers?

- Do ethics get in the way of being a successful salesperson?

- Which guidelines should salespeople consider when confronting situations involving an ethical issue?

- Which laws apply to personal selling?

PROFILE

After graduating from the University of San Francisco where I studied with Professor Jim Prost, I had to find a business that I enjoyed and felt compassionate about. Selling something that I didn't care about just didn't make sense; I knew I wanted to work in some field that would help other people fulfill their dreams. That is why I decided to join a financial planning firm straight out of college; from day one I listened to my clients to help them reach their dreams.

I moved to a boutique investment firm located in the heart of San Francisco's financial district. As a director of wealth management with Global Crown Capital, I have the opportunity to affect others' lives and create lasting relationships. Experience has shown me that when our relationships are built on trust and integrity, they stand the test of time.

There are many factors that can affect success, and many ways to measure success. My approach is to view each day and each meeting with clients as a new challenge: a challenge to create something better, and a challenge to create some long-term value. Without my clients having the confidence and knowledge of my moral and ethical standards, I doubt that I would have been able to create a solid client base.

There is great satisfaction in learning about the visions and dreams of my clients. It is humbling to be privy to information of such meaning and desire. Part of my job is to focus their interests so that they may reach their goals. I believe in defining a road map for success, and that map must be customized for each individual or entity I work with.

The financial services industry is highly regulated because of a number of unfortunate events. People still remember the financial scandals of Enron and WorldCom, which makes establishing relationships of trust more difficult. These events, although unfortunate, I believe are a long-term positive in the marketplace because there are now more regulations and oversight concerning the investment community, which will ultimately protect the investors' interest.

I have the daily task of maneuvering the markets and planning for the future of my clients, while after work I strive to be the best husband and father I can possibly be. For very successful and driven salespeople it is all too easy to become engrossed with work and lose sight of the important aspects of life. My mentors have demonstrated that the best salespeople have a balanced life.

At Global Crown Capital we believe that our actions define who and what we are, and that we must implement strategies that would be acceptable for our own personal financial plans. My clients turn to me for answers and guidance concerning their financial affairs. When meeting with new prospects to grow my practice, it is important to let them know that I care; without that genuine care they will never become a client.

Visit us on the Web at www.globalcrowncapital.com.

"Without my clients having the confidence and knowledge of my moral and ethical standards, I doubt that I would have been able to create a solid client base."

Eric Pollack, Global Crown Capital

ETHICS AND PERSONAL SELLING

Ethics are the principles governing the behavior of an individual or a group. These principles establish appropriate behavior, indicating what is right and wrong. Defining the term is easy, but determining what the principles are is difficult. What one person thinks is right another may consider wrong. For example, 58 percent of sales managers in one poll report believing that sales contests between salespeople do not generate unethical behavior—such as asking customers to take unwanted orders and then return the merchandise after the contest is over—but 42 percent do believe that unethical behaviors are a consequence of sales contests.[1] So the feelings and experiences of sales managers are mixed when it comes to a commonly accepted practice.

What is ethical can vary from country to country and from industry to industry. For example, offering bribes to overcome bureaucratic roadblocks is an accepted practice in Middle Eastern countries but is considered unethical, and illegal, in the United States. Further, an ethical principle can change over time. For example, some years ago doctors and lawyers who advertised their services were considered unethical. Today such advertising is accepted as common practice.

Here are some examples of difficult situations that salespeople face:

- Should you give an expensive Christmas gift to your biggest customer?
- If a buyer tells you it is common practice to pay off purchasing agents to get orders in his or her country, should you do it?
- Is it acceptable to use a high-pressure sales approach when you know your product is the best for the customer's needs?
- Should you attempt to sell a product to a customer if you know a better product exists for that application?
- If you know about the poor performance features of a competing product, should you tell the customer about them?
- How do you handle a customer who has been lied to about your product by one of your competitors?

thinking **it** through

How would you respond to the statements in the preceding list? Why? How do you think your friends and your family would respond?

ETHICS AND PARTNERING RELATIONSHIPS

Ethical principles are particularly important in personal selling. As discussed in Chapter 2, most businesses try to develop long-term, mutually beneficial relationships with their customers. Salespeople are the official representatives of their companies, responsible for developing and maintaining these relationships, which are built on trust. Partnerships between buyers and sellers cannot develop when salespeople behave unethically or illegally.[2] Further, research shows that trust deteriorates rapidly even in well-established relationships if integrity becomes questionable.[3]

Legal principles guide market exchange relationships. The issues governing buying and selling in these relationships are typically straightforward. The terms and conditions are well defined and can easily be written into a traditional contract.

Ethical principles become increasingly important as firms move to partnerships, particularly strategic partnerships. Because of the high levels of investment and uncertainty, the parties in these relationships cannot accurately assess the potential benefits—the size of the pie—accruing from strategic investments in the relationships or the contributions of each party in producing those benefits. Many issues cannot be reduced to contractual terms. For example, a salesperson might make a concession for a buyer with a special problem, anticipating that the buyer will reciprocate on future orders. Thus the parties in a strategic partnership have to trust one another to divide the pie fairly.

A basic principle of ethical selling is that the customer remains free to make a choice. **Manipulation** eliminates or reduces the buyer's choice unfairly. Salespeople can persuade; but with **persuasion,** one is trying to influence the buyer's decision, not force it. Manipulation is unethical; persuasion is not. Keep that difference in mind as you read the rest of this chapter.

FACTORS INFLUENCING THE ETHICAL BEHAVIOR OF SALESPEOPLE

Exhibit 3.1 illustrates the factors that affect the ethical behavior of salespeople. The personal needs of salespeople, the needs of their companies and customers, company policies, the values of significant others, and the salesperson's personal code of ethics affect ethical choices.[4]

Personal, Company, and Customer Needs

Exhibit 3.2 shows how the personal needs of salespeople can conflict with needs of their firms and their customers. Both the salesperson's company and its customers want to make profits. But sometimes these objectives are conflicting. For example, should a salesperson tell a customer about problems his or her firm is having with a new product? Concealing this information might help to make a

Exhibit 3.1
Factors Affecting Ethical Behavior of Salespeople

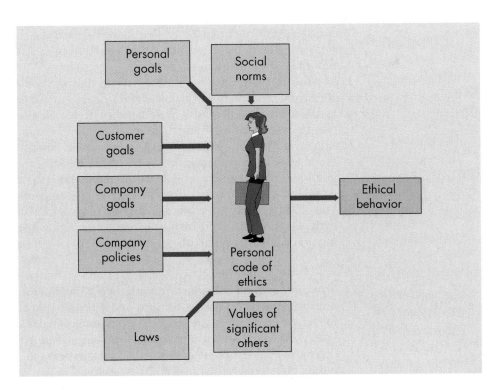

Exhibit 3.2
Conflicting Objectives

Company Objectives	Salesperson Objectives	Customer Objectives
Increase profits.	Increase compensation.	Increase profits.
Increase sales.	Receive recognition.	Solve problems, satisfy needs.
Reduce sales costs.	Satisfy customers.	Reduce costs.
Build long-term customer relationships.	Build long-term customer relationships.	Build relationships with suppliers.
Avoid legal trouble.	Maintain personal code of ethics.	Avoid legal trouble.

sale, increase the company's profits, and enhance the salesperson's chances of getting a promotion and a bonus, but doing so could also decrease the customer's profits when the product does not perform adequately.

Low-balling is one unethical tactic that occurs in large sales. A sales manager who requested anonymity faced an ethical dilemma when his company low-balled a bid. The sale was worth $30 million, but his company adopted a strategy to win the sale by bidding severely below the competition—a number, he says, that would never be sustainable. The company planned to jack up the cost once the customer was committed and the project had started. What surprised this executive was that the unethical strategy came straight from the company's CEO, in spite of this manager's stated objections. The CEO's justification was that the company needed the business and the customer wasn't going to be out anything extra than what the competition was going to charge anyway.[5]

Beth Mitchell, immediately upon graduation, went to work for a company that had a great reputation. The company franchised several businesses, and her job was to find potential franchisees and sell them a franchise. When she starting working at the company, she found that they routinely fired salespeople to avoid paying them commissions and that salespeople were never to admit that any franchisees had failed (they had) and were to browbeat customers until they agreed to purchase. One tactic involved flying prospects to the company's home office and not letting them leave until they had agreed to purchase. Mitchell lasted barely a month before she found another job.

Mitchell's experience is not unusual in that she could solve it only by leaving. Resolving serious ethical problems is difficult, but companies who do resolve ethical issues well experience many benefits. Research shows that a positive ethical climate is related to job satisfaction, commitment to the organization, and intention to stay among salespeople.[6] Organizations that have a positive ethical climate also have salespeople more committed to meeting the organization's goals—somewhat ironic in light of Mitchell's experience.

Ethical conflicts often are not covered by company policies and procedures, and managers may not be available to provide advice. Thus salespeople must make decisions on their own, relying on their ethical standards and understanding of the laws governing these situations.

Company Policies

To maintain good relationships with their companies and customers, salespeople need to have a clear sense of right and wrong so that their companies and customers can depend on them when questionable situations arise. Many companies have codes of ethics for their salespeople to provide guidelines in making ethical decisions. An outline of Motorola's policy appears in Exhibit 3.3. Shell's ethics policy, however, is a book some 20 pages long!

Exhibit 3.3

Ethics Policy for
Motorola Salespeople

Improper Use of Company Funds and Assets

The funds and assets of Motorola may not be used for influential gifts, illegal payments of any kind, or political contributions, whether legal or illegal.

The funds and assets of Motorola must be properly and accurately recorded on the books and records of Motorola.

Motorola shall not enter into, with dealers, distributors, agents, or consultants, any agreements that are not in compliance with U.S. laws and the laws of any other country that may be involved, or that provide for the payment of a commission or fee that is not commensurate with the services to be rendered.

Customer/Supplier/Government Relationships

Motorola will respect the confidence of its customers. Motorola will respect the laws, customs, and traditions of each country in which it operates but, in so doing, will not engage in any act or course of conduct that may violate U.S. laws or its business ethics. Employees of Motorola shall not accept payments, gifts, gratuities, or favors from customers or suppliers.

Conflict of Interest

A Motorola employee shall not be a supplier or a competitor of Motorola or be employed by a competitor, supplier, or customer of Motorola. A Motorola employee shall not engage in any activity where the skill and knowledge developed while in the employment of Motorola is transferred or applied to such activity in a way that results in a negative impact on the present or prospective business interest of Motorola.

A Motorola employee shall not have any relationship with any other business enterprise that might affect the employee's independence of judgment in transactions between Motorola and the other business enterprise.

A Motorola employee may not have any interest in any supplier or customer of Motorola that could compromise the employee's loyalty to Motorola.

Compliance with the code of conduct is a condition of employment. We urge you to read the complete code.

Should any questions remain, you are encouraged to consult your Motorola law department. In the world of business, your understanding and cooperation are essential. As in all things, Motorola cannot operate to the highest standards without you.

Source: Company document.

Values of Significant Others

People acquire their values and attitudes about what is right and wrong from the people they interact with and observe. Some important people influencing the ethical behavior of salespeople are their relatives and friends, other salespeople, and their sales managers. Sales managers are particularly important because they establish the ethical climate in their organization through the salespeople they hire, the ethical training they provide for their salespeople, and the degree to which they enforce ethical standards.[7]

Some people hesitate to pursue a sales career because they think selling will force them to compromise their principles. Research, though, suggests otherwise. One study in the financial services industry showed that salesperson ethical behavior leads to higher customer satisfaction, trust, and loyalty, which mean greater repeat purchases.[8] Another study found similar results for manufacturing firms.[9] As one of our former students now selling commercial real estate told us, "Unethical reps are run out of our industry." Good ethics are good business! Sales managers and salespeople know that.

Laws

In this chapter we examine ethical and legal issues in personal selling. *Laws* dictate which activities society has deemed to be clearly wrong, the activities for which salespeople and their companies will be punished. These laws are reviewed later in the chapter. However, most sales situations are not covered by laws. Salespeople have to rely on their own codes of ethics and/or their firms' and industries' codes of ethics to determine the right thing to do.

A Personal Code of Ethics

Long before salespeople go to work they develop a sense of what is right and wrong—a standard of conduct—from family and friends. Although salespeople should abide by their own codes of ethics, they may be tempted to avoid difficult ethical choices by developing "logical" reasons for unethical conduct. For example, a salesperson may use the following rationalizations:

- All salespeople behave "this way" (unethically) in this situation.
- No one will be hurt by this behavior.
- This behavior is the lesser of two evils.
- This conduct is the price one has to pay for being in business.

Salespeople use such reasoning to avoid feeling responsible for their behavior and being bound by ethical considerations. Even though the pressure to make sales may tempt salespeople to be unethical and act against their internal standards, maintaining an ethical self-image is important. Compromising ethical standards to achieve short-term gains can have adverse long-term effects. When salespeople violate their own principles, they lose self-respect and confidence in their abilities. They may begin to think that the only way they can make sales is to be dishonest or unethical, a downward spiral that can have significant negative effects.

Short-term compromises also make long-term customer relationships more difficult to form. As discussed earlier, customers who have been treated unethically will be reluctant to deal with the salespeople again. Also, they may discuss these experiences with business associates in other companies.

Exhibit 3.4 lists some questions you can ask yourself to determine whether a sales behavior or activity is unethical. The questions emphasize that ethical behavior is determined by widely accepted views of what is right and wrong. Thus you should engage only in activities about which you would be proud to tell your family, friends, employer, and customers.

Your firm can strongly affect the ethical choices you will have to make. What if your manager asks you to engage in activity you consider unethical? There are a number of choices you can make, which are discussed in greater detail in Chap-

Exhibit 3.4
Checklist for Making Ethical Decisions

1. Would I be embarrassed if a customer found out about this behavior?
2. Would my supervisor disapprove of this behavior?
3. Would most salespeople feel that this behavior is unusual?
4. Am I about to do this because I think I can get away with it?
5. Would I be upset if a salesperson did this to me?
6. Would my family or friends think less of me if I told them about engaging in this sales activity?
7. Am I concerned about the possible consequences of this behavior?
8. Would I be upset if this behavior or activity were publicized in a newspaper article?
9. Would society be worse off if everyone engaged in this behavior or activity?

If the answer to any of these questions is yes, the behavior or activity is probably unethical and you should not do it.

ter 16, when we focus on relationships with your manager. From a personal perspective, however, here are three of those choices:

1. *Ignore your personal values and do what your company asks you to do.* Self-respect suffers when you have to compromise principles to please an employer. If you take this path, you will probably feel guilty and be dissatisfied with yourself and your job in the long run.

2. *Take a stand and tell your employer what you think.* Try to influence the decisions and policies of your company and supervisors.

3. *Refuse to compromise your principles.* Taking this path may mean you will get fired or be forced to quit.

You should not take a job with a company whose products, policies, or conduct conflict with your standards. Before taking a sales job, investigate the company's procedures and selling approach to see whether they conflict with your personal ethical standards. The issues concerning the relationship between salespeople and their companies are discussed in more detail in Chapter 16, while methods for evaluating companies are presented in Chapter 17.

SELLING ETHICS AND RELATIONSHIPS

The core principle at work in considering ethics in professional selling is the principle of fairness. The buyer has the right to make the purchase decision with equal and fair access to the information needed to make the decision; further, all competitors should have a fair access to the sales opportunity. Keeping information from the customer or misrepresenting information is not fair because it does not allow the customer to make an informed decision. Kickbacks, bribes, and other unethical activities are unfair to both the customer's organization and to competitors. These and other situations can confront salespeople in their relationships with their customers, competitors, and colleagues (other salespeople).

RELATIONSHIPS WITH CUSTOMERS

Areas of ethical concern involving customers include using deception; offering gifts, bribes, and entertainment; divulging confidential information and rights to privacy; and backdoor selling.

Deception

Deliberately presenting inaccurate information, or lying, to a customer is illegal. However, misleading customers by telling half-truths or withholding important information is a matter of ethics. Frequently salespeople believe it is the customer's responsibility to uncover potential product problems. These salespeople answer questions, perhaps incompletely, and don't offer information that might make a sale more difficult. For example, a salesperson selling satellite communication systems might tell a customer that the system will work in all weather but fail to inform the customer about degradation in quality during storms.

Customers expect salespeople to be enthusiastic about their firm and its products and recognize that this enthusiasm can result in a certain amount of exaggeration as part of the persuasion process. Customers also expect salespeople to emphasize the positive aspects of their products and spend little time talking about the negative aspects. But practicing **deception** by withholding information or telling lies is clearly manipulative, and therefore unethical. Such salespeople take advantage of the trust customers place in them. When buyers uncover these deceptions, they will be reluctant to trust such salespeople in the future.

GOOD ETHICS ARE GOOD BUSINESS

Brad Bischof's most memorable sale took months. One of the nation's largest companies had decided to consolidate its purchases, a decision driven by its supply chain management (SCM) group. That meant that each of two dozen or so business unit managers had to say goodbye to their current vendor and switch to whatever vendor the SCM group decided to choose.

Bischof's organization, Carlson Marketing Group, was none of those current vendors; he was simply one of 30 potential suppliers that started the process. Without someone on the inside as his champion, it was quite a challenge. After several months, SCM cut it to eight, and Carlson made the cut. And that's when the trouble started.

"Most unit managers fought for their vendor, up to a point. But I found myself having to disprove lies about my company on a weekly, almost daily basis," reports Bischof, lies including the poor financial health of his company, past delivery problems, and more. "We met each lie head-on by simply finding data and presenting it to the SCM representatives. We also asked them each time for the source of their information." The SCM group cut the number of potential suppliers from eight to two, and Bischof's Carlson Marketing made the cut. "The lies only got worse, and I found myself spending more time

disproving the false charges than doing meaningful work designing solutions."

The final decision finally came. After six months of spending 70 percent of his time with SCM personnel, the decision was made to implement Carlson Marketing Group. All unit managers agreed to begin implementation, except one; the same one who was the only source of all of the lies about Carlson. This person fought for his former vendor so hard that people began to question why. After an internal investigation, the unit manager left the company.

Was that unit manager on the take? Bischof doesn't know. But he does think the unit manager's strategy backfired. As Bischof reflects, "I think it gave us the opportunity to prove our professionalism. The SCM group realized they needed a vendor they could trust. We proved, over and over, that we were dependable because when we told them we would get information to disprove each allegation, we met or beat each deadline they set." He also refused to knock the competition, focusing instead on what Carlson could do for the customer. Bischof's professional and ethical approach was rewarded with a $15 million sale, the largest of a very successful career.

Source: Brad Bischof, personal communication; used with permission.

Salespeople who fail to give customers complete information about products lose an opportunity to develop trust. By revealing both positive and negative information, salespeople can build credibility. Building Partnerships 3.1 illustrates how being honest and straightforward in a tough situation helped Brad Bischof make the largest sale of his life.

Bribes, Gifts, and Entertainment

Bribes and kickbacks may be illegal. **Bribes** are payments made to buyers to influence their purchase decisions, whereas **kickbacks** are payments made to buyers based on the amount of orders placed. A purchasing agent personally benefits from bribes, but bribes typically have negative consequences for the purchasing agent's firm because the product's performance is not considered in buying decisions.

Taking customers to lunch is a commonly accepted business practice. Most salespeople take customers to lunch occasionally or frequently, and in many instances salespeople use this time to get to know the buyer better rather than pitch business. However, some companies will take customers to sporting events, to play golf, or even on an overnight trip to the company's plant or headquarters. In some cases, these trips can get extreme; the pharmaceutical industry, for example, has come under close governmental regulation for questionable practices regarding exotic, expensive trips for doctors who prescribe certain medication.

Determining which gifts and entertainment activities are acceptable and which are not brings up ethical issues. To avoid these issues, many U.S. companies have policies that forbid employees to accept gifts (more than pencils or coffee cups) or entertainment from suppliers. These firms require that all gifts sent to the employee's home or office be returned. IBM does not allow any gifts, even coffee cups; Wal-Mart, the largest retailer in the world, makes no allowance for entertainment as all contact between buyers and vendors can occur only at business meetings at Wal-Mart's or the vendor's headquarters. On the other hand, many companies have no policy on receiving gifts or entertainment. Some unethical employees will accept and even solicit gifts, even though their company has a policy against such practices.

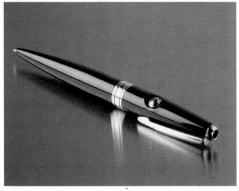

Research shows that nicer gifts, like an expensive pen, are more likely to yield resales; however, gifts that are too nice are too close to bribery to be considered ethical.

I. Boddenberg/Zefa/Masterfile

One reason that salespeople find lavish gift giving so tempting is that it often works. One study compared customer satisfaction and sales with the level of gift given. A $40 gift (gold desk set) resulted in significantly greater repurchases than did a similar $20 gift (silver desk set). But even the silver gift resulted in greater resales than a simple thank-you letter after the initial purchase.[10] Although none of these gifts was too lavish for the situation, the research indicates how effective thank-you gifts can be at influencing future sales.

To develop a productive, long-term relationship, salespeople need to avoid embarrassing customers by asking them to engage in activities they might see as unethical. If a salesperson wants to give a gift out of friendship or invite a customer to lunch to develop a better business relationship, she or he should phrase the offer so that the customer can easily refuse it. For example, a salesperson with a large industrial firm might have this conversation with a customer:

SALESPERSON: John, we have worked well together over the last five years, and I would like to give you something to show my appreciation. Would that be OK?

BUYER: That's very nice of you, but what are you thinking of giving me?

SALESPERSON: Well, I want to give you a Mont Blanc pen. I really enjoy using my pen, and I thought you might like one also. Is that OK?

BUYER: I would appreciate that gift. Thank you.

Buyers typically are sensitive about receiving expensive gifts, according to Shirley Hunter, account manager for Teradata. "It's like getting five dozen roses after a first date. It's embarrassing if anyone finds out, and you have to wonder what's the catch?"[11] Some guidelines for gift giving are as follows:

- Check your motives for giving the gift. The gift should be given to foster a mutually beneficial, long-term relationship, not to obligate or pay off the customer for placing an order.

- Make sure the customer views the gift as a symbol of your appreciation and respect with no strings attached. Never give customers the impression that you are attempting to buy their business with a gift.

- Make sure the gift does not violate the customer's or your firm's policies.

- The safest gifts are inexpensive business items imprinted with the salesperson's company name or logo.

Even when customers encourage and accept gifts, lavish gifts and entertainment are both unethical and bad business. Treating a customer to a three-day fishing trip is no substitute for effective selling. Sales won this way are usually short-lived. Salespeople who offer expensive gifts to get orders may be blackmailed into continually providing these gifts to obtain orders in the future. Customers who can be bribed are likely to switch their business when presented with better offers.

Special Treatment

Some customers try to take advantage of their status to get special treatment from salespeople. For example, a buyer asks a salesperson to make a weekly check on the performance of equipment even after the customer's employees have been thoroughly trained in the operation and maintenance of the equipment. Providing this extra service may upset other customers who do not get the special attention. In addition, the special service can reduce the salesperson's productivity. Salespeople should be diplomatic but careful about undertaking requests to provide unusual services.

Confidential Information

During sales calls salespeople often encounter confidential company information such as new products under development, costs, and production schedules. Offering information about a customer's competitor in exchange for an order is unethical. Many times, though, the request is not that obvious. For example, a customer asks how well your product is selling and you reply, "Great!" The customer then asks, "Well, how is it doing at HEB?" If the customer is told how many cases are sold at HEB, then HEB's right to confidentiality was violated. We'll discuss legal issues about privacy later in this chapter, but ethical issues regarding confidentiality are not always covered by law.

Long-term relationships can develop only when customers trust salespeople to maintain confidentiality. By disclosing confidential information, a salesperson will get a reputation for being untrustworthy. Even the customer who solicited the confidential information will not trust the salesperson, who will then be denied access to information needed to make an effective sales presentation.

Backdoor Selling

Sometimes purchasing agents require that all contacts with the prospect's employees be made through them because they want to be fully informed about and control the buying process. The purchasing agent insists that salespeople get his or her approval before meeting with other people involved in the purchase decision. This policy can make it difficult for a new supplier to get business from a customer using a competitor's products.

Salespeople engage in **backdoor selling** when they ignore the purchasing agent's policy, go around his or her back, and contact other people directly involved in the purchasing decision. Backdoor selling can be very risky and unethical. If the purchasing agent finds out, the salesperson may never be able to get an order. To avoid these potential problems, the salesperson needs to convince the purchasing agent of the benefits to be gained by direct contact with other people in the customer's firm.

Exhibit 3.5 summarizes some research revealing specific sales behaviors that buyers think are unethical or inappropriate. The research suggests that buyers will go out of their way to avoid salespeople who engage in these practices.[12]

Sneaking in the back door to sell behind the purchasing agent's back directly to a user in the buying company is considered unethical and can get a company blacklisted, unable to sell to that buyer again.

RF/Corbis

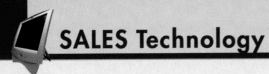

SALES Technology

USING THE COMPANY COMPUTER? KEEP IT PROFESSIONAL!

Communication technology, such as e-mail and the Web, is making it easy for salespeople to communicate with customers and for customers to communicate with various departments within the salesperson's company. These technologies are also making it easy for unethical actions to occur that may seem innocuous.

For example, one salesperson was recently fired because the company computer was used to download pornography from the Internet. Another was fired because he sent a joke to a customer that contained sexual innuendo and she reported it to his company. What is inappropriate in polite company is always inappropriate in e-mail.

While these examples may seem like obvious mistakes, other mistakes may not seem so obvious. For example, no ethical salesperson would purposely violate anti-spamming laws, yet sending blanket e-mails to everyone in a

contact database has yielded spamming complaints from noncustomers and customers alike. Just because you've called on them once does not give you the right to e-mail them repeatedly.

Similarly, there are Web sites where customers can rate the service that a company provided or post complaints about service not provided. Posting fake complaints about competitors and compliments about the salesperson's own company is no more ethical because it is anonymous.

Technology can yield many benefits to salespeople who use it wisely. Using it wisely means remembering that at any time the company can observe how its computers are being used, and customers still want to be treated like people, even if they are on the other end of the Internet.

Exhibit 3.5

Buyers' View of Unethical Sales Behaviors

- Exaggerates benefits of product.
- Passes the blame for something he or she did to someone else.
- Lies about product availability.
- Misrepresents guarantees.
- Lies about competition.
- Sells products that people do not need.
- Makes oral promises that are not legally binding.
- Is not interested in customer needs.
- Answers questions even when he or she does not know the correct answer.
- Sells hazardous products.

Source: Adapted from William Bearden, Thomas Ingram, and Raymond LaForge, *Marketing: Principles and Perspectives* (New York: McGraw-Hill/Irwin, 2004).

RELATIONSHIPS WITH THE SALESPERSON'S COMPANY

Because salespeople's activities in the field cannot be closely monitored, their employers trust them to act in the company's best interests. Professional salespeople do not abuse this trust. They put the interests of their companies above self-interest. Taking this perspective may require them to make short-term sacrifices to achieve long-term benefits for their companies and themselves. Some problem areas in the salesperson–company relationship involve expense accounts, reporting work-time information and activities, and switching jobs. Sales Technology 3.1 illustrates some problems salespeople may have with the use of the company computer.

Expense Accounts

Many companies provide their salespeople with cars and reimburse them for travel and entertainment expenses. Developing a reimbursement policy that prevents salespeople from cheating and still allows them the flexibility they need to cover their territories and entertain customers is almost impossible. Moreover, a lack of tight control can tempt salespeople to use their expense accounts to increase their income.

To do their jobs well, salespeople need to incur expenses. However, using their expense accounts to offset what they consider to be inadequate compensation is unethical. A salesperson who cannot live within the company compensation plan and expense policies has two ethical alternatives: (1) persuade the company to change its compensation plan or expense policy or (2) find another job.

In using the company's expense account, you should act as though you are spending your own money. Eat good food, but don't go to the most expensive restaurant in town. Stay in clean, comfortable, safe lodgings, but not in the best hotel or the best room in a hotel. When traveling, you should maintain the same standards of living and appearance that you do at home.

Reporting Work-Time Information and Activities

Employers expect their salespeople to work full-time. Salespeople on salary are stealing from their employers when they waste time on coffee breaks, long lunches, or unauthorized days off. Even salespeople paid by commission cheat their companies by not working full-time. Their incomes and company profits both decrease when salespeople take time off.

To monitor work activities, many companies ask their salespeople to provide daily call reports. Most salespeople dislike this clerical task. Some provide false information, including calls they never made. Giving inaccurate information or bending the truth is clearly unethical. A failure to get an appointment with a customer is not a sales call. Providing a brief glimpse of a product is not a demonstration.

Switching Jobs

When salespeople decide to change jobs, they have an ethical responsibility to their employers. The company often makes a considerable investment in training salespeople and then gives them confidential information about new products and programs. Over time, salespeople use this training and information to build strong relationships with their customers.

A salesperson may have good reasons to switch jobs. However, if a salesperson goes to work for a competitor, she or he should not say negative things about the past employer. Also, disclosing confidential information about the former employer's business is improper. The ethical approach to leaving a job includes the following:

- Give ample notice. If you leave a job during a busy time and with inadequate notice, your employer may suffer significant lost sales opportunities. Do not be surprised, though, if they escort you out that day. Many companies are concerned about loss of information, as well as lack of productivity of someone who has turned in notice, so the policy may be that you are turned out that day.

- Offer assistance during the transition phase. Help your replacement learn about your customers and territory, if provided the opportunity.

- Don't burn your bridges. Don't say things in anger that may come back to haunt you. Remember that you may want to return to the company or ask the company for a reference in the future. You may even find that the people you worked with move to a company you want to work for or sell to!

- Don't take anything with you that belongs to the company. That includes all of your records and notes on companies you called on, even if you are going to a noncompeting company.

RELATIONSHIPS WITH COLLEAGUES

To be effective, salespeople need to work together with other salespeople. Unethical behavior by salespeople toward their coworkers, such as engaging in sexual harassment and taking advantage of colleagues, can weaken company morale and have a negative effect on the company's reputation.

Sexual Harassment

Sexual harassment includes unwelcome sexual advances, requests for sexual favors, jokes or graffiti, and physical conduct. Harassment is not confined to requests for sexual favors in exchange for job considerations such as a raise or promotion; creating a hostile work environment can be considered sexual harassment. Some actions that are considered sexual harassment are engaging in suggestive behavior, treating people differently because they are male or female, making lewd sexual comments and gestures, joking that has a sexual content, showing obscene photographs, alleging that an employee got rewards by engaging in sexual acts, and spreading rumors about a person's sexual conduct.

Customers as well as coworkers can sexually harass salespeople. Salespeople are particularly vulnerable to harassment from important customers who may seek sexual favors in exchange for their business. Following are some suggestions for dealing with sexual harassment from customers:

Persistent, unwelcome advances are one form of sexual harassment. It is illegal and unethical.

Bob Daemmrich/The Image Works

- Don't become so dependent on one customer that you would consider compromising your principles to retain the customer's business. Develop a large base of customers and prospects to minimize the importance of one customer.

- Tell the harasser in person or write a letter stating that the behavior is offensive, is unacceptable, and must be stopped. Clearly indicate that you are in control and will not be passive.

- Utilize the sexual harassment policies of your firm and your customer's firm to resolve problems. These policies typically state the procedure for filing a complaint, the person responsible for investigating the complaint, the time frame for completing the investigation, and the means by which the parties will be informed about the resolution.

Recent research indicates that sexual harassment is rare; one study found an average of only 1.3 cases per year per company in all areas of the company, not just sales.[13] That study also found, though, that companies are much more worried about making sure their employees have a safe environment in which to work than any fear of lawsuits; in other words, executives want to make sure their people have a pleasant environment in which to work.

Taking Advantage of Other Salespeople

Salespeople can behave unethically when they are too aggressive in pursuing their own goals at the expense of their colleagues. For example, it is unethical to steal leads from other salespeople. Colleagues usually discover such unethical behavior and return the lack of support. Jeff Hostetler, sales director at Tele-Optics, has seen such behavior during tough economic times and likens it to wolves fighting over a chunk of meat. "Not only will reps kill each other, but they will kill the business, too."[14] Such behavior can lead to immediate termination.

RELATIONSHIPS WITH COMPETITORS

Making false claims about competitors' products or sabotaging their efforts is clearly unethical and often illegal. For example, a salesperson who rearranges the display of a competitor's products in a customer's store to make it less appealing is being unethical. This type of behavior can backfire. When customers detect these practices, the reputation of the salespeople and their companies may be permanently damaged.

Another questionable tactic is criticizing a competitor's products or policies. Although you may be tempted to say negative things about a competitor, this approach usually does not work. Customers will assume you are biased toward your own company and its products and discount negative comments you make about the competition. Some customers may even be offended. If they have bought the competitor's products in the past, they may regard these comments as a criticism of their judgment.

LEGAL ISSUES

Society has determined that some activities are clearly unethical and has decided to use the legal system to prevent people from engaging in these activities. Salespeople who violate these laws can cause serious problems for themselves and their companies—problems more serious than just being considered unethical by a buyer. By engaging in illegal activities, salespeople expose themselves and their firms to costly legal fees and millions of dollars in fines.

The activities of salespeople in the United States are affected by three forms of law: statutory, administrative, and common. **Statutory law** is based on legislation passed by either state legislatures or Congress. The main statutory laws governing salespeople are the Uniform Commercial Code and antitrust laws. **Administrative laws** are established by local, state, or federal regulatory agencies. The Federal Trade Commission is the most active agency in developing administrative laws affecting salespeople. However, the Securities and Exchange Commission regulates stockbrokers, and the Food and Drug Administration regulates pharmaceutical salespeople. Finally, **common law** grows out of court decisions. Precedents set by these decisions fill in the gaps where no laws exist.

This section discusses current laws affecting salespeople, but every year important new laws are developed and court decisions rendered. Thus you should contact your firm for advice when a potential legal issue arises.

UNIFORM COMMERCIAL CODE

The **Uniform Commercial Code (UCC)** is the legal guide to commercial practice in the United States. The UCC defines a number of terms related to salespeople.

Agency

A person who acts in place of his or her company is an **agent**. Authorized agents of a company have the authority to legally obligate their firm in a business transaction. This authorization to represent the company does not have to be in writing. Thus, as a salesperson, your statements and actions can legally bind your company and have significant financial impact.

Sale

The UCC defines a **sale** as "the transfer of title to goods by the seller to the buyer for a consideration known as price." A sale differs from a **contract to sell.** Any time a salesperson makes an offer and receives an unqualified acceptance, a contract exists. A sale is made when the contract is completed and title passes from the seller to the buyer.

This buyer is inspecting a shipment of bananas. Because the produce was shipped FOB destination, the buyer is not responsible for the merchandise until it shows up at the buyer's warehouse and can turn down the sale even now if the product is not up to his standard.

Syracuse Newspapers/The Image Works

The UCC also distinguishes between an offer and an invitation to negotiate. A sales presentation is usually considered an **invitation to negotiate.** An **offer** takes place when the salesperson quotes specific terms. The offer specifically states what the seller promises to deliver and what it expects from the buyer. If the buyer accepts these terms, the parties will have established a binding contract.

Salespeople are agents when they have the authority to make offers. However, most salespeople are not agents because they have the power only to solicit written offers from buyers. These written offers, called **orders,** become contracts when they are signed by an authorized representative in the salesperson's company. Sometimes these orders contain clauses stating that the firm is not obligated by its salesperson's statements. However, the buyer usually can have the contract nullified and may even sue for damages if salespeople make misleading statements, even though they are not official agents.

Title and Risk of Loss

If the terms of the contract specify **free on board (FOB) destination,** the seller has title until the goods are received at the destination. In this case any loss or damage incurred during transportation is the responsibility of the seller. The buyer assumes this responsibility and risk if contract terms call for **FOB factory.** The UCC also defines when titles transfer for goods shipped cash on delivery (COD) and for goods sold on consignment. Understanding the terms of the sale and who has title can be useful in resolving complaints about damaged merchandise.

thinking it through

If a salesperson is not an agent, then what is the salesperson? Does not being an agent change the salesperson's obligations to the company in any way? Or to the customer?

Oral versus Written Agreements

In most cases oral agreements between a salesperson and a customer are just as binding as written agreements. Normally, written agreements are required for sales over $500. Salespeople may be the legal representatives of their firms and thus must be careful when signing written agreements.

Obligations and Performance

When the salesperson and the customer agree on the terms of a contract, both firms must perform according to those terms in "good faith." In addition, both parties must perform according to commonly accepted industry practices. Even if salespeople overstate the performance of their products, their firms have to provide the stated performance and meet the terms of the contract.

Warranties

A **warranty** is an assurance by the seller that the products will perform as represented. Sometimes a warranty is called a *guarantee*. The UCC distinguishes between two types of warranties, expressed and implied. An **expressed warranty** is an oral or a written statement by the seller. An **implied warranty** is not actually stated but is still an obligation defined by law. For example, products sold using an oral or a written description (the buyer never sees the products) carry an implied warranty that the products are of average quality. However, if the buyer inspects the product before placing an order, the implied warranty applies only to any performance aspects that the inspection would not have uncovered. Typically, an implied warranty also guarantees that the product can be used in the manner stated by the seller.

Salespeople can create a warranty for their products through inadvertent comments and actions. For example, a chemical company was liable for a product that did not meet the performance standards the salesperson promised, even though the sales brochure contradicted the salesperson's claims for the product. Salespeople can also create an implied warranty when they are knowledgeable about the customer's specific application and recognize that the customer is relying on their judgment.

Salespeople can, but shouldn't, offset the effects of warnings provided by a firm. For example, when securities salespeople indicated that legally required warnings in the documents describing the investment were unimportant and could be ignored, the company offering the securities was liable for millions of dollars when customers were disappointed with the financial returns from the securities.

Problems with warranties often arise when the sale is to a reseller (a distributor or retailer). The ultimate user—the reseller's customer—may complain about a product to the reseller. The reseller, in turn, tries to shift the responsibility to the manufacturer. Salespeople often have to investigate and resolve these issues.

MISREPRESENTATION OR SALES PUFFERY

In their enthusiasm salespeople may exaggerate the performance of products and even make false statements to get an order. Over time, common and administrative laws have defined the difference between illegal misrepresentation and sales puffery. Not all statements salespeople make have legal consequences. However, misrepresentation, even if legal, can destroy a business relationship and may involve salespeople and their firms in lawsuits.

Glowing descriptions such as "Our service can't be beat" are considered to be opinions or **sales puffery.** Customers cannot reasonably rely on these statements. Here are some examples of puffery:

- This is a top-notch product.
- This product will last a lifetime.
- Our school bus chassis has been designed to provide the utmost safety and reliability for carrying the nation's most precious cargo—schoolchildren.
- The most complete line of reliable, economical gas heating appliances.

However, statements about the inherent capabilities of products or services, such as "Our system will reduce your inventory by 40 percent," may be treated as

WALKING THE LINE?

When seniors are your market, walking the line between what is appropriate and what is not can be difficult. One former student described how his family found nearly 4,000 pairs of socks still in their wrappers in the closet at his grandfather's house after they moved him to a nursing home. All was explained shortly after when the family got a phone call from a clerk at a local store. The clerk wanted to know if everything was OK with "Mr. Jones" because he hadn't been in to buy socks lately, something he had done every day for the previous six years! Like many seniors lonely for company, Jones enjoyed the company and attention of the clerks at the store.

Unscrupulous salespeople, however, take advantage of that loneliness and other factors that can influence seniors to make poor decisions. Tyrone Clark, founder of BCA, was barred from selling securities in Massachusetts after creating a seminar designed to sell investments. The seminar was designed to alarm and disturb seniors about their future so that they would make investments with Clark's company.

The state of Alabama assessed a $225,000 penalty against another investment salesperson, Jim Benson Moorehead, and his company AmSouth Investment Services, a division of AmSouth Bank. The problem? Moorehead was accused of misrepresenting the risks associated with variable annuities, either by lying or by failing to disclose important information. While civil suits were also pressed against Moorehead, these cases illustrate the need for extra caution if there is any suspicion that the customer may not have the ability or the knowledge to make an effective decision without reliance on the salesperson. The greater the need for reliance, the greater care that must be taken by the salesperson to help the buyer make the right choice.

Sources: "Mr. Jones," used with permission; Jennifer Gilbert, "The Right Balance," *Sales and Marketing Management*, November 2004, pp. 24–29.

---

statements of fact and warranties. Here are examples of such statements found to be legally binding:

- Mechanically, this oil rig is a 9 on a scale of 10.
- Feel free to prescribe this drug to your patients, doctor. It's nonaddicting.
- This equipment will keep up with any other machine you are using and will work well with your other machines.

Factual statements become particularly strong indicators of an expressed warranty when salespeople sell complex products to unsophisticated buyers. In these situations buyers rely on the technical expertise and integrity of the salespeople. However, when salespeople deal with knowledgeable buyers, the buyers are obligated to go beyond assertions made by the salespeople and make their own investigation of the product's performance.

Bryan Macakanja with Pulte Homes unintentionally made a promise that the company no longer offered. For a short time, Pulte included a free washer and dryer with each house. "Apparently, I missed the e-mail that announced the end of the promotion, and promised a washer and dryer to a couple. They were pretty upset when they found that there were no washer and dryer in their new house." Macakanja honored his promise, though, buying a washer and dryer out of his own pocket. "I made the promise; I had to keep it."[15] This promise could have resulted in a charge of misrepresentation; however, Macakanja was more concerned about the moral than the legal implications. Selling Scenario 3.1 presents two examples where what is unethical was also illegal.

U.S. salespeople need to be aware of both U.S. laws and laws in the host country when selling internationally. All countries have laws regulating marketing and selling activities. In Canada all claims and statements made in advertisements and sales presentations about comparisons with competitive products must pass the **credulous person standard.** This standard means the company and the salesperson have to pay damages if a reasonable person could misunderstand the statement. Thus a statement like "This is the strongest axle in Canada" might be considered puffery in the United States but be viewed as misleading in Canada unless the firm had absolute evidence that the axle was stronger than any other axle sold in Canada.

To avoid legal and ethical problems with misrepresentation, you should try to educate customers thoroughly before concluding a sale. You should tell the customer as much about the specific performance of the product as possible. Unless your firm has test results concerning the product's performance, you should avoid offering an opinion about the product's specific benefits for the customer's application. If you don't have the answer to a customer's question, don't make a guess. Say that you don't know the answer and will get back to the customer with the information.

ILLEGAL BUSINESS PRACTICES

The Sherman Antitrust Act of 1890, the Clayton Act of 1914, the Federal Trade Commission Act of 1914, and the Robinson-Patman Act of 1934 prohibit unfair business practices that may lessen competition. The courts have used these laws to create common law that defines the illegal business practices discussed in this section.

BUSINESS DEFAMATION

Business defamation occurs when a salesperson makes unfair or untrue statements to customers about a competitor, its products, or its salespeople. These statements are illegal when they damage the competitor's reputation or the reputation of its salespeople.

Following are some examples of false statements made about competitors that have been found illegal:

- Company X broke the law when it offered you a free case of toilet paper with every 12 cases you buy.
- Company X is going bankrupt.
- You shouldn't do business with Company X. Mr. Johnson, the CEO, is really incompetent and dishonest.

You should avoid making negative comments about a competitor, its salespeople, or its products unless you have proof to support the statements.

Reciprocity

Reciprocity is a special relationship in which two companies agree to buy products from each other. For example, a manufacturer of computers agrees to use microprocessors from a component manufacturer if the component manufacturer agrees to buy its computers. Such interrelationships can lead to greater trust and cooperation between the firms. However, reciprocity agreements are illegal if one company forces another company to join in the agreement. Reciprocity is legal only when both parties consent to the agreement willingly.

Tying Agreements

In a **tying agreement** a buyer is required to purchase one product in order to get another product. For example, a customer who wants to buy a copy machine is required to buy paper from the same company, or a distributor that wants to stock one product must stock the manufacturer's entire product line. Because they reduce competition, tying agreements typically are illegal. They are legal only when the seller can show that the products must be used together—that is, that one product will not function properly unless the other product is used with it.

Tying agreements are also legal when a company's reputation depends on the proper functioning of equipment. Thus a firm can be required to buy a service contract for equipment it purchases, although the customer need not buy the contract from the manufacturer.

Conspiracy and Collusion

An agreement between competitors before customers are contacted is a **conspiracy,** whereas **collusion** refers to competitors working together while the customer is making a purchase decision. For example, competitors are conspiring when they get together and divide up a territory so that only one competitor will call on each prospect. Collusion occurs when competitors agree to charge the same price for equipment that a prospect is considering. These examples of collusion and conspiracy are illegal because they reduce competition.

Interference with Competitors

Salespeople may illegally interfere with competitors by

- Trying to get a customer to break a contract with a competitor.
- Tampering with a competitor's product.
- Confusing a competitor's market research by buying merchandise from stores.

Restrictions on Resellers

Numerous laws govern the relationship between manufacturers and resellers—wholesalers and retailers. At one time it was illegal for companies to establish a minimum price below which their distributors or retailers could not resell their products. Today this practice, called **resale price maintenance**, is legal in some situations.

Manufacturers do not have to sell their products to any reseller that wants to buy them. Sellers can use their judgment to select resellers as long as they announce their selection criteria in advance. One sales practice considered unfair is providing special incentives to get a reseller's salespeople to push products. For example, salespeople for a cosmetics company may give a department store's cosmetics salespeople prizes based on the sales of the company's product. These special incentives, called **spiffs** (or **push money**), are legal only if the reseller knows and approves of the incentive and it is offered to all of the reseller's salespeople. *Spiff* stands for special promotion incentive fund, and dates back to a time when there was more selling by retail salespeople. Even if legal, though, not everyone agrees that spiffs are ethical.[16]

Using spiffs to promote one product over another, such as one brand of computer over another, is legal, but research shows consumers believe it to be unethical.

Ryan McVay/Getty Images/MGH-DIL

Price Discrimination

The Robinson-Patman Act became law because independent wholesalers and retailers wanted additional protection from the aggressive marketing tactics of large chain stores. Principally, the act forbids price discrimination in interstate commerce. Robinson-Patman applies only to interstate commerce, but most states have passed similar laws to govern sales transactions between buyers and sellers within the same state.

Court decisions related to the Robinson-Patman Act define **price discrimination** as a seller giving unjustified special prices, discounts, or services to some customers and not to others. To justify a special price or discount, the seller must prove that it results from (1) differences in the cost of manufacture, sale, or delivery; (2) differences in the quality or nature of the product delivered; or (3) an attempt to meet prices offered by competitors in a market. Thus a seller must treat all customers equally. If a seller offers a price discount or special service to one customer, the seller must offer the same price or service to all customers. Different prices can be charged, however, if the cost of doing business is different. For example, a customer who buys in large volume can be charged a lower price if the manufacturing and shipping charges for higher-volume orders are lower than they are for smaller orders.

Firms also may not offer special allowances to one reseller unless those allowances are made available to competing resellers. Because most resellers compete in limited geographic areas, firms frequently offer allowances in specific regions of the country.

Privacy Laws

Privacy laws limit the amount of information that a firm can obtain about a consumer and specify how that information can be used or shared. The Gramm-Leach-Bliley Act, passed in 1999, requires written notification to customers regarding privacy policies. Note that the law does not discriminate in how the information was obtained. In other words, the law is the same for a customer who fills out a credit application or a customer who responds to questions from the salesperson. Although this law applies primarily to financial institutions, a second phase of the act became law in 2003, broadening its application. Any company that publishes a privacy policy is expected, by regulation of the Federal Trade Commission, to follow that policy and is liable to prosecution if it uses the information inappropriately.

European Union law is even more stringent than U.S. law. The application of privacy applies to many more settings, and transfer of information is forbidden in nearly all circumstances. Further, the law can apply to information that could be shared among non-EU subsidiaries, which means that in some instances, an account manager in Europe cannot share information with an American colleague.

Do-Not-Call Law

The Federal Do-Not-Call registry took effect in 2003, and limits the conditions under which anyone on the registry may be telephoned at home. A salesperson, for example, cannot call the number of someone on the registry if the person is not already a customer. This registry was set up by the Federal Trade Commission (FTC) under its ability to set rules for commerce, and is an administrative law. However, the FTC has the ability to levy fines against companies and individuals who violate the rules, as some companies have already learned. The rules do not apply to business phones.

INTERNATIONAL ETHICAL AND LEGAL ISSUES

Ethical and legal issues are very complex in international sales. Value judgments and laws vary widely across cultures and countries. Behavior that is commonly accepted as proper in one country can be completely unacceptable in another country. For example, a small payment to expedite the loading of a truck is considered a cost of doing business in some Middle Eastern countries but may be viewed as a bribe in the United States.

Many countries make a clear distinction between payments for lubrication and payments for subordination. **Lubrication** involves small sums of money or gifts, typically made to low-ranking managers or government officials, in countries where these payments are not illegal. The lubrication payments are made to get the official or manager to do the job more rapidly—to process an order more quickly or to provide a copy of a request for a proposal. For example, Halliburton, the company hired to rebuild Iraq, says, "Sometimes, the company (Halliburton) may be required to make facilitating or expediting payments to a low-level government employee or employee in some other countries than the United States to expedite or secure the routine governmental action. . . . Such facilitating payments may not be illegal. . . . Accordingly, facilitating payments must be strictly controlled and every effort must be made to eliminate or minimize such payments."[17] The policy goes on to say that any such payments must have advance authorization from the company's legal department so that there will be no question as to whether the payment is lubrication or subordination. **Subordination** involves paying larger sums of money to higher-ranking officials to get them to do something that is illegal or to ignore an illegal act. Even in countries where bribery is common, subordination is considered unethical.[18]

RESOLVING CULTURAL DIFFERENCES

What do you do when the ethical standards in a country differ from the standards in your country? This is an age-old question. Cultural relativism and ethical imperialism are two extreme answers to this question. **Cultural relativism** is the view that no culture's ethics are superior. If the people in Indonesia tolerate bribery, their attitude toward bribery is no better or worse than that of people in Singapore who refuse to give or accept bribes. When in Rome, do as the Romans do. But is it right for a European pharmaceutical company to pay a Nigerian company to dispose of the pharmaceutical company's highly toxic waste near Nigerian residential neighborhoods, even though Nigeria has no rules against toxic waste disposal?

On the other hand, **ethical imperialism** is the view that ethical standards in one's home country should be applied to one's behavior across the world. This view suggests, for example, that Saudi Arabian salespeople working for a U.S. firm should go through the same sexual harassment training U.S. salespeople do, even though the strict conventions governing relationships between men and women in Saudi Arabia make the training meaningless and potentially embarrassing.

Adopting one of these extreme positions is probably not the best approach. To guide your behavior in dealing with cultural differences, you need to distinguish between what is merely a cultural difference and what is clearly wrong. You must respect core human values that should apply in all business situations but also respect local traditions and use the cultural background to help you decide what is right and what is wrong. For example, exchanging expensive gifts is common in Japanese business relationships, although it may be considered unethical in Western cultures. Most Western firms operating in Japan now accept this practice as an appropriate local tradition. On the other hand, exposing people in less developed countries to hazardous waste is clearly wrong no matter where it takes place. However, selling some fungicides banned in the United States may be acceptable in equatorial countries, because the chemicals may not have the same long-term toxic effects in high-temperature, humid environments.

Research indicates that salespeople, particularly those who operate in foreign cultures, are in significant need of corporate support and guidance in handling cultural ethical differences. Even a high level of personal morality may not prevent an individual from violating a law in a sales context, so it is imperative that companies establish specific standards of conduct, provide ethical training, and monitor behavior to enforce standards as uniformly as possible around the globe.[19]

LEGAL ISSUES

Regardless of the country in which U.S. salespeople sell, they are subject to U.S. laws that prohibit participating in unauthorized boycotts, trading with enemies of the United States, or engaging in activities that adversely affect the U.S. economy. Under the antiboycott law, it is illegal for U.S. firms and their salespeople to be involved in an unauthorized boycott of a foreign country. Any attempt to cooperate in such a boycott must be reported. For example, a large hospital supply company was found guilty of violating this law when it closed its manufacturing plant in Israel to remove its name from an Arab blacklist.

The **Foreign Corrupt Practices Act** makes it illegal for U.S. companies to pay bribes to foreign officials. Violations of the law can result in sizable fines for company managers, employees, and agents who knowingly participate in or authorize the payment of such bribes. However, an amendment to the act permits small lubrication payments when they are customary in a culture.

The U.S. laws concerning bribery are much more restrictive than laws in other countries. For example, in Italy and Germany bribes made outside the countries are clearly defined as legal and tax deductible.

SUMMARY

This chapter discussed the legal and ethical responsibilities of salespeople. These responsibilities are particularly important in personal selling because salespeople may face conflicts between their personal standards and the standards of their firms and customers.

Salespeople's ethical standards determine how they will conduct relationships with their customers, employers, and competitors. Relations with customers involve the use of entertainment and gifts and the disclosure of confidential information. Relations with employers involve expenses and job changes. Finally, salespeople must be careful in how they talk about competitors and treat competitive products.

Many companies have ethical standards that describe the behavior expected of their salespeople. In evaluating potential employers, salespeople should consider these standards.

Salespeople also encounter many situations not covered by company statements and therefore must develop personal standards of right and wrong. Without personal standards, salespeople will lose their self-respect and the respect of their company and customers. Good ethics are good business. Over the long run, salespeople with a strong sense of ethics will be more successful than salespeople who compromise their own and society's ethics for short-term gain.

Statutory laws (such as the Uniform Commercial Code) and administrative laws (such as Federal Trade Commission rulings) guide the activities of salespeople in the United States. Selling in international markets is quite complex, however, because of cultural differences in ethical judgments and laws that relate to sales activities in various countries.

KEY TERMS

administrative law
agent
backdoor selling
bribes
business defamation

collusion
common law
conspiracy
contract to sell
credulous person standard

cultural relativism
deception
ethical imperialism
ethics
expressed warranty
free on board (FOB) destination
FOB factory
Foreign Corrupt Practices Act
implied warranty
invitation to negotiate
kickbacks
lubrication
manipulation
offer
orders

persuasion
price discrimination
privacy laws
reciprocity
resale price maintenance
sale
sales puffery
sexual harassment
spiffs (push money)
statutory law
subordination
tying agreement
Uniform Commercial Code (UCC)
warranty

QUESTIONS AND PROBLEMS

1. There are certainly many ethical and legal issues in selling, as this chapter demonstrates. Do you think there are more in selling than other jobs, such as accounting, finance, retail store management, or the like? Why or why not?

2. For centuries the guideline for business transactions was the Latin term *caveat emptor* (let the buyer beware). This principle suggests that the seller is not responsible for the buyer's welfare. *Pick 4* Is this principle still appropriate in modern business transactions? Why or why not?

3. You are calling on an account when the customer asks if you are going out of business. "Of course not!" you reply. "Why do you ask?" Your competitor, it seems, has been saying that you are within a week of declaring bankruptcy. How do you respond to the customer? What other action should you take?

4. Some professors believe that ethics cannot be taught. Do you agree? Why or why not?

5. What is the relationship between the law and ethics?

6. Your customer asks you what you think of a competitor's product. You know from experience with other customers that it is very unreliable and breaks down frequently. Further, given this particular customer's needs, you expect that it would be an even bigger problem if the customer chose this product. How do you respond? Be specific as to what you would say.

7. Your company has a contact management software system where you enter in all of the information you can about your customers. The

company wants to partner with another firm to comarket products. They want to give your database to the other firm so the other firm can create marketing pieces and e-mail them to your clients. Is this legal? Is it ethical? Why or why not?

8. What is the difference between persuasion and manipulation? Into which of those two categories would you place misrepresentation, and why?

9. For each of the following situations, evaluate the salesperson's action and indicate what you think the appropriate action would be.

   a. A power tool manufacturer begins a program of providing extra incentives to retail clerks in home improvement centers. The salespeople for the power tool company are instructed to contact retail clerks and offer them $10 for each item they sell from the manufacturer's product line. The company instructs the salespeople not to mention this program to the management of the retail stores because they plan to do this in all stores.

   b. In Japan, a young, inexperienced salesperson is given the responsibility for sales. When a buyer confronts the salesperson with a demand for the gift of a nice watch, hinting that no sales are possible without it, the salesperson complies.

   c. A customer asks a salesperson selling small business computers in Canada whether the computer has software for an inventory control system. The salesperson replies that an inventory control software package is available as part of the standard software system that comes with each unit. The salesperson has answered the question truthfully but has failed to mention that the inventory control software is useful only in a few special situations, of which this customer's situation is probably not one.

d. You join a frequent flyer program of American Airlines, and then use American exclusively for all of your business travel, even if it costs 15 percent more, so you can get more miles.

e. The custom of the trade is that competitive firms submit bids based on specifications provided by the buyer; then the buyer places an order with the firm offering the lowest bid. After a salesperson submits a bid, the purchasing agent calls him and indicates the bid is too high; the lowest bid so far is almost 8 percent lower than that. The buyer asks the salesperson to submit another bid at a price at least 10 percent lower.

f. A customer gives a salesperson a suggestion for a new service. The salesperson does not turn in the idea to her company, even though the company's policy manual states that all customer ideas should be submitted with the monthly expense report. Instead, the salesperson quits her job and starts her own business using the customer's suggestion.

g. Jim Hanson is a sales representative for a plastics manufacturer. His company has always had a policy of uniform pricing for all customers. One of his largest customers, Hoffman Container, always tries to bargain for special prices. The buyer is now threatening to use another supplier unless Jim agrees to a special price concession. Jim's sales manager has agreed to the concession. Jim has just gotten a similar-size order from one of Hoffman's competitors at a price 10 percent higher than Hoffman is demanding. What should Jim do? Does Jim have any responsibility to Hoffman's competitor?

h. A few months after joining a company, you learn about a credit card that gives you a 20 percent cash refund on meals at certain restaurants. You get the card and start taking clients to restaurants offering the rebate, pocketing the rebate.

CASE PROBLEMS

case **3.1**

Optima Personnel

Jack Bowen, recent college graduate, sat in a small conference room on his first day with Optima Personnel listening to top sales rep Javier Martinez describe how to sell. Optima Personnel is a matchmaker, matching employers with potential employees for a fee paid by the employer. "You start off by cold-calling, calling people who, when they first hear your voice, think they don't want to talk to you. Then you prove them wrong."

The job is to convince people they want a new job or to convince other people to hire the ones who want the job. "You call a company, and instead of saying that you are a personnel consultant and asking if they have any staffing needs, you say, 'Hi, I'm Javier and I've got a great candidate for your company, came straight from your competitor.' Even though you just made that up, it sounds pretty good, right? And that's the point, you want them to think it sounds good and they want to hear more."

Javier went on to say, "If the company you just called wants to hear more about this candidate, you pick up the phone and call until you find one. Call all the company's competitors if you have to."

Jack interrupted, "But if the company says they're not interested in this competitor's employee, what do you do?"

"That's the beauty of it," laughed Javier. "Ask what they are interested in. You're always looking for jobs that need filling." Javier paused. "Or people who want a job. I use the same approach when calling potential employees. Say, 'I know a company that's looking for someone with your skills and experience.' You say this even though you don't have any such client. You just say it. At the very least, he'll send a résumé so you can add him to your database and you can begin to look for a position."

Questions

1. Apply the checklist in Exhibit 3.4 to this situation. Assume there are ethical issues with Javier's practice. What are they? Why would those issues reflect unethical choices?
2. What arguments would Javier probably use to justify this practice?
3. How widespread do you think such behavior is in this business?

case **3.2**

Perfect Solutions

Perfect Solutions manufactures and distributes chemicals across North America. Usually the company sells to a distributor, who then sells to the customer who uses the chemicals. Bill "Hoot" Jernigan is Nancy Adams's biggest customer. His business, which distributes chemicals in Kansas and Missouri as well as parts of Illinois, represents nearly 15 percent of Nancy's annual sales. Recently Nancy acquired a new account in the same area, Crago Chemicals, which has the potential to be just as large. Her most recent meeting with Hoot, though, went like this:

"Look, Crago Chemicals underbid us on the Hannibal city contract by 10 percent. You must be offering them a better price than us, and I want to know why," said Hoot.

Nancy knew that Crago bid that job with no profit in order to expand into that part of Missouri, and that the price she quoted them was actually 5 percent more than Hoot's. "Hoot, I'm not giving them a better price—they don't buy as much as you do from us so I can't."

"Huh. You'll have to do better than that. You know that the Caterpiller contract is coming up, and it is going to be big. I want to know what they intend to do about it."

"Hoot, if I told you their pricing strategy, as if I knew it, why would you ever trust me with your information?"

"C'mon. I'm your biggest customer. We have to stick together."

"Well, I don't know their strategy."

"Try to find out. And while you're at it, I think I can get the Hudson Pulp and Paper account away from National if you'll give me just a 5 percent discount on those products."

Nancy knew she was as low as she could go pricing wise. But if she gave him a few barrels a month free and marked it down as a trial, that would work. Plus, National was not one of her accounts—adding Hudson would mean another $100,000 in revenue per month.

Questions

1. What should she do about the Crago Chemical situation? Should she try to find out if Crago plans to bid on Caterpillar and if so, what their strategy is?
2. What should she do about the Hudson account?
3. Describe her relationship with Hoot. Where should she go with this account in the future?

ACT! ROLE PLAY

McGillicuddy & Frasier (M&F) is a national distributor of medical equipment. You are calling on Frasier, and everything seems to be going quite well. M&F has 48 salespeople, managed by six sales managers who report to Frasier. Currently they e-mail sales call reports to their managers at the end of each week, and sales are forecast for the following week. Frasier uses these forecasts to manage inventory, but always orders less than forecast because salespeople are overly optimistic. Sales are also lower than he would prefer, and he thinks with better knowledge of what is happening in each account, he could help salespeople perform better.

Time to ask for the order. The seller should summarize how ACT! provides the manager with the ability to summarize the sales team's activities on a daily basis. Salespeople no longer have to e-mail their reports; they simply have to log into ACT! and enter the day's activities. Not only will ACT! give the managers a daily forecast, it will also summarize each rep's performance by level of the sales process. The manager can then use that information to pinpoint how to improve each rep's performance.

Once you've summarized, ask for an order of 55 units. Each buyer will be given a sheet with information as to how to respond.

ADDITIONAL REFERENCES

Abratt, Russell, and Neale Penman. "Understanding Factors Affecting Salespeople's Perceptions of Ethical Behavior in South Africa." *Journal of Business Ethics* 35 (2002), pp. 269–80.

Bowen, Shannon A. "Organizational Factors Encouraging Ethical Decision Making: An Exploration into the Case of an Exemplar." *Journal of Business Ethics* 52 (2004), pp. 311–24.

Bowie, Norman E., and Thomas W. Dunfee. "Confronting Morality in Markets." *Journal of Business Ethics* 38 (2002), pp. 381–93.

Brinkman, Johannes, and Knut J. Ims. "A Conflict Case Approach to Business Ethics." *Journal of Business Ethics* 53 (2004), pp. 123–36.

Canady, Henry. "How Does Your Company Entertain Customers?" *Selling Power,* October 2004, pp. 13–116.

Christie, P. Maria Joseph; Ik-Whan G. Kwon; Philipp A. Stoeberl; and Raymond Baumhart. "A Cross-Cultural Comparison of Ethical Attitudes of Business Managers: India, Korea, and the United States." *Journal of Business Ethics* 46 (September 2003), pp. 263–89.

Fisher, Josie. "Social Responsibility and Ethics: Clarifying the Concepts." *Journal of Business Ethics* 52 (2004), pp. 391–400.

Forte, Amanda. "Business Ethics: A Study of the Moral Reasoning of Selected Business Managers and the Influence of Organizational Ethical Climate." *Journal of Business Ethics* 53 (2004), pp. 167–73.

Kavathatzopoulos, Iordanis. "The Use of Information and Communication Technology in the Training for Ethical Competence in Business." *Journal of Business Ethics* 48 (2003), pp. 43–51.

Ross, William T., and Diana C. Robertson. "A Typology of Situational Factors: Impact on Salesperson Decision-Making about Ethical Issues." *Journal of Business Ethics* 46 (September 2003), pp. 213–35.

Weeks, William A.; Terry W. Loe; Lawrence B. Chonko; and Kirk Wakefield. "The Effect of Perceived Ethical Climate on the Search for Sales Force Excellence." *Journal of Personal Selling & Sales Management* 24 (Summer 2004), pp. 199–214.

BUYING BEHAVIOR AND THE BUYING PROCESS

chapter **4**

part **2**

SOME QUESTIONS ANSWERED IN THIS CHAPTER . . .

- What are the different types of customers?

- How do organizations make purchase decisions?

- Which factors do organizations consider when evaluating products and services?

- Who is involved in the buying decision?

- What should salespeople do in the different types of buying situations?

- Which changes are occurring in organizational buying, and how will these changes affect salespeople?

PROFILE

When I graduated from Texas A&M with a degree in engineering, I knew that I would play some role in purchasing products, but I had no idea how large this role would become. As an engineering manager for the John Deere Ottumwa Works located in Ottumwa, Iowa, I was assigned to a similar John Deere manufacturing factory in Arc-les-Gray, France for nearly two years. These facilities develop and manufacture machinery used in the harvesting of hay and forage. This may seem like an old-fashioned business to be in but, globally, the total hay and forage machinery market is estimated at $2.5 billion. Following my return to the Ottumwa factory, I worked with teams from both factories to standardize and streamline our processes, designs, and components, all with big implications for our suppliers.

The John Deere brand is based on a tradition of quality and reliability. With farm commodity prices currently at 1950s' levels, our customers look to us to provide machines at prices and productivity levels that bring real value to their operations. As a producer, Deere continually looks to our suppliers in the same way. Because the costs of basic commodities such as steel and oil continue to rise, selecting a component supplier challenges us to strike the right balance between quality, cost, reliability, and delivery.

Like other companies, Deere leverages the costs of developing and manufacturing products through worldwide standardization of designs and components. Design centers are located on all continents except Antarctica and Australia. Many of these design centers are developing products that can be produced at other John Deere manufacturing facilities around the world. That standard production means lower costs and higher quality.

To enable manufacturing at multiple worldwide facilities, the product development processes and tools must be the same everywhere. This covers not only the engineering software we use to design products but the manufacturing and sourcing tools as well. Such standardization allows Deere to leverage these activities across all of the diverse product lines. Software tools provide a common look and feel to supplies worldwide, allowing them to view early part drawings, receive quote requests, and return process qualification information much more easily for any John Deere facility in the world.

Many of our products share common components such as bearings, tires, switches, hydraulic pumps, etc. Deere & Company's corporate Supply Management department centralizes many of the procurement activities so that Deere can leverage information on worldwide suppliers. A supplier who does a great job at our France location can use that reputation if trying to earn business in Iowa. In addition, buying for worldwide volume requirements means we can ask for lower prices, better financial terms, or special support during the negotiation.

Suppliers who want to sell to John Deere must not only understand the product needs but must also understand the worldwide sourcing opportunities in their own industries. Many of the Deere suppliers have been under the same pressure and have made efforts to identify alternate manufacturing sources worldwide. The result is to provide Deere with the same product but at a lower cost.

Sales personnel calling on design centers work with Deere to ensure that the components meet the requirements of the product. I've worked with many sales representatives calling on the Ottumwa factory via teleconference with my colleagues in

A supplier who does a great job at our France location can use that reputation if trying to earn business in Iowa.

Marvin Wagner, Engineering Manager

Arc-les-Gray. Such communication is needed if we're to achieve the benefits of global supply management.

For more about Deere & Company, visit us at our Web site at www.johndeere.com

TYPES OF CUSTOMERS

Business is full of a wide variety of customers, including producers, resellers, government agencies, institutions, and consumers. Each of these customer types has different needs and uses a different process to buy products and services. In many situations, salespeople will have only one type of customer; but in other territories, they may have many different types of customers. Thus salespeople may need to use different approaches when selling to different types of customers.

PRODUCERS

Producers buy products and services to manufacture and sell their products and services to customers. Buyers working for producers are involved in two types of buying situations: buying products that will be included in the products the company is manufacturing or buying products and services to support the manufacturing operation.

OEM PURCHASERS

Buyers for **original equipment manufacturers (OEMs)** purchase goods (components, subassemblies, raw and processed materials) to use in making their products. For example, General Motors (GM) buys glass windshields from PPG and uses them in the automobiles GM sells to consumers. The windshields directly affect the performance and cost of GM's cars. GM spends more than $60 billion annually—more than $170 million each day—for products such as steel, upholstery, and tires.

Salespeople selling OEM products need to demonstrate that their products help their customers produce products that will offer superior value. For example, Intel microprocessors have such a strong reputation for quality and performance that personal computer manufacturers advertise that Intel microprocessors are inside their computers.

Most OEM products are bought in large quantities on an annual contract. The purchasing department negotiates the contract with the supplier; however, engineering and production departments play a major role in the purchase decision. Engineers evaluate the products and may prepare specifications for a custom design. The production department works with the supplier to make sure that the OEM products are delivered "just in time."

OEM customers are building long-term relationships with a limited number of OEM suppliers. Thus relationship building with more than one department in a customer firm is particularly important when selling OEM products.

END USERS

When producers buy goods and services to support their own production and operations, they are acting as **end users.** End-user buying situations include the purchase of capital equipment; maintenance, repair, and operating (MRO) supplies; and services. **Capital equipment** items are major purchases, such as mainframe computers and machine tools that the producer uses for a number of years. **MRO supplies** include paper towels and replacement parts for machinery. Services include Internet and telephone connections, employment agencies, consultants, and transportation.

Because capital equipment purchases typically require major financial commitments, capital equipment salespeople need to work with a number of people involved in the purchase decision, including high-level corporate executives. These salespeople need to demonstrate the reliability of their products and their support services because an equipment failure can shut down the producer's operation. Capital equipment buying often focuses on lifetime operating cost rather than the initial purchase price because the equipment is used for a long time. Thus capital equipment salespeople need to present the financial implications as well as the operating features and benefits of their products.

MRO supplies and services are typically a minor expense and therefore are usually less important to businesses than are many other items. Purchasing agents typically oversee MRO buying decisions. Because they often do not want to spend the time to evaluate all suppliers, they tend to purchase from vendors who have performed well in the past.

Although the cost of MRO supplies is typically low, availability can be critical. For example, the failure of a $10 motor in an industrial robot can shut down an entire assembly line. Some professional services, such as accounting, advertising, and consulting, also are important to the company and may be purchased in a manner similar to capital equipment purchases.

RESELLERS

Resellers buy finished products or services with the intention to resell them to businesses and consumers. For example, Barnes & Noble buys large quantities of books from publishers and resells the books to consumers at its retail locations. McKesson Corporation is a wholesaler that buys health care products from manufacturers and resells those products to drugstores. Brazos Valley Equipment is a dealer for John Deere, selling tractors, harvesters, combines, and other agricultural implements to farmers; whereas Dealer's Electric sells lighting, conduit, and other electrical components to electricians and contractors. All of these are resellers, and they buy for similar reasons.

Resellers consider three elements when making decisions about what products to sell: profit margin, turnover, and effort. Resellers want to maximize their return on investment (ROI), which is a function of **profit margin** or how much they make on each sale, **turnover** or how quickly it will sell, and how much effort it takes to sell the product. While a recent study of furniture store owners found that they often focus on either profit margin or turnover, all resellers are interested in putting together an assortment of products that will yield the greatest overall ROI.[1]

Salespeople work with resellers to help them build their ROI. Not only do salespeople help resellers choose which products to sell; they also train resellers on how to sell and service products, build point-of-purchase displays and promotions, and may also help resellers with developing advertising and marketing campaigns to boost sales. For example, with increasing competition between grocery chains, retailers are asking suppliers to create excitement and generate traffic in stores. Eddy Patterson, of STUBB's Legendary Kitchen, created the "Stubb's Tailgater," a mobile merchandising trailer that promotes brand awareness, creating excitement at the stores with music, video, coupons, and samples. "Retailers' expectations for our products' performance continue to escalate. Price is important but not the only thing retailers are demanding," Patterson says. "We need to look at innovative ways that not only help sell our products and create brand awareness but also ways to contribute to the success of our customers, the retailers who sell our products."[2]

Stubbs Legendary Kitchen, a manufacturer of barbecue spices and sauces, sends this barbecue trailer to various stores to help promote their products.

Eddy Patterson, Courtesy STUBB's Legendary Kitchen

Note that the same customer can act as an OEM manufacturer, an end user, and a reseller. For example, Dell Computer makes OEM buying decisions when it purchases microprocessors for its computers, acts as an end user when it buys materials handling equipment for its warehouse, and functions as a reseller when it buys software to resell to its computer customers when they place orders.

GOVERNMENT AGENCIES

The largest customers for goods and services in the United States are federal, state, and local governments, which collectively purchase goods and services valued at more than $1 trillion annually. More than half of these purchases are made by the federal government, making it the largest customer in the world.[3] Government buyers typically develop detailed specifications for a product and then invite qualified suppliers to submit bids. A contract is awarded to the lowest bidder. The government has also developed procedures for buying without a bid, streamlining the process and reducing costs. Studies showed that it could cost the government as much as $90 to $120 just to process an order. Now products and services under $2,500 can be purchased using SmartPay, a credit card limited to government purchasing.[4]

Effective selling to government agencies requires a thorough knowledge of their unique procurement procedures and rules. Salespeople also need to know about projected needs so they can influence the development of the buying specifications. For example, Harris Corporation worked for six years with the Federal Aviation Administration and finally won a $1.7 billion contract to modernize air traffic communication systems. Selling Scenario 4.1 provides more information about selling to the government.

Some resources available to salespeople working with the federal and state governments are these:

- Guidelines for selling to the government published by the U.S. Government Printing Office.

- The *Commerce Business Daily*, which contains all invitations for bids issued by the federal government.

- The National Association of State Purchasing Officials in Washington, D.C., which publishes information on all 50 states, including the availability of vendor guides, registration fees, and how to get on bidder lists.

- The Procurement Automated Source System (PASS), the Small Business Administration database with information on more than 900 federal purchasing agents and prime contractors working on federal contracts.

- FedBizOpps.gov, a Web site listing all business opportunities greater than $25,000. Keep in mind, though, that 90 percent of federal purchasing opportunities are less than $25,000.[5]

Many international salespeople are selling to government agencies, even though private companies may be the biggest buyers of these products and services in the United States. For example, Nortel, a Canadian company that manufactures telephone equipment, sells to private companies such as Verizon and IBM in the United States but to the postal, telephone, and telegraph (PTT) government agencies in many countries in Europe, Asia, and Africa.

SELLING Scenario

SELLING TO THE GOVERNMENT

The United States federal government is the largest buyer in the world, spending more than $250 billion per year with the private sector. Furthermore, while consumer spending may wax and wane depending on factors as varied as the weather and unemployment rates, "federal spending never goes down. Never," says Mark Amtower, a consultant who helps businesses sell to the government. With the need to practice good stewardship of taxpayers' money while at the same time advance social agendas such as the development of minority-owned businesses, though, the government is not an easy customer.

For one thing, companies that want to sell a lot to the government have to undergo a complete inspection by the General Services Administration (GSA). If successful, a special contract, called a *schedule*, is issued by the GSA that makes the seller an approved vendor. If you get a schedule, then 1 percent of all sales to the government must be returned to the GSA. In addition, prices have to be the lowest offered to any account.

Newark Electronics has sold to the government for nearly 70 years, but without a schedule. Small purchases can be made to vendors who aren't on a schedule in certain cases. Although the government has been one of Newark's largest customers, the average order out of their 2,000-page catalog has been $350. They wanted more.

So they filled out the 92-page questionnaire required by the GSA and underwent a five-month inspection. Most of their effort was spent simply coding every item they sell and demonstrating that they could track sales so the GSA could get its 1 percent commission. They also had to document how many of their suppliers were women- or minority-owned. For example, the government set a target that 5 percent of its purchases would be from women-owned businesses, but so far, they've only managed to reach about 3 percent. At the end of the process, Doug DiVenere, sales manager for Newark, had no time to celebrate. After all, the schedule is just a license to start selling; now it's time to make the calls.

Sources: Shane Harris, "Jumping through Hoops," *Government Executive* 34 (July 2002), pp. 78–79; Susan Wilson Solovic, "Federal Procurement Opportunities for Women Business Owners: Good News–Bad News Scenario," *Women in Business* 56 (July/August, 2003), pp. 11–12.

Selling to foreign governments is very challenging. The percentage of domestic product (countries may require that a certain percentage of the product be manufactured or assembled locally) and exchange rates (the value of local currency in U.S. dollars) are as important as the characteristics of the product. Different economic and political systems, cultures, and languages also can make international selling difficult.

INSTITUTIONS

Another important customer group consists of public and private institutions such as churches, hospitals, and colleges. Often these institutions have purchasing rules and procedures that are as complex and rigid as those used by government agencies.

Packaged goods manufacturers, such as Heinz, sell to both resellers (supermarkets) and institutional customers (restaurants and hospitals). These customers have different needs and buying processes. Thus Heinz has one sales force calling on supermarkets and another sales force selling different products to restaurants.

CONSUMERS

Consumers purchase products and services for use by themselves or by their families. Many salespeople sell insurance, automobiles, clothing, and real estate to consumers. However, college graduates often take sales jobs that involve selling to business enterprises, government agencies, or institutions. Thus the examples in this text focus on these selling situations, and this chapter discusses organizational rather than consumer buying behavior.

In the next section we contrast the buying processes of consumers and organizations. Then we describe the buying process that organizations use in more detail, including the steps in the process, who influences the decisions, and how salespeople can influence the decisions.

ORGANIZATIONAL BUYING AND SELLING

Salespeople who sell to consumers and salespeople who call on organizations have very different jobs. Because the organizational buying process typically is more complex than the consumer buying process, selling to organizations often requires more skills and is more challenging than selling to consumers.

COMPLEXITY OF THE ORGANIZATIONAL BUYING PROCESS

The typical organizational purchase is much larger and more complex than the typical consumer purchase. Organizations use highly trained, knowledgeable purchasing agents to make these decisions. Many other people in organizations are involved in purchase decisions, including engineers, production managers, business analysts, and senior executives.

Organizational buying decisions often involve extensive evaluations and negotiations over time. The average period required to complete a purchase is five months, and during that time salespeople need to make many calls to gather and provide information.

For example, Dean Yeck, sales manager with Qwest Communications, had one account with whom he met at least quarterly for over three and a half years, just building a relationship and gathering information until their contract came up for review. When they decided to review the contract before signing a new one, Yeck's entire account team of eight professionals made seven sales calls over the three-month review period to gather more information. In addition to the seven face-to-face meetings, there were four contract negotiating calls. That contract was worth $2.8 million, while another, worth $3.6 million, required 15 sales calls over a 10-month period.

The complexity of organizational purchase decisions means that salespeople must be able to work effectively with a wide range of people working for their customer and their company. For example, when selling a new additive to a food processor such as Nabisco, an International Flavors and Fragrances salesperson may interact with advertising, product development, legal, production, quality control, and customer service people at Nabisco. The salesperson needs to know the technical and economic benefits of the additive to Nabisco and the benefits to consumers.

In addition, the salesperson coordinates all areas of his or her own firm to assist in making the sale. The salesperson works with research and development to provide data on consumer taste tests, with production to meet the customer's delivery requirements, and with finance to set the purchasing terms. (Working effectively within the salesperson's organization is discussed in more detail in Chapter 16.)

The complexity of organizational selling is increasing as more customers become global businesses. For example, Deere & Company has a special department to coordinate worldwide purchases. The department evaluates potential suppliers across the globe for each of its product lines and manufacturing facilities. Further, the company wants to standardize products made in different

If you want to sell a part such as a belt to go on a John Deere harvester made in Ottumwa, Iowa, then you have to also be able to sell and service this plant in Arc-les-Gray, France, too.

Courtesy John Deere & Company

plants. A harvester made in Ottumwa, Iowa, should have the same belt as the same model harvester made at Arc-les-Gray, France. Thus a salesperson selling belts to Deere must work with the corporate buying department as well as with the employees at each manufacturing location around the world.[6] There's no doubt that global competitiveness is a key factor increasing the complexity of organizational buying, but global sourcing is also a key factor in achieving a sustainable competitive advantage.[7]

DERIVED VERSUS DIRECT DEMAND

Salespeople selling to consumers typically can focus on the individual consumer or family needs. Organizational selling often requires salespeople to know about the customer's customers. Sales to OEMs and resellers are based on derived demand rather than direct demand. **Derived demand** means that purchases made by these customers ultimately depend on the demand for their products—either other organizations or consumers. However, manufacturers can influence demand too. For example, McDonalds was selling 625,000 packages of milk per week, and their dairy providers were limited by what McDonalds could sell. McDonalds changed the packaging to attract children's attention and that of their parents. With introduction of the new packaging, sales jumped to over 4 million units per week almost immediately. Not only did this influence demand for milk, it also influenced demand for cases to pack the milk containers in, as well as new bottling equipment.[8] When demand is derived, salespeople must understand the needs of the ultimate user as well as those of the immediate customer.

HOW DO ORGANIZATIONS MAKE BUYING DECISIONS?

To effectively sell to organizations, salespeople need to understand how organizations make buying decisions. This section discusses the steps in the organizational buying process, the different types of buying decisions, and the people involved in making the decisions.[9]

STEPS IN THE BUYING PROCESS

Exhibit 4.1 shows the eight steps in an organizational buying process.

RECOGNIZING A NEED OR A PROBLEM (STEP 1) The buying process starts when someone realizes that a problem exists. Employees in the customer's firm or outside salespeople can trigger this recognition. For example, a supermarket cashier might discover that the optical scanner is making mistakes in reading the bar code labels. Salespeople often trigger the buying process by demonstrating how their products can improve the efficiency of the customer's operation.

DEFINING THE TYPE OF PRODUCT NEEDED (STEP 2) After identifying a problem, organization members develop a general approach to solving it. For example, a production manager who concludes that the factory is not running efficiently recognizes a problem, but this insight may not lead to a purchase decision. The manager may think the inefficiency is caused by poor supervision or unskilled workers.

However, a production equipment salesperson might work with the manager to analyze the situation and show how efficiency could be improved by purchasing some automated assembly equipment. Thus the problem solution is defined in

Exhibit 4.1

Steps in the
Organizational Buying
Process

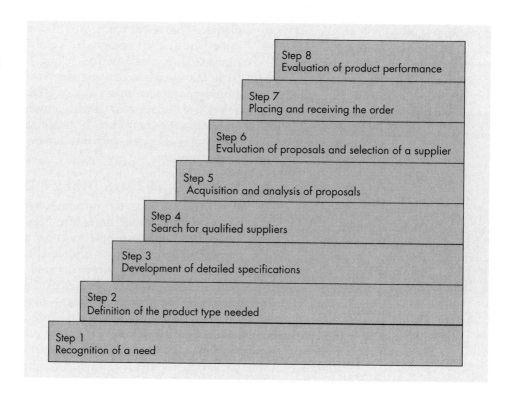

Step 8
Evaluation of product performance

Step 7
Placing and receiving the order

Step 6
Evaluation of proposals and selection of a supplier

Step 5
Acquisition and analysis of proposals

Step 4
Search for qualified suppliers

Step 3
Development of detailed specifications

Step 2
Definition of the product type needed

Step 1
Recognition of a need

terms of purchasing a product or service—the automated assembly equipment needed—and the buying process moves to step 3.

DEVELOPING PRODUCT SPECIFICATIONS (STEP 3)   In step 3 the specifications for the product needed to solve the problem are prepared. Potential suppliers will use these specifications to develop proposals. The buyers will use them to objectively evaluate the proposals.

Steps 2 and 3 offer great opportunities for salespeople to influence the outcome of the buying process. Using their knowledge of their firm's products and the customer's needs, salespeople can help develop specifications that favor their particular product. For example, a Hyster forklift might have superior performance in terms of a small turning radius. Knowing this advantage and the customer's small, tightly packed warehouse, the Hyster salesperson might influence the customer to specify a very small turning radius for forklifts, a turning radius that only Hyster forklifts can provide. Competing salespeople, who first become aware of this procurement after the specifications are written, will be at a severe disadvantage.

SEARCHING FOR QUALIFIED SUPPLIERS (STEP 4)   After the specifications have been written, the customer looks for potential suppliers. The customer may simply contact previous suppliers or go through an extensive search procedure: calling salespeople, asking for a list of customers, and checking with the customers on each supplier's financial stability and performance. Many purchasing agents now use the Internet to find suppliers.

One survey by the Institute for Supply Management indicates that many organizations use the Internet to locate suppliers, and the percentage is rising. Nearly half used the Internet to ask suppliers for proposals, but that figure rose to over 80 percent by the end of 2003. In Canada, the rate of new companies using the Internet to find suppliers is growing much faster than in the United States.[10] Sales

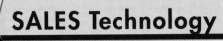

A BRIEF HISTORY OF E-PROCUREMENT

Downsizing is a fact of life in purchasing, a trend for nearly a decade. One could argue that it is due to the fewer supplier relationships businesses need to develop and maintain, but others argue that it is due to increased electronic procurement (e-procurement).

E-procurement actually began long before the Internet existed. In the late 1960s, transportation companies developed electronic interchanges, each with its own proprietary format, to address the amount of documentation needed to get shipments handled properly. Customers had to deal with each format, so they began to push for standards. These standards were developed nearly a decade later.

With the ubiquity of the Internet, these formats moved from proprietary networks to the Web. Other forms of e-procurement have since been created. Exchanges provide places for sellers to offer products for sale, like FreeMarkets and eBay, while reverse auction sites enable buyers a place to offer purchases. These markets, though, are consolidating and declining in number, from 1,500 in 2001 to fewer than 200 today. Such consolidation should not be taken as a sign of decline in importance; rather, it is a sign of market maturation as e-procurement becomes standard operating practice.

Sources: Robert Dwyer and John F. Tanner, *Business Marketing: Connecting Relationships, Strategy, and Learning,* 3rd ed. (New York: McGraw-Hill/Irwin, 2006); Talai Osmonbekov, Daniel C. Bello, and David I. Gilliland, "Adoption of Electronic Commerce Tools in Business Procurement: Enhanced Buying Center Structure and Processes," *Journal of Business & Industrial Marketing* 17 (February 3, 2002), pp. 151–67.

Technology 4.1 illustrates how Internet technology is used to bring buyers and sellers together.

ACQUIRING AND ANALYZING PROPOSALS (STEP 5) In step 5 qualified suppliers are asked to submit proposals. Salespeople work with people in their company to develop their proposal.

EVALUATING PROPOSALS AND SELECTING A SUPPLIER (STEP 6) Next the customer evaluates the proposals. After a preferred supplier is selected, further negotiations may occur concerning price, delivery, or specific performance features. The appendix to this chapter shows a model used in evaluating proposals.

PLACING AN ORDER AND RECEIVING THE PRODUCT (STEP 7) In step 7 an order is placed with the selected supplier. The order goes to the supplier, which acknowledges receipt and commits to a delivery date. Eventually the product is shipped to the buying firm, which inspects the received goods and then pays the supplier for the product. During this step salespeople need to make sure the paperwork is correct and their firm knows what has to be done to satisfy the customer's requirements.

EVALUATING PRODUCT PERFORMANCE (STEP 8) In the final step of the purchasing process, the product's performance is evaluated. The evaluation may be a formal or an informal assessment made by people involved in the buying process.

Salespeople play an important role in this step. They need to work with the users to make sure the product performs well. In addition, salespeople need to work with purchasing agents to ensure that they are satisfied with the communications and delivery.

This after-sale support ensures that the salesperson's product will get a positive evaluation and that he or she will be considered a qualified supplier in future procurement. This step is critical to establishing the successful long-term relationships discussed in Chapter 2. (Building relationships through after-sale support is discussed in more detail in Chapter 14.)

CREEPING COMMITMENT

Creeping commitment means that a customer becomes increasingly committed to a particular course of action while going through the steps in the buying process. As decisions are made at each step, the range of alternatives narrows; the customer becomes more and more committed to a specific course of action and even to a specific vendor. Thus it is critical that salespeople be involved in the initial steps so they will have an opportunity to participate in the final steps.

An example of creeping commitment occurred when Coca-Cola introduced its Diet Coke with lime flavor. As the company examined the market and considered the new product, it brought in potential suppliers for various flavorings. These companies were part of the strategic planning process at Coke. Coke then narrowed the choices among flavorings, which also narrowed the vendor list. So as Coke was developing the new product, it was also making decisions that ultimately led to the selection of the actual supplier.

thinking **it** through

What steps did you go through in making the choice to attend this university? How can you relate your decision-making process to the eight steps in the organizational buying process? Did any decisions you made early in the process affect decisions you made later in the process? What roles did your family and friends play in the decision process?

TYPES OF ORGANIZATIONAL BUYING DECISIONS

Many purchase decisions are made without going through all the steps just described. For example, a Frito-Lay salesperson may check the supply of his or her products in a supermarket, write out a purchase order to restock the shelves, and present it to the store manager. After recognizing the problem of low stock, the manager simply signs the order (step 6) without going through any of the other steps. However, if the Frito-Lay salesperson wanted the manager to devote more shelf space to Frito-Lay snacks, the manager might go through all eight steps in making and evaluating this decision.

Exhibit 4.2 describes three types of buying decisions—new tasks, modified rebuys, and straight rebuys[11]—along with the strategies salespeople need to use in each situation. In this exhibit the "in" company is the seller that has provided the product or service to the company in the past, and the "out" company is the seller that is not or has not been a supplier to the customer.[12]

NEW TASKS

When a customer purchases a product or service for the first time, a **new-task** situation occurs. Most purchase decisions involving capital equipment or the initial purchase of OEM products are new tasks.

Because the customer has not made the purchase decision recently, the company's knowledge is limited and it goes through all eight steps of the buying process. In these situations customers face considerable risk. Thus they typically seek information from salespeople and welcome their knowledge. For example, a

Exhibit 4.2
Types of Organizational
Buying Decisions

	New Task	Modified Rebuy	Straight Rebuy
Customer Needs			
Information and risk reduction	Information about causes and solutions for a new problem; reduce high risk in making a decision with limited knowledge.	Information and solutions to increase efficiency and/or reduce costs.	Needs are generally satisfied.
Nature of Buying Process			
Number of people involved in process	Many	Few	One
Time to make a decision	Months or years	Month	Day
Key steps in the buying process (Exhibit 4.1)	1, 2, 3, 8	3, 4, 5, 6, 8	5, 6, 7, 8
Key decision makers	Executives and engineers.	Production and purchasing managers.	Purchasing agent.
Selling Strategy			
For in-supplier	Monitor changes in customer needs; respond quickly when problems and new needs arise; provide technical information.	Act immediately when problems arise with customers; make sure all of customers' needs are satisfied.	Reinforce relationship.
For out-supplier	Suggest new approach for solving problems; provide technical advice.	Respond more quickly than present supplier when problem arises; encourage customer to consider an alternative; present information on how new alternative will increase efficiency.	Convince customer of potential benefits from reexamining choice of supplier; secure recognition and approval as an alternative supplier.

German company was considering the construction of a new building and asked two Danish firms to act as advisors, including the preparation of bidding specifications. With previous clients, the Danish firms did not have to act as advisors because their customers had enough recent experience to handle it themselves.[13]

From the salesperson's perspective, the initial buying process steps are critical in new-task situations. During these steps the alert salesperson can help the customer define the characteristics of the needed product and develop the purchase specifications. By working with the customer in these initial steps, the salesperson can take advantage of creeping commitment and gain a significant advantage over the competition. The final step, postpurchase evaluation, is also critical. Buyers making a new purchase decision are especially interested in evaluating results and will use this information in making similar purchase decisions in the future.

STRAIGHT REBUYS

In a **straight rebuy** situation, the customer buys the same product from the same source it used when the need arose previously. Because customers have purchased the product or service a number of times, they have considerable knowledge about their requirements and the potential vendors. MRO supplies and services and reorders of OEM components often are straight rebuy situations.

Typically, a straight rebuy is triggered by an internal event, such as a low inventory level. Because needs are easily recognized, specifications have been developed, and potential suppliers have been identified, the latter steps of the buying process assume greater importance.

Some straight rebuys are computerized. For example, many hospitals use an automatic reorder system developed by Baxter, a manufacturer and distributor of medical supplies. When the inventory control system recognizes that levels of supplies such as tape, surgical sponges, or IV kits have dropped to prespecified levels, a purchase order is automatically generated and transmitted electronically to the nearest Baxter distribution center.

When a company is satisfied and has developed a long-term supplier relationship, it continues to order from the same company it has used in the past. Salespeople at in-companies want to maintain the strong relationship; they do not want the customer to consider new suppliers. Thus these salespeople must make sure that orders are delivered on time and that the products continue to get favorable evaluations.

Salespeople trying to break into a straight rebuy situation—those representing an out-supplier—face a tough sales problem. Often they need to persuade a customer to change suppliers, even though the present supplier is performing satisfactorily. In such situations the salesperson hopes the present supplier will make a critical mistake, causing the customer to reevaluate suppliers. To break into a straight rebuy situation, salespeople need to provide very compelling information to motivate the customer to treat the purchase as a modified rebuy.

MODIFIED REBUYS

In a **modified rebuy** situation, the customer has purchased the product or a similar product in the past but is interested in obtaining new information. This situation typically occurs when the in-supplier performs unsatisfactorily, a new product becomes available, or the buying needs change. In such situations sales representatives of the in-suppliers need to convince customers to maintain the relationship and continue their present buying pattern. In-suppliers with strong customer relationships are the first to find out when requirements change. In this case customers provide the supplier's salespeople with information to assist them in responding to the new requirements.

Salespeople with out-suppliers want customers to reevaluate the situation and to actively consider switching vendors. The successful sales rep from an out-supplier will need to influence all the people taking part in the buying decision.

WHO MAKES THE BUYING DECISION?

As we discussed previously, a number of people are involved in new-task and modified rebuy decisions. This group of people is called the **buying center,** an informal, cross-department group of people involved in a purchase decision. People in the customer's organization become involved in a buying center because they have formal responsibilities for purchasing or they are important sources of information. In some cases the buying center includes experts who are not full-time employees. For example, consultants usually specify the air-conditioning equipment that will be used in a factory undergoing remodeling. Thus the buying center defines the set of people who make or influence the purchase decision.[14]

Salespeople need to know the names and responsibilities of all people in the buying center for a purchase decision, and sometimes they need to make sure the right people are participating. For example, Ron Swift, vice president for NCR Teradata, a maker of data warehousing equipment and software, was called in by the marketing director of a cell phone services provider to discuss the problem of customer churn (customers leaving for a competitor). The marketing director believed that better customer information would solve the revenue loss problem, so he wanted to consider a data warehouse in which to store that information. The process advanced without anyone from the information systems department! Fortunately, with Ron's experience, the Teradata team was able to involve the chief information officer and the right people from his area, as well as the financial people needed to understand the budgeting implications. With the right buying team in place, the right system was designed, resulting in a reduction in churn by some 20 percent, and additional revenues of nearly $50 million in only a few years.[15]

Users

Users, such as the manufacturing area personnel for OEM products and capital equipment, typically do not make the ultimate purchase decision. However, they often have considerable influence in the early and late steps of the buying process—need recognition, product definition, and postpurchase evaluation. Thus users are particularly important in new-task and modified rebuy situations. Salespeople often attempt to convert a straight rebuy to a modified rebuy by demonstrating superior product performance or a new benefit to users.

Initiators

Another role in the buying process is that of **initiator,** or the person who starts the buying process. A user can play the role of the initiator, as in "This machine is broken, we need a new one." Or the initiator could be an executive making a decision, such as to introduce a new product (like lime-flavored Diet Coke), which starts the buying process.[16]

Influencers

People inside or outside the organization who directly or indirectly provide information during the buying process are **influencers.** These members of the buying center may seek to influence issues regarding product specifications, criteria for

The buying center for an MRI scanner in a hospital includes the technicians operating the equipment (the users), the radiologists (gatekeepers and influencers), and the hospital administrator (the decision maker).

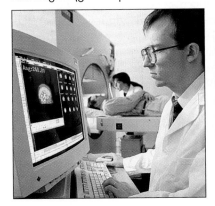

Roger Tully/Stone   Charles Gupton/The Stock Market   Bruce Ayres/Stone

Chapter 4   Buying Behavior and the Buying Process   **99**

evaluating proposals, or information about potential suppliers. For example, the marketing department can influence a purchase decision by indicating that the company's products would sell better if they included a particular supplier's components. Architects can play the critical role in the purchase of construction material by specifying suppliers, even though the ultimate purchase orders will be placed by the contractor responsible for constructing the building. Influence can be technical, such as product specifications, but can also involve the finances and how the decision is made.

Gatekeepers

Gatekeepers control the flow of information and may limit the alternatives considered.[17] For example, the quality control and service departments may determine which potential suppliers are qualified sources.

Purchasing agents often play a gatekeeping role by determining which potential suppliers are notified about the purchase situation and have access to relevant information. In some companies all contacts must be made through purchasing agents. They arrange meetings with other gatekeepers, influencers, and users. When dealing with such companies, salespeople often are not allowed to contact these members of the buying center directly. When purchasing agents restrict access to important information, salespeople are tempted to bypass the purchasing agents and make direct contact. This backdoor selling approach can upset purchasing agents so much that they may disqualify the salesperson's company from the purchase situation.[18] In Chapter 8 we discuss ethical strategies that salespeople can use to deal with this issue.

Deciders

In any buying center one or more members of the group, **deciders,** make the final choice. Determining who actually makes the purchase decision for an organization is often difficult. For straight rebuys the purchasing agent usually selects the vendor and places the order. However, for new tasks many people influence the decision, and several people must approve the decision and sign the purchase order.

In general, senior executives get more involved in important purchase decisions, those that have a greater effect on the performance of the organization. For example, the chief executive officer (CEO) and chief financial officer (CFO) play an important role in purchasing a telephone system because this network has a significant impact on the firm's day-to-day operations.

To sell effectively to organizations, salespeople need to know the people in the buying center and their involvement at different steps of the buying process. Consider the following situation. Salespeople selling expensive intensive care monitoring equipment know that a hospital buying center for the type of equipment they sell typically consists of physicians, nurses, hospital administrators, engineers, and purchasing agents. Through experience, these salespeople also know the relative importance of the buying center members in various stages of the purchasing process (see Exhibit 4.3). With this information the intensive care equipment salespeople know to concentrate on physicians throughout the process, nurses and engineers in the middle of the process, and hospital administrators and purchasing agents at the end of the process.

SUPPLIER EVALUATION AND CHOICE

At various steps in the buying process, members of the buying center evaluate alternative methods for solving a problem (step 2), the qualifications of potential suppliers (step 4), proposals submitted by potential suppliers (step 5), and the

Exhibit 4.3

Importance of Hospital Buying Center Members in the Buying Process for Intensive Care Monitoring Equipment

Step in Buying Process	Physicians	Nurses	Hospital Administrators	Purchasing Engineers	Agents
Need recognition (step 1)	High	Moderate	Low	Low	Low
Definition of product type (step 2)	High	High	Moderate	Moderate	Low
Analysis of proposal (step 5)	High	Moderate	Moderate	High	Low
Proposal evaluation and supplier selection (step 6)	High	Low	High	Low	Moderate

performance of products purchased (step 8). Using these evaluations, buyers select potential suppliers and eventually choose a specific vendor.

The needs of both the organization and the individuals making the decisions affect the evaluation and selection of products and suppliers (see Exhibit 4.4). Often these organizational and personal needs are classified into two categories: rational needs and emotional needs. **Rational needs** are directly related to the performance of the product. Thus the organizational needs discussed in the next section are examples of rational needs. **Emotional needs** are associated with the personal rewards and gratification of the person buying the product. Thus the personal needs of buying center members often are considered emotional needs.

ORGANIZATIONAL NEEDS AND CRITERIA

Organizations consider a number of factors when they make buying decisions, including economic factors such as price, product quality, and supplier service.

Exhibit 4.4

Factors Influencing Organizational Buying Decisions

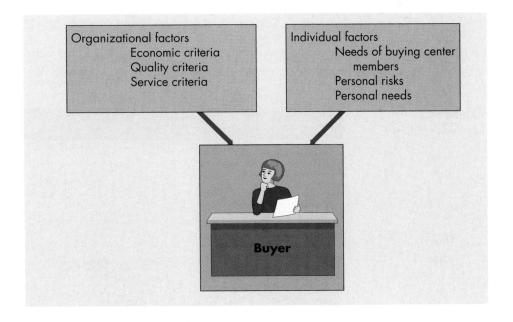

Organizational factors
  Economic criteria
  Quality criteria
  Service criteria

Individual factors
  Needs of buying center members
  Personal risks
  Personal needs

Buyer

Economic Criteria

The objective of businesses is to make a profit. Thus businesses are very concerned about buying products and services at the lowest cost. Organizational buyers are now taking a more sophisticated approach to evaluating the cost of equipment. Rather than simply focusing on the purchase price, they consider installation costs, the costs of needed accessories, freight charges, estimated maintenance costs, and operating costs, including forecasts of energy costs.

Life-cycle costing, also referred to as the *total cost of ownership*, is a method for determining the cost of equipment or supplies over their useful lives. Using this approach, salespeople can demonstrate that a product with a higher initial cost will have a lower overall cost. An example of life-cycle costing appears in Exhibit 4.5. (Approaches salespeople can use to demonstrate the value of their products to customers are discussed in more detail in Chapter 10.)

Quality Criteria

Many firms recognize that the quality and reliability of their products are as important to their customers as price. Firms expect their suppliers to support their efforts to provide quality products. A recent study in Spain indicates that suppliers are evaluated on both the quality of their service and the quality of their products because both impact the quality that the buyer is able to deliver to its customer.[19] Salespeople often need to describe how their firms will support the customer's quality objectives.

To satisfy customer quality needs, salespeople need to know what organizational buyers are looking for. For example, Lionel Dace, of Dace and Dace, was calling on an engineer who was trying to source metal containers. His company had designed a new milkshake machine, and this container was supposed to hold milk inside a milkshake machine. The engineer was beating up Dace over price, and showed him another container from a competitor at a lower price. Dace saw that it was cheaply made using a completely different process than the one he had to offer. The lower-priced version might hold up under moderate use, but Dace thought it just didn't look as good as the machine the engineer and his team had designed. However, Dace had been calling on this buyer for three years and had heard nothing but price, price, price. Out of exasperation, Dace looked at the engineer and said, "Is this really what you want it to look like? Can you be proud of that?" Dace says the buyer was immediately transformed; while he had focused on low price, he really wanted something that looked as sleek as the machine he had designed. Dace got the sale, but perhaps more importantly, the nature of their relationship changed for the better.[20]

Exhibit 4.5
Life-Cycle Costing

	Product A	Product B
Initial cost	$35,000	$30,000
Life of machine	10 years	10 years
Power consumption per year	150 MWh*	180 MWh*
Power cost at $30/MWh	$45,000	$54,000
Estimated operating and maintenance cost over 10 years	$25,000	$30,000
Life-cycle cost	$105,000	$114,000

Note: A more thorough analysis would calculate the net present value of the cash flow associated with each product's purchase and use.

*MWh = megawatt hour

Service Criteria

Organizational buyers want more than products that are inexpensive, perform reliably, and are aesthetically pleasing. They also want suppliers that will work with them to solve their problems. One primary reason firms are interested in developing long-term relationships with suppliers is so they can learn about each other's needs and capabilities and use this information to enhance their products' performance. **Value analysis** is an example of a program in which suppliers and customers work together to reduce costs and still provide the required level of performance.[21]

Representatives from the supplier and the purchasing department and technical experts from engineering, production, or quality control usually form a team to undertake the analysis. The team begins by examining the product's function. Then members brainstorm to see whether changes can be made in the design, materials, construction, or production process to reduce the product's costs but keep its performance high. Some questions addressed in this phase are the following:

- Can a part in the product be eliminated?
- If the part is not standard, can a standard (and presumably less expensive) part be used?
- Does the part have greater performance than this application needs?
- Are unnecessary machining or fine finishes specified?

Salespeople can use value analysis to get customers to consider a new product. This approach is particularly useful for the out-supplier in a straight rebuy situation. Scott Paper Company's salespeople use value analysis to sell hand towels and toilet paper. Because Scott products are of high quality and sell at a premium price, Scott sales representatives have to prove that the products are worth the extra money. The salespeople use value analysis to help purchasing agents determine how much it costs to use the product, rather than how much the product costs. They focus on the price per use, such as the number of dries per case of paper towels, rather than the price per case. Scott even designed a paper towel dispenser to reduce the number of refills needed and thus reduce maintenance labor cost.

INDIVIDUAL NEEDS OF BUYING CENTER MEMBERS

In the preceding section we discussed criteria used to determine whether a product satisfies the needs of the organization. However, buying center members are people. Their evaluations and choices are affected by their personal needs as well as the organization's needs.

Types of Needs

Buying center members, like all people, have personal goals and aspirations. They want to get a raise, be promoted, have their managers recognize their accomplishments, and feel they have done something for their company or demonstrated their skills as a buyer or engineer.

Salespeople can influence members of the buying center by developing strategies to satisfy individual needs. For example, demonstrating how a new product will reduce costs and increase the purchasing agents' bonus would satisfy the purchasing agents' financial security needs. Encouraging an engineer to recommend a product employing the latest technology might satisfy the engineer's need for self-esteem and recognition by his or her engineering peers.

Risk Reduction

In many situations, members of the buying center tend to be more concerned about losing benefits they have now than about increasing their benefits. They place a lot of emphasis on avoiding risks that may result in poor decisions, decisions that can adversely affect their personal reputations and rewards as well as their organization's performance. Buyers first assess the potential for risk, then develop a risk reduction strategy.[22] To reduce risk, buying center members may collect additional information, develop a loyalty to present suppliers, and/or spread the risk by placing orders with several vendors.

Because they know that suppliers try to promote their own products, customers tend to question information received from vendors. Customers usually view information from independent sources such as trade publications, colleagues, and outside consultants as more credible than information provided by salespeople and company advertising and sales literature. Therefore, they will search for such information to reduce risk when a purchase is important.

Advertising, the Internet, and sales literature tend to be used more in the early steps of the buying process. Word-of-mouth information from friends and colleagues is very important in the proposal evaluation and supplier selection steps. Word-of-mouth information is especially important for risky decisions, decisions that will have a significant impact on the organization and/or the buying center member.

Another way to reduce uncertainty and risk is to display **vendor loyalty** to suppliers—that is, to continue buying from suppliers that have proved satisfactory in the past. By converting buying decisions into straight rebuys, the decisions become routine, minimizing the chances of a poor decision. One name for this is **lost-for-good**; for all of the out-suppliers, this account can be considered lost for good because they've cemented this relationship for a long time. Organizations tend to develop vendor loyalty for unimportant purchase decisions, though they will often look to vendors who have proved trustworthy when beginning to search in a risky situation. In these situations the potential benefits from new suppliers do not compensate for the costs of evaluating these suppliers.

The consequences of choosing a poor supplier can be reduced by using more than one vendor. Rather than placing all orders for an OEM component with one supplier, for example, a firm might elect to purchase 75 percent of its needs from one supplier and 25 percent from another. Thus if a problem occurs with one supplier, another will be available to fill the firm's needs. If the product is proprietary-available from only one supplier—the buyer might insist that the supplier develop a second source for the component. Such a strategy is called **always-a-share**, which means that the buyer will always allocate only a share to each vendor.

These risk reduction approaches present a major problem for salespeople working for out-suppliers. To break this loyalty barrier, these salespeople need to develop trusting relationships with customers. They can build trust by offering performance guarantees or consistently meeting personal commitments. Another approach is to encourage buyers to place a small trial order so that the salesperson's company can demonstrate the product's capabilities. On the other hand, the salesperson for the in-supplier wants to discourage buyers from considering new sources, even on a trial basis.

PROFESSIONAL PURCHASING'S GROWING IMPORTANCE

The purchasing profession is undergoing dramatic changes. Companies have recognized the power that effective purchasing can have on the bottom line. For example, if a company can save $5,000 on a purchase, $5,000 is added to net

GOING OUT THROUGH THE BACK DOOR

Travis Bruns is a sales representative for Crown Lift Services in Houston, Texas. In his own words, he describes how he addressed an ethics issue with a buyer.

"Last year I was in a real 'cutthroat' bidding war for a $300,000-plus sales opportunity. Over the course of two months the competitive field had been narrowed down to two organizations . . . mine and the incumbent organization. The customer had set up a set of strict guidelines for the bidding process. One of those was that they had designated a 'point of contact' (POC) that was to be the liaison through which all bids and proposals were to channel through to the VP. My organization and I had truly put our best foot forward on pricing and proposed service after the sale, and although the negotiations had been rough, we were able to sell the value of our solution, retain a fair amount of profit, and were told we had the deal . . . a true 'win–win'. On the final day that the bid was open I received a call from the point of contact asking me to lower my price. I was confused. I inquired about the previous discussions that had taken place, in which we had mutually agreed that the price of our proposal was fair and good. I could hear some level of discomfort if not embarrassment in the POC's voice, so I came right out and asked him, 'I get the sense that you are not comfortable with what is happening here either . . . what happened?'

"He replied, 'Well, Travis, (your competitor) called one of the other managers in the office and was able to find out the pricing in your proposal. He then went around me and called the VP directly and offered a much lower price.

The VP then called me and asked me to get you to lower your price or the other company will get the business.'

"I was dumbfounded. I asked the customer, 'If I cannot lower my price, are you telling me this deal is over for me?'

"'I think so.' he replied.

"'How can that be?' I asked. 'I thought there was a strict procedure that was to be followed in this process, and we followed it. Are you really telling me that my competitor is going to be rewarded for bucking the system? They are going to steal this deal away from us because they were underhanded and broke the rules? I did not think your organization conducted business in this manner.' I was going out on a limb here, but what did I have to lose? I maintained that my best offer was on the table and that I was not willing to compromise my ethics to earn their business.

"The POC agreed with me and was clearly encouraged by the position I was holding. He went to his VP and gave his opinion about how the integrity of their predefined bidding process had been ignored by the other organization. He argued that they should not reward such tactics lest they compromise their own integrity as well. The VP agreed, and we were given the order."

Sometimes sneaking through the back door just lets you out, as Travis's competitor learned.

Source: Travis Bruns, used with permission.

---

income. If sales go up $5,000, of which most is additional costs, only $500 may be added to net income. Building Partnerships 4.1 describes two organizations that have secured major savings in procurement following two different strategies. Most large firms have elevated their directors of purchasing to the level of senior vice president to reflect the increasing importance of this function. Combine recognition of the power of purchasing with technology, and you can see why trends in professional purchasing are changing the business environment. The overall strategy is called *supply chain management*.

SUPPLY CHAIN MANAGEMENT

Supply chain management began as a set of programs undertaken to increase the efficiency of the distribution channel that moves products from the producer's facilities to the end user. More recently, however, supply chain management has become more than just logistics; it is now a strategy of managing inventory while containing costs. Supply chain management (SCM) includes logistics systems such as just-in-time inventory control, as well as supplier evaluation processes such as supplier relationship management systems.

The **just-in-time (JIT) inventory control** system is an example of a logistics supply chain management system used by a producer to minimize its inventory by having frequent deliveries, sometimes daily, just in time for assembly into the final product. In theory each product delivered by a supplier must conform to the manufacturer's specifications every time. It must be delivered when needed, not earlier or later, and it must arrive in the exact quantity needed, not more or less. The ultimate goal is to eventually eliminate all inventory except products in production and transit.[23]

To develop the close coordination needed for JIT systems, manufacturers tend to rely on one supplier. The selection criterion is not the lowest cost, but the ability of the supplier to be flexible. As these relationships develop, employees of the supplier have offices at the customer's site and participate in value analysis meetings with the customer. The salesperson becomes a facilitator, coordinator, and even marriage counselor in developing a selling team that works effectively with the customer's buying center. (The manufacturer and supplier develop a strategic partnership, which we discussed in Chapter 2.)

Resellers are also interested in managing their inventories more efficiently. Retailers and distributors work closely with their suppliers to minimize inventory investments and still satisfy the needs of customers. These JIT inventory systems are referred to as **quick-response** or **efficient consumer response (ECR) systems** in a consumer product distribution channel.[24]

Material requirements planning (MRP) systems are an important element in JIT programs. These systems are used to forecast sales, develop a production schedule, and then order parts and raw materials with delivery dates that minimize the amount of inventory needed, thereby reducing costs. Effective JIT requires that customers inform suppliers well in advance about production schedules and needs.

Automatic replenishment (AR) is a form of JIT where the supplier manages inventory levels for the customer. The materials are provided on consignment, meaning the buyer doesn't pay for them until they are actually used. These types of arrangements are used most often in industrial settings, where the product being consumed is a supply item used in a manufacturing process.[25]

Many firms use elaborate computer systems to keep track of inventories, orders, and deliveries. These systems help firms uncover and eliminate suppliers whose late deliveries and defective products cause scheduling problems. Many customers and suppliers link computer systems, sharing information about sales, production, and shipment and receipt of products. These computer-to-computer linkages between suppliers and buyers are referred to as **electronic data interchange (EDI)**.[26] Exhibit 4.6 illustrates the communications associated with placing orders and receiving products that are transmitted electronically through EDI. Recent research has indicated that the adoption of systems involving both EDI and JIT delivers a number of benefits to the firm, in addition to lower costs. These benefits include greater flexibility in manufacturing, improved stability of supply, and other operating benefits.[27]

SUPPLIER RELATIONSHIP MANAGEMENT

Supplier relationship management (SRM) is a strategy by which organizational buyers evaluate the relative importance of suppliers and use that information to determine with whom they want to develop partnerships. The first step is to identify the **annual spend,** or amount that is spent with each vendor and for what products. One outcome is the ability to consolidate purchases and negotiate better terms (recall Brad Bischof's story in Building Partnerships 3.1). After the rela-

Exhibit 4.6
EDI Transactions

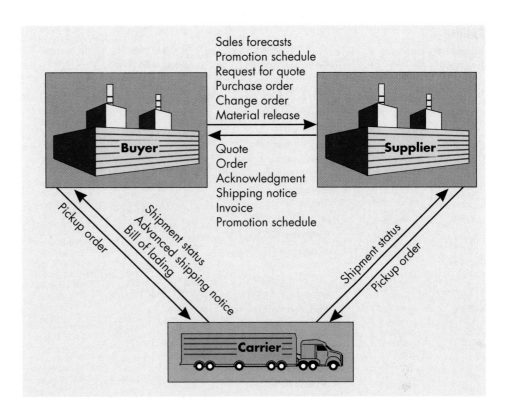

Sales forecasts
Promotion schedule
Request for quote
Purchase order
Change order
Material release

Quote
Order
Acknowledgment
Shipping notice
Invoice
Promotion schedule

Buyer

Supplier

Pickup order

Shipment status
Advanced shipping notice
Bill of lading

Shipment status
Pickup order

Carrier

tive importance is identified, organizational buyers frequently use a formal method, called vendor analysis, to summarize the benefits and needs satisfied by a supplier. When using this procedure, the buyer rates the supplier and its products on a number of criteria such as price, quality, performance, and on-time delivery.[28] Note that the ratings of suppliers can be affected by the perceptions and personal needs of the buyers. Then the ratings are weighted by the importance of the characteristics, and an overall score or evaluation of the vendor is developed. Exhibit 4.7 shows a vendor evaluation form used by Chrysler Corporation. The appendix to this chapter describes the multiattribute model, which is useful in analyzing how members of the buying center evaluate and select products. The model also suggests strategies salespeople can use to influence these evaluations.

Kingfisher pic, a European firm that owns and operates retail stores such as Castorama, uses supplier relationship management software from SAS Institute to track supplier performance.

Jean-Marc Charles/Corbis Sygma

SRM software is being used by companies like Kingfisher plc, a company with some 1,400 stores across 17 countries, and leading European retail brands such as Castorama and BUT. The company's Asia sourcing office in Hong Kong buys over 8,000 products from more than 150 suppliers. SRM software enables the company to identify problems, such as a delivery problem with one vendor in particular. "With the use of that information, we were able to contact the supplier and ask for improvement," says Anthony Sutcliffe, sourcing controller for Kingfisher Asia. Their SRM software is integrated with their EDI software, so they were then able to track that vendor's performance in terms of timeliness and ability to ship the full quantity ordered.[29]

Exhibit 4.7
Sample Vendor Analysis Form

Supplier name: _____ Type of product: _____

Shipping location: _____ Annual sales dollars: _____

	5 Excellent	4 Good	3 Satisfactory	2 Fair	1 Poor	0 N/A
Quality (45%)						
Defect rates	—	—	—	—	—	—
Quality of sample	—	—	—	—	—	—
Conformance with quality program	—	—	—	—	—	—
Responsiveness to quality problems	—	—	—	—	—	—
Overall quality	—	—	—	—	—	—
Delivery (25%)						
Avoidance of late shipments	—	—	—	—	—	—
Ability to expand production capacity	—	—	—	—	—	—
Performance in sample delivery	—	—	—	—	—	—
Response to changes in order size	—	—	—	—	—	—
Overall delivery	—	—	—	—	—	—
Price (20%)						
Price competitiveness	—	—	—	—	—	—
Payment terms	—	—	—	—	—	—
Absorption of costs	—	—	—	—	—	—
Submission of cost savings plans	—	—	—	—	—	—
Overall price	—	—	—	—	—	—
Technology (10%)						
State-of-the-art components	—	—	—	—	—	—
Sharing research & development capability	—	—	—	—	—	—
Ability and willingness to help with design	—	—	—	—	—	—
Responsiveness to engineering problems	—	—	—	—	—	—
Overall technology	—	—	—	—	—	—

Buyer: _____ Date: _____

Comments: _____

Source: Chrysler Corporation.

British auto retailer Dixon has proved the power of SRM. Selling 125,000 vehicles per year across some 60 sites, each with its own local purchasing person, the company has little margin to play with. They buy parts, ramps for service bays, equipment, and a host of other products. Losing any potential margin due to poor purchasing practices was hurting the company's competitiveness.

An analysis using SRM software showed that the company was buying products other than cars from some 17,500 different vendors! One of the first steps that new group purchasing manager John Fowler undertook was to cut that number to 1,200, with plans to further reduce it to only 200. That means consolidating purchases and negotiating contracts at a significant savings. So far, 85 contracts have been signed worth about £35 million, saving about 50 percent over the old decentralized purchasing program. With the other vendors, special arrangements save the company 25–35 percent. The impact has been to add 10 percent directly to annual profit. From the salesperson's perspective, Fowler's actions mean that 17,300 salespeople lost an account. For 200 salespeople, Dixon is now probably their biggest account.[30]

THE INTERNET AND BUSINESS-TO-BUSINESS SELLING

Companies like Amazon.com and eBay that sell products to consumers over the Internet are well known, but the number of business-to-business transactions over the Internet is 10 times greater than the number of business-to-consumer transactions.[31] Electronic ordering through EDI has been a common practice in business for more than 10 years. However, until recently this EDI activity was transacted over private networks that required buyers and sellers to use specialized software to communicate with each other. Now companies are using the Internet to interact with each other. While some information sent over the Internet is not protected, special secure Internet-based networks connecting buyers and suppliers are called **extranets.**

How does the Internet affect salespeople? Most businesses view their Web sites on the Internet as a tool for supporting salespeople rather than replacing them. Buyers will go to supplier Web sites to get information about product specifications and availability, place orders, and check on the status of orders. Some 40 percent of companies buy an average of 14 percent of their total purchases online, with more companies moving to online purchasing.[32] Thus salespeople will be able to spend less time on transactions and more time building relationships.

In some instances, though, buyers do use the Web instead of buying through salespeople. Reverse auctions are one mechanism that buyers use on the Web. A **reverse auction** is an auction in which a buyer offers a contract and sellers bid. Prices fall as sellers compete to win the sale. Reverse auctions work best when the product being purchased can be specified completely and clearly, when the purchase is large enough to attract multiple competitive suppliers, and when the buying company has the infrastructure to support a reverse auction. Buyers are finding you can't just put a product description on the Web and have a reverse auction; it takes planning, accessibility of personnel to answer sellers' questions, and other resources.[33] When it works, though, it can save both money and time. Owens Corning began using reverse auctions in 2001 and conducted over 200 such auctions in 2002, each worth an average of $1 million. Savings averaged 15 percent over procurement through other methods, after accounting for the cost of the reverse auction system.[34] The U.S. Navy saved almost $1 million in its first reverse auction, a reduction of nearly 30 percent over the original price.[35] Heinz has used auctions over 1,000 times, saving more than $60 million. They've found that being completely open and honest with suppliers led to much greater savings and satisfaction because it gave suppliers some flexibility in what they could offer.[36] Reverse auctions can clearly save buyers a great deal of money when buyers know exactly what they need.

thinking **it** through

Review the stages in the decision-making process described earlier in the chapter. Do you go through those stages when making an important purchase? How does the Internet affect the way you buy products and services? What effect does it have on each stage of the process?

SUMMARY

Salespeople sell to many different types of customers, including consumers, business enterprises, government agencies, and institutions. This text focuses on selling to organizations rather than to consumers. Selling to organizations differs from selling to consumers because organizations are more concentrated, demand is derived, and the buying process is more complex.

The organizational buying process consists of eight steps, beginning with the recognition of a need and ending with the evaluation of the product's performance. Each step involves several decisions. As organizations progress through these steps, decisions made at previous steps affect subsequent steps, leading to a creeping commitment. Thus salespeople need to be involved in the buying process as early as possible.

The length of the buying process and the role of various participants depend on the customer's past experiences. When customers have had considerable experience in buying a product, the decision becomes routine—a straight rebuy. Few people are involved, and the process is short. However, when customers have little experience in buying a product—a new task—many people are involved, and the process can be quite lengthy.

The people involved in the buying process are referred to as the buying center. The buying center is composed of people who are initiators, users, influencers, gatekeepers, and deciders. Salespeople need to understand the roles buying center members play to effectively influence their decisions.

Individuals in the buying center are concerned about satisfying the economic, quality, and service needs of their organization. In addition, these people have personal needs they want to satisfy.

Organizations are facing an increasingly dynamic and competitive environment. Purchasing is becoming a strategic weapon with the development of supply chain management and supplier relationship management strategies.

The Internet is playing a much more important role in business-to-business transactions than it plays in the widely publicized business-to-consumer e-businesses. Business-to-business applications of the Internet are designed to support salespeople's ability to build relationships with major customers.

KEY TERMS

always-a-share
annual spend
automatic replenishment (AR)
buying center
capital equipment
creeping commitment
deciders
derived demand
efficient consumer response (ECR)
electronic data interchange (EDI)
emotional needs
end users
extranet
gatekeepers
influencers
initiators
just-in-time (JIT) inventory control

life-cycle costing
lost-for-good
material requirements planning (MRP)
modified rebuy
MRO supplies
new task
original equipment manufacturer (OEM)
producers
profit margin
quick-response system
rational needs
resellers
reverse auction
services
straight rebuy
supplier relationship management
supply chain management

turnover
users
value analysis

vendor analysis
vendor loyalty

ETHICS PROBLEMS

1. You know that the federal government has goals for purchasing from women-owned and minority-owned businesses. You have a product that is innovative and patented, and will save the lives of soldiers that patrol in areas like Iraq. But your business does not qualify as woman-owned or minority-owned because you are a white male, so you are thinking of bringing a partner into the business—your sister. Is this appropri-ate? Or would it be better to license the product to an already certified minority-owned business?

2. You are talking about this class to someone who isn't very familiar with business. When you mention you are studying how people make buying decisions and that this information will help you be a better salesperson, your friend says that you are just trying to learn how to manipulate people more effectively. How do you respond?

QUESTIONS AND PROBLEMS

1. Will salespeople be necessary in the future? Or will the Internet take over? Why or why not? If you see limited application of the Internet, what conditions make purchasing (or selling) over the Internet worthwhile? Does this vary for consumers compared to business buyers?

2. You sell equipment that bends metal pipes or tubes. List all of the products you can think of with bent metal pipes or tubes. Then list the markets from which your demand is derived. What factors are going to influence your business?

3. How would the purchasing decision process differ in the following situations? Which situation is a new task? A modified rebuy? A straight rebuy? How likely is the buyer to get other people in the organization involved? Which types of people are likely to get involved in each decision? Which situation is likely to produce the slowest decision?

  a. The organization is purchasing a custom-designed machine to be used in the manufacturing of automobile engines.

  b. An organization reorders LCD screens that it uses in making medical monitoring equipment from a regular supplier from which it has bought in the past.

  c. The organization is buying an improved and updated microprocessor for its medical monitoring equipment. It is considering its past suppliers as well as some suppliers that it has not bought from before.

4. A retail chain wants to buy new electronic cash registers. Which criteria for evaluating supplier proposals might be used by (a) the purchasing agent, (b) the engineering department, (c) the sales manager, and (d) the head of the legal department? How would this purchase differ from a purchase of cash registers by a company that sells store fixtures and equipment to small retailers?

5. Sally Brown, a purchasing agent, views her decision to buy chemicals used to clean the plant floors as a routine purchase decision. Assume you are a salesperson working for a chemical distributor from which Brown does not currently order. How would you try to make a sale to Brown?

6. Harvey Mackay, noted business author and consultant, says that if you can't be the number one supplier, be number two. Does this make sense if the account is "lost-for-good?" Why or why not? What conditions might change your answer?

7. Why might management place pressure on purchasing agents to buy from the lowest bidder? Why might a purchasing agent ignore this pressure and buy from a higher-priced bidder?

8. Under what conditions might loyalty to a supplier be economically efficient? When might it be inefficient or wasteful?

9. Mitchell's Metal Shop is considering the purchase of a new press, a machine that bends sheet metal. The cost is $10,000, which is about 25 percent of the firm's profit for the quarter. Ford Motor Company is also considering buying about 30 new presses. Discuss how risk is different for Frank Mitchell, owner of Mitchell's Metal Shop, and Ford.

10. You are selling a health care plan to a company. You attend a meeting of people in the company who will participate in the buying decision. Based on the following conversation, which type of buying center person do you think each individual is?

"We need a health plan for our employees. The plan must have doctors who are close to

where our employees work, not close to the plant," says Fred, the plant manager.

"I'll work with you to develop the specifications for the plan," offers Mark, the human resources director.

"I want to make sure that my doctor is covered under the plan," notes Rachael, a production supervisor.

"I will review the plan and let you know what my final decision is," says Shirley, the CEO.

Based on your classification of these people, at which stages in the buying process will each have the most influence?

CASE PROBLEMS

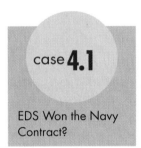

case **4.1**

EDS Won the Navy Contract?

EDS won the U.S. Navy contract to create and install a computer network linking the Navy's 4,000 locations. In 2004, four years after winning the contract, the company has lost over $2 billion on the deal, and many people hardly consider this contract a victory. How could this happen?

In part, the losses stemmed from a lack of experience in selling to the government. Congress delayed the start of the contract by 18 months, asking for additional tests. Once started, the EDS order entry system sabotaged orders by requiring the service person's rank when an order was placed. Because no one told the Navy orders were incomplete, warehouses were full of thousands of PCs waiting for the right paperwork. EDS was also unprepared for transferring 67,000 different software packages, compared to the 5,000 it originally estimated.

The company's return to profitability depends on this one account. The company just hired its third CEO in five years, but no one is certain whether this situation can be turned around.

Questions

1. What caused this fiasco? How could it have been avoided?
2. Assume you are the salesperson responsible for this account. What do you do?

Sources: Gary McWilliams, "Sink or Swim," *The Wall Street Journal* (April 6, 2004), pp. A1 and A10; "The Navy and EDS—Committed to NCI Success" (March 26, 2004), http://www.eds.com/news/news.nmci.eds.success.pdf.

case **4.2**

Atlas Manufacturing

Atlas Manufacturing is a manufacturer of patio and outdoor furniture made of plastic and fiberglass. Patty Boyington, floor supervisor in the plant, has noticed that the downtime on the old extrusion equipment has steadily increased. Extrusion is a method of manufacturing by which fiberglass is pushed through a form to be shaped. Some of the products are made with fiberglass extrusion, while others are made through injected molding, in which liquid plastic is injected into a mold and allowed to harden. The extrusion equipment is averaging about 92 percent uptime (8 percent downtime), which is requiring overtime to meet production quotas. She thinks the cost of overtime is getting so high that it may be offset by buying new equipment. Patty approached Bill McFee, plant manager and Patty's boss, about the situation.

"Not only is it costing us more in overtime," said Patty, "our service calls are costing us more, too. In fact, the last time Frank was here to fix it, he said that parts are getting harder to find."

Bill replied, "I know; that equipment is almost 10 years old. But new equipment is a capital purchase and has to go before the finance committee, and we don't have it in the budget."

"I know," Patty grimaced, "but we're not going to meet our operating budget either."

Later that afternoon, Bill scanned a trade magazine and spotted three ads for equipment. He then went to the Web and found two more potential manufacturers, all of whom sell through distributors. There are two to five distributors per piece of equipment. He knows he needs financial information before he can go to the finance committee, but he doesn't want to waste a lot of time and effort on it either if they aren't going to agree to buy.

Questions

1. What is the likely makeup of the buying center?
2. List the roles in the buying center, based on material in the chapter. What are they likely to want in extrusion equipment?
3. What type of purchase situation is this? What implications will that have if you are a salesperson selling extrusion equipment?

ACT! ROLE PLAY

During the rest of this course, you will be calling on one of three accounts. These accounts are listed here, with some information. Information that you gain on each call can be used in subsequent calls as you practice the skills and apply the concepts introduced in each chapter.

Skylight Productions: Skylight Productions is a company that does special marketing events for clients all across the country. For example, when a PGA golf tournament is in town, Skylight may produce a special event for a client that involves the tournament, some of the players, the client's customers, and so forth. Think party planner for a business.

Binswanger Real Estate: Binswanger is a commercial real estate company located in a major metropolitan town. While Binswanger has a lot of industrial space available, their primary focus is retail development and management. They lease out about 30 per cent of the city's retail space and are the largest retail property manage-

ment firm in town. Clients include stores like Old Navy, Gap, Academy, Radio Shack, and others.

Lincoln Manufacturing: Lincoln makes welding equipment, which is sold through welding supply dealers to users, or directly to large accounts like the government. Lincoln is the second largest welding equipment maker in North America, with operations also in Europe and Asia.

Today you want to try to find out what you can about who is involved in the decision process. You have an appointment arranged with a sales manager, thanks to a lead from an American Marketing Association workshop where you presented a session on sales productivity and software. Start from the beginning: Introduce yourself and your company, thanking the buyer for today's meeting, then tell the buyer you'd like to ask some questions. Ask questions about the buying process, based on what you know from the chapter. After the role play, see if you can chart the buyer's organizational structure and the buying center.

APPENDIX: MULTIATTRIBUTE MODEL OF PRODUCT EVALUATION AND CHOICE

The multiattribute model is a useful approach for understanding the factors individual members of a buying center consider to evaluate products and make choices. The multiattribute model is just one approach that companies can take to making purchases, and is most often used in complex decisions involving several vendors.[37] Many business decisions are straight rebuys, but the original vendor selection decision may have involved a multiattribute approach. The vendor analysis form used by Chrysler (see Exhibit 4.7) illustrates the use of this model in selecting vendors. The model also provides a framework for developing sales strategies.

The multiattribute model is based on the idea that people view a product as a collection of characteristics or attributes. Buyers evaluate a product by considering how each characteristic satisfies the firm's needs and perhaps their individual needs. The following example examines a firm's decision to buy laptop computers for its sales force. The computers will be used by salespeople to keep track of information about customers and provide call reports to sales managers. At the end of each day, salespeople will call headquarters and transmit their call reports through a modem.

PERFORMANCE EVALUATION OF CHARACTERISTICS

Assume the company narrows its choice to three hypothetical brands: Apex, Bell, and Deltos. Exhibit A.1 gives information the company collected about each

Exhibit A.1
Information about
Laptop Computers

Characteristic/Brand	Apex	Bell	Deltos
Reliability rating	Very good	Very good	Excellent
Weight (pounds)	3.0	4.5	7.5
Size (cubic inches)	168	305	551
Speed (clock rate in megahertz)	332	500	400
RAM (in megabytes)	64	64	128
Display visibility	Good	Very good	Excellent
Number of U.S. service centers	140	60	20

brand. Note that the information goes beyond the physical characteristics of the product to include services provided by the potential suppliers.

Each buying center member, or the group as a whole in a meeting, might process this objective information and evaluate the laptop computers on each characteristic. These evaluations appear in Exhibit A.2 as ratings on a 10-point scale, with 10 being the highest rating and 1 the lowest.

How do members of the buying center use these evaluations to select a laptop computer? The final decision depends on the relationship between the performance evaluations and the company's needs. The buying center members must consider the degree to which they are willing to sacrifice poor performance on one attribute for superior performance on another. The members of the buying center must make some trade-offs.

No one product will perform best on all characteristics. For example, Apex excels on size, weight, and availability of convenient service; Bell has superior speed; and Deltos provides the best reliability and internal memory.

IMPORTANCE WEIGHTS

In making an overall evaluation, buying center members need to consider the importance of each characteristic. These importance weights may differ from member to member. Consider two members of the buying center: the national sales manager and the director of management information systems (MIS). The national sales manager is particularly concerned about motivating his salespeople to use the laptop computers. He believes the laptops must be small and lightweight and have good screen visibility. On the other hand, the MIS director foresees using the laptop computers to transmit orders and customer inventory information to corporation headquarters. She believes expanded memory and processing speed will be critical for these future applications.

Exhibit A.2
Performance Evaluation
of Laptop Computers

Characteristic/Brand Rating	Apex	Bell	Deltos
Reliability	5	5	8
Weight	8	5	2
Size	8	6	4
Speed	3	8	6
RAM	3	5	8
Display visibility	2	4	6
Service availability	7	5	3

Characteristic	Importance Weights		Brand Ratings		
	Sales Manager	MIS Director	Apex	Bell	Deltos
Reliability	4	4	5	5	8
Weight	6	2	8	5	2
Size	7	3	8	6	4
Speed	1	7	3	8	6
RAM	1	6	3	5	8
Display visibility	8	5	2	4	6
Service availability	3	3	7	5	3
Overall evaluation					
Sales manager's			167	152	143
MIS director's			130	169	177

Exhibit A.3 shows the importance these two buying center members place on each characteristic using a 10-point scale, with 10 representing very important and 1 representing very unimportant. In this illustration the national sales manager and the MIS director differ in the importance they place on characteristics; however, both have the same evaluations of the brands' performance on the characteristics. In some cases people may differ on both importance weights and performance ratings.

OVERALL EVALUATION

A person's overall evaluation of a product can be quantified by multiplying the sum of the performance ratings by the importance weights. Thus the sales manager's overall evaluation of Apex would be as follows:

$$
\begin{aligned}
4 \times 5 &= 20 \\
6 \times 8 &= 48 \\
7 \times 8 &= 56 \\
1 \times 3 &= 3 \\
1 \times 3 &= 3 \\
8 \times 2 &= 16 \\
3 \times 7 &= \underline{21} \\
&\ 167
\end{aligned}
$$

Using the national sales manager's and MIS director's importance weights, the overall evaluations, or scores, for the three laptop computer brands appear at the bottom of Exhibit A.3. These scores indicate the benefit levels the brands provide as seen by these two buying center members.

VALUE OFFERED

The cost of the computers also needs to be considered in making the purchase decision. One approach for incorporating cost calculates the value—the benefits divided by the cost—for each laptop. The prices for the computers and their val-

	Overall Evaluation (Benefits Points)	Assigned Value	
		Computer Cost	Benefit/Cost
Sales manager			
Apex	167	$1,600	$0.10
Bell	152	1,800	0.08
Deltos	143	1,800	0.08
MIS director			
Apex	130	$1,600	0.08
Bell	169	1,800	0.09
Deltos	177	1,800	0.10

ues are shown in Exhibit A.4. The sales manager believes Apex provides more value. He would probably buy this brand if he were the only person involved in the buying decision. On the other hand, the MIS director believes that Bell and Deltos offer the best value.

SUPPLIER SELECTION

In this situation the sales manager might be the key decision maker, and the MIS director might be a gatekeeper. Rather than using the MIS director's overall evaluation, the buying center might simply ask her to serve as a gatekeeper and determine whether these computers meet her minimum acceptable performance standards on speed and memory. All three laptops pass the minimum levels she established of a 332-megahertz clock rate and a 64-megabyte internal memory. Thus the company would rely on the sales manager's evaluation and purchase Apex laptops for the sales force.

Even if a buying center or individual members do not go through the calculations described here, the multiattribute model is a good representation of their product evaluations and can be used to predict product choices. Purchase decisions are often made as though a formal multiattribute model were used.

thinking **it** through

If you were selling the Bell computer to the national sales manager and MIS director depicted in the text and in Exhibits A.3 and A.4, how would you try to get them to believe that your computer provides more value than Apex or Deltos does? What numbers would you try to change?

IMPLICATIONS FOR SALESPEOPLE

How can salespeople use the multiattribute model to influence their customers' purchase decisions? First, the model indicates what information customers use in making their evaluations and purchase decisions. Thus salespeople need to know the following information to develop a sales strategy:

1. The suppliers or brands the customer is considering.
2. The product characteristics being used in the evaluation.
3. The customer's rating of each product's performance on each dimension.
4. The weights the customer attaches to each dimension.

With this knowledge salespeople can use several strategies to influence purchase decisions. First, salespeople must be sure their product is among the brands being considered. Then they can try to change the customer's perception of their product's value. Some approaches for changing perceived value are

1. Increase the performance rating for your product.
2. Decrease the rating for a competitive product.
3. Increase or decrease an importance weight.
4. Add a new dimension.
5. Decrease the price of your product.

Assume that you are selling the Bell computer and you want to influence the sales manager so that he believes your computer provides more value than the Apex computer. Approach 1 involves altering the sales manager's belief about your product's performance. To raise his evaluation, you would try to have the sales manager perceive your computer as small and lightweight. You might show him how easy it is to carry—how well it satisfies his need for portability. The objective of this demonstration is to increase your rating on weight from 5 to 7 and your rating on size from 6 to 8.

You should focus on these two characteristics because they are the most important to the sales manager. A small change in a performance evaluation on these characteristics will have a large impact on the overall evaluation. You would not want to spend much time influencing his performance evaluations on speed or internal memory because these characteristics are not important to him. Of course, your objectives when selling to the MIS director would be different because she places more importance on speed and internal memory.

This example illustrates a key principle in selling. In general, salespeople should focus primarily on product characteristics that are important to the customer—characteristics that satisfy the customer's needs. Salespeople should not focus on the areas of superior performance (such as speed in this example) that are not important to the customer.

Approach 2 involves decreasing the performance rating of Apex. This strategy can be dangerous. Customers prefer dealing with salespeople who say good things about their products, not bad things about competitive products.

In approach 3 you change the sales manager's importance weights. You want to increase the importance he places on a characteristic on which your product excels, such as speed, or decrease the importance of a characteristic on which your product performs poorly, such as display visibility. For example, you might try to convince the sales manager that a fast computer will decrease the time salespeople need to spend developing and transmitting reports.

Approach 4 encourages the sales manager to consider a new characteristic, one on which your product has superior performance. For example, suppose the sales manager and MIS director have not considered the availability of software. To add a new dimension, you might demonstrate a program specially developed for sales call reports and usable only with your computer.

Approach 5 is the simplest to implement: Simply drop your price. Typically firms use this strategy as a last resort because cutting prices decreases profits.

These strategies illustrate how salespeople can adapt their selling approach to the needs of their customers. Using the multiattribute model, salespeople decide how to alter the content of their presentation—the benefits to be discussed—based on customer beliefs and needs. (Chapter 6 describes adaptive selling in more detail and illustrates it in terms of the form of the presentation—the communication style the salesperson uses.)

ADDITIONAL REFERENCES

Alvarado, Ursula Y., and Herbert Kotzab. "Supply Chain Management: The Integration of Logistics in Marketing." *Industrial Marketing Management* 30 (2001), pp. 183–98.

Anderson, Paul Houman, and Paul Chao. "Country-of-Origin Effects in Global Industrial Sourcing: Toward an Integrated Framework." *Management International Review* 43 (Fourth Quarter, 2003), pp. 339–61.

Bell, Geoffrey G.; Robert J. Oppenheimer; and Andre Bastien. "Trust Deterioration in an International Buyer–Supplier Relationship." *Journal of Business Ethics* 36 (2002), pp. 65–78.

Borders, Aberdeen Leila; Wesley J. Johnston; and Edward E. Rigdon. "Beyond the Dyad: Electronic Commerce and Network Perspectives in Industrial Marketing Management." *Industrial Marketing Management* 30, no. 2, pp. 199–205.

Claycomb, Cindy, and Gary L. Frankwick. "A Contingency Perspective of Communication, Conflict Resolution, and Buyer Search Effort in Buyer–Supplier Relationships." *Journal of Supply Chain Management* 40 (Winter 2004), pp. 18–35.

Evans, Joel R., and Barry Berman. "Conceptualizing and Operationalizing the Business-to-Business Value Chain." *Industrial Marketing Management* 30 (2001), pp. 135–48.

Ford, John; Michael LaTour; and Tony Henthorne. "Cognitive Moral Development and Japanese Procurement Executives: Implications for Industrial Marketers." *Industrial Marketing Management* 29, (November 2000), pp. 589–600.

Gaski, John F., and Nina M. Ray. "Measurement and Modeling of Alienation in the Distribution Channel: Implications for Supplier–Reseller Relations." *Industrial Marketing Management* 30 (2001), pp. 207–26.

Goodman, Lester E., and Paul A. Dion. "The Determinants of Commitment in the Distributor/Manufacturer Relationship." *Industrial Marketing Management* 30 (2001), pp. 287–300.

Hult, G. Tomas M. "Cultural Competitiveness in Global Sourcing." *Industrial Marketing Management* 31 (January 2002), pp. 25–34.

Lee, Don Y. "Power, Conflict, and Satisfaction in IJV Supplier–Chinese Distributor Channels." *Journal of Business Research* 52 (2001), pp. 149–60.

McDonald, Jason B., and Kirk Smith. "The Effects of Technology-Mediated Communication on Industrial Buyer Behavior." *Industrial Marketing Management* 33 (February 2004), pp. 107–24.

McQuiston, Daniel. "A Conceptual Model for Building and Maintaining Relationships between Manufacturers' Representatives and Their Principals." *Industrial Marketing Management* 30 (2001), pp. 165–81.

Mirani, Robert; Deanne Moore; and Johna A. Weber. "Emerging Technologies for Enhancing Supplier–Reseller Partnerships." *Industrial Marketing Management* 30 (2001), pp. 101–14.

Mitchell, Tom. "Cisco Resellers Add Value." *Industrial Marketing Management* 30 (2001), pp. 115–18.

Moon, Junyean, and Surinder Tikoo. "Buying Decision Approaches of Organizational Buyers and Users." *Journal of Business Research* 55 (2002), pp. 293–99.

Park, Jeong, and Michele D. Bunn. "Organizational Memory: A New Perspective on the Organizational Buying Process." *The Journal of Business & Industrial Marketing* 18 (February 3, 2003), pp. 237–58.

Siguaw, Judy A.; Thomas L. Baker; and Penny M. Simpson. "Preliminary Evidence on the Composition of Relational Exchange and Its Outcomes: The Distributor Perspective." *Journal of Business Research* 56 (2003), pp. 311–22.

Simpson, Penny; Judy A. Siguaw; and Thomas L. Baker. "A Model of Value Creation: Supplier Behaviors and Their Impact on Reseller-Perceived Value." *Industrial Marketing Management* 30 (2001), pp. 119–34.

Skarmeas, Dionisis, and Constantine S. Katskikeas. "Drivers of Superior Importer Performance in Cross-Cultural Supplier–Reseller Relationships." *Industrial Marketing Management* 30 (2001), pp. 227–42.

Stoddard, James E., and Edward F. Fern. "Buying Group Choice: The Effect of Individual Group Member's Prior Decision Frame." *Psychology & Marketing* 19, no. 1 (2002), pp. 59–78.

Stremersch, Stefan; Stefan Wuyts; and Ruud T. Frambach. "The Purchasing of Full-Service Contracts: An Exploratory Study within the Industrial Maintenance Market." *Industrial Marketing Management* 30 (January 2001), pp. 1–12.

Strutton, David; Neil Herndon; and Lou E. Pelton. "Competition, Collusion, and Confusion: The Impact of Current Antitrust Guidelines on Competition." *Industrial Marketing Management* 30 (2001), pp. 243–54.

Subroto, Roy; Kiva Sivakumar; and Ian F. Wilkinson. "Innovation Generation in Supply Chain Relationships: A Conceptual Model and Research Propositions." *Journal of the Academy of Marketing Science* 32 (Winter 2004), pp. 61–79.

Tuten, Tracy, and David J. Urban. "An Expanded Model of Business-to-Business Partnership Formation and Success." *Industrial Marketing Management* 30 (2001), pp. 149–64.

Weber, John A. "Partnering with Resellers in Business Markets." *Industrial Marketing Management* 30 (2001), pp. 87–100.

USING COMMUNICATION PRINCIPLES TO BUILD RELATIONSHIPS

chapter **5**

part **2**

**SOME QUESTIONS ANSWERED
IN THIS CHAPTER . . .**

- What are the basic elements in the communication process?

- Why are listening and questioning skills important?

- How can salespeople develop listening skills to collect information about customers?

- How do people communicate without using words?

- What are some things to remember when communicating via technology like phones and e-mail?

- How does a salesperson adjust for cultural differences?

PROFILE

I graduated from Northern Illinois University with a B.S. in marketing with a sales emphasis, and took my selling course from Dr. Rick Ridnour. After college, I went to work for my family's business, BarDan Supply Inc. in Rockford, Illinois. BarDan Supply is a metal fabrication tooling and machinery distributorship with a large customer base across North America. Our company offers products and services for companies to process bar, sheet, and plate steel. I deal primarily with customer service and support for machinery and parts orders as well as servicing local customers in the Rockford, Illinois, area.

Communication is everything in our business. When I am addressing a customer's needs for a part or product they need to make, I have to get it right on the first try or we can lose that customer's business. Asking the right questions in order to establish their needs and solve the issues they might have in making parts helps us establish the critical long-term relationships that not only benefit our company, but benefit the customer with the service they expect as well.

When we build that long-term relationship, it helps to open the door for future business down the road. It could be future tooling and parts business or expansion into new capital equipment to help them grow their business. Our goal at BarDan is to become a "one-stop shop" that today's customer is looking for.

Technology has also become critical to our success. Customers today want immediate contact with their vendors. Be it by e-mail, cell phone, fax, or the Internet, people want to be able to make contact when they need you. It is something that our business has had to employ and accept in order to be one step ahead of our competition and be able to survive in today's business climate.

Being able to communicate and dialogue with my customers is the key to being an effective salesperson. By not getting the important information you need to best assist your customer, you can bet they won't be your customer for too long.

Visit our Web site at: www.bardansupply.com.

"Being able to communicate and dialogue with my customers is the key to being an effective salesperson."

Brad Englin, BarDan Supply

BUILDING RELATIONSHIPS THROUGH TWO-WAY COMMUNICATION

As we discussed in Chapter 2, open and honest communication is a key to building trust and developing successful relationships. To develop a good understanding of each other's needs, buyers and sellers must effectively communicate with each other by actively talking and listening. If the communication is successful, the seller's firm not only will benefit by knowing the customer's current needs but also will see what changes it needs to enact to meet unfilled and future needs.

THE COMMUNICATION PROCESS

Exhibit 5.1 illustrates the **two-way communication** process. The process begins when the sender, either the salesperson or the customer, wants to communicate some thoughts or ideas. Because the receiver cannot read the sender's mind, the sender must translate these ideas into words. The translation of thoughts into words is called **encoding**. Then the receiver must decode the message and try to understand what the sender intended to communicate. **Decoding** involves interpreting the meaning of the received message.

Consider a salesperson who is describing a complex product to a customer. At one point, a perplexed look flits across the customer's face. The salesperson receives this nonverbal message and asks the customer what part of the presentation needs further explanation. The feedback the customer's expression provides tells the salesperson that the message is not being received. The customer then sends verbal messages to the salesperson in the form of questions concerning the operation and benefits of the product.

COMMUNICATION BREAKDOWNS

Communication breakdowns can be caused by encoding and decoding problems and the environment in which the communications occur. The following sales interaction between a copier salesperson and a prospect illustrates problems that can arise in encoding and decoding messages:

> What the salesperson wants to say: We have an entire line of Toshiba copiers. But I think the Model 900 is ideally suited for your needs because it provides the basic copying functions at a low price.

Exhibit 5.1
Two-Way Flow of Information

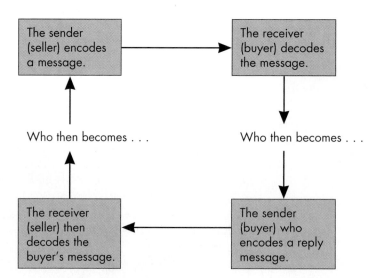

Background noise from traffic can hinder effective communication. The salesperson should attempt to move the discussion to a quieter location so the noise will not distract the customer.

Keith Brofsky/Getty Images/MGH-DIL

What the salesperson says (encodes): The Model 900 is our best-selling copier. It is designed to economically meet the copying needs of small businesses like yours.

What the customer hears: The Model 900 is a low-price copier for small businesses.

What the customer thinks (decodes): This company makes low-price copiers with limited features. They are designed for businesses that don't have much money to spend for a copier. We need a copier with more features. We should invest in a better copier that will meet our future needs.

What the customer says: I don't think I'm interested in buying a copier now.

In this situation the salesperson assumed that price was very important to the prospect, and the prospect thought (incorrectly) that the salesperson's company made only low-price, low-performance copiers.

Communication can also be inhibited by the environment in which the communication process occurs. For example, noises can distract the salesperson and the customer. **Noises** are sounds unrelated to messages being exchanged by the salesperson and the customer, such as ringing telephones or other conversations nearby. To improve communication, the salesperson should attempt to minimize the noises in the environment by closing a door to the room or suggesting that the meeting move to another, quieter place.

Other environmental issues must be dealt with before effective communication can occur. For example, people communicate most effectively when they are physically comfortable. If the room is too hot or too cold, the salesperson should suggest changing the temperature controls, opening or closing a window, or moving to another room. These types of environmental issues and possible solutions will be discussed in Chapters 9 and 10. For now, realize that effective communication can't occur without the proper environment.

thinking it through

Think of a recent face-to-face interaction you had with another person when a communication problem occurred. What caused the miscommunication? Was it a two-way communication with feedback? Did noises affect the interaction?

SENDING VERBAL MESSAGES EFFECTIVELY

Words are tools. Salespeople can use short words and phrases to demonstrate strength and force or to provide charm and grace (like *clean, crisp copies* and *library quiet*).[1] Words in sales presentations should have strength and descriptive quality. Avoid words such as *nice* and *good* and phrases that make you sound like an overeager salesperson such as *a great deal*, *I guarantee you will . . .*, and *No problem!* Also avoid using off-color language, slang, and foul language, even with established customers.[2]

Every salesperson should be able to draw on a set of words to help present the features of a product or service. The words might form a simile, such as *This*

"TROY TRIES HARD, BUT HE'S NOT THE SHARPEST CRAYON IN THE BOX"

"Not the sharpest knife in the drawer." "Lights are on, but nobody's home." "A few bricks short of a load." "Elevator doesn't go to the top." "In the pinball game of life, his flippers were a little farther apart." "A few fries short of a happy meal." What do all of these statements have in common? They're metaphors, denoting one kind of object in place of another—in this case, to describe someone who is not all that smart.

Most salespeople use metaphors (such as "We're making it possible for you to raise the bar in terms of what you can expect from your suppliers" or "Our computerized help desk will be a sturdy bridge to your important customers"). Want some tips for improving their use?

- Use the fewest words possible. For example, say "swimming with sharks," not "swimming in a great big ocean that has a number of sharks swimming around you at the same time."

- Use metaphors that listeners can easily picture. Most people can visualize swimming with sharks around them, but would have more trouble picturing themselves swimming in a pool of asphalt.

- Make sure they're appropriate for the topic. "Swimming with dolphins" wouldn't make quite the same impression as using the word "sharks" if you're trying to convey a predatory situation.

- Make sure they're appropriate for the audience and do not offend. Don't use the shark metaphor when talking to someone whose son was attacked in Florida by a shark. The opening examples could easily be offensive to someone sensitive or someone who has a child with a mental disability.

- Don't overdo their use. It can get distracting if someone talks only in metaphors.

Now you can return to reading the chapter, and learn communication principles that may someday "save your skin"!

Sources: Personal correspondence with Peter J. Leone, Jr., and Scott Luostari; Vincent Muli Wa Kituku, "Tapping the True Power of a Metaphor Requires Creativity," *Presentations*, July 2003, p. 58.

---

battery backup is like a spare tire; a metaphor such as *This machine is a real work-horse*; or a phrase drawing on sensory appeal, such as *smooth as silk* or *strong as steel*. Building Partnerships 5.1 gives some valuable tips for using metaphors.

Words have different meanings in different cultures and even in different subcultures of the United States. In England the hood of a car is called the *bonnet*, and the trunk is called the *boot*. In Boston a *milkshake* is simply syrup mixed with milk, whereas a *frappe* is ice cream, syrup, and milk mixed together. Studies show that about half of blacks over the age of 40 prefer the designation "black," while those 18–39 years old prefer "African American."[3]

Salespeople can paint word pictures to help customers understand the benefits or features of a product. A **word picture** is a story designed to help the buyer visualize a point, as Selling Scenario 5.1 illustrates. To use a word picture effectively, the salesperson needs to paint as accurate and reliable a picture as possible. Also, salespeople cannot assume that all customers will be familiar with trade jargon, and thus need to check with their customers continually to determine whether they are interpreting sales messages properly.[4]

A salesperson's delivery of words affects how the customer will understand and evaluate his or her presentations. Poor voice and speech habits make it difficult for customers to understand the salesperson's message. **Voice characteristics** include rate of speech, loudness, inflection, and articulation.

CAN YOU PAINT A PICTURE?

I work for Lutron Electronics, a high-tech firm that manufactures and designs lighting controls for residential, commercial, and institutional applications, and I call on interior designers, architects, and the EXPO Design Centers (a Home Depot company) to educate them and get them to specify Lutron products.

I like to use word pictures when selling. For example, when trying to get someone to understand the value of a whole-house lighting system, I explain the convenience of having control of lights from a car by telling them, "You leave the house. But you've been gone longer than you thought, it's dark outside and in your home. Maybe you have bags of groceries or other shopping bags you're fumbling with, or even kids. Do you fumble around trying to get into the house and not step on the truck little Johnny left in front of the door?

"Well, now imagine never having to come into a dark house again. With our lighting system, you can turn lights on from your car and create a pathway of light to get you from your garage, down a hall, and into your kitchen, or on into your bedroom—however you normally come into your home, all without doing any special wiring in your home."

I can often win over customers by painting these pictures because these are images they are familiar with. Almost everyone has had these experiences and can easily relate to them. Most people just don't realize they can do something about it.

Source: Barbara Kellgren, used by permission.

In order for the salesperson to communicate with this buyer, he must use words and metaphors that are meaningful and interesting to the buyer.

Digital Vision/Getty Images

Customers have a tendency to question the expertise of salespeople who talk slower or faster than the normal rate of 140 words per minute. Salespeople should vary their rate of speech, depending on the nature of the message and the environment in which the communication occurs. Simple messages can be delivered at faster rates, and more difficult concepts should be presented at slower rates.

Loudness should be tailored to the communication situation. To avoid monotony, salespeople should learn to vary the loudness of their speech. Loudness can also be used to emphasize certain parts of the sales presentation, indicating to the customer that these parts are more important.

Inflection is the tone or pitch of speech. At the end of a sentence, the tone should decrease, indicating the completion of a thought. When the tone goes up at the end of a sentence, listeners often sense uncertainty in the speaker. Use inflection to reduce monotony. However, don't forget to be yourself. The buyer can be turned off if you're obviously just trying to copy the successful communication traits of someone else.[5]

Articulation refers to the production of recognizable sounds. Articulation is best when the speaker opens his or her mouth properly; then the movements of the lips and tongue are unimpeded. When the lips are too close together, the enunciation of certain vowels and consonants suffers.

When asking questions, successful salespeople remember to encourage the buyer to provide a full response. They also avoid asking leading questions that suggest there is only one appropriate answer and remember to ask short, simple questions.

ACTIVE LISTENING

Many people believe effective communication is achieved by talking a lot. Inexperienced salespeople often go into a selling situation thinking they have to outtalk the prospect. They are enthusiastic about their product and company, and they want to tell the prospect all they know. However, salespeople who monopolize conversations cannot find out what customers need.[6] One authority suggests an **80–20 listening rule:** Salespeople should listen 80 percent of the time and talk no more than 20 percent of the time.[7]

People can speak at a rate of only 120 to 160 words per minute, but they can listen to more than 800 words per minute. This difference is referred to as the **speaking–listening differential.** Because of this differential, salespeople often become lazy listeners. They do not pay attention and often remember only 50 percent of what is said immediately after they hear it.

Effective listening is not a passive activity. Salespeople who practice **active listening** project themselves into the mind of the speaker and attempt to feel the way the speaker feels. If a customer says she needs a small microphone, the Sony salesperson needs to listen carefully to find out what the term *small* means to this particular customer, how small the microphone has to be, why she needs a small microphone, and what she will be willing to sacrifice to get a small microphone. Active listening enables the salesperson to recommend a type of microphone that will meet the customer's specific needs.

Active listeners think while they listen. They think about the conclusions toward which the speaker is building, evaluate the evidence being presented, and sort out important facts from irrelevant ones. Active listening also means the listener attempts to draw out as much information as possible. Gestures can motivate a person to continue talking.[8] Head nodding, eye contact, and an occasional *I see*, *Tell me more*, and *That's interesting* all demonstrate an interest in and understanding of what is being said. Take a moment to complete the questionnaire in Exhibit 5.2 to rate your active listening skills.

Suggestions for active listening include (1) repeating information, (2) restating or rephrasing information, (3) clarifying information, (4) summarizing the conversation, (5) tolerating silences, and (6) concentrating on the ideas being communicated.[9]

REPEATING INFORMATION

During a sales interaction the salesperson should verify the information she or he is collecting from the customer. A useful way to verify information is to repeat, word for word, what has been said. This technique minimizes the chance of misunderstandings:

> CUSTOMER: I'll take 20 cases of Nestlé milk chocolate hot cocoa and 12 cases of the rich chocolate.
>
> SALESPERSON: Sure, Mr. Johnson, 20 cases of milk chocolate and 12 cases of rich chocolate.
>
> CUSTOMER: Wait a minute. I got that backward. The rich chocolate is what sells the best here. I want 20 cases of the rich chocolate and 12 cases of the milk chocolate.
>
> SALESPERSON: Fine. Twelve milk chocolate, 20 rich chocolate. Is that right?
>
> CUSTOMER: Yes. That's what I want.

Salespeople need to be careful when using this technique, however. Customers can get irritated with salespeople who echo everything.

Exhibit 5.2
Test Your Active Listening Skills

	My performance could be improved substantially			My performance needs no improvement	
During a typical conversation:					
1. I project an impression that I sincerely care about what the person is saying.	1	2	3	4	5
2. I don't interrupt the person.	1	2	3	4	5
3. I don't jump to conclusions.	1	2	3	4	5
4. I ask probing questions.	1	2	3	4	5
5. I ask continuing questions like "Could you tell me more?"	1	2	3	4	5
6. I maintain eye contact with the person.	1	2	3	4	5
7. I nod to show the person that I agree or understand.	1	2	3	4	5
8. I read the person's nonverbal communications.	1	2	3	4	5
9. I wait for the person to finish speaking before evaluating what has been said.	1	2	3	4	5
10. I ask clarifying questions like "I'm not sure I know what you mean."	1	2	3	4	5
11. I restate what the person has stated or asked.	1	2	3	4	5
12. I summarize what the person has said.	1	2	3	4	5
13. I make an effort to understand the person's point of view.	1	2	3	4	5
14. I try to find things I have in common with the person.	1	2	3	4	5

Scoring: 60–70=Outstanding; 50–59=Good; 40–49=Could use some improvement; 30–39=Could definitely use some improvement; Under 30=Are you listening?

Source: An adaptation of the ILPS scale. Stephen B. Castleberry, C. David Shepherd, and Rick E. Ridnour, "Effective Interpersonal Listening in the Personal Selling Environment: Conceptualization, Measurement, and Nomological Validity," *Journal of Marketing Theory and Practice*, Winter 1999, pp. 30–38.

RESTATING OR REPHRASING INFORMATION

To verify a customer's intent, salespeople should restate the customer's comment in their own words. This step ensures that the salesperson and customer understand each other.

CUSTOMER: The service isn't quite what I had expected.

SALESPERSON: I see, you're a little bit dissatisfied with the service we've been giving you.

CUSTOMER: Oh, no. As a matter of fact, I've been getting better service than I thought I would.

CLARIFYING INFORMATION

Another way to verify a customer's meaning is to ask questions designed to obtain additional information. These can give a more complete understanding of the customer's concerns.

CUSTOMER: Listen, I've tried everything. I just can't get this drill press to work properly.

SALESPERSON: Just what is it that the drill press doesn't do?

CUSTOMER: Well, the rivets keep jamming inside the machine. Sometimes one rivet is inserted on top of the other.

SALESPERSON: Would you describe for me the way you load the rivets onto the tray?

CUSTOMER: Well, first I push down the release lever and take out the tray. Then I push that little button and put in the rivets. Next, I push the lever again, put the tray in the machine, and push the lever.

SALESPERSON: When you put the tray in, which side is up?

CUSTOMER: Does that make a difference?

This exchange shows how a sequence of questions can clarify the problem and help the salesperson determine its cause.

SUMMARIZING THE CONVERSATION

An important element of active listening is to mentally summarize points that have been made. At critical spots in the sales presentation, the salesperson should present his or her mentally prepared summary. Summarizing provides both salesperson and customer with a quick overview of what has taken place and lets them focus on the issues that have been discussed. Summarizing also lets the salesperson change the direction of the conversation.

CUSTOMER: So I told him I wasn't interested.

SALESPERSON: Let me see whether I have this straight. A salesperson called on you today and asked whether you were interested in reducing your costs. He also said he could save you about $125 a month. But when you pursued the matter, you found out the dollar savings in costs were offset by reduced service.

CUSTOMER: That's right.

SALESPERSON: Well, I have your account records right here. Assuming you're interested in getting more for your company's dollar with regard to cell service costs, I think there's a way we can help you—without having to worry about any decrease in the quality of service.

CUSTOMER: Tell me more.

To be an effective listener, the salesperson demonstrates an interest in what the customer is saying and actively thinks about questions for drawing out more information.

Keith Brofsky/Getty Images/MGH-DIL

TOLERATING SILENCES

This technique could more appropriately be titled "Bite your tongue." At times during a sales presentation, a customer needs time to think. This need can be triggered by a tough question or an issue the customer wants to avoid. While the customer is thinking, periods of silence occur. Salespeople may be uncomfortable during these silences and feel they need to say something. However, the customer cannot think when the salesperson is talking. The following conversation about setting a second appointment demonstrates the benefits of tolerating silence:

SALESPERSON: What day would you like me to return with the samples and give that demonstration to you and your team?

CUSTOMER: [obviously thinking]

SALESPERSON: [silence]

CUSTOMER: Okay, let's make it on Monday, the 22nd.

SALESPERSON: Fine, Ms. Quinn. What time would be most convenient?

CUSTOMER: Hmmm . . .

SALESPERSON: [silence]

CUSTOMER: Ten o'clock would be best for me.

CONCENTRATING ON THE IDEAS BEING COMMUNICATED

Frequently what customers say and how they say it can distract salespeople from the ideas the customers are actually trying to communicate. For example, salespeople may react strongly when customers use emotion-laden phrases such as *bad service* or *lousy product*. Rather than getting angry, the salesperson should try to find out what upset the customer so much. Salespeople should listen to the words from the customer's viewpoint instead of reacting from their own viewpoint.

READING NONVERBAL MESSAGES FROM CUSTOMERS

In addition to asking questions and listening, salespeople can learn a lot from their customers' nonverbal behaviors.[10] John Napier, author of the book *Hands*, put it this way: "If language was given to men to conceal their thoughts, then gestures' purpose was to disclose them. Experts on nonverbal behavior say we literally leak our true or masked feelings through our body language and movements."[11] In this section we discuss how salespeople can collect information by observing their customers' **body language**. Later in the chapter we examine how salespeople can use the three forms of **nonverbal communication**—body language, space, and appearance—to convey messages to their customers.

BODY ANGLE

Back-and-forth motions indicate a positive outlook, whereas side-to-side movements suggest insecurity and doubt. Body movements directed toward a person indicate a positive regard; in contrast, leaning back or away suggests boredom, apprehension, or possibly anger. Changes in position may indicate that a customer wants to end the interview, strongly agrees or disagrees with what has been said, or wants to place an order.

FACE

The face has many small muscles capable of communicating innumerable messages. Customers can use these muscles to indicate interest, expectation, concern, disapproval, or approval. The eyes are the most important area of the face. The pupils of interested or excited people tend to enlarge. Thus by looking at a customer's eyes, salespeople can often determine when their presentations have made an impression. For this reason many Chinese jade buyers wear dark glasses so they can conceal their interest in specific items and bargain more effectively. Even the rate at which someone blinks can tell a lot about a person. The average blink rate for a relaxed person is 10 to 20 blinks per minute (bmp). During normal conversation, it increases to about 25 bmp. Bmp over 50, and particularly over 70 bmp, indicates high stress levels.[12]

Eye position can indicate a customer's thought process. Eyes focused straight ahead mean a customer is passively receiving information but devoting little effort to analyzing the meaning and not really concentrating on the presentation. Intense eye contact for more than three seconds generally indicates customer displeasure. Staring indicates coldness, anger, or dislike. Customers look away from the salesperson while they actively consider information in the sales presentation.

The customer in the left panel is giving negative nonverbal signals of arms crossed and no smile. Both buyers and the seller in the right panel are giving positive, nonverbal signals.

Chuck Savage/Corbis

Keith Brofsky/Getty Images/MGH-DIL

When the customer's eyes are positioned to the left or right, the salesperson has succeeded in getting the customer involved in the presentation. A gaze to the right suggests the customer is considering the logic and facts in the presentation, and gazing to the left suggests more intense concentration based on an emotional consideration. Eyes cast down offer the strongest signal of concentration. However, when customers cast their eyes down, they may be thinking, How can I get my boss to buy this product? or How can I get out of this conversation? When customers look away for an extended period, they probably want to end the meeting.

Significant cultural differences dictate the appropriate level of eye contact between individuals.[13] In the United States salespeople look directly into their customers' eyes when speaking or listening to them. Direct eye contact is a sign of interest in what the customer is saying. In other cultures looking someone in the eye may be a sign of disrespect.

- In Japan looking directly at a subordinate indicates that the subordinate has done something wrong. When a subordinate looks directly into the eyes of his or her supervisor, the subordinate is displaying hostility.
- In Muslim countries, eye contact is not supposed to occur between men and women.
- In Korea eye contact is considered rude.
- Brazilians look at people directly even more than Americans do. Americans tend to find this direct eye contact, when held over a long period of time, to be disconcerting.

Skin color and skin tautness are other facial cues. A customer whose face reddens is signaling that something is wrong. That blush can indicate either anger or embarrassment. Tension and anger show in a tightness around the cheeks, jawline, or neck.

The open hands on the left are a positive signal by a salesperson. The intertwined fingers in the middle indicate that the salesperson is expressing his power and authority. On the right the salesperson is playing with his hands, indicating underlying tension.

Michael J. Hruby

ARMS

A key factor in interpreting arm movements is intensity. Customers will use more arm movement when they are conveying an opinion. Broader and more vigorous movement indicates the customer is more emphatic about the point being communicated verbally. Always remember cultural differences. For example, it's rude to cross your arms in Turkey.

HANDS

Hand gestures are very expressive. For example, open and relaxed hands are a positive signal, especially with palms facing up. Self-touching gestures typically indicate tension. Involuntary gestures, such as tightening of a fist, are good indicators of true feelings. The meanings of hand gestures differ from one culture to another. For example, the thumbs-up gesture is considered offensive in the Middle East, rude in Australia, and a sign of OK in France. In Japan the OK sign made by holding the thumb and forefinger in a circle symbolizes money, but in France it indicates that something is worthless.

LEGS

When customers have uncrossed legs in an open position, they send a message of cooperation, confidence, and friendly interest. Legs crossed away from a salesperson suggest that the sales call is not going well. Note that crossing your feet and showing the bottoms of your shoe soles are insulting in Japan.

BODY LANGUAGE PATTERNS

Exhibit 5.3 illustrates the patterns of signals that generally indicate the customer is reacting positively or negatively to a salesperson's presentation. However, no single gesture or position defines a specific emotion or attitude. To interpret a customer's feelings, salespeople need to consider the pattern of the signals via a number of channels. For example, many men are comfortable in informal conversations with their arms crossed. It doesn't necessarily mean they're against you or what you're saying.

In business and social situations, buyers often use nonverbal cues to try to be polite. As a result salespeople often have difficulty knowing what a customer is really thinking. For example, smiling is the most common way to conceal a strong emotion. Salespeople need to know whether a customer's smile is real or just a polite mask. The muscles around the eyes reveal whether a smile is real or polite. When a customer is truly impressed, the muscles around the eyes contract, the skin above the eyes comes down a little, and the eyelids are slightly closed.

Exhibit 5.3

Patterns of Nonverbal
Reactions to
Presentation

Positive Signals	Negative Signals
Uncrossed arms and legs	Crossed arms or legs
Leaning forward	Leaning backward or turned away from you
Smiling or otherwise pleasant expression	Furrowed brow, pursed lips, frowning
Nodding	Shaking head
Contemplative posture	Fidgeting, distracted
Eye contact	No eye contact
Animated, excited reaction	Little change in expression, lifeless

Some other signals that customers may be hiding their true feelings are as follows:

- Contradictions and verbal mistakes. People often forget what they said previously. They may leak their true feelings through a slip of the tongue or a lapse in memory.

- Differences in two parts of a conversation. In the first part of a conversation, a customer may display some nervousness when asked about the performance of a competitor's product and give a flawless response outlining the product's benefits. Later in the conversation, the evaluation of the competitor's product may be much more convoluted.

- Contradictions between verbal and nonverbal messages. For example, facial expression may not match the enthusiasm indicated by verbal comments. Also, a decrease in nonverbal signals may indicate that the customer is making a cautious response.

- Nonverbal signals such as voice tone going up at the end of a sentence, hesitation in the voice, small shrugs, increased self-touching, and stiffer body posture suggest that the customer has concerns.

When customers disguise their true feelings, they are often trying to be polite, not deceptive. To uncover the customer's true feelings and build a relationship, the salesperson needs to encourage the customer to be frank by emphasizing that she or he will benefit from an open exchange of information. Here are some comments a salesperson can make to encourage forthright discussion:

- Perhaps there is some reason you cannot share the information with me.
- Are you worried about how I might react to what you are telling me?
- I have a sense that there is really more to the story than what you are telling me. Let's put the cards on the table so we can put this issue to rest.

SENDING MESSAGES WITH NONVERBAL COMMUNICATION

The preceding section described how salespeople can develop a better understanding of their customers by observing their body language. Salespeople can also use their own body language, spacing, and appearance to send messages to their customers. This section will explore this aspect of body language.

USING BODY LANGUAGE

During a 30-minute sales call around 800 nonverbal signals are exchanged.[14] Astute salespeople use these signals to communicate more effectively with customers. For example, salespeople should strive to use the positive signals shown in Exhibit 5.3. Cooperative cues indicate to customers that the salesperson sincerely wants to help them satisfy their needs. On the other hand, salespeople should avoid using negative cues. These cues will intimidate customers and make them uncomfortable.

Remember this word of warning: The most effective gestures are natural ones, not those you are forcing yourself to perform. A buyer can spot nongenuine nonverbals. Use as much of this information as you can, but don't become so engrossed in following all the rules that you can't be yourself.

Facial Muscles

Nonverbal communication is difficult to manage. Facial reactions are often involuntary, especially during stressful situations. Lips tense, foreheads wrinkle, and eyes glare without salespeople realizing they are disclosing their feelings to a customer. Salespeople will be able to control their facial reactions only with practice.

As with muscles anywhere else in the body, the coordination of facial muscles requires exercise. Actors realize this need and attend facial exercise classes to learn to control their reactions. Salespeople are also performers to some extent and need to learn how to use their faces to communicate emotions.

Nothing creates rapport like a smile. One recent study of tradeshow attendees found that 80 percent were more likely to have a positive perception of a company or product if the seller was smiling.[15] The smile should appear natural and comfortable, not a smirk or an exaggerated, clownlike grin. To achieve the right smile, stand before a mirror or a video camera and place your lips in various smiling positions until you find a position that feels natural and comfortable. Then practice the smile until it becomes almost second nature.

Eye Contact

Appropriate eye contact varies from situation to situation. People should use direct eye contact when talking in front of a group to indicate sincerity, credibility, and trustworthiness. Glancing from face to face rapidly or staring at a wall has the opposite effect. However, staring can overpower customers and make them uncomfortable.

Hand Movements and Hand Shaking

Hand movements can have a dramatic impact. For example, by exposing the palm of the hand, a salesperson indicates openness and receptivity. Slicing hand movements and pointing a finger are very strong signals and should be used to reinforce only the most important points. In most cases pointing a finger should be avoided. This gesture will remind customers of a parent scolding a child. When salespeople make presentations to a group, they often use too few hand gestures. Gestures should be used to drive home a point. But if a salesperson uses too many gestures, acting like an orchestra conductor, people will begin to watch the hands and miss the words.

In terms of shaking hands, salespeople should not automatically extend their hand to a prospect, particularly if the prospect is seated.[16] Shaking hands should be the prospect's choice. If the prospect offers a hand, the salesperson should respond with a firm but not overpowering handshake while maintaining good eye contact. Chances are that you have experienced both a limpid handshake—a hand with little or no grip—and a bone-crunching grip. Either impression is often lasting and negative. Also, if you tend to have sweaty hands, carry a handkerchief.

Women should shake hands in the same manner men do. They should avoid offering their hand for a social handshake (palm facing down and level with the ground, with fingers drooping and pointing to the ground). Likewise, a man should not force a social handshake from a woman in a business setting.

The salesperson selling in an international context needs to carefully consider cultural norms regarding the appropriateness of handshaking, bowing, and other forms of greeting. For example, the Chinese prefer no more than a slight bow in their greeting, whereas an Arab businessperson may not only shake hands vigorously but also keep holding your hand for several seconds. A hug in Mexico communicates a trusting relationship, but in Germany such a gesture would be offensive because it suggests an inappropriate level of intimacy. Germans tend to pump the hand only once during a handshake. Some African cultures snap their fingers after shaking hands, but other Africans would see this act as tasteless. And some Eastern cultures also use the left hand for hygienic purposes, so offering a left hand to them would insult them.

Posture and Body Movements

Shuffling one's feet and slumping give an impression of a lack of both self-confidence and self-discipline. On the other hand, an overly erect posture, such as that of a military cadet, suggests rigidity. Salespeople should let comfort be their guide when searching for the right posture.

To get an idea of what looks good and feels good, stand in front of a mirror and shift your weight until tension in your back and neck is at a minimum. Then gently pull your shoulders up and back and elevate your head. Practice walking by taking a few steps. Keep the pace deliberate, not halting; deliberate, controlled movements indicate confidence and empathy. Note cultural differences like the fact that Japanese value the ability to sit quietly, and can view a fidgety American as uncontrolled.

THE ROLE OF SPACE AND PHYSICAL CONTACT

The physical space between a customer and a salesperson can affect the customer's reaction to a sales presentation. Exhibit 5.4 shows the four distance zones people use when interacting in business and social situations. The **intimate zone** is reserved primarily for a person's closest relationships; the **personal zone** for close friends and those who share special interests; the **social zone** for business transactions and other impersonal relationships; and the **public zone** for speeches, teachers in classrooms, and passersby. The exact sizes of the intimate and personal

Exhibit 5.4
Distance Zones for Interactions

Intimate zone:
0–2 feet

Personal zone:
2–4 feet

Social zone:
4–12 feet

Public zone:
beyond
12 feet

This buyer and seller are in the intimate zone.

Keith Brofsky/Getty Images/MGH-DIL

zones depend on age, gender, culture, and race. For example, the social zone for Latinos is much closer than that for North Americans. Latinos tend to conduct business transactions so close together that North Americans feel uncomfortable.

Customers may react negatively when they believe that salespeople are invading their intimate or personal space. To show the negative reaction, customers may assume a defensive posture by moving back or folding their arms. Although approaching too close can generate a negative reaction, standing too far away can create an image of aloofness, conceit, or unsociability.

In general, salespeople should begin customer interactions at the social zone and not move closer until an initial rapport has been established. If the buyer indicates that a friendlier relationship has developed, the salesperson should move closer.

In terms of touching, buyers fall into two touching groups: contact and noncontact. Contact people usually see noncontact people as cold and unfriendly. On the other hand, noncontact people view contact people as overly friendly and obtrusive. Although some customers may accept a hand on their backs or a touch on their shoulders, salespeople should generally limit touching to a handshake. Touching clearly enters a customer's intimate space and may be considered rude and threatening—an invasion.

APPEARANCE

Physical appearance, specifically dress style, is an aspect of nonverbal communication that affects the customer's evaluation of the salesperson. Two priorities in dressing for business are (1) getting customers to notice you in a positive way and (2) getting customers to trust you. If salespeople overdress, their clothing may distract from their sales presentation. Proper attire and grooming, however, can give salespeople additional poise and confidence.

At one time dressing for work was simple: You just reached in the closet and picked from your wardrobe of blue, gray, and pinstripe suits. Today things are not that simple. With casual days and dress-down Fridays, styles and dress codes vary considerably from office to office. During a given day a salesperson may have to visit his or her company's and customers' offices, each of which may have a different dress code. And sometimes the buyer will have dress codes that even salespeople who visit them must follow. For example, Target has dress codes that apply to salespeople who want to make presentations at their company.[17]

Dr. Vicki West has developed five timeless principles for a salesperson wanting to dress for success.[18] We describe these next.

Principle 1: Consider the Geography

The Temperature   Clothing choices are obviously influenced by *temperature* trends and variations. San Francisco is different from Minneapolis, which is different from Austin, Texas, in humidity, temperature, and weather patterns. These factors dictate the fiber and type of clothing worn. While linen and cotton are cool, warm weather fabrics suitable almost the entire year in the southern part of the United States, they would be appropriate only in the late spring and summer in other locales.

The local cultural norms   Some cities are very formal, and others are known for their casual culture. The economic and business sectors of a community often play a pivotal role in the *local cultural norms* for clothing choices. An example of a cultural norm difference within the short distance of 200 miles that is that between Dallas and Austin, Texas. Dallas is more formal than Austin in most industry sectors. Dallas is known as a "headquarters" town with large regional and national businesses represented. Austin has a large segment of population employed in education, high technology, and the music industry, all of which typically have a younger, more casual workforce.

Principle 2: Consider Your Customers

Their appearance   Customers wear many different types of clothing, which are often dictated by the demands of their profession. Farmers, bankers, high-technology workers, and educators all dress differently depending on the functional demands of their daily work. A salesperson's appearance is certainly impacted by the customers' industry.

Their expectations for your appearance, however, generally reflect their impression of your industry. The salespeople representing the banking industry would be expected to dress differently than salespeople in the music recording industry.

Principle 3: Consider Your Corporate Culture

Norms for your industry should dictate the general parameters for appearance choices. It is obvious that corporate cultures change from time to time. Recently, the trend has been to dress more casually in the hot weather months, even in very conservative industries such as banking and finance. However, the consensus of many industry groups is that it is important to maintain professional business attire on a regular basis, with some exceptions based on geography and a salesperson's customer base.

Principle 4: Consider Your Aspirations

Top levels of your organization generally set the tone for an entire organization. If you aspire to reach a high level in the organization, it would be important to note what expectations your organization might have for your general appearance.

An old rule is to dress *one level above your position.* Watch your immediate superior, who will decide whom to promote. If you want a promotion to the next level in the organization, dress as if you already have the position; then you will be perceived as a good fit for the job.

Principle 5: Consider Your Own Personal Style

Wait until you have the halo effect before making a personal style statement. The "halo effect" refers to the tendency to generalize one positive aspect of your behavior to all aspects of your behavior. This phenomenon can work to your benefit. No one wants to look like a corporate drone with no individual style, but the first week on the job may not be the best time to exercise your personal appearance statement. Wait until you have proved your professional skills, no matter what the industry, before wearing clothing that may be deemed inappropriate to your particular industry.

Be reasonable in your wardrobe choices. Being individualist and memorable can be a very positive decision, depending on the range of choices that are acceptable to a specific industry group. But choosing outrageous or completely unsuitable clothing is probably not in the best interests of your personal career development.

COMMUNICATING VIA TECHNOLOGY

In addition to face-to-face interactions, salespeople communicate with customers by using the telephone, fax, e-mail, and voice mail. As shown in Exhibit 5.5,

Exhibit 5.5

Comparison of Various
Methods of Salesperson
Communications*

	Face-to-face	Telephone	Voice Mail	Fax	E-Mail
Response Time	Fast	Fast	Slow	Slow	Slow
Salesperson Can Use Verbal Communications	Yes	Yes	Yes	No	No
Salesperson Can Hear Buyer's Verbal Communications	Yes	Yes	No	No	No
Salesperson Can Read Buyer's Nonverbal Communications	Yes	No	No	No	No
Quantity of Information Seller Can Send	Highest	Average	Lowest	Varies	Varies
Quantity of Information Buyer Can Send	Highest	Average	None	None	None

*Ratings can vary greatly given the situation.

Developments in technology enable salespeople to improve their communications with customers.

RF/Corbis/MGH-DIL

these methods vary in terms of the interactivity of the communications, the ability to use verbal and nonverbal communication channels, and the quantity of information that can be conveyed. **Response time** is the time between sending a message and getting a response to it.

Telephone and voice mail interactions may not be as effective as face-to-face communication for communicating with customers because the only nonverbal communication that salespeople have access to is voice characteristics. When two people communicate with each other, spoken words play a surprisingly small part in the communication process. Words are responsible for only 40 percent of the information people acquire in face-to-face communication. Voice characteristics account for 10 percent of the message received, and the remaining 50 percent comes from nonverbal communications.[19]

Salespeople need to use the phone correctly and effectively.[20] All of us have used telephones since childhood; many of us have developed bad habits that reduce our effectiveness when talking over the phone. Perfect your phone style by practicing alone before making any calls. Make sure you know what you want to say before placing the call. Many would argue that it is a polite gesture to start by asking, "Is this a good time to talk?" Don't be too rushed to be nice; it is never acceptable to be rude. And don't forget to smile as you talk. Even though the prospect won't see it, she or he will hear it in your enthusiastic tone of voice.

Active listening is as important when conversing over the phone as when conversing in person. Take notes and restate the message or any action you have agreed to undertake. In addition, you will need to encourage two-way communication. If you have ever talked with two-year-olds over the phone, you know that if you ask them a yes-or-no question, they tend to shake their heads yes or no rather than verbalize a response. Similarly, you cannot nod your head to encourage someone to continue talking on the phone. Instead, you must encourage conversations with verbal cues such as *Uh-huh, I see*, or *That's interesting*. Finally, just as in face-to-face conversation, you must be able to tolerate silences so that customers have an opportunity to ask questions, agree or disagree, or relate a point to their circumstances.

It is important to set objectives for your phone call and strategize what you're going to say and why. Here is an example for using the phone to make an appointment:

1. [State customer's name.] Hello, Mr. Peterson? (Pause.)

2. [State your name.] This is Amanda Lowden, with Cisco Systems.

3. [Politely check time.] I hope I didn't catch you in the middle of something urgent or pressing? (Pause.)

4. [State purpose and make presentation.] I'm calling to let you know about our new carrier routing system. I've shown it to several other systems engineers in town, and they found its self-healing and self-defending operating system to be something they wanted to explore further.

5. [Close.] I'd like to meet with you and share some feedback from your business associates. Could you put me on your calendar for 30 minutes next Monday or Tuesday?

6. [Show appreciation and restate time, or keep door open.] Thank you, Mr. Peterson. I'll be at your office at 9 A.M. on Tuesday.

[or]

I appreciate your frankness, Mr. Peterson. I'd like to get back to you in a couple of months. Would that be all right?

Technology makes the transfer of information fast and easy. But it also holds the salesperson at arm's length and makes it difficult to develop rapport. High tech doesn't replace face-to-face interactions; it merely supplements and enhances personal exchanges. Following are some suggestions for salespeople who use high-tech communication:

- Accept the need to communicate through electronic media, but don't be lulled into thinking that immediacy means the same thing as intimacy in communication.

- Learn the customer's preferences and find out which technology tools the customer uses and how she or he likes to communicate. Adapt the content to the customer's preferred communication style. Don't be viewed by your prospect as a spammer![21] Research shows that a seller's poor use of technology tools to communicate with buyers negatively impacts trust, commitment, and their desire to buy from you.[22]

- Avoid "techno overkill." Use electronic communication when speed is critical, but written communication may be better when the customer wants to study the information at his or her leisure.[23]

- Make the communication meaningful. Customers are drowning in information. Don't send junk faxes, and don't send large attachments unless the buyer is expecting them.

- Customize your messages when using technology. Develop a personal hallmark, such as a unique cover for a fax. Use a fresh greeting on your own voice mail each day. Tell callers if a time limit exists for your voice mail, and if possible offer the option to talk to someone immediately.

- Use speed to impress customers. Speed can also be invaluable for damage control. Use technology to exceed a customer's expectations, such as responding immediately to urgent calls via fax or e-mail. E-mail sent to you by customers should be answered by the end of the workday.[24]

- Don't deliver bad news via e-mail; rather, use e-mail to arrange a meeting to discuss the issue.

- Use proper etiquette when leaving voice mail messages, as described in Sales Technology 5.1.

LEAVE A MESSAGE AT THE BEEP . . .

What if in trying to reach the prospect you reach his or her voice mail instead? Here are some tips from experts. If you are making a cold call to set up an appointment, it is usually best not to leave a message. Instead, go to the operator and try to reach the prospect's secretary and find a good time to call back. If you have a referral or have talked to the person before, leave a clear, concise message that includes a suggested time for the person to return your call (so you will know when to expect the call and can be prepared). Speak slowly and distinctly. When leaving a message, don't just talk until the tape runs out. A little casual conversation is fine, but remember that the prospect's time is important. Also, make your message

compelling—for example, "Kris, we just got some new pricing on our heat pump units, and I wanted to share the details with you. But if we hope to get installation before summer, we'll need to act pretty soon. Plus it's expected that our inventory is going to move rather quickly at these prices. If you want to hear the details, call me at (phone number), today if at all possible." Slowly repeat your name and phone number at the end of your message. And remember, never leave bad news on voice mail.

Sources: Howard Feiertag, "Voice-Mail Procedures Reflect Salespeople's Professionalism," *H&MM*, March 15, 2004, p. 12; Kitty O. Locker, *Business and Administrative Communication* (New York: McGraw-Hill, 2006).

This American salesperson needs to recognize the differences between communicating in a high-context Arab culture versus a low-context American culture.

Derek Berwin/The Image Bank

ADJUSTING FOR CULTURAL DIFFERENCES

Salespeople need to recognize that business practices differ around the world. For example, customers in different cultures process verbal and nonverbal information differently. In **low-context cultures** such as the United States, France, and Germany, most of the information that flows between buyer and seller is in the spoken words themselves.[25] As a result, the words must be carefully chosen and extensive details provided via verbal communication, because that is what both sides depend on.

In **high-context cultures** such as Japan, China, Korea, and Mexico, more information is contained in factors surrounding the communication—for example, the background, associations, and basic values of the salesperson and customer. Personal relationships are very important in high-context cultures, and who the salesperson is has as much importance as or more importance than a formal analysis of the product benefits.

Some other differences between high- and low-context cultures are shown in Exhibit 5.8. Studies have shown that the amount of phone and fax communication increases with greater dissimilarity between the buyer and seller in cultural context.[26]

Communication in international selling often takes place in English because English is likely to be the only language salespeople and customers have in common. To communicate effectively with customers whose native language is not English, salespeople need to be careful about the words and expressions they use.

Exhibit 5.8

Differences between High- and Low-Context Cultures

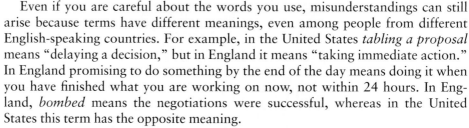

Issue	High Context	Low Context
Person's word	Is his or her bond	Not to be relied on; "get it in writing"
Lawyers	Not very important	Very important
Space	People share common space and stand close to each other	People have a private space around themselves and resent intrusions into their space
Time	Everything is dealt with eventually	Wasting time is to be avoided
Negotiations	Lengthy so that the parties can get a chance to know one another	Accomplished quickly
Competitive bidding	Not very common	Very common

People who use English in international selling should observe the following rules:

- Use common English words that a customer would learn during the first two years of studying the language. For example, use *expense* rather than *expenditure*, or *stop* instead of *cease*.

- Use words that do not have multiple meanings. For example, *right* has many meanings, whereas *accurate* is more specific. When you use words that have several meanings, recognize that nonnative speakers will usually use the most common meaning to interpret what you are saying.

- Avoid slang expressions peculiar to American culture, such as *slice of life*, *struck out*, *wade through the figures*, and *run that by me again*.

- Use rules of grammar more strictly than you would in everyday speech. Make sure you express your thoughts in complete sentences, with a noun and a verb.

- Use action-specific verbs, as in *start the motor*, rather than action-general verbs, as in *get the motor going*.

- Never use vulgar expressions, tell off-color jokes, or make religious references.

Even if you are careful about the words you use, misunderstandings can still arise because terms have different meanings, even among people from different English-speaking countries. For example, in the United States *tabling a proposal* means "delaying a decision," but in England it means "taking immediate action." In England promising to do something by the end of the day means doing it when you have finished what you are working on now, not within 24 hours. In England, *bombed* means the negotiations were successful, whereas in the United States this term has the opposite meaning.

International salespeople need to understand the varying perceptions of time in general and the time it takes for business activities to occur in different countries. For example, in Latin American and Arab countries people are not strict about keeping appointments at the designated times. If you show up for an appointment on time in these cultures, you may have to wait several hours for the meeting to start. Lunch is at 3:00 p.m. in Spain, 12:00 noon in Germany, 1:00 p.m. in England, and 11:00 a.m. in Norway. In Greece no one makes telephone calls between 2:00 p.m. and 5:00 p.m. The British arrive at their desks at 9:30 a.m. but like to do paperwork and have a cup of tea before getting any calls. The French, like the Germans, like to start early in the day, frequently having working breakfasts. Restaurants close at 9:00 p.m. in Norway, just when dinner is starting in Spain. The best time to reach high-level Western European executives is after 7:00 p.m., when daily activities have slowed down and they are continuing to work for a few more hours. However, Germans start going home at 4:00 p.m.

SUMMARY

This chapter discussed the principles of communication and how they can be used to build trust in relationships, improve selling effectiveness, and reduce misunderstandings. The communication process consists of a sender, who encodes information and transmits messages, and a receiver, who decodes the messages. A communication breakdown can occur when the sender does a poor encoding job, when the receiver has difficulty decoding, and when noise and the environment interfere with the transmission of the message.

Effective communication requires a two-way flow of information. At different times in the interaction, both parties will act as sender and receiver. This two-way process enables salespeople to adapt their sales approach to the customer's needs and communication style.

When communicating verbally with customers, salespeople must be careful to use words and expressions their customers will understand. Effective communication is facilitated through the use of word pictures, and by using appropriate voice characteristics like inflection, articulation, and the proper rate of speech and loudness.

Listening is a valuable communication skill that enables salespeople to adapt to various situations. To listen effectively, salespeople need to actively think about what the customer is saying and how to draw out more information. Some suggestions for actively collecting information from customers are to repeat, restate, clarify, summarize the customer's comments, and demonstrate an interest in what the customer is saying.

About 50 percent of communication is nonverbal. Nonverbal messages sent by customers are conveyed by body language. The five channels of body language communication are body angle, face, arms, hands, and legs. No single channel can be used to determine the feelings or attitudes of customers. Salespeople need to analyze the body language pattern composed of all five channels to determine when a customer is nervous, bored, or suspicious.

Salespeople can use nonverbal communication to convey information to customers. In addition to knowing how to use the five channels of body language, salespeople need to know the appropriate distances between themselves and their customers for different types of communications and relationships. Salespeople should learn to use their physical appearance and dress to create a favorable impression on customers.

Finally, two-way communication increases when salespeople adjust their communication styles to the styles of their customers. In making such adjustments, salespeople need to be sensitive to cultural differences when selling internationally and in diverse subcultures.

KEY TERMS

80–20 listening rule
active listening
articulation
body language
decoding
encoding
high-context culture
inflection
intimate zone
loudness
low-context culture

noises
nonverbal communication
personal zone
public zone
response time
social zone
speaking–listening differential
two-way communication
voice characteristics
word picture

ETHICS PROBLEMS

1. Suppose you're a male calling on a male prospect who uses language that is degrading to women. Should you mirror his language to make him like you and feel comfortable dealing with you?

2. Assume you are making a call on a Muslim of the opposite sex. You know that eye contact is not supposed to occur in this situation, but much to your amazement, the buyer continues to look intently into your eyes. You are in an office alone with the buyer. What should you do?

QUESTIONS AND PROBLEMS

1. What are some types of distractions or noise that can affect your ability to listen to the customer? What can you do to reduce these distractions?

2. Have a friend score you using the listening test (Exhibit 5.2) found in this chapter. Compare your friend's score with the one you gave yourself. What can you learn from this?

3. Make a chart with three columns: Items, What I Want This Item to Communicate to Others, and What Others Will Think My Item Is Communicating. In the first column list the following: my hairstyle, the clothing I'm wearing today, and any jewelry or body accents (like earrings). In the second column describe the message you want to communicate with each item. Have someone else fill in the third column, describing what the items communicate to him or her.

4. Develop a word picture that helps explain to a 30-year-old the merits of buying a house instead of renting an apartment.

5. What do the following body language cues indicate?
   a. Tapping a finger or pencil on a desk.
   b. Stroking the chin and leaning forward.
   c. Leaning back in a chair with arms folded across the chest.
   d. Sitting in the middle of a bench or sofa.
   e. Assuming the same posture as the person with whom you are communicating.

6. Word choice is important. Some words, by themselves, may be perceived negatively. Come up with a better word choice that could be more positive for each of the following words: *cost, down payment, deal, objection, cheaper, appointment, commission.*

7. Practice using the speaking–listening differential during a conversation you have with a friend in the next day or so. Report what you learned.

8. Why do you think lawyers wouldn't be as important in a high-context culture, as opposed to a low-context one?

9. Find out what the acceptable clothing styles are for salespeople in the geographic area in which you live. Also, is it acceptable for a salesperson to wear jewelry or body ornaments (such as a tongue-piercing) in your geographic area? What sources did you use to learn the answers to these questions?

10. As a product category, carbonated drinks are referred to with many different labels, depending on where you live: *pop, soda, coke, soda pop,* and so on. Choose the word least like that you normally hear used. Now ask a friend if he or she would like to have a (use the selected word here) and record the reaction to your choice of words.

Jamie Jordon is a salesperson for Hunt-Wesson. He calls on grocery stores, convenience stores, and drugstores, selling products like Hunt's ketchup and soups. A few days ago, in early January, he made a call on Sheree Dhatt, manager of a large regional grocery store chain. In that meeting, Jamie told Sheree about special pricing just released on all Hunt's ketchup purchased between January and March.

Sheree reminded Jamie that she had just placed a rather large order in late December for Hunt's ketchup, and she wondered if her store could still get the discount. The ketchup hadn't even been delivered yet from the distributor.

Jamie didn't know the answer and promised to get back to Sheree as soon as possible. When Jamie got the answer he phoned Sheree right away, but the phone was answered by Sheree's secretary.

SECRETARY: Hello.

JAMIE: Hello, is Sheree there?

SECRETARY: No, she's at one of the stores. Can I help you?

JAMIE: Okay. Well, this is Jamie Jordon.

SECRETARY: How can I help you?

JAMIE: I'm sorry, I should have said, I'm from Hunt-Wesson. Anyway, Sheree had asked me a question and I've got an answer for her.

SECRETARY: Would you like her voice mail?

JAMIE: Sure, that'd be great!

While waiting to be transferred, Jamie flipped open his appointment book and started making a note about another call he was supposed to make later that day. To be honest, he got a little sidetracked and was startled when the receiver blared out.

VOICE MAIL GREETING: Hello, this is Sheree. Leave a message at the beep. Include the time and date you called. Thanks!

JAMIE: Oh, hi. Uh, this is Jamie. From Hunt's. Uh, Jamie Jordon. Sheree? I got that information about the discounts and the answer is no. Can't give them to you because legally you placed your order in December. Sorry. But the pricing is real good and maybe you want to go ahead and order some more. What do you think? Also, I wanted to tell you about a coupon that is going to be coming out in the paper two months from now for our soups. I totally forgot to tell you about it the other day when I was visiting with you. I think you better buy some stock to get ready for the customers who are going to be coming. My recommendation is about 10 cases of each of the better-selling varieties and 5 cases of the others. For each store. Okay? And is that okay about the pricing? I hope so. I talked to my manager . . .

VOICE MAIL SYSTEM: Thank you for your message. Good day.

Then the voice mail system shut down and Jamie heard a dial tone.

Questions

1. Did Jamie do a good job leaving a voice mail message?
2. Rewrite the voice mail message that you would leave in this situation.

Mark Hoffman is a sales representative for Harbor Office Products, an office supply retailer in Manhattan, New York. He has just walked into the office of Maureen Steinnes, the office manager at Bay Digital. Hoffman is 25 years old and has been working for Harbor Office Products for six months. He is dressed in a blue pinstripe suit. Steinnes is about 50 years old and is wearing a pair of slacks and a casual blouse. She is sitting behind her desk, leaning back with her arms crossed.

HOFFMAN [walking around the desk to shake hands with Steinnes]: Good morning, Ms. Steinnes. It's a pleasure to meet you. How are you today?

STEINNES [eye contact is mostly with some papers on her desk]: I'm fine, I suppose. Of course, I was expecting you 15 minutes ago [looking at her watch and sighing]. I have an appointment in 10 minutes, so I don't have much time.

HOFFMAN: I'm only five minutes late. The subway was jammed. You know how it is this time of day.

STEINNES [moving around in her chair and crossing her arms again]: OK. Maybe it wasn't 15 minutes. What can I do for you?

HOFFMAN: I would like to talk to you about our new program for providing office supplies more economically to companies in the telecommunications industry. The program . . .

STEINNES [interrupting, frowning]: Before you waste a lot of time, we just placed a large office supply order with Saratoga Office Supply. We really don't need supplies at this point.

HOFFMAN [blinking rapidly, crossing his arms, speech rate increasing]: That's too bad. Our program could have reduced your office supply costs by 30 percent.

STEINNES [uncrossing arms, leaning forward]: Really?

HOFFMAN [starting to rise and putting on his coat]: Yes, but I guess I'm too late. Well, maybe next time. Goodbye.

Questions

1. How could Hoffman have communicated better with Steinnes by using nonverbal methods?

2. How did Hoffman make a mistake in reading the nonverbal messages sent by Steinnes?

ROLE PLAY

In today's role play interaction, you are still meeting with the same person that you did for Chapter 4 (if you did not do the role play at the end of Chapter 4, you will need to review that information now). That person is telling you about the business. Feel free to ask questions, but your main objective is to listen and understand all you can about the business environment in which he or she operates. Practice active listening skills; after the role play, identify which listening techniques you used. Further, identify the three most important elements about the person's business that you need to understand. Interpret the buyer's body language. Finally, any time you hear jargon, write the word or phrase down.

Note: For background information on these role plays, please see page 27.

To the instructor: Additional information needed to complete the role play is available in the Instructor's Manual.

ADDITIONAL REFERENCES

The Complete Idiot's Guide to Understanding Body Language. New York: Penguin Group (USA) Incorporated, 2004.

Barr, Ann. How to Win the Sale and Keep the Customer: Telephone Sales Scripts, Marketing Letters, Voice Mail, and Email Messages. Philadelphia: Xlibris Corporation, 2003.

Brooks, Bill. "The Power of Active Listening." American Salesman 48 (June 2003), pp. 12–15.

"Forget the Dog & Pony Shows." http://www.chally.com/enews/tip_forgetshows.html (viewed on March 30, 2002).

Feiertag, Howard. "Listening Skills, Enthusiasm Top List of Salespeople's Best Traits." H&MM, (July 15, 2003), pp. 20–21.

Fulfer, Mac. "Nonverbal Communication: How to Read What's Plain as the Nose . . . or Eyelid . . . or Chin . . . on Their Faces." Journal of Organizational Excellence 20 (Spring 2001), pp. 19–27.

Gordon, Kim T. "No Fail E-Mail." Entrepreneur, February 2003, p. 75.

Hackett, Otis. "Hearing Aids: Acronyms That Remind Your Salespeople to Listen." Dealernews, (July 2003), pp. 44–45.

Harvard Business School Press (ed.). Face-to-Face Communications for Clarity and Impact. Boston, MA: Harvard Business School Publishing, 2004.

Holden, Mary T., and Thomas O'Toole. "A Quantitative Exploration of Communication's Role in Determining the Governance of Manufacturer–Retailer Relationships." Industrial Marketing Management 33 (August 2004), pp. 539–48.

Hutcheson, Susanna K. "If You Want Them to Buy . . . Better Listen to What They Need." American Salesman 48 (February 2003), pp. 28–30.

Jacobs, Richard S.; Kenneth R. Evans; Robert E. Kleine III; and Timothy D. Landry. "Disclosure and Its Reciprocity as Predictors of Key Outcomes of an Initial Sales Encounter," Journal of Personal Selling & Sales Management 21, no. 1 (Winter 2001), pp. 51–61.

Knapp, Mark L., and Judith A. Hall. Nonverbal Communication in Human Interaction. Belmont, CA: Wadsworth, 2005.

Lynn, Valerie, and Lynn Manusov. SourceBook of Nonverbal Measures: Going beyond Words. Mahwah, NJ: Lawrence Erlbaum Associates, 2005.

McKenzie, Samuel. "Break Nervous Habits before They Become Distractions." Presentations, (February 2002), p. 62.

Mintu-Wimsatt, Alma, and Jule B. Gassenheimer. "The Moderating Effects of Cultural Context in Buyer–Seller Negotiation." Journal of Personal Selling & Sales Management 20, no. 1 (Winter 2000), pp. 1–9.

Morgan, Nick. Working the Room: How to Move People to Action through Audience-Centered Speaking. Boston: Harvard Business School Press, 2003.

Nelson, Audrey, and Susan K. Golant. You Don't Say: Navigating Nonverbal Communication between the Sexes. New York: Berkley Publishing Group, 2004.

Neuborne, Ellen. "Making E-Mail Work." Sales and Marketing Management, (February 2004), p. 18.

Novinger, Tracy, and Donald Haughey. Communicating with Brazilians: When Yes Means No. Austin, TX: University of Texas Press, 2004.

Page, Charles. Listen . . . It Will Change Your Life. Pacific Grove, CA: Park Place Publications, 2002.

Reid, David A.; Ellen Bolman Pullins; and Richard E. Plank. "The Impact of Purchase Situation on Salesperson Communication Behaviors in Business Markets." Industrial Marketing Management 31, no. 3 (2002), pp. 205–13.

Reilly, Tom. "Less Talking, More Listening." Industrial Distribution 93 (February 2004), p. 65.

Rich, Michael K. "Are We Losing Trust through Technology?" Journal of Business and Industrial Marketing 17, no. 2, pp. 215–22.

"Selling Tips." Sell!ng, July 2003, p. 16.

Shoemaker, Mary E., and Mark C. Johlke. "An Examination of the Antecedents of a Crucial Selling Skill: Asking Questions." Journal of Managerial Issues 14 (Spring 2002), pp. 118–32.

Terminello, Verna, and Marcia Reed. E-Mail: Communicate Effectively. Upper Saddle River, NJ: Prentice Hall, 2002.

Zielinski, Dave. "Cracking the Dress Code." Presentations. (February 2005), pp. 25–33.

ADAPTIVE SELLING FOR RELATIONSHIP BUILDING

chapter **6**

part **2**

**SOME QUESTIONS ANSWERED
IN THIS CHAPTER . . .**

- What is adaptive selling?
- Why is it important for salespeople to practice adaptive selling?
- What kind of knowledge do salespeople need to practice adaptive selling?
- How can salespeople acquire this knowledge?
- How can salespeople adapt their sales strategies, presentations, and social styles to various situations?

PROFILE

I took my personal selling course from Dr. Brian Tietje at California Polytechnic State University, where I earned a BBA degree in marketing in 2001. I am currently an account executive with IGN Entertainment, and sell online advertising for our Web sites to video game companies and agencies. I've learned the importance of adapting to the specific needs of each customer.

For example, one of our clients is one of the most well-known and respected video game publishers in the industry. For years both gamers and the industry had been anticipating the latest installment to one of the most popular game franchises in history. This title was not only important to the publisher, it was important to my company IGN because we knew the power of this game and anticipated a strong marketing push behind this title.

During the advertising planning stage, we told the client the importance of reaching our readers during both the prelaunch and launch periods of the game. Elaborate plans were created at very high spending levels, offering the client the most powerful campaign possible to ensure maximum product exposure and awareness to our visitors.

When we followed up with the client, the following objections were posed:

- The client did not feel that they needed to spend a large amount of money on an advertising presence because the awareness of the game was high due to strong public relations efforts and the popularity of the franchise title— thus there was already huge awareness in the marketplace.

- All ad units needed to be innovative and ground-breaking, just like the game. Therefore, standard advertising units would not work.

The objections were valid, but we worked internally to find an adaptive solution that would meet the advertiser's specific needs and meet our teams' needs.

To face their first objection, we looked at our network of Web sites. The game sites within our network did provide users with much information about the upcoming game. However, we also have a large network of Web sites that includes content sites and channels that do not cover gaming, yet reach a similar demographic. For example, we had recently acquired a movie review Web site called *Rotten Tomatoes* which reaches the mass market audience — a great fit for the game. Our goal was to reach readers of those kinds of sites.

With the help of the advertising product development team, we created a new ad unit never used before. This ad unit helped us overcome the client's first objection and also tied into our second objective, which was new and innovative ad units.

We also thought it was extremely important for the advertiser to have a presence on our gaming Web sites, even though there was a lot of information on the soon-to-be-released game there. We again worked internally with our product development team to create a new advertising unit on the home page of IGN so that on the day of launch, people would be greeted with a new ad unit that highlighted this game.

In addition, we wanted to reach a more targeted audience. The game was going to be available to Playstation 2 users, so we created a new advertisement as well on our Playstation 2 page. The ads on the Playstation 2 page counted down to the day of the launch. This ad would not only get our users excited, it got our advertiser excited!

"I've learned the importance of adapting to the specific needs of each customer."

Katherine Bowe, Account Executive, IGN Entertainment

The response from the client was extremely positive, and we secured ad revenue for a title they almost decided not to promote. It was a success for both the client and IGN.

Visit our Web sites at www.ign.com, www.gamespy.com, www.fileplanet.com, www.teamxbox.com, and www.rottentomatoes.com.

Personal selling is the most effective marketing communication medium because it allows salespeople to tailor their presentations to each customer. They use their knowledge of the customer's buying process (Chapter 4) and finely tuned communication skills (Chapter 5) to learn about their customers and select effective sales strategies. Effective salespeople adapt their selling strategies and approaches to the selling situation. This chapter examines how salespeople can communicate effectively with their customers by practicing adaptive selling.

TYPES OF PRESENTATIONS

Salespeople can choose from a number of presentation types. This text will examine the three most common: (1) the standard memorized presentation, (2) the outlined presentation, and (3) the customized presentation.

STANDARD MEMORIZED PRESENTATION

The **standard memorized presentation**, also called a *canned presentation*, is a completely memorized sales talk. The salesperson presents the same selling points in the same order to all customers. Some companies insist that their inside telemarketing salespeople, for example, memorize the entire presentation and deliver it word for word. Others believe that salespeople should be free to make some minor adjustments.

The standard memorized presentation ensures that the salesperson will provide complete and accurate information about the firm's products and policies. Because it includes the best techniques and methods, the standard memorized presentation can help bring new salespeople up to speed quickly and give them confidence. However, the effectiveness of the standard memorized presentation is limited because it offers no opportunity for the salesperson to tailor the presentation to the needs of the specific customer.

OUTLINED PRESENTATION

The **outlined presentation** is a prearranged presentation that usually includes a standard introduction, standard answers to common objections raised by customers, and a standard method for getting the customer to place an order. An example of an outlined presentation appears in Exhibit 6.1.

An outlined presentation can be very effective because it is well organized. It is more informal and natural than the standard memorized presentation and provides more opportunity for the customer to participate in the sales interaction. It also permits some flexibility in the approach used to present the key points.

CUSTOMIZED PRESENTATION

The **customized presentation** is a written and/or oral presentation based on a detailed analysis of the customer's needs. This type of presentation offers an opportunity to use the communication principles discussed in the last chapter to discover the customer's needs and problems and propose the most effective solu-

Exhibit 6.1

Example of an Outlined Presentation

Scenario: A Procter & Gamble Salesperson Calling on a Grocery Store Manager	
Step in Outlined Sales Presentation	**Say Something Like This**
1. Reinforce past success.	Good morning, Mr. Babcock. I was talking with one of your stockers, and he said that our Crest end-of-aisle display was very popular with customers last weekend. He said that he had to restock it three times. Looks like you made a wise decision to go with that program.
2. Reiterate customer's needs.	I know that profits and fast turns are what you are always looking for.
3. Introduce new Sure antiperspirant campaign.	We have a new campaign coming up for our Sure line.
4. Explain ad campaign and coupon drops.	We will be running a new set of commercials on all three network news programs. . . . Also, we'll be adding an insert in the Sunday coupon section with a 35-cents-off coupon.
5. Explain case allowances.	We are going to give you a $1.20 case allowance for every case of Sure you buy today.
6. Ask for end-of-aisle display and order of cases.	I propose that you erect an end-of-aisle display on aisle 7 . . . and that you order 20 cases.
7. Thank manager for order.	Thank you, and I know the results will be just as good as they were for our Crest promotion.

tion for satisfying those needs. The customer recognizes the sales representative as a professional who is helping to solve problems, not just sell products. The customized presentation allows the salesperson to demonstrate empathy. Cultivating this view is an important step in developing a partnering relationship.

Each of the presentation types just discussed involves a different level of skill, cost, and flexibility. Standard memorized presentations can be delivered at a low cost by unskilled salespeople with little training. On the other hand, the customized presentation can be very costly, requiring highly skilled people to analyze the customer's needs. Salespeople have the greatest opportunity to adapt their presentations to customer needs when using the customized presentation and the least opportunity when using the standard memorized presentation. The next section discusses the importance of adapting sales presentations.

ADAPTIVE SELLING AND SALES SUCCESS

Salespeople practice **adaptive selling** when they react to different sales situations by changing their sales behaviors.[1] An extreme example of nonadaptive selling is using the standard memorized presentation, in which the same presentation is used for all customers. The customized presentation illustrates adaptive selling because the presentation is tailored to the specific needs of the customer.

Adaptive selling is featured in this textbook because this approach forces the salesperson to practice the marketing concept. It emphasizes the importance of satisfying customer needs. And being adaptable increases buyer trust and commitment

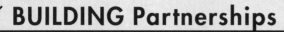

A PECK ON THE CHEEK

I work for Lutron Electronics, a high-tech firm that manufactures and designs lighting controls for residential, commercial, and institutional applications; and I call on interior designers, architects, and the EXPO Design Centers (a Home Depot company) to educate them and get them to specify Lutron products.

My position takes me to southeast Florida twice a month, and the communication that takes place there is different from anywhere else. The store in Miami does a lot of export business with lots of customers from Mexico, Puerto Rico, and South America.

People with Spanish/Hispanic backgrounds have a different idea of proxemics than most Americans. For instance, men and women stand much closer to a stranger than what most Americans find comfortable. Plus, there is a different sense of camaraderie there than at other stores I call on.

Like when I arrive at the Miami store, the sales associates will give me a peck on each cheek—which is a standard greeting in the Spanish world when you see friends. Other locations would probably take this as sexual harassment, but it's not. It's just one more way in which I adapt to the customer's personal style and customs.

Source: Barbara Kellgren, used by permission.

and results in higher sales performance.[2] Building Partnerships 6.1 illustrates how one salesperson builds better customer relationships by adapting her nonverbal communications to the specific sales situation.

The communication principles described in Chapter 5 are required to practice adaptive selling successfully. For example, a Kohler sales representative may believe that a portable generator manufacturer is interested in buying an economical, low-horsepower gasoline motor. While presenting the benefits of a low-cost motor, the sales rep discovers, by observing nonverbal behaviors, that the customer is interested in discussing overall operating costs. At this point the rep asks some questions to find out whether the customer would pay a higher price for a more efficient motor with lower operating costs. Based on the customer's response, the rep may adopt a new sales strategy: presenting a more efficient motor and demonstrating its low operating costs.

It is sometimes hard for people to realize that the world is not made up of people just like them. Many people are much older than you, while some are younger than you. They practice different religions, like different foods, and shop at stores where you would never think of shopping. They have different moral beliefs and different ideas about "the perfect product" and were raised in a totally different way. Their hopes and aspirations don't match yours. Many of them would be shocked to hear what your life's dreams and goals are.

We are not just talking about differences in people in other countries. We are talking about people who live next door to you, who are sitting next to you in your classroom. Men and women can react differently to presentations.[3] Generation Xers are very different from Baby Boomers, who are different from the generations before them.[4] One salesperson reported that grocery stores that cater to migrant farmers in the San Francisco area want a different product mix (such as more demand for Hormel SPAM®) than a grocery store in midtown San Francisco (more demand for upscale, specialty Hormel meat products like Cure81® ham). The sooner you realize that your world is made up of diverse people, the sooner you will realize the importance of becoming adaptive. Selecting the appropriate sales strategy for a sales situation and making adjustments during the interaction are crucial to successful selling.

Salespeople should also adapt to the customer's desire for a specific type of relationship. For example, if a customer is not interested in developing a strategic partnership and is more interested in maintaining a relational partnership, the salesperson should adapt to this desire.

Practicing adaptive selling does not mean that salespeople should be dishonest about their products or their personal feelings. It does mean that salespeople should alter the content and form of their sales presentation so that customers will be able to absorb the information easily and find it relevant to their situation.

thinking **it** through

Do you act act differently when talking to your professor than when you talk to your friends? How do you change your behavior when you go home for school breaks? Do you act differently when you go to a restaurant with a date? With some friends? With your parents? Why?

The advantages and disadvantages of the three types of sales presentations illustrate the benefits and drawbacks of adaptive selling. Adaptive selling gives salespeople the opportunity to use the most effective sales presentation for each customer. However, uncovering needs, designing and delivering different presentations, and making adjustments require a high level of skill. The objective of this textbook is to help you develop the skills and knowledge required to practice adaptive selling.[5]

KNOWLEDGE MANAGEMENT

A key ingredient in effective selling is knowledge.[6] Salespeople need to know about the products they are selling, the company they work for, and the customers they will be selling to. Knowledge enables the salesperson to build self-confidence, gain the buyer's trust, satisfy customer needs, and practice adaptive selling.[7]

This salesperson has acquired an extensive knowledge of the customer's systems.

William Taufic/Corbis

PRODUCT AND COMPANY KNOWLEDGE

Salespeople need to have a lot of information about their products, services, and company.[8] Purchasing agents rate product knowledge as one of the most important attributes of good salespeople. Effective salespeople need to know how products are made, what services are provided with the products, how the products relate to other products, and how the products can satisfy customers' needs. Salespeople also need to know about their competitors' products as well as their own, because they are frequently asked to compare their products to competitors' offerings.[9]

KNOWLEDGE ABOUT SALES SITUATIONS AND CUSTOMERS

Equally important with product and company knowledge is detailed information about the different types of sales situations and customers salespeople may encounter.[10] For example, Nextel salespeople need to be knowledgeable about networking and information technology and have an overall expertise in how businesses operate in order to sell cell phone service to their unique customer types. As Mark Angelino, Senior VP of Sales for Nextel, states, "Our sales philosophy is based on mass customization. It's based on knowledge. Our salespeople have to train, retrain, and train again."[11]

By developing categories of customer types or types of sales situations, salespeople reduce the complexity of selling and free up their mental capacity to think more creatively. The categories salespeople use can focus on the benefits the customer seeks, the person's role in the buying center, the stage in the buying process, or the type of buying situation. For example, a Colgate salesperson might divide buyers into several categories based on their decision-making style. When selling to emotional buyers, this salesperson might need to be more enthusiastic and engage in visual storytelling. When selling to rational buyers, this salesperson might want to stress the financial benefits of purchasing the new toothpaste.

Successful sales managers provide their salespeople with diagnostic feedback.

Ryan McVay/Getty Images/MGH-DIL

HOW TO CREATE KNOWLEDGE

One source of knowledge would be top salespeople in the company you work for. Some firms will collect and share this information with you. For example, a telecommunications company conducted in-depth interviews with its top performers. Through these interviews, it learned about the types of situations these salespeople encountered and what strategies they used in each situation. The company developed role plays for each sales situation and used them when training new salespeople. Such role playing enabled the new salespeople to experience the variety of situations they would actually encounter on the job. The strategies recommended by the top salespeople served as a starting point for the trainees to develop their own sales methods for handling these situations.

Salespeople also create knowledge by getting feedback from sales managers. This can be in the form of **performance feedback** (Did you achieve the goals you set for this call?) or **diagnostic feedback** (Let's talk about why you didn't achieve your goals). Diagnostic feedback provides information about what you're doing right and wrong, instead of just whether you made a sale.

The following example illustrates diagnostic feedback:

SALESPERSON: Why do you think I didn't make the sale?

SALES MANAGER: You stressed the low maintenance cost, but he wasn't interested in maintenance cost. Did you see how he kept looking around while you were talking about how cheap it is to maintain the product?

SALESPERSON: What do you think I should do next time?

SALES MANAGER: You might try spending more time finding his hot button. Maintenance cost isn't it.

Other sources of knowledge include the Web, company sales manuals and newsletters, sales meetings, plant visits, and business and trade publications. Salespeople also collect information about competitors from customers, by visiting competitor displays at trade shows, and from viewing competitors' Web pages.

RETRIEVING KNOWLEDGE FROM THE KNOWLEDGE MANAGEMENT SYSTEM

Salespeople store much of their acquired knowledge in their memory, and as such, retrieval is merely accessing information in that memory. Many companies also have customer relationship management (CRM) systems to support their salespeople. Salespeople use programs like ACT!™ to store and retrieve critical knowledge about accounts, products, and competitors. For example, salespeople for the Houston Aeros hockey franchise use ACT! to store and access information about its customers.[12] They use this knowledge when interacting with customers to develop sales strategies and purchase recommendations.

Hewlett-Packard increases the ease with which its 15,000 salespeople can retrieve knowledge by providing them with an electronic sales partner (ESP). ESP has more than 30,000 documents that salespeople can access electronically from any computer, even during a sales call. These documents include product brochures, competitive information, graphical sales presentations, and answers to frequently asked questions. And, as you can imagine, the ESP system is used extensively: Every 1.2 seconds an HP salesperson accesses the system.[13]

THE SOCIAL STYLE MATRIX: A TRAINING PROGRAM FOR BUILDING ADAPTIVE SELLING SKILLS

To be effective, salespeople need to use their knowledge about products and customers to adapt both the content of their sales presentations—the benefits they emphasize to customers and the needs they attempt to satisfy—and the style they use to communicate with customers. The **social style matrix** is a popular training program that companies use to help salespeople adapt their communication styles.

David Merrill and Roger Reid discovered patterns of communication behaviors, or social styles, that people use when interacting with one another.[14] Merrill and Reid found that people who recognize and adjust to these behavior patterns have better relationships with other people.

Here is a quick preview of what you will learn about the social style training program. As you know, the world is made up of diverse people. For example, some are fast decision makers, while others are very slow to make just about any kind of decision; some like to talk, while others are rather quiet. To make it easier, this system divides all people in the world into four different types or categories (based on just two dimensions). Your goal as a salesperson is to first identify which of those four types you are. Next, you figure out which of the four types your customer is. Finally, you adjust your behavior to mirror or match that of your customer. Now that you have a general idea of how the system works, let's look at it in more detail.

DIMENSIONS OF SOCIAL STYLES

This training program uses two critical dimensions to understand social behavior: assertiveness and responsiveness.

Assertiveness

The degree to which people have opinions about issues and publicly make their positions clear to others is called **assertiveness**. Simply having strong convictions does not make a person assertive; assertive people express their convictions publicly and attempt to influence others to accept these beliefs.

Exhibit 6.2

Indicators of
Assertiveness

Less Assertive	More Assertive
"Ask" oriented	"Tell" oriented
Go-along attitude	Take-charge attitude
Cooperative	Competitive
Supportive	Directive
Risk avoider	Risk taker
Makes decisions slowly	Makes decisions quickly
Lets others take initiative	Takes initiative
Leans backward	Leans forward
Indirect eye contact	Direct eye contact
Speaks slowly, softly	Speaks quickly, intensely
Moves deliberately	Moves rapidly
Makes few statements	Makes many statements
Expresses moderate opinions	Expresses strong opinions

Assertive people speak out, make strong statements, and have a take-charge attitude. When under tension, they tend to confront the situation. Unassertive people rarely dominate a social situation, and they often keep their opinions to themselves. Exhibit 6.2 shows some verbal and nonverbal behavioral indicators of assertiveness.

Responsiveness

The second dimension, **responsiveness**, is based on how emotional people tend to get in social situations. Responsive people readily express joy, anger, and sorrow. They appear to be more concerned with others and are informal and casual in social situations. Less responsive people devote more effort toward controlling their emotions. They are described as cautious, intellectual, serious, formal, and businesslike. Exhibit 6.3 lists some indicators of responsiveness.

CATEGORIES OF SOCIAL STYLES

The two dimensions of social style, assertiveness and responsiveness, form the social style matrix shown in Exhibit 6.4. Each quadrant of the matrix defines a social style type.

Exhibit 6.3

Indicators of
Responsiveness

Less Responsive	More Responsive
Controls emotions	Shows emotions
Cool, aloof	Warm, approachable
Talk oriented	People oriented
Uses facts	Uses opinions
Serious	Playful
Impersonal, businesslike	Personable, friendly
Moves stiffly	Moves freely
Seldom gestures	Gestures frequently
Formal dress	Informal dress
Disciplined about time	Undisciplined about time
Controlled facial expressions	Animated facial expressions
Monotone voice	Many vocal inflections

Exhibit 6.4

Social Style Matrix

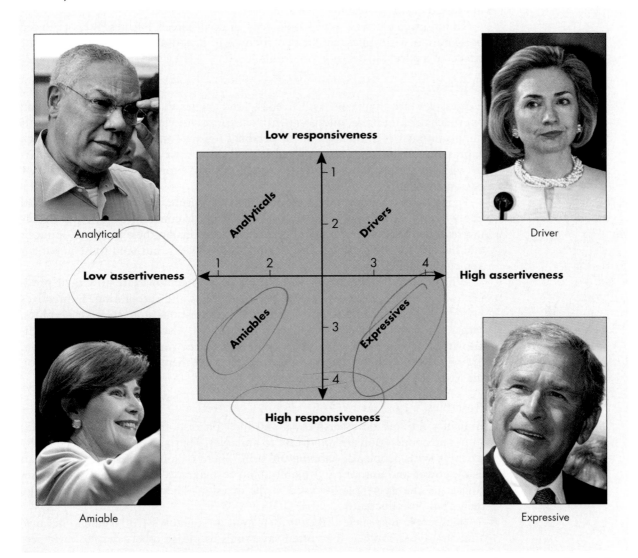

Analytical

Driver

Amiable

Expressive

Low responsiveness

Low assertiveness

High assertiveness

High responsiveness

Analyticals

Drivers

Amiables

Expressives

Some examples of social styles from the political world. Do you agree with where they are placed? Note that all of these people may switch to a different style under certain conditions.

Top left: Roslan Rahman/AFP/Getty Images. Top right: Jacky Naegelen/AP Wide World. Bottom left: Kevin Coombs/Reuters/Corbis. Bottom right: Rick Wilking/Reuters/Corbis

Drivers

Drivers are high on assertiveness and low on responsiveness. The slogan of drivers, who are task-oriented people, might be "Let's get it done now, and get it done my way." Drivers have learned to work with others only because they must do so to get the job done, not because they enjoy people. They have a great desire to get ahead in their companies and careers.

Drivers are swift, efficient decision makers. They focus on the present and appear to have little concern with the past or future. They generally base their decisions on facts, take risks, and want to look at several alternatives before making a decision. As compared to analyticals, who also like facts and data, drivers want to know how the facts affect results—the bottom line. They are not interested in simply technical information.

To influence a driver, salespeople need to use a direct, businesslike, organized presentation with quick action and follow-up. Proposals should emphasize the effects of a purchase decision on profits.

Expressives

Expressives are high on assertiveness and high on responsiveness. Warm, approachable, intuitive, and competitive, expressives view power and politics as important factors in their quest for personal rewards and recognition. Although expressives are interested in personal relationships, their relationships are primarily with supporters and followers recruited to assist expressives in achieving their personal goals.

People with an expressive style focus on the future, directing their time and effort toward achieving their vision. They have little concern for practical details in present situations. Expressives base their decisions on their personal opinions and the opinions of others. They act quickly, take risks, but tend to be impatient and change their minds easily.

When selling to expressives, salespeople need to demonstrate how their products will help the customer achieve personal status and recognition. Expressives prefer sales presentations with product demonstrations and creative graphics, rather than factual statements and technical details. Also, testimonials from well-known firms and people appeal to expressives' need for status and recognition. Expressives respond to sales presentations that put them in the role of innovator, the first person to use a new product.

Amiables

Amiables are low on assertiveness and high on responsiveness. Close relationships and cooperation are important to amiables. They achieve their objectives by working with people, developing an atmosphere of mutual respect rather than using power and authority. Amiables tend to make decisions slowly, building a consensus among people involved in the decision. They avoid risks and change their opinions reluctantly.

Salespeople may have difficulty detecting an amiable's true feelings. Because amiables avoid conflict, they often say things to please others despite their personal opinions. Therefore, salespeople need to build personal relationships with amiables. Amiables are particularly interested in receiving guarantees about a product's performance. They do not like salespeople who agree to undertake activities and then do not follow through on commitments. Salespeople selling to amiables should stress the product's benefits in terms of its effects on the satisfaction of employees.

Analyticals

Analyticals are low on assertiveness and low on responsiveness. They like facts, principles, and logic. Suspicious of power and personal relationships, they strive to find a way to carry out a task without resorting to these influence methods.

Because they are strongly motivated to make the right decision, analyticals make decisions slowly, in a deliberate and disciplined manner. They systematically analyze the facts, using the past as an indication of future events.

Salespeople need to use solid, tangible evidence when making presentations to analyticals. Analyticals are also influenced by sales presentations that recognize their technical expertise and emphasize long-term benefits. They tend to disregard personal opinions. Both analyticals and amiables tend to develop loyalty toward suppliers. For amiables, the loyalty is based on personal relationships; analyticals' loyalty is based on their feeling that well-reasoned decisions do not need to be reexamined.

IDENTIFYING CUSTOMERS' SOCIAL STYLES

Exhibit 6.5 lists some cues for identifying the social styles of customers or prospects. Salespeople can use their communication skills to observe the customer's behavior, listen to the customer, and ask questions to classify the customer. Merrill and Reid caution that identifying social style is difficult and requires close, careful observation. Salespeople should not jump to quick conclusions based on limited information. Some suggestions for making more accurate assessments are as follows:

- Concentrate on the customer's behavior and disregard how you feel about the behavior. Don't let your feelings about the customer or thoughts about the customer's motives cloud your judgment.

- Avoid assuming that specific jobs or functions are associated with a social style (such as he must be an analytical because he is an engineer).

- Test your assessments. Look for clues and information that may suggest you have incorrectly assessed a customer's social style. If you look for only confirming cues, you will filter out a lot of important information.

SOCIAL STYLES AND SALES PRESENTATIONS

In addition to teaching trainees how to assess social style, the Merrill and Reid program also assesses the trainees' social styles. Each person is asked to have a group of his or her customers complete a questionnaire and mail it to the director

Exhibit 6.5
Cues for Recognizing Social Styles

Analytical	Driver
Technical background	Technical background
Achievement awards on wall	Achievement awards on wall
Office is work oriented, showing much activity	No posters or slogans on office walls
Conservative dress	Calendar prominently displayed
Likes solitary activities (e.g., reading, individual sports)	Furniture is placed so that contact with people is across desk
	Conservative dress
	Likes group activities (e.g., politics, team sports)

Amiable	Expressive
Liberal arts background	Liberal arts background
Office has friendly, open atmosphere	Motivational slogans on wall
Pictures of family displayed	Office has friendly, open atmosphere
Personal momentos on wall	Cluttered, unorganized desk
Desk placed for open contact with people	Desk placed for open contact with people
Casual or flamboyant dress	Casual or flamboyant dress
Likes solitary activities (e.g., reading, individual sports)	Likes group activities (e.g., politics, team sports)

of the training program. These responses are used to determine the trainee's style. Trainees frequently are surprised by the difference between their self-perceptions and the perceptions of their customers. To get a rough idea of your own social style, you can complete the assessment in Exhibit 6.6.

Interpreting self-ratings requires great caution. Self-assessments can be misleading because we usually do not see ourselves the same way others see us. When you rate yourself, you know your own feelings, but others can only observe your behaviors. They don't know your thoughts or your intentions. We also vary our behavior from situation to situation. The indicators listed in Exhibits 6.2 and 6.3 merely show a tendency to be assertive or responsive.

Exhibit 6.6
Self-Assessment of Social Styles

Assertiveness Ratings I perceive myself as:				Responsiveness Ratings I perceive myself as:			
Quiet			Talkative	Open			Closed
1	2	3	4	4	3	2	1
Slow to decide			Fast to decide	Impulsive			Deliberate
1	2	3	4	4	3	2	1
Going along			Taking charge	Using opinions			Using facts
1	2	3	4	4	3	2	1
Supportive			Challenging	Informal			Formal
1	2	3	4	4	3	2	1
Compliant			Dominant	Emotional			Unemotional
1	2	3	4	4	3	2	1
Deliberate			Fast to decide	Easy to know			Hard to know
1	2	3	4	4	3	2	1
Asking questions			Making statements	Warm			Cool
1	2	3	4	4	3	2	1
Cooperative			Competitive	Excitable			Calm
1	2	3	4	4	3	2	1
Avoiding risks			Taking risks	Animated			Poker-faced
1	2	3	4	4	3	2	1
Slow, studied			Fast-paced	People-oriented			Task-oriented
1	2	3	4	4	3	2	1
Cautious			Carefree	Spontaneous			Cautious
1	2	3	4	4	3	2	1
Indulgent			Firm	Responsive			Nonresponsive
1	2	3	4	4	3	2	1
Nonassertive			Assertive	Humorous			Serious
1	2	3	4	4	3	2	1
Mellow			Matter-of-fact	Impulsive			Methodical
1	2	3	4	4	3	2	1
Reserved			Outgoing	Lighthearted			Intense
1	2	3	4	4	3	2	1

Mark your answers above. Total the score for each side and divide each by 15. Then plot your scores on Exhibit 6.4 to see what social style you are. For fun, you may want to have several friends also score you.

Source: Based on work by David Merrill and Roger Reid, *Personal Styles and Effective Performance* (Radnor, PA: Chilton, 1981).

Is there one best social style for a salesperson? No. None is "best" for all situations; each style has its strong points and weak points. Driver salespeople are efficient, determined, and decisive, but customers may also find them pushy and dominating. Expressives have enthusiasm, dramatic flair, and creativity but can also seem opinionated, undisciplined, and unstable. Analyticals are orderly, serious, and thorough, but customers may view them as cold, calculating, and stuffy. Finally, amiables are dependable, supportive, and personable but may also be perceived as undisciplined and inflexible.

The sales training program based on the social style matrix emphasizes that effective selling involves more than communicating a product's benefits. Salespeople must also recognize the customer's needs and expectations. In the sales interaction, salespeople should conduct themselves in a manner consistent with customer expectations. Exhibit 6.7 indicates the expectations of customers with various social styles.

Although each customer type requires a different sales presentation, the salesperson's personal social style tends to determine the sales technique he or she typically uses. For example, drivers tend to use a driver technique with all customer types. When interacting with an amiable customer, driver salespeople will be efficient and businesslike, even though the amiable customer would prefer to deal with a more relationship-oriented and friendlier salesperson.

This sales training program emphasizes that to be effective with a variety of customer types, salespeople must adapt their selling presentation to the customer's social style. Versatility is the key to effective adaptive selling.

VERSATILITY

The effort people make to increase the productivity of a relationship by adjusting to the needs of the other party is known as **versatility**. Versatile salespeople—those able to adapt their social styles—are much more effective than salespeople

Exhibit 6.7

Customer Expectations Based on Social Styles

Area of Expectation	Customer's Social Style			
	Driver	Expressive	Amiable	Analytical
Atmosphere in sales interview	Businesslike	Open, friendly	Open, honest	Businesslike
Salesperson's use of time	Effective, efficient	To develop relationship	Leisurely, to develop relationship	Thorough, accurate
Pace of interview	Quick	Quick	Deliberate	Deliberate
Information provided by salesperson	Salesperson's qualifications; value of products	What salesperson thinks; whom he/she knows	Evidence that salesperson is trustworthy, friendly	Evidence of salesperson's expertise in solving problem
Salesperson's actions to win customer acceptance	Documented evidence, stress results	Recognition and approval	Personal attention and interest	Evidence that salesperson has analyzed the situation
Presentation of benefits	What product can do	Who has used the product	Why product is best to solve problem	How product can solve the problem
Assistance to aid decision making	Explanation of options and probabilities	Testimonials	Guarantees and assurances	Evidence and offers of service

who do not adjust their sales presentations. Here is a comparison of behaviors of more versatile and less versatile people:

Less Versatile	More Versatile
Limited ability to adapt to others' needs	Able to adapt to others' needs
Specialist	Generalist
Well-defined interests	Broad interests
Sticks to principles	Negotiates issues
Predictable	Unpredictable
Looks at one side of an issue	Looks at many sides of an issue

How can a salesperson improve his or her versatility? Many companies have sales training programs, using tools like the social style matrix, that help teach salespeople the differences in buyers. Also role playing is used extensively for managers to spot problems in salesperson versatility and to teach new ways to help improve it. For example, sales training might suggest that effective salespeople adjust their social styles to match their customers' styles. In role plays, salespeople with a driver orientation need to become more emotional and less assertive when selling to amiable customers. Analytical salespeople must increase their assertiveness and responsiveness when selling to expressive customers. Exhibit 6.8 shows some techniques for adjusting sales behaviors in terms of assertiveness and responsiveness.

THE ROLE OF KNOWLEDGE

The social style matrix illustrates the importance of knowledge, organized into categories, in determining selling effectiveness through adaptive selling. Sales training based on the social style matrix teaches salespeople the four customer categories or types (driver, expressive, amiable, and analytical). Salespeople learn

Exhibit 6.8
Adjusting Social Styles

Dimension	Adjustment	
	Reduce	Increase
Assertiveness	Ask for customer's opinion.	Get to the point.
	Acknowledge merits of customer's viewpoint.	Don't be vague or ambiguous.
	Listen without interruption.	Volunteer information.
	Be more deliberate; don't rush.	Be willing to disagree.
	Let customer direct flow of conversation.	Take a stand.
		Initiate conversation.
Responsiveness	Become businesslike.	Verbalize feelings.
	Talk less.	Express enthusiasm.
	Restrain enthusiasm.	Pay personal compliments.
	Make decision based on facts.	Spend time on relationships rather than business.
	Stop and think.	Socialize; engage in small talk.
		Use nonverbal communication.

PLEASE DON'T SPIT IN MY FACE!

Steve Waterhouse, of the training firm Waterhouse Group, was looking forward to finally getting a chance to meet with a potential client from Japan. For six months his firm had been carefully working the account with the hopes of gaining a valuable long-term customer. Finally, the moment arrived. It happened at a convention in San Antonio, Texas.

The buyer handed Steve her business card, using the traditional Japanese method: extending it while holding onto both ends. So far, so good. Steve accepted the card and quickly jotted a note on the back of it. When he looked up, the Japanese prospect looked severely shocked and hurt. "I might as well have spit in her face,"

he says. "I quickly put it away and then apologized profusely, but the damage was already done."

Steve and his firm lost the $100,000 deal. All of it. Because of one slip with a business card. In Japan you should show a business card the same respect you would show a person. Writing on the business card was seen as similar to writing directly on the prospect's arm.

Steve and his firm did learn a valuable lesson from this, though. And it's one all should learn: Selling to people from other cultures or subcultures requires adaptability.

Source: "BestPractices: Selling around the World," *Sales and Marketing Management*, May 2001, p. 70.

the cues for identifying them. Salespeople also learn which adjustments they need to make in their communication styles to be effective with each customer type.

SYSTEMS FOR DEVELOPING ADAPTIVE SELLING SKILLS

The social style matrix developed by Merrill and Reid is one of several sales training methods based on customer classification schemes. Rather than using assertiveness and responsiveness, other classification schemes use dimensions like warm–hostile and dominant–submissive; dominance and sociability; relater, socializer, thinker, and director; logical (yellow), emotional (blue), conceptual (orange), and analytical (green); and skeptics, charismatics, thinkers, followers, and controllers.[15]

Regardless of the training system used, it is imperative that salespeople adjust to their audience. Selling Scenario 6.1 provides an excellent example of what can happen when you don't adapt when selling internationally. To repeat, it is also important to adjust your style when selling to diverse cultures even within your own country. For example, Hispanic salespeople may need to alter their communication style when selling to Anglo-American customers.

Expert systems have been developed to assist salespeople in understanding their customers and developing effective sales strategies. An **expert system** is a computer program that mimics a human expert. The program contains the knowledge, rules, and decision processes employed by experts and then uses these elements to solve problems, suggest strategies, and provide advice similar to that of an expert. Sales Technology 6.1 describes one such expert system.

Training methods such as the social style matrix and expert systems are simply a first step in developing knowledge for practicing adaptive selling. They emphasize the need to practice adaptive selling—to use different presentations with different customers—and stimulate salespeople to base their sales presentations on an analysis of the customer. But these methods are limited; they present only a few types of customers, and classification is based on the form of communication (the social style), not on the content of the communication (the specific features and benefits stressed in the presentation).

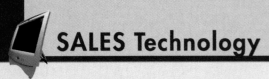

SALES Technology

AN INSIGHTFUL EXPERT SYSTEM

Business Resource Software offers an expert system called Insights for Sales Strategy.™ When using this computer program, salespeople input information about their objectives for an account, the decision makers and the roles they play in the decision, the competitors, the price and benefits of the products, and the salesperson's strategy. The program then analyzes this information, drawing on a knowledge base of sales concepts to suggest a sales strategy for the customer. The output of the program includes an evaluation of the sales strategy, an analysis of the salesperson's strengths and weaknesses with respect to the account, a scoring of the probability of a close, an identification of high-risk factors, and suggested steps for improving strategy.

Source: http://www.brs-inc.com.

Expert systems, like Insights for Sales Strategy, help salespeople understand buyers and develop effective sales strategies.

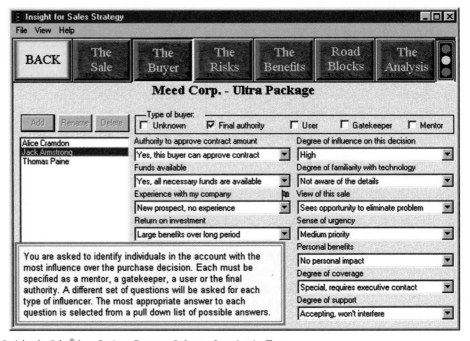

Insights for Sales® from Business Resource Software, Inc., Austin, Texas.

In addition, accurately fitting customers into the suggested categories is often difficult. Customers act differently and have different needs in different sales encounters: A buyer may be amiable in a new-task buying situation and be analytical when dealing with an out-supplier's salesperson in a straight rebuy. Amiable buyers in a bad mood may act like drivers. By rigidly applying the classification rules, salespeople may actually limit their flexibility, reducing the adaptive selling behavior these training methods emphasize.

SUMMARY

Adaptive selling uses one of the unique properties of personal selling as a marketing communication tool: the ability to tailor messages to individual customers and make on-the-spot adjustments. Extensive knowledge of customer and sales situation types is a key ingredient in effective adaptive selling.

To be effective, salespeople need considerable knowledge about the products they sell, the companies for which they work, and the customers to whom they sell. Experienced salespeople organize customer knowledge into categories. Each category has cues for classifying customers or sales situations and an effective sales presentation for customers in the category.

The social style matrix, developed by Merrill and Reid, illustrates the concept of developing categorical knowledge to facilitate adaptive selling. The matrix defines four customer categories based on a customer's responsiveness and assertiveness in sales interactions. To effectively interact with a customer, a salesperson needs to identify the customer's social style and adapt a style to match. The sales training program based on the social style matrix provides cues for identifying social style as well as presentations salespeople can use to make adjustments.

The social style matrix is one example of a categorical scheme salespeople can use to improve their knowledge and adaptability. However, other schemes are used, and some have been incorporated into expert system computer programs.

KEY TERMS

adaptive selling
amiable
analytical
assertiveness
customized presentation
diagnostic feedback
driver
expert system

expressive
outlined presentation
performance feedback
responsiveness
social style matrix
standard memorized presentation
versatility

ETHICS PROBLEMS

1. As a salesperson, aren't you just using tricks when you adjust your presentation based on social styles? Is it ethical to do so? Are there any times when it would be unethical to do so?

2. Knowledge systems are very valuable. Assuming there are no contractual restrictions, is it ethical for a salesperson to take her knowledge system with her to her next job? What if that next job is with a competitor?

QUESTIONS AND PROBLEMS

1. A salesperson stated, "I just can't stand to deal with buyers who have trouble making up their minds. I'd much rather deal with someone who shouts at me and tells me in no uncertain terms what they hate about me or my product." Based on this limited amount of information, what social style would you guess the salesper-

son to be? What would be your response to this salesperson?

2. A salesperson who is amiable is preparing a presentation. What suggestions can you make to improve the salesperson's performance?

3. A salesperson made the following comment: "I hate it when my sales manager makes calls with me. I do so much better when I'm by myself. After the call, she is always telling me what I did wrong." Based on what you learned in this chapter on knowledge systems, what would be your response to this salesperson?

4. "A good salesperson can sell any customer." Do you agree? Why or why not?

5. Would a person with an analytical social style be better at selling than a person with a driver or an expressive style? Why or why not?

6. Some people object to the social style matrix training system because they don't want to "act." Is that a valid objection? What would you say to them?

7. What social styles would you assign to the following people?
   a. President George W. Bush.
   b. Your selling instructor.
   c. The person who sits next to you in this class.
   d. Your best friend.

8. What is the best social style to have if you want to maximize your ability to adapt?

9. Suppose that, during a sales call, a customer says, "I'm not convinced that this new product will sell." How should you respond if this customer is a driver? An expressive?

10. Market research by a commercial cleaning company identified two types of schools. Traditional schools believe that teacher and staff satisfaction is based on the quality of students and that cleaning services are relatively unimportant. Private and charter schools believe that cleaning services are very important because they affect the students' parents' perceptions of the school. What type of sales presentation would you use to sell janitorial services to each of these school types? Which product features and benefits would you emphasize in each case?

CASE PROBLEMS

case **6.1**

Callaway Golf Clubs

You're the head pro at the Marty Irving Country Club in upstate New York. Your country club offers a wide range of golf instruction by yourself and two other pros, including one-week, two-week, and three-day golf camps. You also custom-fit and sell golf clubs made by most of the major golf club manufacturers.

In a few minutes Nate Schroeder, a salesperson from Callaway Golf, is supposed to make a call on you. That's okay with you because you have a few problems to report to him. For one thing, the shaft of the Callaway driver of one of your best customers bent when that customer was on a very important golf outing. Your eyes sparkle as you think of the way you're going to break the news to Nate. He's young, and you enjoy giving Nate a hard time. He seems to be scared of you. And that's just how you like it.

You intend to get right down to business today with Nate, even though Nate always wants to chat about the weather and how things are at the pro shop. You don't have time to chitchat with every salesperson who waltzes though your door.

You smile as you think about the last visit Nate made on you. He kept talking about how other golf pros in the region were adding a new line of clubs offered by Callaway. Who cares what they offer? You see yourself as the expert, able to make your own decisions.

Ah, there's Nate now. You walk directly up to him, looking at your watch as you near him. The first words out of your mouth are, "Well you finally decided to show up! My watch says five after. Thought you were going to get here at 10:00."

Questions

1. Based on information provided in this case, identify "your" (the golf pro's) social style.

2. If you were Nate, what should you do to sell to this golf pro?

Erica Kern is a new salesperson for Tamko Roofing Products. Tamko sells a full range of roofing products for commercial and residential customers. Their products include roll roofing, cements, and coating products, as well as waterproofing products.

Erica has been assigned a territory that includes New Brunswick, Nova Scotia, and Prince Edward Island. Before joining Tamko, Erica worked for CertainTeed, one of the top U.S. manufacturers of roofing products, including extensive waterproofing products. As a result, she is familiar with roofing systems. However, she doesn't have a lot of specific technical knowledge about the Tamko line. Also, she is not familiar with her territory because she has lived only in the southwest part of the United States.

She will be selling primarily to commercial accounts in her new territory. This is similar to what she did at CertainTeed.

Questions

1. What kinds of knowledge does Erica need to do her job effectively?
2. How can she acquire that knowledge?
3. What type of system should she use to store that knowledge and retrieve it as needed?

Source: www.tamko.com, www.certainteed.com

ROLE PLAY

This role play will require some pre-class preparation. Write out a brief outline of how you would describe ACT! to someone who has never seen it. Identify three features of ACT! that you think would benefit your buyer, based on the information you've learned so far this semester. Then write down what you would want to say about each. You will take turns presenting your sales presentations to your buyer. After you give your presentation, determine what the other person's social style was. Identify the hints that the buyer gave you.

If you have been using ACT! role plays all along, you can use the same customer you have called on. If not, you will need to review the Role Play material at the end of Chapter 4. You can also review material about ACT! in the role play case section of the back of this book to understand ACT! and what it does.

When you play the buyer, pick a social style different from your own. Interact with the seller in ways that give clues about your social style. Before the role play starts, think of at least five things you will do to hint at your new social style. Keep in mind that a social style includes both responsiveness and assertiveness, so make sure that your hints combine both dimensions.

After each role play, the salesperson should say what the other person's social style was and what clues were used to make that determination.

Note: For background information on these role plays, please see page 27.

To the instructor: Additional information needed to complete the role play is available in the Instructor's Manual.

ADDITIONAL REFERENCES

Awad, Elias M., and Hassan Ghaziri. *Knowledge Management.* Upper Saddle River, NJ: Prentice Hall PTR, 2003.

Bennet, Alex, and David Bennet. *Organizational Survival in the New World: The Intelligent Complex Adaptive System.* Hartland Four Corners, VT: KMCI Press, 2003.

Bush, Victoria D.; Gregory M. Rose; Faye Gilbert; and Thomas N. Ingram. "Managing Culturally Diverse Buyer–Seller Relationships: The Role of Intercultural Disposition and Adaptive Selling in Developing Intercultural Communication Competence." *Journal of the Academy of Marketing Science* 29, no. 4 (2001), pp. 391–404.

Campbell, Alexandra J. "Creating Customer Knowledge Competence: Managing Customer Relationship Management Programs Strategically." *Industrial Marketing Management* 32 (2003). pp. 375–83.

Chakrabarty, Subhra; Gene Brown; Robert E. Widing II; and Ronald D. Taylor. "Analysis and Recommendations for the Alternative Measures of Adaptive Selling." *Journal of Personal Selling and Sales Management* 24 (Spring 2004), pp. 125–34.

Delvecchio, Susan; Roger McIntrye; and Reid Claxton. "Updating the Adaptive Selling Behaviours: Tactics to Keep and Tactics to Discard." *Journal of Marketing Management* 20 (September 2004), pp. 859–75.

Eveleth, Daniel M., and Linda Morris. "Adaptive Selling in a Call Center Environment: A Qualitative Investigation." *Journal of Interactive Marketing* 16 (Winter 2002), pp. 25–39.

Fang, Tony. "Culture as a Driving Force for Interfirm Adaptation: A Chinese Case." *Industrial Marketing Management* 30 (2001), pp. 51–63.

Harrow, Susan. *Sell Yourself without Selling Your Soul: A Woman's Guide to Promoting Herself, Her Business, Her Product, or Her Cause with Integrity and Spirit.* New York: Harper Collins Publishers, 2003.

"Improve Your Selling Knowledge." *American Salesman* 47. (December 2002), pp. 22–25.

Katsikea, Eva S., and Dionisis A. Skarmeas. "Organisational and Managerial Drivers of Effective Export Sales Organizations." *European Journal of Marketing* 37 (2003), pp. 1723–45.

Kennedy, Karen Norman; Jerry R. Goolsby; and Eric J. Armould. "Implementing a Customer Orientation: Extension of Theory and Application." *Journal of Marketing* 67 (October 2003), pp. 67–81.

Lichtenthal, J. David, and Thomas Tellefsen. "Toward a Theory of Business Buyer–Seller Similarity." *Journal of Personal Selling and Sales Management* 21 (Winter 2001), pp. 1–14.

Marshall, Greg W.; Daniel J. Goebel; and William C. Moncrief. "Hiring for Success at the Buyer–Seller Interface." *Journal of Business Research* 56 (April 2003), pp. 247–55.

Matsuo, Makoto, and Takashi Kusumi. "Salesperson's Procedural Knowledge, Experience and Performance: An Empirical Study in Japan." *European Journal of Marketing* 36 (2002), pp. 840–54.

Miller, Robert B.; Gary A. Williams; and Alden M. Hayashi. *The 5 Paths to Persuasion: The Art of Selling Your Message*. New York: Warner Business Books, 2004.

Park, Jeong-Eun, and Betsy B. Holloway. "Adaptive Selling Behaviors Revisited: An Empirical Examination of Learning Orientation, Sales Performance, and Job Satisfaction." *Journal of Personal Selling and Sales Management* 23 (Summer 2003), pp. 239–52.

Porter, Stephen S., and Lawrence W. Inks. "Cognitive Complexity and Salesperson Adaptability: An Exploratory Investigation." *Journal of Personal Selling & Sales Management* 20, no. 1 (Winter 2000), pp. 15–21.

Sharma, Arun. "Consumer Decision Making, Salespeople's Adaptive Selling and Retail Performance." *Journal of Business Research* 54 (November 2001), pp. 125–29.

Shoemaker, Mary E., and Mark C. Johlke. "An Examination of the Antecedents of a Crucial Selling Skill: Asking Questions." *Journal of Managerial Issues* 14 (Spring 2002), pp. 118–31.

Stump, Rodney L.; Gerard A. Athaide; and Ashwin W. Joshi. "Managing Seller–Buyer New Product Development Relationships for Customized Products: A Contingency Model Based on Transaction Cost Analysis and Empirical Test." *Journal of Product Innovation Management* 19 (November 2002), pp. 439–54.

Verbeke, Willem; Frank Belschak; and Richard P. Bagozzi. "The Adaptive Consequences of Pride in Personal Selling." *Journal of the Academy of Marketing Science* 32 (Fall 2004), pp. 386–402.

PROSPECTING

chapter 7

SOME QUESTIONS ANSWERED IN THIS CHAPTER . . .

- Why is prospecting important for effective selling?

- Are all sales leads good prospects? What are the characteristics of a qualified prospect?

- How can prospects be identified?

- How can the organization's promotional program be used in prospecting?

- How can an effective lead qualification and management system aid a salesperson?

- How can a salesperson overcome a reluctance to prospect?

PROFILE

I graduated from Northern Kentucky University in 2003 with a Bachelor of Science in marketing, and took my personal selling course from Dr. Doris Shaw. Upon graduation, I started working at Parker Marketing Research, a custom research firm, as their sales and marketing coordinator.

I am in charge of new business development and marketing activities that will add to our existing book of business and increase awareness of Parker's research capabilities. A large part of my day is devoted to prospecting to generate leads for our account executives (AE). Prospecting is an important function within Parker because we need to continually add to our current base. Just like in any business, we never know when a current client is going to switch to a competitor or have their research budget cut, which causes a reduction in the number of research projects we do for them in a year.

I approach prospecting by selecting an industry that is in our target market and export a list of prospects from our CRM system called UpShot.® This database contains general information about a prospect's address, phone number, and e-mail address. However, the most important thing I use UpShot for is to track my prospecting activity that has occurred for each prospect.

Once I have exported my list, I select a message that speaks to that industry's needs and send it via e-mail to the prospect. To ensure that the e-mail catches the prospect's attention, I put the prospect's name in the subject line and include a phrase that speaks to their specific needs. After the first e-mail is sent, I send a second e-mail if the prospect hasn't responded. The follow-up e-mail simply asks for a time that the prospect and AE can connect over the phone to learn more about their research needs, shares with them how Parker could be of value, and asks for a referral if they are not the appropriate person we should be contacting. Finally, if there is still no response after the second e-mail is sent, I follow up with outbound telemarketing. This involves a series of three calls, where I simply follow up on the information the AE sent and try to close the call with a time scheduled for the AE and prospect to talk or meet.

The telemarketing aspect of my process can be frustrating at times because I'll call prospects that won't give me the time of day. I just have to remind myself not to take it personally. However, when I do get a lead from my efforts, it gives me an adrenaline rush and makes me realize just how important my job is. So far, my prospecting efforts have generated $388,900 in sales.

Visit our Web site at www.ParkerResearch.com.

"The telemarketing aspect of my process can be frustrating at times because I'll call prospects that won't give me the time of day."

Tasha Stulz, Parker Marketing Research

An important activity for nearly all salespeople is locating qualified prospects. In fact, the selling process generally begins with prospecting. You can be the best salesperson in the world in terms of listening, asking questions, discovering needs, giving presentations, helpfully responding to objections, and obtaining commitment. But if you are calling on the wrong person or organization, none of these skills do you any good! This chapter provides resources to help you prospect effectively and efficiently.

THE IMPORTANCE OF PROSPECTING

Prospecting, the important process of locating potential customers for a product or service, is critical whether you are a new or seasoned sales professional. In fact, many experts note that prospecting is the most important activity a salesperson does.[1]

Why is it so important? Quite simply, the world is constantly changing. Consider the drastic changes in population movements, the creation of new businesses and products, the shifting of businesses to new lines and expansion of old-line companies, and changes in methods of distribution. These changes are resulting in an estimated 15 to 20 percent annual turnover of customers. In addition, salespeople must find new customers to replace those that switch to competitors, go bankrupt, move out of the territory, merge with noncustomers, or decide to do without the product or service. A salesperson often needs to prospect even in existing accounts because of mergers, downsizing by firms, and job changes or retirements of buyers. Sales trainer Joe Girard uses a Ferris wheel metaphor to describe the important process of adding new customers (loading new accounts onto the Ferris wheel) to replace customers you lose (people getting off the Ferris wheel). Without replacing lost accounts, your Ferris wheel will soon be running with no one on board.[2]

Of course, prospecting is more important in some selling fields than in others. For example, the office products salesperson, stockbroker, or real estate sales representative with no effective prospecting plan usually doesn't last long in the business. Sales positions such as these may require 100 contacts to get 10 prospects who will listen to presentations, out of which one person will buy. Each sale, then, represents a great deal of prospecting. It is also important in these fields to prospect continually. Some sales trainers relate this process to your car's gas tank: You don't wait until you are on empty before you fill up!

Some sales positions require less emphasis on locating new contacts. For example, a Procter & Gamble sales representative in a certain geographic area would know all the potential prospects for Crest toothpaste (all the grocery stores, drugstores, convenience stores, and so on) because they are easy to identify. For the same reason, a Du Pont sales rep selling a new line of automobile finishes to auto manufacturers and body shops in Ontario can easily identify all of the main prospects. A Lockheed Martin salesperson assigned exclusively to sell the F-16 tactical fighter jet to Taiwan, South Korea, Greece, and Singapore would not spend any time trying to locate new governments to call on. For these types of sales positions, prospecting as we normally think of it (that is, looking for new leads) is not an important part of the sales process. Nevertheless, salespeople cannot ignore these obvious leads, as the next section discusses. Salespeople still have to assess whether leads are good prospects.

CHARACTERISTICS OF A GOOD PROSPECT

Prospecting actually begins with locating a **lead,** a person or an organization that may or may not have what it takes to be a true prospect. Some salespeople mistakenly consider every lead a prospect without first taking the time to see whether these people really provide an opportunity to make a sale.

To avoid that mistake the salesperson must **qualify the lead.** Qualifying is the process of determining whether a lead is in fact a **prospect.** If the salesperson determines that the lead is a good candidate for making a sale, that person or organization is no longer considered a lead and instead is called a prospect. It should be noted that many leads do not become prospects. Exhibit 7.1 displays the relationship between the steps in the selling process and the terminology we use to refer to the "buyer." Note that qualifying can occur during several stages: prospecting, collecting precall information, making the approach, and discovering needs.

It is important for a salesperson to understand several facts about this movement from being a lead to becoming a prospect. First, the seller should not get ahead of herself and start giving a presentation to a lead. That wouldn't be appropriate until the person has been classified as a prospect. Second, it is interesting to note that often it is the lead who turns himself or herself into a prospect, along with a creeping commitment that indicates an interest in solving his or her problem. Third, the ways in which salespeople strategically move people through the progression outlined in Exhibit 7.1 are important, and will be discussed in more detail in Chapter 15.

Naturally, the amount of time spent trying to determine which leads are prospects varies in different types of selling. It depends on such factors as the type of product or service, the value of the salesperson's time, and the profit per sale. The following five questions help to qualify leads and pinpoint the good prospects:

Does the lead have a want or a need that the purchase of my products or services can satisfy?

Does the lead have the ability to pay?

Does the lead have the authority to buy?

Can the lead be approached favorably?

Is the lead eligible to buy?

Exhibit 7.1

Relationship between the Steps in the Selling Process and the Designation of the "Buyer"

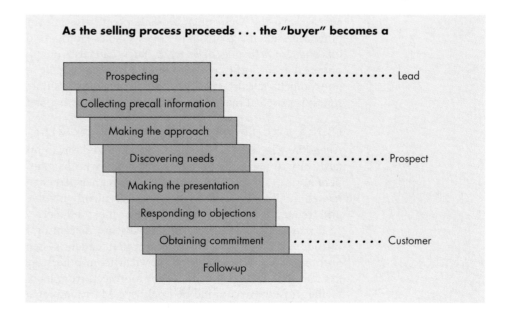

As the selling process proceeds . . . the "buyer" becomes a

Prospecting . . . . Lead

Collecting precall information

Making the approach

Discovering needs . . . . Prospect

Making the presentation

Responding to objections

Obtaining commitment . . . . Customer

Follow-up

These questions can be asked about the person who is a lead, the lead's firm, or both. Chapter 8 discusses how to begin gathering the information needed to answer these questions, and Chapter 9 provides further instruction on how to gather the remaining needed information during actual sales calls. For now, let's look at each question a little more closely.

DOES A WANT OR NEED EXIST?

Research has supplied no infallible answers to why customers buy, but it has found many reasons. As we pointed out in Chapter 4, customers buy to satisfy practical needs as well as intangible needs, such as prestige or aesthetics.

Determining whether leads need a salesperson's products or services is not always simple. Many firms use the telephone or e-mail to assess needs. Sometimes an exploratory interview is conducted to determine whether a lead has needs the seller's products can satisfy. Also, almost everyone has a need for some product lines; for example, practically every organization needs fax machines, computers, Internet access, copiers, paper, and a telephone system.

By using high-pressure tactics, sales may be made to those who do not need or really want a product. Such sales benefit no one. The buyer will resent making the purchase, and a potential long-term customer will be lost. The lead must want to solve his or her problem to be considered a qualified prospect.

DOES THE LEAD HAVE THE ABILITY TO PAY?

The ability to pay for the products or services helps to separate leads from prospects. For example, the commercial real estate agent usually checks the financial status of each client to determine the price range of office buildings to show. A client with annual profits of $100,000 and cash resources of $75,000 may be a genuine prospect for an office building selling in the $200,000 to $250,000 bracket. An agent would be wasting time, however, by showing this client an office building listed at $10 million. The client may have a real desire and need for the more expensive setting, but the client is still not a real prospect for the higher-priced office building if he or she doesn't have the resources to pay for it.

Ability to pay includes both cash and credit. Many companies subscribe to a credit-rating service offered by firms such as Dun & Bradstreet, Moody's, Value Line, and Standard & Poor's. This information is available on CD-ROM and can be accessed via the Web for a fee. Salespeople use information from these sources, often accessed directly from the salesperson's laptop, to determine the financial status and credit rating of a lead. They can also qualify leads with information obtained from local credit agencies, consumer credit agencies such as Experian, noncompetitive salespeople, and the Better Business Bureau. Salespeople are sometimes surprised at their leads' credit ratings. Some big-name firms have poor ratings.

DOES THE LEAD HAVE THE AUTHORITY TO BUY?

A lead may have a real need for a product and the ability to pay for it but lack the authority to make the purchase. Knowing who has this authority saves the salesperson time and effort and results in a higher percentage of closed sales. As discussed in Chapter 4, many people are typically involved in a purchase decision, and frequently it is unclear who has the most influence.

Because of downsizing, more firms are delegating their purchasing tasks to outside vendors. These vendors, often called **systems integrators,** have the authority to buy products and services from others. Systems integrators usually assume complete responsibility for a project, from its beginning to follow-up servicing. An example would be Lockheed Martin acting as a systems integrator for the complete mail-processing system of a new postal sorting facility in Germany.

In that scenario every potential vendor would actually be selling to Lockheed Martin, not to the German government. When systems integrators are involved, salespeople need to delineate clearly who has the authority to purchase. Sometimes the overall buyer (the German government in this example) will retain veto power over potential vendors.

CAN THE LEAD BE APPROACHED FAVORABLY?

Some leads with a need, the ability to pay, and the authority to buy may still not qualify as prospects because they are not accessible to the salesperson. For example, the president of a large bank, a major executive of a large manufacturing company, or the senior partner in a well-established law firm normally would not be accessible to a young college graduate starting out as a sales representative for an investment trust organization. Getting an interview with these people may be so difficult and the chances of making a sale so small that the sales representative should eliminate them as possible prospects.

IS THE LEAD ELIGIBLE TO BUY?

Eligibility is an equally important factor in finding a genuine prospect. For example, a salesperson who works for a firm that requires a large minimum order should not call on leads that could never order in such volume. Likewise, a representative who sells exclusively to wholesalers should be certain the individuals he or she calls on are actually wholesalers, not retailers.

Another factor that may determine eligibility for a particular salesperson is the geographic location of the prospect. Most companies operate on the basis of **exclusive sales territories,** meaning that a particular salesperson can sell only to certain prospects (such as doctors in only a three-county area) and not to other prospects. A salesperson working for such a company must consider whether the prospect is eligible, based on location or customer type, to buy from him or her.

Salespeople should also avoid targeting leads already covered by their corporate headquarters. Large customers or potential customers that are handled exclusively by corporate executives are often called **house accounts.** For example, if Marriott Hotels considers Ingersoll Rand a house account, a Marriott Hotel salesperson (who sets up events and conventions at the hotel) located in New York City should not try to solicit business from one of Ingersoll Rand's divisions located in New York City. Instead, all Ingersoll Rand business would be handled by a Marriott executive at Marriott corporate headquarters.

OTHER CRITERIA

Leads that meet the five criteria are generally considered excellent prospects. Some sellers, however, add other criteria. For example, DEI Management Group instructs its salespeople to classify leads by their likelihood of buying. Salespeople may have a long list of companies that need their product, can pay for it, have authority to buy it, and are approachable and eligible. If, however, these companies have absolutely no interest in buying, the salesperson should look elsewhere.

Criteria can include many things. Some firms look at the timing of purchase to determine whether a lead is really a good prospect. Relevant questions to consider include, When does the prospect's contract with our competitor expire? and Is a purchase decision really pending? How do we know? Still other firms look at the long-term potential of developing a partnering relationship with a lead.[3] Here are some questions to ponder: What is the climate at the organization—is it looking to develop partnering relationships with suppliers? Do any of our competitors already have a partnering relationship there? Answers to these and other questions help a firm determine whether a lead is worth pursuing at this time.

HOW AND WHERE TO OBTAIN PROSPECTS

Prospecting sources and methods vary for different types of selling. A sales representative selling corrugated containers for Tenneco, for example, may use a system different than banking or office products salespeople would use. Exhibit 7.2 presents an overview of some of the most common lead-generating methods. Note that there is some overlap among the methods.

SATISFIED CUSTOMERS

Satisfied customers, particularly those who are truly partners with the seller, are the most effective sources for leads.[4] In fact, some would argue that successful salespeople should be getting about 75 percent of their new business through referrals from customers. Referrals of leads in the same industry are particularly useful because the salesperson already understands the unique needs of this type of organization (If I have sold to a bank already, I have a better understanding of banks' needs). Referrals in some cultures, like Japan, are even more important than they are in North America.

To maximize the usefulness of satisfied customers, salespeople should follow several logical steps.[5] First, they should make a list of potential references (customers who might provide leads) from among their most satisfied customers. This task will be much easier if the salespeople have maintained an accurate and detailed database of customers. Next, they should decide what they would like each customer to

Exhibit 7.2
Overview of Common Sources of Leads

Source	How Used
Satisfied customers	Current and previous customers are contacted for additional business and leads.
Endless chain	Salesperson attempts to secure at least one additional lead from each person he or she interviews.
Networking	Salesperson uses personal relationships with those who are connected and cooperative to secure leads.
Center of influence	Salesperson cultivates well-known, influential people in the territory who are willing to supply lead information.
The Internet	Salesperson uses Web sites, e-mail, Listservs, bulletin boards, forums, roundtables, and newsgroups to secure leads.
Ads, direct mail, catalogs, and publicity	Salespeople use these forms of promotional activities to generate leads.
Shows, fairs, and merchandise markets	Salespeople use trade shows, conventions, fairs, and merchandise markets for lead generation.
Seminars	Salespeople use seminars for prospects to generate leads.
Lists and directories	Salesperson uses secondary data sources, which can be free or fee-based.
Data mining and CRM systems	Salespeople use sophisticated data analysis software and the company's CRM system to generate leads.
Cold calling	Salesperson tries to generate leads by calling on totally unfamiliar organizations.
Spotters	Salesperson pays someone for lead information.
Telemarketing	Salesperson uses phone and/or telemarketing staff to generate leads.
Sales letters	Salesperson writes personal letters to potential leads.
Other sources	Salesperson uses noncompeting salespeople, people in his or her own firm, friends, and so on, to secure information.

Salespeople use referral events to generate leads.

Oil Tennent/Stone/Getty Images

do (such as have the customer write a personal letter of introduction, see whether the customer would be willing to take phone inquiries, have the customer directly contact prospects, or have the customer provide a generic letter of reference). Finally, salespeople should ask the customer for the names of leads and for the specific type of help she or he can provide.[6] And because people have trouble coming up with a list of good leads, salespeople should give their customers time to think of names.

Salespeople sometimes use **referral events**, gatherings designed to allow current customers to introduce prospects to the salesperson, to generate leads. For example, a Merrill Lynch stockbroker might invite a group of current clients to a ski resort for a weekend. The skiing weekend is free for the client if the client brings one or more prospects. Other events that salespeople use include sporting events, theatre visits, dinner at a nice resturant, a short cruise, or golf lessons by a pro. The key is that the gathering should be fun and sociable.[7]

Sometimes customers aren't willing to offer referrals. Why? At times it is because they know that if the salesperson somehow doesn't do a good job, they will be blamed. For this method of prospecting to work, the salesperson must continually keep the referring customer and the prospect fully satisfied. Also, asking for referrals when a new customer signs the order is probably too soon. It is usually best to wait until the new customer has had a chance to use the product and experience both the product's benefits and the level of salesperson service.

Successful salespeople make sure that they keep in touch with their satisfied customers, to make sure they stay satisfied.[8] They do this by maintaining regular communication with the customer through phone calls, mailings, and personal contact. Often this includes sending the customer information that will help the customer do his or her job better. For example, a telecommunications salesperson might send a plumbing contractor information that he found about a potential new building project. While this information has nothing to do with telecommunications, it is very important and helpful for the contractor.

Satisfied customers not only provide leads but also are usually prospects for additional sales. This situation is sometimes referred to as **selling deeper** to a current customer. Salespeople should never overlook this profitable opportunity. Sales to existing customers often result in more profits than do sales to new customers. For example, if a midsized company increased its customer retention by just 5 percent, its profits would double in only 10 years. Chapter 14 explores this topic more fully.

Of course, it is also possible that a customer could be the other kind of a referrer—one who tells others about how poorly you or your product performed.[9] This **negative referral** is not the kind of referral a salesperson is hoping to get, and every effort should be taken to ensure that the customer is satisfied and stays satisfied with the solution offered by the salesperson. This will be discussed in more detail in Chapter 14.

ENDLESS-CHAIN METHOD

In the **endless-chain method**, sales representatives attempt to get at least one additional lead from each person they interview. This method works best when the source is a satisfied customer and partner; however, it may also be used even when a prospect does not buy. For example, at the conclusion of a meeting, the following conversation might ensue:

SELLER: Jim, you told me that you belong to several professional trade associations. Since you said you liked what I'm offering you, maybe you know of some other members who could use my services?

BUYER: Well, you know, maybe Sarah Harkins, and even Josh Smyth, could use this service, too.

SELLER: You know a lot more about these people than I do. If you were me, whom would you call first?

BUYER: Harkins, I guess.

SELLER: When I call Ms. Harkins, may I mention that we are doing some work with you?

Some people object to having their names used as a means of opening the door to friends or business acquaintants. Others, particularly those who trust the salesperson and/or are enthusiastic about the products or services, will not hesitate to provide the names of additional prospects and may even write a letter or card of introduction for the sales representative. The name of a lead provided by either a customer or a prospect, known as a **referred lead,** is generally considered the most successful type of lead. Exhibit 7.3 illustrates how a sales representative successfully used the endless-chain method.

NETWORKING

Networking is the utilization of personal relationships by connected and cooperating individuals for the purpose of achieving goals. In selling, networking simply means establishing connections to other people and then using those networks to generate leads, gather information, generate sales, and so on. Note that networking can, and often does, include satisfied customers.

Networking is crucial in many selling situations.[10] For example, trying to sell in China without successful networking, called *guanxi* in China, would be disastrous. Almost everyone can benefit by networking more actively.

Successful networkers offer a number of practical suggestions.[11] First, call at least two people per day and go to at least one networking event every week to increase your exposure and time with your contacts. You must make a special effort to move outside your own "comfort zone" in a social setting. Learn to mingle with people you don't already know. One expert calls this behavior acting like a host instead of like a guest. Second, spend most of your initial conversation with a new contact talking about his or her business, not yours, and don't forget to learn about the person's nonbusiness interests. Third, follow up with your new contact on a regular basis with cards, notes of congratulations about awards or promotions and articles and information that might help her or him. Whenever you receive a lead from your contact, send a handwritten, personal note thanking the person for the information, regardless of whether the lead buys from you. Whenever possible, send your new contact lead information as well.

Salespeople might want to consider joining Business Network International. With over 3,600 chapters worldwide, BNI is the largest business networking organization in the world, and offers members the opportunity to share ideas, contacts, and most importantly, referrals.[12]

In one particularly important form of networking, the **center-of-influence method,** the salesperson cultivates a relationship with well-known, influential people in the territory who are willing to supply the names of leads. A friend of one of the authors likes to call centers of influence "bell cows" because the rest of the

Exhibit 7.3

Example of the Endless-Chain Method of Prospecting

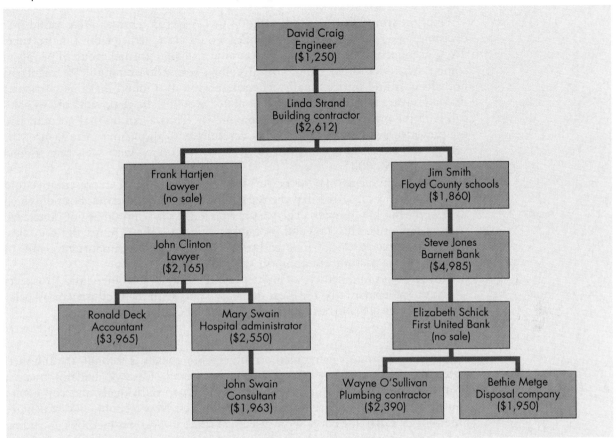

The sales representative used the endless-chain method to produce $25,690 in business (selling fax machines) within a 30-day period. All the sales resulted directly or indirectly from the first referral from an engineer to whom the sales rep had sold a mere $1,250 worth of equipment.

herd follow their lead. This method, like the endless-chain method, works best if the center of influence is already a satisfied customer of the salesperson. Here is the way an industrial cleaning service salesperson used the center-of-influence method when meeting with a well-known and respected maintenance engineer:

Now I've had the chance to explain my service, and you've had the opportunity to learn more about me. I wonder if you will do me a favor? You mentioned that it was probably the best-designed package you've ever seen. I know that as an engineer you wouldn't personally need my services, but can you think of any of your business associates who could benefit from such a plan? Does one come to mind?

In industrial sales situations the centers of influence are frequently people in important departments not directly involved in the purchase decision, such as quality control, equipment maintenance, and receiving. The salesperson keeps in close touch with these people over an extended period, solicits their help in a straightforward manner, and keeps them informed about sales that result from their aid.

The Roper Organization, which has studied centers of influence for more than 45 years, states that they are consistent in one aspect: their degree of activity.

Centers of influence tend to be those who enjoy being very socially involved in their communities. And people in the community not only trust these individuals but also seek their advice.

One true story illustrates the method's use. A Xerox representative found that decision makers from several companies would get together from time to time. These accounts formed a **buying community:** a small, informal group of people in similar positions, often from several companies, who communicate regularly, both socially and professionally. The salesperson also found that one particular decision maker in that group, or community, would share the results of any sales call with the other members of the community. Thus a call on that account had the power of seven calls. By working carefully with this center of influence, the salesperson closed nine orders from the seven accounts, with sales that totaled more than $450,000.

Centers of influence may never buy. One church furnishings representative told of a pastor who suggested that the rep call on two other churches, both of which were in the market for pews. The pastor who made the referral has not purchased pews in more than 10 years and probably will not for many more. But the salesperson continues to spend time with that pastor, who is an important center of influence in the pastoral community.

How do you find centers of influence? Try asking customers and prospects whom they consider to be the most influential person in their industry or association. Then actively cultivate a relationship with the center of influence.

THE INTERNET

Probably the fastest-growing method of generating leads is through the Internet. Successful salespeople are using Web sites, e-mail, listservs, bulletin boards, forums, roundtables, and newsgroups to connect to individuals and companies that may be interested in their products or services. New technologies, which are unfolding at a dizzying pace, allow a selling firm to use various methods, including audio, video (such as showing product demonstrations or plant tours), and text (letters of reference, product specifications, specials, lists of contacts) to provide information to prospects. For example, New Holland, which sells construction and agriculture equipment, uses its Web site to give leads information about products, show them where the nearest dealers are located, and gather their names and addresses if they desire more information.[13] One advantage of Web-based promotions is the number of international leads that can be secured, and New Holland realizes this benefit as well by having the Web site available in five different languages.

Firms use the Web to solicit leads in a number of ways.[14] Foremost, firms make sure their sites are listed on the major and important **search engines,** the tools that individuals use to locate sites. Search engine placement can be one of the most difficult areas of marketing on the Web because many times a search engine does not have a proper category for the products that the firm sells. These have to be continually monitored and updated because the search engines change their criteria regularly. Firms also use banner advertising on other Web sites, either for a fee or on a barter basis. **Banner advertising** consists of ads placed at the top, sides, or bottom of a Web page, encouraging the viewer to visit a different Web site. For example, Marketing Logis-

A company's Web pages help solicit leads for its salespeople.

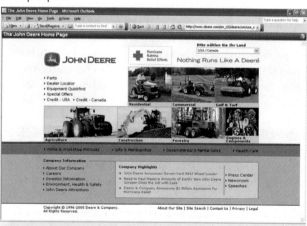

Courtesy Deere & Company, Moline, Illinois, USA.

tics, a firm that sells teaching aids to the early childhood industry, placed banner ads on the CNN Parent Network and CareGuide Web sites. Another way to gather leads on the Internet is to post a message on user group sites or via e-mail to a list the company has purchased.

Firms increasingly take advantage of new software that helps them utilize the Web more effectively in prospecting. For example, Resonate, a Sunnyvale, California, firm, uses ProspectMiner software. ProspectMiner automates a search process (using keywords supplied by Resonate) of multiple search engines and online databases. When it thinks it has found a good prospect for Resonate, the software searches the prospect firm's Web site, gathering key data like financial information, contact information, names of company officers, and important news items. This prospect information is then provided to Resonate salespeople for action.[15]

Firms are also developing **extranets,** Internet sites that are customized for specific target markets. Extranets are usually used to build relationships with current customers, but some companies are also using these sites to generate leads. For example, Turner, a TimesWarner Company, owns TBS, TNT, Cartoon Network, and Turner Classic Movies as well as specialized networks such as Turner South and Boomerang. Turner set up an extranet that's accessible only to media buyers. Buyers are able to access programming information, cable research data, and Turner's salespeople from the site.

Some salespeople have learned how to successfully utilize e-mail to generate leads, a technique called **e-selling.** There are potential drawbacks to using e-mail, however. **Spam,** a term used for unwanted and unsolicited junk e-mail, is causing concern and frustration among Internet users. Although careful marketers target their recipients and the messages they send, some people may still get angry at receiving an unsolicited message. Also, dealing with the replies can be quite time-consuming.

ADS, DIRECT MAIL, CATALOGS, AND PUBLICITY

Firms have developed sophisticated systems to generate inquiries from leads by using advertising and direct mail. For example, Digital Juice sends out direct mail to potential customers for its film and video library. The firm also places advertisements in trade publications, such as *Presentations*. A reader of the ad can request additional information by calling a toll-free number or by returning the reader service card at the back of the magazine. On the reader service card, which is already preaddressed, the interested prospect merely circles the bingo card number for Digital Juice.

Digital Juice can also participate in postcard packs. A **postcard pack** is a group of postcards (usually between 15 and 50 different cards) that provide information from many firms. Each firm has one card, usually describing one product or service. One side of Digital Juice's postcard contains information about a specific product or service (such as Digital Juice's VideoTraxx Film & Video Library). The other side, which is prestamped, carries Digital Juice's address. A company interested in learning more about the product simply fills in its name and address and drops the card in the mail.

Anyone who inquires about Digital Juice's products receives a cover letter, information about the advertised product, and a follow-up inquiry card. A copy of the inquiry goes to the appropriate salesperson. Based on knowledge of the territory, the salesperson decides whether a personal follow-up is appropriate. If the inquirer returns the second inquiry card (frequently called a **bounce-back card**), Digital Juice again notifies the salesperson. Then the salesperson can follow up on the lead.

RADIO ADVERTISING: SOME PROSPECTING TIPS FROM A PRO

As a promotions director at Midwest Communications, I sell radio advertising for Magic 95.7 FM. When you start out in radio advertising sales, you pretty much have to make your own account list. All the people who have been there for five or more years have all the big accounts like car dealers, furniture stores, and grocery stores. For that reason, when you begin your career in sales, the most common word in your vocabulary is prospecting.

So where do I find prospects? Here are a couple of sources I use: (1) With advertising sales I know who is advertising with my competitors. I see their ads in the paper or hear them on competitor radio stations or on TV. The best part about these prospects is that I know they already advertise, so I don't have to convince them to get their names out there; I just have to convince them to first use radio and second use my station. (2) I have created a network of friends (office suppliers, printers, convention center managers, movers, mall managers, and so on) and current clients who know a lot about what is going on in the community. I tap these folks for prospecting info.

(3) Trade shows are an advertising sales heaven. Instead of spending an entire day and a tank of gas driving around town looking for my next client, I can find 200–300 potential clients sitting around just waiting for people to talk to them. (4) Looking at last year's newspapers gives me an idea of which companies have special sales/events and when would be best to call upon them. I buy a copy of our local newspaper. (5) The business section of the paper has a column of business happenings, and I can find out about new businesses, expanding businesses, and the like. (6) I like to set up a referral program with my clients. Every client that gives me the name of a prospect that buys radio from me within two months gets an incentive (approved by my general manager, of course). This way my own clients become my eyes and ears on the street. (7) Our stations run promotions to target a certain group of advertisers or to dovetail with community functions like women's expos, boat shows, and home shows. These promos help me to locate leads.

Source: Angie Main, used by permission.

Many marketing promotions are tied to a toll-free number and the inquirer's fax machine. The prospect calls the toll-free number, talks to a salesperson (or voice mail), and is then asked to supply his or her fax number. The requested information is sent within seconds, often while the salesperson is still on the phone with the prospect.

SHOWS, FAIRS, AND MERCHANDISE MARKETS

Many companies display or demonstrate their products at trade shows, conventions, fairs, and merchandise markets. Sales representatives are present to demonstrate products to visitors, many of whom salespeople have not called on before. Studies show that closing of trade show–generated leads is three times faster than other types of leads.[16] In some cases a manufacturer lives or dies by how well it does in these special selling situations. Keith Clark, a company that manufactures office products such as calendars, depends heavily on the annual national office products association show. Its salespeople report that selling year-round is easier due to the impression the company makes on prospects at the show. Building Partnerships 7.1 talks about one salesperson who successfully uses shows to generate prospects for radio advertising.

Trade shows are short (usually less than a week), temporary exhibitions of products by manufacturers and resellers. In Europe trade shows are called **trade fairs.**[17] Once the show is over, all

Trade shows and fairs help salespeople discover and qualify leads.

Pat Benic/Reuters/Corbis

vendors pack up and leave. Specialty Advertising Association International (SAAI), for example, holds its annual trade show in Dallas each year. Vendors at this show are all manufacturers looking for dealers for their products; the end users of the products are not admitted. Dealers make an entire year's worth of purchases at the SAAI show, so the show is a make-or-break situation for many manufacturers. Comdex, the largest computer trade show in the world, is usually held in Las Vegas. Comdex differs from SAAI's show in that it has a dual audience: vendors exhibit to end users (industrial consumers) as well as to resellers.

Even firms that do not use resellers may have salespeople involved in trade shows. At many trade shows all attendees are customers.[18] For example, the National Association of Legal Secretaries is a professional organization that promotes the welfare of legal secretaries. When it holds its annual convention, it also invites manufacturers of office equipment and other products to exhibit wares. The trade show is an adjunct of the convention, with the audience composed entirely of end users.

Merchandise markets are places where suppliers have sales offices and buyers from resellers visit to purchase merchandise. The Dallas Market Center, for example, hosts separate markets for children's wear, western apparel, linens, and other soft goods. The sellers are the manufacturers or distributors, and they sell only to resellers, not to the public. Sellers may lease showroom space permanently or only during market weeks. Sellers who lease space permanently usually bring in buyers during off-market periods or when no markets are being held.

Buyers visit many vendors during markets, selecting the products they will carry for the next season. In some industries, almost all sales to resellers occur during markets. These industries include hardware, clothing, toys, and furniture. The major furniture markets are held in San Francisco, Toronto, and High Point, North Carolina. The biggest toy show is held annually in New York City. Major clothing markets are held for each season (such as fall and spring) in New York City, Atlanta, Paris, Dallas, and Los Angeles.

Successful salespeople practice adaptive selling (discussed in Chapter 6) when interacting with prospects who stop by their booths or markets.[19] Thus instead of mechanically asking, Are you enjoying the show? or Can I help you with something today? sharp salespeople try to discover whether the lead has a need or a want that they can meet. The seller then provides the lead with helpful information and gathers information that will be used later in further qualifying the lead and preparing for a sales call. Timely follow-up of leads is critical if sales are to follow a show.

SEMINARS

Today many firms use seminars to generate leads and to provide information to prospective customers. For example, a local pharmaceutical representative for Bristol-Myers Squibb will set up a seminar for 8–10 oncologists and invite a nationally known research oncologist to make a presentation. The research specialist usually discusses some new technique or treatment being developed. During or after the presentation, the pharmaceutical representative for Bristol-Myers Squibb will describe how Squibb's drug Taxol® helps in the treatment of ovarian and breast cancer.

What are some key things to keep in mind when planning a seminar? Make sure your seminar appeals to a specialized market and invite good prospects, especially those prospects who might not be willing to see you one-on-one. The subject should be something your attendees have a strong interest in, while your speaker must be considered an authority on the topic. Try to go as high-quality as possible (remember, you're building an image) and consider serving food. Finally, you should take an active role before, during, and after the seminar.

LISTS AND DIRECTORIES

Individual sales representatives can develop prospect lists from sources such as public records, telephone directories, chamber of commerce directories, newspapers, trade publications, club membership lists, and professional or trade membership lists. Secondary sources of information from public libraries also can be useful. For example, industrial trade directories are available for all states. Exhibit 7.4 lists some useful secondary sources for leads.

It is often useful to know the **standard industrial classification (SIC)** code for an industry when researching for leads because many publications are indexed by SIC codes. The SIC system is being replaced by the new **North America industry classification system (NAICS),** which is a uniform classification for all countries in North America.[20]

Salespeople can purchase a number of prospecting directories and lead-generating publications. You can purchase, by geographical area, mailing lists

Exhibit 7.4

Partial List of Secondary Sources of Lead Information*

Source	Description	Website
Annual reports for U.S. firms	Links to most annual reports, as well as home pages	www.reportgallery.com
IndustryLink	Directory of links to industry Web sites	www.industrylink.com
Current Industrial Reports	Measures of industrial activity	www.census.gov/ftp/pub/cir/www/
Thomas Register**	Lists manufacturers, distributors, and service providers by classifications, company profits, and specific product information	www.thomasnet.com
Fortune 500 Information	Details on Fortune 500 firms	www.fortune.com
Inc. 500 Information	Details on the fastest growing small businesses in America, the Inc. 500 list	www.inc.com/inc500/
Encyclopedia of Associations**	Lists 23,000 national associations; more than 20,000 international organizations; 295,000 nonprofit organizations; and more than 92,000 regional, state, and local organizations	www.gale.com
Web Yellow Pages	Contains more than 11 million U.S. business listings	www.bigyellow.com
Business Lists (InfoUSA)**	Contains a complete database on millions of U.S. businesses	www.infousa.com
Middle Market Directory** (Dun & Bradstreet)	Lists 14,000 firms worth between $500,000 and $1 million	www.dnb.com
Hoover's	Provides an excellent search tool for information on businesses	www.hoovers.com
Moody's Industrial Directory**	Contains an annual listing of names, type of business, and a brief financial statement for more than 10,000 publicly held corporations	www.moodys.com
Databases of articles in journals, newspapers, and magazines from search banks like Business Source Premier, Reference USA, and Lexis-Nexis**	Allow you to find articles that have been written about firms and individuals	www.proquest.com www.lexis-nexis.com

*Most libraries own hard copies of some of these resources.

**Must purchase or pay a fee to use.

DATA MINING TOOLS CAN IMPROVE PROSPECTING EFFECTIVENESS

Chubb Group of Insurance Companies had the same problem as most insurance companies: how to prospect to maximize returns on their efforts. Chubb relied primarily on internal sources of data to generate leads, resulting in high costs of acquiring profitable new customers.

Then Chubb began using SAS's business intelligence and data mining tools. With SAS, it was able to combine both internal and external data to start to understand which prospects were most likely to purchase which products and services, and which prospects would be most profitable.

After the software identifies the best leads, agents are provided the information. All salesperson activity is tracked as part of a lead management system. Not only does this allow the system to determine if the data mining was successful, it also helps Chubb determine how effective individual salespeople are at converting leads to sales. The system also tracks lost sales, generating reports to spot trends and situations that might need correcting. For example, if many sales are lost due to certain pricing parameters, then Chubb might change its pricing structure for that segment.

Source: "Return on Intelligence," *Insurance & Technology,* August 2004, p. 16; www.sas.com.

for all gerontologists (specialists in geriatrics), Lions clubs, T-shirt retailers, yacht owners, antique dealers, Catholic high schools, motel supply houses, nudists, multimillionaires, pump wholesalers, and thousands of other classifications. These lists can be delivered as printed mailing labels or on a CD-ROM. Some lists can be secured directly from the Web.

Salespeople should keep in mind that purchased lists can have several drawbacks. The lists may not be current. They may contain some inaccurate information regardless of the guarantee of accuracy. People who are on lists may be targeted by many, many firms and thus be less open to hearing from yet another salesperson. Finally, because lists are easy to obtain and use, some salespeople tend to rely on them exclusively when other methods of prospecting might result in better leads.

Most lists are simply names and telephone numbers. However, prospecting systems can be much more elaborate. For example, construction firms in some large cities can pay to access computerized databases of planned construction projects that meet the user's criteria (type of work to be performed, amount budgeted for the project, method of payment, and so on). Such lists obviously include much more than just names and phone numbers of leads.

In international selling situations, procuring lists can be much more difficult. One of the biggest problems in selling in Mexico under the North American Free Trade Agreement (NAFTA) is that mailing lists and databases simply do not exist. Nor is this phenomenon unique to Mexico; many firms working in international selling environments face similar problems.

DATA MINING AND CRM SYSTEMS

Sophisticated firms are developing interactive **databases** that contain information on leads, prospects, and customers. For example, Pioneer, one of the country's largest producers of seed corn, has a dynamic database of 600,000 farm operators in the United States and Canada that everyone in the firm can access. The system has resulted in better sales prospecting and more tailored sales presentations. Sales Technology 7.1 explains how Chubb Group uses data mining to find the best leads. Chapter 15 more fully examines the issue of databases.

Progressive firms are using **data mining,** which consists of artificial intelligence and statistical tools, to discover insights hidden in the volumes of data in their databases. For example, Eagle Equipment of Norton, Massachusetts, uses iMarket software to target its sales calls to the best prospects. Using the company's database, the software identifies prospects most likely to buy something and then matches that profile against a database of 12 million businesses. The resulting prospect lists are sorted by SIC codes, size, and target categories, ready for the sales force to use in generating new business.[21]

CRM systems are also being tapped to help locate the best prospects to call upon. For example, AMD, the $4.6 billion computer chip maker that competes primarily against Intel, used the CRM system called One-to-One Lead Management to discover the profile of the best prospect. The results so far have been outstanding, with one sale paying for the entire development cost of the system.[22]

COLD CALLING

Before learning about other prospecting methods, college students often assume salespeople spend most of their time making cold calls. In using the **cold canvass method,** or **cold calls** (by call we usually mean a personal visit, not a telemarketing call), a sales representative tries to generate leads for new business by calling on totally unfamiliar organizations. Historically, this method was used extensively. However, cold calling can waste a salesperson's time because many companies have neither a need for the product nor the ability to pay for it. This fact stresses the importance of qualifying the lead quickly in a cold call so as not to waste time. Also, today cold calling is considered rude by many purchasing agents and other professionals.[23] This is especially true if the salesperson is not sensitive to the prospect, as Selling Scenario 7.1 describes.

Salespeople often rate making cold calls as the part of the job they like least. Thus, as mentioned earlier, most firms now encourage their salespeople to qualify leads instead of relying on cold calls. In fact, American Express (Amex) Financial Advisors banned cold calling for its 8,000 salespeople nationwide in late 1995. This policy has forced the reps to use other methods, such as networking and referrals.

Still, some companies use cold calling.[24] And some companies use a selective type of cold calling they refer to as a **blitz:** A large group of salespeople attempts to call on all of the prospective businesses in a given geographical territory on a specified day. For example, an office machine firm may target a specific four-block area in Guadalajara, Mexico; bring in all of the salespeople from the surrounding areas; and then have them, in one day, call on every business located in that four-block area. The purpose is to generate leads for the local sales representative as well as to build camaraderie and a sense of unity among the salespeople.

thinking **it** through

Your company sends you, via e-mail, the names and addresses of leads who registered with your firm's Web site that day. All the leads are in your territory, and your firm expects you to quickly follow up with them. However, your sales manager suggests that such leads are a waste of time. She instructs you to spend your time networking instead: "Networking got me where I am today. It will for you, too!" What would you say in response? What would you do?

A VIEW FROM THE BUYER'S SIDE OF THE TABLE—WHEN PROSPECTING, PLEASE RESPECT MY TIME!

Working at the company headquarters, I know that many sales people will "drop by" while they are at our headquarters. The salesperson may have had a meeting with someone else, which got them access in the building, and then they roam the halls. Some buyers don't mind a "drive by." However, others do. Know what is OK with your customer.

As an example, I was in my doorway about to leave my office to meet with a vice president. I had ended a meeting in my office about three minutes early to give myself the time to get up the three flights of stairs to her (the VP's) office in time. A salesperson stopped me in my doorway, and I explained that I was on my way to an important meeting.

The salesperson said he understood, but proceeded to take my hand and shake it and introduce himself. He continued to say that he was asked to meet with me by another coworker to introduce his services. I continued to explain that I needed to go to my meeting, but I would take his card and call him later. He would not clear the doorway and continued to explain his services, which was "only going to take a minute." I explained that I really didn't have a minute and I would call him later.

He continued to explain his services after I said I didn't have the time. I interrupted him and explained that he needed to allow me to leave my office. His disregard for my time and his desire "to only take a minute of my time" resulted in my being two minutes late for my meeting.

I have meetings back to back every day, including any time considered for lunch. A salesperson stopping by for just a quick minute is enough to make quite an interruption. In this representative's case, I did take his card, and if he would not have stopped me like that, I would have met with him to consider his service.

This salesperson works in a very competitive business. Many groups offer the same services, but I am usually interested in meeting with the different vendors to see if they have any unique feature we have not already evaluated. What did I do in this case? Instead of calling the rep back, I did my homework with the coworker who referred him to me. The project was bid to three vendors. But I didn't bid it to the salesperson that interrupted me in the doorway.

Source: Tracey Brill, used with permission.

SPOTTERS

Some salespeople use **spotters,** also called **bird dogs.** These individuals will, for a fee, provide leads for the salesperson. The sales rep sometimes pays the fee simply for the name of the lead but more often pays only if the lead ends up buying the product or service. Spotters are usually in a position to find out when someone is ready to make a purchase decision. For example, a janitor who works for a janitorial service company and notices that the heating system for a client is antiquated and hears people complaining about it can turn this information over to a heating contractor.

A more recent development is the use of outside paid consultants to locate and qualify leads. Small firms attempting to secure business with very large organizations are most likely to use this approach. For example, Synesis Corporation, a small firm specializing in computerized training, used the services of a consultant to identify and develop leads. The result of one lead was a major contract with AT&T.

Use caution, however, when offering a cash payment to a customer for spotting.[25] Your action may be misconstrued by the customer as exploiting the relationship. Also, some customers' firms may prohibit such behavior. Sometimes it is better to send a personal thank-you note or small gift to the customer instead.

TELEMARKETING

Increasingly, firms are relying on telemarketing to perform many functions sales representatives used to perform. **Telemarketing** is a systematic and continuous program of communicating with customers and prospects via telephone. Telemarketing is not limited to consumer sales; in fact, all the examples in this section involve business-to-business companies. Telemarketing is now used to sell everything from 25-cent supplies to $10 million airplanes.

In **outbound telemarketing** telephones are used to generate and then qualify leads. These calls may be initiated directly by the salesperson, by inside sales representatives (inside sales reps were discussed in Chapter 1),[26] or by third-party vendors. **Inbound telemarketing** uses a telephone number (usually a toll-free number) that leads and customers can call for additional information. Again, the call may be answered by several types of people: the salesperson, an inside salesperson, or a customer service representative.

Progressive firms use telemarketers to qualify leads before sending a salesperson on a call.

Ed Lallo/Index Stock

Firms combine outbound and inbound telemarketing to prospect effectively. For example, Motorola Corporation's Land Mobile Products Sector, which sells mobile communication systems to such diverse entities as contractors, hotels, and police stations, uses outbound telemarketing to generate and then qualify leads for its sales force. Qualified leads are turned over to field sales representatives if the order is large enough to warrant a personal visit to the company. If the prospect needs a smaller system, a separate telemarketing salesperson will handle the account. Motorola also uses inbound telemarketing by providing a toll-free number for people who want more information about a product or service Motorola offers. Because of this excellent telemarketing organization, Motorola's field reps have more time to spend with qualified prospects and more time to develop long-term customer relations.

Although the telephone is a wonderful tool that can enhance productivity, it also has some limitations. Customers often find telephone calls an annoying inconvenience.[27] When telephoning customers—in fact, at all times—salespeople need to respect the customers' privacy concerns and the do not call rules, as discussed in Chapter 3.[28] Attracting and maintaining the customer's attention and interest is harder over the telephone than it is in person, and prospects may even continue to work or read a report or magazine. Also, it can be very hard to actually connect with the prospect on the phone today because many prospects use caller ID or voice mail to screen calls. Finally, saying no is much easier over the phone than in person.

SALES LETTERS

Prospecting sales letters should be integrated into an overall prospecting plan.[29] For example, Xerox salespeople who handle smaller businesses send prospecting sales letters every day. They follow up three days later with a telephone prospecting call and ask for an appointment for a personal visit. The telephone call begins with a question about the letter.

Like the telephone, sales letters have limitations. Once the message is sent, it cannot be modified to fit the prospect's style. The sender also has no chance to alter the message on the basis of feedback. Blanket mailings, then, can seem impersonal. And from time to time anthrax scares have caused many to be wary of any unsolicited mail they might receive, resulting in much mail being thrown away without consideration.[30]

Because people in business receive so much mail, sales letters should be written with care. Think about the amount of junk mail and junk e-mail you receive and how much you throw away or delete without a second glance. It's not surprising that the rate of response from mailings can be as low as 2 percent. Sales letters must stand out to be successful.

One way to make sales letters stand out is to include a promotional item with the mailer. First National Bank of Shreveport, Louisiana, targeted certified public accountants (CPAs) for one mailer. The bank timed the mailers to arrive on April 16, the day after the federal income tax filing deadline. Included in each mailer was a small bottle of wine, a glass, and cheese and crackers—a party kit designed to celebrate the end of tax season. The bank followed up with telephone calls two days later and ultimately gained 21 percent of the CPAs as new customers.

The salesperson must first consider the objective of any written communication (like a sales letter or e-mail message) and the audience. What action does the salesperson desire from the reader? Why would the reader want to undertake that action? Why would the reader not want to undertake the action? These questions help guide the salesperson in writing the letter.

The opening paragraph must grab the reader's attention, just as a salesperson's approach must get a prospect's attention in a face-to-face call. The opening gives the readers a reason to continue reading, drawing them into the rest of the letter. Another way to gain attention is to have a loyal client whom the prospect respects write the introduction (or even the entire letter) for the salesperson. Here's an example of an opening paragraph:

> Thanks for stopping by the Datasource booth at the Strictly Business Computer Expo. I hope you enjoyed the show and had some fun shooting hoops with us! Were you there when one highly energetic attendee shot the basketball clear over into the Microsoft booth and knocked the presenter's Palm™ handheld right out of his hand? You won't believe what he did next! I'll fill you in on the details in a moment, but first I'd like to invite you to something I know you're not going to want to miss.

The next paragraph or two, the body of the letter, considers why the reader would and would not want to take the desired action. Benefits of taking the action should be presented clearly, without jargon, and briefly. The best-presented benefits are tailored to the specific individual, especially when the salesperson can refer to a recent conversation with the reader. A reference such as the following example can truly personalize the letter:

> As you said during our visit at the show, you're looking for a software firm that can work with a small business like yours without making you feel like a second-class citizen. At Datasource, we've committed ourselves to working exclusively with small to midsized firms like yours.

If the salesperson and the buyer do not know each other, part of the body of the letter should be used to increase credibility. References to satisfied customers, market research data, and other independent sources can be used to improve credibility. For example:

> You may have heard that last year we won the prestigious Youcon Achievement Award, presented by the Tennessee Small Business Development Center in recognition for outstanding service specifically to small businesses. In fact, the small businesses themselves are the voters for the award. We're proud of that award because it tangibly reflects the commitment we've shown. And we have dedicated ourselves to continue in that tradition.

The final paragraph should seek commitment to the desired course of action. Whatever the action desired, the letter must specifically ask that it take place.

The writer should leave no doubt in the prospect's mind as to what he or she is supposed to do. The writer should make the action for the prospect easy to accomplish, fully explain why it should be done now, and end with a positive picture. Here's an example:

> So I want to personally invite you to a free lunch seminar at Datasource. You'll hear from our partners on the very latest solutions to your technology challenges. The food promises to be great, and the information will be presented in a casual, small group setting. Please take a moment to reserve your spot at the lunch by visiting our Web site, www.datasource.com, or call 800-343-8764. You'll be glad you did.

A postscript (or PS) can also be effective. Postscripts stand out because of their location and should be used to make an important selling point. Alternatively, they can be used to emphasize the requested action, such as pointing out a deadline.

thinking **it** through   What do you hate most of all about junk mail (e-mail or regular mail)? Can you see any patterns in the way junk mailings present their sales messages? Should a field salesperson adapt some of his or her ideas to an industrial or trade selling situation?

OTHER SOURCES OF LEADS

Many salespeople find leads through personal observation. For example, by reading trade journals carefully, salespeople can learn the names of the most important leaders (and hence decision makers) in the industry. Sellers also read general business publications (such as *BusinessWeek* and *The Wall Street Journal*) and local newspapers. It's easier now because so much of this is available free online. Also, a number of fee-based publications provide the same type of current information.

Nonsales employees within the salesperson's firm can also provide leads. Some companies strongly encourage this practice. For example, Computer Specialists Inc., a computer service firm, pays its nonsales employees a bonus of up to $1,000 for any names of prospective customers they pass along. In one year the program resulted in 75 leads and nine new accounts.

Government agencies can also supply lead information. For example, the Commerce Department identifies some of the hottest prospects for aircraft and aircraft parts, construction materials, computers and home electronics, and so forth around the world. The *Commerce Business Daily* provides information about federal government bid opportunities and can be viewed at http://cbdnet.gpo.gov.

Leads can be found in many other places as well. Salespeople for noncompeting but related products can often provide leads, as can members of trade associations. You can find leads while volunteering in your community, doing things like helping build a house for Habitat for Humanity.[31] Good friends can also provide leads. Of course, one of the best ways to learn about new business opportunities is to keep up with regional, national, and world trends from sources such as *American Demographics* and *World Watch* magazines and industry surveys (Manufacturing USA, Service USA, Standard & Poor's Industry Surveys, U.S. Industrial Outlook, and the like).

Salespeople can get leads during volunteering activities.

Jeff Greenberg/Photoedit

LEAD QUALIFICATION AND MANAGEMENT SYSTEMS

Salespeople need to develop a process for qualifying leads, often called a **lead qualification system.** As mentioned early in this chapter, salespeople must ensure that their leads meet the five basic criteria of a prospect. Let's look more closely at this process.

Many firms view prospecting as a funneling process in which a large number of leads are funneled (or narrowed down) into prospects and some, finally, into customers.[32] To help salespeople use their time wisely, firms will often engage in **prequalification** of leads before turning them over to the field sales force. Sometimes the prequalification process is as simple as purchasing a prequalified list. At other times a firm will use the resources of telemarketers to prequalify leads. For example, PeopleSoft and Microsoft outsource at least part of their telemarketing prospecting.[33]

Salespeople must not only qualify leads but also carefully analyze the relative value of each lead. This part of the process is called a **lead management system,** which will be discussed more fully in Chapter 15.[34] Part of the decision process often includes a valuation of the prospects' expected lifetime customer value, as well as an appraisal of what types of value the selling firm can add to the prospect.[35] Grading prospects and establishing a priority list results in increased sales and the most efficient use of time and energy.

The judicious use of technology makes lead qualification and management more efficient and effective. Most salespeople now use laptops, PCs, personal wireless mobile tools like Palm™ handhelds, and software packages to keep track of leads. And this is often tied into a large, complete corporate system for managing prospects and salespeople's time and territories (Chapter 15 discusses this issue more fully). For example, IBM has tied its lead generation and management system into its CRM system. The results have been better tracking and prioritization of leads and prospects.[36]

Any good lead management system, like IBM's, should evaluate the profitability of sales resulting from various lead-generating activities instead of just counting the number of names a particular method yields. Analysis may show that the present system does not produce enough prospects or the right kinds of prospects. Salespeople may, for example, depend entirely on referred names from company advertising or from the service department. If these two sources do not supply enough names to produce the sales volume and profits desired, other prospecting methods should be considered. A salesperson should not hesitate to scrap time-honored prospecting systems even if they have been used for years in the firm or industry or even by the salesperson's own sales manager.

OVERCOMING A RELUCTANCE TO PROSPECT

People often stereotype salespeople as bold, adventurous, and somewhat abrasive. This view that salespeople are fearless is more fiction than fact.[37] Salespeople often struggle with a reluctance to prospect that persists no matter how well they have been trained and how much they believe in the products they sell. Many people are uncomfortable when they initially contact other people, but for salespeople reluctance to call can be a career-threatening condition.

Research shows a number of reasons for reluctance to call. Reasons include worrying about worst-case scenarios; spending too much time preparing; being overly concerned with looking successful; being fearful of making group presentations, of appearing too pushy, of losing friends or losing family approval, and of using the phone for prospecting; feeling intimidated by people with prestige or

Although it is acceptable to socialize, salespeople must learn not to waste time in the office.

Bruce Ayers/Stone/Getty Images

power, or feeling guilt at having a career in selling; and having a compulsive need to argue, make excuses, or blame others.

A recent study investigated sales call anxiety, of which sales prospecting would be one component. The authors discovered four dimensions of sales call anxiety: a negative self-evaluation by the salesperson ("I will be nervous and forget what I want to say"), imagined negative evaluations from customers ("If I don't know the answers to all of her questions, she's going to think I'm stupid"), a salesperson's physiological symptoms ("I'm sweating and blushing and my hands are cold"), and a desire to perform safety-seeking behaviors (avoiding eye contact, speaking quickly, fiddling with the hands, and ultimately withdrawing from contact with the prospect).[38]

Reluctance to call can and must be overcome to sell successfully. Several activities can help:

- Start by listening to the excuses other salespeople give to justify their call-reluctance behavior. Evaluate their validity. Then identify the excuses you use to avoid making calls and evaluate the validity of those excuses. You'll usually be surprised to find that most excuses really aren't valid.

- Engage in sales training and role-playing activity to improve your prospecting skills and your ability to handle questions and rejections that arise.

- Make prospecting contacts with a supporting partner or sales manager. Just their presence will often provide additional needed confidence (you won't feel so alone).

- Set specific goals for all of your prospecting activity. Chapter 15 will provide more direction in this activity.

- Realize the economic value of most prospecting activities. For example, if you keep good records, you may discover that every phone call you make (regardless of whether that particular prospect buys) results in an average of $22 commission in the long run.

- Stop negative self-evaluations from ruling your behavior. Learn to think positively about the future instead of focusing on your past blunders.

- Remember that you are calling on prospects to solve their needs, not just so you can line your pocket with money. You are performing a vital, helpful, important service to your prospects by calling on them. (If this isn't true, maybe you should find another sales job.)

- Control your perceptions of what prospects might say about you, your company, or your products. You don't know what their reactions will be until you meet with the prospects. Leads do buy from salespeople.

- Learn and apply relaxation and stress-reducing techniques that you can implement before and during prospecting.

- Recount your own prospecting successes, or those of others. Read books by people who have prospected successfully or creatively. Realize that persistence pays off in the long run.

SUMMARY

Locating prospective customers is the first step in the sales process. New prospects are needed to replace old customers lost for a variety of reasons and to replace contacts lost in existing customers because of plant relocations, turnover, mergers, downsizing, and other factors.

Not all sales leads qualify as good prospects. A qualified prospect has a need that can be satisfied by the salesperson's product, has the ability and authority to buy the product, can be approached by the salesperson, and is eligible to buy.

Many methods can be used to locate prospects. The best source is a satisfied customer. Salespeople can also use the endless-chain method, networking, lists and directories, cold canvassing (including blitzes), and spotters. Companies provide leads to salespeople through promotional activities such as the Internet, inquiries from advertising and direct mail, telemarketing, trade shows, merchandise markets, and seminars.

Effective prospecting requires a strong plan that hinges on developing a lead qualification and management system and overcoming reluctance to prospect.

KEY TERMS

banner advertising
bird dog
blitz
bounce-back card
buying community
center-of-influence method
cold call
cold canvass method
databases
data mining
endless-chain method
e-selling
exclusive sales territories
extranet
house accounts
inbound telemarketing
lead
lead management system
lead qualification system
merchandise market
negative referral

networking
North America industry classification system (NAICS)
outbound telemarketing
postcard pack
prequalification
prospect
prospecting
qualifying a lead
referral event
referred lead
search engines
selling deeper
spam
spotter
standard industrial classification (SIC)
systems integrator
telemarketing
trade fair
trade show

ETHICS PROBLEMS

1. Suppose your sales manager says the following to you: "Look, I know how to prospect effectively! After all, I've been selling for 25 years, haven't I? And you're just starting to sell. Okay, here's what I expect you to do. I want you to make 10 cold calls every day. That's all. Just start knocking on doors. Oh yeah, and report them on this call sheet." As you reflect on what he said, you are confused and anxious. You feel there are much better ways of prospecting than just relying on cold calling. What will you do?

What, if anything, will you say to your sales manager?

2. Some people feel obligated to provide a salesperson with at least one referral when a salesperson uses the endless-chain method of prospecting, even though they don't really want to do so. Why? Because they want to be polite. What are the ethical implications of this for the salesperson asking for the referrals? What would you do if you sensed though nonverbal cues that someone was hesitant to offer any names?

QUESTIONS AND PROBLEMS

1. Describe a referral event that could be created, assuming you are an admissions counselor for your college. Your target market for new leads consists of high school students who are in the top 5 percent of their high school class.

2. Negative referrals are certainly not what a salesperson wants. Think of a time when you actually were a negative referral for a product or service or company. Why did you do it? What could the company or salesperson have done to cause you to not be a negative referral?

3. Spam—unrequested and unwanted e-mail—is a real problem. Yet salespeople continue to want to use e-mail to contact leads because it is so efficient.
   a. How can you make sure that you aren't spamming someone?
   b. If you do send unsolicited e-mail, how can you make sure that spam-blocking software won't send your e-mail to the spam-blocked file of a prospect?

4. Assume you are a commercial printer who specializes in printing elaborate four-color books, posters, booklets, and the like. Whom might you use as paid spotters to generate leads?

5. Reluctance to prospect is a real phenomenon. What can you do now (and avoid doing now), while you're in school, to avoid being reluctant to prospect when you become a salesperson?

6. Assume you sell bed pillows. Locate at least one merchandise mart and one trade show or fair where you might be able to display your products.

7. How would you develop a prospect list under the following situations?
   a. You belong to a marketing club that needs to recruit new members.
   b. You sell a new software program that allows the user to fill out any standard business form online, rather than having to use a typewriter.

8. Assume you are starting a career as a stockbroker. Develop a system for rating prospects. The system should contain several important factors for qualifying prospects and scales with which to rate the prospects on these factors. Use the system to rate five of your friends.

9. How can you engage in networking now to increase your odds of landing a good job after you graduate?

10. If you were a salesperson for the following, how would you develop a prospect list?
    a. A new breed of laying hens.
    b. A travel agency specializing in Caribbean vacations.
    c. A manufacturer of an antitheft alarm device for laptops.

CASE PROBLEMS

case **7.1**

3M's Digital Library Assistant

3M is a diversified international company with a wide portfolio of businesses. The company enjoys leading market shares for its products and services, most of which are focused on technical differentiation. Products include everything from touch screen displays, high-speed computing interconnects, and medical products to Scotch® tape and PostIt® notes.

One of 3M's latest products is called a Digital Library Assistant (DLA), a small hand-held unit that is designed for public libraries but could be used by anyone with a collection of books or materials. The DLA, using mobile scanner technology, helps manage the collection in terms of shelving, sorting, and searching for books quickly and easily. For example, it can quickly and easily

- Find lost or missing items in the collection.
- Electronically "read" the collection and give guidance as to how to put it back in order so future users can retrieve the books easily.
- Weed out the collection of materials to be discarded.
- Reshelve items with 100 percent accuracy.
- Confirm that items on a book cart are in proper order before they are taken to the stacks for reshelving.

- Spot errors in the catalog and in the spine labels of books.
- Do all of this by using the existing electromagnetic security system and without any need to retag or mark the entire collection.

Information about more than 1 million items can be downloaded from a library's automation system into the DLA's memory card. The interface between the library's current system and the DLA is seamless and flawless. And of course, the DLA has a comfortable ergonomic design with a swivel antenna that aids in reading books at all levels and in all positions.

3M is ready to market the system to Israel. You have been assigned to prospect for new accounts in that country.

Source: 3M 2000 annual report and 3M Web site (www.3m.com), accessed on March 10, 2002.

Questions

1. Which prospecting methods will you use?
2. How will you qualify the leads you find? Which qualifying factors will be most important?
3. How will you organize your prospecting activities? How will you keep good records?

case **7.2**

Roby's Refurb Center: Developing a Referral Event

Andy Roby is owner and salesperson for Roby's Refurb Center located in your city (or the large city nearest to your university). The company reconditions and refurbishes trucks that are used in the construction and maintenance industries. The company has nearly 30 years of experience in reconditioning trucks, with particular expertise in trucks with extensive hydraulic systems. (Hydraulic systems are what allow machines to do heavy work. They are a series of hoses, pumps, and fluid. The pump pushes the fluid creating extremely high pressures, which then power all kinds of tools.) All service personnel are highly trained and certified by various agencies. Any structural repairs and evaluations are certified by Howell Engineering, also located in your city. This is important because customers realize that engineers are trained to know what will work and what will not hold up over time.

One possible market for Roby's work are tree service companies. These are companies that provide the following types of services to residential, commercial, and municipal customers: tree trimming, tree and stump removal, utility line clearance, emergency storm service, right-of-way clearance, herbicide applications, and disaster recovery services. They also engage in pipeline and railroad clearing services, and some even participate in utility construction and street lighting services. You may have seen the bright orange Asplundh trucks trimming trees by the road—this would be one example of a tree service company.

Over the last several years, Roby's has completely refurbished three trucks that were owned by three different tree service companies in the general area. The refurbishing included installing all new hydraulic hoses, rebuilding all hydraulic cylinders, and replacing all parts that wear. It also included painting the complete chassis, boom, and frame. Any needed engine, transmission, and drive train work was done, and a complete D.O.T. inspection and certification was performed. All five customers seemed to be happy with the results.

Andy would like to prospect for new customers in the tree service industry, but he wants to be wise with his time and money. He is the only salesperson for the firm, and because he has many other duties as owner, his time for prospecting is limited.

Questions

1. Provide a list of company names and addresses for five actual leads in the city where your school is located (or the nearest large city if necessary). Make any assumptions necessary. You don't have to know whether the leads already use the product or service. Explain where you got the list of names.

2. Develop the details of an appropriate referral event, which is a gathering designed specifically for current customers to introduce prospects to Roby's. Give details on the place for the event as well as what will happen during the event. Be creative. Remember that referral events should be fun for current clients as well as leads. Assume that key leaders in most tree service companies in the area, although competitors, meet informally from time to time to discuss new laws and talk about problems they are having.

ROLE PLAY

As a salesperson, how can ACT! help *your buyer* to prospect better? Think about how ACT! might be able to help your buyer develop a comprehensive prospecting system, from lead generation to making the first appointment. Some of the ways ACT! can help is to automate direct mail. Using the database that salespeople create, the marketing department can do a mailing to every contact who meets certain criteria. For example, they can select on industry and send out a letter only to prospects in that industry. Similarly, ACT! provides reporting capabilities. Salespeople can see how effective they are for each method of prospecting, then focus their efforts on the methods that work the best. These are only some ideas—you may want to visit the Web site for more, or think about how the concepts in the chapter can help your account.

Using the same account you've been selling to (Skylight, Lincoln, or Binswanger), write out some questions you'd like to ask your buyer to determine how they prospect now, and how ACT! might help. (Note: If you have not done role plays before, you will need to review the information about the various role play customers that can be found at the end of Chapter 4.) Then role play with your buyer, trying to determine their needs for assistance with prospecting. Once you've identified those needs, give a short presentation as to how ACT! can help. Your professor will pass out buyer sheets.

Note: For background information on these role plays, please see page 27.

To the instructor: Additional information needed to complete the role play is available in the Instructor's Manual.

ADDITIONAL REFERENCES

Batt, Peter J., and Sharon Purchase. "Managing Collaboration within Networks and Relationships." *Industrial Marketing Management* 33 (2004), pp. 169–74.

Bosik, Darren. "So Many Customers, So Little Time." *1to1 Magazine*, (May/June 2002), pp. 39–43.

Blythe, Jim. "Using Trade Fairs in Key Account Management." *Journal of Industrial Marketing Management* 31, no. 7 (2002), pp. 627–35.

Budds, Niall. "Shared Goals Foster Better Lead Management." *Marketing News* 38 (October 1, 2004), pp. 17–18.

Donath, Bob. "Create Lead Reports Management Loves." *Marketing News* (October 1, 2004), p. 5.

Droullard, Kathryn. "Mind Your Manners." *Sales and Marketing Management*, (January 2005), pp. 26–32.

Erffmeyer, Robert C., and Dale A. Johnson. "An Exploratory Study of Sales Force Automation Practices: Expectations and Realities." *Journal of Personal Selling & Sales Management* 21, no. 2 (Spring 2001), pp. 167–75.

Eveleth, Daniel M., and Linda Morris. "Adaptive Selling in a Call Center Environment: A Qualitative Investigation." *Journal of Interactive Marketing* 16 (Winter 2002), pp. 25–39.

Fritzson, Rebecca. *Focus on Buyers: Selling from Your Prospect's Point of View* (iUniverse, Incorporated, 2003).

Frook, John Evan. "How One Manufacturer Converts Leads into Sales." *B to B Magazine* 87 (January 14, 2002), pp. 21–23.

Gombeski, William R. Jr.; David Kanton; Nadine A. Bendycki; and Jeff Wack. "Improve Your Marketing Effectiveness and Net Income through Better Prospecting." *Health Marketing Quarterly* 19, no. 4 (2004), pp. 3–19.

Greco, Susan. "Sales: What Works Now." *Inc. Magazine*, (February 2002), pp. 52–59.

Hogan, Cecilia, and David Lamb. *Prospect Research: A Primer for Growing Nonprofits.* (Boston: Jones & Bartlett Publishers, 2004).

Holmlund, Maria. "Analyzing Business Relationships and Distinguishing Different Interaction Levels." *Industrial Marketing Management* 33 (2004), pp. 279–87.

Kane, Thomas E. *Letters for Lawyers: Essential Communication for Clients, Prospects, and Others.* (Chicago: American Bar Association, 2004).

Kennedy, Karen Norman, and Dawn R. Deeter-Schmelz. "Descriptive and Predictive Analyses of Industrial Buyers' Use of Online Information for Purchasing." *Journal of Personal Selling & Sales Management* 21, no. 4 (Fall 2001), pp. 279–90.

Kimball, D. Scott. *Top Gun Prospecting for Financial Professionals.* (Chicago: Dearborn Trade, 2003).

Leek, Sheena; Peter Naude; and Peter W. Turnbull. "Interactions, Relationships, and Networks in a Changing World." *Industrial Marketing Management* 32 (2003), pp. 87–90.

Lemire, Polly. *The Cold Call Cure: How to Outsmart Your Cold Call Fears and Become a Master at Prospecting for New Business.* (Bloomington, Indiana: AuthorHouse, 2003).

Miller, Robert B.; Stephen E. Helman; and Tad Tuleja. *The New Strategic Selling.* (New York: Warner Business, 2005).

Moran, Gwen. "Quick Pick." *Entrepreneur* 32 (July 2004), p. 70.

Natenberg, Todd. "Referrals: Your Key to Sales Success." *Sell!ng*, (September 2004), p. 9.

Pinar, Musa; Jerry Rogers; and Donald Baac. "An Examination of Trade Show Participation in a Developing Country: An Exploratory Study in Turkey." *Journal of Euromarketing* 11, no. 3 (2002), pp. 33–52.

Schrage, Michael. "Are Customers Selling For You?" *Sales and Marketing Management*, (February 2004), p. 22.

Stevens, Ruth P. "CRM: It's about Prospecting, Too." *1to1 Magazine*, February 2002 (accessed on 3/13/02 at http://www.1to1.com).

PLANNING THE SALES CALL

SOME QUESTIONS ANSWERED
IN THIS CHAPTER ARE . . .

- Why should salespeople plan their sales calls?
- What precall information is needed about the individual prospect and the prospect's organization?
- How can this information be obtained?
- What is involved in setting call objectives?
- Should more than one objective be set for each call?
- How can appointments be made effectively and efficiently?

PROFILE

I graduated from the University of the Sciences in 2003 with a pharmaceutical marketing and management major and a minor in communications. I took my personal selling course from Dr. Glenn Rosenthal. In my last two years of college I participated in a sales internship with Abbott Laboratories and a marketing internship with Crozer-Keystone Health System. During these internships I began to learn the importance of having a plan and executing it efficiently.

The key to a perfect plan, however, is knowing when the plan is working and when changes need to be put into place. As I graduated from college I worked hard, with the help of my professors, to prepare for my upcoming interviews. We planned for everything, from the possible questions that could be asked to the business suit that I would wear. I never felt more prepared in my life. Until I got into the interview.

I immediately realized that even though I had planned everything I was going to do and say, I hadn't counted on the interviewer deviating from my plan. It was then that I realized a good plan needs to be fluid and easily changed, depending on outside circumstances that can arise. After interviewing with several companies, I finally decided to accept a sales position with Pfizer Pharmaceuticals, the leading pharmaceutical company in the industry.

In this industry things are always changing. So it's not surprising that when I first tried to come up with a plan to increase my business I got very frustrated when things didn't stay the same. I asked myself, "Why should I come up with a plan if things never stay the same?" It was then that I finally accepted that a good plan doesn't stay constant but instead is constantly changing to reflect current conditions. Effective planning includes reassessing your goals every so often to make sure they are working for you.

The pharmaceutical industry is one of the most competitive sales positions out there. That is why planning is of the utmost importance. A typical day in this field is spent waiting to see physicians and then trying to expand my time with them. In order to do this effectively I must know my physicians inside and out. I need to know their personality type so I can tailor each presentation specifically toward their interests and needs and base call objectives around this information.

Planning what I will discuss with each physician before I go into the office helps me remain focused on my goals in those few minutes I can spend with the physician. Knowing my objectives beforehand also helps me steer the conversation back if we get off track somehow.

After the call I check how close I came to achieving my objectives and what I will need to do in future calls to bring this physician closer to the goals. Sales representatives who can do this most effectively will be the ones who succeed. As my manager always says, "If you fail to plan, you plan to fail."

Visit our Web site at Pfizer.com.

"I finally accepted that a good plan doesn't stay constant but instead is constantly changing to reflect current conditions."

Rachel Fisher

WHY PLAN THE SALES CALL?

Successful salespeople know that advance planning of the sales interview is essential to achieve in selling. The salesperson should remember that the buyer's time is valuable. Without planning the sales call, a salesperson quite easily may cover material in which the buyer has no interest, try to obtain an order even though that is an unrealistic expectation for this sales call, or strike off into areas that veer from what the buyer actually needs to hear. The result is wasted time and an annoyed prospect. However, by having a clear plan for the call, the salesperson more likely will not only obtain commitment but also win the buyer's respect and confidence.

Salespeople should also remember the value of their own time. Proper planning helps them meet their call objectives efficiently as well as effectively. They then have more time to make additional calls, conduct research on the target customer or other customers, fill out company reports, and complete other necessary tasks. The result is better territory management. (See Chapter 15 for more discussion about time and territory management.)

Of course, planning must fit into the salesperson's goals for the account. Some accounts will have greater strategic importance and thus will require more planning. (See Chapter 2 for a discussion about the types of relationships that a seller can have with a buyer and Chapter 15 about classifying accounts and prospects.) Accounts with which a firm is partnering will obviously need the most planning, whereas smaller accounts may warrant less planning. Also, salespeople must not make planning an end in itself and a way to avoid actually making calls. Exhibit 8.1 provides a flow diagram that shows how the concepts in this chapter are related.

OBTAINING PRECALL INFORMATION

Often the difference between making and not making a sale depends on the amount of homework the salesperson does before making a call. The more information the salesperson has about the prospect, the higher the probability of meeting the prospect's needs and developing a long-term relationship. However, the salesperson must be aware of the costs involved in collecting information. At some point, the time and effort put into collecting information become greater than the benefits obtained. And of course, for some cold calls, there will be little if any precall information collected.

The following dialogue shows what can happen in a sales call made with inadequate precall information:

SALESPERSON: Good morning, Mr. White. I'm Mary Thompson, the new sales rep for McNeil Clothing.

CUSTOMER: My name is Witt, not White.

SALESPERSON: Oh! I'm sorry. I should have asked your secretary to spell your name when I called to make an appointment. I want to show you our new fall line that's just perfect for the growing teen market.

CUSTOMER: Most of our customers are middle-aged. I don't really want to attract teens to my store. They make a lot of noise, and they bother the older customers. To be honest, some of them even kind of scare me!

Exhibit 8.1
A Flow Diagram of the Planning Process

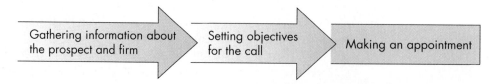

Gathering information about the prospect and firm → Setting objectives for the call → Making an appointment

PLANNING CAN TAKE A LOT OF TIME

As an account representative for PartStock Computer Solutions, Alex Marquette knows firsthand the importance of planning. He relates, "Today's buyers are sharper, more savvy, and focused on saving time and money. They can smell a poorly planned presentation a mile away. Salespeople get only one chance to make a solid first impression. The prospect has hundreds of items on his/her plate, and you're not one of them.

"Recently I spent three weeks developing a solid sales presentation for an important client. I talked with my existing clients, learned why they buy from me, asking what specific benefits we offer that fit their needs. I also talked with our sales staff to develop needs identification questions, a list of possible sales objections, and a fine-tuned list of features and benefits."

As a result of all of this planning, Alex focused on the prospect during the presentations. Not surprisingly, after four sales calls on the prospect, Alex got the business. The planning took a lot of time, but the rewards were outstanding.

Source: Alex Marquette, used with permission.

Gathering information from individuals in the prospect's firm before making a call on the prospect is often a wise investment of time.

RF/Corbis

By not obtaining precall information, this salesperson immediately encountered several embarrassing situations. With such a poor start, the salesperson is unlikely to attain her call objective.

Clearly, a salesperson who has been calling regularly on a prospect or customer may not need to collect a lot of additional information; records and notes from prior calls may be adequate to prepare for the sales call. The same holds true for a new salesperson if the previous one kept good records. But beware! In this fast-paced world, things are changing every day. Consider the following dialogue:

SALESPERSON [walking up to the receptionist of one of his best customers]: Hello, Jim. I'm here to see Toby. I have some information I promised to share with her about our new manufacturing process. She was pretty excited about seeing it!

RECEPTIONIST [looking tired]: Sorry, Jeff. Toby was transferred last week to our Toronto plant. Haven't you heard about our latest reorganization? Just went into effect two weeks ago. I'm still trying to figure it out. It seems that all of our engineering people are moving to the Toronto site.

SALESPERSON [looking confused and worried]: No, I hadn't heard! Well, who took Toby's job? That person really needs to see this information.

RECEPTIONIST: No one took her place. I think they're going to outsource a lot of what she did [starting to pick up the phone for an incoming call]. It's just not going to be the same around here anymore.

The key: Don't assume that your knowledge about the account is automatically up-to-date.

Of course, before you make an initial call on a very important prospect, you will often expend considerable effort on collecting precall information about both the individual prospect and the prospect's company. Don't expect this information gathering to be quick, easy, or cheap, as Selling Scenario 8.1 illustrates.

It is important to learn and maintain current knowledge about both the prospect as an individual and his or her firm. The sections that follow examine these areas more closely. Of course, the salesperson should keep in mind privacy concerns, as related in Chapter 3.

THE PROSPECT/CUSTOMER AS AN INDIVIDUAL

Salespeople should attempt to learn the following types of information about a prospect or a customer:

Personal

- Name (including pronunciation).
- Family status.
- Education.
- Aspirations.
- Interests (such as hobbies) and disinterests.
- Social style (driver or another category—see Chapter 6).

Attitudes

- Toward salespeople.
- Toward your company.
- Toward your product.

Relationships

- Formal reporting relationships.
- Important reference groups and group norms.
- Bonds that the prospect has already formed with other salespeople.[1]

Evaluation of Products/Services

- Product attributes that are important.
- Product evaluation process (see Chapter 4 for details).

THE PROSPECT'S/CUSTOMER'S ORGANIZATION

Information about the prospect's or customer's company obviously helps the salesperson understand the customer's environment. This type of information enables the salesperson to more quickly identify problem areas and respond accordingly.

For example, in a modified rebuy situation, it would not be necessary to educate the prospect about general features common to the product class as a whole. Using the prospect's valuable time by covering material he or she already knows is minimized. Information like the following about the prospect's organization would be helpful:

Demographics

- Type of organization (manufacturing, wholesaling, retailing).
- Size, number of locations.
- Products and services offered.
- Financial position and its future.
- Overall culture of the organization (risk averse, highest ethical standards, forward thinking).

Prospect's Customers

- Types (consumers, retailers, wholesalers).
- Benefits they seek from the prospect's products and services.

Prospect's Competitors

- Who they are.
- How they differ in their business approaches.
- Prospect's strategic position in the industry (dominant, strong, weak).

Historical Buying Patterns

- Amount purchased in the product category.
- Sole supplier or multiple suppliers. Why?
- Reason for buying from present suppliers.
- Level of satisfaction with suppliers.
- Reasons for any dissatisfaction with suppliers or products currently purchased.

Current Buying Situation

- Type of buying process (new task, straight rebuy, or modified rebuy—see Chapter 4).
- Strengths and weaknesses of potential competitors.

People Involved in the Purchase Decision

- How they fit into the formal and informal organizational structure.
- Their roles in this decision (gatekeeper, influencer, or the like).
- Who is most influential.
- Any **influential adversaries** (carry great influence but are opposed to us)?[2]
- Current problems the organization faces.
- Stage in the buying cycle.

Policies and Procedures

- About salespeople.
- About sales visits.
- About purchasing and contracts.

---

thinking it through

It's your first week on the job as a new salesperson. You were given a laptop computer and time and territory management software that the regional manager has tailored specifically for your sales region. Your district sales manager instructs you to fill in all the fields (name, company name, title, who currently buying from, and so on) completely for each new prospect. Most of the information you are asked for seems to make a lot of sense. However, you notice that you are asked to find out each prospect's political party affiliation and the names of each prospect's children. You don't feel comfortable asking for this kind of personal information. What are you going to do?

SOURCES OF INFORMATION

Gathering all the information listed in the preceding sections for every prospect and organization is initially impossible. The goal is to gather what is both possible and profitable. Remember, your time is valuable! Also, you don't want to fall into the trap sometimes referred to as **analysis paralysis,** which is when you prefer to spend practically all of your time analyzing the situation and finding information instead of making sales calls. Salespeople must strike a proper balance between time spent in acquiring information and time spent making calls.

It is important to gather useful information, and not just piles of trivial facts about a prospect. Also, salespeople need to check the quality of any data gathered. One recent survey of salespeople found that 65 percent felt the data they had was outdated or inaccurate.[3] Salespeople must also be concerned about information overload, which can be detrimental to their jobs.[4]

RESOURCES WITHIN YOUR COMPANY

One of the best sources of information can be the records in your own company, especially if your firm has developed a sophisticated database, as described in Chapter 7. The most useful databases include, in addition to standard demographic information, information on any direct inquiries made by the prospect (from direct mail inquiries, through the telemarketing division of your firm, or the like), a sales history on the firm, whether anyone from your company has called on the prospect, and the results of any sales meetings.

Firms are devising many ways to keep the field sales force well informed. Some are using **sales portals,** online databases that include many sources of information in one place.[5] This information can include items like account data, competitor intelligence, and news about the company, the industry, and the economy. All the salesperson has to do is use a single log-on to access all of this information. For example, Continental's salespeople can log onto their company's portal and quickly and easily access key insights about their business customers.[6] Lufthansa airlines salespeople can do the same thing, easily viewing real-time information about key customers.[7] Rubbermaid has asked its entire sales team to record all internal communications and transaction details online.[8] Keebler gives its sales reps an online database of trends, information, and presentation templates.[9]

Even if your firm doesn't have such a database, you should try to gather information about your prospect. For example, wouldn't it be nice to find out before, as opposed to during a sales call, that the prospect used to be a big customer of your firm but quit for some reason?

For important sales, you may well be working with a sales team that interacts with a prospect (a topic more fully addressed in Chapter 16). This team, sometimes called a **selling center,** consists of all people in the selling organization who participate in a selling opportunity. Members of the team may be able to provide or help you secure needed information.

THE INTERNET

Twenty years ago, it took a great deal of time to research and discover information about a prospect. Now, as we mentioned in Chapter 7, a salesperson can learn a wealth of information in a very short time with the Internet.

A first place to look for information would be the prospect company's own Web page. It is amazing what one can find on company Web pages. A recent study of *Fortune* 100 firms discovered that a large percentage had each of the following pieces of information: link to the annual report (100 percent), information about the firm's products and services (99 percent), latest news about the firm (99 percent), a summary about the firm (95 percent), and a statement of values (87 percent).[10]

The sources listed in Exhibit 7.4 would be a good place to start to find information. For example, a salesperson would be able to learn many things about a prospect at www.hoovers.com, Hoover's Web site. The salesperson could easily search by company name, ticker symbol, keywords, or a person's last name for each of the over 42,000 public and private organizations listed, including U.S. and international firms. For each company, there is a brief overview, a company profile, stock quotes, a list of officers, financial data, links to its Web site(s), links to press releases, and a listing of and automatic links to its major competitors. The seller could also peruse news (from Hoover's own files, plus automatic links to all major news services) or easily link to any other major Web search engine to find out more about the company, the market, or specific industries. News articles often include information about the firm's strategy, new product launches, plans for division changes, lawsuits, new investments, competitive challenges, and so on. To learn more about the prospect's industry, the seller can read an analysis of industry sectors, including industry snapshots, key players, trends, definitions, and links to other industry views. There are even online prospecting tools (including databases of leads, requests for proposals from firms, and industry-specific contact information).

Sources like Hoover's Web site are excellent for providing information.

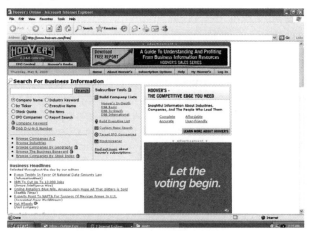

Courtesy of Hoover's, Inc. www.hoovers.com

Keep in mind that much of this information is free (for a fee you can get even more information from Hoover's, including information on over 12 million companies) and comes from just one source. Now multiply that by the thousands of online information sources that a salesperson can access, and you can see that a new problem for salespeople is deciding how to manage all of that information. One reason that firms are starting to build databases and sales portals is to centralize the information that's important to their field sales force.[11]

You can also set up personalized Web pages from many servers that will scan sources for the information you seek and provide periodic updates that can assist your selling and planning efforts. For example, you can set up a personal Web page directly from Netscape that will keep you abreast of the topics you are most interested in.

In addition to checking the Web sources noted in Chapter 7, you may also want to visit the JustSell.com site (www.justsell.com). It contains many helpful links for salespeople, including free company profiles.

SECRETARIES AND RECEPTIONISTS

Secretaries and receptionists in the prospect's firm usually are a rich source of information. Be courteous, however, because secretaries and receptionists are accustomed to having salespeople pry for all sorts of free information. Prioritize your questions and provide justification for asking them. Above all, treat secretaries and receptionists with genuine respect.[12]

NONCOMPETING SALESPEOPLE

Another source for precall information is noncompeting salespeople. In fact, one of the best sources of information is the prospect's own salespeople because they empathize with your situation.[13]

TRADITIONAL SECONDARY SOURCES

Traditional secondary data sources can also be helpful (we described many of them in Chapter 7 when we discussed sources of prospects). Firms such as Standard & Poor's, Hoover's, Wards, and Moody's publish a number of manuals and directories that are available in many public libraries. These sources can help answer questions about brand names, key contacts, historical information, the current situation and outlook for the firm and the industry, location of plants and distribution centers, market shares, and so on.

THE PROSPECT

Much information can be gleaned directly from the prospect. However, don't expect prospects to sit down and answer any and all questions you might have, especially for topics where the information is fairly easy to get (like what products the prospect makes or sells). Prospects don't have time to fill you in on all the details of their business. If you don't know the basics, many prospects will refuse to deal with you.

It is also worth mentioning that, just as you are gathering information about the prospect prior to a meeting, the prospect can and often does collect information about you. Even before the sale your prospect can request price quotes via e-mail. He or she can also view your Web page, as well as your competitors' Web pages. Plus the prospect can easily chat with colleagues via newsgroups and list-servs to learn about you or your firm. Any salesperson who doesn't understand these realities won't be as prepared for the kinds of questions that a prospect might ask or for comments that a prospect might make.

OTHER SOURCES

Many other sources can provide information. Some information may have been gleaned at a trade show the prospect attended. Much information will be in the lists and directories from which the prospect's name came. A center of influence will often be able to provide some information. Occasionally a prospect will be important enough to warrant hiring an outside consultant to collect information, especially if you are gathering precall information for international selling. Although some information about foreign companies is available, much will not be obtainable. Salespeople in the United States are often amazed at the lack of information about foreign companies. Two good sources are the U.S. government's export portal and the U.S. Commercial Service market research library.[14]

SETTING CALL OBJECTIVES

A most important step in planning is to set objectives for the call.[15] Merely stating the objective "I want to make a sale" will not suffice. The customer's decision-making process (see Chapter 4) involves many steps, and salespeople need to undertake many activities as they guide customers through the process.

Yet, as Neil Rackham, an internationally respected sales researcher, notes, "It's astonishing how rarely salespeople set themselves call objectives of any kind—let alone effective ones. Although most books on selling emphasize the importance of clear call objectives, it's rare to see these exhortations turned into practice."[16] Why? Probably because many salespeople want to start doing something instead of "wasting time" planning. But without a plan, they actually increase their chances of wasting time.

As a first step in setting objectives, the salesperson should review what has been learned from precall information gathering. Any call objectives should be based on the results of this review. Also, the seller must keep in mind the relationship the firm wishes to have with the prospect. Not all prospects will or should become strategic partners with the seller's firm. Remember from Chapter 2 that some prospects will simply wish to have a relational partnership or a functional relationship with the seller.

Call objectives should not be created in a vacuum. They should be developed while taking into account the firm's goals, the sales team's goals, and the salesperson's goals. Some experts have even argued for the importance of salespeople maintaining consistency between their personal goals and selling objectives. Regardless of the type of goal you are referring to, the old adage is true: If you don't know where you're going, you may wind up somewhere else.

In their well-received sales training books on strategic selling, Miller and Heiman stress the importance of sales call planning being related to the firm's strategic goals for the account.[17] This important topic is covered in Chapter 15. For now, realize that call objectives are based on strategic decisions about the account.

Even a salesperson who fails to achieve the primary call objective will be encouraged to at least achieve the minimum call objective.

Photodisc Red/Getty Images

CRITERIA FOR EFFECTIVE OBJECTIVES

All objectives should be specific, realistic, and measurable. A call objective that meets only one or two of these criteria will be an ineffective guide for the salesperson. We will now examine each criterion in more detail.

An objective must be *specific* to be effective. It should state precisely what the salesperson hopes to accomplish, who the objective targets are, and any other details (suggested order quantity, suggested dates for future meetings, length of time needed for a follow-up survey, or the like). Specific objectives help the salesperson avoid "shooting from the hip" during the presentation and perhaps moving the prospect along too rapidly or too slowly.

Objectives must also be *realistic*. Inexperienced salespeople often have unrealistic expectations about the prospect's or customer's response in the sales call. For example, if Ford Motor Company currently uses Sony radios on all of its models, a Philips salesperson who expects Ford to change over to Philips radios in the first few sales calls has an unrealistic objective. It is important for sellers to plan objectives for a call that can be accomplished within the time allocated for that sales call. That doesn't mean the objectives should be easy. In reality challenging, but reachable goals, tend to lead to better performance.[18]

For objectives to be realistic, the salesperson needs to consider factors such as cultural influences. For example, some firms have a corporate culture of being extremely conservative. Creating change in such a culture is time-consuming and often frustrating for the seller. The national culture is important in selling to international prospects. When selling to Arab or Japanese businesses, salespeople should plan to spend at least several meetings getting to know the other party. Developing relationships with Chinese businesspeople requires a great deal of entertaining. Selling in Russia is often slowed because of bureaucracy and incredible amounts of red tape. As these examples illustrate, culture is an important consideration in attempts to set realistic call objectives.

Finally, call objectives must be *measurable* so that salespeople can objectively evaluate each sales call at its conclusion and determine whether the objectives were met. This suggests they should be written down. If a salesperson's stated objective is to get acquainted with the prospect or to establish rapport, how can the salesperson assess whether this goal was achieved? How can someone measure "getting acquainted"? To what extent would the salesperson have to be acquainted with the prospect to know that he or she achieved the sales call objective? A more measurable sales call objective (as well as a more specific and realistic one) is something like the following: To get acquainted with the prospect by learning which clubs or organizations she or he belongs to, which sports the prospect follows, what his or her professional background is, and how long the prospect has held the current position. With this revised call objective, a salesperson can very simply determine whether the objective was reached.

An easy way to help ensure that objectives are measurable is to set objectives that require a buyer's response. For example, achievement of the following objective is easy to measure: to make a follow-up appointment with the buyer.

Successful salespeople in almost every industry have learned the importance of setting proper call objectives. Pharmaceutical salespeople for Novartis set clear objectives for each sales call they make to a physician. Then they lay out a series of objectives for subsequent calls so that they know exactly what they hope to accomplish over the next several visits. One industrial products sales manager recommends that her salespeople keep their call objectives in view while they are on the sales call, helping them to focus on the true goals of the sales call. Both of these examples share a common theme: The salesperson needs to set specific, realistic, measurable call objectives. Exhibit 8.2 lists examples of call objectives that meet these criteria.

Some trainers use the acronym SMART to help salespeople remember how to set proper call objections. SMART suggests that call objectives should be **s**pecific, **m**easurable, and **a**chievable but **r**ealistic and **t**ime-based.[19]

SETTING MORE THAN ONE CALL OBJECTIVE

Salespeople have learned the importance of setting multiple objectives for a sales call. Not only do they set a **primary call objective** (the actual goal they hope to achieve) before each sales call; they also set a **minimum call objective** (the mini-

Exhibit 8.2

Examples of Call Objectives

Objectives Related to the Process Leading up to the Sale

- To have the prospect agree to come to the Atlanta branch office sometime during the next two weeks for a hands-on demonstration of the copier.
- To set up another appointment for one week from now, when the buyer will allow me to do a complete survey of her printing needs.
- To inform the doctor of the revolutionary anticlotting mechanism that has been incorporated into our new drug and have her agree to read the pamphlet I will leave.
- To have the buyer agree to pass my information along to the buying committee with his endorsement of my proposal.
- To have the prospect agree to call several references that I will provide to develop further confidence and trust in my office-cleaning business.
- To have the prospect agree on the first point (of our four-point program) and schedule another meeting in two days to discuss the second point.
- To have the prospect initiate the necessary paperwork to allow us to be considered as a future vendor.

Objectives Related to Consummating the Sale

- To have the prospect sign an order for 100 pairs of Levi's jeans.
- To schedule a co-op newspaper advertising program to be implemented in the next month.
- To have the prospect agree to use our brand of computer paper for a trial period of one month.
- To have the retailer agree to allow us space for an end-of-aisle display for the summer promotion of Raid insect repellent.

mum they hope to achieve) because they realize the call may not go exactly as planned (the prospect may be called away or the salesperson may not have all the necessary facts). On the other hand, the call may go better than the salesperson originally thought it would. Thus, although rarely achieved, an **optimistic call objective** (the most optimistic outcome the salesperson thinks could occur) is also set. The optimistic call objective will probably relate to what the salesperson hopes to accomplish for the account over the long term (that is, the account objectives—see Chapter 15).

The primary call objective, for example, of a Nestlé Foods rep might be to secure an order from a grocer for 10 cases of Nestlé Morsels for an upcoming coupon promotion. That is what the seller realistically hopes to accomplish in the call. A minimum call objective could be to sell at least 5 cases of Morsels, whereas an optimistic call objective would be to sell 20 cases, set up an end-of-aisle display, and secure a retail promotional price of $2.89.

Multiple call objectives have many benefits. First, they help take away the salesperson's fear of failure because most salespeople can achieve at least their stated minimum objective. Second, multiple objectives tend to be self-correcting. Salespeople who always reach their optimum objective realize they are probably setting their sights too low. On the other hand, if they rarely meet even their minimum objective, they probably are setting their goals too high.

It is possible to have more than one primary call objective for a single call. For example, several primary objectives a salesperson might hope to accomplish in a single meeting are to sell one unit, be introduced to one other member of the buying center, and have the prospect agree to send along a packet of information to an executive. In this example, if the salesperson genuinely hopes and expects to achieve all three objectives in the next meeting, they will all be considered primary call objectives. To aid in planning the call, some trainers suggest that the salesperson further prioritize these primary objectives into two groups: The most important primary objective is called the primary call objective, whereas the remaining ones become **secondary call objectives.** So, in this example, if selling the product is the most important thing to accomplish in the next meeting, the objectives will be as follows:

Primary call objective:	Sell one unit.
Secondary call objectives:	Be introduced to one other member of the buying center.
	Have the prospect agree to send along a packet of information to an executive.

SETTING OBJECTIVES FOR SEVERAL CALLS

By developing a series of specific objectives for future calls, the salesperson can develop a comprehensive strategy for the prospect or customer. This approach is especially important in a partnering relationship. To illustrate the use of multiple call objectives, Exhibit 8.3 gives a set of call objectives for visits over a period of time. The left side of the exhibit contains the long-term plan and each call objective that the Samsung salesperson developed for Johnson Electronics. Note the logical strategy for introducing the new product, the F104 DVD player. The right side of Exhibit 8.3 shows the actual call results.

The salesperson was not always 100 percent successful in achieving the call objectives. Thus several subsequent objectives needed to be modified. For example, because the meeting on October 10 resulted in the buyer dropping F92 DVD players, the call objectives on November 10 and November 17 need to reflect that Johnson Electronics no longer carries the F92 DVD players. The seller may also

Exhibit 8.3

Multiple Call Objectives of a Samsung Salesperson Selling to Johnson Electronics

Overall Plan Developed on Oct. 1		Actual Call Results	
Expected Date of the Call	**Call Objective**	**Date of Call**	**Call Results**
Oct. 10	Secure normal repeat orders on F88 and F92. Increase normal repeat order of F100 DVD player from three to five units. Provide product information for new DVD product F104.	Oct. 10	Obtained normal order of F88. Steve decided to drop F92 (refused to give a good reason). Purchased only four F100 players. Seemed responsive to F104 but needs a point-of-purchase (POP) display.
Oct. 17	Erect a front-counter POP display for F104 and secure a trial order of two units.	Oct. 18	Steve was out. His assistant didn't like the POP (thought it was too large!). Refused to use POP. Did order one F104. Told me about several complaints with F100.
Nov. 10	Secure normal repeat orders for F88, F92, and F100. Schedule one co-op newspaper ad for the next 30 days featuring F104. Secure an order for F104s.	Nov. 8	Obtained normal orders. Steve agreed to co-op ad but bought only five F104s. Thinks the margins are too low.
Nov. 17	Secure normal repeat orders of F88, F92, and F100. Secure an order for F104s.	Nov. 18	Obtained normal order on F88, but Steve refused to reorder F100. Claimed the competitor product (Sony) is selling much better. Obtained an order of 15 units of F104.

want to add a call objective for October 17: to discuss more about the situation with F92 (because of the outcome of the October 10 meeting) and perhaps try to reintroduce it. This example illustrates the importance of keeping good records, making any necessary adjustments in the long-term call objectives, and then preparing for the next sales call. One sales vice president for a large sales force has some specific advice about setting multiple call objectives:

> The primary objective of the first session is to have another chance to visit. What this allows you to do is have your standards relatively low because you are trying to build a long-term relationship. You should be very sensitive to an opportunity to establish a second visit. What you want to do is identify aspects of the business conversation that require follow-up and make note of them. . . . The key is not the first visit . . . it is the second, the third, the twenty-second visit.[20]

Some industries typically have a long interval between when a prospect is first visited and when an actual sale is consummated. If so, this factor needs to be considered when setting up multiple call objectives and may imply that others get involved in the selling cycle. For example, the typical sale of a Kodak Motion Analysis System, high-speed cameras that can photograph things too fast for the human eye to see, could take several years to close. After having its field sales force demonstrate the camera, the company can use inside sales reps (see Chapter 1 for a description of inside salespeople) to keep the prospects updated in a fashion that is consistent with the prospects' buying time frames. Kodak may also send out newsletters several times a year to prospects. It is important for salespeople to consider the company's other promotional efforts when developing multiple call objectives for a prospect.

When setting multiple call objectives, the salesperson should obviously consider whom to call on in upcoming meetings. Although it seems obvious that the decision maker (who is often a middle manager for many products and services) should be included in those calls, visiting briefly with senior-level managers may also make sense. But what information would you share with the CEO, for example? As discussed in Chapter 1, the answer is the **value proposition,** a written statement (usually one or two sentences) that clearly states how purchasing your product or service can help add shareholder value. The value proposition should be specific and measurable and should be tied to the prospect's mission statement. Meetings to share the value proposition with senior managers probably should include middle managers from the prospect's firm and take no more than 30 minutes.

BUYERS ARE SETTING GOALS ALSO

It's important that salespeople understand that buyers may also be setting objectives for the salesperson's sales call.[21] These objectives are based on perceptions of how the salesperson's product or service can add value, as described in Chapters 1 and 4. Salespeople's job is to discover what customers value and then find ways to improve **customer value** relative to their own products or services.

What are some things that buyers look for to increase value? Purchasing managers continually point to the following areas: on-time delivery, to-spec quality of products, competitive pricing, proper packaging/paperwork, technical support/ service, quality of sales calls, level of technological innovation, and good emergency response. Thus sellers can expect that buyers may set goals for sales calls in these areas.

MAKING AN APPOINTMENT

After gathering precall information and setting objectives, the salesperson's next step is generally to make an appointment. Many sales managers insist that their salespeople make appointments before calling on prospects or customers. Appointments dignify the salesperson and help get the sales process off to a good start by putting the salesperson and the prospect on the same level—equal participants in a legitimate sales interview. Appointments also increase the chances of seeing the right person and having uninterrupted time with the prospect. Building Partnerships 8.1 provides some examples of creative ways to get in and see the prospect.

Experienced sales representatives use different contact methods for different customers. It's also important to point out that attitude (and the salesperson's mood) can have a tremendously important impact on success in making appointments. This section describes how to see the right person[22] at the right time and the right place, how to interact with gatekeepers, and how to gain an appointment.

THE RIGHT PERSON

Some experts emphasize the importance of going right to the top and making the first call on the highest-level decision maker. After carefully studying more than 35,000 sales calls, Neil Rackham offers a radically different view.[23] His research suggests that a salesperson should initially try to call on the **focus of receptivity,** the person who will listen receptively and provide the seller with needed valuable information.[24] Note that this person may not be the decision maker or the one who understands all of the firm's problems. In fact, this person might not even be in the buying center. (See Chapter 4 for details on various people who serve as

TRYING TO GET IN? CREATIVITY MAY BE THE ANSWER

What should you do when a prospect, who you know needs your product, refuses to meet with you? Maybe creativity is the answer. Here are two examples.

Randy Rosler set up a meeting to sell his greeting card company's products to UPS, but UPS's director of marketing had to cancel the meeting and never returned Rosler's calls to set up another meeting. From conversations with the receptionist, Rosler found that the director loved golf. So he bought some golf balls and sent them to the director with a card attached that read "Thought I'd take another swing at it . . ." on the outside, with ". . . as I've been unable to reach you. I'm looking forward to speaking with you soon." on the inside of the card. His next phone call was successful. Rosler got the appointment and UPS's business.

A Moore Wallace rep really wanted to see Steve, an important prospect, but Steve always had an excuse for why he couldn't meet with the rep. In desperation the rep used his creative juices. He decided to send Steve a fresh pineapple every Monday morning. The card attached simply read "From the Pineapple Guy." For seven weeks he sent a pineapple. On Monday of the eighth week, the rep showed up in person at Steve's reception area. When asked who wished to see Steve, the rep said simply, "The Pineapple Guy." Needless to say, the rep was ushered right in.

Sources: Personal contact; Christine Galea, "The Boldest Thing I Did to Make a Sale," *Sales & Marketing Management*, March 2000, p. 64.

Appointments increase the chances of seeing the right person and having uninterrupted time with the prospect.

Michael Keller/Corbis

buying center members.) But this person will talk to the salesperson and provide information.

The focus of receptivity, according to the research, will then lead the salesperson to the **focus of dissatisfaction,** the person who is most likely to perceive problems and dissatisfactions. Finally, the focus of dissatisfaction leads to the **focus of power,** the person who can approve action, prevent action, and/or influence action. Getting to the focus of power too quickly can lead to disaster because the seller has not yet built a relationship and does not really know the buyer's needs. In summary, Rackham notes, "There's a superstition in selling that the sooner you can get to the decision maker the better. Effective selling, so it's said, is going straight to the focus of power. That's a questionable belief."[25]

Buying companies frequently want to manage all interactions between their firms and the salesperson and have set up policies, procedures, and channels to do so. Is it acceptable to bypass these "normal channels" and use a backdoor approach (see Chapter 4) when making calls? In other words, do firms frown on salespeople who bypass the traditional routine? The answer depends on many factors. How important is the account? What are the chances of securing the business? What will the company's reaction be? What damage will be done to the long-term relationship?

Frequently in industrial selling situations, as Chapter 4 described, no one person has the sole authority to buy a product because it is a team buying decision.[26] For example, a forklift sales representative for Clarke may have to see the safety engineer, the methods engineer, the materials-handling engineer, and the general superintendent before selling the product to a manufacturing company. In this case the salesperson should usually try to arrange a meeting with the entire group as well as with each individual.

THE RIGHT TIME

There is little agreement on the subject of the best time for a sales interview: obviously the most opportune time to call will vary by customer and type of selling. The salesperson who calls on wholesale grocers, for example, may find from experience that the best time to call is from 9 a.m. to 11 a.m. and from 1:30 p.m. to 3:30 p.m. A hospital rep, on the other hand, may discover that the most productive calls on surgeons are made between 8:30 a.m. and 10 a.m. and after 4 p.m. For most types of selling, the best hours of the day are from approximately 9 a.m. to 11:30 a.m. and from 1:30 p.m. to 4 p.m.

THE RIGHT PLACE

Meetings can occur just about anywhere. The sales call should take place in an environment conducive to doing business. Such is not always the case, however. For example, salespeople still take customers to topless bars. In addition to distractions, topless bars present a number of problems for the salesperson who uses them to achieve sales. For example, is it ethical to gain business by using such tactics? Also, once a buyer has purchased on the basis of this entertainment, chances are the seller will have to keep it up or lose the customer.

Videoconferencing, meetings in which people are not physically present in one location but are connected via voice and video, seems to be growing in usage.[27] In a variant on videoconferencing, called **Webcasting** or **virtual sales calls,** the meeting is broadcast over the Internet. For example, due to downsizing, emWare, Inc. has only eight salespeople. According to Michael Nelson, CEO of emWare, "Virtual sales calls have become a necessity. And they've turned out to be enormously successful."[28] Salespeople should learn how to plan for such meetings. One key is to carefully plan all technical elements of the presentation and to rehearse them as much as possible (Chapter 10 provides more insight into practicing and avoiding problems).[29]

Videoconferencing makes it easy for a U.S. salesperson to make a presentation in Germany.

Jim Cummins/Taxi/Getty Images

CULTIVATING RELATIONSHIPS WITH SUBORDINATES

Busy executives usually have one or more subordinates who plan and schedule interviews for them. These **screens** (or **barriers,** as salespeople sometimes call them) often make seeing the boss rather difficult. According to one study, decision makers receive over 200 selling contacts per day from business-to-business marketers, so the screen's behavior should not seem unreasonable![30] These screens can also take on the role of gatekeepers for the buying center (Chapter 4 discusses gatekeepers).

Sales strategists have identified several ways to interact with the screen:

Salespeople should work to achieve a friendly relationship with the prospect's subordinates.

Ryan McVay/Getty Images

- The salesperson can work "through the screen." The seller has to convince the gatekeeper that a meeting with the boss is in the boss's best interests.

- The salesperson can go "over the screen." While talking to the screen, the seller drops names of people higher up in the organization. The screen may allow the seller in to see the boss right away for fear of getting into trouble.

- The salesperson can go "under the screen" by trying to make contact with the prospect before or after the screen gets to work (or while the screen is taking a coffee break).

- The seller just bypasses the screen entirely, a strategy that can easily backfire. For example, Oracle learned, the hard way, the impact of having pushy, aggressive salespeople who constantly bypassed screens and formal committees.[31]

thinking **it** through Do you see problems in working over the screen? How about working under the screen? What might these tactics do to long-term relationship development?

TELEPHONING FOR APPOINTMENTS

The phone is most often used to make the initial appointment. Salespeople can save many hours by phoning, or having others phone for them, to make appointments.[32] Chapter 5 provided many insights on how to use the phone effectively.

The goal of the telephone call is to make an appointment, not to sell the product or service. Exhibit 8.4 shows appropriate responses to common objections Xerox copier salespeople encounter when making appointments. Salespeople need to anticipate objections and decide exactly how to respond, as Chapter 11 will more fully discuss.

Exhibit 8.4

Responses to Objections Concerning Appointments

Objection from a Secretary	Response
I'm sorry, but Mr. Wilkes is busy now.	What I have to say will take only a few minutes. Should I call back in a half-hour, or would you suggest I set up an appointment?
We already have a copier.	That's fine. I want to talk to Mr. Wilkes about our new paper-flow system design for companies like yours.
I take care of all the copying.	That's fine, but I'm here to present what Xerox has to offer for a complete paper-flow system that integrates data transmission, report generation, and copiers. I'd like to speak to Mr. Wilkes about this total service.

Objection from the Prospect	Response
Can't you mail the information to me?	Yes, I could. But everyone's situation is different, Mr. Wilkes, and our systems are individually tailored to meet the needs of each customer. Now . . . [benefit statement and repeat request for appointment].
Well, what is it you want to talk about?	It's difficult to explain the system over the telephone. In 15 minutes, I can demonstrate the savings you get from the system.
You'd just be wasting your time. I'm not interested.	The general objection is hiding a specific objection. The salesperson needs to probe for the specific objection: Do you say that because you don't copy many documents?
We had a Xerox copier once and didn't like it.	Probe for the specific reason of dissatisfaction and have a reply, but don't go too far. The objective is to get an appointment, not sell a copier.

Source: Courtesy of Xerox Corporation. Used by permission.

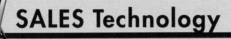

E-MISSIVES: A POWERFUL TOOL IN THE SALES ARSENAL

Want to make friends? Want to cement relationships? Then offer the other party some timely, useful information—called *seeding*. Information is what moves the world today, and your buyer or prospect can use all he or she can get. The information can consist of stories about the client's industry, one of the client's competitors, changes in the political climate as it relates to the prospect, even some research that the client might not have seen.

Because timing is often important, consider sending this information via e-mail. These **e-missives** will be welcomed by the prospect, assuming you've done your homework and the information is truly valuable for him or her. You can scan documents, ads, data, newspaper clippings, or other items as an attachment, always being mindful of copyright laws, of course. Alternatively, you

may want to summarize the information in the e-mail, and then provide a link where the prospect can click to get the information.

This is something you can start doing right now, even while you're still in school. When a guest speaker comes to class, pay attention to the geographic area and industry she or he works in. Then do some research on the Web, find some really useful information, and send it to the guest speaker, along with the normal thank-you for speaking to your class. You'll be happily surprised when you get a return e-mail, thanking you for the great piece of information.

Source: Personal correspondence; Michael Schrage, "The Virtual Newsperson: How E-Mailing Customers Relevant Information Can Build Stronger Relationships," *Sales and Marketing Management*, November 2004, p. 22.

ADDITIONAL PLANNING

A successful salesperson thinks ahead to the meeting that will occur and plans accordingly. For example, salespeople should plan how they intend to make a good first impression and build credibility during the call. It is also important to plan how to further uncover the customer's needs and strengthen the presentation. Salespeople should anticipate the questions and concerns the prospect may raise and plan to answer them helpfully. These issues are discussed in detail in the next several chapters. For now, be aware that these activities should be planned before the meeting begins.

Before making the sales call it is important to practice. How long should a rep spend practicing? Longer than many would think. As Mark Twain once said, "It usually takes more than three weeks to prepare a good impromptu speech." Some have even suggested that for very important presentations, the seller spend 30 minutes preparing and practicing for each one minute of presentation time. While that rule is often broken, it does indicate the importance of planning and practicing the presentation. Of course the time spent in practicing would depend on how much time the seller has plus what the goals of the presentation are.

One other thing that some salespeople do before making the actual sales call is called **seeding:** that is, sending the customer important and useful pieces of information.[33] For example, a rep can constantly search newspapers, magazines, and other sources for material that may be useful for a prospect. This material is sent to the prospect, at intervals, prior to the call, each time with a note saying something like "Jim, I thought you would find this article useful!" This material does not include the selling firm's catalogs, brochures, pricing, and so on. Rather, it is just good, useful information that will help the prospect's business. The result? The prospect views the seller as someone trying to truly be helpful and as someone who really understands the prospect's business. Sales Technology 8.1 describes how a salesperson can use e-mail for this purpose.

SUMMARY

This chapter stressed the importance of planning the sales call. Developing a clear plan saves time for both salespeople and customers. In addition, it helps salespeople increase their confidence and reduce their stress.

As part of the planning process, salespeople need to gather as much information about the prospect as possible before the first call. They need information about both the individual prospect and the prospect's organization. Sources of this information include lists and directories, secretaries and receptionists, noncompeting salespeople, and direct inquiries made by the prospect.

To be effective, a call objective should be specific, realistic, and measurable. In situations requiring several calls, the salesperson should develop a plan with call objectives for each future call. Also, many salespeople benefit from setting multiple levels of objectives—primary, minimum, and optimum—for each call.

As a general rule, salespeople should make appointments before calling on customers. This approach enables the salesperson to talk to the right person at the customer's site.

A number of methods can be used to make appointments. Perhaps the most effective is the straightforward telephone approach.

KEY TERMS

analysis paralysis
barriers
customer value
e-missives
focus of dissatisfaction
focus of power
focus of receptivity
influential adversaries
minimum call objective
optimistic call objective

primary call objective
sales portals
screens
secondary call objectives
seeding
selling center
value proposition
videoconferencing
virtual sales call
Webcasting

ETHICS PROBLEMS

1. Suppose that during your information-gathering phase you identify a very hostile influential adversary named Mike. You know that Mike will do everything possible to see your competitor get the business. In talking about this with your sales manager, she suggests that you find some way to covertly strip Mike of his credibility and thus cause him to be a nonissue. Would you follow your manager's advice? What kinds of things would you be willing to do? What would you be uncomfortable doing?

2. During precall planning, you learn that a very important prospect enjoys being treated by salespeople to visit "gentlemen's clubs." There are several of these strip clubs in your town. Your firm doesn't have any policy about whether you can visit one of these clubs with a client. You've never visited one with a client before. How will these facts impact your planning for your upcoming sales visit to this prospect? What will you do?

QUESTIONS AND PROBLEMS

1. Think about a job you have held. Now think about a manager who worked there. Assume that a salesperson wanted to sell your manager an important product or service. Who would be a good focus of receptivity for this salesperson? Do you think the focus of receptivity would cooperate with the salesperson?

2. Respond to the following statement: Setting call objectives reduces my ability to be adaptable during the call.

3. This chapter listed a number of items of information that a salesperson should find out about a prospect/customer as an individual. Choose a person that you know (but not a best friend) and assume you are selling him or her some important product or service. See how much of the information you can supply from the list in the text.

4. Evaluate the following objectives for a sales call:
   a. Show and demonstrate the entire line of 10 racquetball racquets.
   b. Find out more about competitors' offerings under consideration.
   c. Make the buyer trust me more.
   d. Determine which service the prospect is currently using for pest control and how much it costs.
   e. Have the buyer agree to hold our next meeting at a quieter location.
   f. Get an order for 15 charter boat cruises.
   g. Make the buyer not worry about the fact that our newspaper has been in business only three weeks.

5. Think for a moment about trying to secure a job. Assume you are going to have your second job interview next week with Hormel for a sales position. This interview will take place over the phone with the senior recruiter. You've already had one informational interview on campus. Most candidates go through a set of four interviews. List your primary objective, minimum objective, and optimistic objective for this second interview.

6. Assume you are trying to sell several new models of electronic door locking systems to a hardware store. Your boss listed three possible objectives for your next call: sell two new models, sell five new models, have the prospect watch a demonstration that shows the reliability of the locking systems. Identify the primary objective, the minimum objective, and the optimistic objective.

7. Evaluate the following approach for getting an appointment: Ms. O'Toole, I've not got any calls to make next Thursday. Would it be okay if I stopped by for a few minutes?

8. Although there is no hard and fast rule, list what you think to be the best time of day to call on the following individuals:
   a. A college bookstore manager (to sell backpacks).
   b. A manager at an automotive glass replacement company (to sell a new type of glue).
   c. An apartment complex manager (to sell a new mowing system).
   d. A heating contractor (to sell a new model of heating system).

9. Review the list of prospects in question 8 and identify
   a. The worst time of day to call on each individual.
   b. The worst time of year to call on each individual.

10. Suppose you have graduated, and that you belong to the alumni association of your school. Your association plans to raffle off a number of donated items to raise funds for a new library. To be a success, the event will need many donated raffle prizes.
    a. Which sources will you use to identify potential sponsors?
    b. What information do you need to qualify them properly?

Nomad Technologies, Inc. is the manufacturer of presentation stations, multimedia podiums, and e-learning units. Its products allow users to engage in a large variety of presentation functions, effectively and efficiently. These units contain a wide array of multimedia tools, like DVDs, video projectors, computers, and document cameras. Nomad offers both mobile and permanent audiovisual installations. Some of its most valuable current customers consist of a large number of high schools and universities.

Mike Alfanzo is a salesperson for Nomad. He is currently planning for an important first visit with Hamilton County Circuit Court, in Chattanooga, Tennessee. He will be visiting with Judge Kimberly Prestwood.

Mike would like to provide Kimberly with information about how Nomad products can cut court time in half, thanks to more efficient evidence presentation. Special features of the Nomad units of interest to courtrooms include the following:

- The judge has a separate preview/monitor. This allows the judge to clearly see all evidence presented. The judge can make a ruling on controversial evidence without having to dismiss the jury.
- The judge can have complete control over the presentation. The judge can mute or turn on the video and audio, and can do so in various specific parts of the room (jury, witness box, gallery).
- The presenting attorney can make marks on the presentation materials to highlight information, re-create motion, or show direction.
- The system allows evidence to be presented in every known format, including VHS, DVD, PowerPoint,® document camera, digital camera, media cards, Internet, satellite, cable or closed circuit TV, and so forth.
- The evidence is clear and easy to see.
- Because of efficiency, some courts have been able to process as many as five times the number of cases with Nomad systems versus courts without these systems.

Source: http://www.nomadonline.com/index.cfm, company brochure.

Questions

1. What kind of information should Mike gather about Kimberly before his meeting with her?
2. What kind of information should Mike gather about the Hamilton County Circuit Court before his meeting there?
3. Which sources can Mike use to gather the needed information?

"Look, I've seen a lot of dot-coms come and go," Dr. Crystal Longview exclaimed. "You're here today, with lots of fancy charts and graphs, but tomorrow you'll be gone. And I'll be left to start all over again in developing my course packet of material." She waved the air as if to indicate the meeting was over.

But Connie Faggerty, salesperson for XanEdu, a division of the ProQuest Corporation, wasn't so easily removed. "Look, I hear what you're saying," Connie acknowledged. "I know there have been tons of upsets with dot-coms. But that's not what we are. We have been in business for many, many years. I'm sure you've heard of our former name: Bell & Howell, a well-respected name in higher education."

Dr. Longview sat up a little straighter. "Yes, of course I've heart of B&H. But you're not in here selling movie projectors or slide projectors."

"Right. Because I'm here to sell you what you need. You don't need movie projectors. What I think I heard you say is that you need a way to make it easier for yourself and your distance education students to get the very latest business information available."

After a few more minutes of discussion, Dr. Longview asked Connie to return in a week and meet with a group of three staff people that work in the distance education program of the business school at the university. "To be honest with you, I had never heard of your company before you walked in today. I don't know if my staff members are more up-to-date on this than I am," Dr. Longview said, shaking Connie's hand. "Now that you've piqued my curiosity, I'm going to start checking to see what else is available like this. Well, we'll see you in a week."

XanEdu is a division of the Information and Learning sector of ProQuest. XanEdu provides online access to thousands of periodicals, dissertations, books, and newspapers. All materials are cleared for copyright, thus greatly reducing the time and effort on the part of the instructor. XanEdu offers course packs that are customized for each specific course, making it easier for the professor to ensure that his or her students have access to the latest work in the field. And the course packs are up-to-date, being developed by some of the strongest Web search engines available.

Many XanEdu course packs have been sold to undergraduate students, professors, graduate programs, and distance education programs. Many college students already own PCs, with virtually all having Web access.

Source: http://www.xanedu.com

Questions

1. Assume you are Connie Faggerty. List your call objectives for your next call with the group. Develop a three-call follow-up schedule and list the objectives for each call.
2. What kind of information would you like to have before your next meeting? How could you obtain that information?

ROLE PLAY

This role play continues with the same customer firm that you have been selling to: Skylight, Lincoln, or Binswanger. (If you have not done role plays before, you will need to review the information about the various role play customers that can be found at the end of Chapter 4.)

Congratulations, your buyer has agreed to allow you to meet with the rest of the buying center. Now it is time to plan the sales call. Write out your sales call objectives. In case you need assistance, here is some additional information from your previous calls, and feel free to ask your buyer for additional information. In addition to your call objectives, outline an agenda, or what you plan to do step by step.

> Skylight Productions: You are planning for a sales call with the VP of sales and marketing. You know that the company is growing about 15 percent per year. There are 45 salespeople, managed by one of four regional sales managers.

Binswanger Real Estate: Your sales call will be with the same person plus some of the agents who have contact management software that they bought. The ultimate decision will be made by Mr. Binswanger, but he is likely to buy whatever this group recommends.

Lincoln Manufacturing: You are going to meet with the two VPs of sales. Recall that one manages a sales force of 59 salespeople and sells to distributors, while the other has institutions and government agencies as accounts, with 18 salespeople.

Once you've written your objectives, review them with your group. Make sure they meet the criteria for objectives as specified in the chapter.

Note: For background information on these role plays, please see page 27.

To the instructor: Additional information needed to complete the role play is available in the Instructor's Manual.

ADDITIONAL REFERENCES

Azar, Brian, and Len Foley. *Your Successful Sales Career.* AMACOM, New York, 2004.

Baldauf, Artur; David W. Cravens; and Nigel F. Piercy. "Examining Business Strategy, Sales Management, and Salesperson Antecedents of Sales Organization Effectiveness." *Journal of Personal Selling & Sales Management* 21, no. 2 (Spring 2001), pp. 109–22.

Charan, Ram. *Profitable Growth Is Everyone's Business: 10 Tools You Can Use Monday Morning.* New York: Crown Publishing Group, 2004.

Cohen, Andy. "Best Ways to Get Calls Returned." *Sales and Marketing Management* 154, (March 2002), p. 16.

Hassay, Derek N. "Gender Inclusive Selling Teams: As a Response to the Gender-Based Selection Heuristics of Consumers." In AMA Winter Educator's Conference Proceedings, Geraldine R. Henderson and Marian Chapman Moore. Chicago: American Marketing Association, 2003, pp. 13–19.

Hunter, Gary L. "Information Overload: Guidance for Identifying When Information Becomes Detrimental to Sales Force Performance." *Journal of Personal Selling and Sales Management* 24, (Spring 2004), pp. 91–100.

Lewin, Jeffrey E. "The Effects of Downsizing on Organizational Buying Behavior: An Empirical Investigation." *Journal of the Academy of Marketing Science* 29, no. 2 (2001), pp. 151–64.

Millar, Bill. "Pitching In: Medical Suppliers Are Shifting Emphasis from Selling Products to Becoming Value-Added Service Partners to Physicians." *1to1 Magazine,* (April 2002), pp. 34–38.

Miller, Robert B.; Stephen E. Heiman; Diane Sanchez; and Tad Tuleja. *The New Conceptual Selling: The Most Effective and Proven Method for Face-to-Face Sales Planning.* New York: Warner Business, 2005.

Overholt, Alison. "Virtually There." *Fast Company,* (March 2002), pp. 109–14.

Parinello, Anthony. *Getting to VITO (the Very Important Top Officer): Ten Steps to VITO's Office.* Hoboken, NJ: John Wiley & Sons., 2005.

Peters, Sandra M., and Vincent F. Peters. *Selling to Specialist Physicians.* London: Black Dog Publishing Company, 2004.

Tellefsen, Thomas, and Gloria Penn Thomas. "The Antecedents and Consequences of Organizational and Personal Commitment In Business Service Relationships," *Industrial Marketing Management* 34, (January 2005), pp. 23–37.

Wagner, Judy A.; Noreen M. Klein; and Janet E. Keith. "Buyer–Seller Relationships and Selling Effectiveness: The Moderating Influence of Buyer Expertise and Product Competitive Position." *Journal of Business Research* 56, no. 4 (2003), pp. 295–302.

MAKING THE SALES CALL

chapter **9**

SOME QUESTIONS ANSWERED IN THIS CHAPTER . . .

- How should the salesperson make the initial approach to make a good impression and gain the prospect's attention?

- How can the salesperson develop rapport and increase source credibility?

- Why is discovering the prospect's needs important, and how can a salesperson get this information?

- How can the salesperson most effectively relate the product or service features to the prospect's needs?

- Why is it important for the salesperson to make adjustments during the call?

- How does the salesperson recognize that adjustments are needed?

- How can a salesperson effectively sell to groups?

PROFILE

I started my career with Paychex shortly after completing my Bachelor of Science degree at the State University of New York College at Brockport, where I took my selling course from Dr. Jeff Strieter. I began as an inside sales representative—working in a telemarketing department of Paychex called National Sales Support. My position there required a full day of business-to-business calling all over the United States. During the calls, my focus was to generate interest with business owners in our payroll service with a goal to book an appointment with one of our outside sales representatives. Although my college goal was not to work inside sales, the year I spent at National Sales Support prepared me with the skill set and product knowledge I needed to step into a position in outside sales.

Now I'm an outside sales representative for Paychex. I sell what we refer to as "Core Payroll" to smaller businesses (approximately 1–50 employees). This includes the basics: payroll (actually preparing and printing employee checks), tax payment service (Taxpay), direct deposit, and check reconciliation (Readychex), to name a few.

On an average day I will spend half the day prospecting new business by telemarketing and soliciting referrals as well as maintaining my relationships with the people I network with (Chamber of Commerce, CPAs, banks, and current clients). I try to get in front of one to two new businesses each day, and set two more appointments per day to meet with later in the week.

I recently presented to a prospect I have been trying to meet with for six months. The prospect used a competitor's service. I spent the first five minutes or so building rapport with the client. Because I am selling a *service* to my clients, not a tangible product, it is important that the prospect likes me and trusts me with such an important part of her business. This early conversation also helps me to understand what personality type the prospect is—in this case an analytical.

I then started asking the prospect about her business. As we moved into talking about the payroll, I asked the client to take me through her payroll scenario. As she talked, the prospect let me know problems she was having with her current method. I continued probing to uncover hot buttons. As the prospect talked, I realized that our services would offer significant improvements.

After I felt I had gathered enough information, I moved into my presentation. I briefly discussed the history and setup of my company to build a solid foundation of our security as a payroll company. Then I moved into a scenario of how payroll works at one of my clients—focusing on the features and benefits that would help this prospect. Throughout this scenario I pointed out differences between the services based on what I uncovered the client didn't like about her current provider.

I ended my presentation with a summary of how we can better fit the prospect's needs. Additionally, I provided the prospect with names of businesses I work with in the area so she could verify that I always do a good job at following up with clients and that I offer unsurpassed personal service. To wrap it up, I asked the client, based on the solutions I provided, if we could begin to work together.

Thanks to the way I had proved my abilities at follow-up in the six months prior to the presentation as well as providing an organized presentation that proved Paychex had a better solution for the prospect, I got the business. The client has since referred me to other businesses in the area.

Visit our Web site at www.paychex.com.

"Early conversation also helps me to understand what personality type the prospect is."

Jane Linenfelser, Paychex

Exhibit 9.1
Essential Elements
of the Sales Call

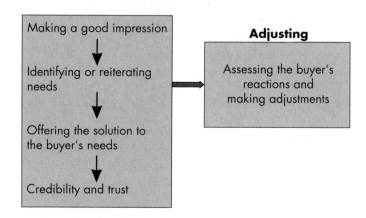

At this point in the sales process, we assume that an appointment has been made, sufficient information about the prospect and his or her organization has been gathered, and the salesperson has developed strong objectives for the call. In this chapter we discuss how to make the actual sales call. The content of an actual sales call depends on the specific situation the salesperson encounters as well as the extent of the relationship the salesperson has already established with the other party.[1] Exhibit 9.1 provides an organizing framework for our discussion. We begin by considering how to make a good impression and begin to develop a long-term relationship. We then examine the initial needs assessment phase of a relationship and how to relate solutions to those needs. Finally, we discuss the relationship between adaptability and successful sales calls.

There are, of course, many conceptualizations of the selling process. For example, one trainer finds value in describing the selling process as the Four A's (**a**cknowledge, **a**cquire, **a**dvise, and **a**ssure).[2] First the seller acknowledges the buyer by greeting/welcoming/honoring and building trust. Next the rep acquires information via needs analysis and a summary of that analysis outlining the agreement between buyer and seller about the current situation and the desired solution. Advising comes next, during which the seller narrows the possible choices to specific options, sells benefits of those options (not just features), watches for buying signals, and asks for the order. Finally, the seller assures the buyer after the sale by enhancing satisfaction with the buying decision and giving proper follow-up and referrals.

Salespeople should use waiting time effectively.

RF/Corbis

MAKING A GOOD IMPRESSION

When salespeople arrive late, make a poor entrance, fail to gain the buyer's interest, or lack rapport-building skills, it is difficult for them to secure commitment and build partnerships.[3] This section discusses how salespeople can manage the buyer's impression of them, a process often termed **impression management.** Most of the information presented here assumes that the salesperson is making a first call on a prospect. However, impression management continues throughout calls.

One of the most important ways to ensure a good first impression is to be well prepared (as we discussed in Chapter 8). Some salespeople prepare a checklist of things to take to the presentation so they won't forget anything.

WAITING FOR A SALES CALL? USE TECHNOLOGY TO GET SOMETHING USEFUL DONE

Salespeople can spend considerable time waiting for appointments. Thanks to technology like cell phones, laptops, PDAs, and satellite Web access, salespeople can use this time wisely and get things done, instead of reading old magazines or looking at others who are waiting.

With laptops, you can check your to-do lists, draft letters and e-mail, work on account planning and strategy, look up information on a prospect, or create the never-ending required reports. If you have satellite Web access, you can accomplish even more. And some waiting areas may even have wireless Web service available for people without satellite service.

With your cell phone, you can make a fast phone call to schedule an appointment, check on messages in your voice mailbox, or check on an order status. But remember to use the cell phone respectfully with regard to others in the waiting room.

However, don't get so caught up in your technology-driven world that you can't close down and walk into that call when your name is called. It takes skill to learn how long your wait might be and what tasks can be undertaken in that period.

WAITING FOR THE PROSPECT

Being on time for a scheduled sales call is critical to avoid giving the buyer a negative impression. With the advent of cell phones, there is practically no good reason for not calling if you're going to be a few minutes late to the appointment.

Every salesperson must expect to spend a certain portion of each working day waiting for sales interviews. Successful salespeople make the best possible use of this time by working on reports, studying new product information, planning and preparing for their next calls, and obtaining additional information about the prospect. And as Sales Technology 9.1 indicates, this activity is getting easier to accomplish in a prospect's waiting room. (Chapter 15 covers time management more fully.)

Some trainers suggest that salespeople not wait for any prospect, under normal circumstances, more than 15 minutes after the appointment time. Why? To demonstrate that the seller's time is also important. Exceptions are necessary, of course, depending on the importance of the customer and the distance the salesperson has traveled. In all cases salespeople should keep the sales call in perspective, realizing that their time is also valuable. Chapter 15 discusses just how valuable that time really is.

When the salesperson arrives, the receptionist may merely say, "I'll tell Ms. Schimpf that you are here." After the receptionist has spoken with Ms. Schimpf, the salesperson should ask approximately how long the wait will be. When the wait will be excessive or the salesperson has another appointment, it may be advisable to explain this tactfully and to ask for another appointment. Usually the secretary either will try to get the salesperson in to see the prospect more quickly or will make arrangements for a later appointment.

VERY FIRST IMPRESSIONS

In the first meeting between a salesperson and a prospect or customer, the first two or three minutes can be very important. Making a favorable first impression usually results in a prospect who is willing to listen. A negative first impression, on the other hand, sets up a barrier that may never be hurdled. Note that one advantage of an existing partnering relationship is that the salesperson has already established a bond and has built a reputation based on his or her prior actions.

Salespeople may make a poor impression without realizing it. They may know their customer's needs and their own product, but overlook seemingly insignificant things that can create negative impressions. As Chapter 5 related, how you dress can affect the message you send to the buyer. Also, studies have shown that the physical attractiveness and gender of salespeople can influence purchase intentions of buyers. And don't forget that according to generation gap experts, it is often quite difficult for a Generation X (born 1965–1978) salesperson to relate to a Baby Boomer (born 1946–1964) buyer, and even harder to relate to a Traditionalist (born 1922–1946) buyer. So what should a seller do to create a good first impression? You should be well groomed and enter confidently (but not cockily) by using erect posture, lengthy stride, and a lively pace; and among the first words out of your mouth should be something like "Thanks for seeing me." And don't forget to smile.[4] Watch what happens when you look at someone and smile. In 99 out of 100 times, you will receive a smile in return.

It is also important to remember prospects' names and how to pronounce them. There are many ways to try to remember someone's name—such as giving your full attention when you hear it and then repeating the name immediately, associating it with someone else you know with the same name, associating it with the person's most prominent feature or trait, using it during the conversation, and writing it down phonetically. Whatever you do, make sure to pronounce the prospect's name correctly.

Some experts argue that the customer's name should be used in the opening statement. Dale Carnegie, a master at developing relationships, said a person's name is "the sweetest and most important sound" to that person. Using a person's name often indicates respect and a recognition of the person's unique qualities. Others disagree with this logic, claiming that using the person's name, especially more than once in any short time, sounds phony and insincere. A compromise is to use the prospect's name in the opening and then to use it sparingly during the rest of the call.

thinking **it** through

You walk into a prospect's office very confidently. Even though you've never met her before, you aren't nervous. You've done your homework and have strong objectives for this meeting. After you introduce yourself to the prospect, you suddenly remember that you left your laptop in your car. And in that laptop is your entire presentation! Your car is several blocks away. What should you do? What would you say to the prospect?

SELECTING A SEAT

When selecting a seat, it is a good idea to look around and start to identify the prospect's social style and status (see Chapter 6). For example, in the United States important decision makers usually have large, well-appointed, private offices. But be careful. In Kuwait, a high-ranking businessperson may have a small office and lots of interruptions. Don't take that environment to mean he or she is a low-ranking employee or is not interested. Wal-Mart buyers conduct interviews with salespeople in quite primitive conditions to help instill the idea that they want the lowest prices they can get.

Asking permission to sit down is usually unnecessary. The salesperson should read the prospect's nonverbal cues to determine the right time to be seated. And note that many calls will not involve sitting down at all, such as talking to a store manager in a grocery store aisle, conversing with a supervisor in a warehouse, or asking questions of a surgeon in a post-op ward.

GETTING THE CUSTOMER'S ATTENTION

Recall from Chapter 6 that there are several types of sales presentations, including standard memorized, outlined, and customized. In this chapter we assume that the salesperson has chosen a customized presentation.

Getting the customer's attention is not a new concept. It is also the goal of many other activities you are familiar with, such as advertising, making new friends, writing an English composition, giving a speech, or writing a letter to a friend.

Time is very valuable to prospects, and prospects concentrate their attention on the first few minutes with a salesperson to determine whether they will benefit from the interaction. The prospect is making a decision: Do I want to give this salesperson 15 minutes of my time? 30 minutes of my time? None of my time? This decision is made even while the salesperson is walking in the door and selecting a seat. One expert noted that "salespeople basically have less than six minutes, according to the studies we've seen, to get credibility with a client."[5] The first few words the salesperson says often set the tone of the entire sales call. The **halo effect** (how and what you do in one thing changes a person's perceptions about other things you do) seems to operate in many sales calls. If the salesperson is perceived by the prospect as effective at the beginning of the call, he will be perceived as effective during the rest of the call, and vice versa.

There are many ways to open a presentation.[6] An **opening** is a method designed to get the prospect's attention and interest quickly and to make a smooth transition into the next part of the presentation (which is usually to more fully discover the prospect's needs). Because each prospect and sales situation is unique, salespeople should be adaptable and be able to use any or a combination of openings.[7] Again, keep in mind that openings are generally less important with partnering customers whom the salesperson has already met. Exhibit 9.2 provides details about a number of possible openings.

DEVELOPING RAPPORT

Rapport in selling is a close, harmonious relationship founded on mutual trust. Ultimately the goal of every salesperson should be to establish rapport with each customer.[8] Often salespeople can accomplish this with some friendly conversation early in the call. Part of this process involves identifying the prospect's social style and making necessary adjustments (see Chapter 6).

The talk about current news, hobbies, mutual friends, and the like that usually breaks the ice for the actual presentation is often referred to as **small talk.** One of the top traits of successful salespeople is the ability to be sociable. Examples include the following:

I understand you went to Nebraska? I graduated from there with a BBA in 2004.

Did you see the Houston Rockets game on TV last night?

I was just chatting with Crystal Mullen, your controller, in the hallway. She said you've decided to join one of your company's softball teams. Fair warning! She and I played on a city league softball team last year, and wow, can she ever pitch a fastball!

Exhibit 9.2
Openings That Salespeople Can Use to Gain Attention

Opening Method	Example	Things to Consider
Introduction opening (simply introduce yourself).	Ms. Hallgren, thank you for seeing me today. My name is Daniel Mundt, and I'm with ServiceMaster.	Simple, but may not generate interest.
Referral opening (tell about someone who referred you to the buyer).	Mr. Schaumberg, I appreciate your seeing me today. I'm here at the suggestion of Ms. Fleming of Acumen Ornamental Iron Works. She thought you would be interested in our line of wrought iron products and railings.	Always get permission. Don't stretch the truth.
Benefit opening (start by telling some benefit of the product).	Mr. Penney, I would like to tell you about a color copier that can reduce your copying costs by 15 percent.	Gets down to business right away.
Product opening (actually demonstrate a product feature and benefit as soon as you walk up to the prospect).	[Carrying a tablet PC into an office] Ms. Hemming, you spend a lot of time on the road as an investigative lawyer. Let me show you how this little handheld item can transform your car (or any place you go) into an efficient, effective office.	Uses visual and not just verbal opening; can create excitement.
Compliment opening (start by complimenting the buyer or the buyer's firm).	I was calling on one of your customers, Jackson Street Books, last week, and the owner couldn't say enough good things about your service. It sure says a lot about your operation to have a customer just start praising you out of the blue.	Must be sincere, not just flattery.
Question opening (start the conversation with a question).	Ms. Borgelt, what is your reaction to the brochure I sent you on our new telemarketing service?	Starts two-way communication.

Customers are more receptive to salespeople with whom they can identify—that is, with whom they have something in common. Thus salespeople will be more effective with customers with whom they establish such links as mutual friends, common hobbies, or attendance at the same schools. Successful salespeople engage in small talk more effectively by first performing **office scanning,** looking around the prospect's environment for relevant topics to talk about.

Be careful, however, when engaging in small talk, or it can be to your detriment. One salesperson told of a client who asked her opinion of the economic outlook. The seller said she thought it was going down. The buyer had a different opinion, and it took months to repair the relationship. It is generally best to avoid controversial topics. Also, especially for first calls on prospects, you want to avoid using trite phrases like How are you doing today? because they don't sound sincere.

Sharing letters from satisfied customers helps a salesperson establish credibility.

SuperStock

Of course, salespeople should consider cultural and personality differences and adapt the extent of their nonbusiness conversation accordingly. For example, an AT&T rep would probably spend considerably less time in friendly conversation with a New York City office manager than with, say, a manager in a rural Texas town. Businesspeople in Africa place such high value on establishing friendships that the norm calls for a great deal of friendly conversation before getting down to business. Chinese customers want a lot of rapport building before they get down to business. Amiables and expressives tend to enjoy such conversations, whereas drivers and analyticals may be less receptive to spending much time in nonbusiness conversation. Also, there could be less need for small talk if the salesperson had utilized the question or product opening when getting the customer's attention.

At this point in the sales call, after gaining the prospect's attention and establishing some rapport, a salesperson will often share his or her goals or agenda for the meeting with the prospect. This step can help build further rapport and trust. For example:

> Just so you know, my goal today is simply to verify what your needs might be and then, as I promised in the phone call, to share with you the results of the lab test we conducted last fall.

WHEN THINGS GO WRONG

Making and maintaining a good impression is important. How nice it would be if the beginning of every call went as smoothly as we have described here. Actually, things do go wrong sometimes. Case 9.2 at the end of this chapter allows you to think about what you would do in some rather awkward situations. You should read the scenarios even if your professor doesn't assign the case.

The best line of defense when something goes wrong is to maintain the proper perspective and a sense of humor. It's probably not the first thing you have done wrong and probably will not be your last. A good example of a call going downhill fast is the following experience, related by a salesperson:

> I pulled my right hand out of the pocket and stuck it forward enthusiastically to shake. Unfortunately, a ball of lint, about the size of a pea, had stuck to the tip of my fingers and was now drifting slowly down onto the document he had been reading. We both watched it descend, as compelling as the ball on New Year's Eve. We shook hands, anyway. I said, "Excuse me," and bent forward to blow the ball of lint off the document. As I did so, I put a dent in the front edge of his desk with my briefcase.[9]

The worst response by this salesperson would be to faint, scream, or totally lose control. A better response would include a sincere apology for the dent and an offer to pay for any repairs. Further, proper planning might have prevented this situation in the first place. If the salesperson had walked into the room with his hands out of his pockets, he would not have picked up the lint.

What if you say something that is truly embarrassing? According to Mark Twain, "Man is the only animal that blushes, or needs to." For example, one salesperson calling on an older buyer motioned to a picture of a very young lady on the buyer's desk. "Is that your daughter?" the seller asked, smiling, "That's my wife," the buyer replied, frowning. The first thing you should do in such a situation is to apologize sincerely. Then change the subject or move on in your presentation. Try to relax and put the incident behind you. And learn this lesson: Next time think before you speak!

Of course, you can get into trouble without even saying a word. As Chapter 5 indicated, you must be careful when using gestures in other cultures because they often take on different meanings.

IDENTIFYING THE PROSPECT'S NEEDS: THE POWER OF ASKING QUESTIONS

Once the salesperson has entered and captured the buyer's attention, it is time to identify the buyer's needs.[10] To begin this process, a salesperson might use transition sentences like the following (assuming a product approach was used to gain attention):

> Well, I'm glad you find this little model interesting. And I want to tell you all about it. But first I need to ask you a few questions to make sure I understand what your specific needs are. Is that okay?

If the buyer gives permission, the salesperson then begins to ask questions about the buyer's needs. Don't be surprised if the buyer is reluctant to provide confidential information. There are many people out there trying to steal valuable company information.[11] The seller has to establish credibility and trust.

Occasionally a salesperson makes the mistake of starting with product information rather than with a discussion of the prospect's needs. The experienced salesperson, however, attempts to uncover the prospect's needs and problems at the start of the relationship. In reality, discovering needs is still a part of qualifying the prospect.

Research continually demonstrates the importance of needs discovery. An analysis by Huthwaite, Inc., of more than 35,000 sales calls in 23 countries over a 12-year period revealed that the distinguishing feature of successful salespeople was their ability to discover the prospect's needs.[12] Discovering needs was more important than opening the call strategically, handling objections, or using closing techniques effectively.

There is an underlying reason for every customer need, and the salesperson must continue probing until he or she uncovers the root problem or need. This process could be called "discovering the root cause of the need" and is graphically illustrated in Exhibit 9.3.

As you discover needs, keep in mind that this process can be uncomfortable for the prospect. The prospect may resent your suggesting that there could be a problem or a better way to do things. When faced with direct evidence that things

Exhibit 9.3
Discovering the Root Cause of the Need

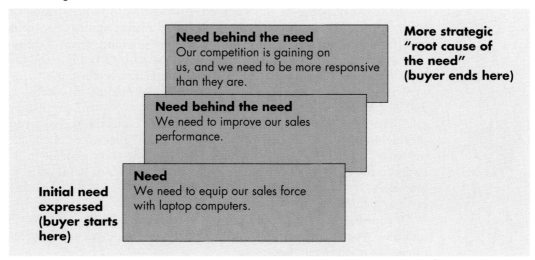

This salesperson needs to discover the prospect's needs before describing the services he offers.

B&M Productions/Taxi/Getty Images

could be better, the prospect may express fear (fear of losing her or his job if things are not corrected, or of things changing and the situation getting worse than it is now). Also, remember that the amount of time and effort needed to discuss needs varies greatly depending on the type of industry, the nature of the product, how well the salesperson and buyer know each other, and so forth. We will come back to this issue after we examine methods of identifying needs.

Chapter 5 covered most of the important communication principles regarding how to effectively ask questions of the prospect and be a better listener. Remember to speak naturally while asking questions. You don't want to sound like a computer asking a set of rote questions. Nor do you want to appear to be following a strict word-for-word outline that you learned in your sales training classes.

We will now briefly describe two of the most widely used systems of needs identification taught to salespeople today.

ASKING OPEN AND CLOSED QUESTIONS

In the first method of needs discovery, salespeople are taught to distinguish between open and closed questions and then encouraged to utilize more open questions. Many highly respected sales training organizations, such as Wilson Learning Corporation and Achieve Global, use this type of approach. **Open questions** require the prospect to go beyond a simple yes-or-no response. They encourage the prospect to open up and share a great deal of useful information. For example:

What kinds of problems have the new federal guidelines caused for your division?

What do you know about our firm?

When you think of a quality sound system, what comes to mind?

Closed questions require the prospect to simply answer yes or no or to offer a short, fill-in-the-blank type of response. Examples include the following questions:

Have you ever experienced computer downtime as a result of an electrical storm?

Is fast delivery important for your firm?

Customers have expressed a desire to have many features, including four channels, AC/DC power, a four-year warranty, and easily upgradable equipment. Which of these are important to you?

In most cases salespeople need to ask both open and closed questions. Open questions help to paint the broad strokes of the situation, whereas closed questions help to zero in on specific problems and attitudes. Some trainers believe simple, closed questions are best at first. Prospects become accustomed to talking and start to open up. After a few closed questions, the salesperson moves to a series of open questions. At some point he or she may revert back to closed questions.

Angie Main, a radio advertising salesperson, likes to ask her prospects the following two open questions to discover their needs:

What misconceptions do people have about your business?

If you could tell people one thing about your business, what would you want to tell them?[13]

Notice how the questions focus on the needs of the prospect rather than the solution (how her radio station can meet those needs).

Exhibit 9.4 contains an illustrative dialogue of a bank selling a commercial checking account to a business. In this sales presentation the salesperson's questions follow a logical flow. Note that follow-up probes are often necessary to clarify the prospect's responses. At the conclusion of asking open and closed questions, the salesperson should have a good feel for the needs and wants of the prospect.

One final suggestion is to summarize the prospect's needs:

> So let me see if I have this right. You are looking for a checking account that pays interest on your unused balance and has a monthly statement. . . . Is that correct?

Summarizing helps to solidify the needs in the prospect's mind and ensure that the prospect has no other hidden needs or wants.

SPIN® TECHNIQUE

The SPIN® method of discovering needs was developed by Huthwaite, Inc., an international research and training organization, after analyzing thousands of actual sales calls.[14] The results indicated that successful salespeople go through a

Exhibit 9.4
Using Open and Closed Questions to Discover Needs

Salesperson's Probe	Prospect's Response
Have you ever done business with our bank before? [closed]	No, our firm has always used First of America Bank.
I assume, then, that your checking account is currently with First of America? [closed]	Yes.
If you could design an ideal checking account for your business, what would it look like? [open]	Well, it would pay interest on all idle money, have no service charges, and supply a good statement.
When you say "good statement" what exactly do you mean? [open]	It should come to us once a month, be easy to follow, and help us reconcile our books quickly.
Uh-huh. Anything else in an ideal checking account? [open]	No, I guess that's about it.
What things, if any, about your checking account have dissatisfied you in the past? [open]	Having to pay so much for our checks! Also, sometimes when we have a question, the bank can't answer it quickly because the computers are down. That's frustrating!
Sure! Anything else dissatisfy you? [open]	Well, I really don't like the layout of the monthly statement we get now. It doesn't list checks in order; it has them listed by the date they cleared the bank.
Normally, what balance do you have on hand in your account? What minimum balance can you maintain? [closed]	About $8,500 now. We could keep a minimum of around $5,000, I guess.
Are you earning interest in your account now? [closed]	Yes, 3 percent of the average monthly balance if we maintain at least a $5,000 balance.
What kind of service charges are you paying now? [closed] *[more questions]*	$25 per month, $.25 per check, $.10 per deposit.
Is there anything else that I need to know before I begin telling you about our account? [open]	No, I think that just about covers it all.

logical needs identification sequence, which Huthwaite labeled **SPIN:** situation questions, problem questions, implication questions, and need payoff questions. SPIN® works for salespeople involved in a **major sale,** one that involves a long selling cycle, a large customer commitment, an ongoing relationship, and large risks for the prospect if a bad decision is made. Major sales can occur anywhere but often involve large or national accounts. For example, both Johnson Wax and Bridgestone Firestone use SPIN® for their major accounts but may use other techniques for smaller accounts.

SPIN® actually helps the prospect identify unrecognized problem areas. Often, when a salesperson simply asks an open question such as "What problems are you having?" the prospect replies, "None!" The prospect isn't lying; he or she just may not realize that a problem exists. SPIN® excels at helping prospects test their current opinions or perceptions of the situation. Also, SPIN® questions may be asked over the course of several sales calls, especially for large or important buyers. An abbreviated needs identification dialogue appears in Exhibit 9.5; it demonstrates all components of SPIN® for a salesperson selling desktop publishing programs.

Situation Questions

Early in the sales call, salespeople ask **situation questions,** general data-gathering questions about background and current facts. Because these questions are very broad, successful salespeople learn to limit them; prospects quickly become bored or impatient if they hear too many of them. Inexperienced and unsuccessful salespeople tend to ask too many situation questions. In fact, many situation-type questions can be answered through precall information gathering and planning. If a salesperson asks too many situation questions, the prospect will think the salesperson is unprepared. Here are some examples of situation questions:

What's your position? How long have you been here?

How many people do you employ? Is the number growing or shrinking?

What kind of handling equipment are you using at present? How long have you had it? Did you buy or lease it?

Exhibit 9.5
Using the SPIN®
Technique to Sell
Desktop Publishing

Salesperson: Do you ever send work out for typesetting? [situation question]

Prospect: Yes, about once a month we have to send work out because we are swamped.

Salesperson: Is the cost of sending work out a burden? [problem question]

Prospect: Not really. It costs only about 5 percent more, and we just add that to the customer's bill.

Salesperson: Do you get fast turnaround? [problem question]

Prospect: Well, now that you mention it, at times the turnaround is kind of slow. You see, we aren't given very high priority because we aren't big customers for the printer. We use them only when we have to, you know.

Salesperson: What happens if you miss a deadline for your customer because the turnaround is slow? [implication question]

Prospect: That happened only once, but it was disastrous. John, the customer, really chewed me out, and we lost a lot of our credibility. As I say, it happened only once, and I wouldn't like it to happen again to John—or any of our customers, for that matter!

Salesperson: If I can show you a way to eliminate outside typesetting without having to increase your staff, would you be interested? [need payoff question]

Prospect: Sure. The more I think about it, the more I realize I have something of a time bomb here. Sooner or later, it's going to go off!

Problem Questions

When salespeople ask about specific difficulties, problems, or dissatisfactions the prospect has, they are asking **problem questions**. The goal is to discover a problem. Here are some examples of problem questions:

Is your current machine difficult to repair?

Have you experienced any problems with the overall quality of your forklifts?

Do your operators ever complain that the noise level is too high?

If a seller can't discover a problem using problem questions, then she might need to ask additional situation questions first, to uncover more issues that might lead to better problem questions.

Implication Questions

Questions that logically follow one or more problem questions and are designed to help the prospect recognize the true ramifications of the problem are **implication questions**. Implication questions cannot be asked until some problem area has been identified (through problem questions). The goal of implication questions is for the prospect to see that the problem they have identified has some serious ramifications and implications that make the problem worthy of being resolved. These questions attempt to motivate the prospect to search for a solution to the problem.

Implication questions relate back to some similar issues that were described in the multiattribute model described in Chapter 4. In the multiattribute model, customers weigh various attributes differently in terms of importance. In the same way, some problems that are identified by problem questions have more weight (are more serious in the eyes of the buyer) than others. The goal of the salesperson is to identify problems that have high importance to the buyer.

Examples of implication questions include these:

What happens if you ship your customer a product that doesn't meet specs?

Does paying overtime for your operators increase your costs?

What does that do to your price as compared to your competitors'?

Does the slowness of your present system create any bottlenecks in other parts of the process?

If the buyer answers these questions in a way that indicates she doesn't see serious implications of the problem identified, then the seller would have to go back and ask additional implication questions, problem questions, and maybe even situation questions. The seller doesn't move ahead to need payoff questions until the prospect sees that there are serious ramifications if she does not solve the problem.

Need Payoff Questions

When salespeople ask questions about the usefulness of solving a problem, they are asking **need payoff questions**. In contrast to implication questions, which are problem centered, need payoff questions are solution centered:

If I can show you a way to eliminate paying overtime for your operators and therefore reduce your cost, would you be interested?

Would you like to see a reduction in the number of products that don't meet quality specifications?

Would an increase in the speed of your present system by 5 percent resolve the bottlenecks you currently experience?

If the prospect responds negatively to a need payoff question, the salesperson has not identified a problem serious enough for the prospect to take action. In that case, the salesperson should probe further by asking additional problem questions, implication questions, and then a new need payoff question.

Conclusions about SPIN®

One critical advantage of SPIN® is that it encourages the prospect to define the need. During the questioning phase the salesperson is focusing on problems and isn't focusing on her product. As a result, the prospect views the salesperson more as a consultant trying to help than as someone trying to push a product.

SPIN® selling has been taught to thousands of salespeople. Many salespeople quickly master the technique, whereas others have more difficulty. The best advice is to practice each component and to plan implication and need payoff questions before each sales call. Also SPIN® works well for buyers that have a real problem (like inventory piling up). It is perhaps more difficult to use when the seller is only discussing an opportunity (no real problems, but my solution could help you make more money).

REITERATING NEEDS YOU IDENTIFIED BEFORE THE MEETING

The extent to which one has to identify needs during any call depends on the success of precall information gathering. The salesperson may fully identify the needs of the prospect before making the sales call. In that case reiterating the needs early in the sales call is advisable so that both parties agree about the problem they are trying to solve. For example:

> Mr. Reed, based on our several phone conversations, it appears that you are looking for an advertising campaign that will position your product for the rapidly growing senior citizen market, at a cost under $100,000, using humor and a well-known older personality, and delivered in less than one month. Is that an accurate summary of your needs? Has anything changed since we talked last?

Likewise, in multiple-call situations, going through a complete needs identification at every call is unnecessary. But it is still best to briefly reiterate the needs identified to that point:

> In my last call we pretty much agreed that your number one concern is customer satisfaction with your inventory system. Is that correct? Has anything changed since we met last time, or is there anything else I need to know?

ADDITIONAL CONSIDERATIONS

How many questions can a salesperson ask to discover needs? It depends on the situation. Generally, as the buyer's risk of making the wrong decision goes up, so does the amount of time the salesperson can spend asking the prospect questions. For example, a Boeing salesperson could address an almost unlimited number of questions to United Air Lines because the airline realizes the importance of having Boeing propose the right configuration of airplane. A salesperson for Johnson Wax calling on a local grocery store, on the other hand, has little time to probe needs before discussing an upcoming promotion and requesting an end-of-aisle display. Regardless of the situation, the salesperson should carefully prepare a set of questions that maximize the use of available time.

Occasionally the prospect will refuse to answer important questions because the information is confidential or proprietary. The salesperson can do little except emphasize the reason for asking the questions. Ultimately, the prospect needs to trust the salesperson enough to divulge sensitive data. Chapters 2 and 14 discuss trust-building strategies.

At times buyers do not answer questions because they honestly don't know the answer. The salesperson should then ask whether the prospect can get the information. If the prospect cannot do so, the salesperson can often ask the buyer's permission to probe further within the prospect's firm.

On the other hand, some buyers not only will answer questions but also will appear to want to talk indefinitely. In general, the advice is to let them talk, particularly in many cultures. For example, people in French-speaking countries tend to love rhetoric, the act and art of speaking; attempts to cut them off will only frustrate and anger them.

thinking it through

Prospects often provide sensitive and confidential information when they reveal facts about their situations and needs. Assume that a prospect at Allied reveals to you her firm's long-term strategy for taking business away from her number one competitor, Baker's. You are close friends with the buyer at Baker's, which is one of your biggest customers. Further assume that Baker's is beginning to lose market share, and you sense that this change will reduce your commissions. You have at best a 50–50 chance of landing Allied's business. Will you share the confidential information with Baker's buyer? What are the long-term consequences of your proposed behavior?

DEVELOPING A STRATEGY FOR THE PRESENTATION

Based on the needs identified, the salesperson should develop a strategy for how best to meet those needs. This process includes sorting through the various options available to the seller to see what is best for this prospect. To do so, the salesperson usually must sort out the needs of the buyer and prioritize them. Decisions have to be made about the exact product or service to recommend, the optimal payment terms to present for consideration, service levels to suggest, product or service features to stress during the presentation, and so on. Chapter 8 also talks about developing a strategy.

Products have many, many features, and one product may possess a large number of features that are unique and exciting when compared to competitive offerings. Rather than overload the customer with all of the great features, successful salespeople discuss only those that specifically address the needs of the prospect. For example, suppose that a Philips salesperson learns from SPIN® questioning that a prospect is looking for a DVD recorder to use only to record new training materials. In this situation the Philips representative should not spend time discussing the DVD recorder's ability to easily record from VCRs. The buyer has no need for this feature. Talking about lots of features of little interest to the customer is a waste of time and is sometimes called **feature dumping**.[15]

OFFERING VALUE: THE SOLUTION TO THE BUYER'S NEEDS

In addition to discovering the buyer's needs, the salesperson often also learns about the decision-making process (who is involved and in what capacity—see Chapter 4 for details), the buyer's time frame for making a decision, and the money budgeted. The seller develops a strategy to effectively communicate a solution to those needs; then it is time to make a presentation that shows how they can be addressed. This step includes relating product or service features that are meaningful to the buyer, assessing the buyer's reaction to what is being said, resolving objections (covered in Chapter 11), and obtaining commitment (the topic of Chapter 12).

The salesperson usually begins offering the solution with a transition sentence, something like the following: Now that I know what your needs are, I would like to talk to you about how our product can meet those needs. The seller's job is then to translate product features into benefits for solving the buyer's needs.

RELATING FEATURES TO BENEFITS

A **feature** is a quality or characteristic of the product or service. Every product has many features designed to help potential customers.[16] A **benefit** is the way in which a specific feature will help a particular buyer and is tied directly to the buying motives of the prospect. A benefit helps the prospect more fully answer the question What's in it for me?[17] (Exhibit 9.6 shows a list of features and sample benefits for a product.) The salesperson usually includes a word or a phrase to make a smooth transition from features to benefits:

> This china is fired at 2,600° F, and what that means to you is that it will last longer. Because it is so sturdy, you will be able to hand this china down to your children as an heirloom, which was one of your biggest concerns.

Exhibit 9.6

An Example of Features and Benefits

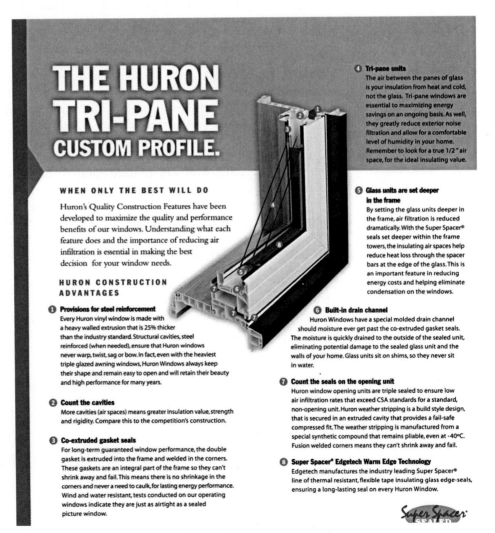

Courtesy of Huron Window Corp., Manitoba, Canada.

This set of golf clubs has shallow-faced fairway woods, which means that you'll be able to get the ball into the air easier. That will certainly help give you the distance you said you were looking for.

Our service hotline is open 24 hours a day, which means that even your third-shift operators can call if they have any questions. That should be a real help to you because you said your third-shift supervisor was inexperienced in dealing with problems.

Some trainers suggest going beyond just mentioning features and benefits. One variation, **FAB,** has salespeople discussing features, **advantages** (why that feature would be important to anyone), and benefits. For example:

This car has antilock brakes (feature), which help the car stop quickly (advantage), which provides the safety you said you were looking for (benefit).

In another variation, **FEBA** (features, evidence, benefits, agreement), salespeople mention the feature, provide evidence that the feature actually does exist, explain the benefit (why that feature is important to the buyer), and then ask whether the buyer agrees with the value of the feature and benefit. For example:

This car has the highest-quality antilock brakes on the market today (feature) as proved by this test by the federal government (evidence). They will provide the safety you said you were looking for (benefit); don't you agree (agreement)?

Buyers are not interested in facts about the product or the seller's company unless those facts help solve their wants or needs.[18] The salesperson's job is to supply the facts and then point out what those features mean to the buyer in terms of benefits. Chapter 10 more fully discusses how to offer proof of assertions.

Exhibit 9.7 illustrates how one trainer incorporates these concepts into a problem/solution model. The customer's needs are called "Business Model." The salesperson knows some of the buyer's needs before the sales call, represented by the first three lines under "Business Model." However, by actively listening (see Chapter 5) the seller learns more needs during the presentation, represented by lines 4 and 5 under "Business Model." Using all identified needs, the seller talks about the relevant features and benefits. While doing this, the salesperson offers proof of these assertions, based on the customer's social style (see Chapter 6). The salesperson also engages in activities to help the buyer realize the importance of meeting his or her needs sooner, providing reasons to buy now. The end result is increased sales and profits for the seller.

Buyers typically consider two or more competitive products when making a purchase decision. Thus salespeople need to know more than just the benefits their products provide. They need to know how the benefits of their products are superior or inferior to the benefits of competitive products. Of course, as you explain the benefits of your service, you must make sure that the prospect is looking for those benefits.

Exhibit 9.7
The Problem/Solution Model

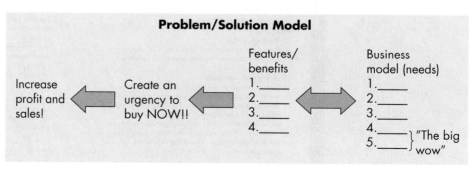

Source: Professor Karl Sooder, used with permission.

Exhibit 9.8

Features and Benefits of Jello Fruit & Cream Bars, as Presented to a Grocery Store

Features	Benefits
Of Importance to the Final Consumer	
Trusted name brand.	Because you trust the Jello brand name, you know that this is a high-quality product.
Only 60 calories per bar.	You can enjoy a treat without worrying about its effect on your weight.
Real fruit in every bite.	You are getting needed nutrition from a snack.
Of Importance to the Grocery Store	
Test marketed for three years.	Because of this research, you are assured of a successful product and effective promotion; thus your risk is greatly reduced.
$10 million will be spent for consumer advertising in the next 18 months.	Your customers will come to your store looking for the product.
40-cent coupon with front positioning in the national Sunday insert section.	Your customers will want to take advantage of the coupon and will be looking in your freezer for the product.

Sometimes, when selling certain commodities, it is important to sell the features and benefits of the seller's firm instead of the product. For example, Ray Hanson sells fasteners such as bolts and nuts. He states, "In the fastener industry I have found that a generic product, such as a nut or bolt, doesn't have too many features and benefits. We talk to our potential customers about the features our company has and how these features could benefit them as our customers."[19]

When selling to resellers, salespeople have two sets of benefits to discuss with the prospect: what the features of the product will do for the reseller and what the product features will do for the ultimate consumer of the product. Covering both sets of features and benefits is important. Exhibit 9.8 illustrates the two sets of features.

ASSESSING REACTIONS

While making a presentation, salespeople need to continually assess the reactions of their prospects. The prospect needs to agree that the benefits described would actually help his or her company. By listening (see Chapter 5 to review how to be a better listener) to what buyers say and observing their body language, salespeople can determine whether prospects are interested in the product. If buyers react favorably to the presentation and seem able to grasp the benefits of the proposed solution, the salesperson will have less need to make alterations or adjustments. But if a prospect does not develop enthusiasm for the product, the salesperson will need to make some changes in the presentation.

Using Nonverbal Cues

An important aspect of making adjustments is interpreting a prospect's reactions to the sales presentation. By observing the prospect's five channels of nonverbal communication, salespeople can determine how to proceed with their presentations. Chapter 5 provides more detailed information about nonverbal cues.

Nonverbal cues help salespeople know when to make adjustments. Can you interpret the cues provided by members of this buying team?

Garry Conner/Index Stock Imagery/PictureQuest

Verbal Probing

As salespeople move through a presentation, they must take the pulse of the situation. This process, often called a **trial close,** will be more fully described in Chapter 12. For example, the salesperson should say something like the following:

How does this sound to you?

Can you see how these features help solve the problem you have?

Have I clearly explained our program to you?

Do you have any questions?

The use of such probing questions helps to achieve several things. First, it allows the salesperson to stop talking and encourages two-way conversation. Without such probing, a salesperson can turn into a rambling talker while the buyer becomes a passive listener. Second, probing lets the salesperson see whether the buyer is listening and understanding what is being said. Third, the probe may show that the prospect is uninterested in what the salesperson is talking about. This response allows the salesperson to redirect the conversation to areas of interest to the buyer. This kind of adjustment is necessary in almost every presentation and underscores the fact that the salesperson should not simply memorize a canned presentation that unfolds in a particular sequence.

Salespeople must listen. Often we hear only what we want to hear. This behavior is called **selective perception,** and everyone is guilty of it at times. For example, read the following sentence:[20]

Finished files are the result of years of scientific study combined with the experience of years.

Now go back and quickly count the number of Fs in that sentence. Most nonnative English speakers see all six Fs, whereas native English speakers see only three (they don't count the Fs in *of* because it is not considered an important word). The point is that once salespeople stop actively listening, they miss many things the buyer is trying to communicate.

Making Adjustments

Salespeople can alter their presentations in many ways to obtain a favorable reaction. For example, salespeople may discover during the sales presentation that the prospect simply does not believe he or she has the appropriate product knowledge. Rather than continue with the presentation, the salesperson should redirect her or his efforts toward establishing credibility in the eyes of the prospect. Salespeople need to continually adapt to the situation at hand.

Other adjustments might require collecting additional information about the prospect, developing a new sales strategy, or altering the style of presentation. For example, a salesperson may believe a prospect is interested in buying an economical, low-cost motor. While presenting the benefits of the lowest-cost motor, the salesperson discovers the prospect is interested in the motor's operating costs. At this point the salesperson should ask some questions to find out whether the prospect would be interested in paying a higher price for a more efficient motor with lower operating costs. On the basis of the prospect's response, the salesperson can adopt a new sales strategy, one that emphasizes operating efficiency rather than the motor's initial price. In this way the sales presentation is shifted from features and benefits based on a low initial cost to features and benefits related to low operating costs. Selling Scenario 9.1 shows what happens when a salesperson doesn't adapt her or his presentation to the prospect.

A VIEW FROM THE BUYER'S SIDE OF THE TABLE— ADAPT YOUR PRESENTATION TO ME!

A person that reported to me, let's call her Sally, saw a product she liked and wanted me to sit in on a pitch from a vendor. Sally put the meeting on my calendar for one hour, but when the time came I only had 30 minutes.

I came to the meeting and explained that I would be able to participate for only 30 minutes, but that Sally would be staying for the remainder of the time. The salesperson began taking me through his sales binder that had a presentation in it. It began with the history of the company.

I explained that I was familiar with the company, but there were certain things that I was interested in learning about their services. I asked him if they could produce two items for me. He said, "Yes, we could," and he would get there in a minute. I patiently waited as he continued to take me through his company history. Now almost 10 minutes had passed.

The next part of his presentation was the work they have done for other companies. This is something that many times I am interested in; however, we were really looking for a vendor for a couple of specific projects, and I wanted to see what they could do for my specific projects. I interrupted the salesperson again from his canned presentation and asked him about my two projects. He said he was almost there.

After showing the work they did for other companies, he began to explain the benefits of working with his company because of their reputation, pricing, service, and so on. I asked again about the two projects, and instead of answering my questions, he continued to follow his canned presentation. I left the meeting after about 20 minutes because I could see he wasn't going to leave his own agenda.

He didn't get the business. Surprised?

Source: Tracey Brill, used with permission.

BUILDING CREDIBILITY DURING THE CALL

To develop a close and harmonious relationship, the salesperson must be perceived as having **credibility;** that is, he or she must be believable and reliable. A salesperson can take many actions during a sales call to develop such a perception.[21]

To establish credibility early in the sales call, the salesperson should clearly delineate the time she or he thinks the call will take and then stop when the time is up. How many times has a salesperson said, "This will take only five minutes!" and 30 minutes later you still can't get rid of him? No doubt you would have perceived the salesperson as more credible if, after five minutes, he or she stated, "Well, I promised to take no more than five minutes, and I see our time is up. How would you like to proceed from here?" One successful salesperson likes to ask for half an hour and take only 25 minutes.[22] Salespeople who learn how to accurately calculate the time needed for a call and then stand by their promises will be much more successful in establishing credibility.

Another way to establish credibility is to offer concrete evidence to back up verbal statements.[23] If a salesperson states, "It is estimated that more than 80 percent of the households in America will own DVD players by 2010," he or she should be prepared to offer proof of this assertion—for instance, hand the prospect a letter or an article from a credible source. Ways to establish credibility are discussed in greater detail in Chapter 10.

Of course, one way to establish credibility is to avoid making statements that do not have the ring of truth to them. For example, some would suggest you

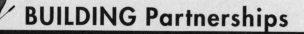
BE CANDID: IT WILL PAY OFF IN THE END

Kyle Townsend works for a car rental agency as a salesperson. He regularly calls on car dealers, body shops, retailers, and finance dealers. He also rents cars to individuals who have rental needs.

His agency does a great job when it comes to renting cars for local use. They are priced competitively, and the agency offers outstanding service. However, Kyle admits that his agency isn't very competitive in the long-distance market.

So when someone comes in, asking the rates and availability for renting a car for a cross-country trip, he is honest. "Look, I can rent you a car, that's not a problem," he states. "But to be honest, we're not going to be price competitive. You're better off dealing with Hertz or National or one of the big national chains, because you'll get a better deal. In fact, here is the phone number of the local Hertz rental agency . . ."

Some customers look at him like he is crazy. He doesn't care. "I know that what I am doing is right. In the long run, it's only going to help my business, not hurt it. Because they know they can trust what I say, they'll be back when their needs are for local rentals."

And that's exactly the case. Kyle's office is one of approximately 50 offices for that rental agency in the state, and each month, each office is rated in terms of profitability. In less than a year Kyle's car rental agency went from 31st in the state to 4th in the state. Being honest and candid does pay off!

Source: Personal communication. All names changed at the request of the salesperson.

should avoid using the phrase "We're the best" or "We're number one." As one skeptical person noted, "Just how many number ones are there in the world, anyway?" Salespeople should also remember that, in addition to damaging credibility, truth-stretching comments can come back to haunt them in the form of legal liability (see Chapter 3 for a review of legal issues).

Many salespeople have found that the most effective way to establish credibility is to make a **balanced presentation** that shows all sides of the situation—that is, to be totally honest. Thus a salesperson might mention some things about the product that make it less than perfect or may speak positively about some exclusive feature of a competitor's product. Will this approach defeat the seller's chances of a sale? No. In fact, it may increase the chances of building long-term commitment and rapport. Building Partnerships 9.1 provides insights about one salesperson who gives balanced presentations. Salespeople can keep customers happy and dedicated by helping them form correct, realistic expectations about the product or service.

Salespeople can build credibility by recognizing subcultural differences, not only in foreign markets but in North America as well. How? By demonstrating sensitivity to the needs and wants of specific subcultures and avoiding biased or racist language. See Chapter 5 for more information on subcultural differences.

In selling complex products, sales representatives often must demonstrate product expertise at the beginning of the sales process—for example, by telling the customer, without bragging, about their special training or education. They can also strengthen credibility with well-conceived, insightful questions or comments.[24]

When selling complicated technical products and services, Todd Graf notes, "You have to keep it simple. Teach as you go. Keep it simple. Make transitions slow and smooth and always ask if they understand (half the time they don't). This is key because they may have to go back and explain some of your features to the decision maker who isn't present in this meeting."[25]

Being willing to say "I'm sorry, I was wrong on that," or "I don't know the answer to that, but I'll get it to you," will also go a long way toward establishing credibility.[26] A seller should never use a word if he or she doesn't know the exact definition. Some buyers may even test the salesperson. Here's an example from a real salesperson who was calling on a doctor:[27]

SALESPERSON: Because product X acts as an agonist at the Kappa receptor, miosis will occur.

DOCTOR: What does *miosis* mean?

SALESPERSON: It means the "stage of disease during which intensity of signs and symptoms diminishes."

DOCTOR: No! *Miosis* means "contraction of the pupils."

SALESPERSON: My definition comes from the 1989 edition of *Taber's Encyclopedic Medical Dictionary*. I would be happy to bring it next time I come in because I wouldn't want you to think I would use a phrase without knowing what it means.

At this point the doctor walked out of the room, and the seller thought she had lost all credibility. Actually, he had just gone out and grabbed a dictionary. The first definition was the contraction of the pupils, and the second was the seller's definition. The salesperson's definition, not the doctor's, fit the use of the term for this medication. The doctor then shook the seller's hand and thanked her for teaching him a new definition of the word. The salesperson's credibility certainly increased.

SELLING TO GROUPS

Selling to groups can be both rewarding and frustrating. On the plus side, if you make an effective presentation, every member of the prospect group becomes your ally. On the down side, groups behave like groups, with group standards and norms and issues of status and group leadership.

When selling to groups, the salesperson must gather information about the needs and concerns of each individual who will attend. Salespeople should discover (for each prospect group member) member status within the group, authority, perceptions about the urgency of the problem, receptivity to ideas, knowledge of the subject matter, attitude toward the salesperson, major areas of interest and concern, key benefits sought, likely resistance, and ways to handle this resistance. Chapter 4 discusses many things that salespeople should consider about buying centers.

Selling to groups requires special skills in monitoring several individuals at once, as well as being able to respond to customers with occasionally conflicting needs.

Digital Vision/MGH-DIL

The salesperson should also discover the ego involvement and issue involvement of each group member. An **ego-involved** audience member perceives the subject matter to be important to his or her own well-being. For example, a person whose job might be eliminated by the introduction of a new computer system would be highly ego involved with regard to the computer system. An **issue-involved** person considers the subject important even though it may not affect him or her personally. For example, an accountant might be interested in what type of new production equipment will be purchased even though the use of that equipment will not affect the accountant in any direct way. Learning the ego involvement and issue involvement of each member in the audience allows the salesperson to adapt portions of the presentation to the specific needs of particular people.

It is important to develop not only objectives for the meeting but also objectives for what the seller hopes to accomplish with each prospect present at the meeting. Planning may include the development of special visual aids for specific individuals present. The seller must expect many more objections and interruptions in a group setting compared to selling to an individual.

An informal atmosphere in which group members are encouraged to speak freely and the salesperson feels free to join the group's discussion usually works best in these situations. Thus an informal location (such as a corner of a large room as opposed to a formal conference room) is preferred. Formal presentation methods, such as speeches, that separate buyers and sellers into them-versus-us sides should be avoided. If the group members decide that the meeting is over, the salesperson should not try to hold them.

Of course, most things you have learned about selling to individuals apply equally to groups. You should learn the names of group members and use them when appropriate. You should listen carefully and observe all nonverbal cues. When one member of the buying team is talking, it is especially important to observe the cues being transmitted by the other members of the buying team to see whether they are, in effect, agreeing or disagreeing with the speaker.

There are several types of group selling situations. If the group meeting is actually a negotiation session, many more things must be considered. As a result, we devote an entire chapter (Chapter 13) to the topic of formal negotiations. Also, sometimes a salesperson makes a call on a prospect with his or her sales manager, someone from technical support, someone from customer support, a sales executive from the firm, or a group from the selling firm. These situations require coordination and teamwork. Because of the importance of the various selling team scenarios, the issue of selling teams is more fully discussed in Chapter 16.

SUMMARY

Salespeople need to make every possible effort to create a good impression during a sales call. The first few minutes with the prospect are important, and care should be taken to make an effective entrance by giving a good first impression, expressing confidence while standing and shaking hands, and selecting an appropriate seat.

The salesperson can use any of several methods to gain the prospect's attention. Salespeople should adopt the opening that is most effective for the prospect's personality style. Also critical is the development of rapport with the prospect, which can often be enhanced by engaging in friendly conversation.

Before beginning any discussion of product information, the salesperson can establish the prospect's needs by using open and closed questions. The SPIN technique is very effective for discovering needs in the major sale. In subsequent calls the salesperson should reiterate the prospect's needs.

When moving into a discussion of the proposed solution or alternatives, the salesperson translates features into benefits for the buyer. The salesperson also makes any necessary adjustments in the presentation based on feedback provided by the buyer's nonverbal cues and by verbal probing.

A close, harmonious relationship will enhance the whole selling process. The salesperson can build credibility by adhering to stated appointment lengths, backing up statements with proof, offering a balanced presentation, and establishing his or her credentials.

When selling to groups, the salesperson must gather information about the needs and concerns of each individual who will attend. The seller should also uncover the ego involvement and issue involvement of each group member. It is important to develop objectives not only for the meeting but also for what the seller hopes to accomplish with each prospect present at the meeting.

Now that you know how to start the sale, discover needs, relate features to specific benefits for the buyer, and build credibility, it is time to look more closely at how to communicate your ideas more effectively. That's the topic of the next chapter, "Strengthening the Presentation."

KEY TERMS

advantages
balanced presentation
benefit
benefit opening
closed questions
compliment opening
credibility
ego-involved
FAB
feature
feature dumping
FEBA
halo effect
implication questions
impression management
introduction opening

issue-involved
major sale
need payoff questions
office scanning
opening
open questions
problem questions
product opening
question opening
rapport
referral opening
selective perception
situation questions
small talk
SPIN®
trial close

ETHICS PROBLEMS

1. Suppose you are calling on a prospect who hands you a brochure illustrating the features and benefits of a competitor's product. You look it over and notice that the brochure is six months old. Since that brochure was printed, your competitor has added some new features that make it much more competitive with what you're offering today. Should you be candid and tell the prospect what you know, even though it will put the competitor's product in a much better light?

2. You suspect that your prospect is overstating the extent of their needs. In fact, after spending a good bit of time with the prospect, you start to get the distinct impression that the prospect is lying and trying to sound important in order to gain information from you about your firm's production process. What should you do?

QUESTIONS AND PROBLEMS

1. Think for a moment about trying to secure a sales job. Assume you are going to have an interview with a district manager with a consumer products firm next week for a sales position. What can you do to develop rapport and build credibility with her?

2. "I don't need to discover my prospect's needs. I sell telephone calling cards to grocery stores and convenience stores. I know what their needs are:

a high profit margin and fast turnover of products!" Comment.

3. Develop the FEBA for one of the features shown in Exhibit 9.8.

4. Assume that you are selling yard maintenance services to a homeowner. Develop a series of open and closed questions to discover the prospect's needs.

5. Assume that you represent your school's placement service. You are calling on a large business nearby that never hires graduates from your college. Generate a list of SPIN® questions, making any additional assumptions necessary.

6. Prepare a list of features and benefits that could be used in a presentation to other students at your college. The objective of the presentation is to encourage them to enroll in the selling course you are taking.

7. Think of a group that you belong to now, or have belonged to in the past. Now assume someone was trying to sell that group something (a product of your choosing). For that specific group, describe the importance of the salesperson listening to and selling to all members of the group. List the different needs and concerns that would probably exist for the various group members.

8. "I always shake hands with anyone I call on. If I didn't shake hands, people would not trust me. Besides, it's common knowledge that you're supposed to shake hands in business settings. It makes you seem more friendly." Comment.

9. In which situations should a salesperson use the prospect's first name? When should a more formal salutation be used?

10. You're selling a new soft drink to a grocery store (choose one). Make a list of features and benefits for the grocery store, as well as a list of features and benefits for the store's customers (the shoppers who come in and buy soft drinks).

CASE PROBLEMS

case 9.1

Nomad Multimedia Stations (Part B)

Nomad Technologies, Inc. is the manufacturer of presentation stations, multimedia podiums, and e-learning units. Its products are designed to allow users to engage in a large variety of presentation functions, effectively and efficiently. These units contain a wide array of multimedia tools, like DVDs, video projectors, computers, and document cameras. Nomad offers both mobile and permanent audiovisual installations. Some of its most valuable current customers consist of a large number of high schools and universities.

Mike Alfanzo is a salesperson for Nomad. Today he will be making his first visit with Hamilton County Circuit Court Judge Kimberly Prestwood, in Chattanooga, Tennessee.

For more details about the Nomad Multimedia Stations, see Case 8.1 and http://www.nomadonline.com/index.cfm.

Questions

1. Develop a set of open and closed questions to fully discover Judge Prestwood's needs.

2. Develop a set of SPIN® questions to discover Judge Prestwood's needs.

case 9.2

What Would You Do?

Lots of crazy things can happen during a sales call. Reflect on the following real-world scenarios and indicate what you feel is the appropriate response or answer to each.

1. You enter the prospect's office and the prospect motions you to have a seat. But the seat is actually a giant two-foot inflated purple ball instead of a chair. You notice that the prospect has an identical ball to sit on behind her desk.

2. You leave with the prospect to head down to production. You are a male and the prospect is a female. As you approach a door, you wonder if you should open the door for the prospect.

3. You are playing golf with your customer and catch the customer cheating. You're not sure if you should call his attention to it.

4. You've not made a call on a particular customer for several months. When you enter her office you notice that she is apparently pregnant: her stomach area is bulging out. Should you mention the fact?

5. You've heard that a female customer of yours got a divorce. Do you refer to her as Miss, Ms., or Mrs.?

6. You're giving a presentation. You lean over to get something out of your briefcase and your coat rips. The prospect starts laughing.

7. You offer your hand for a handshake, and the prospect just looks at you, not offering her hand.

8. You use the referral opening, and the prospect says, "You know, I've never trusted Jim Tollers (the person you used in your referral)."

9. You use the product opening, and the prospect just keeps playing with the product. You are afraid to move on to your presentation without her attention.

10. You state at the beginning, "This will take only 15 minutes"; then the prospect rambles and uses up most of your time in trivial chitchat. At the end of 15 minutes, you haven't accomplished your call objectives.

11. You are at dinner with a prospect, and you accidentally spill soup on your tie or scarf.

Sources: Personal experiences; Kathy Droullard, "Mind Your Manners," *Sales and Marketing Management,* January 2005, pp. 26–32.

ROLE PLAY

Today we are going to start over again, "from the top" as they say in the theatre. Start from the beginning of the sales call, from when you knock on the door through the needs identification stage, ending just before your presentation. All that you have learned in previous role plays about the account continues to hold true. If you've been selling to Skylight, you'll continue to do so, but you are now meeting with a different member of the buying center. The same is true for Binswanger and Lincoln. New buyer sheets will be passed out. You can have the same person play the new role or someone else in class. (Note: If you have not done role plays before, you will need to review the information about the various role play customers that can be found at the end of Chapter 4.)

If your class is divided into groups of three, then the person who is watching should create a tick sheet. Write S, P, I, and N down the left side of the paper. As the salesperson asks a question, tick whether it is a situation, problem, implication, or needs pay-off question. Also, note if and how he or she identified or verified the decision process. Don't forget: At the start of the sales call, identify what type of opening was used (introduction, benefit, product, curiosity, or some other form).

Skylight Products: You will meet with the VP of sales and marketing. This is an appointment that was set up by the regional sales manager you called on earlier. You've never talked to this person before.

Binswanger Real Estate: Mr. Binswanger has asked to see you. You weren't expecting this from your earlier sales calls, but you welcome the opportunity to meet the decision maker. His secretary called and made the appointment.

Lincoln Manufacturing: You are meeting with one of the VPs of sales. The other VP was fired but you don't know why. The meeting was set up by the regional sales manager you called on earlier, who also told you about the firing, but she didn't know what had happened.

Note: For background information on these role plays, please see page 27.

To the instructor: Additional information needed to complete the role play is available in the Instructor's Manual.

ADDITIONAL REFERENCES

Beverland, Michael. "Contextual Influences and the Adoption and Practice of Relationship Selling in a Business-to-Business Setting: An Exploratory Study." *Journal of Personal Selling & Sales Management* 21, no. 3 (Summer 2001), pp. 207–15.

Dixon, Andrea L.; Jule B. Gassenheimer; and Terri Feldman Barr. "Bridging the Distance between Us: How Initial Responses to Sales Team Conflict Help Shape Core Selling Team Outcomes." *Journal of Personal Selling and Sales Management* 22 (Fall 2002), pp. 247–58.

Dixon, Andrea L.; Rosann L. Spiro; and Maqbul Jamil. "Successful and Unsuccessful Sales Calls: Measuring Salesperson Attributions and Behavioral Intentions." *Journal of Marketing,* (July 2001), pp. 64–78.

Eades, Keith M. *The New Solution Selling: The Revolutionary Sales Process That Is Changing the Way People Sell.* New York: McGraw-Hill, 2003.

Fang, Eric. "Goal-Setting Paradoxes? Trade-Offs between Working Hard and Working Smart: The United States versus China." *Journal of the Academy of Marketing Science* 32 (Spring 2004), pp. 188–203.

Fox, Jeffrey J., and Richard G. Gregory. *The Dollarization Discipline: How Smart Companies Create Customer Value . . . and Profit from It.* Hoboken, NJ: Wiley and Sons, 2004.

Miller, William. *ProActive Selling: Control the Process: Win the Sale.* New York: AMACOM, 2003.

Neuborne, Ellen. "Tag-Team Pitches." *Sales and Marketing Management* 154 (March 2002), p. 57.

Parinello, Anthony. *Getting the Second Appointment: How to Close Any Sale in Two Calls!* Hoboken, NJ: John Wiley and Sons, 2004.

Peppers, Don, and Martha Rogers. "Needs Differentiation: The Critical Benchmark in Customer Marketing." *1to1 Magazine,* (April 2002), pp. 52–53.

Sparks, John R., and Charles S. Areni. "The Effects of Sales Presentation Quality and Initial Perceptions on Persuasion: A Multiple Role Perspective." *Journal of Business Research* 55, no. 6 (2002), pp. 517–28.

Szymanski, David M. "Modality and Offering Effects in Sales Presentations for a Good versus a Service." *Journal of the Academy of Marketing Science* 29, no. 2 (2001), pp. 179–89.

Verbeke, Willen, and Richard P. Bagozzi. "A Situational Analysis of How Salespeople Experience and Cope with Shame and Embarrassment." *Psychology and Marketing* 19 (September 2002), pp. 713–41.

Wagner, Ernesto R., and Eric N. Hansen. "A Method for Identifying and Assessing Key Customer Group Needs." *Industrial Marketing Management* 33 (2004), pp. 643–55.

Wagner, Judy A.; Noreen M. Klein; and Janet E. Keith. "Selling Strategies: The Effects of Suggesting a Decision Structure to Novice and Expert Buyers." *Journal of the Academy of Marketing Science* 29, no. 3 (2001), pp. 289–306.

Warner, Fara. "How Fitch Makes Its (Fast) Pitch." *Fast Company,* March 2002, pp. 126–30.

Waterhouse, Steve. *The Team Selling Solution: Creating and Managing Teams That Win the Complex Sale.* New York: McGraw-Hill, 2003.

STRENGTHENING THE PRESENTATION

chapter 10

SOME QUESTIONS ANSWERED IN THIS CHAPTER . . .

- How can salespeople use verbal tools to strengthen the presentation?

- Why do salespeople need to augment their oral communication through tools such as visual aids, samples, testimonials, and demonstrations?

- What methods are available to strengthen the presentation?

- How can salespeople utilize visual aids and technology most effectively?

- What are the ingredients of a good demonstration?

- Is there a way to quantify the salesperson's solution to the buyer's problem?

- How can salespeople reduce presentation jitters?

PROFILE

I graduated from the College of St. Catherine with a BS double major in marketing/management and professional sales and took my personal selling class from Dr. Greg Di Novis. I started with Pfizer in 2002, and my current territory is in northern Manhattan.

During any given day I give nearly a dozen presentations involving several prescription drugs to physicians in my territory. These presentations can range from 30 seconds to a half hour. Because of the short time I have to influence perceptions, I need to make sure my message is accurate, concise, and influential.

I need to be aware of perceptions doctors have of my product, external influences on decision making, and what information they need to make an accurate decision. It is extremely important to be aware of the numerous influences that impact a decision of a doctor. A few of these include competitive actions, governmental restrictions, health insurance policies, and current relationships with competitors.

After discovering this information I need to make presentations that are tailored specifically for that physician to address the issues he or she sees as important. For example, if the physician's biggest concern about prescribing is the safety of the product, I present all the safety data available to the physician so he or she can make an informed decision. The focus of the presentation should be on what is important to the customer, not what is important to me. The customer will pay more attention to what I have to say if it concerns them.

Due to the short amount of time I have to impact my physicians it is imperative to use many tools to reinforce my presentation. While presenting I continually refer to my visuals, which can include marketing materials and clinical information, to reinforce the validity of my information.

Also, people remember more of what they see than what they hear. When I present information to physicians, I show them a graphic summary of the clinical data I am sharing with them along with the full clinical reprint. For example, a graphic of the clinical data may include a large, colorful graph of improvements in pain scores for patients suffering from migraines or an improvement in anxiety scores for patients suffering from an anxiety disorder. I leave the visuals with the doctor after my presentation so they may review them after I am gone. This helps to build the brand within the customers' minds.

Another form of visual tool is to create a mental picture of the patient the physician should be looking for. This may include describing the disruptive symptoms of Alzheimer's disease so the physician can mentally picture what that type of patient may look like in his or her practice.

I also leave samples of my products so that the patient and the physician can see the benefits of my products before purchasing them. Patient education is important to many of my physicians, so I use this as an added value to the patient. I try to keep my physicians as active as possible in the presentation by giving them the samples to look at and allowing them the time to read through the clinical information. I solicit questions from physicians to determine if the information I am giving is important to them, to discover any concerns or questions, and to keep them involved in the conversation. If I am unsure about a question a doctor has, I maintain my credibility by telling them I will get back to them with the correct answer as soon as possible.

The best defense against presentation jitters is to prepare. I prepare and practice the presentations in

> *"The focus of the presentation should be on what is important to the customer, not what is important to me."*
>
> *Amanda Deitz, Pfizer*

advance. Also, I discuss the presentations with others who have experience with the same type of customers to prepare myself for objections or concerns the customer may have. I find it helps to give the presentation to myself several times in a mirror and to others. This allows me to choose appropriate wording and discover behaviors that might distract from my presentation.

By preparing for my presentation I improve my confidence. Confidence in myself and my product will show through and give my customers confidence in me. My goal is to know the information I will be presenting better than anyone. After all, I am the expert for my customer.

View our Web site at www.pfizer.com.

CHARACTERISTICS OF A STRONG PRESENTATION

Communication tools such as visual aids, samples, testimonials, demonstrations, and the use of humor are an important ingredient in most sales calls. Use of such tools focuses the buyer's attention, improves the buyer's understanding, helps the buyer remember what the salesperson said, offers concrete proof of the salesperson's statements, and creates a sense of value.

KEEPS THE BUYER'S ATTENTION

How many times has your mind wandered during classroom lectures while the instructor earnestly discussed some topic? What happened? The instructor lost your attention. In contrast, your attention probably remains higher in a class when the instructor uses visuals and humor effectively, brings in guest speakers, and finds ways to get you actively involved in the discussion.

The same is true of buyer–seller interactions. Unless you can get the buyer actively involved in the communication process and doing more than just passively hearing you talk, the buyer's attention will probably turn to other topics.

The buyer's personality can also affect his or her attention span. For example, one would expect an amiable to listen more attentively to a long presentation than, say, a driver would. Thus an effective salesperson should consider the personality of the prospect and adapt the use of communication aids accordingly (see Chapter 6 for more about personality styles).

IMPROVES THE BUYER'S UNDERSTANDING

Many buyers have difficulty forming clear images from the written or spoken word. An old Chinese proverb says, Tell me—I'll forget. Show me—I may remember. But involve me, and I'll understand. Appeals should be made to as many of the senses (hearing, sight, touch, taste, and smell) as possible. Studies show that appealing to more than one sense, called **multiple-sense appeals**, increases understanding dramatically, as Exhibit 10.1 illustrates. For example, in selling Ben & Jerry's ice cream novelties to a grocery store manager, the salesperson may describe the product's merits—an appeal to the sense of hearing—or show the product and invite the merchant to taste it—appeals to sight, touch, and taste. Appeals to the grocer's fifth sense, smell, are also possible. On the other hand, salespeople who sell machinery are limited to appeals that will affect the buyers' senses of hearing, sight, and touch.

HELPS THE BUYER REMEMBER WHAT WAS SAID

On average, people immediately forget 50 percent of what they hear; after 48 hours they have forgotten 75 percent of the message. This is unfortunate because securing an order often requires multiple visits, and in many situations the

Exhibit 10.1

How We Learn and
Remember

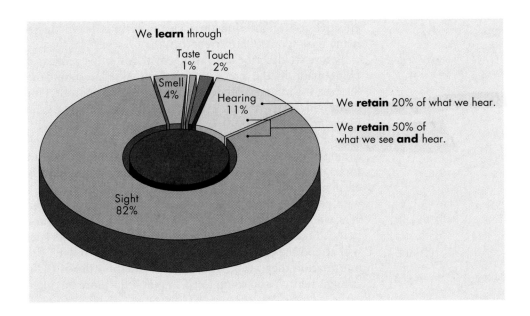

We **learn** through

Taste 1%   Touch 2%

Smell 4%

Hearing 11% — We **retain** 20% of what we hear.

— We **retain** 50% of what we see **and** hear.

Sight 82%

prospect must relay to other people information learned in a sales call. In these circumstances it becomes even more critical for the seller to help the buyer remember what was said.

Even selling situations involving one call or one decision maker will be more profitable if the buyer remembers what was said. Vividly communicated features create such a strong impression that the buyer remembers the seller's claims and is more likely to tell others about them.

Lasting impressions can be created in many ways. One salesperson swallows some industrial cleanser to show that it is nontoxic; another kicks the protective glass in the control panel of a piece of machinery to show that it is virtually unbreakable under even the roughest conditions. Whatever the method used, the prospect is more likely to remember a sales feature if it is presented skillfully in a well-timed demonstration.

OFFERS PROOF OF THE SALESPERSON'S ASSERTIONS

Let's face it: Most people just won't believe everything a salesperson tells them. Many of the communication tools we discuss in this chapter provide solid proof to back up the salesperson's claims. For example, a salesperson can easily claim that a liquid is nontoxic, but the claim is much more convincing if the salesperson drinks some of the liquid in front of the prospect.

CREATES A SENSE OF VALUE

The manner in which a product is handled suggests value. Careful handling communicates value, while careless handling implies that the product has little value. For example, a delicate piece of china will be perceived as more valuable if the salesperson uses appropriate props, words, and care in handling it.

HOW TO STRENGTHEN THE PRESENTATION

Salespeople should ask themselves the following questions: How can I use my imagination and creativity to make a vivid impression on my prospect or customer? How can I make my presentation a little different and a little stronger? With this frame of mind, salespeople will always try to do a better and more effective job of meeting their customers' needs. In this section we explore the many tools available to strengthen the presentation.

Before we describe the various methods, however, it is important to reiterate a point made in the preceding chapter. A seller should not just grab a method because it sounds trendy or because it worked in a previous sales call or because it is highly entertaining. Rather, a seller should strategically select methods and media that will helpfully address the needs of the buyer. This process includes responding to the buyer's unique style (see Chapter 6 to review social styles). For example, expressives like to see strong, intense colors and lots of photos, cartoons, fancy fonts, and positive images (smiles); analyticals prefer visuals that are clean and simple, a list of references, and lots of details; amiables prefer visuals with people in them and a relatively slow-moving presentation; in contrast, drivers want crisp, professional visuals with bold lettering to highlight important points. Strategizing also includes considering elements such as how many people will attend the presentation, which stage of the buying process they are in, what information they need, what type of situation this is (new task, modified rebuy, straight rebuy), and so on (see Chapter 4 for more buying factors to consider).

VERBAL TOOLS

Word Pictures and Stories

The power of the spoken word can be phenomenal.[1] To communicate effectively, the salesperson needs to remember all the hints and tools found in Chapter 5. Word pictures and stories of all types can be effective. Here are some points to keep in mind when using stories:

- It is best to use stories from your own life. If you do borrow one, don't act like it is your personal story.
- Make sure you have a reason for telling the story.
- Use the "hook" of the story to tie back directly into your presentation.
- Be accurate and vivid with the words you choose. Learn to paint a clear picture.
- Pace the story, watching your audience for cues. Use silence and pauses.
- Choose stories that fit your own style. Don't try to be someone you're not.
- Remember, stories can be quite short—even a few sentences.

Humor

Another way a salesperson can help keep the buyer's attention is through the use of humor.[2] The wonderful effects of laughter will put everyone more at ease,[3] including the salesperson. Use humorous stories from your own experience, borrowed humor, or humor adapted from another source. Here are some things to keep in mind:

- Don't oversell the joke (Here's one that'll really break you up!).
- Don't apologize before telling a joke (I wasn't ever good at telling a joke, but here goes.).
- Identify any facts that are absolutely necessary for the punch line of the story to make sense (Jerry Joyner, my next door neighbor who was always sticking his nose in other people's business, . . .).
- Use humor from your own life. Anything you got from e-mail could be circulating widely.
- Enjoy yourself by smiling and animating your voice and nonverbals.

Salespeople should use humor to get and keep the customer's attention.

Copyright © Wonderfile Corporation 2002. All rights reserved.

- Practice telling the joke different ways to see which exact wording works best.
- Make sure your punch line is clear.

Beware of overdoing humor or using off-the-wall or offensive humor.[4] Both can backfire, as one presenter found out when he used the following opening line about an overweight attendee: Pull up two chairs and have a seat. The presenter knew right away that it was a big mistake. Always be cautious about using insider jokes, especially if you're still considered an outsider.

Also, understand that what is funny to one person or group may not be funny to others. Several examples will help you see this point. A foreigner from Egypt may not appreciate someone from America making fun of Egyptian culture—but someone from Egypt can tell that same joke and get plenty of laughs. In recent research involving more than 100,000 people from 70 countries, it was found that men prefer humor about aggression or sexual innuendo, while women prefer humor that involves word play. The same study found that Canadians seem the least likely to laugh at jokes, while Germans laugh the most.[5]

VISUAL TOOLS

A salesperson can use various visually oriented tools to strengthen the presentation. This section explores the content and use of those tools, followed by a discussion of the various media available to display the results.

Graphics and Charts

Graphics and charts help illustrate relationships and clearly communicate large amounts of information.[6] Charts may show, for example, advertising schedules, a breakdown of typical customer profiles, details of product manufacture, profit margins at various pricing points, or the investment nature of purchasing the product.

Charts can easily be customized by including the name of the prospect's company in one corner or by some other form of personalization. Customization helps to project the impression that the presentation is fresh and tailor-made for this prospect.

Following are several important hints for developing charts and related visuals:

- Know the single point the visual should make and then ensure that it accomplishes that point.
- Use current, accurate information.
- Don't place too much information on a visual; on a textual visual, don't use more than five or six words per line or more than five lines per visual. Don't use complete sentences; the speaker should verbally provide the missing details.[7]
- Use bullets (dots or symbols before each line) to more easily differentiate issues and to emphasize key points.
- Don't overload the buyer with numbers. Use no more than five or six columns and drop all unnecessary zeros.
- Clearly label each visual with a title. Label all columns and rows.

- Recognize the emotional impact of colors and choose appropriate ones. An abundance of green connected to a humorous graph might be offensive in Islamic countries, since green is a religious color. In Brazil and Mexico, purple indicates death.

- If possible, use graphics (like diagrams, pie charts, and bar charts) instead of tables. Tables are often needed if actual raw numbers are important; graphics are better for displaying trends and relationships.

- Use consistent art styles, layouts, and scales for your collection of charts and figures. Consistency makes it easier for the buyer to follow along. For Power-Point slides, use 28 point type for the titles and 24 point for the text, using Arial font.[8]

- Check your visuals closely for typographical errors, misspelled words, and other errors.

- Know and obey copyright laws. You can't just grab images off the Web and use them.

thinking **it** through

Computers and the excellent software available today enable anyone to create customized presentations, with the buyer's company logo and name at the top of each visual. As a result, such activity alone might not be enough to give the impression that the buyer is important. In this high-tech world, how else can a seller create the sense that the prospect is of value?

Models, Samples, and Gifts

Visual selling aids such as models, samples, and gifts may be a good answer to the problem of getting and keeping buyer interest. For example, Brink's Locking Systems salespeople carry along a miniature working model of the company's electronic door locks when calling on prison security systems buyers. The model allows the salesperson to show how the various components work together to form a fail-safe security network.

Other salespeople use cross-sectional models to communicate with the buyer. For example, salespeople for Motion Industries use a cutaway model of a power transmission friction reduction product. This model helps the buyer, usually an industrial engineer, to clearly see how the product is constructed, resulting in greater confidence that the product will perform as described.

Depending on the service or product, samples and gifts can make excellent sales aids and help to maintain the prospect's interest after the call. In a Johnson's Wax sales campaign, salespeople called on buyers of major chains to describe the promotion. Salespeople walked into each buyer's office with a solid oak briefcase containing cans of aerosol Pledge, the product to be highlighted during the promotion. During the call the sales representative demonstrated the Pledge furniture polish on the oak briefcase. At the conclusion of the visit, the rep gave the buyer not only the cans of Pledge but also the briefcase. Of course, gift giving must be done with care and not violate the rules of the buyer's company.

Catalogs and Brochures

Catalogs and brochures can help salespeople communicate information to the buyer effectively. The salesperson can use them during presentations and then leave them with the buyer as a reminder of the issues covered. Brochures often summarize key points and contain answers to the usual questions buyers pose.

Firms often spend a great deal of money to develop visually attractive brochures for salespeople. Exhibit 10.2 shows an example of a brochure used by salespeople. Creatively designed brochures usually unfold in a way that enables the salesperson to create and maintain great interest while showing them.

Photos, Illustrations, Ads, and Maps

Photos are easy to prepare, are inexpensive, and permit a realistic portrayal of the product and its benefits. Photographs of people may be particularly effective. For example, leisure made possible through savings can be communicated via photographs of retired people at a ranch, a mountain resort, or the seashore. Illustrations drawn, painted, or prepared in other ways also help to dramatize needs or benefits. Copies of recent or upcoming ads may contribute visual appeal. Detailed maps can be easily developed, for example, to show how a magazine's circulation matches the needs of potential advertisers.

Testimonials and Test Results

Testimonials are statements written by satisfied users of a product or service. For example, company representatives who sell air travel for major airlines have found case histories helpful in communicating sales points. AirCanada recounts actual experiences of business firms, showing the variety of problems that air travel can solve.

The effectiveness of a testimonial hinges on the skill with which it is used and a careful matching of satisfied user and prospect. In some situations the testimony of a rival or a competitor of the prospective buyer would end all chance of closing the sale; in other cases this type of testimony may be a strong factor in obtaining commitment. As much as possible, the person who writes the testimonial should be above reproach, well respected by his or her peers, and perhaps a center of

Exhibit 10.2
A Brochure with Great Visual Appeal

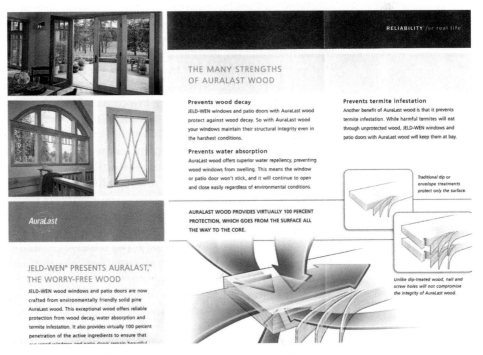

Courtesy of JELD-WEN® Windows & Doors.

influence (see Chapter 7). For example, when selling to certified public accountants (CPAs), a good source for a testimonial would be the president of the state's CPA association.

Before using a testimonial, the salesperson needs to check with the person who wrote it and frequently reaffirm that he or she is still a happy, satisfied customer. One salesperson for Unisys routinely handed all prospects a testimonial from a satisfied customer of a new software package. But, unknown to the salesperson, the "satisfied customer" became an unsatisfied one and actually returned the software. The salesperson kept handing out the letter until one of his prospects alerted him to the situation. He will never know how many other prospects lost interest after contacting that customer.

Salespeople should not just hand out a testimonial to every prospect. Such letters should be used only if they help to address the buyer's needs or concerns. Also, be aware that prospects probably discount testimonials, thinking that the seller is presenting letters only from very satisfied customers.

Salespeople can also use test results to strengthen the presentation. Tests on the product or service may have been conducted by the seller's firm or some third-party organization (such as Consumer Reports or Underwriters Laboratories). Generally, tests conducted by independent, recognized authorities have more credibility for the prospect than tests done by the seller.

Using Media to Display Visuals

Many media are available to display the types of items just mentioned. New media, and improvements to existing media, are being introduced almost every week. Salespeople are encouraged to choose media that are appropriate for the exact situation, and not merely choose a tool because it is new or exciting. Time-honored media, such as portfolios or overhead projectors, may sometimes be appropriate; at other times it may be important to use the most high-tech media available.

Most salespeople have developed a **portfolio,** which is simply a paper-based collection of visual aids, often placed in some sort of binder or container. Salespeople do not intend to use everything in the portfolio in a single call; rather, the portfolio should contain a broad spectrum of visual aids the salesperson can find quickly should the need arise. When showing visuals in your portfolio, make sure the portfolio is turned so the buyer can see it easily. The portfolio should not be placed, like a wall, between you and the buyer. Remember to look at the buyer, not at your visual; maintaining eye contact is always important.

Video is another tool salespeople can use. Salespeople use video to help the buyer see how quality is manufactured into the product (showing the production process at the manufacturing plant), how others use the product or service (showing a group of seniors enjoying the golf course at a retirement resort), promotional support offered with the product (showing the actual upcoming TV commercial for the product), and even testimonials from satisfied users. When using video, make sure the video is fast-paced and relatively short. Don't show more than four minutes of a video at one time.[9]

Salespeople have adopted laptops, tablet PCs, and palm PCs for use in sales calls.[10] For example, Merck pharmaceutical salespeople carry laptops with a database of technical information, as well as complete copies of articles from medical journals. Progressive firms, like Aetna, are investing in **digital collateral management** systems to archive, catalog, and retrieve digital media and text.[11] **Collateral** is the collection of documents that are designed to generate sales, including such items as brochures, sales flyers and fact sheets, and short success stories. Digital collateral management systems simplify the collection and make it

Examples of sales collateral for an excavator.

McGraw-Hill Companies/Jill Braaten, photographer

possible for salespeople to easily secure and adapt these selling tools for specific situations. For example, salespeople access the digital collateral management system when preparing their presentations to easily call up photos, videos, audio files, PowerPoint templates, Web pages, legal documents, streaming media, and just about anything else that has been digitally entered into the system.[12]

Computers not only offer excellent visuals and graphics but also allow the salesperson to perform what-if analyses. For example, when a grocery buyer asked a Procter & Gamble rep what would happen if the new product were sold for $1.69 instead of the $1.75 suggested retail price, the salesperson was able to easily change this number in the Excel spreadsheet program. Instantly all charts and graphs were corrected to illustrate the new pricing point, and comparisons with the competitor's product were generated.

When using computers, be prepared. Have backup batteries, adapters, and copies of CDs or DVDs. Really get to know your hardware and software so you can recover if the system crashes. And make sure both you and your customer can comfortably view the output.

thinking **it** through

You turn the lights down for a PowerPoint computer slide presentation. A few minutes later, you start to panic when your eye catches an unusual jerking movement made by the buyer . . . she's falling asleep! What do you do now?

Images can also be displayed using other media. **Document cameras,** also called **visual presenters,** are similar to traditional overhead projectors, but are also capable of displaying any three-dimensional object without the use of a transparency.[13] **Electronic whiteboards,** or digital easels, are used by salespeople, especially when working with customers who prefer to brainstorm an issue or problem.[14] Hewlett-Packard executives use these to make electronic presentations to remote offices in

Exhibit 10.3

Salespeople Use
Electronic Tools to
Display Important
Information

RF/Corbis

the United States and Europe with their teleconferencing system. Exhibit 10.3 shows an example of a common electronic display tool used by salespeople.

PRODUCT DEMONSTRATIONS

One of the most effective methods of appealing to the buyer's senses is through product demonstrations or performance tests. Customers and prospects have a natural desire to prove the product's claims for themselves. Obviously, the proof is much more satisfying and convincing to anyone who is a party to it.

One enterprising sales representative was having trouble convincing the buyer for a national retailer that the salesperson's company could provide service at all of the retailer's scattered outlets. On the next trip to the buyer, the sales representative brought along a bag of darts and a map marked with the chain's hundreds of stores and service locations. The buyer was invited to throw darts at the map and then find the nearest stores. The test pointed out that the nearest location for service was always within 50 miles. This "service demonstration" helped win the representative's company a multimillion-dollar order.

Another salesperson was selling feeding tubes to a hospital. A nurse took the salesperson to a patient's bed and stated, "Here, you do it. You said it was easier to insert. Let me see you insert it."[15] See Building Partnerships 10.1 for another example of an unusual demonstration scenario.

Some products can be sold most successfully by getting the prospect into the showroom for a hands-on product demonstration. Showrooms can be quite elaborate and effective. For example, Hewlett-Packard (HP) operates a medical marketing center in Germany. Prospects from across Europe can try all of HP's medical products. Patient responses are electronically simulated, which allows medical personnel to test the equipment in mock emergency situations.

Executive briefing centers, rooms set aside to highlight a company's products and capabilities, are the ultimate presentation room. For example, AT&T spent $100 million to build its presentation center. And the payoff is great, with reports of from 70 to 90 percent of business deals discussed in an executive briefing center closing at the centers.[16]

An executive briefing center.

Digital Vision/Getty Images

DON'T THROW MY PLATES AGAINST THE WALL!

I was working as an outside sales rep for a restaurant supply company in southern California. This was my first job out of college. I was one of the youngest employees in the company and the only female sales rep in my region. My largest client was an upscale seafood chain. I had an arranged face-to-face presentation with the general manager and one of the owners, who flew in from the Bay Area for this meeting. I was promoting a high-end plate that was known for not chipping or cracking. Supposedly, it was the most durable plate (and one of the most expensive) on the market.

The manufacturers taught us to demonstrate the plate's durability by dropping it squarely on the base of the plate. If the weight was evenly distributed on the well of the plate, you could drop it on a tile floor and it wouldn't chip or crack. This demo was part of my standard pitch, and the owner had seen it once before. So I set up a lovely table setting of a dozen multicolored plates in an unoccupied room of the restaurant. As soon as I started to drop the first plate, the owner said, "Sit down. I know the drill." He proceeded to toss all 12 plates against the nearest wall, which was covered with leather wallpaper.

Naturally, the plates bounced off the walls and shattered on the tile floor. At first, he was trying to make a point.

Then he started to amuse himself. By the end, both men were laughing hysterically. The general manager said, "That was fun, what else ya got?"

After stammering for a minute, I excused myself to "go get more supplies." I went into the kitchen and got one of the plates they were using at the restaurant at the time. Upon returning, I said, "Let's do a little test," and tossed it at the wall. It disintegrated on the floor. (We had broken a lot of plates in training to observe the difference in materials, so I was relatively sure of the outcome.)

I scooped up the shards of my product and the scraps of their plate and handed them to the owner. I pointed out that my plate had broken into 5 pieces and his had broken into 20. Also, I demonstrated the porousness (which signals a weaker plate) of their current plate, which is not visible if the plate is in one piece. I said "Clearly, my plate is more durable and is made of a stronger material. Also, if it does break, you have a lot less cleanup."

They ordered 200 of my plates.

Source: Sarah Gottry, used with permission.

Here are a number of helpful hints for developing and engaging in effective demonstrations:

- Be prepared. Practice the demonstration until you become an expert.[17] Plan for everything that could possibly go wrong.

- Secure a proper place for the demonstration, one free of distractions for both you and the buyer. If the demonstration is at the buyer's office, make sure you have everything you need (power supply, lighting, and so on).[18] Remember, it can even be an online presentation.[19]

- Check the equipment again to make sure it is in good working order prior to beginning the presentation.[20] Have necessary backup parts and supplies (like paper or bulbs).

- Get the prospect involved in a meaningful way.[21] For example, if you are selling a tractor to a farmer, don't just drive it for him or her; let the farmer drive the tractor. In a group situation, plan which group members need to participate.

- Always relate product features to the buyer's unique needs.

- Make the demonstration an integral part of the overall presentation, not a separate, unrelated activity.

- Keep the demonstration simple, concise, and clear. Long, complicated demonstrations add to the possibility that the buyer will miss the point. Limit technical jargon to technically advanced buyers who you know will understand technical terms.

- Plan what you will do during any dead time—that is, time in which the machine is processing on its own. You can use these intervals to ask the buyer questions and have the buyer ask you questions.

- Find out whether the prospect has already seen a competitor's product demonstration. If so, strategically include a demonstration of features the buyer liked about the competitor's product. Also, plan to show how your product can meet the prospect's desires and do what the competitor's product will not do.

- Find out whether any buyers present at your demonstration have used your product before. Having them assist in the demonstration may be advantageous if they view your product favorably.

- Probe during and after the demonstration. Make sure buyers understand the features and see how the product can help them. Also, probe to see whether buyers are interested in securing the product.

Remember Murphy's law: What can go wrong will go wrong! And occasionally things do go wrong during a demonstration, like when Bill Gates, CEO of Microsoft, was giving the big launch demonstration of Windows 98 and his computer froze. If a demonstration "blows up" for any reason, your best strategy usually is to appeal to fate with a humorous tone of voice: Wow, have you ever seen anything get so messed up? I should run for Congress! Don't let technical glitches embarrass or frustrate you.[22] Life is not perfect, and sometimes things just don't work out the way you plan them. If it will help, remember that prospects also are not perfect and sometimes they mess things up as well. Maintaining a cool and level head will probably impress the prospect with your ability to deal with a difficult situation. It may even increase your chances of a sale because you are demonstrating your ability to handle stress (something that often occurs during the after-sale servicing of an account).[23]

HANDOUTS

Handouts are written documents provided to help buyers remember what was said. A well-prepared set of handouts can be one of the best ways to increase buyer retention of information, especially over longer periods. A common practice is to make a printed copy of the overheads and give that to the buyers at the conclusion of the presentation. Some programs (like PowerPoint) allow you to print several slides on each page.

Others would argue that your use of handouts should be more strategically focused. Thus handouts are not just a last-minute thought, but rather are a tool that needs to be carefully planned at the same time you are preparing your presentation. For example, you could draw a line on a piece of planning paper and on the left side list the things you will do and say during the presentation, while on the right side listing the items that should go into the handout. In that way the two will work together and be complementary.

What things can go into a handout? Complex charts and diagrams can be included. Because you want to keep your presentation visuals relatively simple (see the preceding hints), your handouts can supply more complete, detailed information. You may also want to include some company reports or literature. However, to avoid making the buyer wade through a lot of nonrelevant information, include only important sections. You may even want to highlight sections of the reports. Other items to include are Web addresses with a description of each site, case studies, magazine articles, and yes, even a copy of your presentation slides themselves (with room to take notes if you're going to give the buyer your handout during the presentation). Whatever you choose, here are some tips:

- Don't forget the goal of your meeting. That should drive all of your decisions about what to include in your handouts.
- Make sure the handouts look professional. And use graphics, instead of text, whenever possible.
- Don't cram too much information on a page. White space is fine. Try not to fill more than two-thirds of any page with information.
- Don't drown your prospect in information. Include only helpful information in your handouts.

Handouts are even more important for foreign buyers, especially those who are nonnative English speakers. You might even consider giving them a copy of your handouts before your meeting so they can become more comfortable and familiar with concepts and phrases. Including a glossary, with definitions, will also be appreciated by foreign buyers.

WRITTEN PROPOSALS

In some industries written proposals are an important part of the selling process. Some proposals are simple adaptations of brochures developed by a corporate marketing department. But in industries that sell customized products or require competitive bidding (as many state and local governments do), a written proposal may be necessary for the buyer to organize and compare various offerings.

The RFP Process

A document issued by a prospective buyer asking for a proposal may be called a **request for proposal (RFP),** request for quote (RFQ), or request for bid (RFB). For brevity's sake, we will refer to all of these as RFPs.[24]

The RFP should contain the customer's specifications for the desired product, including delivery schedules. RFPs are used when the customer has a firm idea of the product needed. From the salesperson's perspective, being a part of the specifying process makes sense. Using the needs identification process, the salesperson can assist the customer in identifying needs and specifying product characteristics.[25]

Writing Proposals

Proposals include an **executive summary,** a one- or two-page summary that provides the total cost minus the total savings, a brief description of the problem to be solved, and a brief description of the proposed solution. The summary should satisfy the concerns of an executive who is too busy or unwilling to read the entire proposal. The executive summary also serves to pique the interest of all readers by allowing a quick glance at the benefits of the purchase.

The proposal also includes a description of the current situation in relation to the proposed solution, and a budget (which details costs). Some firms have even developed computer programs to automatically generate sales proposals in response to a set of questions the salesperson answers about a particular customer.[26] This is especially helpful because sometimes buyers use RFPs just to keep their current suppliers in check. In such a case, a seller might want to minimize the amount of time spent responding to an RFP. (A familiar saying in sales is "You can't cash an RFP.")

Presenting the Proposal

Prospects use proposals in many different ways. Proposals can be used to convince the home office that the local office needs the product, or proposals may be used to compare the product and terms of sale with those of competitors. As we mentioned earlier, the intended use will influence the design of the proposal; it will also influence how the salesperson presents the proposal.

When the proposal is going to be sent to the home office, it is wise to secure the support of the local decision maker. Although that person is not the ultimate decision maker, the decision may rest on how much effort that person puts into getting the proposal accepted. Buying centers often use proposals to compare competitive offerings, and the salesperson is asked to present the proposal to the buying committee.

Getting the buyer actively involved during the call is important.

Bill Bachman/e-Stock/PictureQuest

There are several options if you are going to give an oral presentation of your proposal. First, you can give the buyers a copy of the complete proposal before your presentation. During the meeting you would spend about 5 to 10 minutes summarizing the proposal and then ask for questions. Second, if you choose to give the written proposal to the buyers during the oral presentation, you may want to distribute the proposal a section at a time, to avoid having them read ahead instead of listening to your oral presentation.

VALUE ANALYSIS: QUANTIFYING THE SOLUTION

As mentioned in Chapter 4, one of the trends in buying is more sophisticated analyses by buyers. This section explores methods available to help the buyer conduct these types of analyses.

Salespeople can strengthen the presentation by showing the prospect that the cost of the proposal is offset by added value; this process is often called **quantifying the solution** or **value analysis.**[27] Some of the most common ways to quantify the solution are cost–benefit analysis, return on investment, payback period, net present value, and opportunity cost. For retail buyers, the seller usually must prove turnover and profit margins.

Quantifying the solution is more important in some situations than in others. Some products or services (like replacement parts or repairs) pose little risk for the prospect. These products are so necessary for the continuation of the prospect's business that little quantifying of the solution is usually needed. Other products pose moderate risk (such as expanding the production capacity of a plant for an existing successful product) or high risk (like programs designed to reduce costs or increase sales; these present higher risk because it is hard to calculate the exact magnitude of the potential savings or sales). For moderate- and high-risk situations, quantifying the solution becomes increasingly important. Finally, certain products pose super-high risk (brand-new products or services, which are riskier because no one can calculate costs or revenues with certainty). Attempts at quantifying the solution are imperative in super-high-risk situations. In summary, the higher the risk to the prospect, the more attention the salesperson should pay to quantifying the solution.

Cost–Benefit Analysis

Perhaps the simplest method of quantifying the solution is to list the costs to the buyer and the savings the buyer can expect from the investment, often called a **simple cost–benefit analysis.** For this analysis to be realistic and meaningful, information needed to calculate savings must be supplied by the buyer. Exhibit 10.8 shows how one salesperson used a chart to compare the costs and benefits of purchasing a two-way radio system.

In many situations the salesperson does a **comparative cost–benefit analysis** by comparing the present situation's costs with the value of the proposed solution, or the seller's product with a competitor's product. For example, a company with a premium-priced product may justify the higher price on the basis of offsetting costs in other areas. Or if productivity is enhanced, the increased productivity has economic value. Sales Technology 10.1 illustrates the use of a comparative cost–benefit analysis.

Return on Investment

The **return on investment (ROI)** is simply the net profits (or savings) expected from a given investment, expressed as a percentage of the investment:

$$\text{ROI} = \text{Net profits (or savings)} \div \text{Investment}$$

2·3 Questions on Exam

YOU WANT ME TO BUY A PRODUCT THAT COSTS 1,000 TIMES WHAT I'M CURRENTLY USING!?

I was selling to a company that required respiratory protection for some welding conditions. The minimum protection required by OSHA for most welding applications is a filtering face piece that cost as little as $1.50 per employee. As a salesperson with 3M in the Occupational Health and Environmental Safety Division, I was proposing a powered air system that cost about $1,500 per employee. Needless to say, price objections were huge.

I used a CD-ROM program that calculates the hidden costs of eye injuries and workers' compensation–related expenses. I explained to the safety director that by choosing a powered air respiratory system, which is significantly more expensive than the minimum required protection, the company would be able to increase overall productivity. I reasoned that because 3M's face shield would eliminate eye injuries, employees would not be interrupted with trips to a clinic or need eye-related breaks. The cost of sending a worker to a clinic because of an eye injury is large. Eye injuries also mean lost production time and increased insurance costs. An extra benefit would be the added comfort the respirator would provide the employees, allowing them to work at a longer, steadier pace than with an alternative system.

By using a computer program to quantify lost time and production from eye injuries into a dollar figure for the customer, I was able to encourage the customer to consider the larger picture. Through selection of a higher-quality product, savings could be realized from a system that not only met compliance standards but also cut down on workers' compensation costs.

Source: Virginia Wichern, used with permission.

Exhibit 10.8

Cost–Benefit Analysis for a Mobile Radio

	Years 1–5	Year 6+
Monthly Cost		
Monthly equipment payment (five-year lease/purchase)*		$1555.18
Monthly service agreement		339.00
Monthly broadcast fee		+ 533.60
Total monthly cost for entire fleet		$2427.78
Monthly Savings		
Cost savings (per truck) by eliminating backtracking, unnecessary trips (based on $.36/mile × 20 miles × 22 days/month)		$158.40
Labor cost savings (per driver) by eliminating wasted time in backtracking, etc. ($8.00/hour × 25 minutes/day × 22 days/month)		+ 73.33
Total cost savings per vehicle		231.73
Times number of vehicles		× 32
Total monthly cost savings for entire fleet		$7415.36
Monthly savings	$7415.36	$7415.36
Less: monthly cost	− 2427.78	− 872.85
Monthly benefit	4987.58	6542.51
Times months per year	× 12	× 12
Annual benefit	$59,850.96	$78,510.12

*Payment reflects ongoing cost of service agreement and broadcast fees.

Thus if a new product costs $4,000 but saves the firm $5,000, the ROI is 125 percent ($5,000 ÷ $4,000 = 1.25). Many firms set a minimum ROI for any new products, services, or cost-saving programs. Salespeople need to discover the firm's minimum ROI or ROI expectations and then show that the proposal's ROI meets or exceeds those requirements

Payback Period

The **payback period** is the length of time it takes for the investment cash outflow to be returned in the form of cash inflows or savings. To calculate the payback period, you simply add up estimated future cash inflows and divide into the investment cost. If expressed in years, the formula is

$$\text{Payback period} = \text{Investment} \div \text{Savings (or profits) per year}$$

Of course, the payback period could be expressed in days, weeks, months, or any other period.

As an example, suppose a new machine costs $865,000 but will save the firm $120,000 per year in labor costs. The payback period is 7.2 years ($865,000 ÷ $120,000 per year = 7.2 years).

Thus, for the buyer, the payback period indicates how quickly the investment money will come back to him or her and can be a good measure of personal risk. When a buyer makes a decision, his or her neck is "on the line," so to speak, until the investment money is at least recovered. Hence it's not surprising that buyers like to see short payback periods.

We have kept the discussion simple to help you understand the concept. In reality the calculation of the payback period would take into account many other factors, such as investment tax credits and depreciation.

Net Present Value

As you may have learned in finance courses, money left idle loses value over time (a dollar today is worth more than a dollar next week) because of inflation and the firm's cost of capital. Thus firms recalculate the value of future cash inflows into today's dollars (this process is called discounting the cash flows). One tool to assess the validity of an opportunity is to calculate the **net present value (NPV),** which is simply the net value today of future cash inflows (discounted back to their present value today at the firm's cost of capital) minus the investment. The actual method of calculating NPV is beyond the scope of this book, but many computer programs and calculators can calculate NPV quickly and easily.

$$\text{Net present value} = \text{Future cash inflows discounted into today's dollars} - \text{Investment}$$

As an example of the preceding formula, let's assume that a $50 million investment will provide annual cash inflows over the next five years of $15 million per year. The cash inflows are discounted (at the firm's cost of capital), and the result is that they are actually worth $59 million in today's dollars. The NPV is thus $9 million ($59 million – $50 million).

As with ROI and payback period, many firms set a minimum NPV. In no case should the NPV be less than $0. Again, we have kept this discussion quite simple to help you understand the basic concept.

Opportunity Cost

The **opportunity cost** is the return a buyer would have earned from a different use of the same investment capital. Thus a buyer could spend $100 million to buy any of the following: a new computer system, a new production machine, or a controlling interest in another firm.

For large capital outlays, the prospect usually needs to see the return on investment, payback period, and/or net present value.

Lester Lefkowitz/Corbis

Successful salespeople identify other realistic investment opportunities and then help the prospect compare the returns of the various options. These comparisons can be made by using any of the techniques we have already discussed (cost–benefit analysis, ROI, payback period, NPV). For example, a salesperson might help the buyer determine the following information about the options identified:

	NPV	Payback Period
Buying a new telecommunications system	$1.6 million	3.6 years
Upgrading the current telecommunications system	0.4 million	4.0 years

Salespeople should never forget that prospects have a multitude of ways to invest their money.

Selling Value to Resellers

When resellers purchase a product for resale, they are primarily concerned with whether their customers will buy the product and how much they will make on each sale. For example, when the salesperson for Nintendo meets with Wal-Mart to sell video games, he is armed with data showing how much profit is made every time Wal-Mart sells a game, and how fast the games sell. The Wal-Mart buyer uses this information to compare the performance of Nintendo video games with objectives and with other products sold in the same category, such as Microsoft's Xbox and Sony's PlayStation.

Profit Margin   Profit margin is the net profit the reseller makes, expressed as a percentage of sales. It is calculated, and thus influenced, by many factors. For example, if Linz Jewelers bought 100 rings for $1,000 each ($100,000), spent $45,000 in expenses (for advertising, salesperson commission, store rent, and other items) and sold them all at an average price of $3,000 ($300,000 in revenue), then the profit would be $155,000, with a profit margin of 52 percent ($155,000 ÷ $300,000 = .52).

Inventory Turnover   Inventory turnover is typically calculated by dividing the annual sales by the average retail price of the inventory on hand. Thus it measures how fast a product sells relative to how much inventory has to be carried—how efficiently a reseller manages its inventory. The reseller would like to have in the store only the amount needed for that day's sales because inventory represents an investment. Thus large retailers such as Cub Foods receive daily delivery of some products. If the reseller is able to reduce its inventory level, it can invest this savings in stores or warehouses or in the stock market.

For example, if Linz Jewelers usually kept eight rings in stock, inventory turnover would be calculated by dividing total sales in units (100 rings) by average inventory (8 rings). Thus inventory turnover would be 100/8 or 12.5 times. The answer represents the number of times that Linz sold the average inventory level. Another way to calculate this is to divide total sales ($300,000 in the Linz example) by the average price of inventory (eight units at $3,000 or $24,000). The answer is the same, 12.5 times.

A reseller does not necessarily want to increase inventory turnover by reducing the amount of inventory carried. Several negative consequences can result. For example, sales may fall because stockouts occur more frequently and products are not available when customers want to buy them. Expenses can increase because the reseller has to order more frequently. Finally, the cost of goods sold may increase because the reseller pays higher shipping charges and does not get as big a quantity discount.

Sellers provide resellers with information to prove that inventory turnover can be improved by buying from them. They describe their **efficient consumer response (ECR)**, **quick response (QR)**, **automatic replenishment (AR)**, and **just in time (JIT)** inventory management systems designed to reduce the reseller's average inventory and transportation expenses but still make sure that products are available when end users want them.

The September 11, 2001, tragedy created an outpouring of patriotic feelings among Americans. Within 24 hours there was a shortage of American flags, and there is only one major American flag manufacturer. The company had 80,000 flags in inventory on September 11. By the close of business September 12, both Target and Wal-Mart had completely sold out of flags—over 150,000 each. When the stores opened September 13, Wal-Mart had 80,000 more flags, whereas Target had none. How? Wal-Mart's QR system is updated every five minutes, whereas Target doesn't update its inventory system until the stores are closed in the evening. Wal-Mart had an order placed with expedited shipping before the stores closed and before Target knew it was out of flags! Similar situations occurred in other product categories, such as flashlights, batteries, battery-powered radios, bottled water, guns, ammunition, and other products that frightened Americans wanted.[28] As this example illustrates, EDI and ECR systems can give resellers significant competitive advantage.

Electronic data interchange (EDI) is a computer-to-computer transmission of data from a reseller, such as Wal-Mart, to vendors (such as American Flag Co.) and back. Resellers and vendors that have ECR or QR relationships use EDI to transmit purchase orders and shipping information.

Return on Space   A key investment that resellers make is in space—retail store space and warehouse space. A measure that retailers use to assess the return on their space investment is sales per square foot or sales per shelf foot. In a grocery store or a department store, shelf or display space is a finite asset that is used to capacity. Products therefore must be evaluated on how well they use the space allocated to them. For example, if a retailer generates $200 per square foot in sales with Tommy Hilfiger merchandise and only $150 selling Ralph Lauren merchandise, it will increase the space allocated to Tommy Hilfiger and reduce the space allocated to Ralph Lauren. Selling Scenario 10.1 describes how selling to the end user is different than selling to a reseller.

DEALING WITH THE JITTERS

Let's face it. For many people giving a presentation is a frightening experience. Even seasoned salespeople can get the jitters when the presentation is for a very important client or when the prospect has been rude in an earlier meeting. It all comes down to fear: the fear of being embarrassed or failing, the fear of exposing our lack of knowledge in some area, the fear of losing our train of thought. The reasons don't even have to be valid. If you have the jitters, you need to help resolve them.

CONSTRUCTION WORKERS NEED GREAT RADIOS

We were introducing a new DeWalt portable radio. This radio has some great benefits for people on the job site. The heavy-duty construction and roll bars protect it from damage if it is dropped or hit. And that can happen a lot on a job site. Plus, the radio can even be used to charge DeWalt power tools. When we talked to end users, the construction workers and supervisors on job sites, we told them about these and many other benefits. Needless to say, the new product drew a lot of attention.

But then we had to sell the radio to the reseller, in my case to 13 Lowe's home improvement centers in North Carolina and eastern Tennessee. Our presentation was very different than that for the end users. We wanted to convince store managers to feature the radio on an end-aisle display during the Christmas season, which is a very coveted slot. We had to show them how the new radio was going to benefit them, how it was going to increase the inventory turns and profits of their store. Lots of other companies were trying to get their products featured on the end of aisles. So we had to demonstrate how the new radio was going to have a faster sell-through and a higher margin than our competitors' products. By proving superior turnover and profit margins, we were able to prove return on space and secure the coveted spaces we requested. Then our only remaining job was to help the sales associates build the display and keep it stocked—a nice problem to have!

Source: Stan Banks, used with permission.

Here are some tips from the experts on how to reduce presentation jitters:[29]

- Know your audience well.
- Know what you're talking about. Keep up to date.
- Prepare professional, helpful visuals. These not only help your audience understand the presentation, but also can help you remember some important points.
- Be yourself. Don't try to present like someone else.
- Get a good night's sleep.
- For presentations to groups, feed off the energy and enthusiasm of several friendly, happy-looking people in your audience. (Note: That's what professors often do!)
- Recognize the effect of fear on your body and reduce the accompanying stress manifestations by stretching, taking deep breaths to relax breathing, and so on.
- Visualize your audience as your friends—people who are interested and eager to hear what you have to say.
- Psych yourself up for the presentation. Think of the successes you have had in your life (previous presentations that went well or other things you have done well).
- Realize that everyone gets nervous before a presentation at times. It is natural. In fact, it can help you keep from being cocky.
- **Practice, practice, practice!** And finally, practice.

SUMMARY

Strengthening communication with the buyer is important. It helps focus the buyer's attention, improves the buyer's understanding, helps the buyer remember what was said, and can create a sense of value.

Many methods of strengthening communication are available. These include such items as word pictures, stories, humor, charts, models, samples, gifts, catalogs, brochures, photos, ads, maps, illustrations, testimonials, and test results. Media available include portfolios, video, computers, and visual projectors.

A backbone of many sales presentations is the product demonstration. It allows the buyer to get hands-on experience with the product, something most other communication methods do not offer. Handouts and written proposals can also strengthen presentations.

It is often important to quantify the solution so the buyer can evaluate the costs in relation to the benefits he or she can derive from the proposal. Some of the more common methods of quantifying the solution include simple cost–benefit analysis, comparative cost–benefit analysis, return on investment, payback period, net present value, and calculation of opportunity cost, turnover, and profit margins.

All communication tools require skill and practice to be used effectively. Outstanding salespeople follow a number of guidelines to improve their use of visuals, demonstrate their products more effectively, and reduce their nervousness.

KEY TERMS

automatic replenishment (AR)
collateral
comparative cost–benefit analysis
digital collateral management
document cameras
efficient consumer response (ECR)
electronic data interchange (EDI)
electronic whiteboard
executive briefing center
executive summary
handouts
inventory turnover
just in time (JIT)
multiple-sense appeals

net present value (NPV)
opportunity cost
payback period
portfolio
profit margin
quantifying the solution
quick response (QR)
request for proposal (RFP)
return on investment (ROI)
simple cost–benefit analysis
testimonials
value analysis
visual presenters

ETHICS PROBLEMS

1. Men tend to respond more to jokes involving sexual innuendo than women do. Assume this statement is true for a male buyer you are going to call on next Tuesday. You learn that he loves jokes with a sexual bent. Is there any reason you should avoid using a joke with a sexual theme when calling on him?

2. Is encouraging buyers to order a large quantity so they can get a better quantity discount always a good idea? Why or why not?

QUESTIONS AND PROBLEMS

1. Assume you sell laser printers. How would your presentation differ when selling to a business supply store like Office Depot versus selling to an industrial distributor?

2. Assume you plan a demonstration to prove some of the claims you have made for a new luxury automobile model. How would the demonstration be different for each of these three individuals: a person who was very concerned about the environment, an economy-minded person, and a performance-minded person?

3. How could you demonstrate the following products?
   a. A whisper-quiet ceiling fan to a do-it-yourselfer.
   b. The strength of drawers in a new chest of drawers to a furniture retailer.
   c. A highly corrosion-resistant paint for bridges and overpasses to a group of civil engineers.

4. Which communication tools would you use to provide solid proof for the following concerns expressed by prospects?
   a. I don't believe it will sell.
   b. I could never learn how to use that product feature.
   c. Your competitor has a much more modern, state-of-the-art plant than you do.
   d. You look too old to know what the young customers who shop in my store are looking for.

5. This chapter generally described humor as a positive, useful tool for salespeople. When should humor not be used? Are there any times when humor could actually be detrimental to communication effectiveness? Explain.

6. Which communication tools would you use to communicate the following facts?
   a. We have been in business for over 25 years.
   b. As a salesperson, I have been certified by the state to sell this product.
   c. Even though I've been selling this product for only two months, I do possess the necessary product knowledge.
   d. I know our last product was a flop, but this product was developed with extensive test marketing.
   e. Unlike our competitors, my company has never been sued by a customer.

7. Assume that you are selling a new video security system to a manufacturing plant in your town. The system will cost $175,000. It is estimated that the new system will reduce theft and pilferage. You expect losses due to theft to drop by $19,500 each year over the next 10 years. At the manufacturing plant's cost of capital, the discounted cash inflows have a value today of $250,000. Use this information to calculate the following:
   a. Return on investment.
   b. Payback period.
   c. Net present value.

8. Are there products for which resellers wouldn't really be that concerned about turnover?

9. Are there any retail situations for which return on space is not a big deal? How about situations where return on space would be extremely important?

CASE PROBLEMS

case **10.1**

FishyLease

FishyLease is a five-year-old firm that specializes in leasing custom aquarium installations in restaurants, medical offices, homes, and industrial spaces. The firm designs, produces, and installs its unique aquariums to meet the customer's specific needs. They also stock the aquarium with fish and completely service it. Leases start at 12 months, but can run as long as 60 months.

Customers can choose from over 120 exotic fish and aquatic animals for their aquariums. Customers never have to worry about feeding, removing dead animals, cleaning the tank, adding chemicals, or the like. All of that is taken care of by FishyLease.

Aquariums have been designed and built by FishyLease to fit almost every imaginable configuration and need. Some of their most common types of designs include round cylindrical columns, corner units, more traditional-looking table-top aquariums, and a new wave tank, which includes wave-type motion.

Medical offices have often commented on how the aquariums reduce stress for their patients, and even for their staff. Restaurants like the tranquil setting provided by the aquariums. Upscale homeowners rave about the ambiance provided, as well as the ability of aquariums to help relax social gatherings.

Questions

1. Describe how you would use the communication tools described in this chapter to sell a one-year aquarium lease to a hospital or medical office in your area. Make any assumptions necessary.

2. Develop a short (five-minute) slide show that you can use to introduce aquarium leasing to potential buyers at a local trade show for businesses.

case **10.2**

You Think You've
Had a Rough Day?

Here is a list of things that have actually happened to salespeople while they were presenting to a customer.

1. The power goes off in the middle of a computer demonstration, and you lose all of the data you have been inputting for the last eight minutes.

2. The buyer says, "Look, I don't want to see a bunch of pictures and charts! Just tell me how you'll save me money."

3. You involve the prospect by having her help you calculate the savings she will enjoy with your machine. While putting the last number in the calculator, she apparently hits the wrong key. As a result, she calculates the time needed to recoup her investment as 258 years instead of the actual 14 years.

4. You hand the prospect a page from your price book. He takes it, looks at it, opens his desk drawer, and tosses it in. Because your industry has severe price competition, your company's policy forbids you to leave your price sheet with anyone.

5. You are showing your buyer some items in the portfolio, and you accidentally knock it off the desk. The rings open up, and the pages scatter all over the floor.

6. You offer the prospect a sample of your new food product. He tastes it, makes a face, and says, "That's really pretty awful tasting!"

7. You are in the middle of using a computer to demonstrate returns on investment at various pricing points. Suddenly you forget how to call up the next screen. No matter how hard you try, you just can't remember what to do next!

8. You are in the middle of painting a word picture when the buyer is interrupted by a phone call. The call lasts about five minutes. The buyer turns back to you and says, "Now, where were we?"

9. When the salesperson offers his or her hand for a handshake, the prospect doesn't offer his hand in return.
10. As the seller is having a seat, the prospect informs the seller that some catastrophe has just occurred in his or her life. "My child was just hurt at school on the playground"; "My wife just learned she has a possible cancerous growth on her neck"; "I just found out that they are going to be laying off another 400 workers at this plant. I wonder how that is going to impact me!")
11. The prospect asks the seller to have a seat, but then remains standing.
12. The phone rings on the prospect's desk. The prospect picks it up and starts carrying on a spirited conversation.
13. The buyer starts to nod or goes to sleep.

Questions

For each of the situations listed above, answer the following questions.

1. How would you respond?
2. What could the seller have done to prevent getting into this situation?

ROLE PLAY

Today you will present to the same person whose needs you identified in Chapter 9. (If you have not done role plays before, you will need to review the information about the various role play customers that can be found at the end of Chapter 4. If you did not do the role play at the end of Chapter 9, choose one of the three companies to sell to.) If you sold to Skylight, you'll do so again; same with Binswanger and Lincoln. Begin by summarizing the needs with the buyer and gaining agreement that these are all of the needs. Then make your presentation.

As a buyer, do not offer any objections today. Just listen, add your thoughts on how the product might help if asked, and agree. Ask questions if something seems vague or confusing. Further, ask for proof. For example, if the salesperson says everyone loves it, ask to see a testimonial letter or something of that sort.

When you are the odd person out and observing, look for the following:

- Did the seller tie the features to the buyer's needs? Or did the seller present features that were not needed?
- Did the seller try to gain agreement that the buyer recognized and valued the benefit?
- Did the seller use visual aids as proof sources effectively?
- Did the seller use specific language versus general or ambiguous language (for example, it's the best!)?

Note: For background information on these role plays, please see page 27.

To the instructor: Additional information needed to complete the role play is available in the Instructor's Manual.

ADDITIONAL REFERENCES

Bonner, Joseph M., and Roger J. Calantone. "Buyer Attentiveness in Buyer–Supplier Relationships." *Industrial Marketing Management* 34 (January 2005), pp. 53–61.

Chronister, Tom. "Technology Should Not Keep Audiences in the Dark." *Presentations,* May 2002, p. 62.

Cohan, Peter E. "Great Demo!" *How to Create and Execute Stunning Software Demonstrations.* Lincoln, NE: iUniverse, Incorporated, 2003.

Cooper, Brad. "Audience Research Should Take Temperament into Account." *Presentations,* April 2003, p. 54.

Daley, Kevin. "Meeting the Challenges of Group Presenting." *Presentations,* November 2003, p. 66.

Endicott, Jim. "True Creativity Involves More Than Just Pretty Slides." *Presentations,* September 2002, pp. 20–21.

Flint, Daniel J.; Robert B. Woodruff; and Sarah Fisher Gardial. "Exploring the Phenomenon of Customers' Desired Value Change in a Business-to-Business Context." *Journal of Marketing* 66 (October 2002), pp. 102–17.

Gilyard, Burl. "Speaking Volumes." *Presentations,* March 2002, pp. 38–43.

Gonul, Fusun; Franklin Carter; Elina Petrova; and Kannan Srinivason. "Promotion of Prescription Drugs and Its Impact on Physicians' Choice Behavior." *Journal of Marketing* 65 (July 2001), pp. 79–90.

Hill, Julie. "The Attention Deficit." *Presentations,* October 2003, pp. 27–32.

Jaffa, Elliott B. "Powerful Presentations Require a Challenge to Your Comfort Level." *Presentations,* April 2004, p. 50.

Hill, Julie. "The Big Cheese." *Presentations,* May 2002, pp. 29–34.

Jeary, Tony. *Life Is a Series of Presentations.* New York: Simon & Schuster, 2004.

Leech, Thomas. *How to Prepare, Stage, and Deliver Winning Presentations.* New York: AMACOM, 2004.

McGrath, Vicki. "The Eternal Quest to Engage and Involve Your Audience." *Presentations,* September 2002, p. 58.

Mitchell, Sean K. "To Build a Relationship with the Audience, You Need to Get Personal." *Presentations,* March 2003, p. 54.

Morgan, Nick. *Working the Room: How to Move People to Action through Audience-Centered Speaking.* Boston: Harvard Business School Press, 2003.

Nick, Michael J.; Kurt M. Koenig; and Michael Nick. *ROI Selling: Increasing Revenue, Profit, and Customer Loyalty through the 360 Degree Sales Cycle.* New York: Kaplan Professional Company, 2004.

Pierce, Heather. *Persuasive Proposals and Presentations: 24 Lessons for Writing Winners.* New York: McGraw-Hill, 2004.

Porter-Roth, Bud. *Writing Killer Sales Proposals: Win the Bid and Close the Deal.* Irvine, CA: Entrepreneur Press, 2004.

Presentations magazine. Much information is available at its Web site: www.presentations.com.

Pugh, David G. G., and Terry R. Bacon. *Powerful Proposals: How to Give Your Business the Winning Edge.* New York: AMACOM, 2004.

Regenold, Stephen. "The Psychology of Crowds." *Presentations,* August 2004, pp. 21–26.

Robertson, Kelley. "Creating a Powerful Sales Presentation." *Sell!ng,* October 2004, pp. 1–2.

Sawers, Neil. *How to Write Proposals, Sales Letters, and Reports.* Edmonton, AB: The NS Group, 2004.

Simons, Tad. "Presentation Mastery." *Presentations,* June 2004, pp. 28–34.

Stack, Laura. "10 Time-Management Tips to Aid Presenters." *Presentations,* November 2004, p. 50.

Zielinski, Dave. "Oh, No! Not Audience Participation!" *Presentations,* August 2003. pp. 26–32.

Zielinski, Dave. "The Presenter's Pledge." *Presentations,* August 2002, pp. 22–32.

RESPONDING TO OBJECTIONS

chapter **11**

part **3**

SOME QUESTIONS ANSWERED IN THIS CHAPTER . . .

- How should salespeople sell value and build relationships when responding to objections?

- When do buyers object?

- What objections can be expected?

- Which methods are effective when responding to objections?

- How do you deal with tough customers?

PROFILE

I graduated in May 2003 with a degree in business administration from Flagler College in St. Augustine, Florida. My track was sales and marketing, and I took the personal selling course from Dr. Louis Preysz III. During my time at Flagler College, I was very involved with the Society for Advancement of Management, the oldest management society in the world, where I competed during my junior and senior years in the business case competition with several other team members. During this time I learned to come up with objections before the presentation in order to get a jump on the competition. Our teams were awarded back-to-back national championships, and a big part was due to the objection preparation.

Upon graduating, I accepted a position in sales with Jaffe Insurance Concepts in Boca Raton, Florida. The company specializes in long-term care, life insurance, Medicare supplements, and annuities. On my first day my mentor explained to me the importance of objections, especially in the insurance business. My mentor said, "If the buyer does not have any objections, he or she does not have an understanding of the product and will not become a client." That taught me the importance of having a positive attitude about objections.

I had to learn not only to handle the objections in my new job, but also how to bring objections out of the buyer. My mentor promised me that learning this would mean higher sales The first step is to foresee the objections before the sale so during the presentation you can focus on listening and not worry about the answers to the objections.

Once my training had progressed and I had met with several clients, I realized that price was a common objection with most of my prospects. This was true especially for my older clients who are on fixed incomes. As a result, I not only have to discuss the price of our products, but also how certain products are better for certain people. There is a substantial amount of competition in the insurance industry, and it is important for me to set myself apart through client knowledge and service.

As an example of how I handle the price objection, one of my clients was a 52-year-old woman who was single and was interested in making arrangements for long-term care (like assisted living homes and nursing homes). After I finished preparing for the presentation, I met with the woman to discuss the product. Soon after the conversation began I realized that the woman was actually a little unsure of the need for long-term care. Her concern was the cost compared to the benefit: "How do I justify $1,500 per year when I live on a limited single income?" she asked.

I responded, "Most of my clients have similar concerns when we first sit down, but do you realize that one in two Americans will need some form of long-term care in their lifetime?" I then explained that the annual cost of long-term care is approximately $60,000 depending on where you live, and this policy would pay her $250 per day or $91,250 per year. I also explained to her that because of her limited income, if she wanted to protect her standard of living and would like to stay in her home, if and when she needed care, this policy would be crucial in helping her to insure that. Even if the policy was not used for 30 years, she would have invested a total of $45,000, which is still $15,000 less than one year of care. By helpfully responding to this objection I gained her trust. She became one of my best clients.

"I had to learn not only to handle the objections in my new job, but also how to bring objections out of the buyer."

Peter Troup, Jaffe Insurance Concepts

THE GOAL IS TO BUILD RELATIONSHIPS AND SELL VALUE

An **objection** is a concern or a question raised by the buyer. Salespeople should do everything they can to encourage buyers to voice concerns or questions. The worst type of objection is the one the buyer refuses to disclose because a hidden objection cannot be dealt with. Many sales have been lost because salespeople didn't find out the objections or didn't helpfully respond to them.

Salespeople should keep in mind that the goal with regard to objections is the same as with every other part of the sales call: to sell real value to the buyer and to build the kind of relationship that the buyer desires (see Chapter 2). Having a positive attitude about objections is paramount in this regard. Proper attitude is shown by answering sincerely, refraining from arguing or contradicting, and welcoming—even inviting—objections. Objections should be expected and never taken personally.

Simply pretending to be empathetic is useless; buyers can easily see through such pretense. Also, once the buyer gets the idea that the salesperson is talking for effect, regaining that buyer's confidence and respect will be almost impossible. Empathy shows as much in the tone of voice and facial expressions as in the actual words spoken.

The greatest evidence of sincerity, however, comes from the salesperson's actions. One successful advertising agency owner states, "I have always tried to sit on the same side of the table as my clients, to see problems through their eyes." Buyers want valid objections to be treated seriously; they want their ideas to be respected, not belittled. They look for empathetic understanding of their problems. Real objections are logical to the prospect regardless of how irrational they may appear to the salesperson. Salespeople must assume the attitude of helper, counselor, and adviser and act accordingly. To do so, they must treat the prospect as a friend, not a foe. In fact, buyers will feel more comfortable about raising objections and will be much more honest the more they trust the salesperson, the better the rapport, and the stronger the partnering relationship.

The temptation to prove the prospect wrong, to say "I told you so" or "I'm right and you're wrong," is always strong. This kind of attitude invites debate, encouraging—perhaps even forcing—the prospect to defend a position regardless of its merits. Egos get involved when prospects find their positions bluntly challenged. Most will try to defend their own opinions under these circumstances because they do not want to lose face. The sales presentation may then degenerate into a personal duel that the salesperson cannot possibly win. Arguing with, contradicting, and showing belligerence toward a prospect are negative, unwise actions and won't build relationships.

The reality is that salespeople run into more rejection in a day than most people have to absorb in weeks or months. Because of the emotional strain, many see selling as a tough way to make a living. However, salespeople must remember that objections present sales opportunities. People who object have at least some level of interest in what the salesperson is saying. Further, objections provide feedback about what is really on the prospect's mind. Only when this openness exists can a true partnering relationship form. To capitalize on these opportunities, salespeople must show that they welcome any and all objections. Salespeople have to make the prospect believe they are sincerely glad the objection has been raised. This attitude shows in remarks such as the following:

I can see just what you mean. I'd probably feel the same way.

I'm glad you mentioned that, Mr. Atkinson.

That certainly is a wise comment, Ms. Smith, and I can see your problem.

If I were purchasing this product, I'd want an answer to that same question.

Tell me about it.

Maintaining a positive attitude toward objections will go a long way toward building goodwill.

WHEN DO BUYERS RAISE OBJECTIONS?

Salespeople can expect to hear objections at any time during the buyer–seller relationship (see Chapter 4 for a review of the buying process). Objections are raised when the salesperson attempts to secure an appointment, during the approach, during the presentation, when the salesperson attempts to obtain commitment, and during the after-sale follow-up. Objections can also be made during formal negotiation sessions (see Chapter 13).

SETTING UP AN INITIAL APPOINTMENT

Prospects may object to setting the appointment times or dates that salespeople request to introduce the product. This type of objection happens especially when products, services, or concepts are unfamiliar to the buyer. For example, a commercial benefits salesperson for Coast Dental might hear the buyer make the following statement when asked to meet and learn more about a cafeteria-style benefits package: No, I don't need to see you. I've not heard many good things about the use of cafeteria-style packages for dental products. Most employees just get confused! The same types of objections can also occur during the approach.

THE PRESENTATION

Buyers can offer objections during the beginning of the presentation (see Chapter 9). They may not like or believe the salesperson's attention-getting opening statement. They may not wish to engage in small talk or may not agree with statements made by the seller attempting to build rapport. Buyers may object to the salesperson's stated goals for the meeting.

Objections often come up to points made in the presentation. For example, a computer disaster recovery salesperson for Rackspace Managed Hosting might hear this objection: We've never lost a lot of computer data files before! Why should I pay so much money for a service I may never use?

Such objections usually show the prospect's interest; thus they can actually be desirable. Compared to a prospect who just says, No thanks, and never raises his or her concerns, selling is easier when buyers voice their concerns because the salesperson knows where the buyers stand and that they are paying attention.

Buyers sometimes let the salesperson deliver the entire presentation without showing any reaction. Judging the effectiveness of the presentation is difficult in such circumstances.

ATTEMPTING TO OBTAIN COMMITMENT

Objections may be voiced when the salesperson attempts to obtain commitment. For example, an AK Steel salesperson who has just asked the buyer's permission to talk to the buyer's chief engineer may hear this objection: No, I don't want you talking to our engineers. My job is to keep vendors from bugging our employees.

Skill in uncovering and responding to objections is very important at this stage of the sales call. Also, knowing the objections that are likely to occur helps the salesperson prepare supporting documentation (letters of reference, copies of studies, and so on).

Salespeople who hear many objections at this point in the sales call probably need to further develop their skills. An excessive number of objections may indicate a poor job at needs identification and the omission of significant selling points in the presentation. It may also reveal ineffective probing during the presentation to see whether the buyer understands or has any questions about what is being discussed.

AFTER THE SALE

Even buyers who have agreed to purchase the product or service can still raise objections. During the installation, for example, the buyer may raise concerns about the time it is taking to install the equipment, the quality of the product or service, the customer service department's lack of friendliness, or the credit department's refusal to grant the terms the salesperson promised. To develop long-term relationships and partnerships with buyers, salespeople must carefully respond to these objections. After-sale service is more fully discussed in Chapter 14.

COMMON OBJECTIONS

Prospects raise many types of objections. Although listing every objection is impossible, this section attempts to outline the most common buyer objections.

It should be noted that some buyers like to raise objections just to watch salespeople squirm uncomfortably. (Fortunately, most buyers aren't like that!) Seasoned buyers, especially, sometimes like to make life difficult for sellers, particularly for young, nervous sellers. For example, Peggy, a manufacturer's salesperson for Walker Muffler, used to call on a large auto parts store in an attempt to have the store carry her line of mufflers. Jackie, the store's buyer, gave Peggy a tough time on her first two calls. At the end of her second call, Peggy was so frustrated with the way she was being treated that she decided never to call there again. However, as she was walking out of the store, she ran into a Goodyear rep who also called on Jackie to sell belts and hoses. Because the two salespeople were on somewhat friendly terms, Peggy admitted her frustrations to the Goodyear rep. He replied, "Oh, that's just the way Jackie operates. On the third call he is always a nice guy. Just wait and see." Sure enough, Peggy's next call on Jackie was not only pleasant but also productive! Buyers like Jackie usually just want to see the sales rep work hard for the order.

The following sections examine the five major types of objections (objections related to needs, product, source, price, and time), which are summarized in Exhibit 11.1, as well as several other objections that salespeople sometimes hear.

OBJECTIONS RELATED TO NEEDS

I Do Not Need the Product or Service

A prospect may validly state that the company has no need for what the salesperson is selling. A manufacturer that operates on a small scale, for example, may have no use for expensive machinery designed to handle large volumes of work. Similarly, a salesperson who is selling an accounts receivable collection service will find that a retailer that sells for cash does not require a collection service.

Salespeople may encounter objections such as "My business is different" or "I have no use for your service." These objections,

Exhibit 11.1
Five Major Types of Objections

Objections Related to Needs

I do not need the product or service.
I've never done it that way before.

Objections Related to the Product

I don't like the product or service features.
I don't understand.
I need more information.

Objections Related to the Source

I don't like your company.
I don't like you.

Objections Related to the Price

I have no money.
The value does not exceed the cost.

Objections Related to Time

I'm just not interested today.
I need time to think about it.

when made by an accurately qualified buyer, show that the buyer is not convinced that a need exists. This problem could have been prevented with better implication and need payoff questions (see Chapter 9).

If the salesperson cannot establish a need in the buyer's mind, that buyer can logically be expected to object. In **pioneer selling**—selling a new and different product, service, or idea—the salesperson has more difficulty establishing a need in the buyer's mind. For example, salespeople for Citrigel often hear "I don't think we need it" when the buyer is asked to carry a line of biodegradable citrus degreasers.

I've Never Done It That Way Before

Most human beings are creatures of habit. Once they develop a routine or establish a custom, they tend to resist change. Fear or ignorance may be the basis for not wanting to try anything new or different. The buyer's natural tendency to resist buying a new product or changing from a satisfactory brand to a new one can be found behind many objections.

Habits and customs also help to insulate the prospect from certain risks to some degree. For example, suppose you are selling a new line of marine engines to Newton, a newly promoted assistant buyer. If Jane, the previous assistant buyer and now the senior buyer, bought your competitor's product, Newton would appear to take less risk by continuing to buy from your competitor. If Newton buys from you, Jane may think, I've been doing business with the other firm for 15 years. Now, Newton, you come in here and tell me I've been doing it wrong all these years? I'm not sure you're going to be a good assistant buyer.

OBJECTIONS RELATED TO THE PRODUCT

I Don't Like the Product or Service Features

Often the product or service has features that do not satisfy the buyer. At other times the prospect will request features currently not available. Customers may say things like these: It doesn't taste good to me! I was looking for a lighter shade of red, or It took a month for us to receive our last order.

I Don't Understand

Sometimes objections arise because customers do not understand the salesperson's presentation. Because these objections may never be verbalized, the seller must carefully observe the buyer's nonverbal cues. (See Chapter 5 for a discussion of nonverbal communication.) Misunderstandings frequently occur with customers who are unfamiliar with technical terms, unaware of the unique capabilities of a product, or uncertain about benefits arising from services provided with the product, such as warranties. Unfortunately, buyers often will not admit that they do not understand something.

For example, when desktop publishing programs were introduced for personal computers, a salesperson for an IBM distributor gave a presentation to a very busy plant manager of a consumer products firm. The new software would allow the manager to create and produce the plant's monthly newsletter to plant employees in-house, instead of sending the work out to be typeset and printed. The manager, however,

This buyer doesn't understand what the seller is saying.

LWA-Dann Tardif/Zefa/Corbis

did not understand the new product's concept. He thought that the software would create the newsletter but that the firm would still have to send the work out to be typeset and printed. However, he did not want to appear ignorant and simply told the salesperson that he was not interested. The rep never knew that the manager simply had not understood the product until later, when the manager bought a competitor's desktop publishing program.

I Need More Information

Some buyers offer objections in an attempt to get more information. They may have already decided that they want the product or service but wish to fortify themselves with logical reasons they can use to justify the purchase to others. Also, the salesperson may not have provided enough credible proof about a particular benefit.

Conflict may also exist in the buyer's mind. One conflict could be a struggle taking place between the dictates of emotion and reason. Or the buyer may be concerned about the risk, and the seller hasn't sufficiently sold value. The buyer may be trying to decide between two competitive products or between buying and not buying. Whatever the struggle, buyers who object to get more information are usually interested, and the possibility of obtaining commitment is good.

OBJECTIONS RELATED TO THE SOURCE

I Don't Like Your Company

Most buyers, especially industrial buyers, are interested in the sales representative's company because the buyer is put at risk if the seller's firm is not financially sound, cannot continually produce the product, and so forth. These buyers need to be satisfied with the selling company's financial standing, personnel, and business policies. Buyers may ask questions such as these: How do I know that you'll be in business next year? Your company isn't very well known, is it? Why does your company have a bad image in the industry?

Of course, buyers who don't want to be rude may not actually voice these concerns. But unvoiced questions about the sales rep's company may affect their decisions and the long-term partnerships the sales rep is trying to establish.

I Don't Like You

Sometimes a salesperson's personality clashes with a prospect's. Effective salespeople know that they must do everything possible to adjust their manner to please the prospect. At times, however, doing business with some people appears impossible.

Prospects may object to a presentation or an appointment because they have taken a dislike to the salesperson or because they feel they cannot trust the salesperson. Candid prospects may say, "You seem too young to be selling these. You've never worked in my industry, so how can you be trained to know what I need?" More commonly, the prospect shields the real reason and says, "We don't need any."

In some situations, the buyer may honestly have difficulty dealing with a particular salesperson. If the concern is real (not just an excuse), the seller's firm sometimes institutes a **turnover** (**TO**), which simply means the account is given to a different salesperson. Unfortunately, TOs occasionally occur because the buyer has gender, racial, or other prejudices or because the salesperson is failing to practice adaptive selling behaviors.

thinking **it** through

Assume that you have worked as a salesperson for an industrial chemical firm for six months. You have attended a two-week basic selling skills course but have not yet attended any product knowledge training classes. You are making a sales call with your sales manager. The buyer says, "Gee, you look too young to be selling chemicals. Do you have a chemistry degree?" Before you get a chance to respond, your manager says, "Oh, he [meaning you] has already completed our one-month intensive product knowledge course. I guarantee he knows it all!" What would you say or do? What would you do if the buyer later asked you a technical question?

OBJECTIONS RELATED TO THE PRICE

I Have No Money

Companies that lack the resources to buy the product may have been classified as prospects. As indicated in Chapter 7, the ability to pay is an important factor in lead qualification. An incomplete or poor job of qualifying may cause this objection to arise.

When leads say they cannot afford a product, they may have a valid objection. If so, the salesperson should not waste time; new prospects should be contacted.

The Value Does Not Exceed the Cost

Most buyers must sacrifice something (called *opportunity costs*—see Chapter 10) to buy a product. The money spent for the product is not available for other things. When we buy as individuals, the choice may be between the down payment on a new car and a vacation trip; for businesses, it may be between expanding the plant and distributing a dividend to stockholders.

Buyers usually object until they are sure that the value of the product or service being acquired more than offsets the sacrifice. Exhibit 11.2 illustrates this concept. The question of value received often underlies customers' objections.

Exhibit 11.2

Value: The Relationship between Costs and Benefits

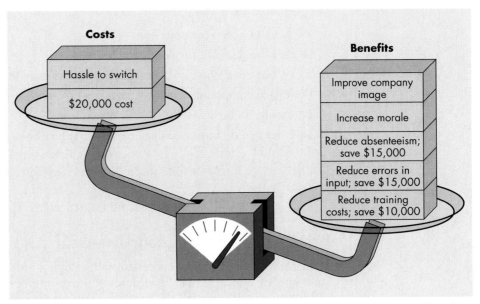

Note: If costs outweigh benefits, the decision will be not to buy. If benefits outweigh costs, the decision will be to buy.

Whatever the price of a product or service, somebody will object that it is too high or out of line with the competition. Here are some other common price objections: I can beat your price on these items. We can't make a reasonable profit if we have to pay that much for the merchandise. I'm going to wait for prices to come down.

Although objections about price occur more often than any other kind of objection, they may be just masks to hide the real reason for the buyer's reluctance. (A more complete discussion of dealing with price objections appears later in this chapter.) Implicit in many price objections is the notion of product or service quality. Thus the buyer who states that your price is too high may actually be thinking, The quality is too low for such a high price.

OBJECTIONS RELATED TO TIME

I'm Just Not Interested Today

Some prospects voice objections simply to dismiss the salesperson. The prospect may not have enough time to devote to the interview, may not be interested in the particular product or service, may not be in the mood to listen, or may have decided because of some unhappy experiences not to face further unpleasant interviews.

These objections occur when salespeople are cold calling (see Chapter 7) or try to make an appointment. Particularly aggressive, rude, impolite, or pesky salespeople can expect prospects to use numerous excuses to keep from listening to a presentation.

I Need Time to Think about It

Buyers often object to making a decision "now." Many, in fact, believe that postponing an action is an effective way to say no. Salespeople can expect to hear objections such as the following, especially from analyticals and amiables (see Chapter 6): I haven't made up my mind. I'd like to talk it over with my partner. Just leave me your literature; I'll study it and then let you know what we decide.

OTHER OBJECTIONS

Listing every possible objection that could occur under any situation would be impossible. However, following are a number of additional objections that salespeople often hear:

We have no room for your line.

There is no demand for your product.

Sorry, but I just don't do business with blacks or women.

I've heard complaints from my friends who use your product.

I prefer to do business with Arab-owned firms.

Sure, we can do business. But I need a little kickback to make it worth my time and trouble.

I believe we might be able to do business if you are willing to start seeing me socially.[1]

It's a lot of hassle in paperwork and time to switch suppliers.

BEHAVIORS OF SUCCESSFUL SALESPEOPLE

With regard to objections, successful salespeople anticipate objections and forestall known concerns, listen without interrupting, evaluate objections before answering, and always tell the truth (see Exhibit 11.3). Responding to objections in a helpful manner requires careful thought and preparation.

They anticipate objections and prepare helpful responses.

They address known problems before the prospect does; that is, they forestall known concerns.

They relax and listen and never interrupt the buyer.

They make sure that the objection is not just an excuse.

They always tell the truth.

ANTICIPATE OBJECTIONS

Salespeople must know that at some time, objections will be made to almost everything concerning their products, their companies, or themselves. Common sense dictates that they prepare helpful, honest answers to objections that are certain to be raised (probably 80 percent or more can be anticipated) because few salespeople can answer objections effectively on the spur of the moment.

Many companies draw up lists of common objections and helpful answers and encourage salespeople to become familiar with these lists. Some firms also videotape practice role plays to help salespeople become more proficient in anticipating objections and responding effectively in each situation. Successful sales representatives may keep a notebook and record new objections they encounter.

FORESTALL KNOWN CONCERNS

Good salespeople, after a period of experience and training, know that certain features of their products or services are vulnerable, are likely to be misunderstood, or are materially different from competitors' products. The salesperson may have products with limited features, may have to quote a price that seems high, may be unable to offer cash discounts, may have no service representatives in the immediate area, or may represent a new company in the field.

In these situations, salespeople often forestall the objection. To **forestall** is to prevent by doing something ahead of time. In selling, this means salespeople raise objections before buyers have a chance to raise them. For example, one salesperson forestalled a concern about the different "feel" of a split computer keyboard (the ones that are split down the middle to relieve stress and strain on the hands and wrists):

> I know you'll find the feel to be different from your old keyboard. You're going to like that, though, because your hands won't get as tired. In almost every split keyboard I've sold, typists have taken only one day to get accustomed to the new feel, and then they swear that they would never go back to their old-fashioned keyboards again!

A salesperson might bring up a potential price problem by saying, "You know, other buyers have been concerned that this product is expensive. Well, let me show you how little it will really cost you to get the best."

Some salespeople do such a good job of forestalling that buyers change their minds without ever going on record as objecting to the feature and then having to reverse themselves.[2] Buyers are more willing to change their thinking when they do not feel constrained to defend a position they have already stated. Although not all objections can be preempted, the major ones can be spotted and forestalled during the presentation. Selling Scenario 11.1 provides an example of forestalling.

Forestalling can be even more important in written proposals (see Chapter 10) because immediate feedback between buyer and seller is not possible. Such forestalled objections can be addressed throughout the proposal. For example, on the page describing delivery terms, the seller could insert a paragraph that begins this way: "You may be wondering how we can promise an eight-day delivery even though we have such a small production capacity. Actually, we are able to . . . because . . ." Another option for forestalling objections in written proposals is to have a separate page or section titled something like "Concerns You May Have with This Proposal." The section could then list the potential concerns and provide responses to them.

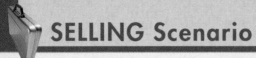

FORESTALL OBJECTIONS THAT YOU KNOW ARE GOING TO COME UP

I work at Swisher International, the company that makes the world-famous Swisher Sweet Cigars. Many, including my prospects, don't know that Swisher also makes chew, which is where I receive about 95 percent of my objections. Swisher's goal is have each salesperson distribute 50 cases of different chews into retail stores. We're given tools to help achieve this (free merchandise, budget to help cut prices if needed). Still, because our brand isn't number one in the market, it's hard to convince prospects to put the chew on their shelves.

My way of handling this objection, which I know is going to come up, was taught to me by Professor John Kratz. His advice was simple. Cover the objection yourself before it is even brought up by the customer. So I start my presentation by saying something like, "I know that our chew product isn't the biggest seller out there, and you're probably wondering why you should carry it. That's a great question and one you should be asking." I then answer the objection by proving that there actually is a market out there, and that this product is 100 percent guaranteed. If it doesn't sell, I'll buy it back. This usually resolves their concerns, and we are able to talk about placement and suggested purchase quantities.

In addition, I've learned the importance of welcoming all objections. Don't back away and become defensive when the prospect objects. Objections truly are a salesperson's friend, because the seller then knows what the issues are.

Source: Christopher Evers, used by permission.

RELAX AND LISTEN—DO NOT INTERRUPT

When responding to an objection, listen first and then answer the objection. Allow the prospect to state a position completely. A wise man said, "He that answereth a matter before he heareth it, it is folly and shame unto him."[3]

Do not interrupt with an answer, even if the objection to be stated is already apparent to you. Listen as though you have never heard that objection before. Unfortunately, too many salespeople conduct conversations somewhat like the following:

> SALESPERSON: Mr. Clark, from a survey of your operations, I'm convinced you're now spending more money repairing your own motors than you would by having us do the job for you—and really do it right!

> CUSTOMER: I wonder if we are not doing it right ourselves. Your repair service may be good. But after all, you don't have to be exactly an electrical genius to be able to . . .

> SALESPERSON: Just a minute now! Pardon me for interrupting, but there's a point I'd like to make right there! It isn't a matter of anyone being a genius. It's a matter of having a heavy investment in special motor repair equipment and supplies like vacuum impregnating tanks and lathes for banding armatures, boring bearings, and turning new shafts.

> CUSTOMER: Yeah, but you don't understand my point. What I'm driving at . . .

> SALESPERSON: I know what you're driving at. And I assure you you're wrong! You forget that even if your own workers are smart cookies, they just can't do high-quality work without a lot of special equipment.

> CUSTOMER: But you still don't get my point! The idea I'm trying to get across—if I can make myself clear on this third attempt—is this: The maintenance workers that we now have doing motor repair work . . .

SALESPERSON: Could more profitably spend their time on plant troubleshooting! Right?

CUSTOMER: That isn't what I was going to say! I was trying to say that between their troubleshooting jobs, instead of just sitting around and shooting the bull . . .

SALESPERSON: Now wait a minute, Mr. Clark. Wait jus-s-t a minute! Let me get a word in here! If you've got any notion that a good motor rewinding job can be done with somebody's left hand on an odd-moment basis, you've got another think coming. And my survey here will prove it! Listen![4]

RF/Corbis

This seller is listening carefully.

Obviously, this type of attitude and interruption is likely to bring the interview to a quick end.

Salespeople should plan to relax as buyers offer objections. It's even OK to plan on using humor in your answers to objections. For example, if the buyer objects to the standard payments and asks how low your company could go, you could respond as follows: Well, if I could get the bank to send you money each month, would you buy it?

After laughing, the seller could talk about the various payment options. Using humor, as in this example, may help defuse the nervousness that both buyer and seller are feeling during this part of the process. For more insight into the use of humor, see Chapter 10.

EVALUATE OBJECTIONS

In order to truly sell value and establish a relationship, the seller must evaluate objections before answering. Objections may be classified as unsatisfied needs (that is, real objections) or excuses. **Excuses** are concerns expressed by the buyer that mask the buyer's true objections. Thus the comment "I can't afford it now" would simply be an excuse if the buyer honestly could afford it now but did not want to buy for some other reason.

A buyer seldom says, "I don't have any reason. I just don't want to buy." More commonly, the buyer gives a reason that appears at first to be a real objection but is really an excuse: "I don't have the money" or "I can't use your product." The tone of voice or the nature of the reason may provide evidence that the prospect is not offering a sincere objection.

Salespeople need to develop skill in evaluating objections.[5] No exact formula has been devised to separate excuses from real objections. Sometimes it is best to follow up with a question:

BUYER: I wish it came in red.

SELLER: If I can get it in red, will you buy it?

If the buyer says yes, you know the concern is real. If the buyer says no, you know the buyer is just offering the objection about color as an excuse.

Circumstances can also provide a clue as to whether the objection is a valid concern. In cold calling, when the prospect says, "I'm sorry, I don't have any money," the salesperson may conclude that the prospect does not want to hear the presentation. However, the same reason offered after a complete presentation has been made and data on the prospect have been gathered through observation and questioning may be valid. Salespeople must rely on observation, questioning, knowledge of why people buy (see Chapter 4), and experience to determine the validity of reasons offered for objections.

ALWAYS TELL THE TRUTH

In dealing with prospects and customers, truthfulness is an absolute necessity for dignity, confidence, and relationship development. Recall that our purpose is to persuade, when appropriate, rather than to manipulate so that the buyer can make the most effective decision. Lying and deception are not a part of a successful long-term relationship. Over time it will be hard to remember which lie you told to which customer. Salespeople should avoid even white lies and half-truths when they answer objections.

Salespeople who tell lies, even small ones, need to recognize they have a problem and then find ways to change. One way to avoid lies is to spend more time gaining knowledge about their products and the products of their competitors.[6] Sellers who do so aren't as tempted to lie to cover up the fact that they don't know some information requested by the prospect. Sellers also should commit to tell the truth, even if competitors don't follow suit. It is simply the right thing to do.

EFFECTIVE RESPONSE METHODS

Any discussion of specific methods for responding to objections needs to emphasize that no perfect method exists for answering all objections completely. Some prospects, no matter what you do, will never believe their objections have been adequately addressed.

In some instances, spending a lot of time trying to convince the prospect may not be wise. For example, when an industrial recycling salesperson contacts a prospect who says, "I don't believe in recycling," the salesperson may better spend available time calling on some of the vast number of people who do.

This section describes seven common methods for responding to objections. As Exhibit 11.4 indicates, the first two, direct denial and indirect denial, are used only when the prospect makes an untrue statement. The next five methods—compensation, referral, revisiting, acknowledgement, and postponement—are useful when the buyer raises a valid point or offers an opinion.

Before using the methods described in this section, salespeople almost always need to probe to help the prospect clarify concerns and to make sure they understand the objection. This method is often called the **probing method.** If the

Exhibit 11.4
Common Methods for Responding to Objections

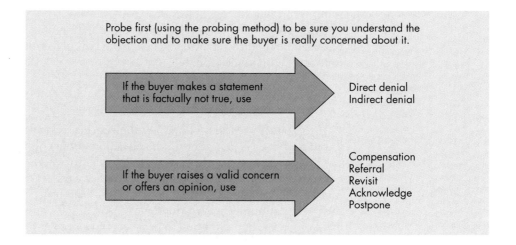

Probe first (using the probing method) to be sure you understand the objection and to make sure the buyer is really concerned about it.

If the buyer makes a statement that is factually not true, use → Direct denial / Indirect denial

If the buyer raises a valid concern or offers an opinion, use → Compensation / Referral / Revisit / Acknowledge / Postpone

prospect says, "Your service is not too good," the salesperson can probe by saying, "I'm not sure I understand," or by asking a question. For example, the seller could ask one or more of the following: Not too good? What do you mean by not too good? Exactly what service are you referring to? Is service very important to you? Can you explain what you mean?

While this probing is usually verbal, it can also include nonverbal probing. For example, Professor Donoho at Northern Arizona University teaches a method called *FSQS*, the *friendly silent questioning stare,* to encourage buyers to elaborate or explain more fully what their concern is.

Many serious blunders have occurred because the salesperson did not understand the question, answered the wrong question, or failed to answer the objection fully. For example, a sales training manager was listening to a representative for a consulting firm talk about her services. At one point in the conversation, the manager asked, "Has anyone in our industry, the electrical products industry specifically, ever used this training package before?" The consultant answered, "Sure, we have sold this package to several firms. Why, just last week I received a nice letter from Colgate that had nothing but good things to say . . ." The manager did not buy the training package; he figured that if the consultant did not even know how to listen, the sales training package she was selling could not be very good either. (Chapter 5 provides many helpful suggestions regarding the art of questioning and probing.)

A salesperson who doesn't know the answer to the buyer's objection might say, "I don't know the answer to that question. But I'll find out and get the answer to you." The seller should paraphrase the question, write it down (this step helps jog the seller's memory as well as demonstrate to the buyer that the seller really intends to follow up), gather the information, and follow up quickly and exactly as promised. If you call the customer with the information and he or she is not available, leave the information on voice mail and then call later to verify that the prospect got the information. And don't forget that it is your responsibility to know most facts, so be prepared the next time for similar and additional questions and concerns. You can be sure your competitor is going to try to have complete answers ready.

thinking **it** through

How can the use of technology (such as databases, computers, and communication technology) help prevent a seller from having to answer, "I don't know the answer to that question. But I'll find out and call you with the information as soon as I can get it"?

DIRECT DENIAL

At times salespeople face objections based on incomplete or inaccurate information of the buyer. They should respond by providing information or correcting facts. When using **direct denial,** the salesperson makes a relatively strong statement to indicate the error the prospect has made. For example:

BUYER: I am not interested in hearing about your guidance systems. Your firm was one of the companies recently indicted for fraud, conspiracy, and price fixing by a federal grand jury. I don't want to do business with such a firm.

SALESPERSON: I'm not sure where you heard that, but it simply is not true. Our firm has never been involved in such activity, and our record is clean. If you would care to tell me the source of your information, I'm sure we can clear this up. Maybe you're confusing us with another firm.

WE CAN LOOK THAT UP, IF YOU LIKE

"But I'm sure it is your company, IGX Systems, whose CEO was indicted on fraud!" What do you say to a prospect who's got your company mixed up with IGX Systems? Why not use your laptop right there in the sales meeting, go online, and prove your point?

There are many ways you can prove that the buyer has incorrect information. You can look up trusted Web sources of news, such as *The Wall Street Journal* online, *The New York Times,* and others. Some of these require you to register before using them, even for free content, so it is best to have this all done before you make sales calls.

You can also go to sites that dispel popular myths. One such site is truthorfiction.com. This site provides proof that many rumors and urban legends are actually myths. For example, one rumor floating around is that Liz Claiborne is a satanist and that all of her profits are going to satanism (the same rumor that was used against Procter & Gamble for years), a myth objectively refuted by the truthorfiction.com. Other sites include http://www.snopes.com and http://www.scambusters.org/legends.html.

You can also use your laptop to log onto your company's computer system to verify information about orders, invoices, shipping times, or return allowances that are disputed by your customer. But remember, no one likes to be told they are wrong. When using technology to prove the facts of your case, do so with care and discretion.

No one likes to be told that he or she is wrong, so the direct denial must be used with caution. It is appropriate only when the objection is blatantly inaccurate and potentially devastating to the presentation. The salesperson must also possess facts to back up such a denial. Using technology to prove the point right on the spot can be effective, as Sales Technology 11.1 indicates.

Direct denial should never be used if the prospect is merely stating an opinion or if the objection is true. For example, direct denial would be inappropriate to this objection: I don't like the feel of simulated leather products. Direct denial should be avoided even for a false statement if the objection is of little importance to the buyer. An indirect denial would be more appropriate in that case.

INDIRECT DENIAL

In the **indirect denial** method, the salesperson denies the objection but attempts to soften the response. The salesperson takes the edge off the response by agreeing with the prospect that the objection is an important one. Prospects expect salespeople to disagree; instead, a salesperson who recognizes the sincerity of the objection will carefully respect the prospect's view. This approach avoids a direct contradiction and confrontation. To begin an answer, a salesperson would do well to agree with the prospect, but only to the extent that the agreement does not weaken the validity of the salesperson's later denial. For example:

BUYER: Your machines break down more often than those of most of your major competitors.

SALESPERSON: I can see why you would feel that way. Just 10 years ago that statement would have been right on target. However, things have changed with our new quality assurance program. In fact, just last year Syncos Ratings, a well-respected independent evaluator of quality in our industry, rated us as number one for fewest breakdowns.

The important features of indirect denial are that salespeople recognize the position of the customer who makes the objection and then continue by introducing substantial evidence. The beginning statement should always be true and assure the prospect that the question is a good one. Examples of opening statements follow:

There is some truth to what you are saying.

With the market the way it is today, I can certainly see why you're concerned about that.

I'll bet 90 percent of the people I call on voice the same concern.

That's really an excellent question, and it allows me to clear up a misconception that perhaps I've given you.

Indirect denial should never be used if the prospect has raised a valid point or is merely expressing an opinion. It can be used for all personality types and is especially effective for amiables and analyticals because they like less assertive salespeople.

COMPENSATION METHOD

Every product has some advantages and some disadvantages compared to competing products. Also, an absolutely perfect product or service has never been developed; the firm always has to make cost–benefit decisions about what features to include.[7]

Buyers note these trade-offs and often object because the salesperson's product is less than perfect. The wise salesperson will admit that such objections are valid and then proceed to show any compensating advantages.[8] This approach is called the **compensation** method of responding to objections. Here is an example:

PROSPECT: This machine has only four filling nozzles. Your competitor's has six nozzles.

SALESPERSON: You're absolutely right. It has only four nozzles, but it costs $4,000 less than the competitor's models, and you said you needed a model that is priced in the lower range. Also, our nozzles are designed for easy maintenance. You have to remove only four screws to get to the filter screens. Most other models have at least 10 screws. Fewer screws will reduce downtime considerably, which is something else you said you were very concerned about.

The compensation method is an explicit use of the multiattribute model discussed in Chapter 4. A low score on one attribute can be compensated for by a high score on another attribute. In fact, the compensation method is often referred to as the **superior benefit method** because the benefit of one attribute overcomes a concern about a less important attribute. The method can be effective for many objections and concerns. It seems most appropriate for analyticals, who are accustomed to conducting trade-off analyses. However, it is useful for all other personality types as well.

Of course, the buyer may not value the compensating advantages, as Building Partnerships 11.1 illustrates. The buyer may really need the features at issue (perhaps the machine must have six nozzles to work with another piece of the prospect's equipment). In such cases salespeople can recommend a different product (from their own line, if available, or from a competitor) or search for other prospects.

Another time that the compensation method may be used is when the prospect says, "I'm just going to think about it. I'll be in touch with you later." The seller can show how acting today more than compensates for the "pain" of making a decision today. These reasons usually include explaining the hidden costs of

A VIEW FROM THE BUYER'S SIDE OF THE TABLE— DON'T USE THE COMPENSATION METHOD ON ME

I was working on a new product launch for a brand expected to be approximately $1 billion in annual sales before the end of its product life cycle. I chose to solicit three bids from vendors for some patient education we needed. A person reporting to me was managing the bid process; let's call him John. I provided John with the names of three companies to begin the bid process.

John called all three companies and came back to me needing some help. One vendor, whom we will call "Unaware," had told John that it would cost us approximately $15,000 for them just to bid for our business. I didn't understand what the charges were for, and John explained that the company wanted to sit in on our patient market research, analyze the research, and provide us with a report along with their sales pitch. I told John that they were welcome to sit in on the market research; however, we were **not** going to pay them to do so. John communicated this to the "Unaware" salesperson, and that salesperson asked John to set up a meeting with me so that it could be better explained to me. I agreed to a 30-minute meeting.

"Unaware" came to the meeting without anything except a notebook. She forgot to even bring the $15,000 bill to review with me. I asked her to take me through the charges, on a copy that John brought to the meeting. We discussed each line item, and it was the same as John had communicated to me. My objection was that I didn't see the benefit in their process for our business because we were creating a market in a patient population that does not have symptoms.

"Unaware" explained that the results of their analysis would be used to develop the materials. "Unaware" not only did not understand our business and didn't ask to clarify or understand the purpose; she also continued to make it look like I was the one that didn't understand. "Unaware" then said that she had already spoken to other members of my team who felt that they do great work. She also said she had developed materials in a project last year for us, and told me about the raving success of those materials.

I then informed "Unaware" that I was well aware of that project last year because I ran that business, and the person they worked with reported to me. I knew every piece they created last year. I explained what I considered strengths and weaknesses of each piece, and I also explained how pieces that she considered successful were not the most successful tools and why. I also explained what I liked about their work, and last I explained that I never had to pay for them to bid for our business in the past.

"Unaware" was stunned. She said she didn't realize I ran that business last year. But she still wasn't listening. She tried to use the compensation method on me by providing examples of tools that they could develop as a result of sitting in on our market research. I explained why not one of those examples would work for our business. The analytic process she wanted to put in place would make sense only for a product on the market or within an established market; it did not make sense for creating the market. She finally understood.

The result? There was no charge for "Unaware" to bid for our business. The "unaware" salesperson later called John and said, "Wow, she's tough, she must be hard to work for." John replied "No, she is not hard to work for. You came completely unprepared, I had to print your own proposal, you provided no examples of what you wanted to do, and it didn't even meet our business needs. Instead, you tried to tell her that other people have been happy with your work so she should be too . . . those people happened to work for her and she knows everything about your work. You didn't listen to me when I gave you the project, you didn't prepare for this meeting, you didn't listen to the product manager, and you weren't even providing an end result that would meet our needs. Based on all of that, I thought she was too easy on you."

They didn't get the business.

Source: Tracey Brill, used with permission.

delaying the decision (it will go off sale, you will be saving money over your current system each month that you have our proposed system, our product may be out of stock when you need it, summer is a particularly good time to install a new system, or the like).

REFERRAL METHOD

When buyers' objections reflect their own attitudes or opinions, the salesperson can show how others held similar views before trying the product or service. In this method, called the **referral method,** or the **feel–felt–found method,** the salesperson goes on to relate that others actually found their initial opinions to be unfounded after they tried the product:

> PROSPECT: I don't think my customers will want to buy a DVD player with all of these fancy features.
>
> SALESPERSON: I can certainly see how you feel. Bob Scott, down the road in Houston, felt the same way when I first proposed that he sell these. However, after he agreed to display them next to his current DVD line, he found that his customers were very interested. In fact, he called me four days later to order more.

A buyer may question the credibility and knowledge of a salesperson. In this situation the salesperson can use the referral method to help resolve those concerns.

Stockbyte/Punchstock Images/MGH-DIL

Those who teach this as the feel–felt–found method highlight the importance of the proper sequence, as well as the person or persons identified in each stage. The sequence should be as follows: I can see how *you* feel . . . *others* felt the same way . . . yet *they* found . . . Inexperienced salespeople often mix up the order or the parties identified (for example, by saying "yet you will find").

Proof of the salesperson's assertion in the form of a testimonial letter strengthens the method; in fact, some trainers refer to this approach as the **third-party-testimony method.** If a letter is not available, the salesperson might be able to supply the name and phone number of the third party. The salesperson should always secure the third party's permission first, however. (See Chapter 10 for suggestions about references.)

Although the referral method can be used for all personality types, it seems most appropriate for expressives and amiables. Both types tend to care about what other people think and are doing.

REVISIT METHOD

When using the **revisit method,** also called the **boomerang method** of responding to objections, the salesperson turns the objection into a reason for buying the product or service. This method can be used in many situations (when making an appointment, during the presentation, when attempting to secure commitment, and in postsale situations):

> BUYER: I don't think these would sell in my gun shop. They're really drab looking.
>
> SALESPERSON: It's interesting that you mention that. In fact, their drab color is probably their best selling point, and the reason you should carry them. You see, when a hunter is in the field, the last thing she wants to do is attract attention to herself. Thanks to the finish we use on this gear . . .

The revisit method requires care. It can appear very pushy and "salesy." This method does have useful applications, however. Often the product or service is actually designed to save the buyer substantial amounts of time or money. If the buyer objects to spending either the time to listen or the money, the revisit method may be a powerful tool to help the buyer see the benefit of investing these resources.

This method works with most personality types. Drivers may require the revisit method more often than other buyers because drivers tend to erect time constraints and other barriers and are less willing to listen to just any salesperson's presentation.

ACKNOWLEDGE METHOD

At times the buyer voices opinions or concerns more to vent frustration than anything else. When this occurs, the best strategy may be to use the **acknowledge method,** also called the **pass-up method.** Simply let the buyer talk, acknowledge that you heard the concern, pause, and then move on to another topic.

> BUYER: Hey, you use Britney Spears in your commercials, don't you? Sure you do. Now I want to tell you that I don't like her style or what she stands for! Kids today need a role model they can look up to. What happened to the kind of role models we used to have?
>
> SALESPERSON: I certainly understand your concern. I remember my dad talking about some of his role models and the respect he had for them. [Pause] What were we talking about? Oh, yes, I was telling you about the coupon drop we are planning.

In this example the salesperson used the acknowledge method because the buyer apparently was just blowing off steam. A buyer who really wanted some response from the salesperson would have used the salesperson's pause to ask a direct question (Can't you change your commercials?) or make a statement. (I refuse to do business with companies that use stars like Britney Spears in their commercials!)

In reality, a salesperson often can do little about some prospects' opinions. What are the chances that this salesperson's firm will pull a $5 million ad campaign just because one buyer objects? It is doubtful that a firm would take such action unless the buyer had tremendous power in the relationship.

Sometimes the salesperson can use the acknowledge method by simply agreeing with the prospect and then moving on, which suggests to the buyer that the concern really should not be much of an issue. For example:

> BUYER: You want $25 for this little plastic bottle?!
>
> SELLER: Uh-huh. That's what they cost . . . [pause] Now do you see the switch on this side? It's used if you ever need to . . .

The acknowledge method should not be used if the objection raised is factually false. Also, it should not be used if the salesperson, through probing, could help clarify the buyer's thinking on the topic. Experience is the key to making such a determination. In general, though, the acknowledge method should be used sparingly.

POSTPONE METHOD

In the early part of a sales interview, the prospect may raise objections that the salesperson would prefer to answer later in the presentation, after discovering the prospect's needs. Using the **postpone method,** the salesperson would ask permission to answer the question at a later time:

> BUYER [very early in the call]: How much does the brass engraving equipment cost?

SALESPERSON: If you don't mind, I would prefer to answer that question in a few minutes. I really can't tell you how much it will cost until I learn more about your engraving needs and know what kinds of features you are looking for.

The prospect will seldom refuse the request if the sales representative appears to be acting in good faith. The sales representative then proceeds with the presentation until the point at which the objection can best be answered.

Some objections are best answered when they occur; others can be responded to most effectively by delaying the answer. Experience should guide the sales representative. The salesperson should take care not to treat an objection lightly or let it appear that he or she does not want to answer the question. Another danger in postponing is that the buyer will be unable to focus on what the salesperson is saying until the concern is addressed. On the other hand, the salesperson is responsible for helping the buyer to critically evaluate the solution offered, and often the buyer can process information effectively only after learning preliminary facts.

Salespeople make the most use of the postponement method when a price objection occurs early in the presentation. However, this method can be utilized for almost any type of objection or question. For example, postponing discussions about guarantees, delivery schedules, implementation time frames, and certain unique product features until later in the presentation is often preferable.

What if the buyer is convinced that he or she deserves the answer right now? Then the salesperson should answer the objection now. Salespeople usually have more to lose by demanding that the buyer wait for information than by simply providing the answer when the buyer strongly requests it. For example:

PROSPECT: What are the delivery schedules for this new product?

SALESPERSON: I would really prefer to discuss that after we talk about our unique production process and extensive quality control measures.

PROSPECT: No, I want to know now!

SALESPERSON: Well, keep in mind that my later discussion about the production process will shed new light on the topic. We anticipate a four-to-five-month delivery time after the contract reaches our corporate headquarters.

USING THE METHODS

The seven methods just discussed appear in sales training courses across all industries and geographic boundaries. To help you more easily distinguish the differences among the various methods, Exhibit 11.5 provides an example of the use of each method for the objection "Your product's quality is too low."

Salespeople often combine methods when answering an objection. For example, a price objection may initially be postponed and then be discussed later, using the compensation method. At other times several methods can be used in one answer. Here is an example:

BUYER: I don't think this product will last as long as some of the other, more expensive competitive products.

SALESPERSON: That's probably the very reason you should buy it [revisit method]. It may not last quite as long, but it is less than half the cost of competitive products [compensation method]. I can certainly understand your concern, though. You know, Mark Hancock felt the way you do. He was concerned about the product's life. But after he used our product for one year, he found that its life expectancy didn't create any problems for his production staff [referral method].

Exhibit 11.5
Responding to
Objections: Using
Each Method

Objection: Your product's quality is too low.

Responses*

Direct denial: That simply is not true. Our product has been rated as the highest in the industry for the last three years.

Indirect denial: I can certainly see why you would be concerned about quality. Actually, though, our product has been rated as the highest in the industry for the last three years.

Compensation: I agree that our quality is not as high as that of some of our competitors. However, it was designed that way for consumers who are looking for a lower-priced alternative, perhaps just to use in a weekend cottage. So you see, our somewhat lower quality is actually offset by our much lower price.

Referral: I can certainly understand how you feel. Mortimer Jiggs felt the same way before he bought the product. But after using it, he found that the quality was actually equal to that of other products.

Revisit: The fact that the quality is lower than in other products is probably the very reason you should buy it. You said that some of your customers are looking for a low-priced product to buy for their grandchildren. This product fills that need.

Acknowledge: I understand your concern. You know, one of the things I always look for is how a product's quality stacks up against its cost. [Pause] Now, we were talking about . . .

Postpone: That's an interesting point. Before discussing it fully, I would like to cover just two things that I think will help you better understand the product from a different perspective. OK?

*These are not necessarily good answers to the stated objection. Also, the choice of method would depend on whether the objection is factual. Thus the replies given in this table are designed simply to differentiate the various methods.

Before moving on with the presentation, the salesperson needs to make sure the buyer agrees that all objections have been completely answered.

Jose Luis Pelaez/Corbis

Before moving on with the presentation, the salesperson needs to make sure that the buyer agrees that all objections have been completely answered. Without this commitment, the salesperson does not know whether the buyer understands the answer or whether the buyer's concerns have been fully addressed. To achieve this commitment, the salesperson can use one or more of the following types of phrases: Did I answer your question? Does that make sense? Do you see why that issue is not as important as you originally thought? I hope I haven't confused you. Do you have any more questions?

OBJECTIONS WHEN SELLING TO A GROUP OF BUYERS

Selling to a group of buyers (see Chapter 9) requires some extra care. If one person offers an objection, the seller should rephrase the question and try to get a sense of whether other buyers share the concern. At times it may make sense to throw the issue back to the group. For example, if a buyer says that the people in his or her department won't attend the type of training sessions being proposed, the seller might respond as follows: Does anyone else have that same problem in their department? You all know your organizational climate better than I do. Have any of you found a way to deal with that issue that you would like to share with us? Any response from the seller should usually be directed to all buyers, not just the one who asked the question. After responding, the seller needs to make sure that all buyers are satisfied with the answer before moving on.

THE PRICE OBJECTION

Price is the perhaps the most frequently mentioned obstacle to obtaining commitment.[9] In fact, about 20 percent of buyers are thought to buy purely on the basis of price (which means that a full 80 percent buy for reasons other than price). As a result, all salespeople need to prepare for price objections. This section relates the concepts covered in this chapter to this common objection.

Price is still an issue even between partnering firms. One leading firm in its industry has estimated that only 3 percent of its orders are sold at list price; the rest are price discounted.[10]

Unfortunately, the first response of many salespeople to a price objection is to lower the price. Inexperienced salespeople, desiring to gain business, often quote the lowest possible price as quickly as possible. They forget that for a mutually beneficial long-term relationship to exist, their firm must make a fair profit. Also, by cutting prices the firm has to sell more to maintain profit margins, as Exhibit 11.6 clearly illustrates.[11]

Exhibit 11.6
Look Before You Cut Prices! You Must Sell More to Break Even

| Cut Price | Present Gross Profit | | | | | |
	5.0%	10.0%	15.0%	20.0%	25.0%	30.0%
1%	25.0	11.1	7.1	5.3	4.2	3.4
2	66.6	25.0	15.4	11.1	8.7	7.1
3	150.0	42.8	25.0	17.6	13.6	11.1
4	400.0	66.6	36.4	25.0	19.0	15.4
5	—	100.0	50.0	33.3	25.0	20.0
6	—	150.0	66.7	42.9	31.6	25.0
7	—	233.3	87.5	53.8	38.9	30.4
8	—	400.0	114.3	66.7	47.1	36.4
9	—	1,000.0	150.0	81.8	56.3	42.9
10	—	—	200.0	100.0	66.7	50.0
11	—	—	275.0	122.2	78.6	57.9
12	—	—	400.0	150.0	92.3	66.7
13	—	—	650.0	185.7	108.3	76.5
14	—	—	1,400.0	233.3	127.3	87.5
15	—	—	—	300.0	150.0	100.0
16	—	—	—	400.0	177.8	114.3
17	—	—	—	566.7	212.5	130.8
18	—	—	—	900.0	257.1	150.0
19	—	—	—	1,900.0	316.7	172.7
20	—	—	—	—	400.0	200.0
21	—	—	—	—	525.0	233.3
22	—	—	—	—	733.3	275.0
23	—	—	—	—	1,115.0	328.6
24	—	—	—	—	2,400.0	400.0
25	—	—	—	—	—	500.0

A business truism says that you can cut, cut, cut until you cut yourself out of business. This can certainly apply to cutting prices in an effort to increase profits. The two don't necessarily go together. For example: Select the gross profit being earned at present from those shown at the top of the chart. Follow the left column down until you line up with the proposed price cut. The intersected figure represents the percentage of increase in unit sales required to earn the same gross profit realized before the price cut. Obviously, it helps to know this figure so you don't end up with a lot of work for nothing.

See for yourself: Assume that your present gross margin is 25 percent and that you cut your selling price 10 percent. Locate the 25 percent column under Present Gross Profit. Now follow the column down until you line up with the 10 percent cut in selling price in column 1. You will need to sell 66.7 percent more units to earn the same margin dollars as at the previous price.

When faced with a price objection, salespeople should ensure that they have up-to-date information, establish the value of the product, and use communication tools effectively.

USE UP-TO-DATE INFORMATION

Successful salespeople make sure they have the most current pricing information available to them. They know not only their prices, but competitors' prices as well. Firms are helping salespeople in this regard. For example, many firms have developed an intranet site for its salespeople. If a salesperson finds that the company's price points are a little higher than the competition, the salesperson can use the intranet site to look for some sales or trade-in program that she or he can leverage to get the deal. It is important for sellers to have correct pricing facts.

ESTABLISH THE VALUE

The product's value must be established before the salesperson spends time discussing price.[12] The value expected determines the price a prospect is willing to pay. Unless the salesperson can build value to exceed the price asked, a sale will not occur. As a rule, value cannot be established during the early stages of the presentation.

Price objections are best handled with a two-step approach. First, the salesperson should try to look at the objection from the customer's viewpoint, asking questions to clarify the customer's perspective: Too high in what respect, Mr. Jones? Could you tell me how much we are out of line? We are usually quite competitive on this model, so I am surprised you find our price high. . . . Are the other quotes you have for the same size engine?

After learning more about the customer's perspective, the next step is to sell value and quality rather than price.[13] Most customers prefer to buy less expensive products if they believe they will receive the same benefits. However, many customers will pay more for higher quality when the quality benefits and features are pointed out to them. Many high-quality products appear similar to lower-quality products; thus salespeople need to emphasize the features that justify a difference.

For example, a Premier Industrial salesperson who sells industrial fasteners and supplies may hear this objection: That bolt costs $750! I could buy it elsewhere for $75. The salesperson should reply, "Yes, but that bolt is inside your most important piece of production equipment. Let's say you buy that $75 bolt. How much employee time and production downtime would it take to disassemble the machine again and replace that one bolt?" The salesperson can then engage in a complete cost–benefit analysis (see Chapter 10) to solidify the point.

Intangible features can also provide value that offsets price. Some of these features are services, company reputation, and the salesperson:

- Good service in the form of faster deliveries, technical advice, and field assistance is but one of the many intangibles that can spell value, savings, and profits to a customer. For example, one company cut its prices in response to buyers' demands. However, the company later found that what the customers really wanted was technical support. As the company cut its prices, it had only reinforced its image as low-priced with little technical support.

- For a customer tempted to buy on price alone, salespeople can emphasize the importance of having a thoroughly reliable source of supply: the salesperson's company. It has been demonstrated time and again that quality is measured by the reputation of the company behind it.

- Customers value sales representatives who go out of their way to help with problems and promotions—salespeople who keep their word and follow through when they start something. These services are very valuable to customers.

USE COMMUNICATION TOOLS EFFECTIVELY

One pharmaceutical salesperson often hears that her company's drug for migraines is too expensive. Her response is to paint a word picture:[14]

DOCTOR: How much does this product cost?

SALESPERSON: It costs about $45. . . . There are 15 doses per bottle, so it ends up about $3 per dose.

DOCTOR: That's too much money!

SALESPERSON: Consider your patients who have to lie in the dark because their headaches are so bad they can't see straight, can't think straight, and are nauseated by migraine pain. A price of $3 is really inexpensive to relieve these patients' pain, wouldn't you agree?

Just telling customers about quality and value is not enough; they must be shown. Top salespeople use the communication tools discussed in Chapter 10 to describe more clearly the quality and value of their products. This process includes activities such as demonstrating the product, showing test results and quality control procedures, using case histories, and offering testimonials.

DEALING WITH TOUGH CUSTOMERS

Sellers need to maintain the positive attitude discussed earlier, even with rude, hard-to-get-along-with prospects. It's not easy, and it's not fun.

Sellers need to realize that we all have bad days. Maybe the buyer is having one. If the rudeness is quite blatant and the seller believes that this behavior is just due to the timing of the visit, the seller might say, "I'm sensing that this might not be the best time to talk. Should we reschedule for another time?"

Salespeople must learn to deal with tough prospects and customers.

Digital Vision/Getty Images

If the buyer continues to be unreasonably rude, you might want to kindly call attention to the fact. After all, to develop a long-term win–win relationship and partnership you both need to be on the same footing. Perhaps saying something like this will clear the air: "I'm sorry, Joe. I don't know quite how to say this. But it seems to me that you wish to argue more than learn about my products. I'll gladly continue if you think we can both approach this problem with professionalism and courtesy." Of course, it is important to keep in mind the various personalities that buyers can have (see Chapter 6) and the adjustments suggested for each.

Also, remember that the buyer's culture often dictates the way he or she will respond to a seller. For example, Germans are known as being thorough, systematic, and well prepared, but they are also rather dogmatic and thus lack flexibility and the desire to compromise. As a result, sellers not accustomed to such a culture could have difficulty dealing with a German prospect who raises a price objection in a strong tone of voice.

SUMMARY

Responding to objections is a vital part of a salesperson's responsibility. Objections may be offered at any time during the relationship between buyer and salesperson. They are to be expected, even welcomed, and they must be handled with skill and empathy.

Successful salespeople carefully prepare effective responses to buyers' concerns. Salespeople need to develop a positive attitude, commit to always telling the truth, refrain from interrupting, anticipate and forestall known objections, and learn how to evaluate objections.

Buyers object for many reasons. They may have no money, or they may not need the product. They may need more information or misunderstand some information already offered. They may be accustomed to another product, may not think the value exceeds the cost, or may not like the product's features. They may want to get rid of the salesperson or may not trust the salesperson or his or her company. They may want time to think or may object for many other reasons.

Effective methods of responding to objections are available, and their success has been proved. Methods exist both for concerns that are not true and for objections that either are true or are only the buyer's opinion. Sensitivity in choosing the right method is vital. Salespeople need to develop skill in responding to price objections and in dealing with tough customers. Nothing will substitute for developing skill in these areas.

KEY TERMS

acknowledge method
boomerang method
compensation method
direct denial
excuses
feel–felt–found method
forestall
indirect denial
objection

pass-up method
pioneer selling
postpone method
probing method
referral method
revisit method
superior benefit method
third-party-testimony method
turnover (TO)

ETHICS PROBLEMS

1. A prospect has just raised an objection about the price of your service, commercial carpet cleaning. You know that the service you are selling usually goes on sale a couple of times each year, but you're not sure when the next time will be. It could be as soon as a few weeks. Should you tell the buyer about the possible lower price?

2. One student in a selling class once said, "Why are we learning these objection-handling methods? These techniques are just to help us manipulate our buyers!" How would you respond?

QUESTIONS AND PROBLEMS

1. Categorize each of the following responses into the five basic types of objections. Then illustrate one way to handle each.
   a. After a sales presentation, the doctor says, "You've made some good points, but your competitor's product can do just about everything yours can do."
   b. After the salesperson answers an objection, the prospect remarks, "I guess your product is all right, but as I told you when you walked in, things are going pretty well for us right now without your product."
   c. After a thorough presentation, the prospect answers, "Whew, that's a lot of money!"

d. The customer says, "I can buy that online for a lot less than what you're selling it for."

2. Bobbie Hightower spent considerable time working with a prospective buyer. She thought a good order would be forthcoming on her next call. A portion of her conversation with the buyer went as follows:

BUYER: You know, I like what I hear about your concrete pumping service. But how can I be sure it will be available on the days that we need it for our next project?

BOBBIE: We've never had any real complaints before. I'm pretty sure they will be easily available.

BUYER: You are sure of that?

BOBBIE: Well, I've never heard of any problems that I can remember.

BUYER [appearing unconvinced and looking at some papers on his desk without glancing up]: I'll let you know later what I plan to do. Thanks for dropping by.

How can you improve on Bobbie's answer to the buyer's concern?

3. Describe the differences between postponing an objection and forestalling an objection.

4. Occasionally a buyer will offer several objections at one time. How would you respond if a buyer made the following comments without pausing: "Say, how long does it take your lab to get the results back to us? And what if we need same-day service sometime? Are your technicians certified? That's important, you know!"

5. Indicate the appropriate action for the sales representative who encounters the following customer attitudes:

a. What if the pretzels don't come out of the pretzel maker in the right form? How hard is it to adjust the machine while it's running?

b. My partner heard I was meeting with you today. She said to me, "Why would you want to talk to them? Their stuff never lasts!"

c. That sounds fine. But there's really no reason to get rid of the pressure washer I have. It works well enough for my purposes.

6. Choose a restaurant in your town. Assume that you work at that restaurant and are planning to make calls to campus club organizations. Assume that the restaurant has a room available for private meetings that will seat 25 people. Your objective is to have officers of the clubs schedule their meetings at the restaurant.

a. Make a list of objections you may expect to encounter.

b. What can you do to meet these objections effectively? List the answer you would propose and label the method used.

7. You expect to hear this objection on your next sales call: Your new product will have more service problems than your competitor's product. How would you attempt to answer the objection in each of the following situations?

a. You are calling on an amiable with whom you have been doing business for four years.

b. You are calling on an expressive for the first time.

c. You are calling on an analytical who bought one of your products three years ago but has bought nothing since.

d. You are calling on a driver who currently uses your competitor's product.

8. You have been describing to a retail security officer and his boss a new security camera that your firm just introduced. The camera has tracking features that make it easier for security officers to review tapes. The security officer says, "I would really like that!" The boss says, "Well, if it's what you think we need, OK. How much does it cost?" At your reply, "This one is $2,498," the boss exclaims, "For that little thing?" What should you say or do?

9. For each of the following objections, provide answers that clearly demonstrate the direct denial and indirect denial methods. Assume each objection is not true.

a. My obstetric patients will never need that service.

b. The cost of replacing the filter will be more than just buying a new unit.

c. I heard that the paint used in manufacturing your unit can cause cancer.

d. I can buy this cheaper online.

10. For each of the following objections, provide answers that clearly demonstrate the compensation method and referral method. Assume all the objections are either true or are the prospect's opinion.

a. Your repossession service costs a lot of money!

b. I don't think our customers will like the new beverage you're selling.

c. Your diesel mechanics aren't certified by the ATSG.

d. My customers have never asked for this brand of dishwasher.

case 11.1

FishyLease Part II

FishyLease is a five-year-old firm that specializes in leasing custom aquarium installations in restaurants, medical offices, homes, and industrial spaces. The firm designs, produces, and installs its unique aquariums to meet the customer's specific needs. They also stock the aquarium with fish and completely service it. Leases start at 12 months, but can run as long as 60 months. See Case 10.1 for more details about this company and the services they offer.

Assume you are a salesperson for FishyLease calling on the owner of a marginally successful restaurant located downtown. Assume that many businesses, including restaurants, have left the downtown area and moved to a new mall located about 20 minutes from the downtown area. Before the mall opening, this restaurant was quite successful.

Questions

1. What objections could the buyer raise? (Use any assumptions necessary to develop this list.)
2. Provide a response to each objection you listed in question 1 (make any assumptions necessary to create your response). Include the name of the method you recommend for each objection.

case 11.2

Lamar Outdoor

Lamar Outdoor Advertising has more than 130,000 structures in 44 states, and reaches over 1,500 markets all over the United States. It offers billboard advertising and transit displays. Lamar helps customers design, produce, and then strategically place the client's advertising message. Its goal is "to be the premier provider of outdoor advertising in each of the markets it serves."

Lamar designers sit down with customers to decide the best way to get the customer's message across. The Lamar team is renowned for their skills in using creativity to deliver messages that are hard-hitting and memorable.

Prices vary depending on the customer's needs. For example, a 14′ × 48′ billboard image (that can be moved to a different billboard location every two months to increase exposure) in Duluth, Minnesota, is $2,700 for a four-month contract.

There are many competitors to Lamar, including other outdoor advertising firms in each market, plus traditional media outlets such as television, radio, and newspaper.

Assume you work for Lamar Outdoor and are calling on your college. Lamar's goal is to secure the school's business for an outdoor ad campaign. You are calling on Shawn Chipley, the college's marketing director.

Source for any quotes, plus information to write this case, came from lamaroutdoor.com.

Questions

1. List objections you think might occur during this first meeting with Shawn. Make any assumptions necessary to develop this list.
2. Describe how you would respond to each objection listed in question 1. Be sure to label the method. Make any assumptions necessary to create your response.

ROLE PLAY

Today you will repeat your role play presentation from Chapter 10. (If you have not done role plays before, you will need to review the information about the various role play customers that can be found at the end of Chapter 4. If you didn't do the role play for Chapter 10, you will need to review that material also, which can be found at the end of Chapter 10.) When you act as the observer today, you should identify what objection-handling method the seller used and if it was done effectively. The professor will give you a sheet to use as a buyer, listing objections for you to use during the role play. When you sell, try to use a variety of objection-handling methods.

Note: For background information on these role plays, please see page 27.

To the instructor: Additional information needed to complete the role play is available in the Instructor's Manual.

ADDITIONAL REFERENCES

Brooks, Bill. "Why Is Your Customer So Difficult?" *American Salesman* 48, no. 7 (July 2003), pp. 20–22.

Cole, Gene H., and Meagan Miner. "Handling Sales Objections." *National Public Accountant* 47, no. 5 (August 2002), pp. 24–26.

Farber, Barry. *Barry Farber's Guide to Handling Sales Objections.* Franklin Lakes, NJ: Career Press, 2004.

Farber, Barry. "Step by Step." *Entrepreneur* 31, no. 3 (March 2003), pp. 66–67.

Gross, T. Scott. *Positively Outrageous Service: How to Delight and Astound Your Customers and Win Them for Life.* New York: Kaplan Professional Company, 2004.

Hinterhuber, Andreas. "Toward Value-Based Pricing—An Integrative Framework for Decision Making." *Industrial Marketing Management* 33, no. 8, pp. 765–78.

Huisken, Brad. "Saving the Sale: Objections, Rejections, and Getting to 'Yes.'" *JCK* 174, no. 1 (January 2003), pp. 62–63.

Joseph, Kissan. "On the Optimality of Delegating Pricing Authority to the Sales Force." *Journal of Marketing* 65 (January 2001), pp. 62–70.

McFarland, Richard G. "Crisis of Conscience: The Use of Coercive Sales Tactics and Resultant Felt Stress in the Salesperson." *Journal of Personal Selling and Sales Management* 23, no. 4 (Fall 2003), pp. 311–26.

Reilly, Tom. "Just Say 'No' to Price Shoppers." *Industrial Distribution* 91, no. 7 (July 2002), p. 54.

Reilly, Tom. "Price Objections: The Salesperson's Bane." *Sell!ng*, December 2003, p. 9.

OBTAINING COMMITMENT

chapter **12**

part **3**

**SOME QUESTIONS ANSWERED
IN THIS CHAPTER . . .**

- How much emphasis should be placed on closing the sale?

- Why is obtaining commitment important?

- When is the best time to obtain commitment?

- Which methods of securing commitment are appropriate for developing partnerships?

- How should pricing be presented?

- What should a salesperson do when the prospect says yes? When the prospect says no?

- What causes difficulties in obtaining commitment, and how can these issues be overcome?

PROFILE

I started my sales career the summer of 1995 selling encyclopedias door to door for The Southwestern Co. in Seguin, Texas. I was still in college at Michigan State and a long way from my home in Panama. That was the toughest job I have ever had, but it reaped very important benefits for me in the long term. While not the same as corporate sales, I certainly learned some important sales fundamentals.

I sold books for three consecutive summers, and then joined Cable & Wireless Panama after graduation. Soon I began to realize that the sales process was not the same as my previous 20-minute presentations. In corporate sales, or selling to other businesses, I was introduced to the concept of "consultative sales," which means that when you sell to companies, it really matters less how our services work compared to how they affect the bottom line. In corporate sales, you become a profitability consultant.

In order to be seen as a consultant to your client it is always important to develop trust. In my experience, trust is developed by being straightforward and a good listener. The client must perceive a genuine interest by the salesperson. A good salesperson deeply understands the customer's business and is able to offer solutions to enterprise, or companywide, problems.

This does not mean that you do not close major sales. It means that the "close" takes a different role. With Southwestern, I was taught that you must "Always Be Closing." With Cable & Wireless Panama, I walk my customer through a series of steps from the first call to the final signature. Each step requires the customer to make a commitment of some kind as we move toward the close of the sale.

To close major deals, you lay the groundwork from the beginning and understand the customer's buying process. Early in the relationship, I draft a process with the client beginning with the end in mind. The customer is clear that you are there to do business, and if all the points are covered, there will be a transaction at the end. Making a sale is easier said than done, but it is very important to clarify expectations with customers, and the earlier the better. The better the selling process is done, including identifying needs, setting expectations, and proving benefits in the presentation, the less effort closing will need at the end.

Visit us on the Web at www.cw.com

"Each step requires the customer to make a commitment of some kind as we move toward the close of the sale."

Juan Silvera

OBTAINING COMMITMENT TODAY

Asking for the buyer's business, often called **closing,** has always received a great deal of emphasis in sales training. Hundreds of books, audiocassettes, videocassettes, and seminar speakers have touted the importance of closing. According to conventional wisdom, the key to success in any sale is to find a method or methods of closing that will make the decision maker say yes. Landy Chase, noted sales trainer, discusses old-style closing this way:

> The idea of "closing" has long been regarded as applying pressure to get a person to buy. This is complete nonsense, and there is no place for this definition of closing in today's business environment. The irony of "closing" is that good closing skills have nothing to do with being pushy.[1]

Others also believe the traditional emphasis on the close damages trust, insults the buyer's intelligence, and raises the possibility of losing commitment altogether.[2] For example, two successful professionals in financial services put it this way:

> The following equation illustrates the closing process: Customer commitment = (Content + Relationship) × Asking. Without the proper content and information (in the sales presentation), the best closing technique in the business will not get a yes. What is more, a customer's willingness to accept that information is heavily influenced by the relationship. The customer will more readily believe the information if the relationship is positive. A healthy combination of information and relationship merely primes the pump for customers to make a buying decision.[3]

Notice their emphasis on customers making a buying decision, rather than the salesperson closing the sale. Buyers want to buy, not to be sold.

Solid research provides strong evidence that questions the value of closing techniques. The research, based on more than 35,000 sales calls over 12 years, has found that in a major sale, reliance on closing techniques actually reduces the chances of making a sale.[4] Further, salespeople who were specifically trained in closing actually closed fewer sales. For very low-priced products (as in door-to-door magazine sales), however, closing techniques may increase the chances of a sale.

So why even cover closing at all? Because there are nonmanipulative and trustworthy ways to gain commitment and because obtaining commitment is critical for the success of salespeople and their firms. Without a buyer's commitment, no sale takes place. Also, buyers rarely volunteer to make the purchase, even when that decision is obviously the right thing to do. One survey of high performers found that they look at a sale as just another way of reaffirming the relationship, meaning that commitment to the relationship is more important than any single sale.[5] This chapter covers the topic of obtaining commitment in a manner that is consistent with the theme of the book: developing and building long-term partnerships.

PART OF THE PROCESS

The process of obtaining commitment occurs throughout the natural, logical progression of any sales call. Recall from Chapter 4 that creeping commitment occurs when a customer becomes committed to a particular course of action throughout the buying process. Salespeople actually gain commitment repeatedly: when asking for an appointment, when checking to see whether all of the customer's needs have been identified, and when asking whether the prospect would like to see a demonstration or receive a proposal. Commitment, of course, is more than just securing an order. As Exhibit 12.1 illustrates, salespeople will attempt to obtain a commitment that is consistent with the objectives of the particular sales call.

Exhibit 12.1
Examples of
Commitments
Salespeople May
Attempt to Obtain

Examples of Presale Commitments

- To have the prospect agree to come to the Atlanta branch office sometime during the next two weeks for a hands-on demonstration of the copier.
- To set up another appointment for one week from now, when the buyer will allow me to do a complete survey of her printing needs.
- To inform the doctor of the revolutionary anticlotting mechanism that has been incorporated into our new drug and have her agree to read the pamphlet I will leave.
- To have the buyer agree to pass my information along to the buying committee with his endorsement of my proposal.
- To have the prospect agree to call several references that I will provide to develop further confidence and trust in my office-cleaning business.
- To have the prospect agree on the first point (of our four-point program) and schedule another meeting in two days to discuss the second point.
- To have the prospect initiate the necessary paperwork to allow us to be considered as a future vendor.

Examples of Commitments That Consummate the Sale

- To have the prospect sign an order for 100 pairs of Levi's jeans.
- To schedule a co-op newspaper advertising program to be implemented in the next month.
- To have the prospect agree to use our brand of computer paper for a trial period of one month.
- To have the retailer agree to allow us space for an end-of-aisle display for the summer presentation of Raid insect repellent.

Obtaining commitment is also important in moving the account through the relationship process. Once a sale is made, salespeople begin to plan for the next sale or for the next level of commitment that indicates a deepening relationship. At the same time, commitment is a two-way street. Salespeople also make commitments to buyers when the sale is made.

THE IMPORTANCE OF SECURING COMMITMENT

Overall, gaining commitment tells the salesperson what to do next and defines the status of the client. For example, gaining a needs identification appointment may mean that you have a "suspect"; at the end of that call, gaining commitment for a demonstration means you have a prospect. Gain an order and you gain a customer. Without gaining commitment, the salesperson may waste time doing the wrong things.

Salespeople need to become proficient in obtaining commitment for several other good reasons. First, if they fail to obtain commitment, it will take longer (more sales calls) to obtain a sale, if at all. Taking more time with one sale means fewer sales overall because you lose time for prospecting and other important activities. Second, assuming the product truly satisfies the prospect's needs, the sooner the prospect buys, the sooner she or he can realize the benefits of the product or service. Third, the company's future success depends on goodwill and earning a profit. Finally, securing commitment results in financial rewards for the salesperson; in addition, meeting needs is also intrinsically rewarding for the seller.

One thing to remember is that if you have done your job well and you have a product that the buyer truly needs, then you deserve the sale. The buyer is not doing you a favor by buying, and expects you to ask for the sale if you've done your work professionally. Not only is gaining commitment important for you and your company, it is the professional thing to do. What is not professional is a high-pressure close; typically, high-pressure closing is necessary (and inappropriate) when the salesperson has not done a good job throughout the entire process.[6]

Before we get into how to obtain commitment, some time should be spent on the importance of terms and conditions of the sale and how these influence the total cost. Sometimes terms are an important need and may be presented early in the call. But we present the credit terms here because often a buyer decides what to buy and then explores the financial terms that are available.

FINANCIAL TERMS AND CONDITIONS

Price is often the last element of the deal to be presented and discussed. Yet it is often one of the most important factors when the buyer makes the decision. The final price is really a function of the terms and conditions of the sale and depends on several factors. For example, Paula Shelton, a salesperson for Cort Furniture in Washington, D.C., encountered a buyer who demanded a 15 percent price cut and several extra benefits or he would cancel a large order. She almost gave in to close the sale but then realized that getting the sale at that price and with the extra services meant that Cort would lose money. So by probing to understand what the buyer needed, she realized that more favorable payment terms would maintain the original price—and she kept the customer.

Factors that affect price are the use of quantity and other discounts, as well as credit and shipping terms. Figuring out the final actual price can be difficult, especially in situations with many options and packages rather than standardized products. Some companies have turned to special software to manage pricing and product complexities, as discussed in Sales Technology 12.1.

DISCOUNTS

Discounts are given for many reasons and may be based on the type of customer (such as wholesaler or retailer, senior citizen or younger adult), quantity purchased, or some other factor. The most common type of discount is the quantity discount.

Quantity discounts encourage large purchases by passing along savings resulting from reduced processing costs. Businesses offer two types of quantity discounts: (1) the single-order discount and (2) a cumulative discount. An office equipment company offering a 10 percent discount on a single order for five or more facsimile machines is an example of a single-order discount. When offering a **cumulative discount,** that same company might offer the 10 percent discount on all purchases over a one-year period, provided the customer purchases more than five fax machines. The customer may sign an agreement at the beginning of the year promising to buy five or more machines, in which case the customer will be billed for each order at the discounted price (10 percent off). If the customer fails to purchase five fax machines, a single bill will be sent at the end of the year for the amount of the discount (10 percent of the single-unit price times the number of fax machines actually purchased). Another method is to bill the customer at the full price and then rebate the discount at the end of the year, based on the actual number of fax machines purchased.

TECHNOLOGY TO HELP CLOSE THE DEAL

Knowing what price to quote should be relatively simple, right? But what if you have several thousand products that can be combined in any number of ways, and all combinations influence the final price? And that price is also a function of the terms offered and other factors? The impact can be significant, such as lost sales due to pricing that is too high or lost revenue because the pricing was too low.

In addition to lost revenue, salespeople lose a great deal of valuable time trying to figure out what to offer customers, in terms of both product and price. That's why so many companies are turning to product and pricing configurators—software that helps salespeople manage the myriad pricing and product combinations. For example, Quantum Corporation is a global leader in computer memory. Their products include highly complex and configurable memory devices, meaning the salesperson can design a product by combining modules. Pricing can vary, depending on whether the buyer is a distributor, user, or OEM. The system Quantum uses, Comergent Configuration Solution software, links to Quantum's man-ufacturing, accounting, and logistics systems so salespeople always have the latest price and product availability.

Crane Pumps & Systems in Piqua, Ohio, turned to Lean Front-End, a product configurator produced by BigMachines. Crane grew rapidly by acquiring nine businesses. Taking orders and taking care of customers meant more than "50 steps in the customer care process—involving too many people, hand-offs, and delays," says Regina Fitzsimmons, team leader with Crane. Lean Front-End changed that by providing a single point of entry into the company's information system for product selection, configuration, quoting, and ordering.

According to Fitzsimmons, Crane is now "miles ahead" of competitors. Letting salespeople focus on finding and serving customers instead of chasing down quotes and trying to figure out solutions has enabled Crane to grow faster than it anticipated.

Sources: Jim Fulcher, "Lean Front-End at Crane Streamlines Customer-Facing Process," *MSI*, August 2004, p. 12; Anonymous, www.comergent.com/banner/config.cfm (accessed March 7, 2005).

CREDIT TERMS

Most U.S. sales are made on a credit basis, with **cash discounts** allowed for early payment. These cash discounts are the last discount taken, meaning that if a quantity discount is also offered, the cash discount is calculated after the quantity discount is taken off. A common discount is 2/10, n/30, which means that the buyer can deduct 2 percent from the bill if it is paid within 10 days from the date of invoice. Otherwise, the full amount must be paid in 30 days. Another common discount is 2/10, EOM, which means that the 10-day period begins at the end of the month. For example, if the customer receives $1,000 worth of supplies on February 15 with terms of 2/10, EOM and pays the bill on March 5, the customer would pay $980 (that is, $1,000 at 2% = $20 discount for paying cash; $1,000–$20 = $980). But if the customer pays on March 11, the bill would be the full $1,000.

SHIPPING COSTS

The terms and conditions of sale include shipping costs. The seller who quotes a **free on board (FOB)** price agrees to load the goods on a truck, freight car, or other means of transportation.

A great many variations exist in the use of FOB, but the term is used to specify the point at which the buyer assumes responsibility for both the goods and the costs of shipping them. Thus FOB destination means that the buyer will take responsibility for the goods once they reach the buyer's location, and the seller will pay the freight.

If Home Made Brands (Newburyport, Massachusetts) receives a shipment FOB origin, then Home Made Brands pays for shipping. FOB destination means that their vendor pays for the shipping.

Spencer Grant/Photoedit

Suppose Johnson Wax quotes an FOB origin price. It will load the truck at its Racine, Wisconsin, plant, but the buyer bears the responsibility for paying for shipping. If Johnson Wax sold a truckload of Raid to Tom Thumb (a grocery chain headquartered in Dallas) under terms of FOB destination, Johnson Wax would pay for shipping and would have the Raid delivered to Tom Thumb's Dallas warehouse, where warehouse personnel would unload the truck.

Another form of FOB is FOB installed, meaning that title and responsibility do not transfer until the equipment is installed and operating properly.[7] In some instances, FOB installed can also mean that operator training must be provided before title transfers. These are important terms because there are significant costs associated with the technical installation and operator training for many pieces of sophisticated equipment. Buyers want to know the total price and what it includes.

The terms and conditions of a sale, including but not limited to price, can often play as important a role as the product itself in determining what is purchased. Creative salespeople understand the terms and conditions they have to work with so that they can meet the needs of their buyers while also meeting the profit objectives of their own companies.

PRESENTING PRICE

Price is often discussed at the end of the presentation simply because the salesperson may not know what that price will be until the final solution is agreed on. Because price is so important to the buyer, it is worth considering how price should be presented.

Most firms set prices after careful study of the competitors' offerings, the value delivered by the product or service, and the cost of providing the product or service. For these reasons the price should represent a reasonable and fair picture of the product's or service's value. Therefore, never apologize for a price or present the price apologetically; rather, present it with confidence.

The late Russ Berry, known as Father Troll because his company made troll dolls popular, related this story about when he began his business. He needed a warehouse because he worked out of his apartment in Manhattan, and there was no room to store inventory. So he knocked on the door of a house that had a sign in the window reading "Garage for rent." He expected to pay $75 a month for the garage, but when the owner of the house said the rent was $50, Berry's response was "$50!" The owner thought Berry was objecting to the price, so he responded, "OK, $35." Berry, as have many other astute businesspeople, learned to always respond with skepticism to the first price offered. Yet in his story, he believed the value of the garage was more than twice what he actually paid for it.[8]

In addition to presenting the price with confidence, remember that price is not the focus of your presentation. The real issue is satisfying the needs of the buyer, of which budget is only one. True, a budget limitation can halt progress toward a sale. The real issue, though, is the total cost of ownership, which means the buyer should also factor in the value of the benefits delivered.

WHEN TO ATTEMPT TO OBTAIN COMMITMENT

Novice salespeople frequently ask themselves these questions: Is there a right time to obtain commitment? How will customers let me know they are ready to buy? Should I make more than one attempt? What should I do if my first attempt fails?

The right time to attempt to gain commitment is when the buyer appears ready, as evidenced by buying signals. Some salespeople say that one psychological moment in each sales presentation affords the best opportunity to obtain commitment, and if this opportunity is bypassed, securing commitment will be difficult or impossible. This belief is not true, however. Seldom does one psychological moment govern the complete success or failure of a sales presentation.

Most buyers will commit themselves only when they clearly understand the benefits and costs of such a decision. At times this point occurs early in the call. A commitment to purchase a large system, however, usually will not occur until a complete presentation and several calls have been made and all questions have been answered.

Buying signals, or indications that the buyer is ready to buy, can be evidenced both in the buyer's comments and nonverbally. Buying signals are also called **closing cues.**

BUYER COMMENTS

A customer's comments often are the best indication that he or she is considering commitment. A prospect will seldom say, "All right, I'm ready to endorse this product to our buying committee." Questions about the product or terms of sale and comments in the form of requirements or benefit statements signal readiness to buy, as do responses to trial closes.

Buyer Questions

Here are some examples of questions that signal readiness to buy:

If I do agree to go with this cooperative advertising program, do you have any ads already developed that I could use?

Do you have any facilities for training our employees in the use of the product?

How soon would you be able to deliver the equipment?

Not all questions signal a readiness to buy. But if the question concerns implementing the purchase and points toward when, not if, the purchase is implemented, the prospect may be getting ready to buy.

Requirements

Requirements are conditions that have to be satisfied before a purchase can take place. For example:

We need a cash discount for a supply order like this.

We need to get this in weekly shipments.

Requirements that are stated near the end of the presentation are need statements that reflect a readiness to buy when they relate to how the purchase will be consummated. As the examples illustrate, requirements relating to financial terms or shipping indicate that the decision to buy the product has been made and now it is time to work out the details.

Benefit Statements

Sometimes prospects offer their own benefit statements, such as these:

Oh, I like the way this equipment is serviced—it will make it much easier on my staff.

Good, that color will match our office decor.

Such positive statements reflect strong feelings in support of the purchase, a sign that the buyer is ready.

Responses to Trial Closes

Salespeople can solicit such comments by continually taking the pulse of the situation with **trial closes,** or questions regarding the prospect's readiness to buy (first discussed in Chapter 9). Throughout the presentation, the salesperson should be asking questions:

> How does this sound to you so far?
>
> Is there anything else you would like to know at this point?
>
> How does this compare with what you have seen of competing products?

Such questions are an important element of any sales process because trial closes serve several purposes, including identifying the customer's proximity to making the decision, gaining agreement on minor points, and creating a true dialogue in which the ultimate close is a natural conclusion. Note that these are more general questions than simply gaining agreement on benefits (discussed in Chapter 9), say as part of a FEBA.

When a seller asks a trial close question, the buyer responds, thus creating a dialogue. Issues can be raised as objections or questions by the buyer, which tell the seller what to cover. Then, because the salesperson has been asking closing questions all along, the final close is just a natural part of the ongoing dialogue, as it should be.

NONVERBAL CUES

As in every phase of the presentation, nonverbal cues serve as important indicators of the customer's state of mind, as discussed in Chapter 5. While attempting to gain commitment, the salesperson should use the buyer's nonverbal signals to better identify areas of concern and see whether the buyer is ready to commit. Facial expressions most often indicate how ready the buyer is to make a commit-

Do the two buyers on the right look like they are ready to commit to a purchase?

© SuperStock

ment. Positive signals include eyes that are open and relaxed, face and mouth not covered with hands, a natural smile, and a relaxed forehead. The reverses of these signals indicate that the buyer is not yet ready to commit to the proposal.

Customers' actions also often indicate readiness to buy or make a commitment. For example, the prospective buyer of a fax machine may get a document and operate the machine or place the machine on the table where it will be used. The industrial buyer may refer to a catalog to compare specifications with competing products. A doctor, when told of a new drug, may pick up the pamphlet and begin carefully reading the indications and contraindications. A retailer considering whether to allow an end-of-aisle display may move to the end of an aisle and scan the layout. Any such actions may be signals for obtaining commitment; they should be viewed in the context of all available verbal and nonverbal cues.

HOW TO SUCCESSFULLY OBTAIN COMMITMENT

To obtain commitment in a nonmanipulative manner, salespeople need to follow several principles, including maintaining a positive attitude, letting the customer set the pace, being assertive instead of aggressive, and selling the right product in the right amounts.

MAINTAIN A POSITIVE ATTITUDE

Confidence is contagious. Customers like to deal with salespeople who have confidence in themselves, their products, and their companies. On the other hand, unnecessary fear can be a self-fulfilling prophecy. The student who fears essay exams usually does poorly; golfers who believe they will miss short putts usually do. So it is with salespeople: If they fear the customer will not accept their proposal, the chances are good they will be right.

One manager related the example of a salesperson selling laundry detergent who unsuccessfully tried to convince a large discount chain to adopt a new liquid version of the product. When the rep's sales manager stopped by the account later in the week to follow up on a recent stockout problem, the buyer related his reasons for refusing the liquid detergent: "Listen, I know you guys are sharp. You probably wouldn't come out with a new product unless you had tons of data to back up your decision. But, honestly, the sales rep who calls on me is always so uptight and apprehensive that I was afraid to adopt the new product! Don't you guys teach them about having confidence?"

LET THE CUSTOMER SET THE PACE

Attempts to gain commitment must be geared to fit the varying reactions, needs, and personalities of each buyer. Thus the sales representative needs to practice adaptive selling. (See Chapter 6 for a complete discussion of adaptive selling.)

Some buyers who react slowly may need plenty of time to assimilate the material presented. They may ask the same question several times or show they do not understand the importance of certain product features. In these circumstances the salesperson must deliver the presentation more slowly and may have to repeat certain parts. Trying to rush buyers is unwise when they show they are not yet ready to commit.

As we discussed earlier in the book, buyers' decision-making styles vary greatly. Japanese and Chinese buyers tend to move more slowly and cautiously when evaluating a proposition. In contrast, buyers working for *Fortune* 500 firms located in the largest U.S. cities often tend to move much more quickly. The successful salesperson recognizes such potential differences and acts accordingly.

WHEN FEAR RULES THE SALES CALL

Building relationships is an important part of selling. Yet making friends and making sales are sometimes two very different things.

George Dudley, cofounder of BSRP, a company that publishes an assessment tool used in the employment of salespeople, says, "For many salespeople, making the initial contact is much more difficult than asking for the sale. Those who avoid making new contacts can fail to grow their sales because they spend too much time with their current accounts." Other research by Willem Verbeke and Richard Bagozzi suggests that another group of salespeople may fear asking for the order, which can delay or cause failure in closing.

Dudley says that those who fear initiating contact may actually be great salespeople if they can learn to deal with their fear. Otherwise, they may look busy but actually do little prospecting. Similarly, salespeople afraid to close average more calls for every sale they do make. "We call them 'friends' or 'professional acquaintances,'" smiles Dudley. "They aren't selling, they're just visiting."

Illiki Rai, publisher of *Rising Women* magazine, says to embrace, rather than fear, rejection. As someone who sells her magazine to potential advertisers regularly, she looks at rejection as an opportunity to learn, but also as a reward of time. She says, "If you consider each rejection as an opportunity to move on to a fresh lead, you will instantly reduce your fear of cold calling." She likens sales to sport fishing; every fish you put back awards you more time to pursue a bigger fish.

Often the fear cannot be rationalized away. While advice such as that offered by Rai may make closing seem like a simple process, for those who have fear, the problem is much more.

The good news is, though, that such fear can be overcome. "Every salesperson has to deal with the fear of rejection," Dudley states. "Learning how can mean the difference between a mediocre or short sales career and unlocking one's true earning potential."

Sources: George Dudley, personal interview, March 7, 2005; Illiki Rai, "Embracing Rejection: Six Strategies to Successful Sales," *Rising Women*, www.risingwomen.com (accessed March 7, 2005); Willem Verbeke and Richard Bagozzi, "Sales Call Anxiety: What It Means When Fear Rules a Sales Encounter," *Journal of Marketing* 64 (July 2000), pp. 88–102.

BE ASSERTIVE, NOT AGGRESSIVE

Marvin Jolson has identified three types of salespeople: aggressive, submissive, and assertive.[9] **Aggressive** salespeople control the sales interaction but often fail to gain commitment because they prejudge the customer's needs and fail to probe for information. Too busy talking to do much listening, they tend to push the buyer too soon, too often, and too vigorously. They might say, I can't understand why you are hesitant, but they do not probe for reasons for the hesitancy.

Submissive salespeople often excel as socializers. With customers they spend a lot of time talking about families, restaurants, and movies. They establish rapport quite effectively. They accept the customers' statements of needs and problems but do not probe to uncover any latent needs or opportunities. Submissive salespeople rarely try to obtain commitment, or they may fear rejection too much, as discussed in Building Partnerships 12.1.

Assertive salespeople are self-confident and positive. They maintain the proper perspective by being responsive to customer needs. Rather than aggressively creating new "needs" in customers through persuasion, they look for buyers who truly need their products and then use questions to acquire information. Their presentations emphasize an exchange of information rather than a one-way presentation. Exhibit 12.2 summarizes the differences among assertive, aggressive, and submissive salespeople's handling of the sales interview.

Exhibit 12.2
How Aggressive, Submissive, and Assertive Salespeople Handle Sales Activities

	Selling Style		
Selling Activity	**Aggressive**	**Submissive**	**Assertive**
Defining customer needs	Believe they are the best judge of customer's needs	Accept customer's definition of needs	Probe for need-related information that customer may not have volunteered
Controlling the presentation	Minimize participation by customer	Permit customer to control presentation	Encourage two-way communication and customer participation
Closing the sale	Overwhelm customer; respond to objections without understanding	Assume customers will buy when ready	Respond to objections, leading to somewhat automatic close

SELL THE RIGHT ITEM IN THE RIGHT AMOUNTS

The chance of obtaining commitment improves when the right product is sold in the right amount. Although this principle sounds obvious, it often is not followed. Sometimes salespeople try to get the biggest order they can. Customers have long memories; they will refuse to do business again with someone who oversells, and they may also lack confidence in someone who undersells.

For example, before attempting to sell two copiers, the office equipment sales representative must be sure that these two copiers, instead of only one copier or perhaps three, best fit the needs of the buyer's office. The chemical company sales representative selling to an industrial firm must know that one tank car of a chemical is more likely to fit the firm's needs than ten 55-gallon drums. The Johnson Wax sales rep who utilizes the firm's Sell to Potential program knows the importance of selling neither too few units (the store will run out of stock during the promotion) nor too many units (the store will be stuck with excess inventory after the promotion). The chances to obtain commitment diminish rapidly when the salesperson tries to sell too many or too few units or the wrong grade or style of product.

Also, salespeople should not rely solely on trial orders. A **trial order** is a small order placed by a buyer to see if the product will work, and should not be confused with a trial close. A trial order is no commitment, and all too often a buyer will agree to a trial just to get rid of the salesperson. Further, if any learning curve is necessary, a customer who agrees to a trial might be unwilling to invest the time necessary to truly learn the product and will not fully realize the benefits. The product will be rejected often because customers don't have time to give fair trials. Trial orders can work well when the product is easy to implement (such as selling a new product to a retailer for resale) or when the benefits can be realized only by seeing the product in use.

EFFECTIVE METHODS

"If closing is seen by so many sales experts as manipulative and insulting, are effective methods those that are manipulative but not insulting?" asked one of our students. It is a fair question, and the answer has two elements. First, the salesperson's purpose is to sell the right product in the right amounts. If the prospect does not need what is being sold, the salesperson should walk to the

This salesperson is too aggressive; in handing the pen to the customer, the salesperson hopes that he will use it to sign the order. Such hokey tricks should be avoided.

Bill Avon/Photoedit

next door and start again. Thus there should never be a need for manipulation (review Chapter 3 for a discussion of manipulation). Second, in addition to selling only what the customer needs, the salesperson should also sell in a fashion consistent with the way the buyer prefers to buy. Therefore, the salesperson should gain commitment in a manner that will help the buyer make the choice, consistent with the principle of persuasion. We use the word *choice* here to mean that the buyer can say no. Salespeople do try to persuade buyers, but with persuasion, the choice remains with the buyer. Manipulative techniques are designed to reduce or eliminate choice; partnering methods are not.

Studying successful methods and techniques enables salespeople to help prospects buy a product or service they want or need. Buyers sometimes have a need or a want but still hesitate to buy the product or service that will satisfy it. For example, an industrial buyer for a candy manufacturer refused to commit to a change in sweeteners, even though she needed better raw material. Why? Because the sweetener rep had met with her on four separate occasions, and the buyer had difficulty remembering all that was said and agreed on. (Apparently, this salesperson was not using a software program like ACT! very effectively.) Had the salesperson used the appropriate method (the benefit summary method, discussed later in this section), commitment might have been obtained. This section describes several of the most important methods for gaining commitment.

DIRECT REQUEST

The most straightforward, effective method of obtaining commitment is simply to ask for it, called the **direct request method.** However, salespeople need to be wary of appearing overly aggressive when using this direct request method. Decisive customers, such as drivers, appreciate getting down to business and not wasting time. Here are some examples:

> Can I put you down for 100 pairs of model 63?
>
> Can we meet with your engineer next Thursday to further discuss this?
>
> Will you come to the home office for a hands-on demonstration?
>
> Can you call the meeting next week?

BENEFIT SUMMARY

Early in the interview salespeople discover or reiterate the needs and problems of the prospect. Then, throughout the presentation, they show how their product can meet those needs. They do this by turning product or service features into benefits specifically for that buyer. As they present each benefit, they ask if that benefit meets the need. When using this approach, called the **benefit summary method,** the salesperson simply reminds the prospect of the agreed-on benefits of the proposal. This nonmanipulative method helps the buyer to synthesize points covered in the presentation to make a wise decision. For example, the salesperson attempting to obtain the buyer's commitment to recommend a proposal to a buying committee might say this:

> You stated early in my visit that you were looking for a product of the highest quality, a vendor that could provide quick delivery, and adequate engineering support.

As I've mentioned, our fasteners have been rated by an independent laboratory as providing 20 percent higher tensile strength than the closest competitor, resulting in a life expectancy of more than four years. We also discussed the fact that my company can deliver fasteners to your location within 3 hours of your request and that this promise holds true 24 hours a day. Finally, I discussed the fact that we have four engineers on staff whose sole responsibility is to provide support and develop specifications for new fasteners for existing customers. Would you be willing to give the information we discussed to the buying committee along with your endorsement of the proposal?

One advantage of the benefit summary method over the direct request method is that the seller can help the buyer remember all the points discussed in the presentation. The summary becomes particularly important in long presentations and in selling situations involving several meetings prior to obtaining commitment. The salesperson cannot assume that the buyer will remember all the major points discussed in the presentation.

BALANCE SHEET METHOD

Sometimes referred to as the *Ben Franklin method* because Franklin described using it to make decisions, the **balance sheet method** aids prospects who cannot make a decision, even though no reason for their behavior is apparent. Such a prospect may be asked to join the salesperson in listing the pros and cons of buying now or buying later, of buying the salesperson's product or that of a competitor, or of buying the product or not buying it at all.

However, like many nonmanipulative sales techniques, this method can insult a buyer's intelligence if used inappropriately. The salesperson may start to obtain commitment with the following type of statement:

You know, Mr. Thacker, Ben Franklin was like you, always anxious to reach the right decisions and avoid the wrong ones. I suppose that's how you feel. Well, he suggested taking a piece of paper and writing all the reasons for deciding yes in one column and then listing the reasons for deciding no in a second column. He said that when you make this kind of graphic comparison, the correct decision becomes much more apparent.

That close may seem manipulative; it certainly sounds silly. A more effective start may be to simply draw a T on a plain piece of paper, place captions on each side of the crossbar, and leave space below for the insertion of specific benefits or sales points. Then just ask the buyer to list pros and cons of making the purchase. For example, assume the product is National Adhesives's hot-melt adhesive used to attach paper labels to plastic Coke bottles. Coca-Cola is currently using a liquid adhesive made by Ajax Corporation. The top of the T might look like this:

Benefits of Adopting the National Adhesives Hot-Melt Method	Benefits of Staying with the Ajax Liquid Adhesives

The salesperson may say something like, "Making a decision like this is difficult. Let's see how many reasons we can think of for your going with the National Adhesives system." The salesperson would write the benefits (not features) in which the customer has shown interest on the left side of the T. Next the salesperson would ask the customer to list reasons to stay with the Ajax adhesive on the right side. When completed, the T lists should accurately reflect all the pros and cons of each possible decision. At that point the buyer is asked, "Which method do you think is the wisest?"

When used properly, the balance sheet method can help hesitant buyers express their feelings about the decision in a manner similar to the multiattribute matrix (Chapter 4), which gives the salesperson an opportunity to deal with those feelings. It is especially appropriate for a buyer who is analytical, but would make less sense for an expressive. However, the balance sheet approach takes time and may appear "salesy," particularly if relatively unimportant benefits are considered to be equal to more important reasons not to buy. Also, the list of benefits of the product being sold will not always outnumber the list on the other side of the T.

PROBING METHOD

In the **probing method** sales representatives initially attempt to obtain commitment by another method, perhaps simply asking for it (the direct request method). If unsuccessful, the salesperson uses a series of probing questions designed to discover the reason for the hesitation. Once the reason(s) becomes apparent, the salesperson asks a what-if question. (What if I could successfully resolve this concern? Would you be willing to commit?) An illustrative dialogue follows:

SALESPERSON: Could we make an appointment for next week, at which time I would come in and do a complete survey of your needs? It shouldn't take more than three hours.

PROSPECT: No, I don't think I am quite ready to take that step yet.

SALESPERSON: There must be some reason why you are hesitating to go ahead now. Do you mind if I ask what it is?

PROSPECT: I'm just not convinced that your firm is large enough to handle a customer of our size.

SALESPERSON: In addition to that, is there any other reason why you would not be willing to go ahead?

PROSPECT: No.

SALESPERSON: If I can resolve the issue of our size, then you would allow me to conduct a survey?

PROSPECT: Well, I wouldn't exactly say that.

SALESPERSON: Then there must be some other reason. May I ask what it is?

PROSPECT: Well, a friend of mine who uses your services told me that often your billing department sends him invoices for material he didn't want and didn't receive.

SALESPERSON: In addition to that, is there any other reason for not going ahead now?

PROSPECT: No, those are my two concerns.

SALESPERSON: If I could resolve those issues right now, would you be willing to set up an appointment for a survey?

PROSPECT: Sure.

This dialogue illustrates the importance of probing in obtaining commitment. The method attempts to bring to the table all issues of concern to the prospect.

The salesperson does not claim to be able to resolve the issues but simply attempts to find out what the issues are. When probing has identified all the issues, the salesperson should attempt to resolve them as soon as possible. After successfully dealing with the concerns of the buyer, the salesperson should then ask for a commitment.

There are many modifications of the probing method. One other way to achieve the same result is the following:

SALESPERSON: Are you willing to buy this product today?

PROSPECT: No, I don't think so.

SALESPERSON: I really would like to get a better feel of where you are. On a scale of 1 to 10, with 1 being absolutely no purchase and 10 being purchase, where would you say you are?

PROSPECT: I would say I'm about a 6.

SALESPERSON: If you don't mind my asking, what would it take to move you from a 6 to a 10?

Also, it is important to always keep cultural differences in mind. For example, if a Japanese businesswoman wants to tell an American salesperson that she is not interested, she might state, "Your proposal would be very difficult," just to be polite. If the seller attempts to use the probing method, the Japanese business-woman may consider the seller to be pushy or a poor listener. In the same way, an Arab businessperson will never say no directly, a custom that helps both sides avoid losing face.[10]

ALTERNATIVE CHOICE

In many situations a salesperson may have multiple options to present to a buyer. For example, Teo Schaars sells diamonds directly from cutters in the Netherlands to consumers in the United States. When he started in sales, he would display several dozen diamonds on a purple damask–covered table. Sales were few until his father, a Dutch diamond broker, suggested that he limit his customers' choices; there were simply too many diamonds to choose from, overwhelming the buyer. Schaars found his father's comments to be wise advice. Now Schaars spends more time probing about budget and desires and then shows only two diamonds at a time, explaining the key characteristics of each. Then he allows the customer to express a preference. Schaars may have to show half a dozen or more diamonds before a customer makes the final decision, but he rarely shows more than two at a time.

OTHER METHODS

Literally hundreds of techniques and methods to obtain commitment have been tried. Exhibit 12.3 lists a number of traditional methods. Most of them, however, tend to be ineffective with sophisticated customers; nevertheless, many can be used in a nonmanipulative manner if appropriate. For example, the minor-point close can be appropriate if there really is a need to choose between two options; the factor that makes the method manipulative is the assumption that the minor choice is the equivalent to making the sale.

No method of obtaining commitment will work if the buyer does not trust the salesperson, the company, and the product. Gaining commitment should not require the use of tricky techniques or methods to force buyers to do something they do not want to do or to manipulate them to buy something they do not need.

Exhibit 12.3
Some Traditional Closing Methods

Method	How It Works	Remark
Minor-point close	The seller assumes it is easier to get the prospect to decide on a very trivial point than on the whole proposition: What color do you like, blue or red?	This method can upset a prospect who feels he or she is being manipulated or tricked into making a commitment. Even unsophisticated buyers easily spot this technique.
Continuous *yes* close	Throughout the presentation, the seller constantly asks questions for which the prospect most logically would answer *yes*. By the end of the discussion, the buyer is so accustomed to saying *yes* that when the order is requested, the natural response is *yes*.	This method is based on self-perception theory. As the presentation progresses, the buyer begins to perceive himself or herself as being agreeable. At the close, the buyer wants to maintain this self-image and almost unthinkingly says *yes*. Use of this method can destroy long-term relationships if the buyer later feels manipulated.
Assumptive close	The seller, without asking for the order, simply begins to write it up. A variation is to fill out the order form as the prospect answers questions.	This method does not even give the buyer the courtesy of agreeing. It can be perceived as being very pushy and manipulative.
Standing-room-only close	This method can be effective if the statement is true. However, if the prospect really does need to act quickly, this deadline should probably be discussed earlier in the presentation to reduce possible mistrust and the feeling of being pushed.	The seller attempts to obtain commitment by describing the negative consequences of waiting. For example, the seller may state, "If you can't decide now, I'll have to offer it to another customer."
Benefit-in-reserve close	First, the seller attempts to obtain commitment by another method. If unsuccessful, the seller says, "Oh, if you order today I can offer you an additional 5 percent for your trade-in."	This method can backfire easily. The buyer tends to think, "If I had agreed to your first attempt to obtain commitment, I would not have learned about this new enticement. If I wait longer, how much better will your offer be?" The buyer may then seek additional concessions in every future sale attempt.
Emotional close	The seller appeals to the buyer's emotions to close the sale. For example, the seller may say, "This really is a good deal. To be honest with you, I desperately need to secure an order today. As you know, I work on a straight commission basis. My wife is going to have surgery next week, and our insurance just won't cover . . ."	Many obvious problems arise with this method. It is an attempt to move away from focusing entirely on the buyer's personal needs. It does not develop trust or respect. Do not use this close!

IF COMMITMENT IS OBTAINED

The salesperson's job is not over when commitment is obtained. In fact, in many ways the job is just beginning. This section describes the salesperson's responsibilities that accrue after the buyer says yes.

NO SURPRISES

Customers do not like surprises, so now is the time to go over any important information they will need to fully enjoy the benefits of the product or service. For example, if you are selling life insurance and a physical is required, give the customer as much detail as possible to prepare him or her for that experience. Or if a company is going to lease a piece of heavy equipment, let the customer know that delivery will occur after a credit check and how long that credit check will take. No customer wants to be kept waiting in the dark, not knowing whether he or she will ever get the new product.

CONFIRM THE CUSTOMER'S CHOICE

Customers like to believe they have chosen intelligently when they make a decision. After important decisions, they may feel a little insecure about whether the sacrifice is worth it. Such feelings are called **buyer's remorse** or **postpurchase dissonance.** Successful salespeople reassure customers that their choice was judicious.[11] For example:

> I know you will enjoy using your new office machines. You can plan on many months of trouble-free service. I'll call on you in about two weeks to make sure everything is operating smoothly. Be sure to call me if you need any help before then.

Or:

> Congratulations, Mr. Jacobs. You are going to be glad you decided to use our service. There is no finer service available. Now let's make certain you get off to the right start. Your first bulletin will arrive on Tuesday, March 2.

One way to help customers feel good about their decision is to assure them that they have made an intelligent choice. Remarks such as the following may also be appropriate:

> You've made an excellent choice. Other stores won't have a product like this for at least 30 days.
>
> You've chosen an excellent model. Did you see it advertised in last week's *Time?*
>
> Your mechanics will thank you for ordering these tools. You will be able to get your work out much faster.

GET THE SIGNATURE

The buyer's signature often formalizes a commitment. Signing the order is a natural part of a well-planned procedure. The order blank should be accessible, and the signing should be treated as a routine matter. Ordinarily, the customer has decided to buy before being asked to sign the order. In other words, the signature on the order blank merely confirms that an agreement has already been reached. The decision to buy or not to buy should not focus on a signature.

The salesperson needs to remember several important points: (1) Make the actual signing an easy, routine procedure; (2) fill out the order blank accurately and promptly; and (3) be careful not to exhibit any excess eagerness or excitement when the prospect is about to sign.

SHOW APPRECIATION

All buyers like to think that their business is appreciated even if they purchase only small quantities. Customers like to do business with salespeople who show that they want the business.

Salespeople may show appreciation by writing the purchaser a letter. This practice develops goodwill, especially after large purchases and with new customers. In some situations a small gift, such as a pen with the selling company's name on it, may also be an effective thank-you. Salespeople should always thank the purchaser personally; the thanks should be genuine but not effusive.

CULTIVATE FOR FUTURE CALLS

In most fields of selling, obtaining commitment is not the end of a business transaction; rather, it is only one part of a mutually profitable business relationship. Obtaining commitment is successful only if it results in goodwill and future commitment. Keep in mind that research shows that it is how the salesperson treats the customer that is the biggest determinant of future sales.[12]

Customers like to do business with salespeople who do not lose interest immediately after securing commitment. What a salesperson does after achieving commitment is called **follow-up.** As Frank DiCarlo, sales director for Calvin Klein, recognizes, "Making the sale is only the beginning." After making the sale, the salesperson must follow up to be sure the product is delivered when promised, set up appropriately, and so forth. We talk more about follow-up in later chapters. The point here is that the sale does not end with the customer's signature on the order form. Research shows that the quality of follow-up service is an important contributing factor in perceptions of salesperson quality and long-term relationships.[13]

REVIEW THE ACTIONS TO BE TAKEN

An important step, particularly when commitment is next in the buying process, is to review what each party has agreed to do. In the case of a multiple-visit sales cycle, the salesperson must review not only what the client will do but also what the salesperson will do to prepare for the next meeting. To be welcomed on repeat calls, salespeople must be considerate of all of the parties involved in buying or using the product. They must pronounce and spell all names correctly, explain and review the terms of the purchase so no misunderstandings will occur, and be sociable and cordial to subordinates as well as those in key positions. In addition, the buyer or user must get the service promised. The importance of this point cannot be overemphasized. Chapter 14 provides detailed information about how to service the account and build a partnership.

IF COMMITMENT IS NOT OBTAINED

Naturally, the salesperson does not always obtain the desired commitment. The salesperson should never take this situation personally (which is easier said than done). Doing everything right does not guarantee a sale. Situations change, and customers who may have really needed the product when everything started may find that other priorities make a purchase impossible, such as illustrated in Selling Scenario 12.1.

Many times, when a buyer says "No," the seller is wise to treat it as "No, not now" rather than "No, never." Adriana Copaceanu started ABC Gifts and Baskets (her company fills baskets with gifts that companies give to their customers) and was looking for her first account. She heard of one business owner who made her own baskets, so Copaceanu called her, only to learn that the buyer had already made all she wanted for the year. So Copaceanu sent her a "thank-you" basket along with company information. The woman called two days later and purchased 150 baskets![14]

"No" can mean "No forever," though, if the rep isn't listening and isn't sensitive to the buyer's needs. Sid Gottlieb, VP of sales and marketing for Corporate Sport, Inc., told a salesperson early in the conversation that he would not be buying anything for about six weeks. She ignored his cue to wrap things up and call back later by showing new items. After nearly 45 minutes, he asked her if she always took this long. Her reply was "I spend as much time as needed to get the order signed." As Gottlieb admits, "Don't assume that a delay or postponement is an automatic no." But that salesperson's lack of sensitivity and inability to listen cost her any future opportunities with Gottlieb.[15]

thinking **it** through | Many students report that asking for the order is the hardest part of selling. Why is it difficult? Does the customer need you to ask for the sale? Have you ever needed a salesperson to ask you to buy? Why or why not?

WHAT DOES "NO" MEAN?

There's a saying in sales that when a buyer says "No," the real meaning is not "No forever" but "No, not right now." The buyer may have a solution that looks better now, but every buyer has to make similar purchases in the future, and you'll get your shot then.

That's what happened to Jon Lawrence, who owns a business of taping presentations made at conferences that the conference sponsors then sell to attendees. "We sell the CDs to the attendees for the customer and then pay the customer a royalty based on the total sales. Our competitor promised to pay a 50 percent royalty, much more than I can pay. You can do that only if you have very old equipment or if you underreport how much was sold to the customer." Sure enough, the client discovered that Lawrence's competitor's accounting didn't add up, and it wasn't long before they asked Lawrence back.

Brad Bischof, an account manager with Carlson Marketing, had a customer who gave him part of his business, but none of his travel and event planning business. With three major events looming and nothing getting done, the client discovered that his travel and event planner had misused deposits to save her own failing business. The client asked Bischof to handle it, even though it was last-minute. Bischof's team worked a miracle, at least in the client's eyes, and completed all three events flawlessly.

A buyer who makes a decision to buy today will have to make that decision again; "No" doesn't have to be "No forever!" Both Lawrence and Bischof advise staying true to one's self and staying close to the customer, and as your reputation grows for doing it the right way, so will the opportunities.

This section describes some common reasons for failing to obtain commitment and offers practical suggestions for salespeople who encounter rejection.

SOME REASONS FOR LOST OPPORTUNITIES

Wrong Attitudes

As discussed earlier in the chapter, salespeople need to have a positive attitude. A fear that obtaining commitment will be difficult may be impossible to hide. Inexperienced salespeople naturally will be concerned about their ability to obtain commitment; most of us have an innate fear of asking someone else to do anything. Some salespeople even fail to ask for the sale because if they never ask, they will never hear no. As a result, they always have more prospects but fewer customers than everyone else. But all salespeople know they need to focus on obtaining commitment to keep their jobs.

Some salespeople display unwarranted excitement when they see that prospects are ready to commit. A salesperson who appears excited or overly eager may display nonverbal cues that suggest dishonesty or a lack of empathy.[16] At this point wary buyers may change their minds and refuse to commit.

One of the main reasons for salespeople's improper attitudes toward obtaining commitment is the historical importance placed on closing the sale. Closing has often been viewed as a win–lose situation (if I get the order, I win; if I don't get the order, I lose). Until salespeople see obtaining commitment as a positive occurrence for the buyer, these attitudes will persist.

Poor Presentation

Prospects or customers who do not understand the presentation or see the benefits of the purchase cannot be expected to buy. The salesperson must use trial closes (see Chapter 9) and continually take the pulse of the interview.

A poor presentation can also be caused by haste. The salesperson who tries to deliver a 60-minute presentation in 20 minutes may skim over or omit important sales points. Forgoing the presentation may be better than delivering it hastily. Further, a sales presentation given at the wrong time or under unfavorable conditions is likely to be ineffective.

Another reason for not obtaining commitment is lack of product knowledge. In fact, lack of product knowledge is often cited as an important barrier to obtaining commitment.[17] If the salesperson does not know what the product does, you can be certain the buyer will not be able to figure it out either.

Poor Habits and Skills

Obtaining commitment requires proper habits and some measure of skill. The habit of talking too much rather than listening often causes otherwise good presentations to fail. Knowing when to quit talking is just as important as knowing what to say. Some salespeople become so fascinated by the sound of their own voices that they talk themselves out of sales they have already made. A presentation that turns into a monologue is not likely to retain the buyer's interest.

DISCOVERING THE CAUSE

The real reasons for not obtaining commitment must be uncovered. Only then can salespeople proceed intelligently to eliminate the barriers. Some firms have developed sophisticated systems to follow up on lost sales. Sales software, such as ACT! or salesforce.com, can also identify points in the selling process where a salesperson may be having difficulty. If the sales cycle involves a demonstration, for example, and the salesperson turns fewer leads into demonstrations, the fault may lie in the needs identification skills of that salesperson.

SUGGESTIONS FOR DEALING WITH REJECTION

Maintain the Proper Perspective

Probably the inexperienced salesperson's most important lesson is that when a buyer says no, the sales process has not necessarily ended. A no may mean "Not now," "I need more information," "Don't hurry me," or "I don't understand." An answer of no should be a challenge to seek the reason behind the buyer's negative response.

In many fields of selling, most prospects do not buy. The ratio of orders achieved to sales presentations may be 1 to 3, 1 to 5, 1 to 10, or even 1 to 20. Salespeople may tend to eliminate nonbuyers from the prospect list after one unsuccessful call. This practice may be sound in some cases; however, many sales result on the second, third, fourth, or fifth call. Dean Yeck, sales manager with Qwest, says one sale took 15 sales calls.[18] When an earlier visit has not resulted in commitment, careful preparation for succeeding calls becomes more crucial.

Another perspective is that when a buyer says no it is because the buyer is not yet fully informed; otherwise, the buyer would have said yes. Consequently, if the buyer has given the salesperson the opportunity to make a presentation, the buyer recognizes that a need exists or is going to exist. What has not happened yet is that match between the offering and the need. At the same time, however, no does not mean "Sell me again right now." It may mean "Sell me again later." Illiki Rai, publisher of *Rising Women* magazine, agrees, noting that when she sells her magazine to prospective advertisers, rejection is often temporary and can lead to referrals as well as future sales opportunities.[19]

The salesperson should have a clear objective for each sales call. When commitment cannot be obtained to meet that objective, the salesperson will often attempt to obtain commitment for a reduced request (a secondary or minimum objective). For example, the salesperson may attempt to gain a trial order instead of an actual order, although, as we discussed earlier, this opportunity should be offered as a last resort.

Recommend Other Sources

A sales representative who uses the consultative selling philosophy (as described in Chapter 6) may recommend a competitor's product to solve the prospect's needs. When recommending other sources, the sales rep should explain why his or her product does not meet the prospect's needs and then provide the name of the competitive product. The goodwill generated by such a gesture should lead to future opportunities when the timing and needs are right.

After recommending other sources, the salesperson usually should ask the prospect for names of people who might be able to buy the seller's product. Also, the salesperson should emphasize the desire to maintain contact with the prospect in the event the seller's firm develops a competitive offering.

Good Manners Are Important

If obtaining commitment fails for any reason, the salesperson should react good-naturedly. Salespeople have to learn to accept no if they expect to call on prospects again. Even if salespeople do not obtain commitment, they should thank prospects for their time. Arguing or showing disappointment gains nothing. The salesperson may plan to keep in contact with these prospects through an occasional phone call, a follow-up letter, or product literature mailings. One salesperson likes to make the following statement at the conclusion of any meeting that does not result in commitment: "I'll never annoy you, but if you don't mind, I'm going to keep in touch."

It is a good idea to leave something behind that will let the prospect contact the salesperson in the future. Many firms use promotional products, such as a pen with the company's name and phone number, as a gift after each call to remind the prospect of the salesperson's company.

Some companies use promotional products, such as pens with the company's name and phone number on them, as something to leave behind and remind the customer of the salesperson's company.

Jeff Greenberg/Photoedit

BRINGING THE INTERVIEW TO A CLOSE

Few buyers are interested in a prolonged visit after they commit. Obviously, the departure cannot be abrupt; the salesperson should complete the interview smoothly. Goodwill is never built by wasting the buyer's time after the business is concluded.

Remember that most sales take several calls to complete. If an order wasn't signed (and often getting an order isn't even the objective of the call; see Chapter 8) and the prospect wishes to continue considering the proposal, the salesperson should leave with a clear action plan for all parties. An example of the kind of dialogue the salesperson might pursue follows:

SALESPERSON: When will you have had a chance to look over this proposal?

BUYER: By the end of next week, probably.

SALESPERSON: Great, I'll call on you in about 10 days, OK?

BUYER: Sure, set up something with my secretary.

SALESPERSON: Is there anything else I need to do for you before that next meeting?

The salesperson should always make sure the next step is clear for both parties. Therefore, review what you will do next, what the customer will do next, and when you will meet again.[20]

Often it is important that you follow up promptly with a thank-you and reminder note after the sales call. Mark Prude, a business consultant, suggests writing a note by hand immediately after the meeting, again reviewing what was said, what is to be done, and confirming the next meeting. By taking this action immediately, he avoids memory lapses, and his follow-up does not pile up! Such letters can also present a professional image and help customers remember the important points of the meeting.[21]

SUMMARY

Commitment cannot be obtained by some magical or miraculous technique if the salesperson has failed to prepare the prospect to make this decision throughout the presentation. Salespeople should always attempt to gain commitment in a way that is consistent with the objectives of the meeting. Obtaining commitment begins with the salesperson's contact with the prospect. It can succeed only when all facets of the selling process fall into their proper place. All sellers need to keep in mind the old saying: "People don't buy products or services; they buy solutions to their problems!"

The process of obtaining commitment is the logical progression of any sales call. Commitment is important for the customer, the seller's firm, and the seller. Commitments should result in a win–win situation for all parties concerned.

Pricing is an important element of any sale and is usually presented at the time of closing. Quantity discounts, payment terms, and shipping terms can affect the final price charged to the buyer as well as influence the decision.

There is no one "right" time to obtain commitment. Salespeople should watch their prospects closely and recognize when to obtain commitment. Successful salespeople carefully monitor customer comments, their buyers' nonverbal cues and actions, and their responses to probes. Comments can be in the form of questions, requirements, benefits, and responses to trial closes.

To successfully obtain commitment, the salesperson needs to maintain a positive attitude, allow the customer to set the pace, be assertive rather than aggressive, and sell the right item in the right amounts. Engaging in these practices will result in a strong long-term relationship between buyer and seller.

No one method of obtaining commitment works best for all buyers. The direct request method is the simplest to use; however, the prospect often needs help in evaluating the proposal. In those instances other methods may be more appropriate, such as the alternative choice, the benefit summary, the balance sheet method, or the probing method. No method of obtaining commitment will work if a buyer does not trust the salesperson.

If commitment is obtained, the salesperson should immediately assure the buyer that the choice was judicious. The salesperson should show genuine appreciation as well as cultivate the relationship for future calls.

If commitment is not obtained, the salesperson should analyze the reasons. Difficulties in obtaining commitment can be directly traced to wrong attitudes, a poor presentation, and/or poor habits and skills. Even if no commitment is obtained, the salesperson should thank the prospect for his or her time.

KEY TERMS

aggressive
assertive
balance sheet method
benefit summary method
buyer's remorse
buying signals
cash discount
closing
closing cues
cumulative discount

direct request method
follow-up
free on board (FOB)
postpurchase dissonance
probing method
requirements
submissive
trial close
trial order

ETHICS PROBLEMS

1. One buyer stated, "All closing methods are devious and self-serving! How can a salesperson use a technique but still keep my needs totally in mind?" Comment. Integrate into your discussion the concepts of persuasion versus manipulation.

2. Which laws govern the obtaining-commitment portion of a sales presentation? (Refer to Chapter 3 if needed.) How can a salesperson stay within these laws while attempting to gain commitment?

QUESTIONS AND PROBLEMS

1. Review the closing methods in Exhibit 12.3 and write out a nonmanipulative and a manipulative version of each. What is the difference?

2. "The ABCs of closing are 'Always be closing.'" Another version is "Close early—close often." What is your reaction to these time-honored statements?

3. Harold Bumpurs, a professional purchasing agent, says he has never noticed any tricky closes. His perception is due not to the smooth closing skills of the salespeople who call on him but to the total skill set they have developed. Prioritize a list of selling skills, from most important to least. How much time should be spent improving commitment-gaining skills as opposed to developing other skills? Why?

4. You are selling institutional refrigerators for use in school cafeterias, restaurants, and so on. After making a presentation that you think went rather well, you request the order and get this reply: "What you say sounds interesting, but I want some time to think it over." You answer, "Well, OK. Would next Tuesday be a good day for me to come back?" How can you improve on your answer?

5. One sales manager who worked for a refrigeration equipment company taught his salespeople the following close: Ask questions that allow you to fill out the contract. Assume the sale is made and hand the contract to the buyer, along with a pen. If the buyer doesn't immediately take the pen, drop it and make the buyer pick it up. Once the buyer has the pen in hand, he or she is more likely to use it to sign the contract, so just wait silently until the buyer does.
   a. Would you label this seller as assertive or aggressive?
   b. Is this a trick or merely dramatization?
   c. How would you respond to this behavior if you were the buyer?

6. The buyer says "No!" and you suspect it is because she doesn't trust you. You have a lot riding on this sale, and you also believe that you have the best solution for the buyer. What do you do?

7. What makes a Lexus worth more than a Honda? How would you convince someone that it is worth more if she or he knew nothing about the various brands of cars? How would the buyer's lack of knowledge influence how you try to gain commitment?

8. A sales manager once told a salesperson, "You know that when Ms. Jacobs told you no, she was saying no to your proposal; she was not rejecting you personally." Why is understanding that statement vital to all salespeople?

9. Most of us have a natural fear of asking someone else to do something. What can you, as a student, do now to reduce such fear?

10. What would you say to a friend to gain his or her commitment to go on a spring break trip? Describe exactly what you would say to your friend, using each of the following methods (make any assumptions necessary):
   a. Alternative choice.
   b. Direct request.
   c. Benefit summary.
   d. Balance sheet.
   e. Probing.

11. A customer is willing to order 100 cases listed at $20 per case to get a 15 percent quantity discount. Terms are 2/10, n30. The customer pays five days after receiving the invoice. How much did the customer pay?

CASE PROBLEMS

case **12.1**

Fischer Electronics

Fischer Electronics manufactures handheld scanning devices that are used in inventory management. Used in any environment where tracking inventory is important, these devices scan the UPC bar code and are used to track movement of products within a warehouse or business. Frank May is calling on Abby Brewster, senior purchasing director for Moore International. Abby has global responsibility for purchasing standardization, and developing a common inventory management system across all of Moore's 32 locations in 12 countries is a task she has to complete this year. His primary call objective is to have Abby agree to set up an appointment in the next several weeks for Frank to present to the supply chain committee that will review proposals and narrow the choices down to three systems.

> FRANK: Our scanning systems can support the digital standards of both the United States and Europe, which means that, with some engineering changes in your computer network, your locations can use the same scanners.
>
> ABBY: Frank, I've really been thinking that the scanners built by Nortel are industry standard. What has Fischer done differently with these scanners?
>
> FRANK: Quality is something we take very seriously at Fischer, but having the best-built old product isn't enough, is it? So we've also built probably the finest engineering staff over the past five years that you'll find anywhere. The result is a product line that was just awarded the Sultan's Engineering Award for Innovation in Egypt only last month.
>
> ABBY: That's impressive, and you're right. A well-built product using yesterday's technology is of no benefit to us. But how important is bicontinental use at the scanning level? Can't we just scan and convert the data into a common format later?
>
> FRANK: Yes, you can, but that's really inconsistent with the overall strategy of minimizing the number of vendors and having global suppliers. Plus, you may have seen a report issued by DataMark that indicates some users have had data problems that were difficult to identify until something goes horribly wrong.
>
> ABBY: I've seen that data from DataMark, as well as an article in the last issue of *Supply Chain Management*. But we've had no plans for such scanners.
>
> FRANK: Why is that?
>
> ABBY: We don't know that it is necessary—we don't think we've got that many locations where scanning is a necessity.

FRANK: What would be considered a significant percentage—of your total sites, I mean?

ABBY: I would guess 50 percent would be acceptable. What are others experiencing?

FRANK: We've got several, maybe four, that have standardized with us globally; another group of about two dozen that use us in the United States or North America. How does that sound?

ABBY: Intriguing, though we're not the same as others.

FRANK: I know. That's why I'd like to set up a meeting with your supply chain team in the near future. But we'll probably also need someone there from logistics, right?

ABBY: Yes, I suppose we would.

FRANK: Will I have your endorsement at the meeting?

ABBY: We'll have to wait and see. I'll need some documentation on the figures you've given me, and I'd like that before we set up the meeting.

Questions

1. What form of closing did Frank use to gain Abby's commitment to the idea? Was that appropriate? Why or why not?

2. List how you would attempt to obtain commitment using three other methods of your choice. Write out exactly what you would say for each method (and be sure to identify the method).

3. Although you have been shown only a portion of the conversation, evaluate Frank's performance in terms of the following:
   a. Selling benefits, not features.
   b. Using trial closes.
   c. Using communication aids to strengthen the presentation.
   d. Responding to objections.
   e. Attempting to gain commitment at the proper time.

case **12.2**

Huffman's ABC Seminar

Huffman Manufacturing is a large manufacturer of retail store fixtures in Montreal and distributes to stores in the eastern half of Canada and the Great Lakes region of the United States. Customers include fashion clothing retailers, hardware stores, garden centers, and restaurants; just about any retail outlet uses Huffman products or something similar. Recently, sales have been stagnant at best, and declining in most areas. To counter the problem, Ms. Huffman, daughter of the firm's founder and VP of sales, brought in noted Canadian sales guru François Carrafour to conduct sales training. After a few opening comments, he asked for salespeople to share their most recent "best" closing story. Jacque Dubois was describing his sales call with Emerald Cloud, a large hotel in Quebec.

JACQUE: I knew we had the best solution for the hotel's retail stores. I wasn't going to take no for an answer. Why, I saved the hotel 15 percent from its costs for last year's redecoration of the restaurant and bar. So when the committee seemed to be hesitating, I pulled out the contract and asked, "Now, will you want the walnut burl display finish or the polished chrome?" And when the head guy said they wanted the polished chrome, I began filling out the contract. After I asked a few more questions, one woman asked, "What are you doing?" I said, "I'm filling out our agreement. I know you're going to really enjoy how this will look in your newsstand at the Emerald." She just swallowed but didn't say anything, and that's when I knew I had it.

CLAUDINE NATALE [interrupting]: Oh, that's nothing. You should have seen me close the Marshall Fine Art Gallery. I handed the buyer the contract, and she just sat there and stared at it. I wasn't going to say anything—I knew that if I did, I lost. I swear, it was dead silence for nearly five minutes. Then she signed it and handed it back to me. I just thanked her and got out of there as fast as I could, before she could change her mind!

In Jean's mind, he could hear his own feeble first attempts at closing. In fact, for Jean's first sale the buyer said, "Well, don't you have a contract or something?" He wondered whether he could get as good at closing as Jacque and Claudine, as he earnestly took notes during the seminar.

Questions

1. Assess the styles of Jacque, Claudine, and Jean. Identify each style. What evidence supports your claim?
2. What would you suggest Jean do? Be as specific as possible and explain your recommendation.

ACT! ROLE PLAY

Once again, you will present your presentation to the same buyer (Skylight, Binswanger, or Lincoln) as you did after Chapters 10 and 11. (If you did not do role plays after those chapters, review that material now.) This time, you will do your presentation, first summarizing the needs and going all the way to asking for the sale. You will have an opportunity to work on presentation, objection handling, and closing skills.

If two people are involved in the sale (a seller and a buyer) while a third observes, the observer should do the following:

1. Identify any objection-handling methods used.
2. Determine whether the seller is focused on benefits or only features.
3. Note when trial closes are used.
4. Identify the closing method used.

The professor will pass out new buyer sheets.

ADDITIONAL REFERENCES

Anderson, James C., and James A. Narus. "Selectively Pursuing More of Your Customer's Business." *Sloan Management Review* 44, no. 3 (2003), pp. 42–49.

Ingram, Thomas N.; Raymond W. LaForge; and Thomas W. Leigh. "Selling in the New Millennium: A Joint Agenda." *Industrial Marketing Management* 31 (2002), pp. 559–77.

Jain, Dipak, and Siddharta Singh. "Customer Lifetime Value Research in Marketing: A Review and Future Directions." *Journal of Interactive Marketing* 16, no. 2 (2002), pp. 34–46.

McCrea, Bridget. "Order Up!" *Industrial Distribution* 92 (May 2004), pp. 60–61.

Niraj, Rakesh; Mahendra Gupta; and Chakravarthi Narasimhan. "Customer Profitability in a Supply Chain." *Journal of Marketing* 65 (July 2001), pp. 1–16.

Reid, David A.; Ellen Bolman Pullins; Richard E. Plank; and Richard E. Buehrer. "Measuring Buyers' Perceptions of Conflict in Business-to-Business Sales Interactions." *Journal of Business & Industrial Marketing* 19 (April 5, 2004), pp. 236–54.

Thakor, Mrugank V., and Ashwin W. Joshi. "Motivating Salesperson Customer Orientation: Insights from the Job Characteristics Model." *Journal of Business Research* 58 (May 2005), pp. 584–601.

Thomas, Jacquelyn S.; Robert C. Blattberg; and Edward Fox. "Recapturing Lost Customers." *Journal of Marketing Research* 41 (February 2004), pp. 31–45.

Van Raaij, Erik M.; Maarten J. A. Vernooij; and Sander van Triest. "The Implementation of Customer Profitability Analysis: A Case Study." *Industrial Marketing Management* 32 (2003), pp. 573–83.

Vargo, Stephen L., and Robert Lusch. "Evolving to a New Dominant Logic in Marketing." *Journal of Marketing* 68, no. 1 (2004), pp. 1–25.

Verbeke, W.; F. Belschak; and R. P. Bagozzi. "The Adaptive Consequences of Pride in Personal Selling." *Journal of the Academy of Marketing Science* 32, no. 4 (2004), pp. 386–402.

FORMAL NEGOTIATING

chapter 13

SOME QUESTIONS ANSWERED IN THIS CHAPTER . . .

- What is negotiation selling? How does it differ from nonnegotiation selling?

- What items can be negotiated in selling?

- What type of planning needs to occur prior to a negotiation meeting? How should a seller set objectives?

- How can the negotiation session be effectively opened? What role does friendly conversation play?

- Which negotiation strategies and tactics do buyers use? How should negotiators respond?

- What are the salesperson's guidelines for offering and requesting concessions?

PROFILE

After receiving my bachelor's degree in agronomy from Universidad de la Republica–Facultad de Agronomia, Montevideo, Uruguay, I came to the United States to begin my sales career. I took the personal selling course from Dr. Thomas Barley at Palm Beach Community College.

My first positions were in environmental services and then insurance. Most recently I began serving as a food broker selling for Andina Food, LLC, purveyors of table olives, bulk olives, and olive oil in the United States and South America. My primary responsibilities are to negotiate contracts with restaurant chains, supermarket chains, retailers, cruise lines, and wholesalers for the sale and delivery of these items. Andina Food also requires me to monitor accounts receivable and market conditions because the company expects to produce and sell 4,400 tons of olive oil, 11,000 tons of packed olives, and 5,500 tons of bulk olives in the current year.

Selling olives and olive oil in the United States begins with customer needs assessment, then submitting preliminary proposals and following up to ensure that all requirements are met. When our preliminary proposals have been accepted, we begin the process of negotiation to gain customer commitment. The details must be carefully articulated at each step in the process and each agreed upon before moving on to the next step. I have to constantly be aware of how our negotiations are progressing compared to Andina Food marketing and contract policies. A thorough knowledge of our clients and our clients' customers, as well as Andina policies, allows me to negotiate a win–win situation.

As an independent food broker selling in a business-to-business environment, I emphasize communication skills to gain customer acceptance. Listening to the customer is the most important communication tool I use because it helps me to understand their communication style. It is important to understand not only a customer's needs but also their behavioral communication requirements. That means I need to adjust my negotiation style to more closely fit the communication style of my customer. I think it is critical to be responsive to our environment, which includes people with different backgrounds than ourselves. When you understand the way another person feels comfortable communicating, you can change your own communication style to make them feel more comfortable. This approach has helped me eliminate much of the distraction that can arise during contract negotiation.

Time is one of a salesperson's most valuable resources, and often negotiations can consume considerable time—so objectives for each negotiation session must be set. Many accounts require us to rewrite our terms and conditions so that they can maintain the flexibility they require for their customers. I must consistently negotiate within specific guidelines set forth by Andina Food and negotiate with our customers a value-added approach that will ensure their satisfaction.

Pricing is a most important consideration in the competitive olive market in the United States. Because Andina olives are grown in a very competitive region in the Andes Mountains in Argentina, we can offer our customers high quality while negotiating prices that represent an excellent value.

What all this means is that I create effective negotiation sessions by listening to my customers and instilling confidence and trust in Andina Food. I try hard to communicate the Andina self-improvement philosophy, which results in not only the best products but also the optimum customer service that will benefit our customers, and their customers.

Visit our Web site at www.andinafood.com.

> *"When you understand the way another person feels comfortable communicating, you can change your own communication style to make them feel more comfortable."*
>
> Joaquin Azanza

We have all engaged in negotiations of some type. Most of these were informal (such as with your parents about attending a concert) and dealt with relatively minor issues, although they may have been intensely important to you at the time. This chapter discusses formal negotiations that occur between buyers and salespeople. The skills you will learn can also be used in your day-to-day negotiations with friends, parents, and people in authority positions.

THE NATURE OF NEGOTIATION

The bargaining process through which buyers and sellers resolve areas of conflict and/or arrive at agreements is called **negotiation.** Areas of conflict may include minor issues (like who should attend future meetings) as well as major ones (such as cost per unit or exclusive purchase agreements). The ultimate goal of both parties should be to reduce or resolve the conflict.

Two radically different philosophies can guide negotiations. In **win–lose negotiating** the negotiator attempts to win all the important concessions and thus triumph over the opponent.[1] This process resembles almost every competitive sport you have ever watched. In boxing, for example, one person is the winner, and the other is, by definition, the loser.

In the second negotiating philosophy, **win–win negotiating,** the negotiator attempts to secure an agreement that satisfies both parties. You have probably experienced social situations similar to this. For example, if you want to attend a football game and your friend wants to attend a party, you may negotiate a mutual agreement that you both attend the first half of the game and still make it to the party. If this arrangement satisfies both you and your friend, you have engaged in win–win negotiating.

The discussion in this chapter assumes that your goal as a salesperson is to engage in win–win negotiating. In fact, this entire book has emphasized developing relationships, which is a win–win perspective. Partners attempt to find solutions that benefit both parties because each is concerned about the other party's welfare.

However, the buyer may be using a win–lose strategy, whereby the buyer hopes to win all major concessions and have the seller be the loser. To help you spot and prepare for such situations, we discuss many of these tactics as well.

NEGOTIATION VERSUS NONNEGOTIATION SELLING

How does negotiation differ from the sales presentations we have discussed up to this point? This textbook has already covered many aspects of negotiating an agreement between buyer and seller. For example, in Chapter 11 we discussed the "negotiations" that occur as the seller is helping the buyer deal with objections. And in Chapter 12 we talked about obtaining commitment, which often requires negotiating on some key points. Importantly, however, we assumed that many, if not most, factors during a regular sales call are constrained, and not open to change or negotiation. For example, the price of Allsteel Energy brand ergonomic seating has been set at $395. The Allsteel salesperson will not lower that price unless, of course, the buyer agrees to purchase large quantities. Even then the buyer will receive just a standard quantity discount as outlined in the seller's price manual. In essence, the salesperson's price book and procedure manual form an inflexible set of rules. If the buyer objects, an attempt to resolve the conflict will occur by using techniques discussed in Chapter 11 (such as the compensation method or the revisit method).

In contrast, if the Allsteel seller enters formal negotiations with the same buyer, the price and delivery schedules will be subject to modification. The buyer neither expects nor wants the seller to come to the negotiation meeting with any standard

Formal negotiations usually involve multiple buyers and multiple sellers.

Frank Herholdt/Stone/Getty Images

price book. Instead, the buyer expects most policies, procedures, and prices to be truly negotiable.

Negotiations also differ from regular sales calls in that they generally involve more intensive planning and a larger number of people from the selling firm. Prenegotiation planning may go on for six months or more before the actual meeting takes place. Planning participants usually cover a wide spectrum of functional areas of the firm, such as production, marketing, sales, human resources, accounting, purchasing, and executive officers.

Finally, formal negotiations generally take place only for very large or important prospective buyers. For example, Nestlé Foods might negotiate with some of the very large food chains, such as Wal-Mart Foods and Cub Foods, but would not engage in a large, formal negotiation session with small local or mom-and-pop grocery stores. Negotiating is an expensive endeavor because it utilizes so much of so many important people's time. The firm wants to invest the time and costs involved in negotiating only if the long-term nature of the relationship and the importance of the customer justify the expense.

WHAT CAN BE NEGOTIATED?

If the customer is large or important enough, almost anything can be negotiated. Salespeople who have not been involved in negotiations before often find it hard to grasp the fact that so many areas are subject to discussion and change. Exhibit 13.1 lists some items that are often negotiated between buyers and sellers.

In reality, no single negotiation session covers all the areas listed. Each side comes to the bargaining table with a list of prioritized issues; only important points for which disagreement exists are discussed.

ARE YOU A GOOD NEGOTIATOR?

All of us are negotiators; some of us are better than others. We have negotiated with parents, friends, professors, and, yes, sometimes even with opponents. However, the fact that you have engaged in many negotiations in your lifetime does not mean you are good at negotiating.

The traits necessary to successfully negotiate vary somewhat, depending on the situation and the parties involved. Some characteristics, however, are almost universal. For example, a good negotiator must have patience and endurance; after two hours of discussing the same issue, the negotiator needs the stamina and willingness to continue until an agreement is reached. Also, a willingness to take risks and the ability to tolerate ambiguity become especially critical in business negotiations because it is necessary to both accept and offer concessions during the meeting without complete information.

Successful salespeople do not always make great negotiators. In fact, negotiating could very well be the most difficult skill for any salesperson to develop. The unconscious reaction of most salespeople in negotiations often ends up

Exhibit 13.1

Items That Are Often Negotiated between Buyers and Sellers

Inventory levels the buyer must maintain.

Inventory levels the seller must keep on hand to be able to restock the buyer quickly.

Details about the design of the product or service.

Web page development.

How the product will be manufactured.

Display allowances for resellers.

Advertising allowances and the amount of advertising the seller does.

Sales promotion within the channel of distribution.

Delivery terms and conditions.

Retail and wholesale pricing points for resellers.

Prices and pricing allowances for volume purchases.

Amount and location of shelf positioning.

Special packaging and design features.

Service levels after the sale.

Disposing of unsold or obsolete merchandise.

Credit terms.

How complaints will be resolved.

Order entry and ease of monitoring orders.

Type and frequency of communication between the parties.

Performance guarantees and bonds.

being the opposite of the correct thing to do. For example, what if, in preparation for the upcoming negotiation session, the customer asks for very detailed specifications about your product? Most salespeople would gladly supply reams of technical data, full glossy pictures, an offer of plant tours, and the like. The problem with that approach lies in the possibility that the customer will pick several features that he or she does not need and then pressure for price concessions. (Look, I don't need that much memory capacity and don't want to pay for something I'm not going to use. So why don't you reduce your price? I shouldn't have to pay for something I'm not planning on ever using!) A salesperson who is a good negotiator would avoid this situation by supplying information to the customer only in exchange for the right to ask the customer more questions and thus gain more information.

People who fear conflict usually are poor negotiators. In fact, some negotiating strategies are actually designed to increase the level of conflict to bring all of the issues to the table and reach an equitable settlement. Along the same lines, people who have a strong need to be liked by all people at all times tend to make very poor negotiators. Other undesirable traits include being closed-minded, unorganized, dishonest, and downright belligerent.

Of course, cultural differences do exist.[2] For example, Brazilian managers may believe competitiveness is more important in a negotiator than integrity. Chinese managers in Taiwan may emphasize the negotiator's rational skills to a lesser extent than his or her interpersonal skills.

As this discussion indicates, being a truly excellent negotiator requires a very careful balance of traits and skills. Take a moment and complete the questionnaire in Exhibit 13.2 to rate your negotiating skills. Don't be discouraged by a

Exhibit 13.2

Negotiation Skills Self-Inventory

Place a check by each item that accurately reflects your personality and traits on an average, normal day.

_____ 1.	Helpful		_____ 20.	Receptive
_____ 2.	Risk taker		_____ 21.	Easily influenced
_____ 3.	Inconsistent		_____ 22.	Enthusiastic
_____ 4.	Persistent		_____ 23.	Planner
_____ 5.	Factual		_____ 24.	Stingy
_____ 6.	Use high pressure		_____ 25.	Listener
_____ 7.	Self-confident		_____ 26.	Controlled
_____ 8.	Practical		_____ 27.	Think under pressure
_____ 9.	Manipulative		_____ 28.	Passive
_____ 10.	Analytical		_____ 29.	Economical
_____ 11.	Arrogant		_____ 30.	Gullible
_____ 12.	Impatient		_____ 31.	Afraid of conflict
_____ 13.	Seek new approaches		_____ 32.	Endurance
_____ 14.	Tactful		_____ 33.	Tolerate ambiguity
_____ 15.	Perfectionist		_____ 34.	Have strong need to be liked
_____ 16.	Stubborn		_____ 35.	Organized
_____ 17.	Flexible		_____ 36.	Honest
_____ 18.	Competitive		_____ 37.	Belligerent
_____ 19.	Gambler			

How to score the checklist:

All of the traits listed are positive except for the following negative traits: 3, 6, 9, 11, 12, 15, 16, 19, 21, 24, 28, 30, 31, 34, and 37. To arrive at a total score, give yourself one point for all positive traits and subtract one point for all negative traits. To interpret your total score: 19–22 = excellent; 15–18 = good; 11–14 = fair.

low score. You cannot easily change personality traits, but the rest of this chapter will suggest ways to improve your skills.

PLANNING FOR THE NEGOTIATION SESSION

Preparation and planning are the most important parts of negotiation, according to many expert sources. In Chapter 8 we discussed how to gather precall information and plan the sales call. All of that material is equally relevant when planning for an upcoming negotiation session—for example, learning everything possible about the buying team and the buyer's organization.

The meetings the salesperson will have with the buyer prior to the actual negotiation session facilitate this learning. The buyer may also be, or have been, a customer of the salesperson, with the upcoming negotiation session designed to review contracts or specify a new working relationship. Even in such scenarios, negotiators will want to carefully review the players and learn as many facts about the situation as possible.

LOCATION

Plan to hold the negotiation at a location free from distraction for both teams. A neutral site, one owned by neither party, is usually best; it removes both teams from interruptions by business associates, and no one has a psychological ("home court") advantage. Experienced negotiators find the middle of the workweek best for negotiations and prefer morning to afternoon or evening (because people are more focused on their jobs rather than after-hours and weekend activities).

TIME ALLOTMENT

As you are probably aware, negotiations can take a tremendous amount of time. Some business negotiations take years. But how much time should be set aside for one negotiation session? The answer depends on the negotiation objectives and the extent to which both sides desire a win–win session. Studies have shown that high time pressure will produce nonagreements and poor outcomes when one or more sides take a win–lose perspective; but if both sides have a win–win perspective, high outcomes are achieved regardless of time pressure.

Sales reps need to set aside time to plan for a negotiation session.

Alan Schein/Corbis

NEGOTIATION OBJECTIVES

Power is a critical element when developing objectives. The selling team must ask, Do we need them more than they need us? What part of our service is most valuable to them? Can they get similar products elsewhere? Optimally, both parties share balanced power, although this situation is rare in practice.

In developing objectives for the session, keep in mind that the seller will almost certainly have to make concessions in the negotiation meeting. Thus setting several objectives, or positions, is extremely important.

The **target position** is what your company hopes to achieve at the negotiation session. Your team should also establish a **minimum position,** the absolute minimum level you will accept. Finally, an **opening position**—the initial proposal—should be developed.

For example, for a Baxter salesperson negotiating the price for a blood collection and transfusion system at a blood bank, the target position could be

SELLING Scenario 13.1

DO YOUR HOMEWORK TO SUCCEED IN NEGOTIATIONS

I work at U.S. Foodservice, one of the largest food service distributors in the United States. We market and distribute more than 43,000 brand items to over 300,000 food service customers, including hotels, restaurants, schools, and the like.

New customer negotiations are relatively easy if I am prepared and I know my company's capabilities. When I go into negotiations I know exactly what we can do and cannot do . . . the bare-bones minimum it takes to be profitable. I know my business as well as their business, and what we need from the customer to have a successful partnership. If we are able to reach an agreement, then it just takes a few more weeks to iron out the details and ship groceries. Most of the time we meet somewhere between bare-bones profitability and high profitability, which is a middle to mid-high profitable account. In a perfect world, negotiations would end there. However, the food service industry is not a perfect world, and negotiations are ongoing.

Negotiations with existing customers are more difficult and can take up to six or eight months to complete. We may revise our amendments to the original contracts a dozen times before reaching an agreement, and then it looks nothing like the original proposal. Existing customers know our business very well and how we operate; they know our company's shortcomings as well as abilities. Bottom line: I better have done my homework and have the backup to show for it.

Sure there are problems and bumps in the road, but my customers have confidence and trust that I will work it out. I think the most important allies you have in sales are trust and communication. If you have these two components, you will succeed—your customers will make sure of that.

Source: Danielle Lord, personal communication; used with permission.

$2,500,000, with a minimum position of $2,000,000 and an opening position of $3,000,000. In negotiations over service levels by Gallovidian Fresh Foods with Cub Foods with regard to fresh vegetables, the seller's opening position might be weekly delivery, the target position delivery twice a week, and the minimum position (the most the seller is willing to do) delivery three times a week.

To allow for concessions, the opening position should reflect higher expectations than the target position. However, the buyer team may consider a very high opening position to be unrealistic and may simply walk away. You have probably seen this happen in negotiations between countries that are at war. To avoid this problem, negotiators must be ready to support that opening position with solid information. Suppose the opening position for a Colgate-Palmolive negotiating team is to offer the grocer a display allowance of $1,000 (with a target position of offering $1,500). The team must be ready to prove that $1,000 is reasonable.

When developing objectives, negotiators need to sort out all issues that could arise in the meeting, prioritizing them by importance to the firm. It is critical to identify all issues and do your homework, as Selling Scenario 13.1 demonstrates. Then the negotiators should develop a set of contingency plans to get a good idea, even before the meeting begins, of their planned reactions and responses to the buyer's suggestions.

Talking over these issues beforehand helps the negotiation team avoid "giving away the store" during the heat of the negotiation session. It also allows the team to draw on the expertise of company experts who will not be present during the session.

The buyer team also develops positions for the meeting. Exhibit 13.3 presents a continuum that shows how the two sets of positions relate. With the positions illustrated, the parties can reach an agreement somewhere between the seller's minimum (S_M) and the buyer's maximum (B_M). However, if B_M falls to the left of

Exhibit 13.3
Comparing Buyer and Seller Price Positions

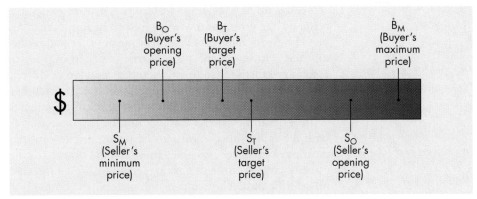

Note: See Howard Raiffa, *The Art and Science of Negotiation* (Cambridge, MA: Belknap Press, 1982) for a more complex discussion of the mathematical formulations designed to predict negotiation outcomes under various states.

S_M (has a lower maximum acceptable price), no agreement can be reached; attempts at negotiation will be futile. For example, if the buyer is not willing to pay more than \$200 (B_M) and the seller will not accept less than \$250 (S_M), agreement is impossible. In general, the seller desires to move as far to the right of S_M (as high a price) as possible, and the buyer desires to move as far to the left of B_M (as low a price) as possible.

Negotiators need to try to anticipate these positions and evaluate them carefully. The more information collected about what the buyer hopes to accomplish, the better the negotiators will be able to manage the meeting and arrive at a win–win decision.

Negotiators create a plan to achieve their objectives. However, the chance of failure always exists. Thus planners need to consider strategy revisions if the original plan should fail. The development of alternative paths to the same goal is known as **adaptive planning.** For example, a firm may attempt to secure a premium shelf position by using any of the following strategies:

- In return for a 5 percent price discount.
- In return for credit terms of 3/10, net 30.
- In return for a 50–50 co-op ad campaign.

The firm would attempt to secure the premium shelf position by using, for example, the first strategy; if that failed, it would move to the second strategy; and so forth. Fortunately, with laptops and software such as Excel® and Lotus 123®, negotiators can quickly calculate the profitability of various package deals for their firms.

Many firms will engage in a brainstorming session to try to develop strategies that will meet the firm's objectives. A **brainstorming session** is a meeting in which people are allowed to creatively explore various methods of achieving goals. Firms also use computer software, such as Negotiator Pro,[3] that is designed specifically to help salespeople prepare for negotiation sessions.

Once again, cultural differences exist. For example, Chinese and Russian businesspeople habitually use extreme initial offers, whereas Swedish businesspeople usually open with a price very close to their target position.

TEAM SELECTION AND MANAGEMENT
So far we have discussed negotiation as though it always involves a team of both buyers and sellers. Usually this is the case. However, negotiations do occur with only two people present: the buyer and the salesperson.

Teams offer both pros and cons. Because of team members' different backgrounds, the group as a whole tends to be more creative than one individual could be. Also, team members can help one another and reduce the chances of making a mistake. However, the more participants, the more time generally required to reach agreement. Also, team members may voice differing opinions among themselves, or one member may address a topic outside his or her area of expertise. Such things can make the seller's team appear unprepared or disorganized.

In general the seller's team should be the same size as the buyer's team. Otherwise the sellers may appear to be trying to exert more power or influence in the meeting. Whenever possible, strive for the fewest team members possible. Unnecessarily large teams can get bogged down in details; also, the larger the team, the more difficult reaching a decision generally becomes.

Each team member should have a defined role in the session. For example, experts are often included to answer technical questions; executives are present as more authoritative speakers on behalf of the selling firm. Exhibit 13.4 lists the types of team members often chosen for negotiations. Many of these people take part in prenegotiation planning but do not actually attend the negotiation session.

Exhibit 13.4
People Who May Serve on the Selling Negotiation Team

Title	Possible Role
Salesperson	Coordinates all functions.
Field sales manager (district manager, regional manager, etc.)	Provides additional local and regional information. Secures necessary local funding and support for planning and presentations. Offers information on competitors.
National sales manager/ vice president of sales	Serves as a liaison with corporate headquarters. Secures necessary corporate funding and staff support for planning and presentation. Offers competitor information.
National account salesperson/ national accounts sales managers	Provide expertise and support in dealing with issues for important customers. Offer information about competitors.
Marketing department senior executives, product managers, and staff	Provide suggestions for product/service applications. Supply market research information as well as information on packaging, new product development, upcoming promotional campaigns, etc. Offer information about competitors.
Chief executive officer/president	Serves as an authority figure. Facilitates quicker decisions regarding changes in current policy and procedures. As a peer, can relate well with buyer's senior officers.
Manufacturing executives and staff	Provide information on current scheduled production as well as the possibility/cost of any modifications in the schedule.
Purchasing executives and staff	Provide information about raw materials inflows. Offer suggestions about possible quantity discounts from suppliers.
Accounting and finance executives and staff	Source of cost accounting information. Supply corporate target returns on investment; cost estimates for any needed changes in the firm under various buying scenarios; and information on order entry, billing, and credit systems.
Information technology executives and staff	Provide information on current information systems and anticipated changes needed under various buying scenarios. Help ensure that needed periodic reports for the buyers can be generated in a timely fashion.
Training executives and staff	Provide training for negotiation effectiveness and conduct practice role plays. Also provide information and suggestions on anticipated necessary buyer training.
Outside consultants	Provide any kind of assistance necessary. Especially helpful if the firm has limited experience in negotiations or has not negotiated with this type of buyer before.

Team members should possess the traits of good negotiators, although it often does not work out that way. For example, many technical experts have no tolerance for ambiguity and may fear conflict. As a result, the team leader needs to help them see clearly what their role is, as well as what they should not get involved in, during the session.

The team leader will manage the actual negotiation session. Because of their intimate knowledge of the buyers and their needs, salespeople often fill this post, rather than the executive on the team. When selecting a team leader, the seller's management needs to also consider the anticipated leader of the buyer team. It is unwise to choose a leader for the selling team who may be intimidated by the buyer's leader.

The team usually develops rules about who will answer what kinds of questions, who should be the first to respond to a concession offered by the buyers, who will offer concessions from the seller's standpoint, and so on. A set of nonverbal and verbal signals is also developed so team members can communicate with one another. For example, they may agree that when the salesperson takes out a breath mint, all team members are to stop talking and let the salesperson handle all issues; or when the executive places her red book inside her briefcase, the team should move toward its target position, and the salesperson should say, "OK, let's look at some alternatives."

BAVARIA/Taxi/Getty Images

The salesperson's team must prepare for an upcoming negotiation session. Remember that the buyer's team is also planning.

To ensure that team members really understand their respective roles and that all rules and signals are clearly grasped, the team should practice. This process usually involves a series of videotaped role play situations. Many firms, such as Standard Register, involve their sales training department in this practice. Trainers, using detailed information supplied by the team, realistically play the roles of the buying team members.

The selling team will likely have many meetings before the negotiation session. These meetings will be internal meetings, with members of the selling team, and also meetings with the buyers. Because not every selling team member can be at all meetings, sometimes it is hard for team members to keep abreast of developments. Sales Technology 13.1 describes one system that helps with this problem.

INDIVIDUAL BEHAVIOR PATTERNS

The team leader needs to consider the personality style of each member of both teams to spot any problems and plan accordingly. Of course, one method would be to sort the members into analyticals, amiables, expressives, and drivers based on the dimensions of assertiveness and responsiveness (see Chapter 6 for a full discussion). Some researchers have developed personality profiles specifically for negotiations. This section presents one of the most widely used sets of negotiation profiles.

After studying actual conflict situations, a number of researchers arrived at a set of basic conflict-handling modes based on the dimensions of assertiveness and cooperativeness.[4] Exhibit 13.5 presents these five modes: competing, accommodating, avoiding, compromising, and collaborating. Note that these five styles are different from the social styles (drivers, amiables, expressives, and analyticals) that we have been using throughout the book. Because all negotiations involve some degree of conflict, this typology is appropriate for use by salespeople preparing for a negotiation session.

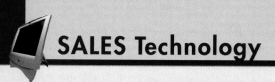

SALES Technology

RECORD THE MEETING SO OTHERS CAN HEAR

In preparing for an upcoming negotiation session, salespeople are usually responsible for putting together a number of meetings with various people from the customer organization, as well as meetings with people in their own firms. The problem is that not all people can be at all meetings. So what's the solution?

Why not record the meeting, with permission of all parties of course? That way, those who can't be at a meeting can benefit from hearing the conversations that were carried on in their absence, as well as any exact verbal agreements reached.

One way to do this is with a simple tape recorder. But then one has to either make copies of the tape and mail them to others, or digitize the recording and then distribute that. Salespeople are busy and don't usually have staff who can do this for them.

It is more convenient to use software and technology to do the task for you. For example, SoniClear offers software called MeetingPro Enterprise, which allows you to record directly to your laptop or desktop computer. Salespeople can easily share the recordings on CD, over a local area network, through e-mail, and on a Web site.

The software also has some helpful note-taking features to make it easier for listeners to locate important points in long meetings. A salesperson can enter agenda items and any predefined notes into the program before the meeting starts. Then while recording the meeting, the salesperson can click to link to those specific agenda items. This creates a table of contents that listeners can use to click to any portion of the meeting. MeetingPro Enterprise also includes features that make it easy to create written minutes of the meeting. Plus, its built-in VoiceBoost Signal Enhancement makes listening to meetings easier and clearer.

Source: www.soniclear.com.

Exhibit 13.5
Conflict-Handling
Behavior Modes

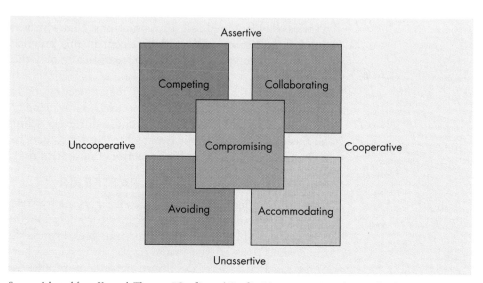

Source: Adapted from Kenneth Thomas, "Conflict and Conflict Management," in *The Handbook of Industrial and Organizational Psychology*, ed. Marvin Dunnett (Skokie, IL: Rand McNally, 1976).

People who resolve conflict in a **competing mode** are assertive and uncooperative. They tend to pursue their own goals and objectives completely at the expense of the other party. Often power oriented, they usually surround themselves with subordinates (often called "yes-men") who go along with their ideas. Team members who use the competing mode look for a win–lose agreement: they win, the other party loses.

Individuals in the **accommodating mode** are the exact opposite of competing people. Unassertive and highly cooperative, accommodators will neglect their own needs and desires to satisfy the concerns of the other party. In fact, they may seek a win–lose agreement, where they are the losers. Accommodators can be spotted by their excessive generosity; their constant, rapid yielding to another's point of view; and their obedience to someone else's order, even if it is obviously not something they desire to do.

Some people operate in the **avoiding mode,** an unassertive and uncooperative mode. These people do not attempt to fulfill their own needs or the needs of others. In essence, they simply refuse to address the conflict at all. They do not strive for a win–win agreement; in fact, they do not strive for any agreement.

The **compromising mode** applies to people "in the middle" in terms of cooperativeness and assertiveness. A compromiser attempts to find a quick, mutually acceptable solution that partially satisfies both parties. A compromiser gives up more than a competing person but less than an accommodating person. In many ways the compromiser attempts to arrive at a win–win solution. However, the agreement reached usually does not maximize the satisfaction of the parties. For example, a compromising person might quickly suggest, Let's just split the difference. Although this sounds fair, a better solution—one that would please both parties more—may be reached with further discussion.

Finally, people in the **collaborating mode** are both assertive and cooperative. They seek to maximize the satisfaction of both parties and hence to reach a truly win–win solution. Collaborators have the motivation, skill, and determination to really dig into an issue or a problem and explore all possible solutions. The best situation, from a negotiation standpoint, would be to have on both teams a number of people who generally use a collaborating mode.

As with the social style matrix described earlier, one person can exhibit different modes in different situations. For example, a buying team negotiator who perceives that his or her position on an issue extremely vital to the long-term welfare of the company is correct may revert from a collaborating mode to a competing mode. Likewise, when potentially heavy damage could occur from confronting an issue, that same buyer might move to an avoiding mode.

People exhibit different conflict-handling modes. Can you spot someone in this photo in the competing mode? The avoiding mode? The collaborating mode?

Mug Shots/The Stock Market

INFORMATION CONTROL

What do buyers do while selling teams engage in preparation? They prepare, too! Keep in mind that buyers have read as many books and attended as many seminars on negotiation as sellers have because this training is one of their best negotiating tools. Buyers try to learn as much as they can about the seller's team and plans, including the seller's opening, target, and minimum positions. Buyers also are interested in the seller's team membership and decision rules. As a result, the selling team leader needs to emphasize the need for security: Don't give everyone access to all information. In fact, many team members (such as technical support) do not need to have complete and exhaustive knowledge of all the facts surrounding the negotiation.

As an example, one *Fortune* 500 firm was negotiating a $15 million deal with one of its customers. The selling team's leader had to leave the room for a few minutes, and while he was gone the plant manager for the selling firm came in. The plant manager, though intending to do no harm, bragged about how his company had already invested $2 million in a prototype and retooling just to prepare for the customer's expected commitment. Needless to say, when the seller's team leader returned to the room, the buyer said he had all the information he needed. Two days later, the buyer was a very tough negotiator, armed with the knowledge that the seller had already committed to the project. It pays to control the flow of information!

THE NEGOTIATION MEETING

Before discussing what occurs in the negotiation meeting, we should note that some buyers will attempt to engage in a win–lose tactic of beginning to negotiate when the other party does not expect it. This tactic has been called **ambush negotiating** or a **sneak attack.** It can occur during meetings prior to the negotiation meeting or even during installation of the new product. For example, during the first week of installation of a new telecommunications system, the buyer may state, "We're going to have to renegotiate the price of this system. Since we signed that contract, we have learned of a new system being introduced by one of your competitors." The seller should never negotiate in such a situation until prepared to deal with the issue completely.

At the negotiation meeting the buyer team and seller team physically come together and deliberate about topics important to both parties, with the goal of arriving at decisions. As mentioned earlier, this meeting usually has been preceded by one or more smaller buyer–seller meetings designed to uncover needs and explore options. Informal phone conversations probably were used to set some aspects of the agenda, learn about team members who will be present, and so on. Also, the negotiation itself may require a series of sessions to resolve all issues.

PRELIMINARIES

Engaging in friendly conversation to break the ice before getting down to business is usually a good idea. Use this time to learn and use the names of all members on the buyer team. This preliminary activity is especially important in many international negotiation meetings. For example, Japanese businesspeople usually want to spend time developing a personal relationship before beginning negotiations, and alcohol is usually a part of this. Not so in Saudi Arabia, where customs dictate strict abstinence.

Every effort should be made to ensure a comfortable environment for all parties. Arranging ahead of time for refreshments, proper climate control, appropriate size of room, adequate lighting, and correct layout of furniture will go far to establish an environment conducive to negotiating.

Most negotiations occur at a rectangular table. Teams usually sit on opposite sides, with the team leaders at the heads of the table. If possible, try to arrange for a round table or at least a seating arrangement that mixes members from each team together. This seating plan helps the parties feel that they are facing a common task and fosters a win–win atmosphere.

If the buyer team has a win–lose philosophy, expect all kinds of ploys to be used. For example, the furniture may be too large or too small or may be uncomfortable to sit in. The buyers may sit in front of large windows to force you to stare directly into sunlight. You may discover that the sellers' seats are all placed beneath heat ducts and the heat is set too high. You should not continue with the meeting until all unfavorable physical arrangements have been set right.

As far as possible the selling team should establish a win–win environment. This environment can be facilitated by avoiding any verbal or nonverbal threatening gestures, remaining calm and courteous, and adopting an attitude of investigation and experimentation. The leader might even comment,

> I can speak for my team that our goal is to reach agreements today that we can all be proud of. We come to this meeting with an open mind and look forward to exploring many avenues toward agreement. I am confident that we will both prosper and be more profitable as a result of this session.

thinking **it** through

What if you do everything in your power to establish a win–win relationship with the buyer team, but the buyers insist on viewing the negotiation session as a series of win–lose maneuvers? That is to say, your team consists mostly of collaborators who are trying to see that both sides are winners, whereas the buyers are mostly in the competing mode where they hope to win and hope you lose. Since they won't play by win–win "rules," should you?

An **agenda,** a listing of what will be discussed and in what sequence, is important for every negotiation session. It helps to set boundaries and keeps everyone on track. Exhibit 13.6 offers an example of a negotiation agenda. The selling team should come to the meeting with a preliminary typed agenda. Don't be surprised when the buyer team also comes with an agenda; in that case the first thing to be negotiated is the agenda itself. In general, putting key issues later in the agenda is advantageous. This approach allows time for each party to learn the other's bargaining style and concession routines. Moreover, agreement has already been reached on some minor issues, which, in a win–win situation, supports an atmosphere for reaching agreement on the major issues.

GENERAL GUIDELINES

To negotiate effectively, the seller team must put into practice the skills discussed throughout this book. For example, listening carefully is extremely important. Careful listening involves not only being silent when the buyer talks but also asking good probing questions to resolve confusion and misunderstanding.

The team leader must keep track of issues discussed or resolved. During complicated negotiations many items may be discussed simultaneously. Also, some issues may be raised but not fully addressed before someone raises a separate issue. The leader can provide great assistance by giving periodic status reports,

Exhibit 13.6
Preliminary Negotiating Session Agenda

Preliminary Agenda
Meeting between FiberCraft and Rome Industrial Inc.
Proposed New Spin Machine for 15 FiberCraft Plants
November 21, 2007

1. Introductions by participants.
2. Agree on the meeting agenda.
3. Issues:
   a. Who will design the new machine?
   b. Who will pay the costs of testing the machine?
   c. Who will have ownership rights to the new machine (if it is ever built for someone else)?
   d. Who will be responsible for maintaining and servicing the new machine during trial runs?
   e. Who will pay for any redesign work needed?
4. Coffee break.
5. Issues:
   a. How and when will the machines be set up in the 15 locations? Who will be responsible for installation?
   b. What percentage will be required for a down payment?
   c. What will the price be? Will there be any price escalation provisions? If not, how long is this price protected?
6. Summary of agreement.

including what has been resolved and the issues being discussed. More important, he or she can map out what still needs to be discussed. In essence this mapping establishes a new agenda for the remainder of the negotiation session.

Once again, cultural differences are important in negotiations. For example, most Canadians and Americans are uncomfortable with silence; most Japanese, on the other hand, are much more comfortable with extended periods of silence. North Americans negotiating with Japanese businesspeople usually find this silence very stressful. Negotiators must prepare themselves for such probabilities and learn ways to reduce stress and cope in this situation.

If negotiations require an interpreter, carefully select someone well-qualified for the job. And don't expect everything you say to be translated correctly. Here are some items that have been translated into English from another language (so you can get a sense of the problem of translation errors):[5]

- In a family-style restaurant in Hong Kong: Come broil yourself at your own table.
- From an Italian hotel in the mountains: Standing among the savage scenery, the hotel offers stupendous revelations. There is a French window in every room. We offer commodious chambers, with balcony imminent to a romantic gorge. We hope you want to drop in. In the close village you can buy jolly memorials for when you pass away.
- In a Moscow newspaper under the heading "INTERPRETING": Let us you letter of business translation do. Every people in our staffing know English like the hand of their back. Up to the minute wise-street phrases, don't you know, old boy!
- In a Sarajevo hotel: Guests should announce abandonment of their rooms before 12 o'clock, emptying the rooms at the latest until 14 o'clock for the use of the room before 5 at the arrival or after the 16 o'clock at the departure will be billed as one more night.

Finally, keep in mind that during negotiations, people need to save **face,** which is the desire for a positive identity or self-concept. Of course, not all people strive for the same face (some want to appear "cool," some "macho," some "crass," and so on). Negotiators will at least try to maintain face and may even use the negotiation session to improve or strengthen this identity.

DEALING WITH WIN–LOSE NEGOTIATORS

Many books have been written and many consultants have grown rich teaching both buyers and sellers strategies for effective negotiating. Unfortunately, many of these techniques are designed to achieve a win–lose situation. We will describe several to illustrate the types of tactics buyers might engage in during negotiations. This knowledge will help the negotiating team defend its position under such attacks.

Both buyers and sellers occasionally engage in the win–lose strategies described here. However, because we are assuming that sellers will adopt a

Exhibit 13.7

What to Do When the Buyer Turns to Win–Lose Strategies

Detach yourself.	Don't respond right away. Instead, give yourself time to think about the issue. Say something like "Hold on, I'm not sure I follow you. Let's go back over what you just said again." Use the time you have gained to rethink your positions and what would be in the best interests of both parties.
Acknowledge their position and then respond.	In using this tool, you are trying to create a favorable climate for your response. You would start off by mentioning that you agree with them by saying something like "Yes, you have a good point there when you said . . ." After agreeing, you then make your point. For example, you might conclude by saying, "and I would like to make sure you continue to have minimal downtime. And for that to happen, you know, we really need to have someone from your firm attend the training." This tool is somewhat similar to the indirect denial and revisit techniques discussed in Chapter 11.
Build them a bridge.	Come up with a solution that incorporates the buyer's suggestion. For example, "building on your idea, what if we . . ." or "I got this idea from something really neat you said at our meeting last Friday." This approach helps the buyer save face.
Warn, but don't threaten.	Sometimes you may have to help the buyer understand the consequences of his or her position. For example, if the buyer indicates that she or he must have a cheaper fabric for the furniture in an office building, you can say, "I know how important the choice of fabric is to your firm's image, but if you choose that fabric, you won't achieve the image you're really looking for. How much will that cost you in lost clients who might not get a sense that you are very successful?" A warning is not the same thing as a threat. A threat is what will happen if you don't get *your* way; a warning is what will happen if they do get *their* way.

win–win perspective, this section focuses on how to handle buyers who engage in these techniques. Exhibit 13.7 presents an effective overall strategy for dealing with win–lose negotiators.

Good Guy–Bad Guy Routine

You have probably seen the **good guy–bad guy routine** if you watch many police movies or TV shows. A tough police detective interrogating the suspect gets a little rough. The detective uses bright lights and intimidation. After a few minutes a second officer (who has been watching) asks his companion to "go out and get some fresh air." While the tough detective (the "bad guy") is outside, the other detective (the "good guy") apologizes for his partner's actions. The good guy goes on to advise the crook to confess now and receive better treatment rather than wait and have the bad guy harass him or her some more.

Negotiators often try the same routine. One member of the buyer team (the bad guy) makes all sorts of outlandish statements and requests:

> Look, we've got to buy these for no more than $15 each, and we must have credit terms of 2/10, net 60. After all the business we've given you in the past, I can't believe you won't agree to those terms!

Then another member of the buyer team (the good guy) takes over and appears to offer a win–win solution by presenting a lower demand:

> Hang on, Jack. These are our friends. Sure, we've given them a lot of business, but remember they've been good to us as well! I believe we should let them make a decent profit, so $15.50 would be more reasonable.

According to theory, the sellers are so relieved to find a friend that they jump on the good guy's suggestion.

As an effective defense against such tactics, the selling team must know its position clearly and not let the buyer's strategy weaken it. Obviously, the selling team needs the ability to spot a good guy–bad guy tactic. A good response might be

> We understand your concern. But based on all the facts of the situation, we still feel our proposal is a fair one for all parties involved.

Lowballing

You may also have experienced **lowballing.** Car dealers have used it for years. The salesperson says, "This car sells for $19,613." After you agree to purchase it, what happens? "Oh, I forgot to tell you that we have to charge you for dealer prep and destination charges, as well as an undercoating already applied to the car. So let's see, the total comes to $20,147. Gee, I'm sorry I didn't mention those expenses before!" Most people go ahead and buy. Why? They have already verbally committed themselves and do not want to go against their agreement. Also, they do not want to start the search process again.

The technique is also used in buyer–seller negotiations in industrial situations. For example, after the sellers have signed a final agreement with the buyer team, one of the buyer team members says, "Oh, I forgot to mention that all of our new contracts must specify FOB destination and the seller must assume all shipping insurance expenses."

The best response to lowballing is to just say no. Remind the buyer team that the agreement has been finalized. The threat of lowballing underscores the importance of getting signatures on contracts and agreements as soon as possible. If the buyers insist on the new items, the selling team will simply be forced to reopen the negotiations. (Try this tactic on car dealers, too!)

A variation of lowballing, **nibbling,** is a small extra, or add-on, the buyer requests after the deal has been closed. Compared to lowballing, a nibble is a much smaller request. For example, one of the buyers may state, "Say, could you give us a one-time 5 percent discount on our first order? That would sure make our boss happy and make us look like we negotiated hard for her." Nibbling often works because the request is so small compared to the entire agreement.

The selling team's response to the nibble depends on the situation. It may be advantageous to go ahead and grant a truly small request that could be easily met. On the other hand, if the buyer team uses nibbling often, granting these requests may need to be restricted. Again, the best strategy is to agree on the seller's position before the meeting begins and set guidelines for potential nibbles. Often the seller grants a nibble only if the buyer agrees to some small concession in return.

Emotional Outbursts

How do you react when a close friend suddenly starts crying, gets angry, or looks very sad? Most of us think, What have I done to cause this? We tend to feel guilty, become uneasy, and try to find a way to make the person stop crying. That is simply human nature.

Occasionally buyer teams will appeal to your human nature by engaging in an **emotional outburst tactic.** For example, one of the buyers may look directly at you, shake his or her head sadly, slowly look down, and say softly,

> I can't believe it's come to this. You know we can't afford that price. And we've been good partners all these years. I don't know what to say.

This statement is followed by complete silence among the entire buyer team. Members hope that you will feel uncomfortable and give in to their demands. In an extreme case one or more buyers would actually walk out of the room or begin to shout or cry.

The selling team, once again, needs to recognize this behavior as the technique it is. Assuming no logical reason exists for the outburst, the negotiators should respond with a gentle but firm reminder of the merits of the offer and attempt to move the buyer group back into a win–win negotiating frame of mind.

Budget Limitation Tactic

In the **budget limitation tactic,** also called a **budget bogey,** the buyer team states something like the following:

> The proposal looks great. We need every facet of the program you are proposing in order for it to work in our business. But our budget allows us only $250,000 total, including all costs. You'll have to come down from $300,000 to that number, or I'm afraid we can't afford it.

This statement may be absolutely true. If so, at least you know what you have to work with. Of course, claims of budget ceilings are sometimes just a ploy to try to get a lower price.

The best defense against budget limitations is to do your homework before going into the negotiation session. Learn as much as you can about budgets and maximums allowed. Have alternative programs or proposals ready that incorporate cost reduction measures. After being told of a budget limitation during the negotiation session, probe to make sure that the claim is valid. Check the possibility of splitting the cost of the proposal over several fiscal years. Probe to find out whether the buyer would be willing to accept more risk for a lower price or to have some of the installation work done by the buyer's staff. You can also help to forestall this tactic by working closely with the buyer prior to the negotiation meeting, providing reasonable ballpark estimates of the cost of the proposal.

Ariel Skelley/Corbis

If a member of the buying team engages in an emotional outburst tactic, the seller should never respond in like fashion.

Browbeating

Sometimes buyers will attempt to alter the selling team's enthusiasm and self-respect by **browbeating** them. One buyer might make a comment like the following:

> Say, I've been reading some pretty unflattering things about your company in *The Wall Street Journal* lately. Seems like you can't keep your unions happy or your nonunion employees from organizing. It must be tough to get out of bed and go to work every day, huh?

If the selling team feels less secure and slightly inferior after such a comment, the tactic was successful.

You should not let browbeating comments influence you or your proposal. That's easier said than done, of course. Presumably you were able to identify in prenegotiation meetings that this buyer had this type of personality. If so, you could prepare by simply telling yourself that browbeating will occur but you will not let it affect your decisions. If you can make it through one such comment, buyers usually will not offer any more because they can see that browbeating will not help them achieve their goals.

One response to such a statement would be to practice **negotiation jujitsu**.[6] In negotiation jujitsu the salesperson steps away from the opponent's attack and then directs the opponent back to the issues being discussed. Instead of striking back, the seller breaks the win–lose attempt by not reacting negatively. The seller may even ask for clarification, advice, or criticism. For example, the salesperson may say,

> We are concerned about our employees and are working to resolve all problems as quickly as we can. If you have any ideas that would help us in this regard, we would appreciate them. . . . Now, we were discussing price . . .

MAKING CONCESSIONS

One of the most important activities in any negotiation is the granting and receiving of concessions from the other party. One party makes a **concession** when it agrees to change a position in some fashion. For example, if your opening price position was $500, you would be granting a concession if you agreed to lower the price to $450.

Based on many successful negotiations in a wide range of situations, a number of guidelines have been formulated to make concessions effectively:[7]

1. Never make concessions until you know all of the buyer's demands and opening position. Use probing to help reveal these.

2. Never make a concession unless you get one in return and don't feel guilty about receiving a concession.

3. Concessions should gradually decrease in size. At first you may be willing to offer "normal size" concessions. As time goes on, however, you should make much smaller ones. This approach helps the prospect see that you are approaching your target position and are becoming much less willing to concede.

4. If a requested concession does not meet your objectives, don't be afraid to simply say, "No. I'm sorry, but I just can't do that."

5. All concessions you offer are tentative until the final agreement is reached and signed. Remember that you may have to take back one of your concessions if the situation changes.

6. Be confident and secure in your position and don't give concessions carelessly. If you don't follow this advice, your buyers may lose respect for your negotiating and business skills. Everyone wants to conduct business with someone who is sharp and who will be in business in the future. Don't give the impression that you are not and will not.

7. Don't accept the buyer's first attempt at a concession. Chances are the buyer has built in some leeway and is simply testing the water.

8. Help the buyer to see the value of any concessions you agree to. Don't assume the buyer will understand the total magnitude of your "generosity."

9. Start the negotiation without preconceived notions. Even though the buyers may have demanded certain concessions in the past, they may not do so in this negotiation meeting.

10. If, after making a concession, you realize you made some sort of mistake, tell the buyer and begin negotiating that issue again. For example, if you made a concession of delivery every two weeks instead of every four

BUILDING Partnerships

YOU WANT WHAT? REQUESTED CONCESSIONS CAN BE QUITE VARIED

Negotiating teams often seek concessions. And sometimes the concessions that are sought and obtained can be quite interesting. For example, take the recent contract between the University of Michigan at Ann Arbor and Nike. Nike wanted exclusive rights to outfit the university's 25 varsity sports teams. Sound easy enough? No way. The negotiations took months to achieve, but a seven-year agreement was finally reached that met both sides' needs. According to the agreement, University of Michigan received the following concessions:

- $1.2 million per year.
- 10 percent of the royalties from licensed University of Michigan products.
- $2 million worth of sports equipment each year.

One of the more interesting concessions dealt with the concern of many Michigan students about the plight of Nike workers in less developed countries. In fact, many students were involved with the Worker Rights Consortium, which demanded that workers in third world countries get better treatment and wages. The final agreement included a concession on Nike's part to include a monitoring process at Nike factories where Michigan-licensed products are produced. Both the University of Michigan and Nike felt the final agreement was the result of win–win negotiating.

Source: Kevin O'Hanlon, "U of Michigan Seals Multimillion-Dollar Deal," *Marketing News*, February 12, 2001, p. 21.

weeks but then realize that your fleet of trucks cannot make that route every two weeks, put the issue back on the table for renegotiation.

11. Don't automatically agree to a "let's just split the difference" offer by the buyers. Check out the offer to see how it compares to your target position.

12. If the customer says, "Tell us what your best price is, and we'll tell you whether we are interested," remain noncommittal. Respond with, "In most cases, a price of $_ is the best we can do. However, if you want to make a proposal, we'll see what we can do."

13. Know when to stop. Don't keep trying to get and get even if you can.

14. Use silence effectively. Studies have shown cultural differences in the negotiator's ability to use silence. For example, Brazilians make more initial concessions (use less silence early) than North Americans, who make more than the Japanese.

15. Plan the session well. In one study of successful negotiators, Neil Rackham found that "80 percent of the concessions obtained during negotiation resulted from things done before the negotiation started."[8]

The granting and receiving of concessions is often very complex and can result in the negotiations taking months or years to complete. Building Partnerships 13.1 describes some of the unusual concessions resulting from negotiations between Nike and the University of Michigan.

Setting the proper environment early in the meeting puts you well on the way to a successful negotiation. Remember to develop an agenda and be aware of win–lose strategies that buyers may use. Offer concessions strategically.

RECAP OF A SUCCESSFUL NEGOTIATION MEETING

This chapter discussed win–win and win–lose negotiation sessions. Seasoned veterans will note that, in some situations, the session could more accurately be classified as **win–win not yet negotiating**. In win–win not yet, the buying team achieves its goals while the selling team doesn't. However, the sellers expect to achieve their goals in the near future, thanks to the results of that negotiation session. For example, Antonio Willars in Monterrey, Mexico, relates the following:

> I was working for the magazine *Revista Motor y Volante* and negotiating with Gonher, a lubricating oil company. At that time, no oil companies advertised in my magazine. So I negotiated an agreement with Gonher with a lower price than I had hoped to achieve, based on the belief that that sale would result in increased business over the long term. Although I didn't achieve my pricing goals in that session, I took a longer-term view. It paid off. That was the first of many, consistent sales to Gonher, all at our regular rates. Plus, many oil companies, such as Quaker State, now advertise in the magazine. So, although I had a "win not yet" outcome in that first meeting, we have now achieved a complete win–win situation.

When the session is over, be sure to get any negotiated agreements in writing. If no formal contract is possible, at least summarize the agreements reached. And don't forget to do postnegotiation evaluation and learn from your mistakes.

thinking it through

How can the use of information technology help keep track of issues during a negotiation session and ensure that all agreements reached during a negotiation session are included in the final written agreement?

Studies have shown that more cooperation exists if both sides expect future interactions. Keep in mind that your goal is to develop a long-term partnership with your buyer. This process can be aided by being levelheaded, courteous, and, above all, honest. Also, do not try to get every concession possible out of your buyer. If you push too hard or too long, the buyer will get irritated and may even walk out. Never lose out on an agreement by being too greedy. Remember your goal: to reach a win–win settlement.

SUMMARY

This chapter described how to engage in win–win negotiating. It also described how buyers may engage in win–lose negotiating.

Almost anything can be negotiated. The areas of negotiation will depend on the needs of both parties and the extent of disagreement on major issues.

A successful salesperson is not necessarily a good negotiator. Important negotiator traits include patience and endurance, willingness to take risks, a tolerance for ambiguity, the ability to deal with conflict, and the ability to engage in negotiation without worrying that every person present will not be on one's side.

As in regular sales calls, careful planning counts. This step involves choosing the location, setting objectives, and developing and managing the negotiating team. The salesperson does not act alone in these tasks, but instead draws on the full resources of the firm.

Preliminaries are important in sales negotiation sessions. Friendly conversation and small talk can help to reduce tensions and establish rapport. Agendas help to set boundaries and keep the negotiation on track. Win–lose strategies that buyers use include a good guy–bad guy routine, lowballing, emotional outbursts, budget limitation, and browbeating. As much as possible, the salesperson should respond to any win–lose maneuvers calmly and with the intent of bringing the other side back to a win–win stance.

Concessions, by definition, will occur in every negotiation. Many guidelines have been established to help negotiators avoid obvious problems. For example, no concession should be given unless the buyer gives a concession of equal value. Also, any concessions given are not formalized until the written agreement is signed; thus all concessions are subject to removal if appropriate.

KEY TERMS

accommodating mode
adaptive planning
agenda
ambush negotiating
avoiding mode
brainstorming session
browbeating
budget bogey
budget limitation tactic
collaborating mode
competing mode
compromising mode
concession
emotional outburst tactic

face
good guy–bad guy routine
lowballing
minimum position
negotiation
negotiation jujitsu
nibbling
opening position
sneak attack
target position
win–lose negotiating
win–win negotiating
win–win not yet negotiating

ETHICS PROBLEMS

1. "Try to get a big concession from your opponent by giving away a small, insignificant concession yourself." Comment.

2. "If your opponent begins to use an unethical tactic, walk out of the room." Comment on this statement.

QUESTIONS AND PROBLEMS

1. Negotiators have been known to lie during an important meeting. How can you tell whether buyers are lying? What should you do if you catch them telling a lie?

2. Suppose you're a salesperson with a local milk producer and you're negotiating with a regional grocer over the number of deliveries you will make to their stores in a given week. Your maximum is nine times a week, your opening is four times a week, and your target is six times a week. After negotiating for some time, the grocer states, "Look, we're not willing to accept anything less than 14 times a week." What do you do now?

3. Assume you're a salesperson who is known for your excellent negotiating skills. You're a true collaborator in every sense of the word. Today you're supposed to engage in a negotiation with an important client. It's taken three months to set up this meeting, and your team of five, including your vice president, is all assembled and ready to walk into the meeting. You are your team's designated leader. Your cell phone rings, and it's a relative, telling you that a very close loved one has passed away unexpectedly. With the news comes a desire to just quit everything. What do you do now?

4. Salesperson E. J. Keeley enjoys meeting people and helping them solve their problems. Although he is excited when he obtains commitment, he really went into selling because he has a strong need to make friends and develop relationships. He is very patient and not averse to taking risks. Because his parents were in the military, he is accustomed to moving a lot and has developed a tolerance for ambiguity and new situations. Do you believe E. J. will make a good negotiator? Why or why not?

5. According to the text, engaging in friendly conversation to break the ice before getting down to business is usually a good idea. When would it not be a good idea?

6. Assume you are going to have your fourth and final job interview with Xerox, an office products firm, next Friday. Knowledgeable friends have told you that because you "passed" the first three interviews, you will be offered the job during the fourth interview. Also, you know that Xerox likes to negotiate with its new hires.

   a. Think about your own needs and desires for your first job (such as salary, expense reimbursement, benefits, geographic location, promotion cycle).

   b. For each need and desire listed, establish your target position, opening position, and minimum position.

   c. Xerox has probably also developed positions that would meet each of your needs and desires. Describe how you might go about discovering these positions before next Friday's meeting.

7. Tamara Lockman, a salesperson for Nabisco, is preparing for an important negotiation session with Safeway, a large, national food chain, regarding an upcoming promotional campaign. Her boss has strongly suggested that he attend the meeting with her. The problem is that her boss is not a good negotiator; he tends to get angry, is unorganized, and tries to resolve conflict by talking nonstop and thus wearing down the buyer team with fatigue. Her boss definitely has a win–lose negotiating philosophy. What should Tamara do?

8. "You are the worst possible person to have to negotiate for yourself. You care too much about the outcome. Always let someone else negotiate for you." State your reaction to this statement. What implications does it have in industrial sales negotiations?

9. During negotiation, buyers make all kinds of statements. What would be your response to the following, assuming each occurred early in the meeting?

   a. We refuse to pay more than $809.00 each. That's our bottom line—take it or leave it!

   b. Come on, you've got to do better than that!

   c. You know, we're going to have to get anything we decide here today approved by our corporate management before we can sign any kind of a contract.

   d. One of our buyers can't make it here for another hour. But let's go ahead and get started and see what progress we can make.

   e. Tell you what, we need to see a detailed cost breakdown for each individual item in your proposal.

10. "As a salesperson negotiator, my buyer's problem becomes my problem." Comment.

CASE PROBLEMS

case **13.1**

Bell Helicopters

Bell Helicopter Textron is a wholly owned subsidiary of Textron, Incorporated. Bell is often cited as building the best helicopters in the world. It also has the reputation of having the best customer service department among helicopter manufacturers.

Bell makes a complete line of helicopters. Satisfied clients include a wide range of commercial users, the military, and law enforcement agencies. For each market segment, Bell manufactures a wide range of helicopters to meet individual needs and budgets.

The first Bell helicopter was placed in law enforcement in 1948 for the New York Police Department. Since then Bell has become a world leader in serving the needs of law enforcement agencies.

Today Praveen Vaidyanathan, a salesperson for Bell, and his team of five engaged in a negotiation session with a homeland security agency, represented by a team of five individuals. The session began pleasantly enough, and Praveen was convinced that an agreement was going to be reached soon in the meeting. In prenegotiation meetings, Praveen had discovered that the agency needed 15 law enforcement helicopters with maximum mission flexibility. The helicopters would need to seat at least six individuals and have capabilities to handle a variety of situations. Based on the needs identified, Praveen had planned the negotiation session intending to sell the agency its 206L-4 Mission helicopter.

The 206L-4 Mission is known for its mission flexibility. It can outmaneuver competitive helicopters in a variety of challenging situations and has the lowest lifetime costs. It seats seven and has a 2,141-pound load capacity. The 206L-4 Mission allows missions to stay airborne longer than most helicopters in its class, up to 4.1 hours before refueling. Because of these characteristics this model is a favorite of SWAT teams across the United States.

Everything was going great until Praveen was asked by Dot Watson, negotiation leader from the agency, for the financial side of things. Praveen opened with the price that the selling team had agreed to in premeeting planning. That's when everything went downhill fast.

"You've got to be kidding!" Dot exclaimed, her face flushing with anger. "You know we can't afford that kind of price! We're talking about taxpayer money here. We're not some IBM or Donald Trump or anyone else who has deep pockets. We're here to protect homeland security." She stood and pointed directly at Praveen. "That includes YOUR security as well, and the security of YOUR family, and yes, even the security of YOUR company, Bell Helicopters. You've got a great helicopter. In fact, we walked into this meeting expecting to do business today. But you're asking too much. Way too much!"

All eyes were on Dot. Slowly, she let her hand drop to her side and sat down, as though dejected and rejected. With bowed head and softened voice she concluded, "We need these helicopters. And we need them now." Quietly she quoted the maximum price that the agency could possibly pay.

Praveen was stunned. He had never seen such an emotional outburst before. He knew the agency was in a state of turmoil and had recently been investigated by a Senate committee regarding charges of overspending. But the number that Dot provided was 10 percent less than Bell's minimum price.

Questions

1. Evaluate the negotiation meeting to this point. How could Praveen have better planned for the meeting?
2. What should Praveen do now? Be explicit and give reasons for your answers. Make any necessary assumptions.

Source: This is a fictitious scenario. Information about Bell came from its Web site, www.bellhelicopter.textron.com.

case 13.2

Identifying Conflict-Handling Modes

This chapter describes a number of basic conflict-handling modes that people use in negotiation. These include competing, collaborating, compromising, avoiding, and accommodating.

Carefully reread the section that describes these modes. For each mode, identify someone you know who falls into the mode and answer the following questions. It will probably help to think of a specific situation that you have observed or have experienced with the person.

Questions

1. How do you know this person has this conflict-handling mode? Identify specific behaviors that you have observed or heard about to support your assertion about this person.
2. How do you (and others) interact with this person during a conflict situation? In other words, what do you do? How do you respond to this person's behavior? Is your approach effective?
3. Would you like to have this person on your team during an important negotiation session? Why or why not?

ACT! ROLE PLAY

Break up into pairs; one person will serve as a buyer and the other as an ACT! salesperson. The buyer is the VP of sales for the Houston regional office of DHL shipping. DHL is an international carrier that does overnight express package delivery (like FedEx), package delivery (like UPS), and international shipping. They can ship anything anywhere. There are 54 salespeople employed, with six sales managers reporting to the VP. The salespeople use a card system, whereby they get the buyer's business card and staple it to an index card on which they can keep their notes. The company plans to add five salespeople per year until it doubles in size, with a new sales manager every other year. Sales force turnover is 15 percent per year, and often the cards are not turned over or are incomplete. One other problem is that growth is not meeting targets. Managers train their sales teams, but reps complain that it isn't what they need. Managers don't know what they need because they don't know where in the sales process that reps are not effective. ACT! can provide pipeline analysis as well as better reporting of activity and results, a key need. Each rep generates about $1 million in shipping revenue per year.

Reps are not particularly computer literate. They don't use computers to keep track of their accounts now. They do have laptops, which they can use to access shipping records via a wireless Internet connection.

As a rep or as a buyer, take a few minutes to determine your opening and target positions on such factors as price, training, service, and anything else you can think of. Both of you can use information about ACT! found in the role play section at the end of the book or on the ACT! Web site to determine your position and negotiating strategy. In your planning, include the use of a win–lose tactic, but be willing to move back to win–win if the other person responds appropriately. No additional information will be provided by the instructor.

Note: For background information about these role plays, please see page 27.

To the instructor: Additional information needed to complete the role play is available in the Instructor's Manual.

ADDITIONAL REFERENCES

Atkinson, William. "Forget Dog & Pony Shows." *Purchasing* 133 (February 2004), pp. 34–37.

Bazerman, Max H. *Negotiation, Decision Making and Conflict Mangement*. Northampton, MA: Edward Elgar Publishing, 2005.

Benoliel, Michael, and Linda Cashdan. *Done Deal: The World's Best Negotiators Get You What You Want*. Avon, MA: Adams Media Corporation, 2005.

Busch, Karl R. "Increasing Your Power in a Single-Source Negotiation." *Inside Supply Chain Management*, January 2002, pp. 6–8.

Chamoun-Nicholas, Habib. *Deal: Guidelines for a Flawless Negotiation*. Kingwood, TX: Keynegotiations, 2004.

Dietmeyer, Brian J. *Strategic Negotiation: A Breakthrough Four-Step Process for Effective Business Negotiation*. Chicago: Dearborn Trade, 2004.

Fisher, Roger, and William Ury. *Getting to Yes: Negotiating Agreement without Giving In*. 2nd ed. Boston: Houghton Mifflin, 1991.

Gelfand, Michele J., and Jeanne M. Brett. *The Handbook of Negotiation and Culture*. Palo Alto, CA: Stanford University Press, 2004.

Green, Ida. *Soft Power Skills: Women and Negotiations*. Bloomington, IN: AuthorHouse, 2004.

Kaeter, Margaret, and Angelique Pinet. *Everything Negotiating Book*. Avon, MA: Adams Media, 2005.

Keller, Wendy. *Secrets of Successful Negotiating for Women*. Franklin Lakes, NJ: Career Press, 2004.

Lum, Grande. *The Negotiation Fieldbook*, New York: McGraw-Hill, 2004.

Luo, Yadong. "Partnering with Foreign Businesses: Perspectives from Chinese Firms." *Journal of Business Research* 55, no. 6 (2002), pp. 481–93.

Menard, Robert A. II., "Unwritten Negotiation Rules." *Selling*, March 2004, p. 9.

Mnookin, Robert H.; Andrew S. Tulumello; and Scott R. Peppet. *Beyond Winning: Negotiating to Create Value in Deals and Disputes."* Boston: Harvard University Press, 2004.

Reardon, Kathleen. *The Skilled Negotiator: Mastering the Language of Engagement.* San Francisco: Jossey-Bass, 2004.

Strelecky, John. "Take 3 Simple Steps to Mastering Negotiations." *Selling,* September 2004, p. 8.

Thompson, Leigh L. *Mind and Heart of the Negotiator.* Upper Saddle River, NJ: Prentice Hall, 2004.

"Walk Away the Winner during Sales Negotiations." *Selling,* June 2004, p. 8.

Zarkada-Fraser, Anna, and Campbell Fraser. "Moral Decision Making in International Sales Negotiations." *Journal of Business & Industrial Marketing* 16, no. 4 (2001), pp. 274–93.

Zhao, Jensen J. "The Chinese Approach to International Business Negotiation." *The Journal of Business Communication* 37 (July 2002), pp. 209–37.

AFTER THE SALE: BUILDING LONG-TERM PARTNERSHIPS

chapter **14**

SOME QUESTIONS ANSWERED IN THIS CHAPTER . . .

- How important is service after the sale?
- How should salespeople stay in contact with customers?
- Which sales strategies stimulate repeat sales and new business in current accounts?
- Which techniques are important to use when handling complaints?

part **3**

PROFILE

I truly enjoy being a salesperson. I have learned that I should never promise a customer what I cannot deliver. I sell myself and I do not want to damage my credibility. Credibility is the key to building long-term partnerships with my clients. It also helps me to retain and grow my customer base. That trust and overall experience opens new doors into other groups inside an organization for increased sales.

I first began selling in the wireless industry in a four-county area in the northern part of the state. After two successful years, I accepted a position selling to the larger corporate customers. I moved my family to a larger city and was given an existing account. This company was only doing a fraction of the business of which they were capable using our services, though my management thought we were well positioned in the account. When I took the account over, my customer was in the middle of negotiating one of the largest contracts in their company's history in another area of their business. The executive VP of purchasing was traveling and needed to keep in touch with the home office at all times to stay abreast of the negotiations. During his travel he lost his communication service for a few hours and was unable to reach key people as the negotiating process reached the critical stages.

This did not set well for us as a communications supplier. In fact, it damaged our current relationship with their executive management team to the point that they began looking for an alternative vendor for their wireless needs.

While there was no doubt that their search for an alter-native was a major problem, I viewed this as an opportunity to show what we could do. I immediately set out to assess the problem, why it occurred, and how we could prevent this from ever happening in the future. I put a plan of action together that included a list of all their executive people along with their wireless numbers. These numbers were checked for proper provisioning in our system immediately. Then each month we would check to make sure that nothing had changed that would affect their service when traveling. I presented this plan of action and solution to the customer. The trust in our relationship was still damaged however. They began to order a competitor's product and services.

Our service was better, but I had to prove it. They weren't going to just take my word that we were better. I immediately pulled together our team and implemented a process that would lead to becoming the benchmark to measure our competitors. The executive exposure that this situation created led to more opened doors inside my customer, and I overcame the doubt that had been created. When I won back their trust, my company and I were again viewed as a strategic partner inside the company, but now at a higher level than before. I enjoyed the results by signing a long-term contract with my customer and increasing our revenues more than 250 percent.

My plan required that my company live up to the promises I made. Knowing what promises to make, what promises can be kept, and what promises make a difference are critical to my success. But it takes more than promises to keep customers; it takes keeping promises.

Visit us on the Web at www.cingular.com

"It takes more than promises to keep customers; it takes keeping promises."

Jim Allgood, Cingular

THE VALUE OF CUSTOMERS

Many people believe the emphasis in selling is on getting the initial sale. For most salespeople, however, sales increases from one year to the next are due to increasing the revenue from existing accounts, not from getting new accounts. Even in industries where purchase decisions are made infrequently, salespeople gain a competitive advantage by maintaining strong relationships with their customers. Eventually, when buying decisions need to be made, those customers look to people they know. For example, when Turner Broadcasting (CNN, TNT, and other stations) purchases satellite time for television broadcasting from Hughes Telecommunications, the contract is for the entire life of the satellite (15 years or longer). Hughes may launch only a couple of satellites each year, but it is important that the Hughes salesperson maintain a high-quality relationship with Turner so that revenue is optimized through maximum customer satisfaction.

This chapter integrates the knowledge you have already gained in selling to new prospects with the material covered in Chapter 2 on building partnerships so that you can learn how to sell to the same accounts over the long term. The chapter also discusses how to handle unhappy customers.

Customers are, of course, the primary revenue source for companies. As we discussed in Chapter 2, customers are worth more in terms of revenue than some salespeople recognize. For example, a car salesperson may think only of the immediate sale, but each customer is potentially worth hundreds of thousands of dollars in revenue over the salesperson's lifetime. Exhibit 14.1 illustrates the value of a small law office over a twenty-year period for just a few salespeople. For example, if an office equipment/supply salesperson sold all of the copiers and office supplies needed during those twenty years, total revenue would be over $80,000! If the salesperson thinks in terms of just one sale, however, the customer is worth only about $5,000.

thinking **it** through

How much do you spend on clothing each month? Now multiply that figure by 12. Assuming that you shop in the same places during the four years you will be in college, multiply that result by 4. The total is the amount of your clothing purchases over your college career. Does anyone treat you like a $1,000 customer, or are you treated like a $20 customer? How would you expect to be treated differently if the store recognized your true value?

Exhibit 14.1
Selected Expenses for a Small Law Firm over a 20-Year Period

Item	Cost	Total
Copiers	5 @ $5,000	$25,000
Copying supplies	$50 per month	12,000
Fax machines	5 @ $2,000	10,000
Fax supplies	$20 per month	4,800
Telephone systems	3 @ $1,000	3,000
Other office supplies	$100 per month	24,000
Office furniture	$5,000	5,000
Total over 20 years		$83,800

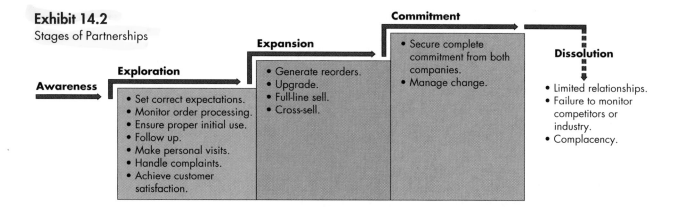

Exhibit 14.2
Stages of Partnerships

Awareness

Exploration
- Set correct expectations.
- Monitor order processing.
- Ensure proper initial use.
- Follow up.
- Make personal visits.
- Handle complaints.
- Achieve customer satisfaction.

Expansion
- Generate reorders.
- Upgrade.
- Full-line sell.
- Cross-sell.

Commitment
- Secure complete commitment from both companies.
- Manage change.

Dissolution
- Limited relationships.
- Failure to monitor competitors or industry.
- Complacency.

Research shows that successfully retaining customers is important to all companies. Manufacturers that set explicit targets for customer retention and make extraordinary efforts to exceed these goals are 60 percent more profitable than those without such goals or that fail to track loyalty.[1] Yet another study finds that the average company loses 20–50 percent of its customer base every year.[2] Salespeople are critical to the process: Another study finds that it takes only a slight dip in attention from the salesperson to lead to a willingness to consider alternative sources.[3]

We have already discussed the importance of good service in generating referrals and of becoming a trusted member of the community in which your buyers operate so you can acquire more customers (see Chapter 7). The value of satisfied customers is so high that it makes good business sense to build the strongest possible relationships.

As we discussed in Chapter 2, relationships go through several stages, beginning with awareness and ending in dissolution. In this chapter we focus on the three stages between awareness and dissolution—exploration, expansion, and commitment—as illustrated in Exhibit 14.2. As you read the rest of the chapter, you will see how trust is built and maintained throughout the life of the partnership.

EXPLORATION

In the exploration stage, the relationship is defined through the development of expectations for each party. The buyer tests the seller's product, how the seller responds to requests, and other similar actions after the initial sale is made. A small percentage of the buyer's business is given to minimize the risk in case the vendor cannot perform. When the vendor performs well, trust is developed, as is a personal relationship.

Beginning the relationship properly is important if the relationship is going to last a long time. Keep in mind that the customer is excited about receiving the benefits of the product as promised by the salesperson. An unfavorable initial experience with the product or with the company may be extremely difficult to overcome. Beginning the relationship properly requires that the salesperson set the right expectations, monitor order processing, ensure proper use of the product, and assist in servicing the product.

SET THE RIGHT EXPECTATIONS

The best way to begin a relationship is for each party to be aware of what the other expects. To a large degree, customers base their expectations on sales presentations.

This salesperson is training the customer on how to use the product properly. Getting customers off to the right start is essential to building long and satisfying relationships.

Bonnie Kamin/Photoedit

Salespeople should make sure customers have reasonable expectations of product performance. If the salesperson exaggerates the capabilities of the product or the company, the customer will be disappointed. Admitting there has been a misunderstanding will not satisfy a customer who has registered a complaint. Avoiding complaints by setting proper expectations is best. Long-term relationships are begun by making an honest presentation of the product's capabilities and eliminating any misconceptions before the order is placed.

MONITOR ORDER PROCESSING

Although many people may work on an order before it is shipped, the salesperson is ultimately responsible, at least in the eyes of the customer, for seeing that the product is shipped when promised. Salespeople should keep track of pending orders and inform buyers when the paperwork is delayed in the customer's plant. Orders placed directly with a salesperson should be transmitted to the factory immediately. Also, progress on orders should be closely monitored. If problems arise in filling the order, the customer should be informed promptly; on the other hand, if the order can be filled sooner than promised, the customer should be notified so that proper arrangements can be made.

Fortunately, computers have made the sales representative's job easier. Salespeople can use handheld terminals and laptop PCs to check on inventory or the status of an order. For example, Northeast Utilities account executives use customer relationship management software to monitor the billing cycle and ensure that sales are being processed properly.[4] Progressive firms have introduced automated order systems that allow the customer to sign a pad on the computer; the signature is sent to the company electronically, avoiding delays that might result if the contract were mailed.

Many firms, such as GE and Baxter Healthcare, facilitate automatic placement of orders by having their own computers talk to customers' computers. This technology, called **electronic data interchange** (EDI—see Chapter 10), boosts the productivity of both the salespeople and the purchasing managers they call on. As a result, salespeople spend less time writing orders and more time solving problems; buyers save on ordering and inventory costs. Computerized communication for order placement is particularly useful when managing a customer's needs worldwide. Problems arising from elements such as time zones and language barriers are minimized.

Monitoring order processing and other after-sale activities is critical to developing a partnership. Studies continually show that buyers are displeased with most salespeople in this respect. Colonial Life and Accident Insurance, a company that sells insurance to other companies, uses a quarterly Service Report Card that customers complete, rating the salesperson's after-sale activities. The data are available to the salespeople—and to customers, no matter the results. Colonial recognizes the importance of good customer care in retaining customers.[5]

ENSURE PROPER INITIAL USE OF THE PRODUCT OR SERVICE

Customer dissatisfaction can occur just after delivery of a new product, especially if the product is technical or requires special installation. Customers unfamiliar with the product may have problems installing or using it. They may even damage the product through improper use. Many salespeople visit new customers right after initial deliveries to ensure the correct use of the product. In this way they can also help the customer realize the full potential benefits of the product.

Some buyers may know how to use the basic features of a product or service, but if it is not operating at maximum efficiency, the wise salesperson will show the buyer how to get more profitable use out of it. Many firms have staffed a customer service department to aid salespeople in this task. It is still the salesperson's responsibility, however, to make sure that the customer service department takes proper care of each new customer.

To be most effective, the salesperson should not wait until the user has trouble with the product. The fewer the difficulties allowed to occur, the greater will be the customer's confidence in the salesperson and the product.

FOLLOW UP

The first follow-up a salesperson should perform after the sale is a call to say thank you and to check whether the product is working appropriately. Some salespeople use specialty advertising, or gifts imprinted with their company's name, to say thanks. These items are generally small enough to avoid concerns about bribery and can include desk clocks, pens, and the like. But salespeople should also follow up regularly with their accounts to stay in touch with any changing needs or possible problems. In fact, failing to follow up is a major complaint that buyers have about salespeople.

Joe Hunter, owner of Karr-Hunter Pontiac, told us that his dealership does several hundred dollars' worth of printing every month. He tried four printers before he finally found one who would call him every few weeks. Joe wanted that kind of follow-up to avoid running out of forms. Regular follow-up prompts Joe to check his stock and to order printing before he runs out. Regular follow-up with satisfied customers also promotes opportunities for securing references. Regular follow-up can be accomplished via a personal visit, the telephone, or even e-mail and regular mail.

Personal visits can be the most expensive form of follow-up because of travel time and because the sales call will last longer than one conducted through other means. A personal visit, though, can be extremely productive because the salesperson can check on inventories, the performance of the machine, or other aspects that can be accomplished only at the customer's site. In addition, a customer may be more likely to disclose information, such as a minor complaint or compliment, in a personal setting than over the phone. Regular personal visits can also build trust, a key component needed to move the relationship forward.

Between personal visits, it is often a good idea to make contact via telephone. A salesperson can make 12 or more such calls within an hour, efficiently checking on his or her clients. Telephone calls are two-way communication, giving the customer an opportunity to voice any concerns and minimizing intrusion. Contact management software, such as ACT!, can help salespeople schedule telephone follow-ups.

Iomega Corporation sells digital storage solutions and uses e-mail newsletters (called e-missives; see Chapter 8) to keep in touch with customers.[6] These newsletters can be personalized with both the salesperson's and the customer's names, which helps maintain a sense of commitment to the relationship. Customers' replies to the e-mail go straight back to the rep.

Many companies provide form letters or thank-you cards to encourage their salespeople to follow up on new sales. Salespeople can also create their own form letters and use their contact management software to generate the most appropriate mailing list. The problem, though, is that these are still form letters. Creative use of certain fields in contact management software like ACT!, however, enables salespeople to add a personalized paragraph, creating that special touch that can dramatically increase the impact of such a letter. E-mail is also becoming a common form of customer contact, with customers appreciating the opportunity to choose when to read and respond to the salesperson's contact.

Following up with customers signals that the salesperson is dependable and customer oriented. Although the objective may be to create a functional relationship rather than a strategic partnership, such follow-up is still necessary to remind customers that you are the salesperson with whom they want to do business.

HANDLE CUSTOMER COMPLAINTS

Handling complaints is critical to developing goodwill and maintaining partnerships. Complaints can occur at any time in the partnering process, not just during the exploration stage; but they may be more important in the early stages of a partnership. Attempts to establish partnerships often collapse because of shortsightedness in handling customer complaints. Some firms spend thousands of dollars on advertising but make the mistake of insulting customers who attempt to secure a satisfactory adjustment.

Complaints normally arise when the company and its products do not live up to the customer's expectations. Assuming the proper expectations were set, customers can be disappointed for any of the following reasons: (1) the product performs poorly, (2) it is being used improperly, or (3) the terms of the sales contract were not met. Although salespeople usually cannot change the product or terms, they can affect these sources of complaints, minimizing them by setting proper expectations and ensuring proper use.

One study showed that when a company fails in its dealings with a complainant, the latter will tell 10 people, on average, about the bad experience; those who are satisfied tell only four to five others. Also, for every dissatisfied person who complains, an estimated 50 more simply stop buying the product.[7]

Another study found that you have a 40 percent chance of winning back a customer who is upset, so it is worth the effort.[8]

Most progressive companies have learned that an excellent way to handle customer complaints is through personal visits by sales representatives. Thus the salesperson may have total responsibility for this portion of the company's public relations. Salespeople who carry this burden must be prepared to do an effective job.

Complaints cannot be eliminated; they can only be reduced in frequency. The salesperson who knows complaints are inevitable can learn to handle them as a normal part of the job. The following discussion presents some techniques for responding to complaints; Exhibit 14.3 provides an overview.

Encourage Buyers to Tell Their Stories

Some customers can become angry over real or imaginary grievances. They welcome the salesperson's visit as an opportunity to voice complaints. Other buyers are less emotional in expressing complaints and give little evidence of irritation or anger, but the complaint is no less important. In either case customers need to tell their stories without interruption. Interruptions add to the irritation of emotionally upset buyers, making it almost impossible to arrive at a settlement that is fair to all parties.

Customers want a sympathetic reaction to their problems, whether real or imagined. They want their feelings to be acknowledged, their business to be recognized as important, and their grievances handled in a friendly manner. An antagonistic attitude or an attitude that implies the customer is trying to cheat the

Exhibit 14.3

Responding to Complaints

- Encourage buyers to tell their story.
- Determine the facts.
- Offer a solution.
- Follow through with action.

Exhibit 14.4

Handling Rude or Irate Customers

1. Follow the Golden Rule—treat your customer the way you would like to be treated, no matter how difficult the client becomes.
2. Prove you listened—paraphrase the customer's concern, recognizing the customer's feelings along with the facts.
3. Don't justify, excuse, or blame others—be positive and thank the customer for bringing the problem to your attention so you can resolve it.
4. Do the hard things first—the faster they get done, the more your customer will appreciate you and your efforts.
5. Call back if the customer hangs up.
6. Give the customer someone else to call, but only in case you are not available— don't pass the buck!

company seldom paves the way for a satisfactory adjustment. You can probably relate to this feeling if you have ever had to return a defective product or get some kind of adjustment made on a bill. Exhibit 14.4 suggests ways to handle irate customers.

Good salespeople show they are happy the grievance has been brought to their attention. After the customer describes the problem, the salesperson may express regret for any inconvenience. An attempt should then be made to talk about points of agreement. Agreeing with the customer as far as possible gets the process off to the right start.

Determine the Facts

It is easy to be influenced by a customer who is honestly making a claim for an adjustment. An inexperienced salesperson might forget that many customers make their case for a claim as strong as possible. Emphasizing the points most likely to strengthen one's case is human nature. But the salesperson has a responsibility to his or her company, too. A satisfactory adjustment cannot be made until all the facts are known.

Whenever possible, the salesperson should examine, in the presence of the customer, the product claimed to be defective. Encouraging the customer to pinpoint the exact problem is a good idea. If the defect is evident, this step may be unnecessary. In other instances, make certain the complaint is understood. The purpose of getting the facts is to determine the cause of the problem so the proper solution can be provided.

Experienced salespeople soon learn that products may appear defective when actually nothing is wrong with them. For example, a buyer may complain that paint was applied exactly as directed but repainting became necessary in a short time; therefore, the paint was no good. However, the paint may have been spread too thin. Any paint will cover just so much area. If the manufacturer recommends using a gallon of paint to cover 400 square feet with two coats and the user covers 600 square feet with two coats, the product is not at fault.

On the other hand, salespeople should not assume product or service failure is always the user's fault. They need an open mind to search for the facts in each case. In one instance, the paint spilled out of the bucket all over the buyer's truck while taking it back to Home Depot to register a complaint that the paint was too thin—like painting with milk. The Home Depot customer service representative refused to believe the buyer that the paint had spilled (even though the paint-covered truck was in the Home Depot parking lot), assuming the buyer used it and was trying to get it for free. The buyer agreed that it was reasonable to require him to take the claim up with the manufacturer, but the Home Depot clerk's assumption that the missing paint was used and not spilled cost Home Depot a $10,000/year customer. Some companies have the policy that the customer is always right, in which case there is no need to establish responsibility. Although there is still a need to determine the cause so the right solution can be offered, do not assume the customer is to blame.

In this phase of making an adjustment, salespeople must avoid giving the impression of stalling. The customer should know that the purpose of determining the facts is to permit a fair adjustment—that the inquiry is not being made to delay action or avoid resolution.

Offer a Solution

After the customer tells his or her story and the facts are determined, the next step is to offer a solution. At this time the company representative describes the process by which the company will resolve the complaint, and the rep should then gain agreement that the proposed solution is satisfactory.

Company policies vary, but many assign the responsibility for settling claims to the salesperson. Other companies require the salesperson to investigate claims and recommend a settlement to the home office. Salespeople are in the best position to make adjustments fairly, promptly, and satisfactorily, especially if the customer and salesperson are geographically distant from the home office. Permitting salespeople to only recommend a course of action, though, assures the customer of attention from a higher level of management, increasing the likelihood that the customer will accept the action taken.

Whatever the company policy, the customer desires quick action and fair treatment and wants to know the reasons for the action. Most customers are satisfied if they quickly receive fair treatment. Customers are seldom convinced of the fairness of a solution that isn't exactly what they wanted unless the reasoning behind the decision is explained to them. Nothing discourages a customer more than having action postponed indefinitely or being offered vague promises. Although some decisions may take time, the salesperson should try to expedite action. The opportunity to develop a partnership may be lost if the time lapse is too great, even though action is taken in the customer's favor.

Some salespeople make disparaging remarks about their own companies or managers in an effort to shift the blame. Blaming someone else in the company is a poor practice because this behavior can cause the customer to lose faith in both the salesperson and the company. Moreover, if the customer does not like the proposed solution, the salesperson trusted to make an adjustment or recommendation should shoulder the responsibility. Any disagreement on the action taken should be ironed out between the salesperson and the home office staff. When reported to the customer, the action must be stated in a sound, convincing manner.

The action taken may vary with the circumstances. Some possible settlements when a product is unsatisfactory are

1. Replace the product without cost to the customer.
2. Replace the product and share the costs with the customer.
3. Instruct the customer on how to proceed with a claim against a third party (for example, the paint manufacturer in the Home Depot situation).
4. Send the product to the factory for a decision.

Occasionally customers make claims they know are unfair. Although they realize the company is not at fault, they still try to get a settlement. Fortunately, relatively few customers do this. To assume that a customer is willfully trying to cheat the company would be unwise. He or she may honestly see a claim as legitimate even though the salesperson can clearly tell that the company is not at fault. The salesperson does well, then, to proceed cautiously and, if any doubt exists, to treat the claim as legitimate.

A salesperson convinced that a claim is dishonest has two ways to take action. First, he or she can give the buyer an opportunity to save face by suggesting that a third party may be to blame. For example, if a machine appears not to have been oiled for a long time, a salesperson may suggest, "Is it possible that your maintenance crew neglected to oil this machine?" Second, the salesperson can unmask the fraudulent claim and appeal to the customer's sense of fair play. This procedure may cause the loss of a customer. In some cases, however, the company may be better off without that customer.

Answers to the following questions often affect the action to be taken:

- What is the dollar value of the claim? Many firms have established standard procedures for what they classify as small claims. For example, one moving and storage firm considers any claim under $200 to be too insignificant to investigate fully; thus a refund check is issued automatically for a claim under this amount. Firms may also have a complete set of procedures and policies developed for every size of claim.

- How often has this customer made claims? If the buyer has instituted many claims in the past, the company may need to not only resolve the specific complaint but also conduct a more comprehensive investigation of all prior claims. Such a probe may reveal systematic flaws in the salesperson's company, product, or procedures. For example, Pinacor (a $5 billion technology distributor) identified a pattern of shipping complaints from one customer. By creating extra inventory, Pinacor was able to meet the customer's higher demands and then applied the same solution to other customers. The result was an overall increase in sales.[9]

- How will the action taken affect other customers? The salesperson should assume that the action taken will be communicated to other prospects and customers. If the complaining customer is part of a buying community (discussed in Chapter 7), chances are very good that others will learn about the resolution of the claim. Thus the salesperson must take actions necessary to maintain a positive presence in that community, possibly even providing a more generous solution than the merits of the case dictate.

The solution that will be provided must be clearly communicated to the customer. The customer must perceive the settlement as fair. When describing the settlement, the salesperson should carefully monitor all verbal and nonverbal cues to determine the customer's level of satisfaction. If the customer does not agree with the proposed action, the salesperson should seek ways to change the settlement or provide additional information about why the settlement is fair to all parties.

Follow Through with Action

A fair settlement made in the customer's favor helps to resell the company and its products or services. The salesperson has the chance to prove what the customer has been told for a long time: that the company will devote time and effort to keeping customers satisfied.

The salesperson who has authority only to recommend an adjustment must take care to report the facts of the case promptly and accurately to the home or branch office. The salesperson has the responsibility to act as a buffer between the customer and the company. After the claim is filed, contact must be maintained with the customer to see that the customer secures the promised settlement.

The salesperson also has a responsibility to educate the customer to forestall future claims. After a claim has been settled to the customer's satisfaction is a fine time to make some suggestions. For example, the industrial sales representative may provide a new set of directions on how to oil and clean a machine.

Achieve Customer Satisfaction

Although complaints always signal customer dissatisfaction, their absence does not necessarily mean customers are happy. Customers probably voice only 1 in 20 of their concerns. They may speak out only when highly dissatisfied, or a big corporation's buyer may not be aware of problems until the product's users vent their frustration. Lower levels of dissatisfaction still hurt sales. Salespeople should continuously monitor customers' levels of satisfaction and perceptions of product performance because customer satisfaction is the most important reason for reordering at this stage in the relationship.

When the customer is satisfied, an opportunity for further business exists. Complaints and dissatisfaction can occur at any time during the relationship, but handling complaints well during the exploration stage is one way to prove that the salesperson is committed to keeping the customer's business. When customers sense such commitment, whether through the handling of a complaint or through other forms of special attention, they may be ready to move to the expansion stage.

EXPANSION

The next phase of the buyer–seller relationship is expansion. When a salesperson does a good job of identifying and satisfying needs and the beginnings of a partnership are in place, the opportunity is ripe for additional sales. For example, Craig Murchison, account manager for ABCO, a printing company, was given a small job as his first sale to Acclivus. When he proved that ABCO could save Acclivus money by reducing waste, he was given bigger jobs. Over time, greater trust developed, and he was ultimately awarded all of Acclivus's business. With greater trust, the salesperson can focus on identifying additional needs and providing solutions. In this section we discuss how to increase sales from current customers to expand the relationship. Keep in mind, however, that the activities of the exploration stage (monitoring order processing, handling complaints, and so on) still apply.

There are several ways to maximize the selling opportunity each account represents. These include generating reorders, upgrading, full-line selling, and cross-selling.

GENERATING REPEAT ORDERS

In some situations the most appropriate strategy is to generate repeat orders. For example, Cargill provides salt and other cooking ingredients to Kelloggs. The best strategy for the Cargill salesperson may be to ensure that Kelloggs continues to buy those ingredients from Cargill. Several methods can be used to improve the likelihood of reorders. We will discuss each method in turn.

Be Present at Buying Time

One important method of ensuring reorders is to know how often and when the company makes decisions. For example, one salesperson uses contact management software like ACT! to track his customers' purchases. By simply sending them a letter a week before their usual purchases, he has been able to generate an 85 percent reorder rate—without making a personal visit.[10]

Buyers do not always have regular buying cycles, which can make it difficult for salespeople to be present at buying time. In these situations the seller still wants to be present in the buyer's mind. Two items that can help keep the seller present are catalogs and specialty advertising items. Catalogs are useful for buyers, who will usually refer to them when ready to buy. Specialty advertising items, such as pens or desk calendars, also aid buyers in reordering, especially if the toll-free number is easy to find. Florida Furniture Industries has used desk calendars for more than 70 years to remind furniture store buyers of whom to call when inventories are low.

Providing good service may include helping stores (left) or industrial distributors (right) take inventory or merchandize products.

Spencer Grant/PhotoEdit

John Boykin/PhotoEdit

Help to Service the Product

Most products need periodic maintenance and repair, and some mechanical and electronic products require routine adjustments. Such service requirements offer salespeople a chance to show buyers that the seller's interest did not end with the delivery of the product. Salespeople should be able to make minor adjustments or take care of minor repairs. If they cannot put the product back into working order, they must notify the proper company representative. They should then check to see that the repairs have been completed in a timely manner and to the customer's complete satisfaction.

As we discuss in Chapter 16, part of the salesperson's job is getting to know the company's maintenance and repair people. These repair people can act as the salesperson's eyes and ears when they make service calls. When a good relationship is established with service personnel, salespeople can learn of pending decisions or concerns and take the necessary action.

Helping to service the product is just as important—and maybe more so—when the product is a service, as Jim Allgood discovered. As he says in the opening profile, he had to make sure that his company provided the highest-quality cell phone service to this client by getting engineering involved, and then prove to the client that his company had delivered.

thinking **it** through

Some customers take advantage of salespeople by trying to have them perform almost all of the routine maintenance on a product for free. What can you as a salesperson do to curb such requests? How do you know where to draw the line?

Provide Expert Guidance

An industrial buyer or purchasing agent may need help in choosing a proper grade of oil or in selecting a suitable floor cleaner. A buyer for a retail store may want help developing sales promotion ideas. Whether the buyer needs help in advertising, selling, or managing, good salespeople are prepared to offer worth-

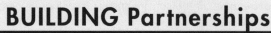
HARD WORK *PLUS* EXPERTISE PAY OFF

Becky Cole's first job out of college was to sell ice cream through Wal-Mart for Southwest Dairy. The ice cream was a new product specifically for diabetics called LeCarb. "When I first started visiting Wal-Marts all over the United States, I had no credibility of my own. To managers in New England, I was only a young girl with a cute Southern accent; to managers in the South, I was just another kid fresh out of college." Managers would put her off with comments like "I'll improve the display later" or "I'll make sure it gets restocked tomorrow." Her reply was always, "No problem, I'll do it now for you." Cole adds, "Of course the product was usually in the very back of their huge warehouse freezers that were never warmer than −12°. I would dig back there and get everything done during my visit. When the managers saw me get back there and actually get my hands (or gloves) dirty, I gained a whole new level of respect from them."

She also provided marketing expertise, albeit expertise she learned from other Wal-Marts. "When I visited the store in Blackstone, Virginia, the frozen food manager was raving about his sales. I documented how he marketed his product, so when I heard the objection, 'The product is not moving at all in my store, so I don't see why it deserves good placement,' I had a great response. I would say, 'Billy is having incredible sales in Blackstone, VA, because he sets it up this way.' Being a young female that called on middle-aged tough guys all day who work in freezers, I found that I could make them budge if another tough guy changed *and* he was selling the product better. Another manager in Villa Rica, Georgia, explained to me that he took the product to his staff meeting and that made a huge difference. I was having people from Ruidoso Downs, New Mexico, to Sunnyside, Washington, make the same changes that were happening on the east coast because I had the data to prove they worked."

Southwest Dairy initially told her the job was supposed to last only a few weeks, just long enough to get the product established. The dairy soon realized that they needed her expertise as much as Wal-Mart did, turning a temporary job into a permanent one.

Source: Becky Cole, personal correspondence; used with permission.

while suggestions or services. Building Partnerships 14.1 illustrates how taking care of the customer can pay off.

The salesperson usually prospers only if the buyer prospers. Obviously, unless buyers can use a product or service profitably or resell it at a profit, they have no need to continue buying from that product's seller. One expert suggests finding non–selling-related ideas to offer your customers. When you use your industry expertise to solve problems or develop opportunities for your clients that do not involve the sale of your product, you add value to the relationship, which can ultimately help you expand your business within the account.

Many firms have developed a team approach to providing guidance and suggestions. For example, Verizon uses a systems approach to help develop and maintain the communication systems of its major accounts. The major account service team (MAST) is composed of marketing (as chairperson), engineering, service, supply, and traffic representatives. This interdepartmental approach brings together all skills required to provide expert guidance and suggestions to meet the expanding, sophisticated needs of large customers.

Standard Register's philosophy for success in the highly competitive field of selling business forms includes expert advice. Its forms management program makes the company a business partner with, rather than merely a supplier to, its major accounts. Customers are shown how to control the costs of buying and using forms by such practices as redesigning existing forms, grouping forms for

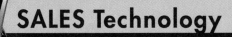
WHY GO WIRELESS?

With all of the information salespeople have to manage, they quickly learn that they can't know it all. That's where the Web comes in handy. With online product catalogs, salespeople can access product information, even if they are selling from a list of 5,000 products. But customers aren't always downtown in skyscrapers. How does a rep access the information then?

Tom Hurt, a representative for United Pipe and Supply in Portland, Oregon, was calling on a residential landscape contractor who was at a job site trying to turn a barren acre of countryside into a manicured lawn, complete with sprinklers and lighting. "The contractor didn't know what product to use on this particular project," Hurt says. Hurt, though, had wireless access to the Web from his laptop. "We were able to, out in this undeveloped field, from my pickup truck, log onto manufacturers' Web sites to get information about product performance," he says. The customer liked what he saw, and Hurt was able to close the sale and deliver the goods in less than three hours.

Roger Diamond, with Technology Sales & Marketing in Indianapolis, has had similar experiences. When trying to cover Wisconsin, Minnesota, North and South Dakota, and the Upper Peninsula of Michigan, he's often in the car, driving around in the wide open spaces. "It's not uncommon while I'm on the road to have a customer call me with a bill of materials and ask for a quote. While I'm still in my car, I can jump on the Internet, access a manufacturer's extranet, gather the needed information, plug in a multiplier, and turn it all around within an hour. And that's all from my car with no need for me to be in the office."

With near-immediate turnaround, wireless access enables salespeople to take better care of their customers. The result is greater cross-selling, as customers seek out salespeople they can rely on.

Sources: Jennifer Gilbert, "No Strings Attached," *Sales and Marketing Management* July 2004, p. 22; Anonymous, "The Future Is Now for Wireless," *Agency Sales*, February 2005, pp. 6–10.

more economical ordering, keeping records of quantities on hand and on order, and keeping track of the dollar value of the inventory. Standard Register's customers welcome such advice, and the result is a high reorder rate.

Provide Special Assistance

Salespeople are in a unique position to offer many types of assistance to the buyer. This section briefly mentions a few types of assistance salespeople can give their customers.

Salespeople engage in many activities. For example, salespeople for Cott Beverages, a Canadian maker of private-label soft drinks for companies like Wal-Mart, work as consultants, offering advice on product design and store layout.[11] Salespeople at Simmons help set up mattress displays in furniture stores. Makita power tool salespeople provide free demonstrations for customers of hardware stores. Most salespeople who sell to resellers will tidy up the shelves and physically restock them from the stockroom supplies. Salespeople also help train the reseller's employees in how to sell the products to the final consumers.

Gail Walker of Marquis Communications, a trade show and special events service agency, worked in the customer's booth at a trade show when one of the customer's salespeople got sick. She worked as hard as if she were one of the firm's employees. Providing such special assistance is one hallmark of excellence in selling. Good relationships are built faster and made more solid by the salesperson who does a little something extra for a customer, performing services over and above his or her normal responsibilities. Sales Technology 14.1 illustrates how wireless communications are helping some salespeople take better care of their customers.

UPGRADING

Similar to generating reorders is the concept of upgrading. **Upgrading,** also called *upselling,* is convincing the customer to use a higher-quality product or a newer product. The salesperson seeks the upgrade because the new or better product serves the needs of the buyer more effectively than the old product did.

Upgrading is crucial to companies like Hobart. According to industry statistics, 60 percent of equipment like what Hobart makes, sold to restaurants and institutional users, will be replacements, not new installations. As a result, post-sale service is more important than ever, and service reps work closely with salespeople so opportunities for upgrading can be identified.[12]

When you upgrade, it is a good idea to emphasize during the needs identification phase that the initial decision was a good one. Now, however, needs or technology have changed, and the newer product fits the customer's requirements better. Otherwise, the buyer may believe that the seller is trying to take advantage of the relationship to foist a higher-priced product.

FULL-LINE SELLING

Full-line selling is selling the entire line of associated products. For example, a Xerox copier salesperson may sell a copier but also wants to sell the dry ink and paper the copier uses and a service contract. Or a Campbell Soup Company salesperson will ask a store to carry cream of potato soup as well as tomato soup.

The emphasis in full-line selling is on helping the buyer realize the synergy of owning or carrying all of the products in that line. For example, the Xerox salesperson may emphasize the security in using Xerox supplies, whereas the Campbell rep will point out that sales for all soups will increase if the assortment is broader.

CROSS-SELLING

Cross-selling is similar to full-line selling except the additional products sold are not directly associated with the initial products. For example, cross-selling occurs when a Xerox salesperson attempts to sell a fax machine to a copier customer or when a Campbell Soup Company rep sells spaghetti sauce to a soup buyer. Cross-selling involves leveraging the relationship with a buyer to identify needs for additional products; estimates are that it costs five times less to cross-sell to an existing client than to acquire a new client.[13] Again, trust in the selling organization and the salesperson already exist; therefore, the sale should not be as difficult as it would be with a new customer, provided the needs exist. Astra Pharmaceutical cross-sells through multiple reps. Because of the technical knowledge required to sell pharmaceuticals, a separate rep is needed for each product, but they use e-mail and other technology to leverage their knowledge about their doctor customers.[14]

Cross-selling and full-line selling require additional training, as illustrated in Exhibit 14.5. Some attempts at cross-selling, though, can resemble the initial sale because the buying center may change. For example, the spaghetti sauce buyer may not be the same person who buys soups. If that is the case, the salesperson will have to begin a relationship with the new buyer, building trust and credibility.

Convincing a retailer to carry all of Campbell's soups is full-line selling; convincing the retailer to also carry Prego spaghetti sauce is cross-selling. Cross-selling leverages existing relationships in order to increase account share, or the percentage of a customer's business that you can earn.

Michael Newman/Photoedit

Exhibit 14.5

Seven Tips for Effective Cross-Selling

1. *Product knowledge:* Salespeople have to know all of their company's products. When companies introduce new cross-selling opportunities, training is needed to learn the new product lines.

2. *Cross-selling skills:* Salespeople must know how to identify the appropriate decision maker, how to leverage current relationships, and how to use other cross-selling skills. Cross-selling often requires additional training.

3. *Incentives:* Many salespeople are afraid of losing the first piece of business by asking for too much, so incentives can help make it worthwhile to ask.

4. *Reasonable quotas or goals:* The first goal when implementing a cross-selling strategy is to get salespeople to simply ask for the opportunity. Goals that are too tough encourage salespeople to force the cross-sale.

5. *Results tracking:* Effective organizations track results by individual and by sales team to identify cross-selling success. Many companies use contact management software like ACT! or salesforce.com for results tracking.

6. *Timing:* Creating a promotion campaign to support cross-selling efforts, particularly when seasonality is an issue, can make a cross-selling strategy successful. Timing also refers to making sure that training occurs before the program starts.

7. *Performance appraisals:* Salespeople need feedback to identify where and how in the process to improve.

Source: Vicki West, PhD, and Jan Minifie, PhD. Used by permission.

COMMITMENT

When the buyer–seller relationship has reached the commitment stage, there is a stated or implied pledge to continue the relationship, as we discussed in Chapter 2. Formally, this pledge may begin with the seller becoming a **preferred supplier,** which is a much greater level of commitment than those levels discussed in Chapter 12. Although preferred-supplier status may mean different things in different companies, in general it means that the supplier is assured of a large percentage of the buyer's business and will get the first opportunity to earn new business. For example, at John Deere, only preferred suppliers are eligible to bid on new product programs. Thus preferred supplier is one term used for "partnership."

DaimlerChrysler classifies its relationships with suppliers into four categories. The first is transactional, or what we called *solo exchange* in Chapter 2. The second is coordinative, in which DaimlerChrysler may sign an annual contract. These two types of relationships are operational in nature. The next two are more strategic, with selective partnership being the first level. Suppliers are integrated into product development processes and work closely with DaimlerChrysler to develop effective interfaces. Alliances, or strategic partnerships, go even further, with integration of departments across the two companies, investment in joint assets, and joint concept development taking place. Such commitment is rare; few companies are strategic partners.[15]

What does it take to become a preferred supplier? PPG, as part of its Supplier Added Value Effort or SAVE program, uses several criteria (listed in Exhibit 14.6). In some cases a PPG preferred supplier is a distributor, not a manufacturer. In these situations the supplier and PPG work in tandem to find the best manufacturers at the lowest prices, with the result being increases in sales volume and better volume discounts. PPG gets the lowest price possible at the required service level, and the distributor makes more profit. Clearly this is a win–win opportunity.

Note that upgrading, full-line selling, cross-selling, and handling complaints will continue to occur during the commitment stage. Because a commitment has been made by both parties to the partnership, however, expectations are greater.

Exhibit 14.6

Examples of Supplier Criteria to Sell to PPG

Hard Savings

- Payment terms, such as cash discounts
- Improve process
  Cycle time reduction (shorter order/delivery cycles, for example)
- Inventory management
  Vendor inventory management
- Quality and innovation
  Variability reduction—no defects, and no adjustments needed to make products fit our applications
- Supply chain management
  Optimal packaging—light packaging that reduces shipping costs while still protecting the product

Soft Savings

- Commercial
  Minority-owned vendors
- Global initiatives
  New markets—provide access to new markets, either by partnering into new markets or by adjusting products to fit needs of new markets
- Improve process
  Improve safety or environmental procedures
- Quality and innovation
  Training
- Supply chain management
  Bar coding—can reduce the time our employees take to process a shipment

Source: http://www.ppg.com/crp_purchasing/$ave/ measurement_grid.htm, accessed April 12, 2005.

Handling complaints properly, appropriately upgrading or cross-selling, and fulfilling new needs are even more important because of the high level of commitment made to the partner.

Many buyers evaluate suppliers on criteria similar to those used by PPG (see Exhibit 14.6). Although the salesperson may not have the ability to influence corporate culture, she or he plays an important role in managing the relationship and leading both sides into commitment.

SECURING COMMITMENT TO A PARTNERSHIP

When firms reach the commitment stage, elements in addition to trust become important. Trust may be operationalized in the form of shared risk, such as Baxter International's agreements with some customers to share savings or expenses for joint programs. Along with the dimensions of trust such as competence, dependability, and honesty (or ethics), there must be commitment to the partnership from the entire supplying organization, a culture that fits with the buyer's organizational culture, and channels of communication so open that the seller and buyer appear to be part of the same company. In fact, one seller and buyer considered exactly that question. Mead and Pillsbury representatives asked each other, "If we were one company, what would we do differently?" The result was a level of commitment far greater and with more impact.[16]

COMMITMENT MUST BE COMPLETE

Commitment to the relationship should permeate both organizations, from top management to the secretary who answers the phone. This level of commitment means devoting the resources necessary to satisfy the customer's needs, even anticipating needs before the buyer does. As one buyer in the chemical industry says, "What we tend to find is that companies are out of synchronization between what they are selling and what (we) want. . . . They try to sell you bulk chemicals when what you want is service, systems, and programs."[17] As other authors say, "There's a balance between giving and getting. . . . When companies ask their customers for friendship, loyalty, and respect, too often they don't give those customers friendship, loyalty, and respect in return."[18] It is often the responsibility of the salesperson to secure commitment from his or her own company. Senior management must be convinced of the benefits of partnering with a specific account and be willing to allow the salesperson to direct the resources necessary to sustain the partnership. (Chapter 16 explores the process of building the internal partnerships the salesperson needs to coordinate those resources.)

Commitment also requires that all employees be empowered to handle the needs of the customer. For example, if the customer has a problem with a billing process, administration should be willing to work with the partner to develop a more satisfactory process. In a partnership the customer should not have to rely on only the salesperson to satisfy its needs.

COMMUNICATION

In the exploration stage, availability must be demonstrated (we already discussed the example of toll-free hot lines and voice mail to allow the seller's organization to respond quickly to customer calls). But in the commitment phase of a partnership, the seller must take a proactive communication stance. This approach means actively seeking opportunities to communicate at times other than when the salesperson has something to sell or the customer has a problem to resolve.

Partners are usually the first to learn of each other's new products, many times even codeveloping those products.[19] Part of the commitment between suppliers and their customer partners is the trust that such early knowledge will be kept confidential. Partners want to know what is coming out soon so they can make appropriate plans. But what happens if the new product is delayed or needs to have some bugs worked out? That happened to Jeff Meisner, president of Skyline DFW, a distributor of Skyline trade show displays. Skyline introduced a new product, but Meisner added a few weeks to the launch date just in case the product wasn't ready. He then did an e-mail campaign to let customers know about the new product. Several were interested and placed orders. A manufacturing delay pushed back the delivery date by several months, which could have caused Meisner significant problems with customers who had ordered the new product. Fortunately, he had warned them about the possibility of a delay when each customer placed an order, and he had a "Plan B" in place. The result was that all of these partners were taken care of in the manner they've come to expect from Meisner.[20]

Salespeople should also encourage direct communication among similar functional areas. In previous stages the two firms communicated through the buyer and the salesperson. If multilevel selling occurred, it occurred at even levels—that is, vice presidents talking to one another. But when two firms commit to a partnership, the boundaries between them, at least in terms of communication, should blur, as illustrated in Exhibit 14.7.

The buyer's production department, for example, should be able to communicate directly with the seller's engineering department rather than going through the salesperson, if production needs to work on a change in the product design. Although the salesperson would want to be aware of a product design change and ensure that engineering responded promptly to the customer's concern, direct communication means more accurate communication and a better understanding of the customer's needs. A better solution is more likely to result when there is direct communication.

CORPORATE CULTURE

Corporate culture consists of the values and beliefs held by senior management. A company's culture shapes the attitudes and actions of employees and influences the development of policies and programs.[21] For example, consider the following scene. In a large room with concrete floors are a number of cubicles built out of plywood. In each cubicle are a card table, two folding chairs, and a poster that says, "How low can you go?" Such is the scene in Bentonville, Arkansas, the corporate headquarters of Wal-Mart, where salespeople meet their buyers for Sam's Club and Wal-Mart. That room reflects Wal-Mart's culture of the lowest possible price.

A similar culture of constantly seeking ways to drive down costs is necessary for a seller to develop a partnership with Wal-Mart. A single salesperson will not change a company's corporate culture to secure a partnership with a buyer, but the salesperson must identify the type of culture both organizations hold and

Exhibit 14.7

Direct Communication between Partners
In traditional settings, companies communicate through a single buyer or purchasing agent and the salesperson.
Partners, though, allow direct communication between members of the selling and buying companies.

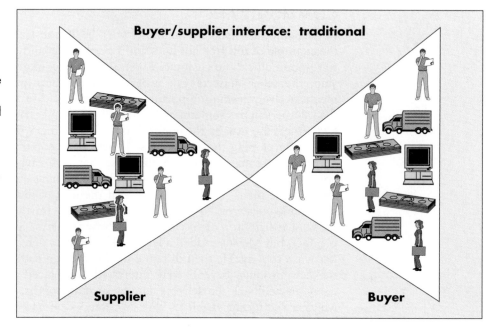

Buyer/supplier interface: traditional

Supplier

Buyer

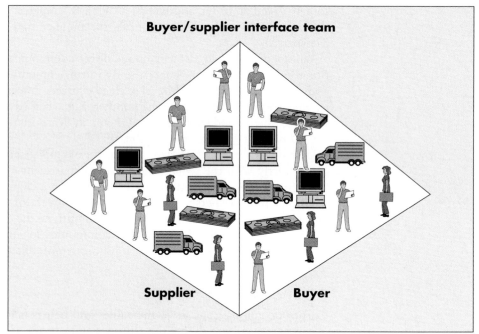

Buyer/supplier interface team

Supplier

Buyer

assess fit. Although a perfect match is not necessary, the salesperson must be ready to demonstrate that there is a fit. Offering lavish entertainment to a Wal-Mart buyer, for example, would not demonstrate a fit. Telling the buyer that you are staying at a Circle-6 Motel might.

Companies have often sought international partners as a way to enter foreign markets. Wal-Mart partnered with Cifra when the U.S. retailer entered the Mexican market. Cifra provides distribution services and products to Wal-Mart for Sam's Club and Wal-Mart stores located in Mexico City, Monterrey, and Guadalajara. In partnering with companies from other countries, country culture differences as well as corporate culture differences can cause difficulties.

Though not attempting to change a company's culture, the salesperson who seeks a partnering relationship seeks change for both organizations. In the next section we discuss what types of changes salespeople manage and how they manage those changes.

THE SALESPERSON AS CHANGE AGENT

To achieve increasing revenue in an account over time, the salesperson acts as a **change agent,** or a cause of change in the organization. Each sale may involve some type of change, perhaps a change from a competitive product or simply a new version of the old one. Partnering, though, often requires changes in both the buying and selling organizations.

For example, American Distribution Systems (ADS), a pharmaceutical distributor, and Ciba-Geigy, a pharmaceutical manufacturer, took six months to implement a joint operating plan that integrated systems of both companies. ADS created a cross-functional team that re-created ADS systems to function as part of Ciba-Geigy. At the same time, Ciba-Geigy had to share information and other resources to take full advantage of the benefits of the relationship. In this instance both buyer and seller had to change significantly for the partnership to work.

Change is not easy, even when it is obviously beneficial. The objective is to manage change, such as changing from steel to iron pipe, in the buyer's organization while giving the appearance of stability. Two critical elements to consider about change are its rate and scope. The **rate of change** refers to how quickly the change is made; the **scope of change** refers to the degree to which the change affects the organization. Broad changes affect many areas of the company, whereas narrow changes affect small areas. In general, the faster and broader the change, the more likely it will meet with resistance, as illustrated in Exhibit 14.8.[22]

To overcome resistance to change, the salesperson should consider several decisions. The first decision involves finding help in the buying organization for selling the proposal. Other important decisions are positioning the proposal, determining the necessary resources, and developing a time-based strategy.

Champions

First, the choice of one or more champions must be made. **Champions,** also called advocates or internal salespeople, work for the buying firm in the areas most affected by the proposed change and work with the salesperson to make the

Exhibit 14.8

Change and Resistance
Resistance to change is greatest when the scope is broad and the rate of change is fast.

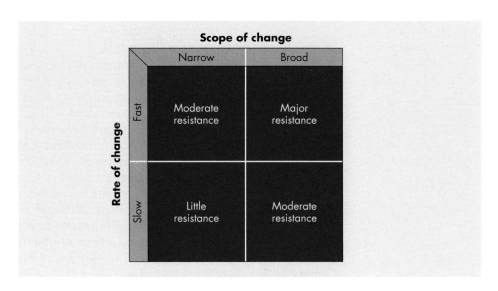

proposal successful. These champions can build momentum for the proposal by selling in arenas or during times that are off limits to the salesperson. For example, a champion may sell for the salesperson during a company picnic in a casual conversation with a coworker.

It is also important to recognize that the change in status from preferred supplier to strategic partner may also require a champion. Champions not only help persuade the firm to change but also help implement the change once the decision has been made.[23] Thus champions are very important to salespeople.

Salespeople can help potential champions by giving them all of the knowledge they need. Knowledge builds confidence; champions will have the courage to speak up when they are certain that they know what they are talking about. Salespeople can also motivate champions to participate fully in the decision process by showing how the decision meets their needs as well as the overall needs of the company.

Positioning the Change

Positioning the change is similar to positioning a product in mass marketing, as you may have learned in a principles of marketing course. In this case, however, the salesperson examines the specific needs and wants of the various constituencies in the account to position the change for the greatest likelihood of success. For example, Benson Bakery makes bread for restaurants. It was considering the purchase of equipment that would allow it to make bread and freeze it at the request of Steak and Ale, one of its major accounts. Hobart, which manufactures such equipment, could have positioned its equipment as delivering the best-quality product (marketing's concern) or as being the easiest to use and maintain (manufacturing's concern). Because manufacturing was not the key area in this decision, such a positioning may have been fatal.

Because salespeople are highly proactive in finding areas for improvement (or change) in their partners' organizations, positioning a change may determine who is involved in the decision. For example, suppose the IBM representative who calls on your school recognizes that the student computer labs are getting out of date. Is a proposal for new equipment primarily the domain of the computer services department, or is it the domain of faculty who teach computing classes? If the computer services department favors IBM but the users favor Apple, the IBM rep will be better served by positioning the change as the responsibility of the computer services department. Positioning the proposed change appropriately may spell success or failure for the proposal.

Determining the Necessary Resources

The customer's needs may be beyond the salesperson's expertise. For example, Fram, a maker of auto parts, may be working with CarQuest, an auto parts retailer, to develop a major advertising program that will highlight their growing partnership. Such a change may require some selling to the advertising department at CarQuest. The Fram account representative will use the expert advice of Fram's own advertising department, its marketing research department, and probably its marketing management as well. These experts may visit CarQuest with the account rep and help secure that change in CarQuest's advertising focus.

The salesperson must assess the situation and determine what resources are needed to secure the buyer's commitment. Although the preceding example discusses allocation of personnel, salespeople must manage other resources as well, such as travel and entertainment budgets or sample supplies. (We discuss how to build internal partnerships to effectively coordinate company resources in Chapter 16.)

Exhibit 14.9
Time Line for Fram/CarQuest

Month 1	Month 2	Month 3	Month 4	Month 5	Month 6
Visit director of marketing.	Visit merchandising manager and director of advertising.	Visit director of marketing.	Arrange tour of Fram facilities for VP or retail, director of marketing, and advertising and merchandising managers.	Submit plan to director of marketing.	Implement advertising program.
Primary objective: determine marketing needs.	Primary objective: secure support in principle.	Primary objective: specify objectives for new advertising plan and secure commitment in principle.	Primary objective: obtain commitment for review of plan.		
Minimum objective: secure permission to see merchandising and advertising.					

Developing a Time-Based Strategy

The salesperson must determine a strategy for the proposed change and set that strategy against a time line. This action accomplishes several objectives. First, the strategy is an outline of planned sales calls, with primary and minimum call objectives determined for each call. Second, the time line estimates when each call should occur. Of course, objectives and planned times will change depending on the results of each call, but this type of planning is necessary to give the salesperson guidance for each call, determine when resources are to be used, and make sure each call contributes to strategic account objectives.

For example, the Fram salesperson may determine that calls need to be made on five individuals at CarQuest. A time-based strategy would indicate which person should be visited first and what should be accomplished during that visit, as well as the order of visits to the remaining four members of the buying center. The strategy would also alert the salesperson as to when the advertising personnel were needed. Exhibit 14.9 illustrates such a time line.

DISSOLUTION

Too often salespeople believe that once a customer has committed to a partnership, less work is needed to maintain that relationship. That belief, however, is untrue. One study found that 55 percent of all strategic partnerships dissolve within 3 to 5 years, and the rest have a further life expectancy of only 3.5 years.[24] Salespeople who subscribe to the belief that partnerships require less work fall victim to one or more common problems. As discussed in Chapter 2, the final stage for partnerships is dissolution, or breakup, but this stage can occur at any point, not just after commitment. Several potential problems, including maintaining few personal relationships, failing to monitor competitor actions or the industry, and falling into complacency, can lead to dissolution.

LIMITED PERSONAL RELATIONSHIPS

Salespeople tend to call on buyers they like; it is natural to want to spend time with friends. The result is that relationships are cultivated with only a few individuals in the account. Unfortunately for such salespeople, buyers may leave the organization, transfer to an unrelated area, or simply not participate in some decisions. Truly effective salespeople attempt to develop multiple relationships within an account.

Dun & Bradstreet calls this building customer relationships "high and wide." The company, which gathers and markets business data, believes it must be perceived as a value-added supplier, eventually becoming a strategic partner. The only way that Dun & Bradstreet believes it can reach the partnership level is to understand the senior executive's strategic perspective as well as that of the managers who implement programs. Dun & Bradstreet identified $26.5 million in additional sales in the first year of using the high-and-wide relationship strategy.[25]

FAILING TO MONITOR COMPETITOR ACTIONS

No matter how strong the partnership is, competition will want a piece of the business. And no matter how good the salesperson is, there will still be times when the account is vulnerable to competitor action. Accounts are most vulnerable when a personnel change occurs (especially if the rep has developed relationships with a limited number of people in the account), when technology changes, or when major directional changes occur, such as a company starting a new division or entering a new market.

The successful salesperson, however, monitors competitor action even when the account seems invulnerable. For example, an insurance agency had all of the insurance business at a state university in Texas for more than 10 years but failed to monitor competitor action at the state capital and lost the account when another insurance agency found a sympathetic buyer in Austin. The loss of this one account cut annual earnings by more than 70 percent.

Monitoring competitor action can be as simple as checking the visitor's log at the front desk to see who has dropped by or keeping up with competitor actions and asking buyers for their opinions. Frequently, developing relationships with the many potential influencers in an account will also keep salespeople informed about competitor actions. As each person is visited, questions and comments about competitors will arise, indicating the activity level of competition.

Monitoring competition also means thinking about the benefits competitors offer, what their products do, and what their selling strategies are. When salespeople understand what the competition offers, they can position their own company's unique capabilities more effectively. It is not enough to know where competitors have made calls; good salespeople also know what the competition is saying.

FAILING TO MONITOR THE INDUSTRY

Similar to failing to monitor competition is a failure to monitor the industry in which either the salesperson or the customer operates. Salespeople often assume that the responsibility of monitoring the industry lies with someone else, either higher-ups in their own company or with the customer. But salespeople who fail to monitor both industries stand to miss opportunities that change creates. As an extreme example, what would happen to the advertising agency's account executive if the Internet were ignored?

How does the professional salesperson monitor the industry? By reading trade magazines and by attending trade shows and conferences. The Moore-Wallace account manager who serves American Airlines reads airline and travel trade magazines, such as *Meetings & Conventions,* to understand the industry trends that will influence American's business. It's not enough to know your company's industry; with strategic partners, you must also know their industry.

FALLING INTO COMPLACENCY

Perhaps the most common thief of good accounts is complacency. In sales terms, **complacency** is assuming that the business is yours and will always be yours. It is failing to continue to work as hard to keep the business as you did initially to earn the business. For example, Coca-Cola was the sole supplier to El Volcan, the stadium for the professional soccer team Los Tigres in Monterrey, Mexico. After many years the stadium's concessions manager began to become annoyed with Coca-Cola because service seemed lackadaisical. As a result, the contract was put out to bid; Pepsi responded with a significantly better offer and won the business.

Monty Covington, vice president of sales for Grocery Supply Co. (GSC), schedules annual account reviews with key accounts. In these reviews, he and the account manager ask the customer to evaluate GSC's performance and to identify strategies that can help both companies continue to grow. These annual reviews do not allow GSC to become complacent.

To avoid complacency, salespeople should regularly audit their own customer service. Here are some questions a salesperson may want to consider:

- Do I understand each individual's personal characteristics? Do I have these characteristics in my computer file on each account?
- Do I maintain a written or computerized record of promises made?
- Do I follow up on every customer request promptly, no matter how insignificant it may seem?
- Do I follow up on deliveries, make sure initial experiences are positive, and ensure that all paperwork is done correctly and quickly?
- Have I recently found something new that I can do better than the competition?

CONFLICT

Not all dissolution is the result of conflict, as you can see from the types of reasons that most often lead to dissolution. But conflict between buyer and seller can occur, and when it does, the issues can be much more complex than the "usual" complaint.

Tom Bassett, corporate purchasing manager for Century Business Services (Independence, Ohio), notes that customer–supplier conflict is sometimes the result of conflicting policies within the customer's organization, and even conflict between parts of the organization.[26] A salesperson can moderate such conflict by helping the customer develop appropriate policies; one salesperson even brought in her own purchasing VP to consult with one of her clients.

Trust-destroying conflicts, though, can be avoided with several steps. First, start with a clear product description. If the product is a component part or critical for other reasons, and the potential for ambiguity exists, write out a clear description. Services providers are especially vulnerable to ambiguity in the sales process. Another important element is to define who has authority to do what—both for the customer and for the selling organization. For example, it has to be clearly understood who can authorize change orders if the product specs have to be modified. Both of these ideas require clear documentation, but good documentation is critical should such a dispute reach the courts.[27]

While conflict can result in the dissolution of a partnership, more common is dissatisfaction due to complacency by the seller.

Owen Franken/Corbis

WINNING BACK LOST CUSTOMERS

A great deal of research shows that customer satisfaction is not the same as customer loyalty. Even the most satisfied customer may leave if there is no attitudinal loyalty. Of course, many who leave do so because they are dissatisfied; but does that have to mean that the customer is forever lost?

AT&T didn't want to think so. It analyzed the value of customers it lost and identified 30 different segments based on customer value. One segment, though, was so valuable that AT&T called it the "Dream Segment." Creating a "Dream Team" of salespeople, AT&T began a campaign using historical customer data and effective questioning techniques to identify customer needs. The result was a win-back rate of 25 percent; more important, revenue win-back was 50 percent, meaning that AT&T not only won back a good number of accounts, the ones recaptured actually spent twice as much as before.

Jackie Floyd, a sales consultant in Dallas, was devastated after receiving notification that her biggest account would not renew its contract. "Funding didn't come through for continuing a contract," she says, "partly because the CEO didn't think that what we did was valuable." Her primary contact, though, assured Floyd that the work was valuable and to not lose hope. He helped her put together a review of what the consulting agency had done over the past two years, documenting the payback. At a meeting intended to serve as a conclusion to the relationship, she presented the data. Before the meeting was over, the CEO changed his mind—Floyd was back as in the budget.

Floyd says, "I learned something very important—don't assume the client knows how valuable our work is." Like AT&T, she also learned to never give up. Many good customers can be won back.

Sources: Anonymous, "AT&T Case Study," http://www.resonatesolutions.com.au/pdfs/cs_at_t.pdf, accessed April 15, 2005; Jackie Floyd, personal correspondence, used with permission.

Recognize that complaints can be the beginning of major conflict. We discussed complaint handling as part of the exploration stage, but keep in mind that poor handling of complaints leads to the dissolution stage! Complaints in later stages are likely to lead to full-blown conflict if trust is not carefully salvaged. To repair damage to trust in a conflict, one consultant recommends the following seven steps (compare to the complaint-handling process discussed earlier):

1. Observe and acknowledge what has happened to lead to the loss of trust.
2. Allow your feelings to surface, but take responsibility for your actions.
3. Gain support—offer your peer a chance to save face and gain agreement on any mitigating circumstances.
4. Put the experience in the larger context to affirm your commitment to the relationship.
5. Shift the focus from assigning blame to problem solving.
6. Implement the solution.
7. Let go and move on.

Keep in mind that while the relationship may be between two organizations, even the deepest strategic partnership is ultimately the responsibility of two people.[28]

Whatever the reason for dissolution, all is not necessarily lost. Customers who defect or buy from other vendors sometimes return. Jim Allgood's story at the start of this chapter is an illustration of a customer who began to defect but was won back. Selling Scenario 14.1 discusses the importance of win-back strategies.

SUMMARY

Developing partnerships has become increasingly important for salespeople and their firms. Salespeople can develop partnerships and generate goodwill by servicing accounts properly and by strategically building relationships. Both salespeople and buyers benefit from partnering.

Many specific activities are necessary to ensure customer satisfaction and to develop a partnering relationship. The salesperson must maintain the proper perspective, remember the customer between calls, build perceptions of trust, monitor order processing, ensure the proper initial use of the product or service, help to service the product, provide expert guidance and suggestions, and provide any necessary special assistance.

The best opportunities to develop goodwill are usually provided by the proper handling of customer complaints. Sales representatives should encourage unhappy customers to tell their stories completely, fully, and without interruption. A sympathetic attitude to a real or an imaginary product or service failure cannot be overemphasized. After determining the facts, the salesperson should implement the solution promptly and monitor it to ensure that proper action is taken.

The appropriate solution will depend on many factors, such as the seriousness of the problem, the dollar amount involved, and the value of the account. A routine should be developed to handle all complaints fairly and equitably.

In the expansion phase of the relationship, key sales activities are generating repeat orders, upgrading, cross-selling, and full-line selling. The goal is to achieve a partnership, in which case the seller is often designated a preferred supplier.

At this level of relationship, it is important that both organizations commit to the relationship from top to bottom, with open communication directly between appropriate personnel in both organizations. At this point, salespeople become change agents as they work in both organizations to seamlessly integrate the partnership.

Sometimes, however, relationships break up. When partnerships dissolve, usually there are multiple reasons for the breakup. For example, when a salesperson leans too heavily on a few personal relationships and those people leave, or when the salesperson fails to monitor competitive actions, then the buying organization may feel less commitment to the relationship. Other reasons for dissolution include failing to monitor changes in the industry and simply becoming complacent. Winning a customer back, though, is still a possibility and should be pursued when appropriate.

KEY TERMS

champion
change agent
complacency
corporate culture
cross-selling
electronic data interchange

full-line selling
preferred supplier
rate of change
scope of change
upgrading

ETHICS PROBLEMS

1. How can a salesperson lose by overselling a customer?
2. The fairest solution to a customer's complaint is one that turns out to be against company policy, though certainly not against the law or unethical in any way. If you tried to do it, the chances are you could get away with it. What would you do?

QUESTIONS AND PROBLEMS

1. Mega-Soft introduced a new version of its accounting software that didn't allow users to transfer their old data to the new program easily. Articles appeared in magazines that identified the problem, and the company fixed the problem; but considerable damage to the company's reputation may have occurred as a result. The fix was a patch that customers could download from the Mega-Soft Web site, which would then allow for easier transfer. How would you deal with this problem if a customer brought it up? How would you respond if a prospect brought it up?

2. Explain how active listening can be applied to a situation in which a customer makes a complaint. What can applying this art accomplish? What forms of active listening might actually cause *more* problems?

3. Your company has just introduced a new product. To determine whether the product could perform a customer's application, you asked the head of the service department, who said that it would. But after delivery, it is clear that the new product will not perform that application. What should you do? Does the stage of the buyer–seller relationship matter?

4. Should a salesperson handle all complaints so that customers are completely satisfied? Explain why or why not. Would your answer change if you were in the exploration stage versus the commitment stage?

5. Some research suggests that how salespeople handle complaints is more important than whether there are problems. In fact, handling complaints well is one way to win loyalty. So should a company not fix a problem that it knows will lead to some complaints, thus giving its reps a chance to satisfy those complaints?

6. What is your reaction to the statement "The customer is always right"? Is it a sound basis for making adjustments and satisfying complaints? Can it be followed literally? Why or why not?

7. Your roommate or spouse complains that you don't do your share of the housework. Your friend complains that you never seem to have any free time anymore. What have you learned in this chapter that you could use to restore these relationships? In previous chapters? If the answer is that you have learned nothing, justify that answer. If you have learned useful techniques, explain how they would apply to the two situations.

8. How do you know when full-line selling, upgrading, or cross-selling strategies are appropriate?

9. What are the various ways a salesperson can provide a potential champion with knowledge to build confidence? What types of knowledge will the champion need?

10. Cellular phone companies like Jim Allgood's have a high disconnect rate. Why do they lose so many customers? What can a salesperson do to avoid these problems?

CASE PROBLEMS

case **14.1**

Incredible
Manufacturing

Ryan Nemec, account manager for Incredible, faced a huge dilemma: what to do with Landon Equipment, a company that had recently placed its first order with promises of many more big ones. Landon makes equipment for the food industry, products like milk shake machines that sometimes have to be custom-designed to fit a limited space in a fast-food restaurant. Incredible Manufacturing is a contract manufacturer, meaning that it makes component parts under contract to original equipment manufacturers or assemblers. For Landon, Incredible was making a special iced tea brewing machine that made sweet tea without needing someone to add the sugar, a popular product for Southern fast-food chains. Nemec had just cashed the first commission check on what promised to be a long-term sale to Landon when he got this call.

LANDON: Ryan, this is Bob Landon. We got a call from Bush's Chicken that the machines we shipped are leaking sugar into the tea when they want unsweet tea. When we looked at the machines we still had in stock, we found that the seals are missing on all of the sugar dispensers, allowing sugar to leak into the tea whether they want it or not.

NEMEC: Well, that isn't a good thing.

LANDON: (Voice rising with exasperation) No, it isn't! What are you going to do about it?

NEMEC: I'm not sure, I need to find out what we can do.

LANDON: I'll tell you what you should do. Ship me the seals and we'll install them—plus drop-ship seals directly to the Bush's Chicken stores and have someone install them. As for the 500 we have in stock, you'll have to rebate us 10 percent for our trouble.

Nemec promised to see what he could do. Now that he had talked things over with his boss, Marge Cooper, the director of sales, he was despondent. She told him in no uncertain terms that the company would not do what Landon wanted. The profit margin was only 10 percent to begin with. Fortunately, there were only five machines shipped to Bush's.

Questions

1. Nemec's commission is 10 percent. Should he offer to either pay Landon the 10 percent or return it to the company?
2. On further investigation, it was clear that the fault belonged to the drafter who drew the designs for the product. That meant the fault was entirely Incredible's. Does that change your answer to question 1?
3. What other alternatives does Nemec have? How can such a problem be avoided in the future? Is it even reasonable to assume Nemec has any responsibility once the order is turned in?

case **14.2**

Turning It Around

Sandy Hutto, manager of Performance Personnel, held the phone away from her ear. The customer was shouting loudly enough to be heard across the room. Performance Personnel places workers in temporary jobs, earning a fee from the company that hires the workers.

"We deal with human beings; that's our product," notes Hutto. "And in this particular case, the people we sent to work for this account let us down. But as far as our client was concerned, it was Performance Personnel that let them down."

The client, a major insurance company, had a data entry job that would take four temporary employees about three weeks to complete, including three days of training. Because of the training and the tight deadline, Hutto had asked for a three-week commitment from each person.

Unfortunately, one person's father died, and she quit to be with her family. Another found a permanent job and quit, leaving two people to finish the job in less than two weeks. The customer wasn't interested, though, in why they left; the only thing the customer knew was that there was a deadline and it wasn't going to be met.

Hutto offered to come to the customer's office and discuss alternatives, but the customer wanted none of that. "The last thing I heard before he hung up on me was, 'Sandy, we can't depend on Performance Personnel. We're going to another agency.'" But whether he wanted to see her or not, Hutto developed two possible solutions and drove straight to her client's office.

"He still didn't want to see me when I arrived," she said. "But I had two options and asked him to just look at them."

"Each option would take care of his biggest concern, which was getting people trained and productive in order to meet the deadline. And in each option we absorbed any additional cost." Hutto also reminded her client of everything that Performance Personnel had done right. But as she notes, "The biggest factor, though, was that I personally and immediately went to see him. He knew then how much his business meant to me." Hutto not only saved that job, she won all of the company's business.

Source: Sandra Hutto, used with permission.

Questions

1. Why was it so impressive to the buyer that Sandy personally and immediately went to see him? What did this action communicate?
2. Her decision to present two options was important and strategic. Why?
3. Write out exactly what you would plan to say to just get the buyer's permission to present the two options if you were Sandy and had to make this call. Be prepared to role-play.

ACT! ROLE PLAY

Today you will receive a telephone call from one of your accounts. The account is Limo Ceramics, a company that manufactures industrial ceramics and sells them worldwide. There is one plant in St. Albans, Vermont, and one in Montpellier, France. With 12 salespeople in the United States and 6 in Europe, the company does about $50 million a year in gross revenue. It bought 20 copies of ACT! from you, which were received about two weeks ago. Training was done through an independent certified ACT! trainer, one in the United States and one in France. The vice president of sales was the decision maker and the only person you met. The primary needs were to get better forecasting so the plant would not fall behind or schedule things wrong, leading to stockouts or overruns; to get more customer information so you can market directly to customers and get them to prefer Limo for all of their needs; and to reduce the amount of time spent on paperwork by salespeople.

Each of you will take turns being the buyer and the seller. If divided into teams of three, the third person will observe. Your professor will give you a sheet to use when you are the buyer.

ADDITIONAL REFERENCES

Frankwick, Gary L.; Stephen S. Porter; and Lawrence A. Crosby. "Dynamics of Relationship Selling: A Longitudinal Examination of Changes in Salesperson–Customer Relationship Status." *Journal of Personal Selling & Sales Management* 21 (Spring 2001), pp. 145–46.

Fredette, Michael. "Learning from the Other Side." *Purchasing Today,* April 2001, pp. 44–53. This article presents an interesting perspective of relationships and salespeople from the buyer's side.

Haytko, Diana L. "Firm-to-Firm and Interpersonal Relationships: Perspectives from Advertising Agency Account Managers." *Journal of the Academy of Marketing Science* 32 (Summer 2004), pp. 312–29.

Homburg, Christian, and Bettina Rudolph. "Customer Satisfaction in Industrial Markets: Dimensional and Multiple Role Issues." *Journal of Business Research* 52 (2001), pp. 15–33.

Hultman, Claes M., and Eleanor Shaw. "The Interface between Transactional and Relational Orientation in Small Service Firms' Marketing Behaviour: A Study of Scottish and Swedish Small Firms in the Service Sector." *Journal of Marketing Theory & Practice* 11 (2003), pp. 36–52.

Jap, Sandy. "The Strategic Role of the Salesforce in Developing Customer Satisfaction across the Relationship Lifecycle." *Journal of Personal Selling & Sales Management* 21 (Spring 2001), pp. 95–108.

Johnson, Julie; Hiram C. Barksdale Jr.; and James S. Boles. "The Strategic Role of the Salesperson in Reducing Customer Defection in Business Relationships." *Journal of Personal Selling & Sales Management* 21 (Spring 2001), pp. 123–34.

Liu, Annie H., and Mark P. Leach. "Developing Loyal Customers with a Value-Adding Sales Force: Examining Customer Satisfaction and Perceived Credibility of Consultative Salespeople." *Journal of Personal Selling & Sales Management* 21 (Spring 2001), pp. 147–56.

Pillai, Kishore G., and Arun Sharma. "Mature Relationships: Why Does Relational Orientation Turn into Transaction Orientation?" *Industrial Marketing Management* 32 (2003), pp. 643–51.

Thomke, Stefan, and Eric Von Hipple. "Customers as Innovators: A New Way to Create Value." *Harvard Business Review,* April 2002, pp. 74–81.

Ulwick, Anthony. "Turn Customer Input into Innovation." *Harvard Business Review,* January 2002, pp. 91–97.

Wilson, David. "Deep Relationships: The Case of the Vanishing Salesperson." *Journal of Personal Selling & Sales Management* 20 (Winter 2000), pp. 53–61.

MANAGING YOUR TIME AND TERRITORY

SOME QUESTIONS ANSWERED
IN THIS CHAPTER . . .

- Why is time so valuable for salespeople?

- What can you do to "create" more selling time?

- What should you consider when devising a territory strategy?

- How does territory strategy relate to account strategy and building partnerships?

- How should you analyze your daily activities and sales calls?

- How can you evaluate your own performance so that you can improve?

PROFILE

I learned from Susan Emens, professor at Kent State, that managing your own territory is like managing your own business—sounded like a dream job to me. There is no one to watch over your shoulder, no clocking in or out, no timed breaks or lunches. Basically, you do what you want, when you want. Five years ago when I accepted an outside sales position selling custom design carpet, I thought it couldn't get any better than this. I was given a sales quota based on the market potential of my territory, and it was my responsibility to figure out how to make those numbers. I was given a list of accounts from the previous salesperson and I would set the appointments accordingly. Make the calls, make the sales. This shouldn't be difficult, right?

I set as many appointments as I could in a week, not allowing much office time. After all, I thought the more calls I could make, the better chance I had to make quota. I also had some additional responsibility with this position: weekly call logs, project tracking, lead follow-up, expense reports, business plans, customer plant tours, local trade shows, and the list goes on. With Pittsburgh, Cleveland, and upstate New York as my territory, I did quite a bit of traveling. By the end of the week, I noticed that a lot of the required paperwork was not getting done. What started out to be Saturday mornings of paperwork led to working through Sunday evenings. Before I knew it, the five-day workweek turned into seven. Was this the dream job I thought it was?

After five years, I learned to work smarter than ever before. You never want to put all of your eggs in one basket; however, you need to understand where the majority of your business is coming from and focus your attention there. Now as regional sales manager, I'm managing 15 salespeople and covering the eastern half of the United States for Lonseal. Managing my time wisely is more important than ever; but at the same, the salespeople I manage need to also manage their time wisely. I want my salespeople to focus on the right customers and grow the business within target accounts, rather than making sales calls on anyone and everyone. If we're to grow the business, we have to do so intelligently. My biggest mistake as a new salesperson was the idea that the *quantity* of calls was more important than the *quality,*

Visit us on the Web at www.Lonseal.com.

"My biggest mistake was the idea that the quantity *of calls was more important than the* quality.*"*

Susan Flaviano, Lonseal

THE VALUE OF TIME

The old axiom "Time is money" certainly applies to selling. If you work eight hours a day for 240 days in a year, you will work 1,920 hours that year. If you earn $40,000, each of those hours will be worth $20.83. An hour of time would be worth $26.04 if your earnings climb to $50,000. Looking at your time another way, you would have to sell $260 worth of product per hour to earn $50,000 if you earned a 10 percent commission!

The typical salesperson spends only 920 hours a year in front of customers. The other 1,000 hours are spent waiting, traveling, doing paperwork, or attending sales meetings. Thus as a typical salesperson, you really have to be twice as good, selling $520 worth of products every hour to earn that $50,000 commission.

The lesson from this analysis is clear: Salespeople must make every hour count to be successful. Time is a resource that cannot be replaced if wasted. But time is just one resource, although a critical one, at the salesperson's disposal.

Managing time and territory is often a question of how to allocate resources. Allocating resources such as time is a difficult management process; but when done well, it often spells the difference between stellar and average performance. Many times it is difficult to know what is really important and what only seems important. In this chapter we discuss how to manage your time. Building on what you have learned about the many activities of salespeople, we also provide strategies for allocating resources among accounts—that is, managing your territory.

THE SELF-MANAGEMENT PROCESS

The self-management process in selling has four stages. The first stage is setting goals, or determining what is to be accomplished. The second stage is allocating resources and determining strategies to meet those goals. In the third stage the salesperson implements the time management strategies by making sales calls, sending direct mail pieces, or executing whatever action the strategy calls for. In the fourth and final stage, the salesperson evaluates performance to determine whether the goals will be reached and the strategies are effective, or whether the goals cannot be reached and the strategies must change. This process is illustrated in Exhibit 15.1 and will serve as an outline for this chapter.

SETTING GOALS

THE NEED FOR GOALS

The first step in managing any worthwhile endeavor is to consider what makes it worthwhile and what you want to accomplish. Salespeople need to examine their careers in the same way. Career goals and objectives should reflect personal ambitions and desires so that the individual can create the desired lifestyle, as illustrated in Exhibit 15.2.[1] When career goals reflect personal ambitions, the salesperson is more committed to achieving those goals.

To achieve career objectives, salespeople must set sales goals. These sales goals provide some of the means for reaching personal objectives. Sales goals also guide the salesperson's decisions regarding which activities to perform, when to perform those activities, whom to see, and how to sell.

The salesperson who lacks goals will drift around the territory, wasting time and energy. Sales calls will be unrelated to objectives and may be minimally productive or even harmful to the sales process. The result will be poor performance and, eventually, the need to find another job.

Exhibit 15.1
The Self-Management Process

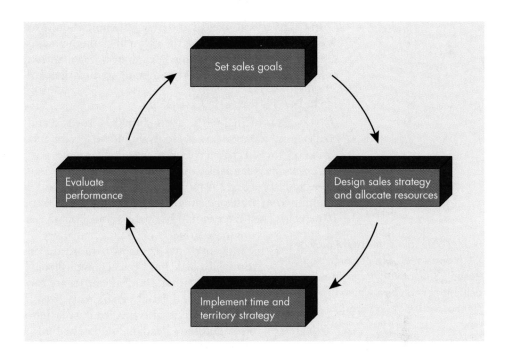

Exhibit 15.2

The Relationship of Goals

Career goals are devised from lifestyle objectives. Sales goals should reflect career goals. While activities lead to sales, performance goals are usually set first. Then, using conversion goals, activity goals are set.

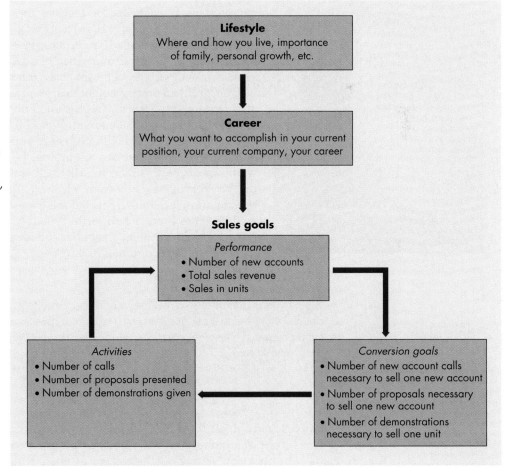

In Chapter 8 you learned that salespeople should set call objectives so that the activities performed during the call will bring them closer to those objectives. The same can be said for setting sales goals: When sales goals are set properly and adhered to, the salesperson has a guide to direct his or her activities.

THE NATURE OF GOALS

As you read in Chapter 8, goals should be specific and measurable, reachable yet challenging, and time based. Goals should be specific and measurable so the salesperson knows when they have been met. For example, setting a goal of making better presentations is laudable, but how would the salesperson know if the presentations were better or worse? A more helpful goal would be to increase the number of sales resulting from those presentations. The best goal would be a specific increase, such as 10 percent. Then there would be no question about the achievement of the goal.

Goals should also be reachable yet challenging. One purpose of setting personal goals is to motivate oneself. If goals are reached too easily, little has been accomplished. Challenging goals, then, are more motivating. But if the goals are too challenging, or if they are unreachable, the salesperson may give up.

Goals should also be time based; that is, goals should have deadlines. Putting a deadline on the goal provides more guidance for the salesperson and creates a sense of urgency that can be motivating. Without a deadline, the goal is not specific enough, and the salesperson may be able to drag on forever, never reaching the goal but thinking progress is being made. Imagine the motivational difference between setting a goal of a 10 percent increase in sales with no deadline and setting a goal of a 10 percent increase for the next month. The first instance lacks a sense of urgency, of needing to work toward that goal now. Without a deadline, the goal has little motivational value.

One problem some people have is periodically creating goals and then forgetting them. Goals should be written down and then posted. For example, each month Will Pinkham has a goal for selling five new accounts (Will sells office equipment for Ikon Office Solutions). At the start of each month, he puts a new list on the wall over his desk, and as he sells each new account, he adds it to the list starting at the bottom. He starts the list at the bottom to remind himself that his goal is to sell five; so when he sells one, his goal becomes four, and so forth. Probably not all goals should be posted in highly public areas, but the idea is to keep the goal in front of you so it continues to direct your activities.

Putting a deadline on a goal provides the professional salesperson with a time-based goal, increasing the likelihood of achievement and providing another element of feedback on progress.

Jose Luis Pelaez/Zefa/Corbis

thinking **it** through

What types of goals have you set for yourself in your college career? For specific classes? How would these goals meet the criteria of specific and measurable, reachable yet challenging, and time based? How do you keep these goals in front of you? What would you do differently now?

TYPES OF SALES GOALS

Salespeople need to set three types of sales goals: performance, activity, and conversions (refer to Exhibit 15.2). Although many salespeople focus only on how many sales they get, setting all three types of goals is necessary to achieve the highest possible success.

Exhibit 15.3

Goal Calculations

Monthly earnings goal (performance goal):	$6,000
Commission per sale:	$750
$6,000 earnings ÷ $750 per sale = 8 sales	
Monthly sales goal (performance goal):	8
Closings goal (conversion goal):	10%
8 sales × 10 prospects per sale = 80 prospects	
Monthly prospect goal (performance goal):	80
Prospects per calls goal (conversion goal):	1 in 3
80 prospects × 3 calls per prospect = 240 calls	
Monthly sales calls goal (activity goal):	240
240 calls ÷ 20 working days per month = 12 calls	
Daily sales calls goal (activity goal):	12

Performance Goals

Goals relating to outcomes are **performance goals.** In sales, outcomes such as the size of a commission or bonus check, the amount of sales revenue generated or number of sales generated, and the number of prospects identified are common performance goals. For example, the salesperson in Exhibit 15.3 set a performance goal of $6,000 in commissions and another performance goal of eight sales. Revenue quotas are an example of goals set by the company, but each salesperson should also consider setting personally relevant goals. For example, you may want to set higher goals so you can achieve higher earnings. People are more committed to achieving goals they set themselves; that commitment makes achieving them more likely. Performance goals should be set first because attaining certain performance levels is of primary importance to both the organization and the salesperson.

Personal development goals, such as improving presentation skills, are important to long-term professional growth and are a form of performance goals. Every person, whether in sales or other fields, should have some personal development goals. Reaching those goals not only will improve overall job performance but also will increase personal satisfaction. Like all performance goals, however, these goals should meet the criteria of being specific, challenging, and time based. Further, it helps to make these goals measurable. For example, if you set improving presentation skills as a performance goal, some outcome such as increased sales or fewer objections should occur that you can measure to determine if your skills are truly improving.

Activity Goals

Salespeople also set activity goals. **Activity goals** are behavioral objectives: the number of calls made in a day, the number of demonstrations performed, and so on. Activity goals reflect how hard the salesperson wants to work. The company may set some activity goals for salespeople, such as a quota of sales calls to be made each week. Exhibit 15.3 lists two activity goals: 240 sales calls per month and 12 calls per day.

All activity goals are intermediate goals; that is, achieving them should ultimately translate into achievement of performance goals. As Times Mirror Cable Television discovered by auditing sales performance, activity goals such as 10 prospecting calls per day are needed for the salespeople to achieve the overall performance goals. Activity goals help salespeople decide what to do each day, but those goals must ultimately be related to making sales.

However, activity goals and performance goals are not enough. For example, a salesperson may have goals of achieving 10 sales and making 150 calls in one month. The salesperson may get 10 sales but make 220 calls. That salesperson had to work much harder than someone who managed to get 10 sales in only 150 calls. That is why salespeople should also set conversion goals.

Conversion Goals

Conversion goals measure a salesperson's efficiency. Conversion goals reflect how efficiently the salesperson would like to work, or work smarter. Unlike performance goals, conversion goals express relative accomplishments, such as the number of sales relative to the number of calls made or the number of customers divided by the number of prospects. The higher the ratio, the more efficient the salesperson. Exhibit 15.3 lists two conversion goals: closing 10 percent of all prospects and finding one prospect for every three calls. In the preceding example a rep who made 10 sales while making 150 calls could make 4 or 5 more sales by making 220 calls because that rep makes a sale every 15 calls.

Conversion goals are important because they reflect how efficiently the salesperson uses resources, such as time, to accomplish performance goals. For example, Freeman Exhibit Company builds custom trade show exhibits. Customers often ask for booth designs (called *speculative designs*) before making the purchase to evaluate the offerings of various competitors. Creating a custom booth design is a lot of work for a designer, and the cost can be high, but it does not guarantee a sale. If a salesperson has a low conversion rate for speculative designs, overall profits will be lower because the cost for the unsold designs must still be covered. If the rep can increase the conversion rate, the overall costs for unsold designs will be lower, hence increasing profits.

Working harder would show up in an increase in activity; working smarter should be reflected in conversion goals. For example, a salesperson may be performing at a conversion rate of 10 percent. Reaching a conversion goal of 12 percent (closing 1 out of 8 instead of 1 out of 10) would reflect some improvement in the way the salesperson operates—some method of working smarter.

Measuring conversions tells salespeople which activities work best. For example, suppose a salesperson has two sales strategies. If A generates 10 sales and B generates 8 sales, the salesperson may think A is the better strategy. But if A requires 30 sales calls and B only 20, the salesperson would be better off using strategy B. Thirty sales calls would have generated 12 sales with strategy B.

Comparing your performance with the best in your organization is a form of **benchmarking**.[2] Benchmarking can help you see where you are falling short. For example, if your conversion ratio of leads to appointments (the number of leads needed to get one appointment) is the same as that of the top seller but you are closing only half of your spec designs and that person is closing 80 percent, you know you are losing sales at the spec design stage. You can then examine what that person does to achieve the higher conversion ratio.

SETTING SALES GOALS

Performance and conversion goals are the basis for activity goals. Suppose a sale is worth $250 in commission. A person who wants to earn $2,000 per month (a performance goal) needs to make eight sales each month. If the salesperson sees closing 1 out of 10 prospects as a realistic conversion goal, a second performance goal results: The rep must identify 80 prospects to yield eight closings. If the rep can identify one prospect for every three sales calls (another conversion goal), 240 sales calls (an activity goal) must be made. Assuming 20 working days in a month, the rep must make 12 sales calls each day (another activity goal). Thus activity goals need to be the last type of goals set because they will be determined by the desired level of performance at a certain rate of conversion.

Even though the conversion analysis results in a goal of 12 calls each day, that conversion rate is affected by the strategy the salesperson employs. A better strategy results in a higher conversion rate and better allocation of time, one of many important resources that must be allocated properly to achieve sales goals. We discuss how to allocate resources in the next section.

ALLOCATING RESOURCES

The second stage of the time and territory management process is to develop a strategy that allocates resources properly. These resources are allocated to different sales strategies used with different types of accounts with the purpose of achieving sales goals in the most effective and efficient manner possible.

RESOURCES TO BE ALLOCATED

Salespeople manage many resources. Some of these are physical resources, such as free samples, demonstration products, trial products, brochures, direct mail budgets, and other marketing resources. Each of these physical resources represents a cost to the company, but to the salesperson they are investments. Salespeople consider physical resources as investments because resources must be managed wisely to generate the best possible return. Whereas financial investments may return dividends or price increases, the salesperson's investments should yield sales.

A key resource that salespeople manage is time. Time is limited, and not all of a salesperson's work time can be spent making sales calls. Some time must be spent attending meetings, learning about new products, preparing reports for management, traveling to sales calls, and handling other nonselling duties; in fact, nonselling activities can take up to 70 percent of a salesperson's time. Thus being able to manage time wisely is important. As we discuss in the next chapter, salespeople also coordinate many of the company's other departments to serve customers well. Salespeople must learn how to allocate these resources in ways that generate the greatest level of sales.

WHERE TO ALLOCATE RESOURCES

For salespeople the allocation of resources is often a question of finding the customers or companies that are most likely to buy and then allocating selling resources to maximize the opportunities they offer. As you may have learned in your principles of marketing course, some market segments are more profitable than others. And just as the company's marketing executive tries to determine which segments are most profitable so that marketing plans can be directed toward those segments, salespeople examine their markets to allocate their selling resources.

Maximizing the opportunity means finding profitable ways to satisfy the greatest number of customers, but not necessarily everybody. Fast Industries, a specialty plastics manufacturer, decides which customers it wants to keep based on profit plans, adjusting service levels and sales strategies to fit not only the customer's need but also the profit requirements.[3] In the following section we discuss how to analyze the market to identify potential customers who are most likely to buy so that resources will be allocated properly.

ACCOUNT CLASSIFICATION AND RESOURCE ALLOCATION

Not all customers have the same buying potential, just as not all sales activities produce the same results. The salesperson has to concentrate on the most profitable customers and minimize effort spent with customers that offer little opportunity for profitable sales. The proportion of unprofitable accounts is usually greater than one would think. As a rule, 80 percent of the sales in a territory come from only 20 percent of the customers. Therefore, salespeople should classify customers on the basis of their sales potential to avoid spending too much time and other resources with low-potential accounts, thus helping to achieve sales goals.

Customer management is not just a time management issue. Managing customers includes allocating all the resources at the salesperson's disposal in the most productive manner. Time may be the most important of these resources, but salespeople also manage sample and demonstration inventories, direct mail budgets, printed materials, and other resources.

ABC Analysis

The simplest classification scheme, called **ABC analysis,** ranks accounts by sales potential. The idea is that the accounts with the greatest sales potential deserve the most attention. Using the 80/20 rule, the salesperson identifies the 20 percent of accounts that (could) buy the most and calls those A accounts. The other 80 percent are B accounts, and noncustomers (or accounts with low potential for sales) are C accounts. Eli Lilly (pharmaceuticals company) classifies physicians and Johnson Wax classifies retail stores this way. Federal Express studied buying habits of its customers and realized that 1 percent of its accounts generated 50 percent of revenue; it might call these A++ accounts! An example of an account analysis appears in Exhibit 15.4. As you can see, Sam Thompson has used esti-

Exhibit 15.4
Account Classification

Salesperson: Sam Thompson	A. Analysis of Call Pattern: 2006				
Customer Type	Number of Customers Contacted	Number of Calls	Average Calls per Customer	Sales Volume	Average Sales per Call
A	15	121	8.1	$212,515	$1,756
B	21	154	7.3	115,451	750
C	32	226	7.0	78,010	345
D	59	320	5.4	53,882	168
Total	127	821		$460,859	561

B. Annual Territory Sales Plan (dollars in thousands)

Account	Actual Sales			2007 Estimated Potential Sales	Forecast	Number of Calls Allocated	Classification
	2004	2005	2006				
Allied Foods	$100	$110	$150	$250	$150	48	A
Pic N-Save	75	75	90	300	115	48	A
Wright Grocers	40	50	60	175	90	24	B
H.E.B.	20	30	30	150	30	24	B
Piggly Wiggly	10	10	25	100	55	18	C
Sal's Superstore	0	0	30	100	80	18	C
Buy-Rite	0	0	0	80	75	18	C
Tom Thumb	0	10	20	75	70	18	C
Apple Tree	0	5	12	60	60	12	D
Buy Lo	0	0	10	60	50	12	D
Whyte's Family Foods	10	8	9	50	40	12	D

While this little store may appear smaller than Lowe's, the astute salesperson would determine each business's sales potential before classifying either as an A, B, or C account.

© Erv Schowengerdt

© Erv Schowengerdt

mated potential to classify accounts so that he can allocate sales calls to accounts with the greatest potential.

Classification schemes can be used to generate call plans. Tom McCarthy, a sales representative for Hilton, realized that he was spending way too much time with one account. He really liked the buyer, but nothing was getting sold. Wondering if he was wasting time with other accounts, he examined all of 300 accounts and classified them into four categories. The top 20 percent were A accounts, B and C accounts were the next two groups of 30 percent, and the bottom 20 percent were labeled D accounts. A accounts were given 12 calls per year (once a month), and D accounts might get called on once a year. From then on, his sales increased steadily because he knew where to go.[4]

ABC classification schemes work well only in industries that require regular contact with the same accounts, such as consumer packaged goods and pharmaceuticals. Some industries (plant equipment, medical equipment, and other capital products) may require numerous sales calls until the product is sold. After that sale, another sale may be unlikely for several years, and the number of sales calls may diminish. Then the A, B, and C classification may not be as helpful.

Salespeople in some industries find grid and customer relationship analysis methods more useful than ABC analysis. They have learned that simply allocating sales activities on the basis of sales potential may lead to inefficiencies. For example, satisfied customers may need fewer calls to maximize great potential than accounts of equal potential that are loyal to a competitor.

Grid Analysis

The **sales call allocation grid** classifies accounts on the basis of the company's competitive position with an account, along with the account's sales potential. As with ABC analysis, the purpose of classifying accounts through grid analysis is to determine which accounts should receive more resources. Using this method, each account in a salesperson's territory falls into one of the four segments shown in Exhibit 15.5. The classification is determined by the salesperson's evaluation of the account on the following two dimensions.

First, the **account opportunity** dimension indicates how much the customer needs the product and whether the customer is able to buy the product. Some factors the salesperson can consider when determining account opportunity are the account's sales potential, growth rate, and financial condition. This rating is

Exhibit 15.5
Sales Call Allocation Grid

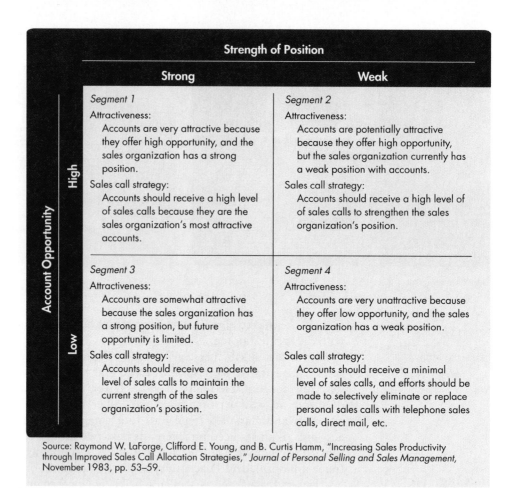

		Strength of Position	
		Strong	**Weak**
Account Opportunity	**High**	**Segment 1** Attractiveness: Accounts are very attractive because they offer high opportunity, and the sales organization has a strong position. Sales call strategy: Accounts should receive a high level of sales calls because they are the sales organization's most attractive accounts.	**Segment 2** Attractiveness: Accounts are potentially attractive because they offer high opportunity, but the sales organization currently has a weak position with accounts. Sales call strategy: Accounts should receive a high level of of sales calls to strengthen the sales organization's position.
	Low	**Segment 3** Attractiveness: Accounts are somewhat attractive because the sales organization has a strong position, but future opportunity is limited. Sales call strategy: Accounts should receive a moderate level of sales calls to maintain the current strength of the sales organization's position.	**Segment 4** Attractiveness: Accounts are very unattractive because they offer low opportunity, and the sales organization has a weak position. Sales call strategy: Accounts should receive a minimal level of sales calls, and efforts should be made to selectively eliminate or replace personal sales calls with telephone sales calls, direct mail, etc.

Source: Raymond W. LaForge, Clifford E. Young, and B. Curtis Hamm, "Increasing Sales Productivity through Improved Sales Call Allocation Strategies," *Journal of Personal Selling and Sales Management,* November 1983, pp. 53–59.

similar to ABC analysis and is a measure of total sales potential. Again, the idea is that accounts with the greatest opportunity deserve the greatest resources.

Second, the **strength of position** dimension indicates how strong the salesperson and company are in selling the account. Some factors that determine strength of position are the present share of the account's purchases of the product, the attitude of the account toward the company and the salesperson, and the relationship between the salesperson and the key decision makers in the account. The strength of position helps the salesperson understand what level of sales is likely in the account. The account opportunity may be tremendous, say, $1 million. But if the account has always purchased another brand, the salesperson's strength of position is weak, and his or her real potential is something much less than $1 million.

The appropriate sales call strategy depends on the grid segment into which the account falls. Accounts with high potential and a strong position are very attractive because the salesperson should be able to sell large amounts relatively easily. Thus these attractive accounts should receive the highest level of sales calls. For example, if you have an account that likes your product and has established a budget for it, and you know that the customer needs 300 units per year, you may consider that a segment 1 account (assuming 300 units is a high number) and plan to allocate more calls to that account. But if a competitor has a three-year contract with the account, you might be better off spending less time there. The account may buy 3,000 units per year, but you have little chance of getting any of

WHOSE ACCOUNT IS IT?

Knowing what to say when is an important part of selling. Ever since NCR, Singer Sewing Machine, and other leading manufacturers began conducting sales training in the late 1800s, companies have wanted to increase sales by controlling sales strategy. More recently, technology is making close to total control possible. Consider the potential impact of contact management technology: Sales managers for companies like Konica-Minolta use such technology to review their salespeople's notes about upcoming calls and suggest a sales strategy or ask to join in the sales call.

Sales strategy suggestions can even be programmed into a notebook computer. Jim Dickie, CSO Insight, describes one pharmaceutical company that provides a notebook computer to each salesperson. When a doctor offers an objection, the rep clicks on the appropriate icon, and the

appropriate clinical study comes up to respond to the doctor's objection. The system can then prompt the salesperson to ask follow-up questions.

Dickie's research shows that companies that can provide salespeople with greater "customer message management," or control over selling strategy, have 25 percent more salespeople achieving quota than those without customer message management. Furthermore, they are 3.4 times more likely to close a prospect. These salespeople are told what to say when, based on what is known to work. And it does work.

Sources: Jeff Fernandes, Konica-Minolta, interviewed April 4, 2004; Jim Dickie, "Sales and CRM," presented to the Center for Professional Selling, October 29, 2002; Jim Dickie, "Increasing Sales Effectiveness by Blending CMM and CRM," Defy the Limits Vol. 5 (San Francisco: Montgomery Research).

---

that business. By classifying the account as a segment 2, you would recognize that the most appropriate strategy is to strengthen your position in the account. The sales call allocation grid, then, aids salespeople in determining where, by account, to spend time in order to meet sales goals. In some companies, management is using technology for greater control over account strategy, as you can see in Selling Scenario 15.1.

THE GRID AND CURRENT CUSTOMERS   The sales call allocation grid is a great tool for analyzing current customers. Recall the value of a customer that was discussed in Chapter 14; many businesses experience little or no profit in the first year of a customer relationship. But over time profit grows if the salesperson is able to grow sales in the account, find ways to reduce the cost to serve the account (for example, shipping more can mean reduced shipping costs), and so on.

In a landmark study of the paper and plastics industry, the key to a company's profit was found to be customer share, not market share. **Customer share,** also called **account share,** is the average percentage of business received from a company's accounts. The analysis of companies in that industry indicated that even if a company was the dominant supplier to a group of buyers, another company could be more profitable if it served fewer customers but had all of their business.[5] Since that study, numerous studies have found similar insights. As a result, many companies are looking for how to increase account share, rather than the number of accounts.[6]

CUSTOMER RELATIONSHIP MANAGEMENT SOFTWARE

Use of computers and sales force automation software, such as ACT!, has grown tremendously over the past few years. Companies have found great productivity gains by creating one database of customers rather than separate databases used

MANAGING CUSTOMER RELATIONSHIPS

Over the past 20 years the average cost of a sales call has actually fallen, while at the same time compensation of salespeople has risen faster than the inflation rate. One important reason for companies' ability to more efficiently utilize their salespeople has been technology advances that offer better customer management strategies.

First called *sales force automation (SFA),* the class of software that now helps salespeople and their organizations manage customers is called *customer relationship management (CRM),* and it has been integrated more fully into the overall company operations. IBM has a monstrous sales force with over 35,000 salespeople. Add 40,000 service and support personnel who need access to customer information, and the need for CRM solutions becomes incredible. "It's not just sharing information across the sales team, but the service team as well," says Cher de Rossiter, CRM project executive at IBM. Key to the CRM strategy is making sure the appropriate cost-to-serve channel, whether a field salesperson, a telephone salesperson, or a combination with the Internet, meets the needs of the customer.

Volvo Rents, a construction equipment rental company with 54 franchise offices, uses technology to profile and select potential clients. "We pick our customers before they pick us," says Nick Mavrick, vice president of global strategy and development. Volvo Rents built its CRM system on the premise that not all customers have an equal impact on profitability: Mavrick estimates that 13 percent of the company's customers generate 87 percent of its revenue. The approach has paid off for Volvo Rents: Its customer base more than doubled in one year, from 23,000 in 2003 to 50,000 in 2004, and high-frequency customers tripled in that time. "Customers in the highest-frequency category spend almost four times what the lowest-frequency customers do," Mavrick says. "Those are the customers we want." CRM software helps Volvo Rents find those customers.

Sources: David Myron, "Big CRM Plans from Big Blue," *Customer Relationship Management,* April 2002, p. 13; Sara Calabro, "The Ones You Want," *Sales and Marketing Management,* March 2005, p. 16.

by salespeople, the credit department, and the service department. A single database enables the company to understand the buying history of an account that might use a field salesperson to place one order but order another product through the Internet. Using customer relationship management (CRM) software, a more complete grid analysis can then be conducted to understand the account's needs. Sales Technology 15.1 discusses CRM software in more detail.

Another application for CRM software is *pipeline analysis.* Recall that in Chapter 7 we discussed how accounts can move through stages, from lead to suspect to prospect to customer. ACT!, for example, can complete a pipeline analysis, telling the salesperson how well she is moving accounts from one stage to the next.

Konica-Minolta compiles data from its CRM database to create marketing campaigns that support the field sales force. For example, the company will create a profile of the organizations most likely to buy a specific product using the account records submitted by salespeople. Konica-Minolta uses that profile to generate a mailing list to introduce customers to the product. Salespeople are then given a prospecting list for making follow-up sales calls.

INVESTING IN ACCOUNTS

Planning based on customer analysis should result in more effective use of the opportunities presented by accounts. This improvement relates to the improved use of time, which is allocated to the appropriate accounts. But developing good strategies entails more than developing good time use plans; strategies require other resources as well.

Salespeople invest time, free samples or trials, customer training, displays, and other resources in their customers. Boise Cascade, for example, classifies customers as Most Valuable Customer, Most Growable Customer, Migrators, or Opportunity, also known as Below Zeroes, based on their profitability and potential profitability.[7] This knowledge helps salespeople determine where to invest resources—time, samples, displays, and so forth. Sales costs, or costs associated with the use of such resources, are not always costs in the traditional sense, but rather investments in customers—the asset that generates nearly all of a firm's revenue. Viewed from this perspective, formulating a strategy to allocate resources to maintaining or developing customers becomes vitally important.

IMPLEMENTING THE TIME MANAGEMENT STRATEGY

Time is a limited resource. Once spent, it cannot be regained. How salespeople use their time often means the difference between superstar success and average performance. Susan Flaviano, the Milliken salesperson profiled at the start of this chapter, offers the following tips for managing your time as a salesperson; keep these in mind as you read through this section:

- Start early. Get a jump start to the day before anyone else. Then you control the day without the day controlling you.
- Manage responsiveness. Although responsiveness is key to being successful, you cannot let the customer calls, e-mails, and voice mails consume your day. We now have the ability to respond immediately, but it is important to choose specific times during the day to reply to correspondence.
- Schedule in advance. Flaviano sets most of her appointments one week in advance, which helps her stay on target. Usually, if there is not a set commitment, it is easy to justify staying in the office to get caught up on paperwork.
- Use down time wisely. If you have a canceled appointment or extra time over lunch, or you arrive to an appointment early, use this time to plan or follow up. With laptops and sophisticated project tracking tools, you can use this time anywhere and reduce the amount of time in your office or at home on Saturday catching up on paperwork.

Remember that your time is worth $30 to $40 an hour, but only if you use it to sell. Use it to hone a golf game or spruce up the yard, and opportunities to sell disappear. Although no manager really knows how a salesperson uses time, when the results are posted, accurate conclusions can be drawn.

thinking **it** through

How do you plan your time now? Do you use a computer to help manage your time? How much of your time is planned by others, and how much of it are you free to allocate? How do you make sure you use your time wisely?

DAILY ACTIVITY PLANNING

To be effective time planners, salespeople must understand their own work habits. For example, some people tend to procrastinate in getting the day started, whereas others may want to knock off early. If you are a late riser, you may want to schedule early appointments to force yourself to get started. On the other hand, if your problem is heading for home too early, schedule late appointments so that you work a full day.

Thad Davis, with JetPowered Group, had the opposite problem—often working more than 14 hours a day, he had no personal life. He began spending 15 minutes each evening, planning the next day's activities. He even schedules time in his planner for working, and he's found that by planning the night before, he's much more focused. He believes that he's gained 45 minutes a day. "Before, I used to get to my desk, look at the computer, and realize I have fifteen thousand things to do. What do I start on first?" Davis says. "Now I'm just better focused."[8]

GUIDELINES

Salespeople need to include time for prospecting and customer care in their daily activities. Some minimize the time for such activities because they think sales do not occur on such calls, but prospects and happy customers feed future sales. IKON, an office equipment dealer, requires salespeople to handle customer care calls before 9 a.m. and after 4 p.m. and to schedule prospecting activities between 10 a.m. and noon and between 2 p.m. and 3 p.m. Scheduled appointments are worked in when customers require them. The company bases these guidelines on its experience with buyers and when they are available.

Such planning guides are designed to maximize **prime selling time,** the time of day at which a salesperson is most likely to see a buyer. Prime selling time depends on the buyer's industry. For example, a good time to call on bankers is late afternoon, after the bank has closed to customers. However, late afternoon is a bad time to call on physicians, who are then making rounds at the hospital or trying to catch up on a full day's schedule of patients. Prime selling time should be devoted to sales calls, with the rest of the day used for nonselling activities such as servicing accounts, doing paperwork, or getting information from the home office.

Prime selling time can also vary from country to country. In the United States prime selling time is usually 9 a.m. to 4 p.m. with the noon hour off for lunch. In Mexico lunch starts and ends later, generally from 12:30 to 2:00 p.m.; offices may not close until 7 p.m. or later. In Great Britain prime selling time starts later; a British Telecom rep may not begin making calls until 10 a.m.

PLANNING PROCESS

A process exists to help you plan your daily activities, with or without the aid of planning guides. This process can even help you now, as a student, take more control of your time and use it effectively.

As Exhibit 15.6 shows, you begin by making a to-do list. Then you determine the priority for each activity on your list. Many executives rank activities as A, B, or C, with A activities requiring immediate action, B activities being of secondary importance, and C activities being done only if time allows.[9] You can correlate these A, B, and C activities with the A, B, and C accounts discussed earlier, as well as activities such as paperwork and training. Prioritizing activities helps you choose which activities to perform first.

Note, however, the difference between activities that seem urgent and activities that truly are important. For example, when the phone rings, most people stop whatever they are doing to answer it. The ringing phone seems urgent. Activities such as requests from managers or even customers may have that same sense of urgency; the desire to drop everything else to handle the request is called the "tyranny of the urgent." And the "urgent" can get overwhelming: a study by Pitney-Bowes shows the average U.S. office worker sends and receives 52 phone messages, 36 e-mails, 36 pieces of mail, 14 faxes, and eight pager messages per day.[10] Yet, like most phone calls, even requests from customers may be less important than other tasks.[11] Successful businesspeople learn to recognize what is truly urgent and prioritize those activities first.

Exhibit 15.6
Activities Planning
Process

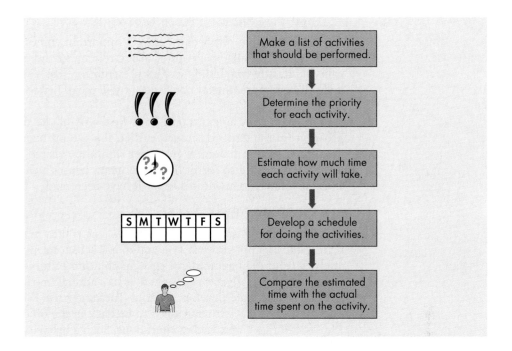

The next step in the planning process is to estimate the time required for each activity. In sales, as we mentioned earlier, time must be set aside for customer care and prospecting. The amount of time depends on the activity goals set earlier and on how long each call should take. However, salespeople often have unique activities, such as special sales calls, demonstrations, customer training, and sales meetings, to plan for as well. Time must also be set aside for planning and paperwork.

The next step, developing an effective schedule, requires estimating the amount of time such activities will require. As follow-up, be sure to compare how long an activity actually took with how long you thought it would take. Comparing actual time to planned time with the aid of planning devices such as a DayRunner or DayTimer (paper-based calendars and planners) or computer software like ACT! can help you plan more accurately in the future.

Using the Computer for Planning

Many of the same customer management programs that salespeople use to identify and analyze accounts incorporate time-planning elements. This software can generate to-do lists and calendars through a tickler file or by listing certain customer types. A **tickler file** is a file or calendar that salespeople use to remember when to call specific accounts. For example, if customer A says to call back in 90 days, the computer will remind ("tickle") the salesperson in 90 days to call that customer. Or if the company just introduced a product that can knock out competitor B, the computer can generate a list of prospects with products from competitor B; the salesperson then has a list of prospects for the new product.

Platinum Technology equipped its salespeople with WisdomWare, a software package that creates knowledge bases. A *knowledge base* includes all the product knowledge that a salesperson needs to know, tips on what the competition is up to, and other pertinent information. As salespeople learn in the field, they add their findings to the knowledge base, which is then shared with all other salespeople at Platinum. Then each salesperson can use WisdomWare for account and territory planning.[12]

Need for Flexibility

Although working out a daily plan is important, times will arise when the plan should be laid aside. You cannot accurately judge the time needed for each sales call, and hastily concluding a sales presentation just to stick to a schedule would be foolish. If more time at one account will mean better sales results, the schedule should be revised.

To plan for the unexpected, your first visit of the day should be to a prime prospect (in the terms discussed earlier, this would be an A account or activity); then the next best potential customer should be visited (provided the travel time is reasonable); and so forth. If an emergency causes a change of plans, at least the calls most likely to result in sales will have been made.

MAKING MORE CALLS

Making daily plans and developing efficient routes are important steps toward better time use. But suppose you could make just one more call per day. Using our analysis from the beginning of this chapter and Exhibit 15.3, this change would mean 240 more calls per year, which is like adding one month to the year!

Some salespeople develop an "out Tuesday, back Friday" complex. They can offer many reasons why they need to be back in the office or at home on Monday and Friday afternoons. Such a behavior pattern, however, means the salesperson makes 20 to 30 percent fewer calls than a salesperson who works a full week. Scott Woolford, national sales manager at M.D. Industries, a health care supply company, took a big account away from a competitor on a Friday afternoon. The buyer had a problem with the competitor's delivery schedule, and Woolford was able to guarantee delivery the next day—Saturday. Working a full week really paid off for Woolford.[13]

To get the most out of a territory, the sales representative must make full use of all available days. For example, the days before or after holidays are often seen as bad selling days. Hence, while the competition takes those extra days off, the salesperson can be working and making sales calls he or she would otherwise miss. The same reasoning applies to bad weather: It reduces competition and makes things easier for the salesperson who doesn't find excuses to take it easy. On the other hand, good weather can tempt the salesperson to the golf course, doing yard work, or otherwise avoiding the job. No matter the weather, the professional salesperson continues to work.

Salespeople can use certain techniques to increase the time they spend in front of customers selling instead of traveling. For example, Lisa Paolozzi found herself working 15-hour days and was on the verge of quitting her sales job at FIND/SVP, a market research and consulting firm. One day, while flipping through her calendar, she realized, "I was all over the map. I was going on the number of appointments I needed, but I was so unorganized." Now she uses many time management techniques to organize herself and provide structure, with the result that she holds her company's record for the most sales in a year.[14] She uses routing and zoning techniques, as well as the computer. For example, mapping software can save valuable time when traveling in an unfamiliar area. Rather than getting lost and calling the customer from the car for directions, she now relies on mapping software to help her find the account on the first try.

Salespeople who make calls in bad weather often find that their competition has taken the day off, leaving the field wide open for those who want to succeed.

Steve Bly/Zephyr

Routing

Routing is a method of planning sales calls in a specific order to minimize travel time. Two types of sales call patterns, routine and variable, can be more efficient with effective routing. Using **routine call patterns,** a salesperson sees the same customers regularly. For example, Eli Lilly pharmaceutical salespeople's call plans enable them to see all important doctors in their territory at least once each six weeks. Some doctors (those who see large numbers of certain types of patients) are visited every two weeks. The salesperson repeats the pattern every six weeks, ensuring the proper call level.

Variable call patterns occur when the salesperson must call on accounts in an irregular order. In this situation the salesperson would not routinely call on each account within a specified period. Routing techniques are useful, but the salesperson may not repeat the call plan on a cyclical basis.

The four types of routing plans, **circular routing, leapfrog routing, straight-line routing,** and **cloverleaf routing,** are illustrated in Exhibit 15.7. If an Eli Lilly salesperson used the cloverleaf method (with six leaves instead of four) for a routine

Exhibit 15.7

Types of Routing Plans

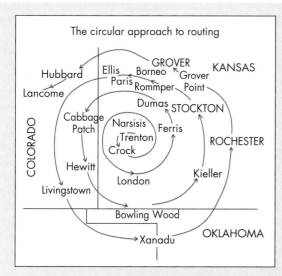

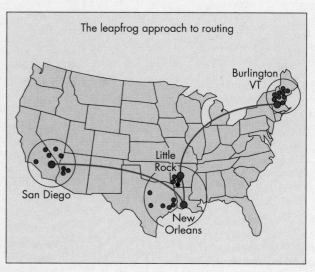

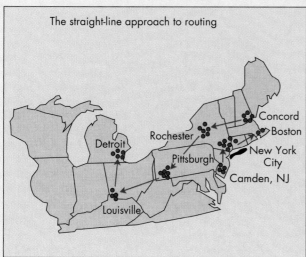

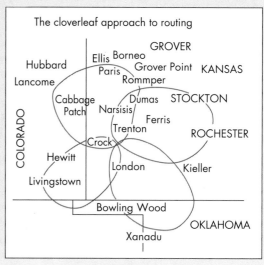

call pattern, every sixth Tuesday would find that salesperson in the same spot. But a salesperson with variable call patterns could use the cloverleaf method to plan sales calls for an upcoming week and then use the straight-line method the next week. The pattern would vary depending on the demands of the customers and the salesperson's ability to schedule calls at convenient times.

Zoning

Zoning means dividing the territory into zones, based on ease of travel and concentration of customers, to minimize travel time. First the salesperson locates concentrations of accounts on a map. For example, an office supply salesperson may find that many accounts are located downtown, with other concentrations around the airport, in an industrial park, and in a part of town where two highways cross near a rail line. Each area is the center of a zone. The salesperson then plans to spend a day, for example, in each zone. In a territory zoned like the one in Exhibit 15.8, the salesperson might spend Monday in zone 1, Tuesday in zone 2, and so forth.

Zoning works best for compact territories or for situations in which salespeople do not call regularly on the same accounts. (In a large territory, such as the entire Midwest, a salesperson is more likely to use leapfrog routes, but the principle is similar.) Calling on customers that are in a relatively small area minimizes travel time between calls.

Salespeople can also combine zoning with routing, using a circular approach within a zone, for example. When zones are designed properly, travel time between accounts should be minimal.

Using E-Mail and Telephone

Customer contacts should not always be in-person sales calls. As many companies have learned, some sales objectives can be accomplished over the phone or through e-mail. For example, some customer care calls can be handled by simply sending the customer an e-mail and asking whether everything is OK. The customer may appreciate the e-mail more than a personal visit because it can be read

Exhibit 15.8
Zoning a Sales Territory
A salesperson may work
in zone 1 on Monday,
zone 2 on Tuesday,
and so forth.

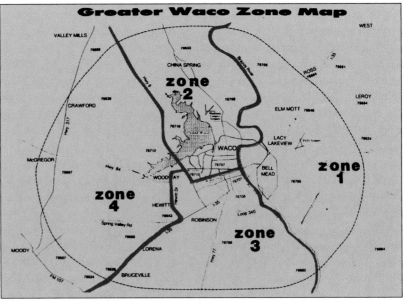

Source: *Waco Tribune Herald*

BUILDING E-RELATIONSHIPS

Are personal sales calls going the way of the house call? Many have wondered about the future of professional selling in an era where anything can be purchased by computer. Ben Dixon, a 35-year veteran of sales, says that first, a salesperson had to sign in at the customer's location and wait with 50 other salespeople to see buyers. "Now," he says, "as a result of everything from voice mail, e-mail, and the need for appointments, when you get to the customer's location you can't even get a game of pool going because no one else is there." Does that mean that sales are all done by computer?

There's no question that sales have changed, and salespeople have changed with them. Ram Ramamurthy, who sells digital imaging services for Sri IIST, maintains that the need for personal relationships is still there, but also notes that many personal relationships start electronically. "We take important documents and scan them—our clients trust us with very important documents like 70 years of high

school transcripts for the state of Louisiana." That level of trust does require a personal relationship, "but the relationship (with the buyer for Louisiana) started with an e-mail reply to a Web posting describing the job and what they needed."

Understanding which accounts need what form of communication—personal visits, telephone calls, and e-mail, and when—is an important skill for today's salesperson. As Ramamurthy notes, "I can 'see' a lot more people by e-mail than in person, but building trust means they need to see me in person."

Sources: Anonymous, "Reps Learn the Value of Evolving with the Profession: A Veteran Perspective," *Agency Sales* 34 (October 2004), pp. 11–14; Ram Ramamurthy, personal correspondence, used with permission; John F. Tanner Jr., Christophe Fournier, Sandrine Hollet, and Juliet Poujol, "The Future of Selling," AM/AMA Biennial Global Conference, presented July 2005.

and responded to when the customer has time and doesn't take him or her away from other pressing responsibilities. The salesperson may be able to make more customer care calls by e-mail, increasing the number of contacts with customers. Keep in mind, though, that not all customer care activities should be handled by e-mail or phone. Recall from Chapter 14 that there are many reasons, such as reorders and cross-selling, to continue to make sales calls in person to current customers.

Similarly, the telephone and direct mail can be used profitably for prospecting, as we discussed in Chapter 7. More calls, or customer contacts, can be made equally effectively with judicious use of e-mail and the telephone. Building Partnerships 15.1 provides additional tips regarding the use of e-mail and telephone.

HANDLING PAPERWORK AND REPORTS

Every sales job requires preparing reports for management. All salespeople complain about such paperwork, but it is important. As we will discuss later, paperwork can provide information that helps a salesperson determine what should be improved. The information also helps management decide what types of marketing plans work and should be used again. Therefore, every salesperson should learn to handle paperwork efficiently.

Paperwork time is less productive than time spent selling to customers, so completing it quickly is important. Salespeople can do several things to minimize the impact of paperwork on their prime selling time.

First, salespeople should think positively about paperwork. Although less productive than selling, it can increase their productivity and the productivity of the company's marketing programs by facilitating a detailed review of selling activities and marketing programs.

Second, salespeople should not let paperwork accumulate. We once knew a salesperson who never did expense reports. He finally offered a summer intern 10 percent if she would complete his expense reports for the previous 12 months. This deal cost him $600; in addition, he was essentially lending the company $500 per month, interest free.

Routine reports should be completed daily. Nonproductive time (like time spent waiting for a customer) can be used for paperwork. Call reports and account records should be updated immediately after the call so that important points are remembered and any follow-up actions can be planned.

Finally, salespeople should set aside a block of nonselling time for paperwork. The quickest way to do this job is to concentrate on it and avoid interruptions. Setting aside a small amount of time at the beginning or end of each day for writing thank-you and follow-up notes and completing reports saves prime selling time for selling activities while ensuring that the salesperson keeps up with paperwork.

Using the Computer to Handle Paperwork and Communications

Many companies, such as McGraw-Hill, give their salespeople laptop or notebook computers. These computers can be hooked up to the company's network to access customer information and process other paperwork automatically. Salespeople who travel can then complete their paperwork while in a hotel, an airport waiting area, and other places. Allied Beverages, a California beer distributor, requires salespeople to input orders three times a day, which they do through wireless Internet. Confirmation is text-messaged back to the rep's cell phone. Such speedy order entry means that not only do reps spend less time with paperwork, but the product is loaded and ready for transport at the end of the day.[15]

Salespeople calling on overseas accounts can also file reports or check the status of orders, even though the home office in another time zone may be closed for the night. Computers can help international selling organizations operate smoothly by reducing communication barriers between the field and the home office. Computers and fax machines enable salespeople to communicate with colleagues and customers all around the world, despite significant time differences.

Some customer relationship management packages, like ACT!, include territory management capabilities. These packages allow salespeople to track their performance by calculating conversion rates, commissions, expenses, and other important figures. Such technology enables salespeople to file reports quickly. Samsung's 100 U.S. field salespeople file their call reports nightly, describing what they saw in the stores they visited that day. Product placement on the stores' shelves, training effectiveness of the stores' salespeople, and other details are e-mailed to sales management every evening, and then forwarded to the marketing department so that marketing plans can be adjusted accordingly. Such quick reporting and adept change have enabled Samsung to grow some 30-plus percent in just one year.[16]

To manage your time wisely, you must exploit a scarce resource in the most effective manner possible. Your objective is to make as many quality calls as possible by reserving prime selling time for selling activities. Routing, zoning, goal setting, and other methods of planning and scheduling time will help you maximize your prime selling time.

Many companies now provide their salespeople with wireless notebook computers so they can access customer information and complete paperwork in the field.

Getty Images

EVALUATING PERFORMANCE

Success in sales is a result of how hard and how smart a salesperson works. Unlike many other workers, however, salespeople have a great deal of control over both how hard and how smart they work. Evaluating performance is the component of self-management that provides direction for how hard the salesperson should be working as well as an opportunity to determine which strategies work best.

POSTCALL ANALYSIS

At the end of each call, many salespeople take a moment to write down what occurred and what needs to be done, perhaps using a printed form (see Exhibit 15.9) or entering the information into a territory management program. Information such as the customer's purchase volume, key people in the decision process, and current vendors is important to have, but so is personal information such as the fact that the buyer's three children play soccer. The salesperson can use that information when preparing for the next call.

Remember the plan you made for each sales call? That plan included one or more objectives. Postcall analysis should include reflecting on whether those objectives were reached. The professional salesperson not only looks for specific areas to improve but also evaluates the success of the overall sales call.

Exhibit 15.9
Postcall Analysis Form

COMPANY NAME: _____	Date: _____
Contact name: _____	STATUS:
Decision maker's name: _____	A—Current
Office address: _____	account
_____	B—Current
	prospect
Office phone: _____	C—Competitor
First contact date: _____	D—Dormant
Next contact date: _____	E—Not interested
Ranking: (Hot) 5 4 3 2 1 (Cold)	INITIAL
Notes:	CONTACT:
	D—Direct mail
	T—Telephone
	C—Cold call

COMPANY NAME: _____	Date: _____
Contact name: _____	STATUS:
Decision maker's name: _____	A—Current
Office address: _____	account
_____	B—Current
	prospect
Office phone: _____	C—Competitor
First contact date: _____	D—Dormant
Next contact date: _____	E—Not interested
Ranking: (Hot) 5 4 3 2 1 (Cold)	INITIAL
Notes:	CONTACT:
	D—Direct mail
	T—Telephone
	C—Cold call

COMPANY NAME: _____	Date: _____
Contact name: _____	STATUS:
Decision maker's name: _____	A—Current
Office address: _____	account
_____	B—Current
	prospect
Office phone: _____	C—Competitor
First contact date: _____	D—Dormant
Next contact date: _____	E—Not interested
Ranking: (Hot) 5 4 3 2 1 (Cold)	INITIAL
Notes:	CONTACT:
	D—Direct mail
	T—Telephone
	C—Cold call

COMPANY NAME: _____	Date: _____
Contact name: _____	STATUS:
Decision maker's name: _____	A—Current
Office address: _____	account
_____	B—Current
	prospect
Office phone: _____	C—Competitor
First contact date: _____	D—Dormant
Next contact date: _____	E—Not interested
Ranking: (Hot) 5 4 3 2 1 (Cold)	INITIAL
Notes:	CONTACT:
	D—Direct mail
	T—Telephone
	C—Cold call

ACTIVITY ANALYSIS

When planning their time, salespeople set certain activity goals. They use these goals not only as guidelines but also to evaluate their own performance. At the end of each day, week, and month, salespeople should review their activities in relation to the goals they set. Goals would be written down or entered into ACT! at the time they are set—say, Sunday evening when planning the following week. Then on Friday evening, the actual activities from each day would be tallied and totaled for the week and compared to the goals. The salesperson could evaluate whether more calls of a certain type are needed in the following week.

Merrill Lynch, for example, recommends that new brokers make 100 telephone calls each day (calls count even if no one answers). Frank Baugh, a new broker in central Texas, made 7,544 calls in his first 92 working days, or 82 calls per day. His goal is now 120 calls per day to bring his average up to 100 in the next quarter.

PERFORMANCE ANALYSIS

Salespeople also need to evaluate performance relative to performance goals set earlier. For example, they often evaluate sales performance in terms of percentage of quota achieved. Of course, a commission or a bonus check also tells the salesperson if the earnings goal was met.

An earnings goal can be an effective check for overall performance, but salespeople also need to evaluate sales by product type, as outlined in Exhibit 15.10. Salespeople who sell only part of the product line may be missing opportunities for cross-selling or full-line selling, which means they have to work harder to achieve the same level of sales as the salesperson who successfully integrates cross-selling and full-line selling in the sales strategy.

Exhibit 15.10

Sales Evaluation Measures

Evaluation Measure	Calculation	How to Use It
Conversion rate 　For total performance 　By customer type 　By product type	$\dfrac{\text{Number of sales}}{\text{Number of calls}}$	Are your strategies effective? Do you need to improve by working smarter (i.e., a better strategy to improve your hit rate)? Compare yours to your company and/or industry average.
Sales achievement	$\dfrac{\text{\$ actual sales}}{\text{\$ sales goal}}$	Is your overall performance where you believe it should be? Are you meeting your goals? Your company's goals?
Commission	$\dfrac{\text{\$ actual commission}}{\text{\$ earnings goal}}$	
Sales volume (in dollars) 　By customer type		Where are you most effective? Do you need help with a customer type?
By product category		Are you selling the whole line?
By market share		How are you doing relative to your competition?
By new customers		Are you building new business?
By old customers		Are you servicing your accounts properly?
Sales calls 　Prospecting calls 　Account calls 　Sales presentations 　Call frequency by 　customer type		Are your efforts in the right place?

PRODUCTIVITY ANALYSIS

Salespeople also need to identify which strategies work. For example, if using a certain strategy improved the ratio of appointments to cold calls made, that approach should be continued. Otherwise, the salesperson should change it or go back to a previous approach. Frank Baugh, the Merrill Lynch broker, tried several approaches before settling on one that works well for him. Of course, Baugh keeps good records so he knows what works and what does not.

The **conversion ratio,** or number of sales per calls, is an important measure of effectiveness. Conversion ratios should also be calculated by account type; for example, a conversion ratio for type A accounts should be determined. Other conversion ratios can also pinpoint effective strategies and areas that need improvement.

SUMMARY

A sales territory can be viewed as a small business. Territory salespeople have the freedom to establish programs and strategies. They manage a number of resources, including physical resources such as sample inventory, displays, demonstration equipment, and perhaps a company vehicle. More important, they manage their time, their customers, and their skills.

Managing a territory involves setting performance, activity, and conversion goals. Salespeople use these goals to allocate time to various activities and to manage customers.

To manage customers well, salespeople must analyze their potential. Accounts can be classified using the ABC method or the sales call allocation grid. These analyses tell how much effort should be put into each account. Some organizations use CRM software to conduct these analyses on the entire customer database, which helps identify patterns within a territory. Salespeople can use these patterns to develop account sales strategies.

More calls (working harder) can be accomplished by moving nonselling activities, such as paperwork, to nonselling time. Also, selling time can be used more efficiently (working smarter). For example, routing and zoning techniques enable the salesperson to spend more prime selling time in front of customers instead of behind the steering wheel of a car.

Effective planning of the salesperson's day requires setting aside time for important activities such as prospecting and still making the appropriate number of sales appointments. Using the full workweek and employing technology such as telephones, computers, and fax machines can help the salesperson stay ahead of the competition.

Finally, salespeople must manage their skills. Managing skills involves choosing how to make sales calls and improving the way one sells. Improvement requires that salespeople first understand what they do well and what needs improvement. Evaluating their performance can give them that insight.

KEY TERMS

ABC analysis
account opportunity
account share
activity goals
benchmarking
circular routing

cloverleaf routing
conversion goals
conversion ratio
customer share
leapfrog routing
performance goals

prime selling time
routine call patterns
routing
sales call allocation grid
straight-line routing

strength of position
tickler file
variable call patterns
zoning

ETHICS PROBLEMS

1. After reading this chapter, a salesperson protests, "That's no fun. I like to play golf every other afternoon. If I have to hustle every minute of every day, then forget it. I'll get another job!" What would you tell this salesperson? Would it matter if this salesperson was paid salary or straight commission?

2. One company's culture is "flashy," meaning salespeople are expected to wear expensive suits, expensive jewelry and watches, and drive expensive cars. Assume you are about to graduate and go to work for this company. Consider this culture and relate it to your goals—how might this culture influence your goals? Is that influence healthy? Why or why not?

QUESTIONS AND PROBLEMS

1. Look over the profile of Susan Flaviano at the start of the chapter. Do you think her experience is normal for people new to a career in sales? Did it hurt her or help her to go through that learning process? Why do you think it hurt or helped?

2. Many salespeople work out of their homes and have described how tempting it is to work longer and to put off paperwork until the weekends because it is so convenient. What problems might succumbing to such temptation cause? What safeguards can the salesperson put into place?

3. Compare and contrast the special problems of self-management for a computer salesperson who works in a computer store with those of a computer salesperson who calls on customers in their offices.

4. Shakespeare wrote, "To thine own self be true." How would you apply this statement to your planning and development activities?

5. Which factors are important for classifying customers? Why? How would these factors change depending on the industry?

6. Distinguish between routing and scheduling and between routing and zoning. Explain how routing and scheduling can interact to complement the planning of an efficient day's work.

7. How might a pharmaceutical salesperson increase the number of calls made per day? A construction equipment salesperson? A financial services representative? A representative who sells golf clubs to retailers and pro shops?

8. Sales managers know that making more sales calls results in more sales. Should sales managers encourage salespeople to continually increase the number of calls made each week? Explain your answer.

9. One recruiter told a class that students are used to getting feedback on how they are doing every couple of months, but salespeople do not get a "final grade" until a year has gone by. He claims that students have a hard time making that adjustment when they enter the work world. What do salespeople do to know where they stand at any given time? What do you do now that helps you know where you stand in your classes? Why is such knowledge important?

10. Do you ever find yourself "burning the midnight oil" to study or finish an assignment? What self-management principles could you use to avoid all-nighters? Is any software available to help you manage your time as a student?

case **15.1**

Growing Clifton Feeds

Keith "Spanky" McFarland sells MRO (maintenance, repair, and operations) products. MRO products, sold to the maintenance and operations crews in manufacturing plants, can consist of nuts and bolts, wire, tape, electrical outlets and connectors, and other types of hardware used to repair equipment, utilities, and other things around the plant. As he drove home, he reflected on Clifton Feeds and Products, the last call of the day.

Clifton Feeds and Products is a manufacturer of feed and other products for livestock. They began as a manufacturer of horse feed for horse racing when the founder won three horses in a poker game and didn't like any of the commercial feed on the market. He hired an equine scientist from Texas A&M to conduct studies on equine performance and in short order found people asking why his horses outperformed all the others. As the company grew, it developed lines of feed for poultry, cattle, sheep, and goats. The acquisition of several companies added product lines such as feed buckets, feed storage bins, and other products that make feeding easier and more effective.

Spanky sold MRO items to one of those newly acquired companies in Lampasas, Texas before it was acquired and had continued to serve them after the merger. The account was not that large—a C account that he called on once every 90 days or so. Most of the time, he took care of them by phone. But today Jack Davis, the purchasing agent, told Spanky that Clifton was creating two divisions, consolidating the manufacturing plants into one division and the mills into another. Davis also said that he was moving to create a central purchasing office in Austin at company headquarters and would issue a request for quotes for an annual contract for the manufacturing division. They wanted one company providing MRO items for all four Clifton product manufacturing plants. Spanky already had some sales at the two feed mills in addition to the Lampasas plant, but none at the other plants in spite of trying. He also knew that the maintenance managers at the other plants liked to buy from three vendors, splitting the business. Further, he knew that the electrician at one plant liked to get his parts from a local electrical parts distributor. He estimated that if he had all of the business at the plants, it would be his third or fourth largest account.

Questions

1. Assess the overall Clifton account in terms of the sales effort allocation grid. What about the mills and the manufacturing plants as separate divisions?
2. Is the manufacturing division a suspect or prospect? Why? How would you assess that division in terms of the sales effort allocation grid?

case **15.2**

McGraw-Hill

Pierce Totten is a salesperson for McGraw-Hill, the company that publishes this textbook. Pierce works from Minneapolis–St. Paul; his territory includes northern Minnesota and the following accounts:

Bemidji State, Bemidji: This school has 12 faculty members in the business administration program. It offers five majors: finance, generalist, management, marketing, and small business. It is a small school with approximately 400 undergraduate business students.

Central Lakes College, Brainerd: There are 11 faculty members at the Brainerd campus of Central Lakes in the business department. The school offers eight majors: finance, management, marketing, accounting, information systems, insurance, economics, and entrepreneurship in a two-year associate program. This pre-BBA program can be combined with programs at schools such as St. Scholastica. The school has 350 students at the Brainerd campus and another 100 taking courses online.

Lake Superior College, Duluth: There are approximately 8,500 students at Lake Superior. The business department has 10 full-time faculty members and offers 19 majors in the bachelor's program. There are approximately 30 adjunct professors who teach one class each, but in almost all cases, the full-time faculty decide what books they use.

University of Minnesota–Duluth: There are over 9,000 students total at UMD. The school of business and economics has over 40 faculty members (full-time) in four departments, and approximately 60 percent of all undergraduates are business majors.

St. Cloud University, St. Cloud: There are five departments offering 10 majors at St. Cloud. Over 70 faculty teach in the undergraduate program, serving approximately 3,500 students.

Source: Based on information and a scenario suggested by Dr. Jeff Totten, Southeastern Louisiana University, and a sales representative from another textbook publisher.

Questions

1. Plan an appropriate schedule for Pierce.
2. What are the three most important issues that Pierce needs to consider in scheduling his time? Why are these issues so important?

Map of Pierce Totten's Territory

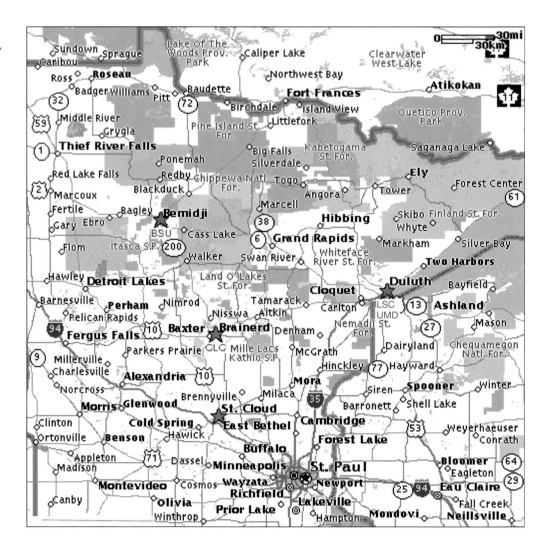

ACT! ROLE PLAY

Six months ago you went through your accounts and determined that how you've allocated your effort is not consistent with the potential of each account and your relative position. In one instance, Bellamy Buildings, you've got a great relationship with the CIO (chief information officer or head of information technology) and have called on her once or twice a month. There are, however, only 24 salespeople there; and Bellamy is not growing, so there isn't much opportunity. You have decided that this is an account you no longer plan to visit in person but will check in by phone.

Another account, Franklin Production, merits more calling. It had 34 salespeople six months and has 44 now. Because Franklin continues to grow and has indicated that it may grow through acquisi-

tion of other companies, you've decided to visit it once or twice a month.

Majestic Mint, a manufacturer of collectibles, has been a tough account to understand. It has 120 salespeople who call on retailers around the country, and they use a paper-based system to keep track of accounts. Orders are placed on special handheld computer devices that download them at night. The VP of sales says that's all they need, but the VP of marketing wants more information for a CRM marketing strategy. Today you will visit the VP of marketing to determine if you want to continue with this account.

Your professor will give you buyer sheets for your turn as a buyer.

ADDITIONAL REFERENCES

Buchwald, Art. "Selecting the Correct Sales Tool." *Customer Relationship Management,* November 2001, pp. 27–28. This is a good, short article on selecting a CRM software system.

DeCormier, Ray, and Arthur Beirn. "Corporate Policies to Include Micro Activity Goals Can Affect Sales Urgency in Salespeople, Prospects, and Customers." *Industrial and Commercial Training* 35 (April 5, 2003), pp. 220–23.

Deeter-Schmelz, Dawn, and Karen Norman Kennedy. "Buyer–Seller Relationships and Information Sources in an E-Commerce World." *The Journal of Business & Industrial Marketing* 19 (2004), pp. 188–205.

Donaldson, Bill; Nikos Tzokas; and Mike Saren. "The Sale Never Closes: How Closer Relationships between Buyers and Sellers Change the Role of the Salesperson." *The Journal of Selling and Major Account Management* 3 (Winter 2001), pp. 31–43.

Harman, Harry A.; Gene Brown; Robert E. Widing II; and Kevin L. Hammond. "Exploring the Sales Manager's Feedback to a Failed Sales Effort." *The Journal of Business & Industrial Marketing* 17 (2002), pp. 43–56.

Larpsiri, Ravipa and Mark Speece. "Technology Integration: Perceptions of Sales Force Automation in Thailand's Life Assurance Industry," *Marketing Intelligence & Planning* 22 (2004), pp. 392–409.

Matsuo, Makoto, and Takashi Kusumi. "Salesperson's Procedural Knowledge, Experience and Performance: An Empirical Study in Japan." *European Journal of Marketing* 36 (2002), pp. 840–57.

Murphy, William H. "In Pursuit of Short-Term Goals: Anticipating the Unintended Consequences of Using Special Incentives to Motivate the Sales Force." *Journal of Business Research* 57 (November 2004), pp. 1265–79.

Nonis, Sarath A. and Jeffrey K. Sager. "Coping Strategy Profiles used by Salespeople: Their Relationships with Personal Characteristics and Work Outcomes." *The Journal of Personal Selling & Sales Management* 23 (Spring 2003), pp. 139–52.

Verbeke, Willem; Frank Belschak; and Richard P Bagozzi. "The Adaptive Consequences of Pride in Personal Selling." *Journal of the Academy of Marketing Science* 32 (Fall 2004), pp. 386–403.

MANAGING WITHIN YOUR COMPANY

chapter **16**

SOME QUESTIONS ANSWERED IN THIS CHAPTER . . .

- Which areas of the company work with salespeople to satisfy customer needs?

- How do salespeople coordinate the efforts of various functional areas of the company?

- How do salespeople work with sales managers and sales executives?

- How do company policies, such as compensation plans, influence salespeople?

- How do salespeople work within the company to resolve ethical issues?

- What is the organizational structure, and how does it influence salesperson activities?

PROFILE

Do you feel like you participate in group work in just about every business class you have taken? I felt the same way when I was a marketing student at the University of Central Florida studying sales with Dr. Karl Sooder, and I thought the group work was in preparation for marketing-related jobs. But I knew I wanted to be a sales professional and wondered why group work was necessary. I had no idea how much the skills I would learn from working in groups would apply to my career as a medical sales representative at Cardinal Health.

Most of Cardinal Health's $65 billion of revenue are in distribution of pharmaceuticals and medical supplies. I do not work in the distribution side of the company; I specialize in a segment of medical products and services called convertors products, which includes all of the Cardinal Health surgical drapes, gowns, standard packs, face masks, and sterilization products. In any given account, which includes hospitals and surgery centers, there can be 20 medical products and services representatives. Included in the achievement of my quota are sales from distribution representatives and custom pack representatives; everyone benefits from others' sales.

The distribution representatives can sell my products or my competitors' products to the customer, but they have an incentive of a higher gross profit percentage for selling Cardinal Health self-manufactured products, such as Convertors products. In most cases, the distribution representative will sell the customers whatever brand they want, so I have to be proactive to get my products into the facility. In order to increase my success, I have to work closely with the customer and the distribution representative. Once I build a strong relationship with my distribution representatives, they will bring leads to me. I have a great relationship with some of my distribution representatives, which is helpful because I am the first person that comes to their mind when a customer needs any of the products I specialize in. Recently I had one of my distribution representatives come to me with a lead about a customer who was using a competitor's sterilization products, which were going on backorder. With the lead from my distribution representative, I was able to get my product put in place of the competitor's.

Other internal relationships that are critical to my success are relationships with some of the other medical products and services reps that work on the same accounts as I do. Recently, one of my customers informed me they had ongoing problems with a competitor's instrument, so I contacted the V. Mueller representative (another Cardinal Health company), who solved the problem for the customer. That customer was so grateful that they converted their entire protective apparel line to Convertors, without even looking into pricing. This satisfied my customer's needs, help to build rapport with my customer, and also built the internal relationship with the other representative from Cardinal Health. Within the next month that V. Mueller representative brought two leads to me.

By building close internal relationships with other sales representatives within my company, it not only benefits my sales, it also satisfies the customers. The relationships I have with my distribution representatives and other sales representatives from Cardinal Health have contributed to my success—I am currently ranked third out of 53 Convertors representatives. As you can see, skills learned from group work pertain not only to marketing careers; sales professionals can benefit from group work skills just as much as, if not more than, marketing professionals.

Visit us on the Web at www.cardinalhealth.com.

"By building close internal relationships with other sales representatives within my company, it not only benefits my sales, it also satisfies the customers."

Amy Boynton, Cardinal Health

BUILDING INTERNAL PARTNERSHIPS

To effectively coordinate the efforts of various areas of a company, a salesperson must develop partnerships with the individuals in those areas. **Internal partnerships** are partnering relationships between a salesperson and another member of the same company. These partnerships should be dedicated to satisfying customer needs.

THE IMPORTANCE OF INTERNAL PARTNERSHIPS

By definition, a sales representative represents something. Students often think the title means that the salesperson represents only a company or a product, but at times the salesperson must represent the customer to the company. For example, the salesperson may have to convince the warehouse manager to ship a customer's product next to meet a special deadline. The salesperson does not have the authority to order the manager to ship the product; he or she must use persuasion. Or the rep may have to negotiate with production to get a product manufactured to a customer's specifications. Sometimes success in landing a sale may depend on the salesperson's ability to manage such company efforts.

This ability to work with groups inside the company can directly affect the rep's pocketbook. One of the authors, while selling for a major corporation, had an opportunity to earn a large bonus by making 30 sales. He had 31 orders, but a sale wasn't a sale until the product was delivered. Unfortunately, two orders were delivered after the deadline, and he did not get the bonus. In tracking down the slow deliveries, the hapless salesperson learned that the order entry clerk had delayed processing the orders. A little probing uncovered the reason: She was upset with the way he prepared his paperwork! Her performance was evaluated on how quickly an order was delivered, but his sloppy paperwork always slowed her down and got her into trouble. Delaying work on his orders was her way of getting his attention.

It worked! For several months after that, he enlisted her help in filling out the paperwork properly before he turned it in. After that, she never had a problem with his orders. And, when necessary to meet a customer's requirements, she would prioritize his orders.

THE ROLE OF SALES

Salespeople not only sell a company, its products, and its services to customers but also sell their customers' needs to their companies. Carrying the customer's voice across the organization is one of the most important functions of the sales force. Although many companies work to increase the customer contact time for support personnel so that they will understand customers, often the only person who really understands what the customer needs and why, is the salesperson. The salesperson's ability to carry the voice of the customer across the organization is key to any firm.[1]

Watlow Electric Manufacturing, a manufacturer of industrial heaters, has salespeople regularly fill out a Voice of the Customer information sheet. These sheets are compiled and distributed around the organization to ensure that the company's processes of design, producing, delivering, and invoicing are consistent with what the customer wants.[2] But when companies do not have a formal voice of the customer process, salespeople still have a responsibility to their customers to ensure that the company is responsive to their changing needs.

In addition, salespeople must adapt to satisfy the needs and desires of those who influence sales performance. Salespeople who develop strong internal partnerships are successful because they meet the needs of their partners. Building Partnerships 16.1 describes how one company has been successful because of strong internal partnerships.

TEAMWORK GETS THE JOB DONE

Should one customer drive change in an organization? Probably not, but when a customer is an exemplar of what could be done in an entire market, a partnership is just the vehicle to make such a change possible.

It began with an innocuous request. In 1991 Microsoft needed some help with a trade show, so David Gauthreaux, Freeman Companies account executive, helped them out. Freeman decorates exhibit halls for special meetings and trade shows, along with providing other services to the exhibition industry. Dressed in jeans, Gauthreaux worked side by side with Microsoft personnel to get the show ready. But nothing more seemed to come from it; so the next year his manager said, "Why not drive over and see if you can sell Microsoft some signs?"

Selling a few signs turned into handling 500 to 600 projects a year, developing a pretty tight partnership along the way. Getting from a few signs to 500 projects a year, though, required a different Freeman. Originally, "every part of Freeman, whether it was an operating division like AVW (selling and renting audiovisual equipment) or Freeman Transportation or even just a local office of Freeman Exhibits, was operating like it was its own company. But, like many large companies, Microsoft wanted one Freeman," says Gauthreaux. So he would take each Microsoft request, call the appropriate part of Freeman, order whatever was needed, and ask them to send him the invoice. "Then I would consolidate all of their charges and send them one bill."

Microsoft, though, wanted more integration. They wanted one unified set of policies, for example, about how their material would be handled from show to show. They also wanted to be able to use materials from one show to the next, and they wanted parts of Freeman to work together to come up with solutions when show design needed to be integrated. "I became a change agent," laughs Gauthreaux, "representing their needs to Freeman."

Microsoft was just one of many potentially large accounts, so it was not hard for Freeman management to recognize the need for integration. Getting it done, though, took a while. The result was a complete makeover in how Freeman operates, changing from a lot of little companies with one owner to one company serving the customer. "Now we can do nearly everything: design, installation, electrical, audiovisual, transportation, decorating, the works. And we do it as one team."

The transition hasn't always been easy, but Microsoft has been there to help. "If we weren't good at what we do, we would have never gotten this far with Microsoft. What made it work was Microsoft realized that we are accountable, meaning we do what we say and we warn them if there are any problems." Gauthreaux also isn't shy about sending Microsoft to other vendors when they need something Freeman doesn't do. "I don't worry about losing their business because they know we, the whole company, will take care of them." Because that's what happens when partners work together.

SELLING INTERNALLY

To service customers well, salespeople must often rely on personnel in other areas of the firm to do their respective jobs properly. But how well those other employees assist salespeople may be a function of the relationship the salesperson has already established with them. That relationship should be a partnership, just like the one the salesperson wants to establish with appropriate customers. To establish the appropriate partnership, the salesperson must invest time in understanding the customer's needs and then work to satisfy those needs.

thinking **it** through

Consider the impact electronic forms of communication have had on your life so far. How do such forms of communication help build internal partnerships, particularly when a salesperson is stationed far away from company headquarters? How can such forms of communication hinder a salesperson's efforts to build internal partnerships?

Exhibit 16.1

Seven Principles of Selling Internally

1. Understand that it's your problem. **Accept responsibility** for gaining the support of the internal staff.
2. **Appeal to a higher objective.** For example, show how what you are asking for meets an important company objective.
3. Probe to find out and **understand the personal and professional needs** of the internal customer. Use SPIN® and active listening techniques.
4. Use arguments for support that adequately **address internal customers' needs** as well as your own. Use your presentation skills.
5. Do not spend time or energy resenting the internal customers' inability to understand or accept your sense of urgency. Rather, spend this time fruitfully by trying to figure out how you can better communicate your needs in a manner that will **increase the internal customers' sense of urgency** to the level you need.
6. **Never personalize** any issues. Don't call names, blame the person in public, or hold a grudge.
7. Be prepared to **negotiate.**

As summarized in Exhibit 16.1, the first step of selling laterally is to recognize that it is the salesperson's responsibility to develop relationships with other departments. Rarely do other departments have an incentive to take the initiative. Salespeople who expect other workers to serve them are frustrated by the lack of support they receive. The better perspective is, How can I serve them so we can serve the customer better?

Use questioning skills such as SPIN® to understand the personal and professional needs of personnel in other departments. Salespeople have excellent communication skills but sometimes fail to use these skills when dealing with internal customers and support groups. SPIN and active listening are just as important to understanding the needs of colleagues as they are to satisfying customer needs. For example:

SALESPERSON: What do you do with these credit applications? (Situation)

CREDIT REP: We key the information into the computer system, and then it is processed by a credit company each night. The next morning we get a report that shows who has been approved and who hasn't. That's why it is so important to have a clean copy.

SALESPERSON: So the quality of the copy we give you is a problem? (Problem)

CREDIT REP: That's right.

SALESPERSON: What happens when you can't read the copy we give you? (Implication)

CREDIT REP: We put in incorrect information, which can result in a customer's credit application being rejected when it should have been accepted.

SALESPERSON: What happens when that happens? (Implication)

CREDIT REP: That's when we call you. Then we get the right information and reenter it. But we get in trouble because the approval cycle was made longer, and you know that the goal is to have a customer's order shipped in three days. We can't meet that goal if we're still working on their credit application.

SALESPERSON: So you need legible applications—and probably e-mail would be better than handwritten, right? (Needs payoff)

CREDIT REP: Yes, that would help a lot.

Keep in mind too that the salesperson cannot simply order a colleague to do what the salesperson wants, such as approving a customer's credit application. But if a salesperson can show that doing what he or she wants will also meet the needs of the colleague, the salesperson is more likely to receive the desired aid. Just as when selling to an external customer, persuasion requires the salesperson to meet the other person's needs as well. For example, if a salesperson can show a plant manager how an expedited order will result in a higher profit margin, thereby more than covering the plant manager's higher costs and helping that manager make production targets, both the plant manager's needs and the customer's needs will be met.

People from other departments, except for billing and customer service, do not have direct contact with the customer. Therefore, they do not feel the same sense of urgency the customer or the salesperson feels. Successful internal sellers can communicate that sense of urgency by relating to the needs of the internal customer. Just as they do with external customers, salespeople need to communicate the need to act now when they sell internally. They need to secure commitment to the desired course of action. Also, just as with external customers, the salesperson should be sure to say thank you when someone agrees to provide the support requested.

Selling to internal customers also means keeping issues professional. Personal relationships can and should be developed. But when conflicts arise, focus on the issue, not the person. Personalizing conflict makes it seem bigger and harder to resolve. For example, rather than saying, "why won't you do this?" ask, "if you can't do this, how can we resolve the customer's concern?" This type of statement focuses the other individual on resolving the real problem rather than arguing about company policy or personal competence.

Be prepared to negotiate. Remember from Chapter 13 that negotiation is a set of techniques to resolve conflict. Conflicts between salespeople and members of the firm representing other areas will occur, and negotiation skills can be used to respond to conflicts professionally.

Salespeople must work with many elements of their organization. In fact, few jobs require the boundary-spanning coordination and management skill that the sales job needs. In the next section we examine the many areas of the company with which the salesperson works, what their needs are, and how they partner with the salesperson to deliver customer satisfaction.

COMPANY AREAS IMPORTANT TO SALESPEOPLE

The sales force interacts with many areas of the firm. Salespeople work with manufacturing, sales administration, customer service, and personnel. In some industries requiring customization of products, engineering is an important department for salespeople. Finance can get into the picture as well when that department determines which customers receive credit and what price is charged. In addition, salespeople work with members of their own department and the marketing department.

MANUFACTURING

Grafo Regia S.A. is a packaging and labeling firm in Monterrey, Mexico. Its clients include companies such as Kellogg, and it prints labels and boxes that are used around the world. A key competitive advantage for Grafo Regia is its ability to deliver small or large orders faster than its competitors. Because the primary competitive advantage is based on manufacturing, the sales managers and salespeople spend a great deal of time in the factory learning the manufacturing processes. More important, these salespeople have established personal relationships with workers at every level in the plant. Salespeople even play on manufacturing softball teams in a local corporate league, even though they may have to fly from Kellogg's headquarters in Battle Creek, Michigan, to make a game.

These personal relationships help Grafo Regia respond quickly to customer needs. If Kellogg needs to change a Frosted Flakes package to include a promotion involving the San Antonio Spurs just for the San Antonio market, Grafo Regia can do it faster than anyone else. One main reason is that manufacturing and sales are on the same team and are not viewed as separate entities.

Salespeople who develop internal partnerships with people in areas such as manufacturing and service can count on their internal partners for support.

Walter Hodges/Photodisc Red/Getty Images

Bill Lai/The Image Works

In general, manufacturing is concerned with producing product at the lowest possible cost. Thus in most cases manufacturing wants long production runs, little customization, and low inventories. Customers, however, want their purchases shipped immediately and custom-made to their exact specifications. Salespeople may have to negotiate compromises between manufacturing and the customer. Salespeople should also develop relationships with manufacturing so that they can make accurate promises and guarantees to customers.

ADMINISTRATION

The functions of order entry, billing, credit, and employee compensation require each company to have an administrative department. This department processes orders and sees that the salesperson gets paid for them. Employees in this area (as discussed earlier) are often evaluated on how quickly they process orders and how quickly the company receives customer payment. Salespeople can greatly influence both processes and realize substantial personal benefit for themselves.

The credit department is an important part of administration. Understanding the needs of the credit department and assisting it in collecting payments can better position the salesperson to help customers receive credit later. A credit representative who knows you will help collect a payment when a problem arises is more likely to grant credit to one of your customers. Some companies do not pay commission until after the customer has paid to ensure that salespeople sell to creditworthy accounts. These companies, such as Robert Half International, believe a close working relationship between sales and credit is critical to the financial health of the company.[3]

SHIPPING

The scheduling of product shipments may be part of sales administration or manufacturing, or it may stand alone. In any case salespeople need the help of the shipping department. When salespeople make special promises to expedite a delivery, they actually must depend on shipping to carry out the promise. Shipping managers focus on costs, and they often keep their costs under control by planning efficient shipping routes and moving products quickly through warehouses. Expedited or special-handling deliveries can interfere with plans for efficient shipping. Salespeople who make promises that shipping cannot or will not fulfill are left with egg on their faces. That's why Andrea Kinnard, sales representative for Konica-Minolta in Fort Worth, has been known to help load a delivery truck so that a customer could get a much-needed copier.

CUSTOMER SERVICE

Salespeople also need to interact with customer service. The need for this relationship should be obvious, but many salespeople arrogantly ignore the information obtained by customer service representatives. A technician who fixes the company's products often goes into more customers' offices or plants than the salesperson does. The technician often has early warning concerning a customer's switch to a competitor, a change in customer needs, or failure of a product to satisfy. For example, if an IBM technician spies a competitor's computer in the customer's office, the technician can ask whether the unit is on trial. If a good working relationship exists between the technician and the salesperson, the technician will warn the salesperson that the account is considering a competitive product. Close relationships and support of customer or technical service representatives mean not only better customer service but faster and more direct information flow to the salesperson. This information will help the salesperson gain and keep customers.

Salespeople, in turn, can help customer service by setting reasonable expectations for product performance with customers, training customers in the proper use of the product, and handling complaints promptly. Technicians are evaluated on the number of service calls they make each day and how long the product works between service calls, among other things. Salespeople can reduce some service calls by setting the right expectations for product performance. Salespeople can also extend the amount of time between calls by training customers in the proper use of the product and in preventive maintenance. An important byproduct of such actions should be higher customer satisfaction.

MARKETING

Sales is part of marketing in some firms and separate from marketing in others. Marketing and sales should be highly coordinated because their functions are closely related. Both are concerned with providing the right product to the customer in the most efficient and effective manner. Sales acts as the eyes and ears of marketing, while marketing develops the promotions and products that salespeople sell. Salespeople act as eyes and ears by informing the marketing department of competitor actions, customer trends, and other important market information. Marketing serves salespeople by using that information to create promotional programs or design new products. Marketing is also responsible for generating leads through trade show exhibiting, direct mail programs, advertising, and public relations.

Unfortunately, not all marketing and sales departments just naturally get along. Only 27 percent of marketing executives believe salespeople deliver the same message promoted by marketing.[4] Several other studies have shown that sales and marketing departments fail to communicate, don't trust each other, and even sabotage each other.[5] The biggest problem seems to be a lack of communication.[6] In yet another study the lack of communication led to misunderstandings concerning responsibility and roles for each department. Neither sales nor marketing knew who was responsible for developing strategies, marketing and sales plans, and tactics.[7] Proactive salespeople, however, won't wait for marketing managers to make the first move. Rather than complain about poor marketing programs, these salespeople and sales managers prefer to participate in marketing decisions and keep communication lines open. When sales and marketing work together, salespeople have better programs with which to sell.

SALES

Within any sales force, there may be several types of salespeople. As you learned in earlier chapters, global account managers may work with the largest accounts while other representatives handle the rest of the customers, and the salesperson must interact with certain sales executives and sales managers. How these people work together is the subject of the next section.

PARTNERS IN THE SALES ORGANIZATION

The sales function may be organized in many different ways, but no matter how it is organized, it is rarely perfect. Usually some customer overlap exists among salespeople, meaning several salespeople have to work together to serve the needs of one account. Customer needs may require direct customer contact with the sales executive as well as the salesperson. At the same time, the salesperson must operate in an environment that is influenced by the policies and procedures created by that same sales executive and executed by the salesperson's immediate manager. In this section we examine how the activities of sales management affect salespeople.

SALES MANAGEMENT

Salespeople should understand the roles of both sales executives and field sales managers. Salespeople who are able to develop partnerships with their managers will have more resources available to perform at a higher level.

The Sales Executive

The sales executive is the manager at the top of the sales force hierarchy. This person is a policy maker, making decisions about how the sales force will accomplish corporate objectives. Sales executives play a vital role in determining the company's strategies with respect to new products, new markets, sales forecasts, prices, and competition. The executives determine the size and organization of the sales force, develop annual and long-range plans, and monitor and control sales efforts. Duties of the sales executive include forecasting overall sales, budgeting, setting sales quotas, and designing compensation programs.

Size and Organization of the Sales Force The sales executive determines how many salespeople are needed to achieve the company's sales and customer satisfaction targets. In addition, the sales executive must determine what types of salespeople are needed. For example, it is the sales executive who determines whether global account management is needed. Many other types of salespeople can be selected, which we will discuss later in this chapter. For now, keep in mind that the sales executive determines the level of customer satisfaction necessary to achieve sales objectives and then designs a sales force to achieve those goals. How that sales force is put together is important because salespeople often have to work together to deliver appropriate customer service and successfully accomplish sales goals.

Forecasting Sales executives use a number of techniques to arrive at sales forecasts. One of the most widely used techniques is **bottom-up forecasting,** or simply adding each salesperson's own forecast into a forecast for total company sales. At each level of management, the forecast would normally be adjusted based on the manager's experience and broader perspective. This technique allows the information to come from the people closest to the market: the salespeople. Also, the forecast comes from the people with the responsibility for making those sales. But salespeople tend to be optimistic and may overestimate sales, or they may underestimate future sales if they know their bonuses depend on exceeding forecasts or if they think their quotas will be raised. Wise managers quickly realize when salespeople are underestimating forecasts, though the salespeople may be able to obtain significant earnings the first time. Such behavior, though, is not only unethical—it creates many problems for the organization.

Salespeople are especially important to the forecasting process when the executive is attempting to forecast international sales. Statistics used in the United States to forecast sales are often not available in other countries or, if available, may be unreliable. Companies in Europe operate in so many different countries that the only consistent numbers available may come from the sales force. One candy company found that its salespeople provided the best forecast possible, in part because they were closest to the customer but also because each country's data were collected and compiled in different ways, making comparisons impossible.[8]

Expense Budgets   Managers sometimes use expense budgets to control costs. An expense budget may be expressed in dollars (for example, the salesperson may be allowed to spend up to $500) or as a percentage of sales volume (such as expenses cannot exceed 10 percent of sales). A regional manager or salesperson may be awarded a bonus for spending less than the budget allocates. However, such a bonus may encourage the salesperson to underspend, which could hurt sales performance. For example, if a salesperson refuses to give out samples, customers may not be able to visualize how the product will work; thus some may not buy. The salesperson has reduced expenses but hurt sales.

Although salespeople may have limited input into a budget, they do spend the money. Ultimately it is the salesperson's responsibility to manage the territorial budget. The salesperson not only has control over how much is spent and whether expenditures are over or under budget but also, and more important, decides where to place resources. Recall from Chapter 15 that these resources, such as samples and trial units or direct mailers, are investments in future sales. If they are used unwisely, the salesperson may still meet the expense budget but fail to meet his or her sales quota.

Control and Quota Setting   The sales executive faces the challenge of setting up a balanced control system that will encourage each sales manager and salesperson to maximize his or her individual results through effective self-control. As we have pointed out throughout this text, salespeople operate somewhat independently. However, the control system management devises can help salespeople manage themselves more effectively.

Quotas are a useful technique for controlling the sales force. A **quota** represents a quantitative minimum level of acceptable performance for a specific period. A **sales quota** is the minimum number of sales in units, and a **revenue quota** is the minimum sales revenue necessary for acceptable performance. Often sales quotas are simple breakdowns of the company's total sales forecast. Thus the total of all sales quotas equals the sales forecast. Other types of quotas can also be used. Understanding quotas is important to the salesperson because performance relative to quota is evaluated by management.

Profit quotas or **gross margin quotas** are minimum levels of acceptable profit or gross margin performance. These quotas motivate the sales force to sell more profitable products or to sell to more profitable customers. Some companies assign points to each product based on the product's gross margin. More points are assigned to higher-margin products. The salesperson can then meet a point quota by selling either a lot of low-margin products or fewer high-margin products. For example, assume an office equipment company sells fax machines and copiers. The profit margin (not including salesperson compensation) on copiers is 30 percent but only 20 percent on fax machines. Copiers may be worth three points each, whereas faxes are worth two. If the salesperson's quota is 12 points, the quota can be reached by selling four copiers, or six faxes, or some combination of both.

One challenge sales managers face is recognizing that performance quotas can negatively influence a customer orientation as salespeople put the need to make quota ahead of their customers' needs.[9] One type of quota that can avoid this dilemma is an activity quota. **Activity quotas,** similar to the activity goals we discussed in the preceding chapter, are minimal expectations of activities for each salesperson. The company sets these quotas to control the activities of the sales force. This type of quota is important in situations where the sales cycle is long and sales are few because activities can be observed more frequently than sales. For example, for some medical equipment, the sales cycle is longer than one year, and a salesperson may sell only one or two units each quarter. Having a monthly sales target in this case would be inappropriate, but requiring a certain minimum number of calls to be made is reasonable. The assumption made by management is that if the salesperson is performing the proper activities, sales will follow—with the customer's needs in mind. Activities for which quotas may be established include number of demonstrations, total customer calls, number of calls on prospects, or number of displays set up.

Compensation and Evaluation   An important task of the sales executive is to establish the company's basic compensation and evaluation system. The compensation system must satisfy the needs of both the salespeople and the company. You, as a salesperson, need an equitable, stable, understandable system that motivates you to meet your objectives. The company, however, needs a system that encourages you to sell products at a profitable price and in the right amounts.

Salespeople want a system that bases rewards on effort and results. Compensation must also be uniform within the company and in line with what competitors' salespeople receive. If a competitor's salespeople earn more, you will want to leave and work for that competitor. But your company expects the compensation system to attract and keep good salespeople and to encourage you to do specific things. The system should reward outstanding performance while achieving the proper balance between sales results and costs.

Compensation often relates to quotas. As with quotas, salespeople who perceive the system as unfair may give up or leave the firm. A stable compensation system ensures that salespeople can reap the benefits of their efforts, whereas a constantly changing system may lead them to constantly change their activities but never make any money. A system that is not understandable will be ignored.

The sales executive decides how much income will be based on salary or incentive pay. The salesperson may receive a **salary,** a regular payment regardless of performance, or **incentive pay,** which is tied to some level of performance. There are two types of incentives: commission and bonus. A **commission** is incentive pay for an individual sale, whereas a **bonus** is incentive pay for overall performance in one or more areas. For example, a bonus may be paid for acquiring a certain number of new customers, reaching a specified level of total sales in units, or selling a certain amount of a new product.

Sales executives can choose to pay salespeople a straight salary, a straight commission, or some combination of salary, commission, and/or bonus. Most firms opt for some combination of salary and bonus or salary and commission. Fewer than 4 percent pay only commission, and slightly fewer than 5 percent pay only salary. Exhibit 16.2 illustrates how various types of compensation plans work.

Under the **straight salary** method, a salesperson receives a fixed amount of money for work during a specified time. The salesperson is assured of a steady income and

Exhibit 16.2
How Different Types of Compensation Plans Pay

		Amount Paid to Salesperson			
Month	Sales Revenue	Straight Salary	Straight Commission*	Combination†	Point Plan**
January	$50,000 6 copiers 10 faxes	$3,500	$5,000	$1,500 (salary) 3,000 (commission) 4,500 (total)	$3,800
February	$60,000 6 copiers 15 faxes	3,500	6,000	1,500 (salary) 3,600 (commission) 5,100 (total)	4,800
March	$20,000 2 copiers 5 faxes	3,500	2,000	1,500 (salary) 1,200 (commission) 2,700 (total)	1,600

*Commission plan pays 10 percent of sales revenue.
†Commission portion pays 6 percent of sales revenue.
**Copiers are worth three points, faxes are worth two, and each point is worth $100 in commission.
Note: These commission rates are used only to illustrate how compensation schemes work. Point plans, for example, do not necessarily always yield the lowest compensation.

can develop a sense of loyalty to customers. The company also has more control over the salesperson. Because income does not depend directly on results, the company can ask the salesperson to do things in the best interest of the company, even if those activities may not lead to immediate sales. Straight salary, however, provides little financial incentive for salespeople to sell more. For example, in Exhibit 16.2, the salesperson receives $3,500 per month, no matter how much is sold.

Straight salary plans are used when sales require long negotiation, when a team of salespeople is involved and individual results cannot be measured, or when other aspects of the marketing mix (such as advertising) are more important than the salesperson's efforts in generating sales (as in trade selling of consumer products). Most sales trainees also receive a straight salary.

A **straight commission** plan pays a certain amount per sale and includes a base and a rate but not a salary. The **commission base,** the item from which commission is determined, is often unit sales, dollar sales, or gross margin. The **commission rate,** which determines the amount paid, is expressed as a percentage of the base (such as 10 percent of sales or 8 percent of gross margin) or as a dollar amount (like $100 per sale). Exhibit 16.2 illustrates two straight commission plans: One pays 10 percent of sales revenue, and the other is a point plan that pays $100 per point (using the copier and fax example we discussed previously).

Commission plans often include a draw. A **draw** is money paid to the salesperson against future commissions, in essence a loan that guarantees a stable cash flow. For example, in Exhibit 16.3 the salesperson receives a draw of $3,000 per

Exhibit 16.3
An Example of a Draw Compensation Plan

Month	Draw	Commission Earned	Payment to Salesperson	Balance Owed to Company
January	$3,000	$0	$3,000	$3,000
February	3,000	5,000	3,000	1,000
March	3,000	4,500	3,500	

month. No commissions were earned during January, but the salesperson still received $3,000. In February the rep earned $5,000, but $2,000 went to pay back some of the draw from January, and the rep received only $3,000. In March the rep earned $4,500, of which $1,000 finished paying off the balance from January. Thus the rep was given $3,500 in March.

Straight commission plans have the advantage of tying the salesperson's compensation directly to performance, thus providing more financial incentive for the salesperson to work hard. However, salespeople on straight commission have little company loyalty and certainly are less willing to perform activities, such as paperwork, that do not directly lead to sales. Xerox experimented with such a plan but found that customer service suffered, as did company loyalty among salespeople.

Companies that do not emphasize service to customers or do not anticipate long-term customer relationships (like a company selling kitchen appliances directly to consumers) typically use commission plans. Such plans are also used when the sales force includes many part-timers because part-timers can earn more when their pay is tied to their performance. Also, part-timers may need the extra motivation straight commission can provide.

Under a bonus plan, salespeople receive a lump-sum payment for a certain level of performance over a specified time. Bonuses resemble commissions, but the amount paid depends on total performance, not on each individual sale. Bonuses, awarded monthly, quarterly, or annually, are always used with salary and/or commissions in **combination plans.** Combination plans, also called salary-plus-commission plans, provide salary and commission and offer the greatest flexibility for motivating and controlling the activities of salespeople. The plans can incorporate the advantages and avoid the disadvantages of using any of the basic plans alone.

The main disadvantage of combination plans lies in their complexity. Salespeople confused by this complexity could unknowingly perform the wrong activities, or sales managers could unintentionally design a program that rewards the wrong activities. Using the earlier office equipment example, if faxes and copiers were worth the same commission (for example, $100 per sale), the salesperson would sell whatever was easiest to sell. If faxes were easier to sell than copiers, the firm may make less money because salespeople would expend all of their effort selling a lower-profit product unless the volume sold made up for the lower margin. Even then, however, the firm may be stuck with a warehouse of unsold copiers.

Compensation is one of the toughest issues that sales managers have to address. When market conditions change rapidly, the issue is even tougher, as those in the steel industry found out. Selling Scenario 16.1 describes the compensation issues the industry faced when prices doubled quickly.

thinking **it** through

As a buyer, under which plan would you prefer your salesperson to work? Which would you prefer if you were a salesperson? What conflicts might occur between buyer and seller because of the type of compensation plan?

FIELD SALES MANAGERS

Salespeople report directly not to a sales executive, but to a **field sales manager.** Field sales managers hire salespeople, evaluate their performance, train them, and perform other important tasks. Salespeople find it useful to partner with their man-

DOUBLE THE PRICE—DOUBLE THE INCOME!

In just a few months during 2004, steel prices suddenly doubled. Those companies in the steel industry who paid straight commission suddenly found salespeople happily selling half as much but making the same, while other salespeople who maintained steady sales were suddenly earning more than anyone in the company!

That's why Earle M. Jorgensen Co. put a cap on earnings. Morale problems were created by the salespeople's sudden wealth, a wealth they really had no part in earning. Other employees were unhappy about the sudden disparity in compensation.

Fewer than 8 percent of steel distributors pay straight commission. Most pay salary plus commission or bonus. One such company is Loeffel Steel, which didn't change its compensation plan. The result was "some pretty happy

salespeople" according to president Maurice Loeffel Jr. But he also said that the increase in sales meant salespeople would have to beat that increase in the coming year to earn a bonus.

So what happened in 2005? Prices fell some 20 percent over six straight months. But that's still placing prices at high levels historically, and while demand in some sectors is soft, demand in other areas may enable good salespeople to meet those higher targets. One thing is for certain: Changing economic conditions can quickly influence a salesperson's compensation.

Sources: Tim Triplett, "Salespeople Face Tough Encore," *Metal Center News* 45 (February 2005), p. 6; Tim Triplett, personal correspondence, April 26, 2005, used with permission.

agers because the managers often represent the salespeople to other parts of the organization. Also, the salesperson often has to sell the manager first on any new idea before the idea can be pitched to others in management. Building a partnering relationship with managers can go a long way toward getting ideas accepted.[10]

Evaluating Performance

Field sales managers are responsible for evaluating the performance of their salespeople. The easiest method of evaluating performance is to simply add up the amount of sales that the salesperson makes. But sales managers must also rate their salespeople's customer service level, product knowledge, and other, less tangible qualities. Some companies, such as FedEx, use customer satisfaction surveys to evaluate salespeople. In other companies the manager rates each salesperson, using evaluation forms that list the desired aspects. (An example of an evaluation form appears in Exhibit 16.4.) Such evaluations help managers determine training needs, promotions, and pay raises.

The records and reports salespeople submit also play an important role in communicating their activities to the sales manager. The manager then uses these reports to evaluate performance in a manner similar to the way the salesperson would. But these written reports are not enough; sales managers should also make calls with salespeople to directly observe their performance. These observations can be the basis for recommendations for improving individual performance or for commending outstanding performance. Other information, such as customer response to a new strategy, can be gained by making calls. This information should be shared with upper management to improve strategies.

Training

The sales manager trains new hires and provides refresher training for experienced salespeople. To determine what refresher training they need, managers

Exhibit 16.4
Behavioral Observation
Scale (BOS)

	Almost Never						Almost Always
1. Checks deliveries to see whether they have arrived on time.	1	2	3	4	5	6	7
2. Files sales reports on time.	1	2	3	4	5	6	7
3. Uses promotional brochures and correspondence with potential accounts.	1	2	3	4	5	6	7
4. Monitors competitors' activities.	1	2	3	4	5	6	7
5. Brushes up on selling techniques.	1	2	3	4	5	6	7
6. Reads marketing research reports.	1	2	3	4	5	6	7
7. Prospects for new accounts.	1	2	3	4	5	6	7
8. Makes service calls.	1	2	3	4	5	6	7
9. Answers customer inquiries when they occur.	1	2	3	4	5	6	7

often use information gathered while observing salespeople making sales calls. Content of training for new salespeople may be determined by a sales executive, but the field sales manager is often responsible for carrying out the training.

Professional salespeople constantly seek to upgrade their skills; here, a group at Infocus Systems is reviewing a role play sales call.

Mark Richards/PhotoEdit

Most experienced salespeople welcome training when they perceive that it will improve their sales. Unfortunately, salespeople often view training as an inconvenience that takes away from precious selling time. Steve Herzog, president of Herzog & Associates of Knoxville, Tennessee, says that ongoing skill training of experienced salespeople is part of a "trend toward creating an environment that consistently brings out the best in all personnel." Salespeople who take advantage of such training are far more likely to progress in their career.

You should continue to welcome training, no matter how successful you are. It always offers the opportunity to improve your performance, or at least achieve the same level with less effort. Also, as you will see in Chapter 17, continuing to learn is important to the salesperson who is part of a learning organization.

MANAGING ETHICS IN SALES

Salespeople, particularly those within certain industries, have earned a reputation that is unfavorable. Most salespeople, though, want to act ethically. Because we have emphasized throughout this book methods of selling that help people solve problems and satisfy needs, we believe it is important to understand what companies do to encourage ethical behavior and how salespeople should work with their sales management partners to choose ethical options. First we discuss the sales executive's role in making ethics policy. Then we cover the roles of the field sales manager and the salesperson in implementing that policy.

ETHICS AND THE SALES EXECUTIVE

Part of a sales executive's job is to determine corporate policy concerning what is considered ethical and what is not and how unethical behavior will be investigated and punished. In addition, the sales executive must ensure that other policies, such as the performance measurement and compensation policies, also support the ethics of the organization. Performance measurement and compensation policies that reward only outcomes may inadvertently encourage salespeople to act unethically because of pressure to achieve and a culture supporting the credo "the end justifies the means." But when behavioral performance measurement systems are also in place, the compensation system can reward those who do things the right way. In addition, research shows that closer relationships with ethical managers also support ethical behavior.[11] Although unethical behaviors may result in short-term gain (and therefore may accidentally be rewarded in an outcome-only compensation scheme), they can have serious long-term effects, such as loss of customers, unhappy salespeople who quit, and other negative outcomes.[12]

Sales executives must therefore develop a culture that creates behavioral norms regarding how things should be done and what behaviors will not be tolerated. Such a culture can be enhanced through the development of formal policy, training courses on ethics, ethics review boards, and an open-door policy. **Open-door policies** are general management techniques that allow subordinates to bypass immediate managers and take concerns straight to upper management when the subordinates perceive a lack of support from the immediate manager. Open-door policies enhance an ethical culture because salespeople can feel free to discuss troublesome issues that involve their managers with someone in a position to respond. Two versions are **ethics review boards** and ethics officers, both of which provide expert advice to salespeople who are unsure of the ethical consequences of an action. Ethics review boards may consist of experts inside and outside the company who are responsible for reviewing ethics policies, investigating allegations of unethical behavior, and acting as a sounding board for employees. One ethics officer, David Reid of Texas Instruments, says that most of the calls he gets from salespeople concern giving gifts to customers, but he also hears about issues between sales managers and salespeople.[13]

Salespeople also have the right to expect ethical treatment from their company. Fair treatment concerning compensation, promotion policies, territory allocation, and other actions should be delivered. Compensation is probably the area with the most common concerns, although problems can arise in all areas. Compensation problems can include slow payment, hidden caps, or compensation plan changes after the sale.

For example, one company paid its salespeople a straight commission of about 10 percent. When a salesperson sold one major account $11 million worth of product, the company changed her commission plan to a salary plus commission to cut her payment. In another example a company refused to pay a salesperson all of his commission because he earned more than the vice president of

Like Tiger Woods, sales managers are role models whether they want to be or not. As role models, it is imperative that they model ethical behavior at all times.

Michael Newman/Photoedit

sales. The company claimed there was a **cap**, or limit, on earnings. Caps are not unethical; what was unethical was that the salesperson was not made aware of the cap prior to selling. Although some problems do occur, most companies want to hire and keep good salespeople, and most businesspeople are ethical.

thinking **it** through | Should schools have ethics review boards? What advantages would such boards have for the student? For the teacher? Would salespeople reap the same types of benefits if their companies had ethics review boards?

ETHICS AND THE FIELD SALES MANAGER

Salespeople often ask managers for direction on how to handle ethical problems, and the sales manager is usually the first person to investigate complaints of unethical behavior. Field sales managers can provide a role model for salespeople by demonstrating ethical behavior in role plays during training or when conducting sales calls in the field. Sales managers should also avoid teaching high-pressure techniques and manipulative methods of selling.

RESPONDING TO UNETHICAL REQUESTS

Salespeople, however, may find themselves facing a sales manager who encourages them to engage in unethical behavior. When that situation occurs, a salesperson has several ways to avoid engaging in such behavior.[14] Perhaps the most obvious option is to find another job, but that is not always the best solution. If the organizational culture supports the unethical request, however, finding another job may be the only choice. Exhibit 16.5 lists choices available to the salesperson.

Another way to handle unethical requests is to blow the whistle, or report the behavior, if the salesperson has adequate evidence (if adequate evidence is not available, sometimes simply threatening to blow the whistle may work). If this course of action is followed, the salesperson must be ready to accept a perception of disloyalty, retaliation by the manager, or other consequences. However, if senior management is sincere in efforts to promote ethical behavior, steps should be taken to minimize those negative outcomes. If an open-door policy or an ethics review board exists, the salesperson can take the concern to higher levels for review. For example, the salesperson could say, I'm not sure that is appropriate. I'd like to get the opinion of the ethics review board. If the action is unethical, the sales manager may back down at that point. It is also possible that the manager will try to coerce the salesperson into not applying to the ethics review board; if that is the case, another course of action may prove to be a better choice.

Another strategy is to negotiate an alternative. This response requires the salesperson to identify an alternative course of action with a high probability of success. For example, if a sales manager tells the salesperson to offer a prospect a bribe, the salesperson should be prepared to prove that a price reduction would be just as effective. A similar tactic is to simply ignore the request.

Exhibit 16.5

Strategies for Handling Unethical Requests from a Manager

- Leave the organization or ask for a transfer.
- Negotiate an alternative course of action.
- Blow the whistle, internally or externally.
- Threaten to blow the whistle.
- Appeal to a higher authority, such as an ethics officer or ethics review board, or a senior executive if ethics offices do not exist.
- Agree to the demand but fail to carry it out.
- Refuse to comply with the request.
- Ignore the request.

The salesperson may say to the manager that the request was carried out, when in fact it was not; the potential problem with this approach is that the salesperson has admitted to carrying out an unethical act (even though she or he did not), which can lead to future problems. Finally, the salesperson can simply deny the request. Denial can be a dangerous action in that it opens the salesperson to possible retaliation, particularly retaliation that is not obviously linked to the denial, such as denying access to training or reducing the size of the salesperson's territory.

thinking **it** through | Is it ethical to lie to your manager and say that you will engage in the unethical behavior that your manager demanded when you know you won't? Is all fair when you are combating a request to engage in unethical behavior?

The salesperson's choice of action will depend on how much proof is available, what alternative actions to the unethical action exist, and the type of relationship with the manager. Other factors to consider include the ethical climate of the organization and whether an open-door policy exists. The salesperson, however, is always in control of his or her behavior and should never rationalize a behavior by placing responsibility on the sales manager.

SALESPEOPLE AS PARTNERS

Many types of salespeople exist, including telemarketing representatives, field salespeople, product specialists, and account specialists. Often there is some overlap in responsibilities; when overlap occurs, companies should have policies that facilitate serving the customer.

GEOGRAPHIC SALESPEOPLE

Most sales departments are organized geographically. A **geographic salesperson** is assigned a specific geographic territory in which to sell the company's products and services. Companies often combine geographic territories into larger branches, zones, or regions. For example, Eli Lilly has geographic regions that include 50 or more salespeople. Each Lilly salesperson has responsibility for a specific geographic area. For example, one rep may call on physicians in a portion of Dallas, using zip code boundaries to determine the territory; that rep may have all physicians in zip codes 75212, 75213, 75218, 75239, 75240, and 75252. Geographic salespeople may also work with account managers, product specialists, inside salespeople, and other members of the company's sales team.

ACCOUNT SALESPEOPLE

Companies may organize salespeople by account in several ways. The most extreme example is to give a salesperson the responsibility to sell to only one company but at every location of that company in the country or the world. In another common form of specialization, some salespeople develop new accounts while others maintain existing accounts. Developing new accounts requires different skills than maintaining an already sold account. One RCA radio communications division uses field salespeople to develop new accounts and a telemarketing sales force to maintain the accounts. The field salespeople must identify prospects from noncustomers and sell the product. Once the RCA product has been installed, the account becomes the responsibility of the telemarketing sales force.

Similar customers often have similar needs, whereas different types of customers may have very different needs for the same product. In such cases salespeople may specialize in calling on only one or a few customer types, although they sell the same products. NCR has different sales forces calling on manufacturing companies, retailers, and financial companies. Andritz, an international heavy machinery company, has salespeople who sell only to paper producers and other salespeople who sell only to wastewater treatment plants, even though the same product is being sold. Some Procter & Gamble salespeople call on central buying offices for grocery store chains; others call on food wholesalers.

Companies also divide their customers on the basis of size. Large customers, sometimes called **key accounts,** may have a salesperson assigned only to that account; in some cases a small sales force is assigned to one large account. In some firms one company executive coordinates all the salespeople who call on an account throughout the nation or the world. These executives are called **national account managers (NAMs)** or **strategic account managers (SAMs).** These account managers are more than salespeople; they are business executives. Carlson Hotels created a position for national account managers, then trained them on consultative selling so that needs would be paramount rather than price. Now companies like DaimlerChrysler consider Carlson to be a partner, not just a vendor.[15]

Strategic account managers manage large teams of salespeople. Atrion, for example, is a relatively small provider of telephone equipment and services competing against the likes of AT&T, Nokia, and others. Using a team approach, the company responded to a request for proposals from Security Lock for a new telephone switch. Unlike competitors, Atrion's team of salespeople and engineers took the time to understand Security Lock's needs. "What separated Atrion from every other company was that they weren't just interested in selling us a system. They came in and wanted to learn our business first," said Barry Silver, Security Lock's director of information technology. "They took two to three times as long with us as the others. They went way over and above the standard questions about how many users and locations we had." The result was a much larger sale of the telephone switch, a local area network, and a wide-area network.[16]

The local geographic rep's responsibility may involve coordinating delivery with the local customer. This coordination may also require customer training on the product or working with a local store manager to set up displays, plan inventories, and so on. Local reps should also look for sales opportunities in the customer's location and provide this information to the SAM. They often become the eyes and ears of the SAM and provide early notice of opportunities or threats in the account, just as a service rep does for the geographic rep. Hewlett-Packard's enterprise systems group, for example, revamped its compensation to include division profit as one performance outcome for all salespeople. This change was to encourage all salespeople, local and strategic, to work together.[17] SAMs often report directly to the vice president of sales or to a director of global sales, as illustrated in Exhibit 16.6, but work with geographic reps.

As described in Chapter 7, a **house account** is handled by a sales or marketing executive in addition to that executive's regular duties, and no commission is paid on any sales from that account. House accounts are often key accounts, but not all key accounts are house accounts. The main difference is that house accounts have no "true" salesperson. Wal-Mart has negotiated to be a house account with some suppliers with the expectation that those suppliers will pass on to Wal-Mart what they do not have to pay in commission or salary. General Dynamics attempted the same strategy when buying, but abandoned the plan upon realizing that lower costs also meant reduced service.

Exhibit 16.6

SAMs in the Sales Force
Although SAMs and
geographic salespeople
have different immediate
managers, they still
work together. SAMs
coordinate the efforts of
geographic reps within
local buying offices of
global accounts.

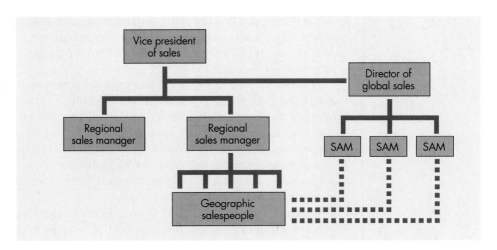

Somewhat different is the mega-account strategy used at Motorola. The top 20 international accounts are actually managed by Motorola's CEO, who works directly with the CEO in each account. These accounts are a form of house account, but the CEO has sales responsibility and sales goals to achieve.

PRODUCT SPECIALISTS

When companies have diverse products, their salespeople often specialize by types of products. Johnson & Johnson, which sells baby products, has two specialized sales forces: the disposable products sales force and the toiletries sales force. Hewlett-Packard has separate sales forces that specialize in selling computers, electronic test instruments, electronic components, medical test equipment, or analytical test equipment. Each sales force has its own regional, district, and area sales managers. Insuror's of Texas has salespeople who specialize in auto insurance, others who specialize in homeowner's insurance, and still others who specialize in medical and disability insurance. However, all of Insuror's salespeople operate under the same sales management structure. Regardless of the management structure, sometimes the technical knowledge requirements are so great that organizing territories by product makes sense.

In addition to having management responsibilities similar to those for geographic reps, product salespeople must coordinate their activities with those of salespeople from other divisions. Success can be greater for all involved when leads and customer information are shared. For example, a Hewlett-Packard test instrument salesperson may have a customer who is also a prospect for electronic components. Sharing that information with the electronic components rep can help build a relationship that can pay off with leads for test instruments.

INSIDE VERSUS OUTSIDE

Our discussion to this point has focused on outside salespeople, called **field salespeople**—that is, salespeople who sell at the customer's location. **Inside salespeople** (first identified in Chapter 1) sell at their own company's location. Inside salespeople may handle walk-in customers or be telemarketing salespeople, or they may handle both duties. For example, a plumbing supply distributor may sell entirely to plumbers and employ inside salespeople who sell to those plumbers who come into the distributorship to buy products.

As we discussed in Chapter 7, the job of some telemarketing is to provide leads for field salespeople. Other types of telemarketing salespeople include account managers, field support reps, and customer service reps. A telemarketer who is an account manager has the same responsibilities and duties a field salesperson does except that all business is conducted over the phone. ProBusiness, a division of ADP, conducts all of its business with account managers who cover accounts only by phone.[18]

A **field support rep** is a telemarketer who works with field salespeople and does more than prospect for leads. For example, field support reps at RPG Digital Imaging do Web research, make phone calls to gather information and develop contacts, and build rapport with prospects. The field support rep may also cross-sell, upgrade, or seek reorders. Together with RPG field salespeople, field support reps develop account strategies, handle customer concerns, and perform similar duties.[19] We discuss these representatives further when we discuss team selling strategies shortly.

Customer service reps (CSRs) are inbound salespeople who handle customer concerns. **Inbound** means they respond to telephone calls placed by customers, rather than **outbound,** which means the telemarketer makes the phone call (prospectors, account managers, and field support telemarketers are outbound reps). For example, if you call the 800 telephone number on the back of a tube of Crest toothpaste, you will speak with an inbound customer service rep. Many companies are now using customer service reps to identify cross-selling and upselling opportunities, either by sending leads to field salespeople or closing the sales themselves. The insurance industry, for example, is seeing a change in how CSRs are viewed, as they engage in more cross-selling.[20]

SALES TEAMS

A growing number of companies are adopting a team approach to sales.[21] This concept is being used by companies that recognize they can best build partnerships by empowering one person, the account manager, to represent the organization. In **team selling** a group of salespeople supports a single account. Each person on the team brings a different area of expertise or handles different responsibilities. As you see in Exhibit 16.7, each specialist can be called on to team up with the account managers.

Exhibit 16.7

Team Selling Organization
In team selling, product specialists work with account managers, who have total account responsibility. Product specialists are responsible for sales and service of only a limited portion of the product line and may work with several account managers.

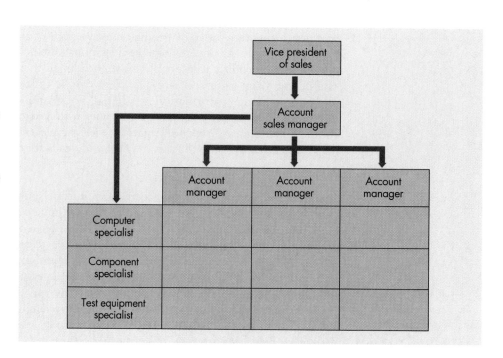

Many companies use teams to work with large accounts. There may be members of management, finance, manufacturing, and engineering on the account team.

Keith Brofsky/Getty Images/MGH-DIL

Before adopting team selling, companies may have had one salesperson for each product line. Xerox, for example, once had separate copier, duplicator, supplies, fax machine, printer, computer workstation, and communication network salespeople all calling on the same buyer. These reps would pass in customers' lobbies without recognizing one another. Customers grew tired of seeing as many as seven salespeople from Xerox. Now one account manager calls on the buyer and brings in product specialists as needed.

Xerox uses permanent teams, whereas Anderson Development Company, a chemical company, forms teams as needed. The company may involve engineers, scientists, quality control managers, and others in the process. In both cases, though, salespeople are responsible for coordinating the efforts of the specialists and determining who is brought in at what point in the sale.[22]

In an extension of team selling, **multilevel selling,** members at various levels of the sales organization call on their counterparts in the buying organization. (As charted in Exhibit 16.8, for example, the vice president of sales calls on the vice president of purchasing.) Multilevel selling can take place without a formal multilevel sales team if the account representative requests upper-level management's involvement in the sale. For example, you may ask your company's vice president of sales to call on the vice president of operations at a prospect's company to secure top-level support for your proposal.

Another type of sales team is made up of the field rep and the field support rep (see Exhibit 16.9). Some companies use one telemarketer for each field salesperson,

Exhibit 16.8

Forming Sales Teams for Multilevel Selling

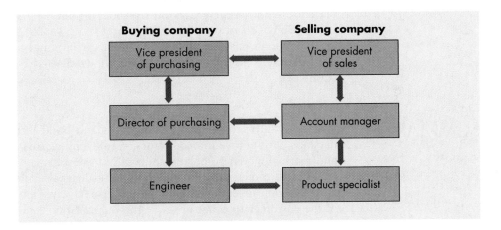

Exhibit 16.9

Inside/Outside Sales Team
Sometimes an inside rep or a field support rep works with accounts over the phone, and his or her partner, the field rep, makes calls at the customer's location.

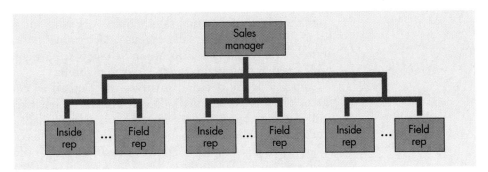

TECHNOLOGY AND TEAMWORK

Technology has greatly facilitated the growth of teams because it provides quick communication to anyone in the world. Technology enables communication among people in different time zones: Conversations can be conducted via e-mail over a period of days, with none of the parties required to be in the office or on the phone at the same time. Voice-over IP, or telephone conversations over the Internet, and products like Web-Ex® that allow for computer presentations to be made on any computer virtually anywhere have made conference calls inexpensive and productive. E-mail is used to keep the sales team informed, and companies are using instant messages and bulletin boards to communicate internally and with customers.

Jack Sands, president of Intrep, has some 60-plus salespeople working out of their homes across the country make phone calls to prospects. He can host meetings of the entire company by conference call, then use Web-Ex® to make a presentation to his sales team. Daily communication is possible via chat or instant messaging. When a customer asks a sales rep a question or poses an objection and the sales rep doesn't know how to respond, it can be posted on the chat, and another sales rep can provide input via instant message. Such quick response can enable the first salesperson to respond more quickly to the customer. Keeping the team in touch increases the salesperson's connections to the company and decreases the feelings of being out there all alone, even though they rarely see each other face-to-face.

whereas other companies have several salespeople working with a telemarketer. The telemarketer performs as many selling tasks as possible over the telephone. But when a sales call is needed at the customer's location, the field support rep makes the appointment for the field rep. Such is the case with IBM.com, a division of IBM that provides software and technology consulting. Good communication and joint planning are necessary to avoid overbooking the field rep, as well as to prevent duplication of effort.

Technology has played a key role in promoting good communication and joint planning. In Sales Technology 16.1 we discuss how technology influences teamwork.

SUMMARY

Successful salespeople manage resources and build internal partnerships—partnerships with people in order entry, credit, billing, and shipping, as well as sales and marketing. These partnerships allow salespeople to keep the promises they make to customers when someone else must carry out those promises.

Salespeople in learning organizations also have a responsibility to carry the voice of the customer to other areas of the organization. Successful learning organizations are more adept at adapting to changing customer needs and developing successful products when salespeople fulfill their role of speaking for the customer.

In the sales organization salespeople work with and for a sales executive and a field sales manager. The sales executive determines policy and maintains financial control over the sales organization. Salespeople participate in the development of forecasts that the sales executive uses in planning.

Another policy decision involves the method of compensation for the sales force. The four basic methods are straight salary, straight commission, bonus, and a combination plan. Straight commission plans provide strong financial incentive for salespeople but give the company little control over their activities. Salary plans give greater control to the company but offer less incentive for salespeople to work hard.

Sales executives are also responsible for creating a culture that supports ethical activities. Policies (such as open-door policies) can encourage salespeople to act ethically. Ethical review boards are also useful in reviewing ethics policies, investigating potential ethics violations, and counseling salespeople who have concerns about the ethics of possible actions. Sometimes, however, salespeople face unethical requests from their managers. If that occurs, salespeople can choose from several courses of actions, such as blowing the whistle or appealing to an ethics review board.

Partnerships must be built within the sales force, too. Some examples include team selling with product specialists, inside and outside teams, and multilevel selling.

KEY TERMS

activity quota
bonus
bottom-up forecasting
cap
combination plans
commission
commission base
commission rate
customer service rep
draw
ethics review board
field sales manager
field salespeople
field support rep
geographic salesperson
gross margin quota
house account
inbound

incentive pay
inside salespeople
internal partnerships
key accounts
multilevel selling
national account manager (NAM)
open-door policy
outbound
profit quota
quota
revenue quota
salary
sales quota
straight commission
straight salary
strategic account manager (SAM)
team selling

ETHICS PROBLEMS

1. It took you four months to find a job, and you were almost out of money when you finally landed your position. But today your boss asked you to do something unethical. You aren't sure what the corporate culture is yet because you are new at the company. How do you respond?

2. Your largest and most faithful customer wants its order shipped early. You could do that, but it would mean that a new, small account's order would be delayed. What will you do? In another situation you have an order from an account with the potential to be your biggest. But shipping tells you the product will be delayed one week, and credit refuses to allow the customer to pay COD on the first order, which is what the customer specifically requested. What will you do? What could you have done to prevent these problems?

QUESTIONS AND PROBLEMS

1. Discuss how economic conditions can influence salesperson compensation (review Selling Scenario 16.1, "Double the Price—Double the Income!"), as well as quotas. How might managers avoid problems due to economic cycles? What are the impacts on salespeople?

2. A company that rents office equipment to businesses pays its salespeople a commission equal to the first month's rent. However, if the customer cancels or fails to pay its bills, the commission is taken back, even if the customer cancels 10 months later. Is this policy fair? Why or why not? Why would the company have this plan?

3. Outside of sales, what is the most important area that salespeople work with inside the organization? Why is that the most important?

4. What is the role of the geographic salesperson in a national or strategic account? Assume that you are a NAM. What would you do to ensure the support of geographic reps? How would that support differ if you were a product specialist and worked in a team situation? As a product specialist, how would you get the support of the account manager?

5. Consider your own experience in group work at school. What makes groups effective? How can you translate what you have learned about group work into working as part of a sales team? What difference would there be in your answer if you were a global account manager versus a sales manager?

6. Some companies are using contact management software to observe salespeople's activities and to supervise salespeople more closely. Some salespeople, though, are not supervised closely—as long as they close enough sales, the company is satisfied. To what extent should salespeople be allowed to manage themselves? What risks do you take as a sales manager when you allow self-management among salespeople? How can you minimize those risks?

7. A sales manager gets one too many complaints about pushy salespeople, poor follow-up after the sale, and a lack of customer care, and wonders if the compensation plan is to blame. What can a manager do with compensation to promote greater customer service? Are there other ways to motivate good customer service?

8. Many wise people, such as Steven Covey, say to worry about the things you can control and not to worry about the things you can't control. What does that mean for a salesperson, when so many promises a salesperson makes are actually fulfilled by someone else?

9. An experienced salesperson argues against salaries: "I don't like subsidizing poor performers. If you paid us straight commission, we'd know who could make it and who couldn't. Sure, it may take awhile to get rid of the deadwood; but after that, sales would skyrocket!" Explain why you agree or disagree with this statement.

10. Assume you are only making about 75 percent of quota. How would you respond if you felt you were making as many calls as possible during the workweek, yet your manager demanded that you make more? The manager's reasoning is that if you make more, you will sell more. How would your response change if you were selling twice your sales quota?

CASE PROBLEMS

case **16.1**

Flow Master Controls

Flow Master Controls, a manufacturer of heating and air conditioning control systems, has the following compensation program. Reps are paid a $1,500 draw per month, with straight commission paid on a point system and a bonus based on quota performance. The Digital Master, Flow Master's newest product, does much the same thing as the older Flow Master, but 30 percent faster and with greater accuracy. The point system is shown in Table 1:

Table 1

Product	Points/Sale	Quota
Digital Master	50	4 (units per month)
Flow Master	40	5
Hydrameter	35	6
Quadrameter	25	8
Triplex Scanner	5	45

Reps are paid $5 per point, or $5,165 plus a bonus of $500, if they sell quota for each product, for a total of $5,675. The total number of points to reach each month is 1,035, but reps have to reach quota for each product to get the bonus. Tables 2–4 show the performance of the district:

Table 2

Product	Quota	Number Sold
Digital Master	40	22
Flow Master	50	78
Hydrameter	60	63
Quadrameter	80	82
Triplex Scanner	450	479

Table 3

Name	Digital Master	Flow Master	Hydrameter	Quadrameter	Triplex Scanner	Total Points
McMahon	3	11	7	9	52	1,320
Davis	5	6	7	9	53	1,255
Foreman	2	9	7	11	46	1,210
Wu	4	8	6	8	48	1,160
Sanchez	3	8	7	6	48	1,105
Gruber	2	8	6	7	48	1,045
Sakamoto	1	8	6	8	48	1,020
Flora	1	7	7	8	47	1,010
Ricks	1	7	5	8	45	930
Dixon	0	6	5	8	44	835
Total	22	78	63	82	479	

Table 4

Sales Call	Digital Master	Flow Master	Hydrameter	Quadrameter	Triplex Scanner	Total Points
Quota	20	20	10	10	10	70
Foreman	28	16	11	9	10	75
Gruber	24	24	8	8	7	71
District average	27.2	18.6	9.5	10.4	9.7	75.4

Questions

1. Evaluate the district's sales performance. Draw conclusions (Just where are we doing well? Doing poorly?) but don't fix anything yet. Justify your conclusions.
2. Compare the performance of Foreman and Gruber. What are some possible explanations for the poor Digital Master sales?
3. The VP of sales says the problem is a compensation plan problem. How would you fix it?
4. The company is planning to create a new position of product specialist. This salesperson will work with territory salespeople and will have a sales quota for Digital Master only. The product specialist salesperson will work with one sales team (8 to 12 salespeople) and, once a territory rep has identified a Digital Master prospect, the rep will bring in the product specialist. How should the compensation plan be adjusted? Why?
5. The VP of sales managed to get the product specialist idea approved by the CEO, even though the CEO argued that the salespeople were just too lazy to make the effort to sell the Digital Master. Lower the compensation on it to the territory reps, and everyone will sell the Flow Master at its lower price, the CEO says. The best way to get more Digital Master sales is to cut compensation on the Flow Master to 20 points. What do you think should be done? Why?

case **16.2**

Specialty Delivery

Amanda Castillo sat back and thought, "This is one too many." She had just hung up the phone with one of her customers, El Tapatio, who had just gotten another shipment of the wrong produce. Castillo represents Specialty Fruits & Vegetables, a company that sells imported fruits and vegetables to ethnic restaurants so that they can make authentic Mexican and Latin American dishes. Lately Anna Diaz, the new manager of shipping, seems to have everything in disarray.

"Freddie, we've got to do something," she complained to Freddie Duron, owner of Specialty Fruits & Vegetables. "I just got a call from El Tapatio and their delivery today is all wrong."

"Well, what are you going to do?" he replied.

"I'm going to take them enough to get through today, but they'll need a full delivery tomorrow."

"But what about the produce that's there now?" he asked. "You need to bring that back or we'll lose some of that produce!"

"Me? I can't bring it all back! It won't fit in my Honda!" she exclaimed. "Plus, I need to make sales calls, not deliveries! Besides, this is the second time this week that Anna has messed up one of my deliveries!"

"The problem must be with you, because none of the others have complained."

"That's because they've not had as big a mistake as the ones she's made with my accounts," Castillo shot back.

"Just get this taken care of," glowered Duron.

What should Castillo do? How should your answer differ if Castillo is paid straight commission versus salary plus commission or a straight salary?

ACT! ROLE PLAY

You've just gotten back from KB Homes, one of the fastest-growing home builders in the United States. KB Homes is considering ACT! for all its salespeople, and it has raised a number of questions that you need to answer. If successful, this sale could be as big as 1,000 units. But KB wants to know several things:

1. Can you create a kiosk that will allow customers who visit KB's model homes to input their own data directly into a file that will load with ACT!?

2. KB wants a license that includes all upgrades for three years, something that ACT! hasn't done. Company policy is that customers pay for upgrades (they don't pay for patches or fixes to bugs).

3. KB wants permission to send a rep to ACT!'s corporate headquarters to make a presentation to all ACT! employees about KB Homes. Employees who work in the field will be mailed a DVD presentation about KB Homes.

Each student will take turns playing the salesperson. The first question has to be addressed by the chief engineer. The second has to be addressed by the legal department. The final question has to be solved by the chief operations officer. If there are three people in a group, take turns observing. Your instructor will provide you with sheets for your role as one of the other ACT! managers.

ADDITIONAL REFERENCES

Deeter-Schmelz, Dawn R., and Rosemary P. Ramsey. "An Investigation of Team Information Processing in Service Teams: Exploring the Link between Teams and Customers." *Journal of the Academy of Marketing Science* 31 (Fall 2003), pp. 409–24.

Fang, Eric; Robert W. Palmatier; and Kenneth R. Evans. "Goal-Setting Paradoxes? Trade-Offs between Working Hard and Working Smart: The United States versus China." *Journal of the Academy of Marketing Science* 32 (Spring 2004), pp. 188–203.

Homburg, Christian; John P. Workman; and Ove Jensen. "A Configurational Perspective on Key Account Management." *Journal of Marketing* 66, April 2002, pp. 38–61.

Joshi, Ashwin W., and Sheila Randall. "The Indirect Effects of Organizational Controls on Salesperson Performance and Customer Orientation." *Journal of Business Research* 54 (2001), pp. 1–9.

Kivetz, Ran. "The Effects of Effort and Intrinsic Motivation on Risky Choice." *Marketing Science* 22 (2003), pp. 477–502.

Marshall, Greg W.; Felicia G. Lassk; and William C. Moncrief. "Salesperson Job Involvement: Do Demographic, Job Situational, and Market Variables Matter?" *Journal of Business & Industrial Marketing* 19 (2004), pp. 337–49.

Pullig, Chris; James G. Maxham III; and Joseph F. Hair Jr. "Salesforce Automation Systems: An Exploratory Examination of Organizational Factors Associated with Effec-

tive Implementation and Salesforce Productivity." *Journal of Business Research* 55 (2002), pp. 410–15.

Schultz, Roberta J., and Kenneth R. Evans. "Strategic Collaborative Communication by Key Account Representatives." *Journal of Personal Selling & Sales Management* 22 (Winter 2002), pp. 23–31.

Schwepker, Charles H. Jr., and David J. Good, "Marketing Control and Sales Force Customer Orientation." *Journal of Personal Selling & Sales Management* 24 (Summer 2004), pp. 167–79.

Schwepker, Charles H. Jr., and David J. Good. "Understanding Sales Quotas: An Exploratory Investigation of the Consequences of Failure." *The Journal of Business & Industrial Marketing* 19 (2004), pp. 39–52.

Smaros, Johanna, and Markus Hellstrom. "Using the Assortment Forecasting Method to Enable Sales Force Involvement in Forecasting: A Case Study." *International Journal of Physical Distribution & Logistics Management* 34 (2004), pp. 140–54.

Tremblay, Michael; Jerome Cote; and David B. Balkin. "Explaining Sales Pay Strategy Using Agency." *Transaction Cost and Resource Dependence Theories* 40 (November 2003), pp. 1651–64.

Workman, John P.; Christian Homburg; and Ove Jensen. "Intraorganizational Determinants of Key Account Management Effectiveness." *Journal of the Academy of Marketing Science* 31 (Winter 2003), pp. 3–22.

MANAGING YOUR CAREER

chapter **17**

part **4**

SOME QUESTIONS ANSWERED IN THIS CHAPTER . . .

- Which entry-level jobs are available to new college graduates?

- Where do I find these jobs?

- How should I go about getting interviews, and what should I do when I have an interview?

- Which selection procedures besides interviews might I go through?

- Which career paths are available in sales?

- How can I prepare myself for a promotion into management?

PROFILE

College is a time to dream, to wonder about the future and your role in it. As a sophomore in college at State University of New York at Brockport, I had four solid years of retail experience on my hands. My success stemmed from taking ownership of my sales approach and product, which led me to believe I would be a great outside sales representative.

I dreamed of being successful, but I also knew I had to prepare for success. That meant adding business-oriented activities to my résumé, so I became vice president of the Marketing Club and was the first to raise my hand when my Sales Management Professor, Dr. Jeffrey Strieter, needed a research assistant. He became my mentor and shared with me that the best jobs out of college are sales positions.

I took a new course called Business Careers, which requires students to dress professionally, write résumés and cover letters, conduct career research, and attend job fairs. In preparation for the job fair, I worked with several professors to revise the final copy of my résumé. I focused on meeting the decision makers who would help me choose a sales position that would best suit me. When I came across a Paychex, Inc., recruiter, he stood out from the rest. His positive energy and enthusiasm for sales and opportunity informed me of the genuine corporate culture for which this company has a reputation.

I received many calls for interviews after the job fair and went on three. Before any interviews, I researched the company to learn about the opportunities available within the company. Paychex, Inc., required math tests, group setting interviews, single interviews, and interviews over the phone. When asked what motivates me, I responded, "My own personal success: setting a goal for my success and obtaining it." The entry-level position involved telemarketing at one of the local offices for one year, and then I could pursue a promotion anywhere in the country if I exceeded my sales quotas. I always wanted to move out of New York, so I knew this could be an exciting opportunity. A day after my college graduation and four interviews later, I was offered a position as a telemarketing sales representative booking appointments for outside sales reps.

I spent one year working in Rochester, New York, dialing the phones every day to seek potential clients to meet with a field representative to present our payroll services. In the meantime, I researched all cities across the country and wanted to find my ideal place to live and work. Because of the beautiful beach climate and growing business, I made it a goal to pursue an outside sales position in San Diego, California. It was a challenge to differentiate myself from other candidates across the country, especially because the sales office in San Diego had never promoted from my department. I was asked to push for very high numbers. I interviewed over the phone with multiple managers in San Diego, and they wanted to make certain of my interest in San Diego while also trying to sense whether I would be a good fit for the office. During the interviewing process, I was always persistent in order to get what I wanted. I also networked with the outside field reps in San Diego to get the word out that I was interested and how successful I would be. I used an online roommate finder to make sure I had someone to live with when I finally got the promotion. By the end of the summer, I received the phone call from the Southern California manager that I had the job. It required two weeks of sales school and passing an exam before I could fly to my new home in San Diego for the first time.

I have now been living in San Diego for the past eight months and living my dream. With preparation, hard work, and opportunity, dreams do come true.

Visit us on the Web at www.paychex.com

"The best jobs out of college are sales positions."

Amy Mancini, Paychex, Inc.

Landing that first career position is an exciting moment! However, the job search is just the first task in managing your career. Like the chess player who is thinking two or three moves ahead, you too must think about subsequent opportunities. Also like the chess player, you must maintain some flexibility so that you do not checkmate your career if one strategy does not work.

Sales is a great place to begin a career. Just ask Jeffrey Immelt, CEO of General Electric. Immelt was competing with two other executives for the top spot when Jack Welch announced his retirement. Analysts and insiders alike say it was Immelt's sales experience and long history with customers that made him the top choice.[1] Because salespeople must represent the entire company, they learn about many aspects of the business and get to know people in various parts of the company. All of this knowledge can be put to use later in a career.

OPPORTUNITIES IN SELLING

Selling offers many opportunities. Over 5 million people are engaged in nonretail sales, with growth of over 12 percent expected in the next decade.[2] This fast-paced growth bodes well for marketing students because most marketing careers begin in sales. Growth is especially strong in health care and pharmaceuticals, real estate, manufacturing, and office equipment and services.[3]

Corporate executives clearly recognize the importance of selling experience in any marketing career, as evidenced by people like Jeffrey Immelt. Many people have also found career satisfaction by staying in sales throughout their working lives.

Whether the career is sales or any other field, similar questions apply when searching for a job. In this chapter the focus is on the search for a sales position and how to land the first job. We examine how companies make hiring decisions and offer tips on how to build selling and management skills while managing a career.

MAKING A GOOD MATCH

The keys to being successful and happy lie in finding a good match between what you need and desire in a position and the positions companies offer.[4] The first step, then, is to understand yourself, what you need, and what you have to offer. Then you must consider what each company needs and what each has to offer. As Exhibit 17.1 illustrates, a good match means that your needs are satisfied by what the company offers and that what you offer satisfies the company's needs.

UNDERSTANDING YOURSELF

Shakespeare said, "To thine own self be true"; but to be true to yourself, you must know who you are, what you need, and what you can offer others.[5] Knowing these things about yourself requires substantial self-examination. We will pose some questions that can help you follow Shakespeare's suggestion.

Understanding Your Needs

The first step in making a good match between what you have to offer and a company's position is to determine what you need. Important questions to consider include the following:

1. *Structure:* Can you work well when assignments are ambiguous, or do you need a lot of instruction? Do you need deadlines that others set, or do you

Exhibit 17.1

A Good Match between Salesperson and Company

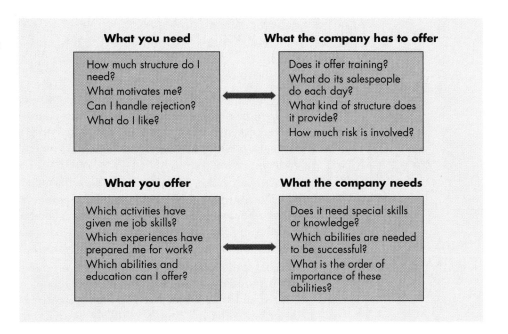

What you need

How much structure do I need?

What motivates me?

Can I handle rejection?

What do I like?

What the company has to offer

Does it offer training?

What do its salespeople do each day?

What kind of structure does it provide?

How much risk is involved?

What you offer

Which activities have given me job skills?

Which experiences have prepared me for work?

Which abilities and education can I offer?

What the company needs

Does it need special skills or knowledge?

Which abilities are needed to be successful?

What is the order of importance of these abilities?

set your own deadlines? If you are uncomfortable when left on your own, you may need structure in your work life. Many sales positions, such as missionary and trade sales, are in a structured environment with well-defined procedures and routines. Other positions require the salesperson to operate with little guidance or structure.

2. *Motivation:* Will financial incentives, personal recognition, or simply job satisfaction get you going? Probably it will be some combination of the three, but try to determine the relative value of each to you. Then you can weigh compensation plans, recognition programs, and other factors when considering which sales position is right for you. You may want to review the section on compensation plan types in Chapter 16 to aid in determining which plan best suits your needs.

Many companies, such as Konica-Minolta, reward top sales performers every year with an exotic trip.

Caroline von Tuempling/Iconica/Getty Images

3. *Stress and rejection:* How much stress can you handle? Are you a risk taker, or do you prefer more secure activities? What do you do when faced with stress? With rejection? These are important questions in understanding what you need from a sales position. For example, capital equipment sales jobs can be high-stress positions because sales are few and far between. Other jobs may require you to wade through many rejections before landing a sale. If you thrive on that kind of challenge, the rewards can be gratifying. Some sales positions, though, involve working only with current customers, and salespeople incur little outright rejection. Every grocery store, for example, will carry at least some Procter & Gamble products.

4. *Interest:* What do you find interesting? Mechanical or technical topics? Merchandising? Art or fashion? You cannot sell something that bores you. You would just bore and annoy the customer.

Understanding What You Have to Offer

Other resources that can help you understand the person you are may be available through your college's placement center. You must also take inventory of what you bring to the job:

1. *Skills:* What activities and experiences taught you certain skills? What did you learn from those experiences and your education that you can apply to a career? Keep in mind that it is not the activities in which you participated that matter to hiring companies; it is what you learned by participating that counts.

2. *Knowledge:* College has provided you with many areas of knowledge, but you have also probably learned much by participating in hobbies and other interests. For example, you may have special computer knowledge that would be useful in selling software, or you may have participated in a particular sport that makes you well suited to sell equipment to sporting goods stores.

3. *Qualities and traits:* Every person has a unique personality. What part of your personality adds value for your potential employer? Are you detail oriented and systematic? Are you highly creative? In other words, what can you bring to the job that is uniquely you? Exhibit 17.2 lists traits of top salespeople, according to a study conducted for *Sales & Marketing Management* magazine.

Your answers to these questions will generate a list of what you have to offer companies. Then, when you are in an interview, you can present features that make you a desirable candidate.

When to Ask These Questions

Unfortunately, many students wait until just before graduation before seriously considering what type of career they desire. According to one career services director, students who start a search while in school will find a job three times faster than those who start after graduation. Although it is not always realistic to expect every student to map out a life plan prior to senior year, asking questions such as these as early as possible can guide a student to better course selection, better use of learning opportunities, and, ultimately, a better career decision. Then the student can begin actively searching for the job at the beginning of the senior year so that graduation signals the beginning of a career, not a career search.

Consider too what type of career and what type of difference you want to make. Building Partnerships 17.1 describes the difference you can make as a salesperson.

UNDERSTANDING THE COMPANY

While developing a good feel for who you are and what you have to offer companies, you should also explore what is available and which companies offer positions that appeal to you. As you can see in Exhibit 17.3, numerous sources provide information regarding positions and growth opportunities in various industries and specific companies. Don't forget, though, that the best

Exhibit 17.2
Traits of Top Salespeople

1. Strong ego: able to handle rejection with healthy self-esteem.
2. Sense of urgency: getting it done now.
3. Ego driven: obsessive about being successful.
4. Assertive: being firm without being aggressive (see the discussion in Chapter 12).
5. Willing to take risks: willing to innovate.
6. Sociable: good at building relationships.
7. Abstract reasoner: able to handle complex selling situations and ideas.
8. Skeptical: a healthy bit of suspicion, not counting on commission until the sale is really a sale.
9. Creative: able to set oneself apart from the competition.
10. Empathic: able to place oneself in the buyer's shoes.

Source: Adapted from Erika Rasmusson, "The Ten Traits of Top Salespeople," *Sales & Marketing Management,* August 1999, pp. 34–37.

IN THE PRESENCE OF THE TRULY GREAT

In life, we rarely come in contact with someone who is truly great. Pat Tillman, the NFL player who walked away to serve in the U.S. Army, was one of those people. So was Christopher Reeve. To that list, add Tom McCart.

To be sure, all he did was sell air conditioning. Yet in 1986, his first year in the business, he sold over $1 million *one house at a time*. It isn't just the sales record, though, that makes him unusual. Two things cause McCart to stand out—what he had to overcome, time after time, and the way he made his records.

Born into a poor family, his first home had a dirt floor and no indoor plumbing. He overcame polio as a child, but dropped out of school. After a career in the Army, he applied for the sales job only so he could get unemployment. To his surprise, he was hired. In that first year, he was given 337 leads of which he closed 303!

Was it hard-selling manipulation that got him the sales, or the fact that he knew what it was like to live without air conditioning? With a philosophy of "Stop selling and help people to buy," it is no wonder that he was able to find buyers when others struggled to cover quota.

But he didn't just make sales: he built people. Even though he was on straight commission, he volunteered to tutor five other salespeople. He provided free on-site consulting to companies who could not afford consulting but needed it. Through articles and free seminars at trade shows, he taught the industry how to serve customers more effectively.

Then tragedy struck. Not once, but three times. A serious car accident took him out of the field for nearly a year. Then he was diagnosed with Lou Gehrig's disease. In 2003, came another diagnosis, this time cancer. Most people would quit, but not the truly great. In McCart's case, he continued to train other salespeople to sell by that same credo, even long after he spent his days virtually paralyzed, strapped into a wheelchair.

Facing challenges that would make most people give up, McCart had this to offer. "What makes my situation easy to accept is that we were born to die. I had polio as a child. I was never supposed to walk. I walked for 50 years. It's not how many times you get knocked down. It's how many times you're willing to get up." Tom McCart's legacy is not in the sales numbers he posted, but in the number of people's lives made better because he was their salesperson or their trainer. Truly, one of the great.

To learn more about Tom McCart, visit http://www.nosecrets.com/abouttom.htm.

Sources: Greer, Charlie, "Air Conditioning, Heating & Refrigeration News." 222 (May 31, 2004), pp. 22–24; Greer, Charlie, personal correspondence, used by permission.

Exhibit 17.3
Sources of Job Information

Source	Example
Government	U.S. Industrial Outlook
Research services	Standard & Poor's Industry Surveys
Industry associations	Christian Booksellers' Association
Professional organizations	Sales and Marketing Executives International
General magazines	*BusinessWeek, Money*
Trade magazines	*Sales & Marketing Management, Selling Power*
Placement services	University placement office; nonfee private agencies such as Personnel One
Personal sources	Friends, relatives, industry association executives at trade shows, recruiters at career fairs
Web sites	marketingjobs.com

sources are personal; be sure to talk over job opportunities with your friends, friends of your parents, and your professors. Use term papers as an excuse to call professionals in a field that interests you. Join trade and professional associations now—these offer great networking opportunities. As someone who has studied sales, you should use your prospecting skills, too. Let's discuss how to evaluate what you learn about the companies and their positions.

What the Company Has to Offer

When you meet a salesperson or sales manager, you should ask about compensation and recognition programs, training, career opportunities, and other information to determine whether the company truly offers benefits to satisfy your needs. You should also explore daily activities of the salesperson, likes and dislikes about the job, and what that person thinks it takes to succeed. This information will help you determine whether a match exists.

For example, if you need structure, you should look for a sales position in which your day is structured for you. Any industry that relies on repeated sales calls to the same accounts is likely to be highly structured. Industries with a structured sales day include consumer packaged goods sales (Procter & Gamble, Quaker Oats, and the like) and pharmaceutical sales (Novartis, Eli Lilly Company, and so forth). Even these sales positions, however, offer some flexibility and independence. Office and industrial equipment sales provide much less structure when the emphasis is on getting new accounts.

Knowing your comfort level with risk and your need for incentives should help you pick a company with a compensation program that is right for you. If you need the security of a salary, look for companies in trade sales, equipment sales, pharmaceuticals, or consumer packaged goods. But if you like the risk of straight commission, which can often be matched with greater financial rewards for success, explore careers in areas such as convention sales, financial services, and other straight-commission jobs.

Other factors to consider include the size of the company and its promotion policies, particularly if the company is foreign. Many companies have a "promote from within" policy, which means that whenever possible they fill positions with people who already are employees. One example is Worldwide Express, a company that sells for DHL in the United States (DHL is a shipping and overnight express company based in Belgium). Alex BeMent was promoted after working at Worldwide Express for only six months to managing three salespeople, with responsibility for growing the office to five or more. Such policies are attractive if you seek career growth into management. A company that is foreign owned, however, may prefer to staff certain positions with people from its home country.

Take advantage of interests you already have. If you are intrigued by medical science, seek a medical sales position. If merchandising excites you, a position selling to the trade would be appropriate. A bar of soap by itself is not exciting, but helping customers find ways to market that bar of soap is.

What the Company Needs

At this point in your job search, you may have narrowed your selection to a group of industries or companies. At a minimum you have a good picture of what a company should offer to land you as a salesperson. The next step is to find a company that needs you. Finding out what a company needs will require some research, but you will find this step fun and rewarding.

In general, companies look for three qualities in salespeople: good communication skills, self-motivation, and a positive and enthusiastic attitude.[6] Al Lynch,

Career fairs, such as this one at a hotel during spring break, can be a great opportunity to find internships or permanent sales positions.

Daytona Beach News-Journal/Roger Simms/AP Wide World

former CEO of JCPenney International, adds to this list quantitative skills and an ability to ask the right questions.

Companies in certain industries may also desire related technical skills or knowledge, such as medical knowledge for the field of pharmaceutical sales or insurance knowledge to enter that field. All companies need salespeople with computer skills because the computer is increasingly being used to track and manage accounts, communicate internally, and perform other important activities. If you want to enter a field requiring specialized knowledge or skills, now is the time to begin acquiring that knowledge. Not only will you already have the knowledge when you begin to search for a position; you will also have demonstrated self-motivation and the right kind of attitude by taking on the task of acquiring that knowledge and skill.

THE RECRUITING PROCESS

Early in this book we discussed the buying process so that you would understand the purchase decision buyers make. Now we will look at the recruiting process so that you will understand how companies will view you as a candidate for a sales job or any other position.

SELECTING SALESPEOPLE

In recent years companies have made considerable progress in screening and selecting salespeople. Most have discarded the myth that there is a "sales type" who will be successful selling anything to anybody. Instead, they seek people who match the requirements of a specific position, using various methods to gain information and determine whether a good match will be made.

APPLICANT INFORMATION SOURCES

To determine whether a match exists between the job requirements and the applicant's abilities, information about the applicant must be collected. Companies use five important sources of information: application forms, references, tests, personal interviews, and assessment centers. We describe these five sources from the perspective of the company so you can understand how they are used to make hiring decisions. We also explain how you should use these sources of information so you can present yourself accurately and positively.

The **application form** is a preprinted form that the candidate completes. You have probably already filled these out for part-time jobs. The form should include factual questions concerning the profile the company established for the position. Responses on the form are also useful for structuring the personal interview. Résumés provide much of the same information application forms do but are often too individualized for easy comparison. For this and other reasons, companies must supplement résumés with an application form (we discuss résumés in greater detail later in this chapter).

Contacting **references,** or people who know the applicant, is a good way to validate information on the application form. References can also supplement the information with personal observations. The most frequently contacted references are former employers. Other references are coworkers, leaders of social or religious organizations, and professors. You should be aware that some organizations try to develop relationships with faculty so they can receive leads on excellent candidates before visiting the placement office. Professors recommend students who have demonstrated the qualities the recruiting companies desire.

When you select references, keep in mind that companies want references that can validate information about you. Choose references that provide different information, such as one character reference, one educational reference, and one work-related reference.

Experienced sales managers expect to hear favorable comments from an applicant's references. More useful information may be contained in unusual comments, gestures, faint praise, or hesitant responses that may indicate a problem. Before you offer someone's name as a reference, ask that person for permission. At that time you should be able to tell whether the person is willing to give you a good recommendation.

Intelligence, ability, personality, and interest **tests** provide information about a potential salesperson that cannot be obtained readily from other sources. Tests can also correct misjudgments made by sales managers who tend to act on "gut feelings." Although tests were widely criticized in the early 1980s for failing to predict success better than other sources did, recent studies indicate that assessment tests are growing in popularity once more, in part because of their improved predictive power.[7] The new assessment tests, however, are more accurate when they are specifically related to sales and the situations potential salespeople may encounter.

Several types of tests may be given. H.R. Challey Inc. designs tests to determine a person's psychological aptitude for different sales situations. BSRP offers a test that measures a salesperson's call reluctance, or fear of initiating contact. IBM requires sales candidates to demonstrate technical aptitude through a test, while Skyline requires a test that indicates the individual's ability to handle details. Like many companies, KB Homes requires candidates to pass a math test because of the importance of calculating price correctly. Still other tests indicate a candidate's ethical nature. Companies may require candidates to take tests in all of these categories.

The important point to remember about tests is to remain relaxed. If the test is a valid selection tool, you should be happy with the outcome no matter what it is. If you believe the test is not valid—that is, does not predict your ability to succeed in that job—you may want to present your feelings to the recruiter. Be prepared to back up your line of reasoning with facts and experiences that illustrate you are a good candidate for the position.

Interviews, or personal interaction between recruiter and candidate, are an important source of information for recruiters. Companies now give more attention to conducting multiple interviews in the selection process because sometimes candidates show only slight differences. Multiple interviews can improve a recruiter's chances of observing the differences and selecting the best candidate. We cover interviews in more detail later in the chapter.

Companies sometimes evaluate candidates at centrally located **assessment centers.** In addition to being used for testing and personal interviews, these locations may simulate portions of the job. Simulating the job serves two purposes. First, the simulation lets managers see candidates respond to a joblike situation. Second, candidates can experience the job and determine whether it fits them. For example, Merrill Lynch sometimes places broker candidates in an office and simulates two hours of customer telephone calls. As many as half of the candidates may then decide that being a stockbroker is not right for them, and Merrill Lynch can also evaluate the candidates' abilities in a lifelike setting.

Companies use many sources of information in making a hiring decision, perhaps even asking for a copy of a videotaped presentation you may make for this class. These sources are actually selling opportunities for you. You can present yourself and learn about the job at the same time, continuing your evaluation of the match.

SELLING YOUR CAPABILITIES

With an understanding of the recruiting process from the company's point of view, you can create a presentation that sells your capabilities and proves you have the skills and knowledge the company wants. Preparing the résumé, gaining an interview, and presenting your capabilities in the interview are important activities that require sound planning to present yourself effectively.

PREPARING THE RÉSUMÉ

The résumé is the brochure in your marketing plan. As such, it needs to tell the recruiter why you should be hired. Physician Sales and Service (PSS), for example, gets 300 resumes for sales positions each month; having a résumé that stands out from that crowd is difficult. There are, however, a lot of companies like PSS that prefer to hire inexperienced salespeople, so don't let a lack of experience create anxiety or lead to misrepresentation on your résumé.[8] Whether you choose the conventional style or the functional style of résumé, the purpose is to sell your skills and experience.

Conventional Résumés

Conventional résumés are a form of life history, organized by type of experience. The three categories of experience most often used are education, work, and activities/hobbies (see the example in Exhibit 17.4). Although it is easy to create conventional résumés, it is also easy to fail to emphasize important points. To avoid making this mistake, follow this simple procedure:

- List education, work experience, and activities.
- Write out what you gained in each experience that will help you prove you have the desired qualities.
- Emphasize what you learned and that you have the desired qualities under each heading.

For example, the résumé in Exhibit 17.4 is designed for a student interested in a sales career. Note how skills gained in this class are emphasized in addition to GPA and major. The candidate has also chosen to focus on customer service skills gained as a camp counselor, a job that a recruiter would otherwise overlook. Rather than just listing herself as a member of the soccer team, the candidate highlights the leadership skills she gained as captain.

Functional Résumés

Functional résumés reverse the content and titles of the conventional résumé, organizing by what the candidate can do or has learned rather than by types of experience. As you can see in Exhibit 17.5, an advantage of this type of résumé is that it highlights more forcefully what the candidate can do.

When preparing a functional résumé, begin by listing the qualities you have that you think will help you get the job. Narrow this list to three or four qualities, and then list activities and experiences to prove that you have those skills and abilities. The qualities are the headings for the résumé; the activities and experiences show that you have those qualities. One difficulty with this type of résumé is that one past job may relate to several qualities. If that is the case, emphasize the activity within the job that provided you with the experience for each specific quality.

GAINING THE INTERVIEW

Students should begin examining different industries as early as possible, as we suggested earlier. As graduation looms closer and the time for serious job hunting arrives, your knowledge of the industries and companies that interest you will put

Exhibit 17.4
Conventional Résumé
Example

Cheryl McSwain

After June 1:
435 Wayward View, Apt. B
State College, PA 10303
203/555-1289

Present Address:
612 Homer
Aurora, CO 86475
804/555-9183

Career Objective: Sales in the telecommunications industry

Education:
Colorado University, Boulder, Colorado
Bachelor of Business Administration, June 2005
Marketing
GPA: 3.25 on 4.0 scale

Major Subjects: Other Subjects:
Personal Selling   Microcomputing
Sales Management   Local Area Networks Management
Industrial Marketing   Telecommunications

Emphasized selling and sales management in computing
and telecommunications. Learned SPIN, social styles, and
other adaptive selling techniques. Studied LANWORKS
and Novell network management.

Work Experience: Sales representative, *The Lariat* (CU campus newspaper)
Practiced sales skills in making cold calls
and selling advertising
Fall 2001 to present

Counselor, Camp Kanatcook
Learned customer service and leadership skills
Summers, 2002, 2003, 2004

Scholarships and Honors:
University Merit Scholar ($2,000/year, two years)
Top sales student, spring 2005
Dean's List, three semesters

Activities:
Member, Alpha Delta Pi Sorority
Rush chair, 2004
Motivated members to actively recruit; interviewed candidates
for selection
Homecoming float chair, 2002
Managed float building; sorority awarded second in float competition
Women's soccer team, four years
Captain, 2004–2005
Led team to conference championship, fall 2004

you a step ahead. You will also understand the process the company will go through in searching for a new salesperson.

Using Personal Contacts

More important, you have already begun to make personal contacts in those fields—contacts you can now use to gain interviews. The same salespeople and sales managers who gave you information before to help you with term projects will usually be happy to introduce you to the person in charge of recruiting. Contacts you made at job fairs and trade shows can also be helpful.

thinking **it** through

Many students feel uncomfortable asking for favors from people they barely know, such as asking an acquaintance to forward a resume to a decision maker or set up an interview. How can you overcome such feelings of discomfort? Why would someone want to help you find places to interview? What obligations do you have to people who provide you with the names of job contacts?

Exhibit 17.5
Functional Résumé
Example

Cheryl McSwain

After June 1:
435 Wayward View, Apt. B
State College, PA 10303
203/555-1289

Present Address:
612 Homer
Aurora, CO 86475
804/555-9183

Career Objective: Sales in the telecommunications industry

Sales and Customer Service Experience:
Studied SPIN and adaptive selling techniques in personal selling.
Sold advertising in *The Lariat*, campus newspaper. Responsibilities included
making cold calls, presenting advertising strategies, and closing sales.
Performed customer service tasks as camp counselor at Camp Kanatcook.
Served as the primary parent contact during drop-off and pick-up periods,
answering parent queries, resolving parental concerns, and handling similar
responsibilities.

Management and Leadership Experience:
Studied situational management in sales management.
Served as rush chair for sorority. Responsible for motivating members to
recruit new members and developed and implemented a sales training seminar
so members would present the sorority favorably within university guidelines.
Managed homecoming-float project. Sorority awarded second place in float
competition.
Captained the women's varsity soccer team to a conference championship.

Telecommunications Skills and Experience:
Studied LANWORKS and Novell network management in
telecommunications.
Designed, as a term project, a Novell-based LAN for a small
manufacturing business.
Purchased and installed a six-computer network in a family-owned
wholesaling business.

Scholarships and Honors:
University Merit Scholar ($2,000/year, two years)
Top sales student, spring 2005
Dean's List, three semesters

Using Employment Postings

Responding to Web postings or newspaper advertisements can also lead to job interviews. You will need to carefully interpret employment postings and then respond effectively to them.

All ads are designed to sell, and employment ads are no exception. But what sounds great may not be wonderful in reality. Here are some phrases often found in such ads and interpretations of them:[9]

Independent contractor: You will work on straight commission with no employee benefits. You will probably receive no training and little, if any, support.

Earn up to $___ (or *Unlimited income* or *Our top rep made $500,000 last year*): You need to know what the average person makes and what the average first-year earnings are, not what the top rep made or the upper limit. The job could still be desirable, but you need to find out what reality is before accepting a position.

Sales manager trainee: This is another title for sales representative. Don't be put off or overly encouraged by high-sounding titles.

The Internet is a great source of leads for jobs; however, recruiters report receiving hundreds, and sometimes, thousands of résumés for every job they post. If you really want a job with a particular company, approach it like a sales opportunity and use your prospecting and relationship building skills.

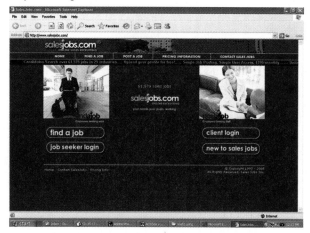

Courtesy SalesJobs.com

Bonuses paid weekly, Daily commissions, or *Weekly commissions:* These are high-pressure jobs and probably involve high-pressure sales.

Ten salespeople needed now!: That's because everyone quit. This company uses salespeople and then discards them.

You should look for two things in an ad: what the company needs and what it has to offer. The company should provide concrete information concerning training, compensation plan (although not necessarily the amount), amount of travel to expect, and type of product or service you will sell. You should also expect to find the qualifications the company desires, including experience and education. If you do not have the experience now, call and ask how to get it. Be specific: What companies should I pursue that will give me the experience you are looking for?

Responding to Postings

Many postings and ads will ask you to write or e-mail and may not list the company's name. A blind box number is given when the company name is not included in a newspaper ad; the box number is usually at the address of the newspaper. For example, the ad may say to send a résumé to Box 000, care of the *Dallas Morning News*. Don't be put off by the lack of company name; the posting or ad may be placed by a company such as IBM that would otherwise receive a large number of unqualified applicants. Companies use blind postings and blind box numbers for many legitimate reasons.

Many blind ads now ask you to e-mail your résumé. Similarly, when responding to Internet ads, like those on Monster.com, you may not know who the employer is. Do not let that put you off; however, if you already have a sales job and you are looking for a change, you may not want to reply to blind ads. One of our students did that; he was fired when it turned out the company in the ad was his own employer. Sales Technology 17.1 discusses additional considerations when using the Internet to find a job.

Writing the Cover Letter

When you write in response to a posting, you are writing a sales letter. Like any sales letter, it should focus on what you can do for the company, not what you expect from it. The letter should start with an attention getter. Here is one example:

> In today's economy, you need someone who can become productive quickly as a territory representative. Based on your posting at Monster.com, I believe that I am that person.

This attention getter is direct, focuses on a probable need, and refers to the posting. The probability of getting a response to this cover letter is far greater than if you simply said,

> Please consider me for the territory representative position you posted at Monster.com.

The attention getter tells why you should be considered.

The body of the letter should center on two or three reasons you should be hired. For example, if you have the qualities of self-motivation and leadership,

A MILLION GREAT JOBS—ONE LIFE!

Sometimes Internet job sites to a graduating college senior can be like a candy store to a little kid. So many opportunities, but you have only one nickel! While it is fun to dream about all of the opportunities, keep in mind that recruiters get hundreds, and sometimes a thousand, résumés for each posting.

Keeping the résumé simple is one way to get noticed. According to Eric Martinez, veteran sales recruiter working with sales candidates at Salesjobs.com, one mistake college students make is to put too much detail. "All they want to know is if you can sell." Highlight activities and jobs that included selling or related activities.

Don't just cut and paste that résumé into an online form, however. Special formatting for a resume may not come across properly when the recruiter looks at it online. The formatting may not come across properly unless saved as rich text.

Martinez also suggests writing a cover letter for each online posting. "At Salesjobs.com, probably 90 percent of all postings are made by the sales manager personally. That means your cover letter and your e-mail go directly to the person who will make the decision," says Martinez. He suggests saving your cover letter in the same document as the résumé. "Use the cover letter to show that you know something about the company and the industry."

E-mail addresses like *myvixen* and *partystupid* may be fine in college but not when you're looking for a job. "E-mail addresses should be professional—first name, last name, and a number are fine," notes Martinez. Although Martinez recognizes that many people apply for sales jobs, "It's the little things, like an e-mail address, that can help you get that dream job."

---

devote two paragraphs relating each to the position. Use your résumé as proof. For example:

> A territory representative position often requires self-motivation. As you can see from the attached résumé, I demonstrated self-motivation as a sales representative for the campus newspaper, as a volunteer for the local food bank, and as a member of the Dean's Honor Roll during two of the last four semesters.

The letter should close with a request for action. Ask for an interview and suggest times you are available. For example:

> Please call me to arrange an interview. My schedule allows me to meet with you on Tuesday or Thursday afternoon.

An alternative is to state that you will call:

> I will call you early next week to discuss my potential as a salesperson for XYZ Corporation.

No response does not necessarily mean you have been rejected; follow up with a phone call if you do not hear anything within a week. One former student got a job because he called to verify that the sales manager had received his résumé. She had never seen it but was impressed enough with the student's phone call to arrange an appointment. Sometimes e-mail is lost or delayed, and you would not want a company to miss out on the opportunity to hire you because of a computer glitch!

One hiring manager, Ryan Donovan with Text 100 Corp., points out a few mistakes he sees far too often. For example, when applicants apply by e-mail, they change their addresses so quickly that Donovan can't reply. To make it worse, these candidates provide e-mail as their only contact method. Another beef he has is attaching a résumé or other documents in a format he can't open.[10]

Exhibit 17.6

Frequently Asked Interview Questions

1. What are your long-range and short-range goals and objectives? When and why did you establish these goals, and how are you preparing yourself to achieve them?
2. What do you consider to be your greatest strengths and weaknesses?
3. Why did you choose the career for which you are preparing?
4. How do you think a friend or professor who knows you well would describe you?
5. Why should I hire you?
6. In what ways do you think you can make a contribution to our company?
7. Do you think your grades are a good indication of your academic achievement?
8. What major problem have you encountered, and how did you deal with it?
9. What do you know about our company? Why are you seeking a position with us?
10. If you were hiring a graduate for this position, what qualities would you look for?

THE INTERVIEW

Many students do not realize how much competition exists for the best entry-level sales positions, or perhaps they do not know what companies look for in new employees. Students often act as though they are shopping for a job. Job shoppers, however, are not seriously considered by recruiters, who are usually astute enough to quickly pick up on the student's lack of interest. If the job shopper does become interested, it is probably too late because the recruiter has already discounted this applicant. Like it or not, you are really competing for a job. As in any competition, success requires preparation and practice.

Preparing for the Interview

Students who know something about the company and its industry lead the competition. You have already looked for company and industry information in the library, in business reference books, and in periodicals. You visited the company's Web site. You have also interviewed the company's customers, salespeople, and sales managers. You can use this knowledge to demonstrate your self-motivation and positive attitude, two of the top three characteristics sales managers look for in sales candidates. You will find it easier to demonstrate the third top characteristic, communication skills, with the confidence you gain from proper preparation.

In addition to building knowledge of the "customer," you must plan your responses to the questions you will be asked. Exhibit 17.6 lists standard interview questions.

Scenario questions are popular with recruiters. These questions ask what the candidate would do in a certain situation involving actions of competitors (for example, What would you do if a customer told you something negative about your product that you knew to be untrue, and the customer's source of information was your competitor?). Such questions test ethics regarding competitors and the ability to handle a delicate situation. Scenario questions also test the candidate's response to rejection, ability to plan, and other characteristics. You can best prepare for these types of questions with this class and by placing yourself in the situations described in the cases and exercises in this book. You may also want to review the questions at the ends of the chapters.

The sales field has several unusual characteristics, such as travel, that influence the type of questions asked. For example, if significant travel is part of the position, you may be asked, Travel is an important part of this job, and you may be away from home about three nights per week. Would you be able and willing to travel as the job requires? However, some questions are illegal, and you do not have to answer them—such as What is your marital status? Do you plan to have a family? Will that affect your ability to travel? Exhibit 17.7 lists some questions that are illegal, as well as legal questions that you may have to answer.

What do you do when you face an illegal question? One thing you should do is report the incident to your school's career services personnel if the interview is taking place on campus or as a result of the campus career services center. But when actually asked the question, you have several choices. One is to inquire, "Why do you ask? Is that important?" You may find that it is a question asked by

Exhibit 17.7

Examples of Legal and Illegal Questions

Subject	Legal Questions	Illegal Questions
Name	Have you ever used another name?	What is your maiden name?
Residence	Where do you live?	Do you own or rent your home?
Birthplace or national origin	Can you, after employment, verify your right to work in the United States?	Where were you born? Where were your parents born?
Marital or family status	Statement of company policy regarding assignment of work of employees who are related. Statement of company policy concerning travel: Can you accept this policy?	With whom do you reside? Are you married? Do you plan a family?
Arrest or criminal record	Have you ever been convicted of a felony? (Such a question must be accompanied by a statement that a conviction will not necessarily disqualify the applicant.)	Have you ever been arrested?

Source: Baylor University Career Services Center.

an interviewer out of personal curiosity, and the interviewer may not have realized the question was inappropriate. Another response is to simply reply, "I'm sorry, I would prefer not to answer that question." If probed, you can state that you believe the question is not legal, but you will check with career services later; if the question is legal, you will answer it later. If the interviewer is simply ignorant, you will probably get an apology, and the interview will move on. Otherwise, you've identified a company where you may not wish to work. Your final option is, of course, to go ahead and answer the question.

At some point during the interview, the recruiter will ask whether you have any questions. In addition to the standard questions concerning pay, training, and benefits, you should prepare questions that are unlikely to have been answered already. For example, suppose your research has uncovered the fact that the company was recently awarded the Malcolm Baldrige Award for Quality; you might plan to ask what the company did to win that award.

You may also want to plan questions about the interviewer's career, how it got started, and what positions he or she has held. These questions work best when you are truly interested in the response; otherwise you might sound insincere. Answers to these questions can give you a personal insight into the company. Also, you may often find yourself working for the interviewer, so the answers to your questions may help you decide whether you like and can work with this person.

Other important subjects to ask about are career advancement opportunities, typical first-year responsibilities, and corporate personality. You also need to know how financially stable the company is, but you can find this information for public firms in the library. If the firm is privately owned, ask about its financial stability.

Finally, it may seem trivial, but shine your shoes! You are interviewing for a professional position, so look professional. Recruiters have told us about students showing up for an interview dressed in cut-off shorts and a T-shirt or looking hung over. Those interviews were over before they began. If you do not look the part now, an interviewer will not see you in the part.

During the Interview

The job interview is much like any other sales call. It includes an approach, needs identification, presentation, and gaining commitment. There are, however, several important differences because both parties are identifying needs and making presentations.

The Approach   Social amenities will begin the interview. You will not need the same type of attention getter that you would on a cold call. However, you may want to include an attention getter in your greeting. For example, use a compliment approach, such as "It must be very exciting to work for a Malcolm Baldrige award winner."

Needs Identification   One difference between sales calls and job interviews is that both parties have needs they have individually defined before the meeting (in a sales call, SPIN® helps you to assist the buyer in defining needs). A question such as "Are you willing to relocate?" is used not to define needs so much as to determine whether the company's needs will be met. You should prepare questions that will help you learn whether the company's offer will meet your needs.

Take notes during the interview, especially when asking about the company, so that you can evaluate whether your needs will be met. Carry a portfolio with extra résumés and blank paper and pen for note taking. You may want to ask, "Do you mind if I take notes? This information is important to me, and I don't want to forget anything."

Try to determine early whether your interviewer is a sales manager or a personnel manager. Personnel managers may have a difficult time telling you about the job itself, its daily activities, and so forth; they may be able to outline only things such as training and employee benefits. Sales managers, however, can tell you a lot about the job, perhaps to the point of describing the actual territory you will work in.

Personnel managers do not like being asked about salary; you will find that many people will advise you not to ask about money in the first interview. On the other hand, you are making an important decision. Why waste your time or theirs if the salary is much lower than your other alternatives? Sales managers are less likely to object; but just in case, you may want to preface a question about earnings by saying, Compensation is as important a consideration for me as training and other benefits when making a decision. Can you tell me the approximate earnings of a first-year salesperson? You will probably get a range rather than a specific figure. You could also wait until a later meeting to ask about earnings.

People who prefer security desire compensation plans with an emphasis on salary. Other people like the potential rewards of straight commission. If either is important to you, ask about the type of compensation plan in the first meeting. For example, you should ask, "What type of compensation plan do you offer: salary, straight commission, or a combination of salary plus commission or bonus?"

Presentation   Features alone are not persuasive in interviews, just as features alone do not persuade buyers to purchase products. Recall the FEBA technique presented in Chapter 9, which stands for feature, evidence, benefit, agreement. Cheryl McSwain (see Exhibit 17.4) might say, "I was a camp counselor for three summers at Camp Kanatcook (feature), as you can see on my résumé (evidence). This experience taught me customer service skills that you will appreciate when I sell for you (benefit), don't you agree?"

For example, Adam Caplan, a student at the Kellogg School (Northwestern University), was interviewing with Joseph Vansyckle of Drugstore.com and was asked how he handles stress in the work environment. Adam recounted his competitive tennis experience, saying, "During the point, I'm utterly focused and have a killer instinct, but when the point is over, it's very important for me to relax, to think about something else . . . before I get up again for the next point. Focused and relaxed—I apply that to my work and have found that it leads to success." He then related this experience to the job at Drugstore.com and how that characteristic would help him deal with work stress. Afterward, Vansyckle said that answer "was genius." The answer provided all three components: the feature (focus), evidence (tennis experience), and benefit (how he applies it to work stress).[11]

If asked to describe yourself, use features to prove benefits. Recruiters will appreciate specific evidence that can back up your claims. For example, if you say you like people and that is why you think you would be a good salesperson, be prepared to demonstrate how your love of people has translated into action.

Many students carry portfolios into interviews. A **portfolio** is an organized collection of evidence of one's career.[12] For example, a portfolio might contain letters of reference, a résumé, thank-you letters from customers, a paper about an internship, a strategic plan created for a business policy class, or even photographs of the homecoming float for which you were chairperson. Some of our students offer videos of their sales calls from this class as part of their portfolio. Portfolios are one method of offering proof that you can deliver benefits.

thinking **it** through   How would you describe yourself in terms of features? What needs would be satisfied by those features so they could become benefits? What would go on your Web site or in your portfolio to prove your features? How could you use a Web site to market yourself?

Keep in mind that the interviewer also will be taking notes. Writing down answers takes the interviewer longer than it takes for you to speak. Once the question is answered sufficiently, stop and allow the interviewer time to write. Many applicants believe they should continue talking; the silence of waiting is too much to bear. Stay silent, however; otherwise, you may talk yourself out of a sale.

Gaining Commitment   Because sales positions usually require skill at gaining commitment, sales managers will want to see whether the candidate has that skill. Be prepared to close the interview with some form of gaining commitment: I'm very excited about this opportunity. What is our next step?

Be sure to learn when you can expect to hear from the company, confirm that deadline, and write it down. You may want to say, So I'll receive a call or a letter within the next two weeks. Let's see, that would be the 21st, right?

Asking for commitment and confirming the information signal your professionalism and your organizational and selling skills.

SPECIAL TYPES OF INTERVIEWS

You can face many types of interviews: disguised interviews, stress interviews, and panel interviews, among others. **Disguised interviews,** or interviews in which the candidate is unaware that the interviewer is evaluating the candidate, are common at college placement offices. In the lobby you may meet a **greeter,** probably a recent graduate of your college, who will try to help you relax before a scheduled interview and offer you an opportunity to ask questions about the job and the company. Although you can obtain a lot of good information from a greeter, you may want to save some questions for the real interview. You may also want to repeat some questions in the interview to check for consistency. Keep in mind that the greeter is also interviewing you, even though the meeting seems like friendly conversation. Keep your enthusiasm high and your nerves low.

A **stress interview** is designed to place the candidate under severe stress to see how the candidate reacts. Stress interviews have been criticized as being unfair because the type of stress one experiences on a job interview often differs from the type of stress one would actually face on the job. Still, many reputable companies believe it appropriate to try to determine how a candidate reacts to stress because stress is a real part of just about every sales position. One tactic is to ask three questions at once and see how the candidate answers; another is to ask, "How are you going to lose money for me?" (translation: What mistakes have you made in the past and what might you do in the future?) or other reversed versions of appropriate questions.[13] While questionable in terms of measuring the appropriate form of stress, these methods are less questionable than the following: The interviewer asks the applicant to reveal something personal, such as a time when the person felt hurt. Once the situation has been described, the interviewer may mock the applicant, saying the situation wasn't that personal or that hurtful and surely the applicant can dig deeper. Another stress tactic is to ask the interviewee to sell something such as a pencil or a table.

You probably will not see stress interviews at a college placement office, but you could face one at some point in the job-hunting process. You may find it helpful to deal with a stress interview by treating it as a game (say to yourself, She's just trying to stress me out; I wonder how far she will go if I don't react). Of course, you may simply refuse to play the game, either by terminating the interview or by changing the subject. If you terminate the interview, you will probably not get the job.

Panel interviews require special tactics by the candidate to keep all interviewers involved.

Michael Newman/PhotoEdit

In **panel interviews** you will encounter multiple interviewers. During a panel interview try to make eye contact with each interviewer. Focus on each person for at least three seconds at a time; anything less than that and you are simply sweeping the room. When asked a question, begin your answer by directing it to the questioner but then shift your attention to the group. By speaking to the group, you will keep all interviewers involved and avoid a two-person conversation. You may want to review how to sell to a group, discussed in Chapter 9.

Group interviews are similar to panel interviews but include several candidates as well as several interviewers. Group interviews may take place in a conference room or around a dinner table. If you find yourself in a group interview, avoid trying to top the stories of the other candidates. Treat social occasions during office or plant visits as interviews and avoid alcohol or overeating. As with stress interviews, the key is to maintain your cool while being yourself. You cannot do that if you overindulge.

FOLLOW-UP

Regardless of the type of interview, you should send a thank-you note shortly afterward. Send one to the greeter, if possible (thus you will probably want to get this person's business card). If you had a panel interview, find out who the contact person is and write to that person. After thanking the person in the first paragraph, write a paragraph that summarizes the interview. Focus your summary on the reasons you should be hired. In the final paragraph reiterate your thanks and end with an assumptive statement, such as "I look forward to seeing you again."

If you do not hear by the target date, contact the person. Call if the interviewer was a sales manager; write if a personnel manager spoke with you. Sales managers will appreciate the saleslike perseverance; personnel managers may not. Within another week, call the personnel manager also. Simply ask for the status of your application rather than whether you got the job. The process of deciding may have taken longer than expected, or other situations may have caused delays. You need to know where you stand, however, so that you can take advantage of alternatives, if possible.

INTERVIEWING NEVER ENDS

Even if you spend your entire career with one company, your job interviewing days are not over after you land that first job; you will interview for promotions as well. Some companies even interview candidates for admission to management development programs. The same techniques apply in all of these cases. You will still need to prepare properly, conduct the interview professionally, close for some level of commitment, and follow up.

MANAGING YOUR CAREER GOALS

An important aspect of career management is to set life-based objectives and then use them to determine your career objectives. Balance between family and work goals is necessary, or one or several negative consequences could occur, such as divorce or success without fulfillment. Ross Glatzer faced the conflicting loyalties of his career and family, deciding that a two-year sabbatical was needed to meet his family's needs. One survey reported that a lack of balance was one of the top reasons that managers resigned, were terminated, or were poorly evaluated.[14]

Balance, then, is important when setting career goals. Career decisions must be compatible with family and personal objectives. Keeping life goals in mind and remembering your reasons for setting those goals will help you map out a career with which you can be happy.

SALES BLOOPERS

Closing those big deals can be thrilling. Sales, though, is like improvisational theater; while it can be exciting and wonderful when things are going well, mistakes can easily occur, turning a great performance into a dud.

One sales consultant wore a Casio watch to an appointment with the training department at Fossil. He thought the appointment went great. Afterward, they wouldn't return his calls. Was it because he wore a competitor's product? He'll never know because the company won't talk to him. But SBC, official telecommunications sponsor of the Dallas Stars, was not too happy when the VP of sales for the Stars was using an Alltel phone. Fortunately, he was waiting for delivery of the SBC phone, so things were smoothed out.

Other mistakes are, perhaps, more comical and easy to overcome. Bill Maxwell was a new college graduate and a newlywed with little money when he got his first sales job. So he borrowed $1,000 from his parents to buy several business suits. "I found one that I liked and it fit really well, so I bought it in two different colors," he says. Getting dressed in the dark so as not to wake his wife, he didn't realize that the pants he put on didn't match the coat until he was at the customer's office. "I couldn't just reschedule, but it's hard to impress upon someone that

you can handle the details of satisfying their needs when you can't dress yourself!" Still, Maxwell says the customer laughed along with him, told stories of his own newlywed days, and is now one of Bill's best accounts.

Darren Jennings's biggest gaffe involved an Indian restaurant. "My customer loves curry, and we went to a restaurant that he chose. He insisted on ordering the meal, one of his favorites, for both of us." But Jennings didn't realize the dish included cilantro, to which he is allergic. "I saw it, and I knew I shouldn't eat it. But to be nice, I ate some, trying to avoid the cilantro." By the end of the meal, Darren's face and neck were red and blotchy, as well as very itchy. "It was obvious something was wrong; fortunately, it just looks bad, it isn't life-threatening." When he explained what happened in response to a question from the customer, the customer said, "You should have told me!"

Salespeople constantly take risks, some of which pay off while others crash and burn. But everyone will make mistakes. As Jennings says, "You realize you can relax and not worry about being perfect all of the time. The mark of a true professional is how you overcome mistakes, not whether you never make one."

MAKING THE TRANSITION FROM COLLEGE TO CAREER

That first year after college is a unique and important time in anyone's life. How this transition is handled can have a big influence in whether you reach success or experience disappointment. Although a life's work is not created or ruined in the first months, a poor start can take years to overcome. It is not just a matter of giving up student attitudes and behaviors; making the transition also requires taking the time to understand and earn the rights, responsibilities, and credibility of being a sales professional. You will make mistakes during that transition; everyone does (see Selling Scenario 17.1). But as many successful salespeople have learned, it isn't whether you make mistakes, but rather whether you learn from them.

Many new hires want to make a great first impression, so they charge ahead and fail to recognize that the organization was there long before they were and has already developed its own way of doing things. The first thing to do is learn the organization's culture, its values, and the way things are done there.

Another important aspect of the first year is that you are under a microscope. Your activities are watched closely as management and your peers try to decide whether you are someone on whom they can depend. Demonstrate a mature willingness to learn, plus respect for those with experience. Part of this mature willingness to learn means you hold your expectations in check and keep your promotion hopes realistic. Remember too that recruiters tend to engage in puffery when presenting the opportunities and benefits of a company. Although the recruiter said it may be possible to earn a promotion in six months, the average may be much longer.

Seek a partnership with your manager. Although partnership implies a peer-level relationship and you do not have the experience to be a true peer with your manager, use the same partnering skills with him or her that you would use with customers. Find out what your manager needs and wants and then do it. Every workday is a test day except that you sometimes write the questions. Just like your professor, your manager wants the answers, not the problems. Give your boss solutions, and you will be well on the way to a partnership. Other salespeople can also help, as you can see in Building Partnerships 17.1.

DUAL CAREER PATH

When you start out in sales, many career options are open. Career paths can alternate between sales and marketing or follow a route entirely within sales or entirely within marketing. You may even wind up as chief executive officer of a major global corporation. Exemplifying how you might pursue various positions, Exhibit 17.8 depicts the various career paths for salespeople at TAC–Americas. Note that in addition to sales management opportunities, they have opportunities in marketing and product development that all begin in sales.

CONTINUE TO DEVELOP YOUR KSAs

Knowledge, skills, and abilities, or **KSAs,** are the package that you offer your employer. You just spent four or five years and a lot of money developing a set of KSAs; but like any asset, your KSAs will begin to decay if you do not continue to invest in them. Because you are the person in your company to whom your career means the most, many companies, such as Advance Realty, have recognized that ownership of development belongs to the person, not to the company, and have turned training into self-directed development programs. Advance Realty provides

Exhibit 17.8
Sales Advancement at Tours Andover Controls

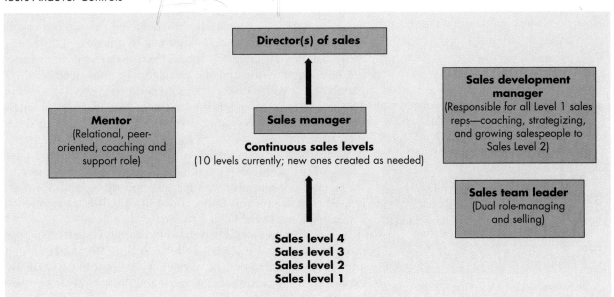

each salesperson a budget to spend on training, and it is up the salesperson to determine where.[15] Even if your company has not formalized development into a self-directed program or if the development program does not provide many options, take the time and effort to invest in yourself so that you can grow in your career. As the philosopher Eric Hoffer said, "In times of change, the learners inherit the earth, while the learned find themselves beautifully equipped to handle a world that no longer exists."[16]

Lifelong learning is important in today's learning organization. Continuing sales training is one of the top training topics, behind only leadership and general business skills.[17] Although many companies have downsized, it is the versatile, well-educated employee who not only keeps a job but also grows a career.

Lifelong learning can be an important factor in not only improving your position but also enjoying what you do. Once you have a position within an organization, your objective will be to develop yourself to get a promotion and then to be successful in that promotion. (To get the promotion after that, you will need to do well in the job you are seeking.) You should take several significant actions in each position along the way. The first action is to understand your options because sales can often lead to various positions.

Sources of Improvement

Most companies continue to train their salespeople after basic sales training, but most training of experienced salespeople is product related rather than sales skills related. If you want to improve your selling skills, you may have to actively seek assistance.

The first place to start is with the field sales manager. When that person works with you in your territory, solicit feedback after each call. During these curbside conferences, you can learn a great deal about what you are doing from an objective observer.

Peers provide another source. Who is successful in the company? When gathered together for a sales meeting, many successful salespeople pick one another's brains for new ideas and strategies. Offer to work with them in their territories for a day or so to learn from them. In most situations they will be flattered and helpful. Pulte Homes, for example, has a mentoring program that matches up successful salespeople with younger reps. Pulte hires about 75 percent of its sales force straight out of college, so mentoring is an important aspect of getting these new salespeople adjusted. Like many other companies, Pulte has found that this arrangement benefits both the mentor and the protégé.[18] Noncompeting salespeople in professional organizations such as Sales and Marketing Executives, an international organization of salespeople and marketing managers, will also be flattered to share their tips with you.

Bookstores offer a wealth of material for developing sales skills. Many good books remind salespeople of the basics of selling and present advanced methods of selling and negotiating. Be sure to save this book, too, as you will want to refer to it when you are in the field.

Sales seminars and CDs are also available. Seminars, such as those offered by Zig Ziglar, Dale Carnegie, Wilson Learning, and Tom Hopkins, can be very motivating. However, many experienced salespeople desire more than just motivation; they look for seminars that also teach new ways to present and gain

Learning doesn't end with college. Motorola customers and employees, for example, attend training classes at the Galvin Center, the company's training center in Chicago.

Reproduced with permission from Motorola, Inc. © 2002 Motorola, Inc.

commitment, as well as other sales skills. When they cannot attend seminars, they purchase CDs. They can listen while driving, using what would have been unproductive time to improve their skills.[19]

Another source of improvement is an industry association. Many industries and professions offer certification programs, which not only require that you improve and update your knowledge and skills, but also offer proof to your customers that you have made that effort. In the promotional products industry, for example, one-third of buyers surveyed said that certification of the salespeople who sold to them was an important factor when choosing vendors.[20] Certification was one measure of service quality that these buyers used when comparing suppliers.

In this course you have begun to develop your interpersonal persuasion, or selling, skills. Whether or not you plan a career in sales, you owe it to yourself to continue to develop these skills.

Learn Your Current Job

Learn all you can about the job you have now. Many people want promotions as fast as they can get them, regardless of their readiness. But consider that you will probably be managing the people who will be holding your current job. To be truly effective as their manager, you should learn all you can about the job of the people you hope to manage while in the best position to do so: while you are one of them.

Learn the Job You Want Next

A manager once said, "In order to become a manager, you must first be a manager." He meant that promoting someone is easier when that person already has the characteristics the position requires—that is, already acts like a manager—rather than having only potential.

Several ways exist for you to learn about the job you desire. First, solicit the help of people who hold the job now. Many companies expect managers to develop their people. Take advantage of that fact; ask for the help of such managers. Find out what they did to prepare themselves and what you should do.

Second, volunteer to take on special projects that will demonstrate your leadership and organizational abilities. Taking projects off the hands of your manager can also let you see the manager's responsibilities. Look for ways you can contribute to the overall sales team to show your commitment to the organization, your ability to lead and develop others, and your management skills.

MANAGING STRESS

Selling can be a stressful career. For example, with three days left in the month, Richard Langlotz, a sales manager at Konica-Minolta, faced a sales team that lost $100,000 in business. One sale alone, worth $60,000, would have made the team's quota, but that account delayed its order for a few months. The other prospects decided to go with the competition. Suddenly it looked as though Langlotz was going to finish the month well below quota. To top it off, one of his salespeople quit. What did he do? "I took my sales team to a pizza place," Langlotz says. He thought about calling a meeting and getting tough with his team, but he realized they already had enough stress and didn't need any more from him. At the pizza parlor, without any prompting from him, each salesperson examined his or her prospect lists and determined how the team was going to move sales forecast for the next month into the current month. The team was successful, and Langlotz says he learned a valuable lesson. "When you have good people doing their best, they don't need more stress from their manager."

Exhibit 17.9

Coping with Situational Stress

Use imaging: Close your eyes and imagine yourself past the source of stress. Try to feel the actual sensation of what it will be like when the stress is gone.

Exercise: Exercise can moderate feelings of stress. When situational stress occurs over time, schedule exercise breaks.

Take breaks: Take a walk, phone a friend, do something. If working on a stressful project, take regular stress breaks. Combine imaging techniques with breaks to increase the stress-reducing power of breaks.

Rest: In addition to breaks, be well rested when the situation arises. If you have a major presentation, get a good night's rest beforehand.

Prepare: If the situation involves future performance, prepare and practice. Prepare for every contingency, but don't let the tension build by thinking only of things going wrong.

Recover: Plan time for postsituation recovery before you charge into the next high-stress situation. Doing two major presentations in one day, for example, may not allow the recovery time you need to do well in the second presentation.

Peter Callaghan, VP of Maximizer Software, agrees. The company offers, among other things, a massage therapist once a week to help salespeople deal with stress, such as meeting quotas.[21] Many salespeople liken sales to a roller coaster ride, with great emotional highs when sales are good but emotional lows when sales are poor.

For some people, coping with stress results in changing jobs. Changing jobs may be the right thing for some people to do. Others turn to less healthful releases, such as absenteeism, drugs, alcohol, and so forth.[22] All jobs have some stress; managing that stress is important to leading a happy and healthy life. However, managing stress does not always mean removing the cause of stress. Sometimes, as with the loss of a loved one, most people find they must manage stress because they cannot remove or change its cause. Two types of stress common to salespeople because of the unique nature of sales positions are situational stress and felt stress.

SITUATIONAL STRESS

Situational stress is short-term anxiety caused by a situational factor.[23] You may face situational stress when waiting to make a sales presentation for your class, for example. The best strategy to deal with situational stress is to leave the situation or remove the situational factor causing the stress, but that approach is not always possible. You cannot, for example, simply tell your instructor that you are too stressed to sell in class today, so you are leaving! One technique for managing situational stress is to imagine that the situational factor has been removed (see Exhibit 17.9 for more ideas). In class, imagine that you have already finished your role play. Mentally consider that feeling of relief you get when you know you have done a job well. Sometimes imagining success can reduce feelings of stress.

In sales situational stress may be caused by impending presentations, deadlines for closing orders (as in Richard Langlotz's case), and similar situations. Situational stress can cause stage fright in even the most experienced salespeople. One price of success is that situational stress will continue to occur, but successful salespeople learn to control their feelings about situational stress.

FELT STRESS

Felt stress lasts longer than situational stress because the causes are more enduring. **Felt stress** is psychological distress or anxiety brought about by job demands or constraints encountered in the work environment.[24] Perhaps the most common form of felt stress is role stress, or feelings of stress caused by the salesperson's role.

Role stress is brought about by role conflict, role overload, and/or role ambiguity. **Role conflict** occurs when two partners demand incompatible actions of the salesperson. For example, Cameron Dube with Servall Packaging Industries once had a customer who was dissatisfied with a new machine. "While I was in [the customer's] office, I heard two sets of voices, my customer's and my boss's," he said. "The customer wanted something I knew the company wouldn't pay for."[25] Conflict occurred with the salesperson caught in the middle. **Role ambiguity** occurs when the salesperson is not sure what actions are required. The salesper-

Exhibit 17.10

Reducing Role Stress

Prioritize: Set your own priorities so that when different people place conflicting expectations on you, your preset priorities determine where your actions will go.

Seek support: Enlist support of your priorities from your spouse, your manager, and other key people. By focusing on goals and priorities, you can reduce conflict over specific activities.

Reset expectations: By prioritizing and seeking support, you can reset expectations of various constituencies so that they are in harmony. Communicate and gain agreement on what you are capable of doing so that others' expectations of you are realistic.

Act and move on: Once you have made a decision to act, don't dwell on the conflict. Act and move on.

son may not be sure what is expected, how to achieve it, or how performance will be evaluated and rewarded. **Role overload** is what happens when the role demands more than the person can perform. Asking a new salesperson to make the same types of presentations to high-level accounts that a veteran would make could cause role overload.

In general, the best way to handle role stress is to increase role accuracy (see Exhibit 17.10 for specific ideas). When the problem is role ambiguity, simply asking for further instruction or reviewing training materials may be helpful. Coaching and other management support can also be requested.

Role conflict and role overload, however, require prioritizing activities. In the example of the salesperson who feels stress due to conflict between the customer's and the manager's demands, the salesperson must decide whose needs will be met. Once that decision is made, further stress can be avoided by refusing to dwell on the conflict. Note that the conflict is still there (both parties have conflicting demands), but the effect on the salesperson is minimized.

In either case a strong partnership with the sales manager can greatly aid in reducing stress. When a partnership is formed between a sales manager and a salesperson, the salesperson has a better understanding of the demands of the job, which activities should receive priority, and how the job should be performed. Partners also have access to more resources and more information, which can help remove some of the organizational constraints that can bring about stress.[26]

Strong sales skills can also reduce feelings of stress. Mastery of the job will reduce feelings of stress because the salesperson is in control of the situation.

SUMMARY

A sales career offers many opportunities for growth and personal development, but that career has to start somewhere. That is the purpose of the job search: to find a good match between what you need and have to offer and what a company needs and has to offer.

To achieve a match that results in mutual satisfaction, you must first understand who you are, specifically what you need and what you have to offer. You can ask yourself a number of questions to stimulate your thinking about the type of person you are and what you will need from a sales position. In addition, as you review your experiences in school, work, and other activities, you can identify the skills and characteristics that you have to offer.

Finding industries and companies with the characteristics you desire will require you to apply your marketing research skills. The library contains many sources of information that will help you. Personal sources can also be useful in providing information as well as leads for interviews, as can the Internet.

Sources for job interviews include the campus placement office, personal contacts, and advertisements. Résumés are personal brochures that help sell a candidate. Writing effective cover letters will help you get interviews off campus, whereas the interview itself is similar to a sales call. Plan questions that demonstrate your knowledge of and interest in the company. Also, plan to ask for information that will help you make your decision. Follow up after the interview to demonstrate your desire and perseverance.

You are the person in the company to whom your career means the most. Therefore, you must actively manage your own career. Set career goals that are compatible with family and personal objectives. Keeping the reasons for these career goals in front of you will enable you to make better decisions.

Learn the job you have now. You may someday manage people who have this job; the better you know it, the better you will be at managing it. To become a manager, you must first be a manager. Learn the manager's job as well, and volunteer for activities and projects that will let you demonstrate your management ability.

Stress can occur in any job. Situational stress is short-term, whereas felt stress is longer-term. For many people, the key to managing stress is to reduce the influence stressors have because the causes of stress often cannot be eliminated.

Sales offers a challenging and exciting career. The opportunities are so varied that almost anyone can probably fit into some sales position. Even if you choose a career in another field, take advantage of the material in this chapter. You should find these job search and career management tips helpful in any field. Good luck!

KEY TERMS

application form
assessment center
conventional résumé
disguised interview
felt stress
functional résumé
greeter
group interview
interview
KSAs

panel interview
portfolio
references
role ambiguity
role conflict
role overload
role stress
situational stress
stress interview
tests

ETHICS PROBLEMS

1. You are interviewing for your dream job. Suddenly the interviewer notices your wedding ring and compliments you on it. But then he says, "You know, this job requires a lot of travel. What is your spouse going to say to that?" You answer the question, and he replies, "That's great, now, when you don't have kids. You don't have kids, do you? Because it is tough to be successful if you don't get the travel done." What do you do?

2. Some people recommend signing up for as many interviews as possible, reasoning that the experience will be helpful when you find a company with a job you really want. (And who knows? You might find a job you like.) Is this practice ethical? Why or why not? Are companies ethical when they come to campus and interview, even though a job is not available, just to maintain a presence on campus?

QUESTIONS AND PROBLEMS

1. What would you do differently if you were being interviewed by an amiable, a driver, an analytical, or an expressive? What about a panel interview with one driver and one amiable? One analytical and one expressive?

2. Is a résumé the only document you should take into an interview? What other things might help document your capabilities?

3. Analyze yourself. List your strengths and weaknesses. What type of sales would best suit you? Why? Are you qualified for that job? If not, what do you need, and how would you go about getting it? How would you express your career objective in one sentence? If you are thinking of two or more industries, rewrite the career objective as you would for a résumé to be sent to recruiters in each industry.

4. The chapter suggests joining a trade or professional association now. How can the organization help you determine whether you are pursuing the right position? How could you network through the association?

5. What do you think the biggest challenges will be for you in making the transition from college to a career? Why will those be difficult? What do you think the common transition challenges are, and what can you do to prepare for those challenges?

6. Answer the questions in Exhibit 17.6 as you would in a sales job interview.

7. Your summer internship in a sales job was a bad experience. Your biggest complaint was that the sales manager seemed incompetent. In spite of this negative experience, you like sales, so you are interviewing for a sales position. What would you say if asked why you do not seek full-time employment with the summer internship firm?

8. The chapter discusses finding successful salespeople and learning from them. Another important career tactic is to find a mentor. How would you find or select a mentor? What characteristics would you want to see in a mentor?

9. How does partnering reduce stress? Could multiple partnerships lead to role conflict? If so, what should the salesperson do when such conflict arises?

10. What stresses do you have now? How do you deal with stress? What healthy methods to handle stress do you use? What are some ways you respond to stress that may not be so healthy?

CASE PROBLEMS

case **17.1**

Finding a Job

While studying for the final exam for the sales class, a group of students began talking about jobs. "I just don't think I could do sales," said Marian. "I don't think I could either go cold-calling or try to call people on the phone I don't know and try to sell them something."

"I think I could," replied Tony. "I just don't know what I want to sell. It has to be something I believe in." Murmurs of agreement followed. "And I want to have something different every day—I don't think I could sit behind a desk with the same old routine."

"I'm more like Marian," said Bobbie. "I don't think I could do a lot of cold-calling, but I'd like to be in sales anyway. Maybe something where they come to me or I see the same people. I'm good with people once I get to know them."

"I heard a lot of companies start you out on the phones first," Darrell noted. "Like IBM. You start out on the phones and if you're good, then you get to go out into the field."

Questions

1. What kinds of jobs would Tony be suited for? Bobbie? Can Bobbie's fears be overcome, or should she just find a job that doesn't involve cold-calling?

2. Using the Web, find a position each student can apply for. Print the ad; then on the same sheet (write on the back if you need to), justify your choice.

3. Pick one of the four positions you used in question 2 for yourself. Why is that a good fit for you?

case **17.2**

Help Wanted

You found these ads on Monster.com:

US—PA—Philadelphia—SALESPERSON

Local territory selling packaging products to manufacturers. Straight salary plus bonus, car allowance, full med & dent. No overnight. Exp. preferred, 3 mo. training. E-mail résumé to Sales1@crummer.com.

US—Nationwide—SALES PROFESSIONAL

Selling network systems to small businesses. 20% travel. Opening new market. Sales exp. helpful, not nec. Must have some computer or telephone exp., college degree. 6 mo. tng. in NY. Co. car. Straight sal. first yr., sal. plus comm. after. E-mail résumé to Ms. R. Weinberg, RWein@wedocomputers.com.

Questions

1. What characteristics do you have that might work well in these positions? What characteristics do you think are necessary to succeed in these jobs? Why?

2. Tausha Aldridge from Crummer called and wants to interview you tomorrow. You never heard of the company until you saw the ad. How will you learn more about it?

3. It turns out that Crummer is a division of a U.S.–based *Fortune* 500 company, whereas Wedo is a distributor for several Japanese manufacturers. Crummer employs 535 salespeople; Wedo employs 47 salespeople. What are the advantages and disadvantages of working for Crummer? For Wedo?

ACT! ROLE PLAY

Congratulations—you just got promoted! Now you have to replace yourself by hiring a college graduate to take over your sales territory. Given everything you've learned about ACT! this semester and what you know about sales, take a few minutes to identify the three most important features a salesperson should bring to the job and the questions you'd ask to determine if the candidate had those features. Then take turns interviewing each other in your group. There is no candidate information to be provided—each student will play himself or herself when playing the candidate role.

ADDITIONAL REFERENCES

Bhuian, Shahid N. Bulent Menguc, and Rene Borsboom. "Stressors and Job Outcomes in Sales: A Triphasic Model versus a Linear-Quadratic-Interactive Model." *Journal of Business Research* 58, (February 2005), pp. 141–52.

Bush, Victoria, and Thomas N. Ingram. "Building and Assessing Cultural Diversity Skills: Implications for Sales Training." *Industrial Marketing Management* 30 (2001), pp. 65–76.

Castleberry, Stephen B., and Rick M. Ridnour. "Anticipatory Socialization: A Longitudinal Case Study of Salespeople Hired from College." *The Journal of Selling and Account Management* 4 (Autumn 2001), pp. 53–69.

DelVecchio, Susan; James Zemanek; Roger McIntyre; and Reid Claxton. "Updating the Adaptive Selling Behaviours: Tactics to Keep and Tactics to Discard." *Journal of Marketing Management* 20 (September 2004), pp. 859–71.

Dixon, Andrea L.; Rosann L. Spiro; and Lukas P. Forbes. "Attributions and Behavioral Intentions of Inexperienced Salespersons to Failure: An Empirical Investigation." *Journal of the Academy of Marketing Science* 31 (Fall 2003), pp. 459–67.

"The 50 Best Companies to Sell For." *Selling Power,* October 2001, pp. 101–5.

Gohmann, Stephan F.; Robert M. Barker; David J. Faulds; and Jian Guan. "Salesforce Automation, Perceived Information Accuracy, and User Satisfaction." *The Journal of Business & Industrial Marketing* 33, no. 1 (2005), pp. 23–32.

Grapentine, Terry. "Segmenting the Sales Force." *Marketing Management* 14 (January/February 2005), pp. 32–37.

Jantan, M. Asri; Earl D. Honeycutt Jr.; Shawn T. Thelen; and Ashraf M. Attia. "Managerial Perceptions of Sales Training and Performance." *Industrial Marketing Management* 33 (October 2004), pp. 667–80.

Leach, Mark P., and Annie H. Liu. "Investigating Interrelationships among Sales Training Evaluation Methods." *Journal of Personal Selling & Sales Management* 23 (Fall 2003), pp. 325–37.

Manna, Dean R., and Alan D. Smith. "Exploring the Need for Emotional Intelligence and Awareness among Sales Representatives." *Marketing Intelligence & Planning* 22, no. 1 (2004), pp. 66–83.

McElroy, James, and Thomas DeCarlo. "Physical Attractiveness on Cognitive Evaluations of Saleswomen's Performance." *Journal of Marketing Theory and Practice* 9 (Summer 2001), pp. 84–96.

Moncrief, William C., and Greg W. Marshall. "The Evolution of the Seven Steps of Selling." *Industrial Marketing Management* 34 (January 2005), pp. 13–26.

Randall, James, and Cindy Randall. "A Current Review of Hiring Techniques for Sales Personnel: The First Step in the Sales Management Process." *Journal of Marketing Theory and Practice* 9 (Spring 2001), pp. 80–93.

Rozell, Elizabeth J.; Charles E. Pettijohn; and R. Stephen Parker. "Customer Oriented Selling: Exploring the Roles of Emotional Intelligence and Organizational Commitment." *Psychology & Marketing* 21 (June 2004), pp. 405–17.

Tsai, Ming-Tien, and Chia-Mei Shih. "The Influences of Organizational and Personal Ethics on Role Conflict among Marketing Managers: An Empirical Investigation." *International Journal of Management* 22, March 2005, pp. 54–61.

Walsh, Stephen M. "Call Reluctance: The Dark Side of Professional Selling?" *Southern Business Review* 29 (Spring 2004), pp. 23–32.

ROLE PLAY CASE 1

STUBB'S BAR-B-Q

Stubb's Bar-B-Q is an Austin, Texas, manufacturer of barbecue sauces and marinades. Founder C. B. Stubblefield states on the Web site, "My recipes are known throughout Texas and the world as the best in barbecue, and I've put my heart and soul into each one. With my picture on the label and my recipe inside, you can be sure you're getting the finest quality available. Simply put, my life is in these bottles."

Stubb's offers a wide variety of products (see its Web site for the most up-to-date list of products and prices):

Product	Suggested Retail Price	Reseller Case Prices (When Buying Fewer Than 20 Cases in a Single Order)
Stubb's Smokey Mesquite Bar-B-Q Sauce	$3.85	6 for $18
Stubb's Legendary Bar-B-Q Sauce (comes in original, mild, and spicy varieties)	$3.85	6 for $18
Stubb's Marinades (come in pork, beef, and chicken varieties)	$4.25	6 for $21
Stubb's Spice Rubs (come in Bar-B-Q, Rosemary Ginger, Chili Lime, and Herbal Mustard varieties)	$3.50	12 for $36
Stubb's Liquid Smokes (come in Hickory and Mesquite flavors)	$1.85	12 for $16
Stubb's Bar-B-Q Baste Moppin' Sauce (comes in original and inferno varieties)	$4.25	6 for $21
Stubb's Chicken Wing Sauces (come in original and inferno varieties)	$4.25	6 for $21

Stubb's recommends that cooks try the three-step system to excellent barbecuing. First use the rubs before cooking. Then, while cooking, use the Moppin' Sauce to baste the food. Third, pour warmed Bar-B-Q sauce over the meat when it is ready to be served. The Liquid Smokes are offered for customers who want to add a natural hickory or mesquite smoky flavor to meats.

Stubb's offers noncumulative quantity discounts for resellers (the total number of cases can be based on mixed items; thus a reseller that buys 10 cases of Spice Rubs in any varieties and 11 cases of Moppin' Sauce in any varieties would get the additional 5 percent discount):

Quantity Purchased	Discount
Fewer than 20 cases	Standard reseller case prices
21–100 cases	An additional 5 percent off reseller case prices
Over 100 cases	An additional 10 percent off reseller case prices

Stubb's also offers a number of promotions for resellers. Resellers that set up an end-of-aisle display of at least 50 cases of a mix of sizes and flavors earn an extra $1 case discount on all cases purchased. For resellers that advertise Stubb's products in the newspaper, there is a 50 percent co-op payment for the actual portion of the page cost of the advertisement. Thus, if a grocery store runs a newspaper ad that includes one-eighth of a page for Stubb's products, Stubb's will reimburse the grocery store for 50 percent of the cost of one-eight of the ad.

Source: http://www.buystubbs.com/stublegbarbq.html. For more up-to-date information, please visit the Web site.

SITUATION 1   KROGER SUPERMARKETS—CORPORATE HEADQUARTERS (RESELL SITUATION)

Kroger owns and operates over 2,500 supermarkets in 32 states under the chain names of Kroger, Ralphs, Dillons, Smith's, King Soopers, Fry's, QFC, City Market, Hilander, Owen's, Jay C, Cala Foods/Bell Markets, Kessel Food Markets, Pay Less, Baker's, and Gerbes. It also owns multidepartment stores (such as Fred Meyer, Fry's Marketplace, Smith's Marketplace, Kroger Marketplace) and price-impact warehouse stores (Food 4 Less, Foods Co).

The Kroger supermarket chain stores are combination food and drug stores designed to draw customers within a three-mile radius. These Kroger supermarkets include specialty departments like whole health sections, pharmacies, and pet centers; many offer fresh seafood and organic produce.

You are a salesperson for Stubb's. You are calling the corporate headquarters grocery buyer of the Kroger supermarket chain stores (which does not include the multidepartment or price-impact warehouse stores). Kroger's has not carried Stubb's products in the past. Your goal is to have Kroger's corporate headquarters approve the offering of at least some Stubb's products in its stores and stock them in Kroger's distribution warehouses. Assume that the final decision about which product will be offered in individual stores is up to the local store manager.

Source: www.hoovers.com, http://www.kroger.com/operations_grocery_about.htm. See Kroger's Web site for more up-to-date information if desired.

SITUATION 2   KROGER SUPERMARKETS—LOCAL SUPERMARKET (RESELL SITUATION)

Kroger owns and operates over 2,500 supermarkets in 32 states under the chain names of Kroger, Ralphs, Dillons, Smith's, King Soopers, Fry's, QFC, City Market, Hilander, Owen's, Jay C, Cala Foods/Bell Markets, Kessel Food Markets, Pay Less, Baker's, and Gerbes. It also owns multidepartment stores (such as Fred Meyer, Fry's Marketplace, Smith's Marketplace, Kroger Marketplace) and price-impact warehouse stores (Food 4 Less, Foods Co).

The Kroger supermarket chain stores are combination food and drug stores designed to draw customers within a three-mile radius. These Kroger supermarkets include specialty departments like whole health sections, pharmacies, and pet centers; many offer fresh seafood and organic produce.

You are a salesperson for Stubb's. You are calling the grocery manager of a local Kroger supermarket. Assume that Kroger's corporate headquarters has approved the offering of Stubb's products and that Kroger's carries them in its distribution centers. However, this Kroger supermarket has never carried Stubb's products in the past. Your goal is to have this store manager approve the offering of at least some Stubb's products in her or his store. Note: If the store manager agrees to offer Stubb's, he or she will simply order the products from the Kroger's distribution center.

Source: www.hoovers.com, http://www.kroger.com/operations_grocery_about.htm. See Kroger's Web site for more up-to-date information if desired.

SITUATION 3   WAGNER'S IGA GROCERY STORE (RESELL SITUATION)

Wagner's IGA is a full-service, locally owned grocery store located in Minister, Ohio, that has been in operation since 1922. The store includes bakery, deli, meat, grocery, produce, seafood, frozen food, and beer/wine/liquor departments. The store also offers special services including a branch for a local bank, a gift shop, dry cleaning drop-off and pickup, a fax/copy machine, film drop-off, and postal products. The store carries several brands of barbecue sauce but has never carried Stubb's.

You are a salesperson for Stubb's. Your goal is to introduce Stubb's products to the grocery store manager and secure a sale of at least some of the products.

Source: http://www.wagnersiga.com/about.html. See this Web site if more up-to-date information is desired.

SITUATION 4   7-ELEVEN CONVENIENCE STORES (RESELL SITUATION)

7-Eleven, Inc. is the largest chain in the convenience retailing industry with headquarters in Dallas, Texas. There are over 5,800 7-Eleven® stores in the United States and Canada, with over 22,000 stores in other countries throughout the world.

7-Eleven carries a wide assortment of products and services designed to serve people who want quick service at reasonable prices. Products include hot ready-to-eat foods, fresh foods, frozen treats, fountain drinks, magazines, gasoline, newspapers, beverages, dairy products, selected grocery items, and so forth.

You are a salesperson for Stubb's. Your goal is to introduce Stubb's Legendary Bar-B-Q sauce to the grocery buyer of a regional franchise of 7-Eleven stores located in Louisiana and to secure at least a trial order.

Source: www.7-Eleven.com. See the Web site for more up-to-date information as desired.

SITUATION 5   HOME DEPOT – CORPORATE HEADQUARTERS (RESELL SITUATION)

Home Depot is the world's largest home improvement retailer and the second largest retailer in the United States. In addition to selling many items for do-it-yourselfers like electrical and plumbing supplies, hardware, hand tools, and paint, it also sells a limited number of outdoor living products that include items such as barbecue grills, grill accessories, and grill cleaning and cooking tools. During grilling season it carries a few of the best-selling brands of barbecue sauce next to the grills.

You are a salesperson for Stubb's. You are calling the corporate headquarters buyer for outdoors products at the Home Depot. Home Depot has not carried Stubb's products in the past. Your goal is to have Home Depot's corporate headquarters approve the offering of at least some of Stubb's products in its stores, and carry the products in the Home Depot's distribution warehouse. Assume that the final decision about which products will be offered in individual stores is up to the local store manager.

Source: www.homedepot.com. See the Web site for more up-to-date information as desired.

SITUATION 6   HOME DEPOT—INDIVIDUAL STORE (RESELL SITUATION)

Home Depot is the world's largest home improvement retailer and the second largest retailer in the United States. In addition to selling many items for do-it-yourselfers like electrical and plumbing supplies, hardware, hand tools, and paint, it also sells a limited number of outdoor living products that include items such as barbecue grills, grill accessories, and grill cleaning and cooking tools. During grilling season it carries a few of the best-selling brands of barbecue sauce next to the grills.

You are a salesperson for Stubb's. You are calling on the outdoors department manager for one Home Depot store. Assume that the Home Depot corporate headquarters has approved the offering of Stubb's products and carries them in the Home Depot distribution center. However, this Home Depot has never carried Stubb's products in the past. Your goal is to have this outdoors department manager approve the offering of at least some Stubb's products in her or his store. Note: If the store manager agrees to offer Stubb's, he or she will simply order the products from the Home Depot distribution center.

Source: www.homedepot.com. See the Web site for more up-to-date information as desired.

SITUATION 7   CRACKER BARREL—CORPORATE HEADQUARTERS (RESELL SITUATION)

Cracker Barrel Old Country Store operates over 500 full-service, country-style restaurants and gift shops, which are found in most states. Most stores are located next to interstate highways, but several stores are so unique that they are considered tourist destinations.

The restaurants serve all three meals and feature home-style country cooking. All meals are fully prepared on site using Cracker Barrel's own recipes. The stores are constructed in a rustic design and include separate retail areas. The retail portions sell a wide variety of items including hand-blown glassware, cast iron cookware, toys, apparel, and wood crafts. The stores also sell old-fashioned candies, jellies, and other food items.

You are a salesperson for Stubb's. Your goal is to introduce Stubb's products to the grocery buyer of Cracker Barrel at corporate headquarters and secure an agreement that allows the offering of at least some Stubb's products in the stores. Assume that the final decision about which product will be offered in individual Cracker Barrel stores is up to the local store manager. Also assume that the local store manager, if interested, would buy the products directly from Stubb's.

Source: http://www.crackerbarrel.com/ See the Web site for more up-to-date information as desired.

SITUATION 8   CRACKER BARREL—LOCAL STORE (RESELL SITUATION)

Cracker Barrel Old Country Store operates over 500 full-service, country-style restaurants and gift shops, which are found in most states. Most stores are located next to interstate highways, but several stores are so unique that they are considered tourist destinations.

The restaurants serve all three meals and feature home-style country cooking. All meals are fully prepared on site using Cracker Barrel's own recipes. The stores are constructed in a rustic design and include separate retail areas. The retail portions sell a wide variety of items, including hand-blown glassware, cast iron cookware, toys, apparel, and wood crafts. The store also sells old-fashioned candies, jellies, and other food items.

You are a salesperson for Stubb's. You are calling on the store manager of a local Cracker Barrel. Assume that the corporate headquarters of Cracker Barrel has approved the offering of Stubb's products. However, this Cracker Barrel has never carried Stubb's products in the past. Your goal is to have this local manager approve the offering of at least some Stubb's products in her or his store. Note: If the store manager agrees to offer Stubb's, he or she will need to purchase the products directly from Stubb's because the Cracker Barrel distribution center does not stock Stubb's products.

Source: http://www.crackerbarrel.com/ See the Web site for more up-to-date information as desired.

SITUATION 9   T.G.I. FRIDAYS

T.G.I. Friday's (TGIF) is a chain of restaurants located around the globe. There are 530 TGIF's in the United States, with 256 company-owned and the remainder being franchises. There are also 229 TGIF's in international locations spread throughout 57 different countries. TGIF's can be found in 49 states.

TGIF's is a sit-down restaurant that offers drinks, special brunch menus, kid's menus, party platters, and special diet menus. Its regular menus include a variety of appetizers as well as a wide selection of entrees including chicken, pasta, steaks, salads, ribs, shrimp, fish, burgers, and specialty sandwiches. Many of the items are barbecued and tex-mex style.

You are a salesperson for Stubb's calling on the corporate headquarters of TGIF's. TGIF's has never carried your sauce, and you have not called on the chain before. Your goal is to have TGIF's have Stubb's sauce available for customers to use with their meals, either as a standard item placed on dining tables or available on request. Note: You are not requesting that TGIF's sell Stubb's products to customers.

Source: http://www.tgifridays.com. See TGIF's Web site for more up-to-date information if desired.

SITUATION 10   SOUTHERN BELLE RIVERBOAT

The Southern Belle Riverboat offers dinner cruises, daily lunch cruises, and day-time sightseeing cruises. Passengers get to enjoy the cruise either outside on the decks or inside in air-conditioned comfort. The Southern Belle is also available for private cruises.

Each night has a different theme. Monday is pizza night, Tuesday is BBQ night (with BBQ beef, corn on the cob, baked beans, cole slaw, and dinner rolls), Wednesday is prime rib night, and Thursday through Sunday are Dixeland nights with prime rib and shrimp creole. Lunch menus include sandwiches, baked beans, chips, and dessert. Groups can also request special meals.

You are a salesperson for Stubb's calling on the chef of the Southern Belle. Your goal is to have the chef consider using Stubb's barbecue products as she prepares meals that use barbecue sauce and marinades. You would also like Stubb's products to be available if patrons request them during a meal. Note: You are not requesting that the Southern Belle sell Stubb's products to customers.

Source: http://www.chattanoogariverboat.com/www. See the Southern Belle's Web site for more up-to-date information if desired.

ROLE PLAY CASE 2   ACT!

ACT! is award-winning contact management software that integrates personal databases on accounts with calendar management, word processing, and other computer applications. From the salesperson's perspective, the software helps keep track of account information, such as address and contact information, information about the buying center, what the account buys, and even buyers' birthdays and other personal information. The salesperson can also track performance, activity, and conversions.

A sales manager, however, can use the software to monitor what the salespeople are doing. If the sales rep synchronizes with the company's ACT! the sales rep's records are stored on a central server. The manager can then access all of the salesperson's records and generate reports, either for a single salesperson or for the entire sales team. The manager can use this information to pinpoint parts of the sales process where a rep may need more training, more activity, or other support. The manager can also generate forecasts, which can help manage inventory. See the ACT! Web site for case studies that illustrate how companies have used ACT!

Key competitors for ACT! include GoldMine (www.frontrange.com), Maximizer (www.maximizer.com), salesforce.com, and Salesnet.com. A good idea might be to visit each competitor's Web site to learn about how contact management software benefits the sales force, as well as understand the advantages and disadvantages of each program.

When you visit the ACT! Web site, you can determine current retail pricing for single users as well as quantity discounts. Note that any quantity discounts require shipping to one location—if a customer wants it shipped directly to multiple sites, each order is treated as a separate order for the quantity discount. As a salesperson, you can also offer your accounts terms of 2/10 n30 (which they can't get via the Web site). Trade discounts are 50 percent off single-user pricing for a reseller (no matter the quantity, though anything over 1,000 units can receive a negotiated price that you have to get approved), along with a co-op advertising copayment. If the reseller features the product in a newspaper ad, then up to $100 will be paid to the reseller. Payment is in the form of a credit applied to any outstanding invoices. Resellers also get a "shelf-talker,"—a small tag that can be taped to the shelf and hangs out with a $50 rebate offer for any copy of Gold-Mine that is sent in, along with a receipt for ACT!. This GoldMine trade-in special ends after the current month.

Read through all of the following situations, as there is occasionally additional product or competitive information that you might find useful.

RESELLER SITUATIONS
CENTER CITY OFFICE DISCOUNTERS

This chain of 16 stores is similar to Office Depot. The company also has a field sales force that sells office supplies to larger customers. The 16 stores are spread out over a five-state area. You are meeting with the software buyer for the first time after telephoning for an appointment, and you know that Center City carries GoldMine because you saw it as you walked through one of the stores before today's meeting.

HOURGLASS COMPUTER SERVICE CENTER

Primarily a computer service center, this small company has begun also offering software and building computers for its customers. The company just hired its first outside salesperson to call on larger accounts; previously it had been strictly a retail outlet where people brought computers in for repair. You are just dropping in today.

HARD'N SOFT

You are calling on Ms. Hardin, the owner of Hard'N Soft. This company sells customized computer solutions directly to companies, many times taking off-the-shelf software like ACT! and configuring it to the customer's needs. You made a cold call on the account last week, and the owner set up today's appointment. You know that Hard'N Soft have sold Salesnet.com in the past, and you suspect that it is harder to sell and configure than ACT! Salesnet.com requires that a company have a standard sales process, which not all companies have. The software then has to be configured to fit that process.

SAV-ON OFFICE SUPPLY

The national headquarters of Sav-On Supply just approved ACT!, but that doesn't mean that local regions or stores have to carry it. Your company gives Sav-On an additional 5 percent discount because of the company's size, but the store has to order 24 copies and give the product two facings. None of the stores in your territory carries ACT! yet. Today you are meeting with the manager of the largest Sav-On in your territory, with the goal of getting that person to carry ACT! in that store. You believe if that manager will adopt ACT! the others in your territory will follow suit. Sav-On has carried GoldMine and Maximizer, which are still approved products. You called and arranged the meeting.

CENTRAL OFFICE SUPPLY

This downtown office supply distributor has been in business for over 100 years. The company has a large sales force and a large downtown retail store. It has the largest selection of office furniture in town. A traditional retailer with a solid Web presence, the company is known to be very forward-thinking in spite of its age and its traditional downtown location (there are no other retail outlets). Today you have an appointment to see the computer department manager.

USER SITUATIONS
SHIPP BELTING

This company buys belting material and makes customized belts for industrial and agricultural equipment. Shipp sews, staples, glues, or weaves belts together based on the customer's needs, and sometimes installs the belts on the equipment. The company has been in business for over 100 years and is now run by a great-grandchild of the original founder, whom you met at a Rotary meeting. The two of you got to talking about what you do, and you arranged today's meeting. You know that Shipp has six salespeople scattered throughout the state.

WBAP

This Disney radio station has 12 salespeople who call on potential advertisers in the metropolitan area. You have an appointment with the sales director. You checked, and Disney does not have a national agreement with ACT! or any other software provider as far as your company knows. When you talked with the sales director over the telephone when you set up the appointment, you were told that some reps have their own laptops and other reps use Blackberries exclusively, and there is no standard software used by the reps. One uses ACT! They do have access to a desktop on a network at the WBAP office.

AUSTIN MANUFACTURING

Austin Manufacturing is a contract manufacturer, meaning that it makes products that go into other companies' products. For example, Austin manufactures the cases in which home air conditioner compressors and fans are installed for the leading home air conditioner company. You don't know much about the company, but the director of sales easily agreed to an appointment when you made a cold call.

AXXIS DENTAL

This dental products distributor is less than 10 years old but already has a national sales force of some 44 salespeople. The company's salespeople call directly on dental labs, dental schools, hospitals, prison dental offices, and the armed forces (individual dental offices are too small to warrant a sales call). Axxis is headquartered here; you have an appointment with the vice president of sales, who agreed to meet with you after the two of you met at a chamber of commerce networking event.

TATA

Tata is a large company headquartered in India, offering many services such as contract manufacturing and call center outsourcing, as well as manufacturing cars, trucks, tractors, and other products. The commercial vehicle division has just opened up its first U.S. office here in your territory to begin exporting those vehicles from India to the United States. You read about the new office in the local business section of your newspaper and called the office to make an appointment with the vice president of sales.

ENDNOTES

CHAPTER 1

1. Wendell Berry, *The Unsettling of America*, 3rd ed. (San Francisco: Sierra Club Books, 1996).
2. For details on how a sales firm engages in mass customization, see Valerie Popeck, "Delivery Services Go the Extra Mile," *1to1 Magazine*, January/February 2005, pp. 38–39.
3. John Gaffney and Christopher Helm, "Less Talk, More Action," *1to1 Magazine*, October 2004, p. 23.
4. See Molly Stein, "Making the Call: Why Effective Selling Is a Critical Part of Every Profession," *Duluthian*, March/April 2005, pp. 12–15.
5. Lawrence G. Friedman, *Go to Market Strategies* (Woburn, MA: Butterworth-Heinemann, 2002).
6. See Don Peppers and Martha Rogers, "Introducing Return on Customer," *1to1 Magazine*, April 2004, p. 50; Don Peppers and Martha Rogers, "Trust Stakes Its Claim to Customer Value," *1to1 Magazine*, November/December 2004, p. 50.
7. Scott Reeves, "'Do Not Call' Revives Door-to-Door Sales," *Marketing News*, December 8, 2003, p. 13.
8. Mila D'Antonio, "Connecting to Success," *1to1 Magazine*, September 2003, p. 21; John M. Chew Coe, "Developing a B-to-B Data Strategy: Choosing the Right Elements for Your Database is a Crucial Step," *Direct* 14, no. 4, March 15, 2002, p. 42.
9. See John Gaffney, "Finding the Right Fit," *1to1 Magazine*, March 2005, pp. 18–21.
10. Marilyn Kennedy Melia, "The E-volving Salesman," *Chicago Tribune*, June 11, 2000; "Click First, Buy Later," *Marketing News*, May 21, 2001, p. 5; Marijo Puleo and Jenny Belser, "Is Sales an Endangered Species?" *1to1 Magazine*, May/June 2003, pp. 46–47.
11. The Alexander Group, Inc., SalesTime Maker, Software Services, February 8, 2002, http://tools.saleslobby.com/perfMgmt/2001 STM Presentation.pdf.
12. Glenn R. Price, used by permission.
13. Lou Pritchett, *Stop Paddling and Start Rocking the Boat* (New York: Harper Business, 1995),
14. Don Peppers and Martha Rogers, "Getting Ready for Your Customer Close-Up," *1to1 Magazine* October 2004, p. 50.
15. Penny Righthand, "Selling with Passion," *Advisor Today*, August 2003, p. 78.
16. W. H. Weiss, "Demonstrating Creativity and Innovation," *Supervision* 63, March 2002, pp. 6–9; Susan A. Friedman, "Ten Steps to a Successful Trade Show," *Marketing Health Services* 22, Spring 2002, pp. 31–32.
17. Jill E. Perry-Smith and Christina E. Shalley, "The Social Side of Creativity: A Static and Dynamic Social Network Perspective," *Academy of Management Review* 28, no. 1 (2003), pp. 89–106.
18. Tad Simons, "The Confidence Game," *Presentations*, November 2004, pp. 25–31.
19. See Mike Gorman, "The Emotionally Effective Salesperson," Professional Remodeler, September 2003, p. 77; Tom Reilly, "The Emotional Side of Selling," *Industrial Distribution*, July 2004, p. 54.
20. Daniel Goleman, *Working with Emotional Intelligence* (New York: Bantam, 1999).
21. See also Jane Z. Sojka and Dawn R. Deeter-Schmeltz, "Enhancing the Emotional Intelligence of Salespeople," *Mid-American Journal of Business* 17 (Spring 2002), pp. 43–50.
22. *Occupational Outlook Handbook*, 2004–2005 edition, U.S. Department of Labor, Bureau of Labor Statistics.

CHAPTER 2

1. Thomas Wotruba, "The Evolution of Personal Selling," *Journal of Personal Selling & Sales Management* (Summer 1991), pp. 1–12; William C. Moncrief and Greg W. Marshall, "The Evolution of the Seven Steps of Selling," *Industrial Marketing Management* 34 (January 2005), pp. 13–22.
2. George W. Dudley, and John F. Tanner Jr., *The Hard Truth about Soft Selling* (Dallas: Behavioral Science Research Press, 2005).
3. Werner J. Reinartz, and V. Kumar, "The Impact of Customer Relationship Characteristics on Profitable Lifetime Duration," *Journal of Marketing* 67, no. 1 (2003), pp. 77–99; Rajkumar Venkatesan and V. Kumar, "A Customer Lifetime Value Framework for Customer Selection and Resource Allocation Strategy," *Journal of Marketing* 68, no. 4 (2004), pp. 106–25.
4. Mark Uncles, Grahme R. Dowling, and Kathy Hammond, "Customer Loyalty and Customer Loyalty Programs," *Journal of Consumer Marketing* 20, no. 4 (2003), pp. 294–316.
5. Sandy Jap and Barton Weitz, "A Taxonomy of Long-Term Relationships" (working paper, College of Business Administration, University of Florida, 1996); F. Robert Dwyer, Paul Schurr, and Sejo Oh, "Developing Buyer–Seller Relationships," *Journal of Marketing*, April 1987, pp. 11–27. Lloyd M. Rinehart, James A. Eckert, Thomas J. Page Jr., and Thomas Atkin, "An Assessment of Supplier–Customer Relationships," *Journal of Business Logistics* 25, no. 1 (2004), pp. 25–63.
6. Chuck Salter, "The Soft Sell," *Fast Company* (January 2005), pp. 72–73.
7. Robert W. Armstrong and Siew Min Yee, "Do Chinese Trust Chinese? A Study of Chinese Buyers and Sellers in Malaysia," *Journal of International Marketing* 9:3 (2001), pp. 63–86.
8. Felix T. Mavondo and Elaine M. Rodrigo, "The Effect of Relationship Dimensions on Interpersonal and Interorganizational Commitment in Organizations Conducting Business between Australia and China," *Journal of Business Research* 52 (2001), pp. 111–21.

9. Daniel Fries, "Have Trust and Confidence," *Purchasing Today,* April 2001, p. 68.

10. Achim Walter and Thomas Ritter, "The Influence of Adaptations, Trust, and Commitment on Value-Creating Functions of Customer Relationships," *Journal of Business & Industrial Marketing* 18, no. 415 (2003), pp. 353–65.

11. Annie H. Liu and Mark P. Leach, "Developing Loyal Customers with a Value-Adding Sales Force: Examining Customer Satisfaction and the Perceived Credibility of Consultative Salespeople," *Journal of Personal Selling & Sales Management* 21, no. 2 (2001), pp. 147–56.

12. "Eastman Kodak Brings Training into Sharper Focus," *Sales & Marketing Management,* September 1992, p. 62.

13. Erin Strout, "To Tell the Truth," *Sales & Marketing Management* 154, no. 7 (2002), pp. 40–48.

14. Chuck Salter, "The Soft Sell," *Fast Company* (January 2005), pp. 72–73; Jon M. Hawes, Kenneth E. Mast, and John E. Swan, "Trust Earning Perceptions of Sellers and Buyers," *Journal of Personal Selling & Sales Management* (Spring 1989), pp. 1–8.

15. Lisa Cross, "Establishing Customer Loyalty," *Graphic Arts Monthly* 76, no. 9 (2004), pp. 39–42.

16. Tracy L. Tuten and David J. Urban, "An Expanded Model of Business-to-Business Partnership Formation and Success," *Industrial Marketing Management* 30 (2001), pp. 149–64.

17. D. Ross Brennan, Peter W. Turnbull, and David T. Wilson, "Dyadic Adaptation in Business-to-Business Markets," *European Journal of Marketing* 37, no. 11/12 (2003), pp. 1636–68; Ik-Whan Kwon and Taewon Suh, "Factors Affecting the Level of Trust and Commitment in Supply Chain Relationships," *Journal of Supply Chain Management* 40 (Spring 2004), pp. 4–15.

18. Betsy Cummings, "Dodging Dishonesty," *Sales & Marketing Management* 157, no. 2 (2005), p. 10.

19. Coreen Bailor, "Listening, with Interest," *Customer Relationship Management* 9 (February 2005), pp. 28–33.

20. Eilene Zimmerman, "Quota Busters," *Sales & Marketing Management* 153 (January 2001), pp. 58–63.

21. Scott Widmier, "The Effects of Incentives and Personality on Saleperson's Customer Orientation," *Industrial Marketing Management* 31, no. 7 (2002), pp. 609–16.

22. Anonymous, "Changing Compensation Plans," *Agency Sales* 31 (July 2001), pp. 48–49.

23. Zimmerman, "Quota Busters," p. 58.

24. Dwyer, Schurr & Oh.

25. Reinartz and Kumar, "The Impact of Customer Relationship Characteristics."

26. Michael D. Johnson, and Fred Selnes, "Customer Portfolio Management: Toward a Dynamic Theory of Relationships," *Journal of Marketing* 68, no. 2 (2004), pp. 1–17.

27. Dennis Campbell and Frances Frei, "The Persistence of Customer Profitability: Empirical Evidence and Implications from a Financial Services Firm," *Journal of Service Research* 7, no. 2 (2004), pp. 107–124.

28. Thomas Vollman and Carlos Cordon, "Building Successful Customer–Supplier Alliances," *Long Range Planning* 31:5, 1998, pp. 684–94.

29. Betsy Cummings, "Give 'em What They Want," *Sales & Marketing Management* 154, no. 3 (2002), p. 12.

30. Glen L. Urban, and John R. Hauser, "Listening In to Find and Explore New Combinations of Customer Needs," *Journal of Marketing* 68, no. 2 (2004), pp. 72–87.

CHAPTER 3

1. Erin Strout, "Are Your Salespeople Ripping You Off?" *Sales & Marketing Management,* February 2001, pp. 57–62.

2. Sergio Roman and Salvador Ruiz, "Relationship Outcomes of Perceived Ethical Sales Behavior: The Customer's Perspective," *Journal of Business Research* 58 (April 2005), pp. 439–51.

3. Geoffrey G. Bell, Robert J. Oppenheimer, and Andre Bastien, "Trust Deterioration in an International Buyer–Seller Relationship," *Journal of Business Ethics* 36 (2002), pp. 65–78.

4. Willem Verbeke, Cok Ouwerkerk, and Ed Peelen, "Exploring the Contextual and Individual Factors on Ethical Decision Making of Salespeople," *Journal of Business Ethics* 15, Fall 1996, pp. 1175–87.

5. Betsy Cummings, "Ethical Breach," *Sales and Marketing Management* 156 (July 2004), p. 10.

6. Charles W. Schwepker, Jr., "Ethical Climate's Relationship to Job Satisfaction, Organizational Commitment and Turnover Intention in the Salesforce," *Journal of Business Research* 54 (2001), pp. 39–52.

7. Eberhard Schnebel and Marge Bienert, "Implementing Ethics in Business Organizations," *Journal of Business Ethics* 53 (2004), pp. 203–11.

8. Sergio Roman "The Impact of Ethical Sales Behaviour on Customer Satisfaction, Trust and Loyalty to the Company: An Empirical Study in the Financial Services Industry," *Journal of Marketing Management* 19 (2003), pp. 915–39.

9. Stephen S. Batory, William Neese, and Anne H. Batory, "Ethical Marketing Practices: An Investigation of Antecedents, Innovativeness and Business Performance," *Journal of American Academy of Business* (March 2, 2005), pp. 135–42.

10. Dawn Myers, "You Get What You Give So Make It Good," *Promotional Products Business,* June 1998, pp. 105–11.

11. Shirley Hunter, personal correspondence; used with permission.

12. William Bearden, Thomas Ingram, and Raymond LaForge, *Marketing: Principles and Perspectives* (New York: McGraw-Hill/Irwin, 2004).

13. Anonymous, "Exclusive IOMA Survey: How Employers Address Sexual Harrassment," *HR Focus* 78 (12), pp. 3–5.

14. Christopher Stewart, "Desperate Measures," *Sales and Marketing Management* 155 (September 2003), p. 32.

15. Bryan Macakanja, personal correspondence; used with permission.

16. Tara J. Radin and Carolyn E. Predmore, "The Myth of the Salesperson: Intended and Unintended Consequences of Product-Specific Sales Incentives," *Journal of Business Ethics* 36 (2002), pp. 79–92.

17. Halliburton, "Sensitive Transactions," http://www.halliburton.com/about/sensitive_transactions.jsp (accessed February 8, 2005).

18. Meryl Davids, "Global Standards, Local Problems," *Journal of Business Strategy,* January/February 1999, pp. 22–35; Sak Onkvisit and John Shaw, "International Corporate Bribery: Some Legal, Cultural, Economic, and Ethical–Philosophical and Marketing Considerations," *Journal of Global Marketing* 42 (1991), pp. 5–20.

19. O. C. Ferrell, Thomas N. Ingram, and Raymond W. LaForge, "Initiating Structure for Legal and Ethical Decisions in a Global Sales Organization," *Industrial Marketing Management* 29 (2000), pp. 555–64.

CHAPTER 4

1. Mary Anne Raymond, John Mittelstaedt, Christopher Hopkins, and John F. Tanner Jr., "Retailer Merchandising Decisions: Using Retailer Perceptions to Develop a Multi-Level Competitive Strategic Profit Model," *Journal of Marketing Management* (Forthcoming).

2. Eddy Patterson, personal correspondence; used with permission.

3. U.S. Department of Commerce, *Statistical Abstracts of the United States*, 119th ed. (Washington, DC: U.S. Government Printing Office, 1999), p. 115.

4. Mark Del Franco, "Thanks, Uncle Sam," *Catalog Age* 20 (November 2003), pp. 1–3.

5. Susan W. Solovic, "Federal Procurement Opportunities for Women Business Owners: Good News—Bad News Scenario," *Women in Business* 56, no. 4 (2004), 11–12.

6. Marvin Wagner, personal correspondence received February 16, 2005, used with permission.; G. Tomas M. Hult, "The Effect of Global Leadership on Purchasing Process Outcomes," *European Journal of Marketing* 32, (November/December 1998), pp. 1029–32.

7. G. Tomas M. Hult, "Culture Competitiveness in Global Sourcing," *Industrial Marketing Management* 31 (January 2002), pp. 25–34.

8. Anonymous, "Cream O'Weber Thinks Outside the Box for McDonalds," *Dairy Foods: Innovative Ideas for Dairy Processors*, www.dairyfoods.com (posted January 10, 2005).

9. Robert Dwyer and John F. Tanner Jr., *Business Marketing: Connecting Strategy, Relationships, and Learning* 3rd ed. (New York: McGraw-Hill/Irwin, 2006).

10. Julie Roberts, "Great Expectations: E-Procurement and Work Processes," *Purchasing Today*, October 2001, pp. 24–30.

11. For a very interesting look at satisfaction by role in the buying center and by buy-class, see Jeanne Rossomme, "Customer Satisfaction Measurement in a Business-to-Business Context: A Conceptual Framework," *Journal of Business & Industrial Marketing* 18 (February 3, 2003), pp. 179–96.

12. For a revised and expanded taxonomy of buying situations, see Michele Bunn, "Taxonomy of Buying Decision Approaches," *Journal of Marketing*, January 1993, pp. 38–56.

13. Maria Anne Skaates, Henrikki Tikkanen, and Jarno Lindblom, "Relationships and Project Marketing Success," *Journal of Business & Industrial Marketing* 17, no. 5 (2002), pp. 389–406.

14. Dwyer and Tanner, *Business Marketing: Connecting Strategy, Relationships, and Learning.*

15. Ron Swift, personal correspondence; used with permission.

16. Stefan Stremersch, Stefan Wuyts, and Ruud T. Frambach, "The Purchasing of Full-Service Contracts: An Exploratory Study within the Industrial Maintenance Market," *Industrial Marketing Management* 30 (January 2001), pp. 1–12.

17. Geok Theng Lau, Mohammed A. Razzaque, and Angeline Ong, "Gatekeeping in Organizational Purchasing: An Empirical Investigation," *Journal of Business & Industrial Marketing* 18, no. 1 (2003), pp. 82–104.

18. Frank Bingham, Charles Quigly, and Povert Valvo, "Back-Door Selling: A Descriptive Model," in *Enriching Marketing Practice and Education*, ed. Elenora Stuart and Ellen Moore (Atlanta: Southern Marketing Association, 1997), pp. 244–48.

19. Javier Gonzalez-Benito, Angel R. Martinez-Lorente, and Barrie G. Dale, "A Study of the Purchasing Management System with Respect to Total Quality Management," *Industrial Marketing Management* 32 (2002), pp. 443–54.

20. Lionel Dace, personal interview, February 18, 2003.

21. David Sprague, "Adding Value and Value Analysis to TQM," *Journal for Quality and Participation,* January/February 1996, pp. 70–72.

22. Margy Conchar, George Zinkhan, Cara Peters, and Sergio Olavarrieta, "An Integrated Framework for the Conceptualization of Consumers' Perceived-Risk Processing," *Journal of the Academy of Marketing Science* 32, no. 4 (2004), pp. 418–37.

23. Vijay R. Kannan and Keah Choon Tan, "Just in Time, Total Quality Management, and Supply Chain Management: Understanding Their Linkages and Impact on Business Performance," *Omega* 33 (April 2005), pp. 153–74.

24. Peter Duchessi, Charles M. Schaninger, and Thomas Nowak, "Creating Cluster-Specific Purchase Profiles from Point-of-Sale Scanner Data and Geodemographic Clusters: Improving Category Management at a Major U.S. Grocery Chain," *Journal of Consumer Behaviour* 4 (December 2004), pp. 97–118.

25. Roberta Duffy, "Value through Integration," *Purchasing Today*, March 2001, pp. 36–40.

26. Elizabeth Baatz, "How Tools Unlock Supply Value," *Purchasing Magazine*, April 22, 1999, pp. 28–31.

27. Andreas I. Nicolaou, "Adoption of Just-In-Time and Electronic Data Interchange Systems and Perceptions of Cost Management Systems," *Accounting Information Systems* 3 (2002), pp. 35–62.

28. Hank Darlington, "How to Pick the Best Vendor Partners for Your Business," *Supply House Times* 46 (February 2004), pp. 52–53; C. Muralidharan, N. Anantharaman, and Srinath G. Deshmukh, "Vendor Rating in Purchasing Scenario: A Confidence Interval Approach," *International Journal of Operations & Production* 21 (September 10, 2001), pp. 1305–26.

29. Matt Barnason, "Keeping Suppliers Competitive," *SAS.com* (Third Quarter 2003), pp. 15–16.

30. Jane Simms, "On the Road to Success," *Supply Management* 8 (November 13, 2003), pp. 30–31.

31. Mark Brunelli, "Consultants See BIG Future for E-Commerce," *Purchasing Magazine*, October 21, 1999, pp. S83–S86.

32. Thomas N. Martin and John C. Hafer, "Internet Procurement by Corporate Purchasing Agents: Is It All Hype?" *Advanced Management Journal* 67 (Winter 2002), pp. 41–48.

33. Larry R. Smeltzer and Amelia S. Carr, "Electronic Reverse Auctions: Promises, Risks, and Conditions for Success," *Industrial Marketing Management* 32 (2003), pp. 481–88.

34. Anonymous, "Owens Corning Builds Major Savings from Reverse Auctions," *Supplier Selection & Management Report* 1 (March 2002), pp. 13–14.

35. Anonymous, "U.S. Navy Saves Nearly $900,000 Using eBreviate Auction" (press release, A. T. Kearney Procurement Solutions, 2001).

36. Geraint John, "Smart Saucing," *Supply Management* 23 no. 9 (2004), p. 40.

37. Simeon Chow and Reed Holden, "Toward an Understanding of Loyalty: The Moderating Role of Trust," *Journal of Managerial Issues* 9 (Fall 2000), pp. 275–98.

CHAPTER 5

1. Stephen D. Boyd, "For a More Powerful Performance, Say It Short, and Say It Well," *Presentations*, January 2003, p. 62.
2. Melinda Ligos, "Does Image Matter?" *Sales and Marketing Management*, March 2001, p. 56.
3. Kitty O. Locker, *Business and Administrative Communication* (New York: McGraw-Hill, 2006), p. 50.
4. See Tad Simons, "Buzzword Abuse Is More Than Just Annoying—It Can Be Dangerous," *Presentations*, April 2003, p. 6; Tad Simons, "Are You a Buzzword Abuser?" *Presentations*, April 2003, pp. 30–34.
5. Monica I. Wofford, "You Don't Have to Be Perfect To Be Effective as a Speaker," *Presentations*, December 2004, p. 90.
6. Lee Witherell, "Keep Selling to Old Customers Like They're New," *Marketing*, July 24, 2003, p. 16.
7. Richard Buckingham, "Hear What Your Clients Are Actually Saying," *Customer Once, Client Forever*, as displayed at http://search.epnet.com/login.aspx?direct=true$AuthType=cookie,ip,url,uid&db+buh&an=9327498 (accessed on 12/1/2004).
8. See Stephen D. Boyd, "Giving Voice and Gestures More Power in Presentations" *Presentations*, June 2004, p. 58.
9. See Lucette Comer and Tanya Drollinger, "Active Empathetic Listening and Selling Success: A Conceptual Framework," *Journal of Personal Selling and Sales Management* 9 (Winter 1999), pp. 15–29; C. David Shepherd, Stephen Castleberry, and Rick Ridnour, "Linking Effective Listening with Salesperson Performance: An Exploratory Study," *Journal of Business & Industrial Marketing* 12 (1997), pp. 315–32; Stephen Castleberry and C. David Shepherd, "Effective Interpersonal Listening and Personal Selling," *Journal of Personal Selling & Sales Management*, Winter 1993, pp. 35–50; Stephen B. Castleberry, C. David Shepherd, and Rick E. Ridnour, "Effective Interpersonal Listening in the Personal Selling Environment: Conceptualization, Measurement, and Nomological Validity," *Journal of Marketing Theory and Practice*, Winter 1999, pp. 30–38.
10. Lori Patel, "Is She Buying Your Pitch?" *Business 2.0*, October 2002, p. 34.
11. Dave Zielinski, "Body Language Myths," *Presentations*, April 2001, p. 39.
12. Zielinski, "Body Language Myths," p. 42.
13. See Locker, *Business and Administrative Communication*, p. 301.
14. John Perry, "Palm Power in the Workplace," *The American Salesman* 46 (October 2001), p. 22.
15. Julia Chang, "Selling in Action," *Sales & Marketing Management* 156 (May 2004), p. 22.
16. Dale Carnegie, a noted sales training consultant, would disagree with this advice. He suggests that not offering a handshake shows a lack of assertiveness.
17. Dave Zielinski, "Cracking the Dress Code," *Presentations*, February 2005, p. 28.
18. All material presented in the five principles was written by Vicki L. West; used by permission.
19. Owen Hargie, *The Handbook of Communication Skills*, 2nd ed. (London: Routledge, 1997)
20. "Phone Sales," *Sell!ng*, September 2004, p. 10.
21. David Wallace, "Navigating the E-mail Minefield," *1to1 Magazine*, April 2004, pp. 26–27.
22. Jason B. MacDonald and Kirk Smith, "The Effects of Technology-Mediated Communication on Industrial Buyer Behavior," *Industrial Marketing Management* 33 (2004), pp. 107–16.
23. See for example, Cynthia J. Bean, James S. Boles, and Cynthia Rodriguez Cano, "Electronic Mail Appraisal: A Buyer and Seller Survey," *Journal of Business and Industrial Marketing*, 18 (2003), pp. 419–34.
24. Kathryn Droullard, "Mind Your Manners," *Sales and Marketing Management*, January 2005, p. 28.
25. See Locker, *Business and Administrative Communication*, pp. 296, 297.
26. See also Bert Rosenbloom and Trina Larsen, "Communication in International Business-to-Business Marketing Channels: Does Culture Matter?" *Industrial Marketing Management* 32 (2003), pp. 309–15.

CHAPTER 6

1. David A. Reid, Ellen Bolman Pullins, and Richard E. Plank, "The Impact of Purchase Situation on Salesperson Communication Behaviors in Business Markets," *Industrial Marketing Management* 31 (2002), pp. 205–13.
2. Stephen S. Porter, Joshua L. Wiener, and Gary L. Frankwick, "The Moderating Effect of Selling Situation on the Adaptive Selling Strategy—Selling Effectiveness Relationship," *Journal of Business Research* 56 (April 2003), pp. 275–81.
3. Dave Zielinski, "From the Playground to the Podium: What Men and Women Can Learn from Each Other," *Presentations*, May 2004, pp. 22–26.
4. Lynne C. Lancaster and David Stillman, *When Generations Collide*, (New York: Harper Business, 2003).
5. See Michael Beverland, "Contextual Influences and the Adoption and Practice of Relationship Selling in a Business-to-Business Setting: An Exploratory Study," *Journal of Personal Selling & Sales Management* 21, no. 3 (Summer 2001), pp. 207–15.
6. Barry Farber, "Pump It Up," *Entrepreneur* 32 (February 2004), pp. 73–74; Andrew Adamson, "Salespeople Should Know What They Sell," *Cabinet Maker*, September 10, 2004, p. 6; "Selling to the CIO," *Computerworld* 38 (6/7/2004), p. 48.
7. See Richard S. Jacobs, Kenneth R. Evans, Robert E. Kleine III and Timothy D. Landry, "Disclosure and Its Reciprocity as Predictors of Key Outcomes of an Initial Sales Encounter," *Journal of Personal Selling & Sales Management* 21, no. 1 (Winter 2001), pp. 51–61.
8. Larry Blaine, "The Challenge of Selling," *American Salesman* 49 (July 2004), pp. 14–17; "Be a Sales Superstar: Know Products and People," *Selling*, July 2004, p. 5; Howard Feiertag, "Sales Folks Should Concentrate on Value to Improve Business," *Hotel and Motel Management* 219 (2/2/2004), p. 6.
9. Customers are also gaining knowledge on their own. See, for example, Karen Norman Kennedy and Dawn R. Deeter-Schmelz, "Descriptive and Predictive Analyses of Industrial Buyers' Use of Online Information for Purchasing," *Journal of Personal Selling & Sales Management* 21, no. 4 (Fall 2001), pp. 279–90.
10. See Susi Geiger and Darach Turley, "Grounded Theory in Sales Research: An Investigation of Salespeople's Client Relationships," *Journal of Business and Industrial Marketing* 18 (2003), pp. 580–94.

11. John Gaffney, "What Will You Bring to the Table?" *1to1 Magazine*, January/February 2005, p. 36.

12. Marji McClure, "Contact Management Provides Sales and Service for Houston Aeros," *1to1 Magazine*, July/August 2003, pp. 12–13.

13. Henry Canady, "ESP at HP," *Selling Power*, September 1997, pp. 76–81.

14. David Merrill and Roger Reid, *Personal Styles and Effective Performance* (Radnor, PA: Chilton, 1981); Robert Bolton and Dorothy Bolton, *Social Style/Management Style* (New York: AMACOM, 1984); Robert Bolton and Dorothy Bolton, *People Styles at Work: Making Bad Relationships Good and Good Relationships Better* (New York: AMACOM, 1996).

15. For example, see Robert B. Miller, Gary A. Williams, and Alden M. Hayashi, *The 5 Paths to Persuasion: The Art of Selling Your Message.* (New York: Warner Business Books, 2004).

CHAPTER 7

1. It is even important for nonprofit organizations. See, for example, Cecilia Hogan and David Lamb, *Prospect Research: A Primer for Growing Nonprofits* (Boston: Jones & Bartlett, 2004).

2. "Treasuring Talent and Customer Insight," *1to1 Magazine*, May/June 2004, p. 33.

3. Maria Holmlund, "Analyzing Business Relationships and Distinguishing Different Interaction Levels," *Industrial Marketing Management* 33 (2004), pp. 279–87.

4. Michael Schrage, "Are Customers Selling for You? Your Best Clients Can Often Be Your Best Salespeople," *Sales and Marketing Management*, February 2004, p. 22.

5. Bill Brooks, "7 Power-Packed Prospecting Pointers," *American Salesman* 48 (October 2003), pp. 8–11.

6. Customers may or may not want to provide names. See Julie T. Johnson, Hiram C. Barksdale Jr., and James S. Boles, "Factors Associated with Customer Willingness to Refer Leads to Salespeople," *Journal of Business Research* 56, no. 4 (2003), pp. 257–63.

7. Bill Cates, "Referral Events Build Your Practice," *On Wall Street*, January 2004, p. 78.

8. "Digging Deeper," *Sales and Marketing Management*, February 2004, p. 8.

9. Terry L. Mayfield, "The Other Type of Referral," *Sell!ng*, July 2004, pp. 12–13.

10. Barry Farber, "Meet and Potatoes," *Entrepreneur*, February 2002, pp. 89–90.

11. For example, see Howard Feiertag, "Networking Groups Help Broaden Contacts, Increase Business," *H&MM*, December 8, 2003, p. 12.

12. See bni.com for more information.

13. See http://www.newholland.com.

14. "Lead Generator," *Sales and Marketing Management* 156 (January 2004), p. 16.

15. See http://www.update.com/products/pm_en.html.

16. John A. Fugel, "Trade Show Know-How; Turning Prospects into Sales," *Rural Telecommunications* 23 (May/June 2003), pp. 48–49.

17. Jim Blythe, "Using Trade Fairs in Key Account Management," *Industrial Marketing Management* 31, (October 2002), pp. 627–34.

18. Kathleen Conroy, "Use Trade Shows to Introduce Products, Market, and Prospect," *Sell!ng*, January 2004, p. 5.

19. Daniel Tynan, "Tricks of the Trade Show," *Sales and Marketing Management* 156, (January 2004), p. 27.

20. For information on SIC and NAICS codes, see the following: An excellent listing of Web resources is available at www.d.umn.edu/~jvileta/naics.html; 1997 NAICS codes are at http://www.census.gov/epcd/naics/naicscod.txt ; SIC codes are at www.osha.gov/oshstats/sicser.html.

21. Jill Duman, "Striking Gold," *Customer Relationship Management*, November 2001, pp. 59–60.

22. Ruth P. Stevens, "CRM: It's about Prospecting, Too," *1to1 Magazine*, February 2002 (accessed on 3/13/02 at http://www.1to1.com).

23. "Positive Prospecting," *Sales and Marketing Management* 156 (January 2004), p. 16.

24. For some hints on how to do cold calling more effectively, see Polly Lemire, *The Cold Call Cure: How to Outsmart Your Cold Call Fears and Become a Master at Prospecting for New Business* (Bloomington, Indiana: AuthorHouse, 2003).

25. Andy Cohen, "Success with Referrals," *Sales and Marketing Management* 155 (September 2003), p. 12.

26. Wendy Weiss, "Sell!ng Tips," *Sell!ng*, February 2004, p. 8.

27. See Paul J. Batista, "Telemarketing and the TCPA: Let the Seller Beware," *Journal of the Academy of Marketing Science* 31, no. 1 (2003), pp. 97–98.

28. See Bill Cates, "Turning Do Not Call into Referrals," *On Wall Street*, October 2003, p. 78.

29. See for example, Thomas E. Kane, *Letters for Lawyers: Essential Communication for Clients, Prospects, and Others* (Chicago: American Bar Association, 2004).

30. Denny Hatch, "Anthrax: Sleeping with the Enemy: How Are Direct Marketers Coping?" *Target Marketing* 25 (January 2002), pp. 15–20.

31. Marlene Caroselli, "Fill the Bill—and Other Great Prospecting Ideas," *Sell!ng*, February 2002, p. 11.

32. For the classic treatment of the funneling process, see Robert B. Miller, Stephen E. Heiman, and Tad Tuleja, *The New Strategic Selling* (New York: Warner Business, 2005).

33. Victoria Murphy, "Dialing for Tech Dollars," *Forbes* 174 (November 15, 2004), p. 64.

34. See also Alyssa Dver, "Taking the Lead," *Bank Marketing* 35 (December 2002), pp. 28–32.

35. Niall Budds, "Shared Goals Foster Better Lead Management," *Marketing News* 38 (October 1, 2004), pp. 17–18.

36. Ruth P. Stevens, "CRM: It's about Prospecting, Too," *1to1 Magazine*, February 2002 (accessed on 3/13/02 at http://www.1to1.com).

37. Bill Brooks, "Ways You Can Conquer Call Reluctance," *American Salesman* 48 (August 2003), pp.19–21.

38. Willem Verbeke and Richard P. Bagozzi, "Sales Call Anxiety: Exploring What It Means When Fear Rules a Sales Encounter," *Journal of Marketing* 64 (July 2000), pp. 88–101.

CHAPTER 8

1. See Thomas Tellefsen and Gloria Penn Thomas, "The Antecedents and Consequences of Organizational and Personal Commitment in Business Service Relationships," *Industrial Marketing Management* 34 (January 2005), pp. 23–37.

2. These are also called "red flags." See Robert B. Miller, Stephen E. Heiman, Diane Sanchez, and Tad Tuleja, *The*

New Conceptual Selling: The Most Effective and Proven Method for Face-to-Face Sales Planning (New York: Warner Business, 2005).

3. Harry Campbell, "Smarter Selling," *Sales and Marketing Management,* (December 2004), p. 10.

4. Gary L. Hunter, "Information Overload: Guidance for Identifying When Information Becomes Detrimental to Sales Force Performance," *Journal of Personal Selling and Sales Management* 24 (Spring 2004), pp. 91–100.

5. Mila D'Antonio, "Connecting to Success," *1to1 Magazine,* (September 2003), p. 22.

6. Mila D'Antonio, "Continental's Data Warehouse Pilots a Customer-Focused Enterprise," *1to1 Magazine,* (January/February) 2005, pp. 24–25.

7. Larry Dobrow, "Customer Value Is on Lufthansa's Radar," *1to1 Magazine,* (January/February 2005), p. 16.

8. "Best Practices," *1to1 Magazine,* (January/February 2005), p. 11.

9. Stephen Regenold, "Case Study: A Cracker of a Presentation," *Presentations,* (February 2002), p. 18.

10. Stephen B. Castleberry, "The Web as an Information Source for Sales Recruits: Its Effectiveness in Aiding Anticipatory Socialization of Salespeople," *Industrial Marketing Management,* in press (2002).

11. This description was accurate at the time the book went to press. One thing is obvious: The Web changes daily. Don't be surprised if this site has different offerings on the day you visit.

12. Michelle Nichols, "Crashing Past the Gatekeepers—Part Two," *BusinessWeek Online,* (April 24), 2002.

13. See Nichols, "Crashing Past the Gatekeepers."

14. http://www.export.gov.

15. Stephan Schiffman, *Sales Don't Just Happen* (Chicago: Dearborn Trade, 2002).

16. Neil Rackham, *Major Account Sales Strategy* (New York: McGraw-Hill, 1989), p. 39.

17. For their latest book on the topic, see Robert B. Miller, Stephen E. Heiman, Diane Sanchez, and Tad Tuleja, *The New Conceptual Selling: The Most Effective and Proven Method for Face-to-Face Sales Planning* (New York: Warner Business, 2005).

18. Matthew May, "Create Goals That Inspire Productivity, Profitability," *Sell!ng,* (April 2004), p. 2.

19. See Sarah Cook, "Learning Needs Analysis: Part I: What Is Learning Needs Analysis?" *Training Journal,* (January 2005), pp. 64–68.; Garry Platt, "Smart Objectives: What They Mean and How to Set Them," *Training Journal,* (August 2002), pp. 23–26.

20. Jim Hersma, personal correspondence. Used with permission.

21. See, for example, Tim Breithaupt, *10 Steps to Sales Success* (New York: AMACOM, 2003).

22. See Troy Korsgaden, "Getting It Right! Sell the Appointment First and Your Products Will Be Sold to the Right People," *Advisor Today,* (January 2004), p. 22.

23. Neil Rackham, *Major Account Sales Strategy* (New York: McGraw-Hill, 1989).

24. Michelle Nichols, "Salespeople Who Need People," *BusinessWeek Online,* (November 4), 2002.

25. Rackham, *Major Account Sales Strategy,* p. 30.

26. Steve Waterhouse, *The Team Selling Solution: Creating and Managing Teams That Win the Complex Sale* (New York: McGraw-Hill, 2003).

27. Janelle Barlow, Peta Peter, and Lewis Barlow, *Smart Videoconferencing: New Habits for Virtual Meetings* (San Francisco: Berrett-Koehler Publishers, 2002).

28. Alison Overholt, "Virtually There," *Fast Company,* (March 2002), p. 112.

29. John J. Champa, *Videoconferencing Skills* (Mason, OH: South-Western Educational & Professional, 2003).

30. Betsy Cummings, "Do Customers Hate Salespeople? Only If They Commit One of These Deadly Sins of Selling," *Sales and Marketing Management,* (June 2001), pp. 44–51.

31. Ian Mount, "Out of Control," *Business 2.0,* (August 2002), pp. 38–44.

32. See Todd Natenberg, "Virtual Selling: Double Your Sales in Half the Time," *Sell!ng,* (November 2004), p. 9; "Turn Appointments into Sales," *Sell!ng,* (June 2004), p. 2.

33. Robert Brenner, "Leading Contenders," *Sales and Marketing Management,* (October 2004), p. 14.

CHAPTER 9

1. Building partnerships and strong relationships is a process that starts when a lead is identified and continues throughout all postsale service and future calls.

2. Based on personal correspondence with Karl Sooder. Used with permission.

3. Of course, many aspects of first impressions, such as race and gender, are outside the control of the salesperson.

4. But be careful if you're just pretending. See Alicia A. Grandey, "When the Show Must Go On: Surface Acting and Deep Acting as Determinants of Emotional Exhaustion and Peer-Rated Service Delivery," *Academy of Management Journal* 46 (February 2003), pp. 86–96.

5. Betsy Cummings, "In Their Shoes," *Sales and Marketing Management,* October 2004, p. 37.

6. For more examples, see Ted Pollock, "How to Command the Prospect's Attention," *American Salesman* 48 (August 2003), pp. 22–26.

7. Some would even suggest that the goal of the opening is to take control of the conversation. See, for example, Jeffrey Gitomer, "Key to the Cold Call Is Take Control of the Conversation," *Warsaw Business Journal,* April 8–14, 2002, p. 12.

8. See Jeffrey Gitomer, "Want to Make a Sale? First Establish Rapport," *Prague Business Journal* 7 (April 29, 2002), p. 9.

9. This classic example can be found, along with other humorous ones, in Ken Delmar, *Winning Moves* (New York: Warner, 1984), p. 4.

10. See "Do You Know What Motivates Your Customers?" *1to1 Magazine,* March 2005, p. 50.

11. Michael Fielding, "Damage Control: Firms Must Plan for Counterintelligence," *Marketing News,* September 15, 2004, pp. 19–22.

12. Neil Rackham, *SPIN Selling* (New York: McGraw-Hill, 1988)

13. Angie Main, used with permission.

14. Rackham, SPIN Selling.

15. Anita Sirianni, "Talking Trash on 'Feature Dumping,'" *Proofs,* September 2004, p. 70.

16. "Sales Basics," *Sell!ng,* September 2004, p. 14.

17. "Emphasize the Benefits of Your Products and Services," *Teller Sense,* January 1, 2003, pp. 1–7.

18. "Getting and Selling the Benefits of Benefits," *Cabinet Maker,* November 2003, p. 6.

19. Ray Hanson, personal correspondence. Used by permission.

20. Nancy J. Adler, *International Dimensions of Organizational Behavior* (Boston: Kent Publishing, 1986), p. 55.

21. Credibility can obviously be strengthened in other ways. See, for example, Amy Moerke, "Parties with Purpose: How to Build Credibility with Clients through Social Outings," *Sales and Marketing Management,* May 2004, p. 18.

22. Jim Hersma, personal correspondence. Used with permission.

23. Sam Manfer, "How to Reach Corporate Leaders and Establish Relationships," *American Salesman,* June 2003, pp. 15–17.

24. John R. Graham, "Talking Our Way Out of Sales," *American Salesman,* July 2002, pp. 14–18.

25. Todd Graf, personal correspondence. Used with permission.

26. Nancy R. Mandell, "What to Do When Nobody's Buying What You're Selling," *On Wall Street,* February 2003, pp. 32–37.

27. Tracey Brill, personal correspondence. Used with permission.

CHAPTER 10

1. Dave Zielinski, "Handle with Care: How to Say the Right Thing, at the Right Time, in the Right Way Whatever the Occasion," *Presentations,* March 2003, pp. 26–32.

2. See for example, John L. Elman, "Laughter Is Everywhere," *Advisor Today,* September 2002, p. 122.

3. Even when using high-tech presentations. See Michael Kerr, "Adding Humor to High-Tech Presentations Has Some Serious Advantages," *Presentations,* November 2002, p. 82.

4. See Chris Sandlund, "You Think That's Funny?" *Entrepreneur,* December 2002, p. 101.

5. Julie Hill, "Laugh Lab," *Presentations,* March 2002, p. 18.

6. See "Give Your Presentations a Boost with Effective Graphics," *Sell!ng,* June 2004, p. 14.

7. See for example, Marilyn M. Helms, "The Key to a Strong Presentation Is in the Details," *Presentations,* May 2003, p. 58.

8. For more details on how to prepare PowerPoint slides, see Julie Hill, "The Writing on the Wall," *Presentations,* February 2004, pp. 37–40; Geetesh Bajaj, "Get the Most out of Your PowerPoint Files," *Presentations,* February 2003, pp. 38–42; Terry Wall, "PowerPoint Pitfalls That Can Kill an Audience's Will to Stay Awake," *Presentations,* October 2004, p. 46; Julie Terberg, "Full Images Offer a Unique and Effective Alternative to Bullet Points," October 2004, pp. 18–19; Patty Civalleri, "Quick-Masked Heading, Striking Audio Create Dramatic Opening Slide," *Presentations,* May 2004, pp. 16–18; Patty Civalleri, "Big and Bold Photos Bring Attention to the Topic," *Presentations,* March 2004, pp. 20–21.

9. See Tim Zaun, "There's More Than One Way to Use Video," *Presentations,* December 2003, p. 78.

10. Stephen Regenold, "Tablet PCs: Your New Best Friend," *Presentations,* February 2003, pp. 28–36.

11. See for example, Marji McClure, "A Template for Innovation," *1to1 Magazine,* April 2003, pp. 24–31.

12. For more examples, see Mila D'Antonio, "Connecting to Success," *1to1 Magazine,* September 2003, pp. 20–24.

13. See Stephen Regenold, "New Respect for Doc-Cams," *Presentations,* July 2004, pp. 34–38.

14. Julie Hill, "All A-Board," *Presentations,* September 2004, pp. 37–40.

15. Personal correspondence.

16. Tad Simons, "The Room," *Presentations,* June 2002, pp. 42–48.

17. See Dave Zielinski, "Perfect Practice," *Presentations,* May 2003, pp. 30–36.

18. See Richard T. Kasuya, "Dealing with a Presentation-Room Nightmare," *Presentations,* February 2003, p. 54.

19. See Daniel Tynan, "Virtual Meetings in Real Time," *Sales and Marketing Management,* July 2004, pp. 20.

20. See Dave Zielinski, "Techno Stressed? Don't Let Your Gadgets and Gizmos Get You Down," *Presentations,* February 2004, pp. 28–35.

21. See also Michael Schrage, "The Dynamic Demo," *Sales and Marketing Management,* May 2004, p. 26.

22. See Dave Paradi, "When Technology Fails, Be Ready," *Presentations,* July 2004, p. 42.

23. See Tad Simons, "First Aid for Podium Emergencies," *Presentations,* November 2003, pp. 24–29.

24. See Robert A. Potter, "Requests for Proposal," *Sell!ng,* July 2003, p. 5.

25. See Barry Farber, "Decent Proposals," *Entrepreneur,* October 2002, p. 93.

26. Pragmatech Software (http://www.pragmatech.com/) does this. See also Carol Ann Wharton, "Proposing Higher Sales," *1to1 Magazine,* October 2002, pp. 44–49.

27. Ultimately, the goal of much of this is to reduce customer risk. See Dean A. Goettsch, "Reduce Customer Risk to Get More Sales," *Sell!ng,* October 2004, p. 8.

28. Mark Hurd, "What Is CRM?" presentation at Baylor University, February 19, 2002.

29. See Mark Merritt, "Taming the Beast Within," *Presentations,* March 2002, pp. 29–36.

CHAPTER 11

1. See "Ask the Etiquette Doctor," *Sales and Marketing Management,* May 2004, p. 66.

2. Salespeople can forestall known concerns, but shouldn't bring up issues that aren't even a problem with a particular prospect. Thus the need for good precall information gathering becomes obvious. See "Think Like a Customer to Make Buying From You a Cinch," *Sell!ng,* November 2004, p. 8.

3. Solomon, the Bible, Proverbs 18:13.

4. *Increase Your Selling Power* (Pittsburgh: Westinghouse Electric Corporation), sec. 3, pp. 4–5.

5. See Brad Huisken, "Saving the Sale: Objections, Rejections and Getting to 'Yes,'" *JCK,* January 2003, pp. 62–63.

6. See Bill Brooks, "Why Is Your Prospect So Difficult?" *American Salesman,* July 2003, pp. 20–22.

7. See Michelle Nichols, "What the Art of Selling Is Not," *BusinessWeek Online,* June 19, 2002.

8. See Bill Brooks, "Ten Ways to Add Value and Defeat Price Objections," *American Salesman,* November 2003, pp. 3–6.

9. See Tom Reilly, "Why Do You Cut Prices?" *Industrial Distribution,* June 2003, p. 72.

10. Personal correspondence; name of firm and industry withheld by request.

11. See Erin Strout, "Ask S&MM," *Sales and Marketing Management,* May 2001, p. 74; Andy Cohen, "Don't Succumb to Price Pressures," Sales and Marketing Management, March 2001, p. 14.

12. See Robert Menard, "'Cost' Is About More Than the Price," *Sell!ng,* July 2003, p. 9.

13. See Barry Farber, "Selling Added Value: A Few Tips," *CRN,* January 13, 2003, p. 14A.

14. Tracey Brill, personal correspondence. Used with permission.

CHAPTER 12

1. Landy Chase, "Building a Professional Sales Organization," *The American Salesman* 50 (January 2005), pp. 3–6.

2. Mark Borkowski, "How to Succeed in Closing Deals, Without Closing," *Canadian Electronics* 19 (May 2004), p. 6.

3. Benson Smith and Tony Rutigliano, "Getting Customers to Commit," *Advisor Today* 98 (May 2003), p. 78.

4. Neil Rackham, *SPIN Selling* (New York: McGraw-Hill, 1988), pp. 19–51.

5. Janet Arrowood, "Closing the Sale," *Advisor Today* 99 (June 2004), p. 42.

6. Joan Leotta, "Effortless Closing," *Selling Power,* October 2001, pp. 28–31.

7. Mary Lu Harding, "Total Cost of Ownership—Capital Equipment," *Purchasing Today,* September 2001, pp. 16–17.

8. Russ Berry, "You're Always Selling," presented as executive in residence, Baylor University's Center for Professional Selling, October 19, 1995.

9. Marvin A. Jolson, "Selling Assertively," *Business Horizons,* September/October 1984, pp. 71–77.

10. See Sergey Frank, "Global Negotiating: Vive les Differences!" *Sales & Marketing Management,* May 1992, p. 67.

11. Mack Heaton, "Why Aren't You Closing Your Sales?" *Air Conditioning, Heating, & Refrigeration News* 223 (December 20, 2004), p. 23.

12. Michael W. Preis, "The Impact of Interpersonal Satisfaction on Repurchase Decisions," *Journal of Supply Chain Management* 39 (Summer 2003), pp. 30–44.

13. Karin A. Venetis, and Pervez N. Ghauri, "Service Quality and Customer Retention: Building Long-Term Relationships," *European Journal of Marketing* 38 (11/12), pp. 1577–93.

14. Adriana Copaceanu, "A Basketful of Sales," *Selling Power,* October 2001, p. 56.

15. Steve Atlas, "Warm and Fuzzy Tips from Buyers for Closing More Sales," *Selling Power,* (October 2001) pp. 74–78.

16. Joseph J. Lukacs, "Ten Steps to Effective Closing," *National Underwriter, Life & Health* 108 (November 1, 2004), pp. 12–13.

17. Margaret Kane, "Why Most Cross-Selling Efforts Flop," *ABA Banking Journal* 97 (February 2005), pp. 64–65.

18. Dean Yeck, personal correspondence, used with permission.

19. Illiki Rai, "Embracing Rejection: Six Strategies to Successful Sales," *Rising Women,* www.risingwomen.com (accessed March 7, 2005).

20. Linda Richardson. "Close the Deal." *Advisor Today* 98 (November 2003), p. 78.

21. Mark Prude, "Making the Transition from College to Life," presented at Baylor University, September 27, 2004.

CHAPTER 13

1. Robert Menard, "Win–Win Negotiating Is Not the Only Way," *Selling,* February 2004, p. 9.

2. See Jenson J. Zhao, "The Chinese Approach to International Business Negotiation," *The Journal of Business Communication* 37, July 2002, pp. 209–37.

3. Beacon Expert Systems, Inc., 35 Gardner Rd., Brookline, MA (617) 738-9300. Information can be found at www.negotiatorpro.com/npro/negprosof.html.

4. The information in this section was developed from Kenneth Thomas, "Conflict and Conflict Management," in *The Handbook of Industrial and Organizational Psychology,* ed. Marvin Dunnette (Skokie, IL: Rand McNally, 1976). For another model of negotiation orientations, see Bradley W. Brooks and Randall L. Rose, "A Contextual Model of Negotiation Orientation," *Industrial Marketing Management* 33 (2004), pp. 125–33.

5. "Fractured English," *Have a Good Day,* January 1997, pp. 1–2.

6. See Roger Fisher and William Ury, *Getting to Yes: Negotiating Agreement without Giving In,* 2nd ed. (Boston: Houghton Mifflin, 1991).

7. Robert Menard, "Sometimes You Must Concede to Proceed," *Selling,* September 2003, p. 9; Kelley Robertson, "Offer a Trade, Not a Discount," *Selling,* June 2004, p. 10.

8. Neil Rackham, "Winning the Price War," *Sales and Marketing Management,* November 2001, p. 26.

CHAPTER 14

1. Deloitte & Touche Survey, reported in *Selling Power,* October 2001, p. 17.

2. Gary L. Frankwick, Stephen S. Porter, and Lawrence A. Crosby, "Dynamics of Relationship Selling: A Longitudinal Examination of Changes in Salesperson–Customer Relationship Status," *Journal of Personal Selling & Sales Management* 21, Spring 2001, pp. 135–146.

3. John Tashek, "How to Avoid a CRM Failure," *eWeek* 18:40, October 15, 2001, p. 31.

4. Tricia Campbell, "Service with a :-)," *Sales & Marketing Management,* March 1999, pp. 63–68.

5. Laura J. Hester, "Worksite Marketing: Maintaining and Expanding the Customer Base," *LIMRA's MarketFacts Quarterly* 23 (Fall 2004), pp. 52–54.

6. Chad Kaydo, "As Good as It Gets," *Sales & Marketing Management,* March 2000, pp. 55–60.

7. The Forum Corporation, "Why Do Customers Stop Buying?" *Sales & Marketing Management,* January 1998, p. 14.

8. Chris Taylor, "The Art of the Winback," *Sales and Marketing Management* 157 (April 2005), pp. 30–34.

9. Malcolm Fleschner, "Bold Goals," *Selling Power,* June 1999, pp. 54–59.

10. Stephanie Gruner, "How Can I Increase Sales?" *Inc.,* March 1997, p. 103.

11. Andrea Zoe Aster, "Good Drinks Come in Smart Packaging," *Marketing* 109 (October 11, 2004), pp. 13–15.

12. Bruce Peeling, "Partnering Service with Sales," *Foodservice Equipment & Supplies* 57 (2004), p. 54.

13. Nancy Feig, "The Cross-Sales Puzzle: Putting the Right Pieces in Place," *Community Banker* 13 (July 2004), p. 30.

14. Don Peppers and Martha Rogers, "Growing Revenues with Cross-Selling," *Sales & Marketing Management,* June 1999, p. 24.

15. Stephan M. Wagner, and Roman Boutellier, "Capabilities for Managing a Portfolio of Supplier Relationships," *Business Horizons* (November/December 2002), pp. 79–88.

16. Neil Rackham, "The Pitfalls of Partnering," *Sales & Marketing Management,* April 2001, pp. 32–33.

17. Keith Thompson, Helen Mitchell, and Simon Knox, "Organisational Buying Behaviour in Changing Times," *European Management Journal* 16:6, pp. 698–795.

18. Susan Fournier, Susan Dobscha, and David Glen Mick, "Preventing the Premature Death of Relationship Marketing," *Harvard Business Review,* January/February 1998, pp. 42–51.

19. Robert Dwyer, and John F. Tanner Jr., *Business Marketing: Connecting Strategy, Relationships, and Learning* 3rd ed., (New York: McGraw-Hill/Irwin, 2005).

20. Jeff Meisner, personal correspondence, April 22, 2005; used with permission.

21. Gilbert A. Churchill, Neil M. Ford, Orville C. Walker, Jr., Mark Johnston, and John F. Tanner, Jr., *Sales Force Management* (San Francisco: McGraw-Hill, 2000).

22. Paul Kelly, *Situational Selling* (New York: AMACOM, 1988).

23. Achim Walter, "Relationship Promoters: Driving Forces for Successful Customer Relationships," *Industrial Marketing Management* 28, 1999, pp. 537–51.

24. Joe Sperry, "Recommended Reading," *NAMA Journal,* Fall 1998, p. 26.

25. John Schanck, "Dun & Bradstreet Shortens Sales Cycle for High-End Solutions," *Acclivus Update,* October 1999, pp. 1–5.

26. Tom Bassett, "Managing Conflict with Suppliers," *Purchasing Today,* December 2001, pp. 7–9.

27. Richard Porterfield, "The Basics of Avoiding Disputes," *Purchasing Today,* March 2001, p. 8.

28. John Yuva, "Trust and Business Go Hand-in-Hand," *Purchasing Today,* July 2001, pp. 49–53.

CHAPTER 15

1. Renee Zemanski, "A Matter of Time," *Selling Power,* October 2001, pp. 80–82.

2. Tim Lukes and Jennifer Stanley, "Bringing Science to Sales," *Marketing Management* 13 (October 2004), pp. 36–42.

3. Art Weinstein, "Customer-Specific Strategies—Customer Retention: A Usage Segmentation and Customer Value Approach," *Journal of Targeting, Measurement and Analysis for Marketing* 10 (March 2002), pp. 250–69.

4. Tom McCarthy, "Spend Time in Relation to Potential," *Lodging Hospitality* 59 (June 2003), p. 22.

5. Adel El-Ansary and Waleed A. El-Ansary, *Winning Customers, Building Accounts: Some Do It Better than Others* (Jacksonville, FL: Paper and Plastics Education and Research Foundation, 1994).

6. Tiffany Perkins-Munn, Lerzan Aksoy, Timothy L. Keiningham, and Demitry Estrin, "Actual Purchase as a Proxy for Share of Wallet," *Journal of Service Research* 7 (February 2005), pp. 245–57.

7. Michael E. Kennedy and Alfred M. King, "Using Customer Relationship Management to Increase Profits," *Strategic Finance* 85 (March 2004), pp. 36–43.

8. Betsy Cummings, "Change Your Life: Pad the To-Do List," *Sales and Marketing Management* 155 (December 2003), p. 59.

9. Steve Atlas, "Time to Organize," *Selling Power,* November/December 2001, pp. 35–38.

10. Michael Goldstein, "Getting Out from Under," *Successful Meetings,* October 1999, p. 28.

11. Joan Leotta, "Time Tyrants," *Selling Power,* April 2000, pp. 117–20.

12. Thomas Petzinger, Jr., "Bob Schmonsee Has a Tool for Better Sales and It Ignores Excuses," *Wall Street Journal,* March 26, 1999, p. B1.

13. T. J. Becker, "How to Make the Most of Downtime," *Selling,* October 1995, pp. 54–56.

14. Stuart Miller, "Beating the Clock—and Records," *Sales & Marketing Management,* February 1997, pp. 20–21.

15. Jeff Cioletti, "The Art (and Science) of Communication," *Beverage World,* August 15, 2004, pp. 60–61.

16. Andy Cohen, "Winds of Change," *Sales and Marketing Management* 155 (May 2004), pp. 44–51.

CHAPTER 16

1. John F. Tanner, Michael Ahearne, Thomas Leigh, Charlotte Mason, and William Moncrief, "CRM in Sales Intensive Settings: A Review and Research Agenda," *Journal of Personal Selling & Sales Management;* (forthcoming 2005) Ranchana Rajatanavin, and Mark Speece, "The Sales Force as an Information Transfer Mechanism for New Service Development in the Thai Insurance Industry," *Journal of Financial Services Marketing* 8 (March), pp. 244–59.

2. Joseph S. Hoff, "Three Who Listen to the Voice of Customer," *Electrical Apparatus* 57 (October 2004), p. 17.

3. Paula Streit, "Small Steps, Big Rewards: Seven Tips for Enhancing Credit and Collections through Improved Communication," *Business Credit* 106 (November/December 2004), pp. 16–17.

4. Sara Calabro, "The Same Team," *Sales & Marketing Management* 157 (April 2005), p. 14.

5. Robert Dwyer and John F. Tanner Jr., *Business Marketing: Connecting Strategy, Relationships, and Learning,* 3rd ed., (New York: McGraw-Hill/Irwin, 2005).

6. Anonymous, "Selling Events Internally and to Customers," *Folio* 33 (November 2004), pp. 35–37.

7. Jo Yandle and Jim Blythe, "Intra-Departmental Conflict between Sales and Marketing: An Exploratory Study," *The Journal of Selling and Major Account Management* 2, Spring 2000, pp. 13–31.

8. Johanna Smaros and Markus Hellstrom, "Using the Assortment Forecasting Method to Enable Sales Force Involvement in Forecasting: A Case Study," *International Journal of Physical Distribution & Logistics Management* 34 (2004), pp. 140–57.

9. Charles H. Schwepker, Jr. and David J. Good, "Marketing Control and Sales Force Customer Orientation," *The Journal of Personal Selling & Sales Management* 24 (Summer 2004), pp. 167–84.

10. Thomas G. Brashear, Chris Manolis, and Charles M. Brooks, "The Effects of Control, Trust, and Justice on Salesperson Turnover," *Journal of Business Research* 58 (March 2005), pp. 241–57.

11. William H. Murphy, "In Pursuit of Short-Term Goals: Anticipating the Unintended Consequences of Using Special Incentives to Motivation the Sales Force," *Journal of Business Research* 57 (November 2004), pp. 1265–77.

12. Sean Valentine and Gary Fleischman, "Ethics Training and Businesspersons' Perceptions of Organizational Ethics," *Journal of Business Ethics* 52 (July 2004), pp. 391–409.

13. Julia Chang, "Breaking the Silence," *Sales & Marketing Management* 154 (December 2003), 54.

14. Much of this section is based on the work of Richard P. Nielsen, "What Can Managers Do about Unethical Management?" *Journal of Business Ethics,* Vol. 6, 1987, pp. 309–20, and on "Negotiating as an Ethics Action (Praxis) Strategy," *Journal of Business Ethics,* Vol. 9, 1989, pp. 383–90.

15. Julia Chang, "Change Agents," *Sales & Marketing Management* 157 (April 2005), pp. 24–28.

16. Timothy Long, "Demand Generator," *CRN* (February 7, 2005), p. 12.

17. Pui-Wing Tam, "Man on the Hot Seat at H-P's Struggling Enterprise Unit," *The Wall Street Journal* (Eastern Edition, August 19, 2003), p. B1.

18. Julia Chang, "Staying Interactive," *Sales & Marketing Management* 157 (January 2005), p. 22.

19. Steve Atlas and Elise Atlas, "Team Approach," *Selling Power,* May 2000, pp. 126–28.

20. Julie Gallagher, "Customer Consolidation," *Insurance & Technology* 29 (August 2004), pp. 24–29.

21. Dawn R. Deeter-Schmelz and Rosemary P. Ramsey, "An Investigation of Team Information Processing in Service Teams: Exploring the Link between Teams and Customers," *Journal of the Academy of Marketing Science* 31 (Fall), pp. 409–24; Barry Higgins, "Sales Teams Have Growing Appeal," *National Underwriter* 107 (August 11, 2003), p. 32.

22. Clay Boswell, "Anderson Development Builds Specialties but Sticks to Custom," *Chemical Market Reporter* 265 (June 7, 2004), p. 17.

CHAPTER 17

1. Eileen Zimmerman, "So You Wanna Be a CEO," *Sales and Marketing Management,* January 2002, pp. 31–35

2. Occupational Outlook 2004, http://www.bls.gov/oco/home.htm.

3. Julia Chang and Brian Yeado, "Where the Jobs Are," *Sales & Marketing Management* 155 (June 2003), p. 32.

4. Andy Holloway, "Finding the Right Fit." *Canadian Business* 75 (November 25, 2002), pp. 119–22.

5. Lewis C. Rogers, "Sales Interview Preparation," Orioncareernetwork.com, May 16, 2001.

6. Eugene Johnson, "How Do Sales Managers View College Preparation for Sales?" *Journal of Personal Selling and Sales Management,* Summer 1990, pp. 69–72; Cliff Enico, "Essential Characteristics for Sales Success," SAM, May/June 2001, pp. 62–63.

7. George W. Dudley, and Shannon L. Goodson, *Earning What You're Worth? The Psychology of Sales Call Reluctance,* (Dallas: Behavioral Science Research Press, 1999).

8. Betsy Cummings and Jennifer Gilbert, "Growing Pains," *Sales & Marketing Management* 156 (August 2004), pp. 22–29.

9. Gene Garofalo and Gary Drummond, *Sales Professional's Survival Guide* (Englewood Cliffs, NJ: Prentice Hall, 1987).

10. Margaret Littman, "Good Economy, Bad Candidates," *Marketing News,* April 10, 2000, pp. 12–13.

11. Dana James, "A Day in the Life of a Corporate Recruiter," *Marketing News,* April 10, 2000, pp. 1, 11.

12. Lucy Aitken, "Me and My Portfolio," *Campaign,* May 14, 2004, pp. 36–37; Denny E. McCorkle, Joe F. Alexander, James Reardon, and Nathan D. Kling, "Developing Self-Marketing Skills: Are Marketing Students Prepared for the Job Search?" *Journal of Marketing Education* 25 (December 2003), pp. 196–207.

13. Vadim Liberman, "Manager's Tool Kit," *Across the Board,* January/February 2002, pp. 78–79.

14. Michael Adams, "Family Matters," *Sales & Marketing Management,* March 1998, pp. 61–66.

15. Robin Suttell, "Professional Development on a Budget," *Buildings* 9 (March 2005), pp. 52–56.

16. Diane McGrath, "Continuous Learning," *Update,* Fourth Quarter 1998, p. 8.

17. Brandon Hall, "The Top Training Priorities for 2005," *Training* 42 (February 2005), pp. 22–27.

18. Anonymous, "Pulte Homes: Recruiting & Mentoring," *Professional Builder* 70 (April 2005), p. NHQ20.

19. Jessalynn Brinkmeyer, "Productive Car Time," *Sales & Marketing Management* 157 (April 2005), p. 46.

20. Rick Ebel and Alan D. Fletcher, "Who Are Today's Buyers and What Do They Really Want?" *Promotional Products Business,* January 1999, pp. 71–84.

21. Julia Chang, "Pressure Points," *Sales & Marketing Management* 157 (April 2005), p. 18.

22. Betsy Cummings, "Sales Ruined My Personal Life," *Sales and Marketing Management,* November 2001, pp. 45–50.

23. John F. Tanner, Jr., Mark G. Dunn, and Lawrence B. Chonko, "Vertical Exchange and Salesperson Stress," *Journal of Personal Selling and Sales Management,* Spring 1993, pp. 27–35.

24. Ibid.

25. Andy Cohen, "Facing Pressure," *Sales & Marketing Management,* April 1997, pp. 30–38.

26. Praveen Agrawwal, John F. Tanner Jr., and Stephen B. Castleberry, "Factors Associated with Propensity to Leave the Organization: A Study of Salespeople," *Marketing Management Journal* 14, no. 1 (2004), pp. 90–102.

GLOSSARY

80-20 listening rule a guideline that suggests salespeople should listen 80% of the time and talk 20% of the time.

ABC analysis Evaluating the importance of an account. The most important is an A account, the second most important is a B account, and the least important is a C account.

accommodating mode Resolving conflict by being unassertive and highly cooperative. When using this approach, people often neglect their own needs and desires to satisfy the concerns of the other party.

account opportunity Another term for the sales potential dimensions of the sales call allocation grid.

account share See *customer share.*

acknowledge method Responding to an objection by letting the buyer talk, acknowledging that you heard the concern, and then moving on to another topic without trying to resolve the concern.

active listening Process in which the listener attempts to draw out as much information as possible by actively processing information received and stimulating the communication of additional information.

activity goals Behavioral objectives, such as the number of calls made in a day.

activity quota A type of quota that sets minimal behavioral expectations for a salesperson's activities. Used when the sales cycle is long and sales are few. Controls activities of salespeople.

adaptive planning The development of alternative paths to the same goal in a negotiation session.

adaptive selling Approach to personal selling in which selling behaviors and approaches are altered during a sales interaction or across customer interactions, based on information about the nature of the selling situation.

administrative law Laws established by local, state, or federal regulatory agencies, such as the Federal Trade Commission or the Food and Drug Administration.

adoption process Steps that a person or an organization goes through when making an initial purchase and then using a new product or service.

advantages Why a feature would be important to someone.

after-tax cash flows Used to evaluate a purchase; ensures that the company has enough cash to pay for the purchase.

agenda Listing of what will be discussed, and in what sequence, in a negotiation session.

agent Person who acts in place of his or her company. See also *manufacturers' agents.*

aggressive Sales style that controls the sales interaction but often does not gain commitment because it ignores the customer's needs and fails to probe for information.

always-a-share A buyer who will always allocate only a share to each vendor, never giving one vendor all of the business (see *lost-for-good*).

ambush negotiating A win–lose tactic used by a buyer at the beginning of, or prior to, negotiations when the seller does not expect this approach.

amiable Category in the social style matrix; describes people who like cooperation and close relationships. Amiables are low on assertiveness and high on responsiveness.

analysis paralysis When a salesperson prefers to spend practically all of his or her time analyzing the situation and gathering information instead of making sales calls.

analytical Category in the social style matrix; describes people who emphasize facts and logic. Analyticals are low on assertiveness and responsiveness.

annual spend The amount that is spent with each vendor and for what products.

application form Preprinted form completed by a job applicant.

approach Method designed to get the prospect's attention and interest quickly.

articulation The production of recognizable speech.

assertive Sales manner that stresses responding to customer needs while being self-confident and positive.

assertiveness Dimension of the social style matrix that assesses the degree to which people have opinions on issues and publicly make their positions clear to others.

assessment center Central location for evaluating job candidates.

attitudinal loyalty Is an emotional attachment to a brand, company, or salesperson.

automatic replenishment (AR) A form of just-in-time inventory management where the vendor manages the customer's inventory, and automatically ships and stocks products at the customer's location based on mutually agreed-upon standards.

avoiding mode Resolving conflict in an unassertive and uncooperative manner. In this mode people make no attempt to resolve their own needs or the needs of others.

awareness phase The first phase in the development of a buyer–seller relationship, in which salespeople locate and qualify prospects and buyers consider various sources of supply.

backdoor selling Actions by one salesperson that go behind the back of a purchaser to directly contact other members of the buying center.

balanced presentation Occurs when the salesperson shows all sides of the situation—that is, is totally honest.

balance sheet method Attempts to obtain commitment by asking the buyer to think of the pros and cons of the various alternatives; often referred to as the *Ben Franklin method.*

banner advertising Ads placed at the top, sides, or bottom of a Web page, encouraging the viewer to visit a different website.

barriers Buyer's subordinates who plan and schedule interviews for their superiors; also called *screens.*

behavioral loyalty The purchase of the same product from the same vendor over time.

benchmarking A process of comparing your activities and performance with those of the best organization or individual in order to improve.

benefit How a particular feature will help a particular buyer.

benefit opening Approach in which the salesperson focuses on the prospect's needs by stating a benefit of the product or service.

benefit summary method Obtaining commitment by simply reminding the prospect of the agreed-on benefits of the proposal.

bird dog Individual who, for a fee, will provide the names of leads for the salesperson; also called a *spotter.*

blitz Canvassing method in which a large group of salespeople attempt to make calls on all prospective businesses in a given geographic territory on a specified day.

body language Nonverbal signals communicated through facial expressions, arms, hands, and legs.

bonus Lump-sum incentive payment based on performance.

bottom-up forecasting Forecast compiled by adding up each salesperson's forecast for total company sales.

bounce-back card Card returned from a lead that requests additional information.

boundary-spanning employees Those employees who cross the organizational boundary and interact with customers or vendors.

brainstorming session Meeting in which people are allowed to creatively explore different methods of achieving goals.

bribes Payments made to buyers to influence their purchase decisions.

browbeating Negotiation strategy in which buyers attempt to alter the selling team's enthusiasm and self-respect by making unflattering comments.

budget bogey Negotiation strategy in which one side claims that the budget does not allow for the solution proposed; also called *budget limitation tactic.*

budget limitation tactic See *budget bogey.*

business defamation Making unfair or untrue statements to customers about a competitor, its products, or its salespeople.

buyer's remorse The insecurity a buyer feels about whether the choice was a wise one; also called *post-purchase dissonance.*

buying center Informal, cross-department group of people involved in a purchase decision.

buying community Small, informal group of people in similar positions who communicate regularly, often both socially and professionally.

buying signals Nonverbal cues given by the buyer that indicate the buyer may be ready to commit; also called *closing cues.*

canned presentation See *standard memorized presentation.*

canned sales pitch See *standard memorized presentation.*

cap A limit placed on a salesperson's earnings.

capital equipment Major purchases made by a business, such as computer systems, that are used by the business for several years in its operations or production process.

cash discount Price discount given for early payment in cash.

center-of-influence method Prospecting method wherein the salesperson cultivates well-known, influential people in the territory who are willing to supply lead information.

champion Person who works for the buying firm in the areas most affected by the proposed change and works with the salesperson for the success of the proposal; also called *advocate* or *internal salesperson.*

change agent Person who is a cause of change in an organization.

circular routing Method of scheduling sales calls that includes using circular patterns from the home base in order to cover the territory.

closed questions Questions that can be answered with a word or short phrase.

closing Common term for obtaining commitment, which usually refers only to asking for the buyer's business.

closing cues See *buying signals*.

cloverleaf routing Method of scheduling sales calls that involves using loops to cover different portions of the territory on different days or weeks; on a map it should resemble a cloverleaf.

cold call See *cold canvass method*.

cold canvass method Prospecting method in which a sales representative tries to generate leads for new business by calling on totally unfamiliar organizations; also called *cold calls*.

collaborating mode Resolving conflict by seeking to maximize the satisfaction of both parties and hence truly reach a win–win solution.

collateral Collection of documents that are designed to generate sales, and include such items as brochures, sales flyers and fact sheets, and short success stories.

collusion Agreement among competitors, made after contacting customers, concerning their relationships with customers.

combination plan Compensation plan that provides salary and commission; offers the greatest flexibility for motivating and controlling the activities of salespeople.

Commerce Business Daily Publication that contains all the invitations for bids issued by the federal government.

commission Incentive payment for an individual sale; often a percentage of the sale price.

commission base Unit of analysis used to determine commissions: for example, unit sales, dollar sales, or gross margin.

commission rate Percentage of base paid or the amount per base unit paid in a commission compensation plan: for example, a percentage of dollar sales or an amount per unit sold.

commitment phase The fourth stage in the development of a buyer–seller relationship in which the buyer and seller have implicitly or explicitly pledged to continue the relationship for an extended period.

common law Legal precedents that arise out of court decisions.

comparative cost-benefit analysis A comparison of the buyer's current situation's costs with the value of the seller's proposed solution. Can also be a comparison-the seller's product with a competitor's product.

compensation method Method used to respond helpfully to objections by agreeing that the objection is valid, but then proceeding to show any compensating advantages.

competence Whether the salesperson knows what he or she is talking about.

competing mode Resolving conflict in an assertive and noncooperative manner.

complacency Assuming the business is yours and will always be yours.

compliment opening Approach in which the salesperson begins the sales call by complimenting the buyer in some fashion.

compromising mode Resolving conflict by being somewhat cooperative and somewhat assertive. People using this approach attempt to find a quick, mutually acceptable solution that partially satisfies both parties.

concession Occurs when one party in a negotiation meeting agrees to change his or her position in some fashion.

consequence questions Questions that illustrate the consequences of a disadvantage in a competitor's product.

conspiracy Agreement among competitors, made prior to contacting customers, concerning their relationships with customers.

consultative selling philosophy Form of customized presentation in which salespeople identify the prospect's needs and then recommend the best solution, even when the best solution does not include the salesperson's own products or services.

contest Trade promotion a firm uses to increase sales by rewarding top salespeople with trips, extra money, or merchandise.

contract to sell Offer made by a salesperson that received an unqualified acceptance by a buyer.

conventional résumé Form of life history organized by type of work experience.

conversion goals Measures of salesperson efficiency.

conversion ratio Similar to a batting average; calculated by dividing performance results by activity results (for example, dividing the number of sales by the number of calls).

corporate culture The values and beliefs held by a company and expressed by senior management.

coupon clippers People who like to send off for product information, even though they have no intention of ever buying the product or service.

creativity The trait of having imagination and inventiveness and using it to come up with new solutions and ideas.

credibility The characteristic of being perceived by the buyer as believable and reliable.

credible commitments Tangible investments in a relationship that indicate commitment to the relationship.

credulous person standard Canadian law stating that a company is liable to pay damages if advertising and sale presentation claims and statements about comparisons with competitive products could be misunderstood by a reasonable person.

creeping commitment Purchase decision process that arises when decisions made early in the process have significant influence on decisions made later in the process.

cross-selling Similar to full-line selling except that the additional products sold are not directly associated with the initial products.

cultural relativism A view that no culture's ethics are superior to those of another culture's.

cumulative discount Quantity discount for purchases over a period of time; the buyer is allowed to add up all the purchases to determine the total quantity and the total quantity discount.

curiosity approach Arousing interest by making an unexpected comment that piques the prospect's curiosity.

customer-centric Making the customer the very center of everything that the selling firm does. See also *customer orientation.*

customer intentions survey Method of forecasting sales in which customers are asked how much they intend to buy over the forecasting period.

customer orientation Selling approach based on keeping the customer's interests paramount.

customer relationship management (CRM) See *relationship marketing.*

customer service rep Inbound salesperson who handles customer concerns.

customer share The percentage of business received from a company's accounts. Also called *account share* or *share of wallet.*

customer value The customer's perception of what he or she wants to have happen in a specific use situation, with the help of a product or service offering, in order to accomplish a desired purpose or goal.

customized presentation Presentation developed from a detailed and comprehensive analysis or survey of the prospect's needs that is not canned or memorized in any fashion.

databases Contain information on leads, prospects, and customers.

data mining The use of artificial intelligence and statistical tools to discover hidden insights in the volumes of data in a database.

deal Promotional discount offered by a manufacturer to a retailer, often (but not always) in exchange for featuring a product in a newspaper ad and/or a special display.

deception Unethical practice of withholding information or telling white lies.

deciders Buying center members who make the final selection of the product to purchase.

decoding Communication activity undertaken by a receiver interpreting the meaning of the received message.

dependability Whether the salesperson will live up to promises made; is not something a salesperson can demonstrate immediately.

derived demand Situation in which the demand for a producer's goods is based on what its customers sell.

diagnostic feedback Information given to a salesperson indicating how he or she is performing.

digital collateral management Systems which archive, catalog, and retrieve digital media and text. Used by salespeople to create presentation.

direct denial Method of answering objections in which the salesperson makes a relatively strong statement indicating the error the prospect has made.

direct request method Attaining commitment by simply asking for it in a straightforward statement.

disadvantage questions Questions that ask a customer to articulate a specific problem.

disguised interview Discussion between an applicant and an interviewer in which the applicant is unaware that the interviewer is evaluating the applicant for the position.

dissolution The process of terminating the relationship; can occur because of poor performance, clash in culture, change in needs, and other factors.

distribution channel Set of people and organizations responsible for the flow of products and services from the producer to the ultimate user.

document cameras Also called *visual presenters;* are similar to traditional overhead projectors in their ability to display transparencies. However, because they are essentially cameras, document cameras are also capable of displaying any three-dimensional object without the use of a transparency.

dormant accounts Accounts that have not purchased for a specified time.

draw Advance from the company to a salesperson made against future commissions.

driver Category in the social style matrix; describes task-oriented people who are high on assertiveness and low on responsiveness.

efficient customer response (ECR) system Distribution system that drives inventory to the lowest possible levels, increases the frequency of shipping, and automates ordering and inventory control processes without the problems of stockouts and higher costs.

ego-involved Refers to the perception of an audience member that presented subject matter is important to his or her own well-being. For a contrast, see *issue-involved.*

elaboration questions Questions that are positive requests for additional information rather than simply verbal encouragement.

electronic data interchange (EDI) Computer-to-computer linkages between suppliers and buyers for information sharing about sales, production, shipment, and receipt of products.

electronic whiteboard A digital version of an easel.

e-missives Timely, useful information that a seller provides to a buyer. This information might have nothing to do with the seller or the seller's product. The goal is to help make friends with the buyer and cement the relationship.

emotional intelligence The ability to effectively understand and use your own emotions and those of people with whom you interact. Includes four aspects: (1) knowing your own feelings and emotions as they are happening, (2) controlling your emotions so you do not act impulsively, (3) recognizing your customer's emotions (called *empathy*), and (4) using your emotions to interact effectively with customers.

emotional needs Organizational and/or personal needs that are associated with some type of personal reward and gratification for the person buying the product.

emotional outburst tactic Negotiation strategy in which one party attempts to gain concessions by resorting to a display of strong emotion.

encoding Communication activity undertaken by a sender translating his or her thought into a message.

encouragement probes Questions or nonverbal signals that encourage customers to reveal further information.

end users Businesses that purchase goods and services to support their own production and operations.

endless-chain method Prospecting method whereby a sales representative attempts to get at least one additional lead from each person he or she interviews.

e-selling Utilizing e-mail to generate leads.

ethical imperialism The view that the ethical standards that apply locally or in one's home country should be applied to everyone's behavior around the world.

ethics Principles governing the behavior of an individual or a group.

ethics review board May consist of experts inside and outside the company who are responsible for reviewing ethics policies, investigating allegations of unethical behavior, and acting as a sounding board for employees.

evaluative feedback Information to a salesperson indicating how he or she is performing.

exclusive sales territories Method that uses a prospect's geographic location to determine whether a salesperson can sell to that prospect.

excuses Concerns expressed by the buyer that are intended to mask the buyer's true objections.

executive briefing center Presentation rooms set aside to highlight a company's products and capabilities.

executive summary In a written proposal, a summary of one page or less that briefly describes the total cost minus total savings, the problem to be solved, and the proposed solution.

expansion phase The third phase in the development of a relationship, in which it takes a significant effort to share information and further investigate the potential relationship benefits.

expense budget Budget detailing expenses; may be expressed in dollars or as a percentage of sales volume.

expert opinions Method of forecasting sales that involves averaging the estimates of several experts.

expert system Computer program that mimics a human expert.

exploration phase The second phase in the development of a relationship, in which both buyers and sellers explore the potential benefits and costs associated with the relationship.

expressed warranty Warranty specified through oral or written communications.

expressive Category in the social style matrix; describes people who are both competitive and approachable. They are high on assertiveness and responsiveness.

extranets Secure Internet-based networks connecting buyers and suppliers.

FAB When salespeople describe the features, advantages (why that feature is important), and benefits of their product or service.

face A person's desire for a positive identity or self-concept.

factual questions Questions that ask for factual information and usually start with who, what, where, how, or why.

fax Electronic document transfer device; short for *facsimile*.

feature (1) Quality or characteristic of the product or service. (2) Putting a product on sale with a special display and featuring the product in advertising.

feature dumping To talk about lots of features of little interest to the customer which is a waste of the buyer's time.

FEB Stands for feature, evidence, benefit; technique useful in interviewing.

FEBA A method of describing a product or service where salespeople mention the feature, provide evidence that the feature actually does exist, explain the benefit (why that feature is important to the buyer), and then ask whether the buyer agrees with the value of the feature and benefit.

feedback See *diagnostic feedback* and *evaluative feedback.*

felt stress Persistent and enduring psychological distress brought about by job demands or constraints encountered in the work environment.

field sales manager First-level manager.

field salespeople Salespeople who spend considerable time in the customer's place of business, communicating with the customer face to face.

field support representative Telemarketer who works with field salespeople and does more than prospect for leads.

flip chart A large easel-type chart placed on the floor; used in making presentations to a group.

FOB (free on board) Designates the point at which responsibility shifts from seller to buyer.

FOB destination The seller has title until the goods are received at the destination.

FOB factory The buyer has title when the goods leave the seller's facility.

focus of dissatisfaction The person in the organization who is most likely to perceive problems and dissatisfactions; leads to the focus of power.

focus of power The person in the organization who can approve, prevent, or influence action.

focus of receptivity The person in the organization who will listen receptively and provide a seller with valuable information; leads to the focus of dissatisfaction.

follow-up Activities a salesperson performs after commitment is achieved.

Foreign Corrupt Practices Act Law that governs the behavior of U.S. business in foreign countries; restricts the bribing of foreign officials.

forestall To resolve objections before buyers have a chance to raise them.

free on board See *FOB.*

full-line selling Selling the entire line of associated products.

functional relationship Series of market exchanges between a buyer and a seller, linked together over time. These relationships are characterized as win–lose relationships.

functional résumé Life history that reverses the content and titles of a conventional résumé and is organized by what a candidate can do or has learned rather than by types of experience.

gatekeepers Buying center members who influence the buying process by controlling the flow of information and/or limiting the alternatives considered. Sometimes called *barriers* or *screens.*

geographic salesperson Salesperson assigned a specific geographic territory in which to sell all the company's products and services.

global account manager (GAM) Sales executive responsible for coordinating sales efforts for one account globally.

good guy–bad guy routine Negotiation strategy in which one team member acts as the "good guy" while another team member acts as the "bad guy." The goal of the strategy is to have the opposing team accept the good guy's proposal to avoid the consequences of the bad guy's proposal.

goodwill Value of the feelings or attitudes customers or prospects have toward a company and its products.

go-to-market strategies The various options that firms have to sell their products. Examples include the Internet, franchises, telemarketers, agents, value added resellers, field salespeople, and so on.

greeter Interviewer who greets the applicant and may conduct a disguised interview.

gross margin quota Minimum levels of acceptable profit or gross margin performance.

group interview Similar to *panel interview* but includes several candidates as well as several interviewers.

guaranteed price Price guaranteed to be the lowest. If the price falls, the buyer is refunded the difference between the original and new prices for any inventory still in stock.

halo effect How one does in one thing changes a person's perceptions about other things one does.

handouts Written documents provided to buyers before, during, or after a meeting to help them remember what was said.

high-context culture Culture in which the verbal part of communication carries less of the information in a message than the nonverbal parts. The sender's values, position, and background are conveyed by the way the message is expressed. Examples of high-context cultures include Japan, France, and Spain.

honesty Combination of truthfulness and sincerity; highly related to dependability.

house accounts Accounts assigned to a sales executive rather than to the specific salesperson responsible for the territory containing the account.

implication questions Questions that logically follow one or more problem questions (in SPIN®); designed to help the prospect recognize the true ramifications of the problem.

implied warranty Warranty that is not expressly stated through oral or written communication but is still an obligation defined by law.

impression management Activities in which salespeople engage to affect and manage the buyer's impression of them.

inbound Salespeople or customer service reps who respond to calls placed to the firm by customers rather than placing calls out to customers.

inbound telemarketing Use of the telephone, usually with a toll-free number, that allows leads and/or customers to call for additional information or to place an order.

incentive pay Compensation based on performance.

indirect denial Method used to respond to objections in which the salesperson denies the objection but attempts to soften the response by first agreeing with the prospect that the objection is an important one.

inflection Tone of voice.

influencers Buying center members inside or outside an organization who directly or indirectly influence the buying process.

influential adversaries Individuals in the buyer's organization who carry great influence and are opposed to the salesperson's product or service.

initiator The person who starts the buying process.

inside salespeople Salespeople who work at their employer's location and interact with customers by telephone or letter.

integrated marketing communications Coordinated communications programs that exploit the strengths of various communication vehicles to maximize the total impact on customers.

internal partnerships Partnering relationships between a salesperson and another member of the same company for the purpose of satisfying customer needs.

internal selling A communication process by which salespeople influence other employees in their firms to support the salespeople's sales efforts with customers.

interview Personal interactions between candidates and job recruiters for the purpose of evaluating job candidates.

intimate zone That physical space around a buyer that is reserved primarily for a person's closest relationships. See also social zone, public zone, and personal zone.

intrinsic motivation Motivation stimulated by the rewards salespeople get from simply doing their job.

introduction opening Approach method in which salespeople simply state their names and the names of their companies.

inventory turnover Measure of how efficiently a retailer manages inventory; calculated by dividing net sales by inventory.

invitation to negotiate The initiation of an interaction, usually a sales presentation, that results in an offer.

issue-involved Refers to the perception by an audience member that a subject is important although it may not affect him or her personally. For a contrast, see *ego-involved*.

job descriptions Formal, written descriptions of the duties and responsibilities of a job.

just-in-time (JIT) inventory control Planning systems for reducing inventory by having frequent deliveries planned just in time for the delivered products to be assembled into the final product.

keiretsu Group (more than two) or family of Japanese companies that form strategic partnerships to jointly develop plans to exploit market opportunities and to share the risks and rewards of their investments.

key accounts Large accounts, usually generating more than a specified amount in revenue per year, that receive special treatment.

kickbacks Payments made to buyers based on the amount of orders they place for a salesperson's products or services.

KSAs Acronym for knowledge, skills, and abilities, or, are the package that a candidate offers an employer.

lead A potential prospect; a person or organization that may have the characteristics of a true prospect.

lead management system The part of the lead process in which salespeople carefully analyze the relative value of each lead.

lead qualification system A process for qualifying leads.

lead user Company that faces and resolves needs months or years ahead of the rest of the marketplace.

leapfrog routing Method of scheduling calls that requires the identification of clusters of customers; visiting these clusters and "leaping" over single, sparsely located accounts should minimize travel time from the sales office to customers.

life-cycle costing Method for determining the cost of equipment or supplies over their useful life.

lifetime customer value (LCV) The sum of the customer's purchases over their entire life.

likability Behaving in a friendly manner and finding a common ground between the buyer and seller.

list price Quoted or published price in a manufacturer's catalog or price list from which buyers may receive discounts.

lost-for-good A buyer who gives all business to one vendor is considered lost-for-good for all of the out-suppliers, because the buyer has cemented this relationship for a long period of time (see *always-a-share*).

lowballing Negotiation strategy in which one party voices agreement and then raises the cost of that agreement in some way.

low-context culture Culture in which the verbal part of communication carries more of the information in a message than the nonverbal parts. The sender's values, position, and background are conveyed by the content of the message. Examples of low-context cultures include the United States, Canada, Germany, and Switzerland.

lubrication Small sums of money or gifts, typically paid to officials in foreign countries, to get the officials to do their job more rapidly.

major sale Sale that involves a long selling cycle, a large customer commitment, an ongoing relationship, and large risks for the buyer if a bad decision is made.

manipulation (Salesperson) practices that eliminate or reduces the buyer's choice unfairly.

manufacturers' agents Independent businesspeople who are paid a commission by a manufacturer for all products and services the agents sell.

market (1) Mall where manufacturers show and sell products to retailers. (2) A short period of time when manufacturers gather to sell products to retailers.

market exchange Relationship that involves a short-term transaction between a buyer and a seller who do not expect to be involved in future transactions with each other.

marketing mix Elements used by firms to market their offerings: product, price, place (distribution), and promotion. Personal selling is part of the promotion element.

material requirements planning (MRP) Planning system for reducing inventory levels by forecasting sales, developing a production schedule, and ordering parts and raw materials with specific delivery dates.

minimum call objective Minimum that a salesperson hopes to accomplish in an upcoming sales call.

minimum position Negotiation objective that states the absolute minimum level the team is willing to accept.

missionary salespeople Salespeople who work for a manufacturer and promote the manufacturer's products to other firms. Those firms buy products from distributors or other manufacturers, not directly from the salesperson's firm.

modified rebuy Purchase decision process associated with a customer who has purchased the product or service in the past but is interested in obtaining additional information.

MRO supplies Minor purchases made by businesses for maintenance and repairs, such as towels and pencils.

multiattribute model Model describing how information about a product's performance on various dimensions is used to make an overall evaluation of the product.

multichannel strategy When a firm uses various go-to-market strategies at the same time.

multilevel selling Strategy that involves using multiple levels of company employees to call on similar levels in an account; for example, the VP of sales might call on the VP of purchasing.

multiple-sense appeals Appealing to as many of the senses (hearing, sight, touch, taste, and smell) as possible.

mutual investments Tangible investments in the relationship by both parties (seller and buyer).

national account Prospect or customer that is covered by a single, national sales strategy; may be a house account.

national account manager (NAM) Sales executive responsible for managing and coordinating sales efforts on a single account nationwide.

need payoff questions Questions that ask about the usefulness of solving the problem.

needs satisfaction philosophy Form of customized presentation in which the prospect's unique needs are identified and then the salesperson shows how his or her product or service can meet those needs.

negative referral A customer who tells others about how poorly your or your product performed.

negotiation Decision-making process through which buyers and sellers resolve areas of conflict and arrive at agreements.

negotiation jujitsu Negotiation response in which the attacked person or team steps away from the opponent's attack and then directs the opponent back to the issues being discussed.

net present value (NPV) The investment minus the net value today of future cash inflows (discounted back to their present value today at the firm's cost of capital).

net price The price the buyer pays after all discounts and allowances are subtracted.

net sales Total sales minus returns.

networking Establishing connections to other people and then using those networks to generate leads, gather information, generate sales, and so on.

new task Purchase decision process associated with the initial purchase of a product or service.

nibbling Negotiation strategy in which the buyer requests a small extra or add-on after the deal has been closed. Compared with lowballing, a nibble is a much smaller request.

noise Sounds unrelated to the message being exchanged between a salesperson and a customer.

nonverbal communication Nonspoken forms of expression—body language, space, and appearance—that communicate thoughts and emotions.

North America industry classification system (NAICS) A uniform classification system for all businesses for all countries in North America.

objection Concern or question raised by the buyer.

offer Specific statement by a seller outlining what the seller will provide and what is expected from the buyer.

office scanning Activity in which the salesperson looks around the prospect's environment for relevant topics to talk about.

one-way communication Methods of communication, such as e-mail messages and letters, that have low levels of interactivity.

open-door policy General management technique that allows subordinates to bypass immediate managers and take concerns straight to upper management when the subordinates feel a lack of support from the immediate manager.

opening position The initial proposal of a negotiating session.

opening A method designed to get the prospect's attention and interest quickly and make a smooth transition into the next part of the presentation. Examples include introduction, product, question, referral and so on.

open questions Questions for which there are no simple yes–no answers.

opinion questions Questions that ask for a customer's feelings on a subject.

opportunity cost The return a buyer would have earned from a different use of the same investment capital.

optimistic call objective The most optimistic outcome the salesperson thinks could occur in a given sales call.

orders Written orders that become contracts when they are signed by an authorized representative in a salesperson's company.

original equipment manufacturer (OEM) Business that purchases goods (components, subassemblies, raw and processed materials) to incorporate into products it manufactures.

outbound Salespeople, customer service reps, prospectors, account managers, and field support telemarketers who place phone calls out to customers.

outbound telemarketing Using the telephone to generate and qualify leads to determine whether they are truly prospects or not; also used to secure orders and provide customer contact.

outlined presentation Systematically arranged presentation that outlines the most important sales points. Often includes the necessary steps for determining the prospect's needs and for building goodwill at the close of the sale.

panel interview Job interview conducted by more than one person.

participative leadership Style of leadership that allows followers to make a contribution to decision making.

partnership Ongoing, mutually beneficial relationship between a buyer and a seller.

payback period Length of time it takes for the investment cash outflows to be returned in the form of cash inflows or savings.

performance feedback A type of feedback that salespeople often get from their supervisors that focuses on the seller's actual performance during a sales call.

performance goals Goals relating to outcomes, such as revenue.

personal selling Interpersonal communication process in which a seller uncovers and satisfies the needs of a buyer to the mutual, long-term benefit of both parties.

personal zone That physical space around a buyer that is reserved for close friends and those who share special interests. See also *public zone, social zone,* and *intimate zone.*

persuasion (Salesperson) practices designed to influence the buyer's decision, not manipulate it (see *manipulation*).

pioneer selling Selling a new and different product, service, or idea. In these situations the salesperson usually has difficulty establishing a need in the buyer's mind.

portfolio Collection of visual aids that can be used to enhance communication during a sales call.

postcard pack Cards that provide targeted information from a number of firms; this pack is mailed to prospective buyers.

postpone method Objection response technique in which the salesperson asks permission to answer the question at a later time.

postpurchase dissonance See *buyer's remorse.*

preferred supplier Supplier that is assured a large percentage of the buyer's business and will get the first opportunity to earn new business.

prequalification To help salespeople use their time wisely, firms determine whether leads are qualified before even turning them over to the field sales force.

price discrimination Situation in which a seller gives unjustified special prices, discounts, or special services to some customers and not to others.

primary call objective Actual goal the salesperson hopes to achieve in an upcoming sales call.

prime selling time Time of day at which a salesperson is most likely to be able to see a customer.

privacy laws Laws that limit the amount of information that a firm can obtain about a consumer and specify how that information can be used or shared.

probing method Method to obtain commitment in which the salesperson initially uses the direct request method and, if unsuccessful, uses a series of probing questions designed to discover the reason for the hesitation.

problem questions Questions about specific difficulties, problems, or dissatisfactions that the prospect has.

Procurement Automated Source System (PASS) A Small Business Administration database that contains information on federal purchasing agents working on federal contracts.

producer Firm that buys goods and services to manufacture and sell other goods and services to its customers.

product opening Approach in which the salesperson actually demonstrates the product features and benefits as soon as he or she walks up to the prospect.

production era A business era, prior to 1930, in which firms focused on making products with little concern for buyers' needs and developing products to satisfy those needs. The role of salespeople in this era was taking orders.

productivity goals Objective concerning how efficiently a salesperson works, such as sales per call. Efficiency measures indicate an output divided by an input.

profit margin The net profit the reseller makes, expressed as a percentage of sales.

profit quota Minimum levels of acceptable profit or gross margin performance.

prospect A lead that is a good candidate for buying what the salesperson is selling.

prospecting The process of locating potential customers for a product or service.

public zone That physical space around a person in which listening to speeches, and interacting with passerbys is comfortable for that person. See also *personal zone, intimate zone,* and *social zone.*

push money (PM) Money paid directly to the retailer's salespeople by the manufacturer for selling the manufacturer's product. See also *spiffs.*

qualifying a lead The process of determining whether a lead is in fact a prospect.

quantifying the solution Showing the prospect that the cost of the proposal is offset by added value.

question opening Beginning the conversation with a question or stating an interesting fact in the form of a question.

quick-response (Q) system Minimizing order quantities to the lowest level possible while increasing the speed of delivery to drive inventory turnover; accomplished by prepackaging certain combinations of products.

quota Quantitative level of performance for a specific time period.

rapport Close, harmonious relationship founded on mutual trust.

rate of change A critical element to consider about change; refers to how fast change is occurring.

rational needs Organizational and/or personal needs that are directly related to product performance.

reciprocity Special relationship in which two companies agree to buy products from each other.

references People who know an applicant for a position and can provide information about that applicant to the hiring company.

referral event Gatherings designed to allow current customers to introduce prospects to the salesperson in order to generate leads.

referral opening Approach in which the name of a satisfied customer or friend of the prospect is used at the beginning of a sales call.

referral method Method of helpfully responding to objections in which the salesperson shows how others held similar views before trying the product or service.

referred lead Name of a lead provided by either a customer or a prospect of the salesperson.

reflective probes Neutral statements that reaffirm or repeat a customer's comment or emotion, allowing the salesperson to dig deeper and stimulate customers to continue their thoughts in a logical manner.

relational partnership Long-term business relationship in which the buyer and seller have a close, trusting relationship but have not made significant investments in the relationship. These relationships are characterized as win–win relationships.

relationship behaviors Actions taken by a manager to deal with a subordinate's feelings and welfare, develop support, or build the salesperson's self-confidence or commitment to the job or organization.

relationship manager The role of salespeople in the partnering era to manage the firm's resources to develop win–win relationships with customers.

relationship marketing Creating the type of relationship that best suits the customer's need, which may or may not require a partnership.

request for proposal (RFP) Issued by a potential buyer desiring bids from several potential vendors for a product. RFPs often include specifications for the product, desired payment terms, and other information helpful to the bidder. Also called *request for bids* or *request for quotes.*

requirements Conditions that must be satisfied before a purchase can take place.

resale price maintenance Contractual term in which a producer establishes a minimum price below which distributors or retailers cannot sell their products.

resellers Businesses, typically distributors or retailers, that purchase products for resale.

response time The time between sending a message and getting a response to it.

responsiveness The degree to which people react emotionally when they are in social situations. One of the two dimensions in the social style matrix.

retail salespeople Salespeople who sell to customers who come into a store.

return on investment (ROI) Net profits (or savings) expected from a given investment, expressed as a percentage of the investment.

revenue quota The minimum amount of sales revenue necessary for acceptable performance.

reverse auction An auction but instead of a seller offering a product and buyers bidding, a buyer offers a contract and sellers bid; prices fall as sellers compete to win the sale.

revisit method Responding to objections by turning the objection into a reason for acting now.

role ambiguity The degree to which a salesperson is not sure about the actions required in the sales role.

role clarity The degree to which a salesperson understands the job and what is required to perform it.

role conflict The extent to which the salesperson faces incompatible demands from two or more constituencies that he or she serves.

role overload When the role (or job) demands more than the person can perform.

role stress The psychological distress that may be a consequence of a salesperson's lack of role accuracy.

routine call patterns Method of scheduling calls used when the same customers are seen regularly.

routing Method of scheduling sales calls to minimize travel time.

salary Compensation paid periodically to an employee independently of performance.

sale The transfer of title to goods and services by the seller to the buyer in exchange for money.

sales call allocation grid Grid used to determine account strategy; the dimensions are the strength of the company's position with the account and the account's sales potential.

sales era A business era, from 1930 to 1960, in which firms focused on increasing demand for the products they produced. The role of salespeople in this era was persuading customers to buy products by using high-pressure selling techniques.

sales-force intensive organization Firms whose go-to-market strategy relies heavily on salespeople.

sales portals On-line data bases that include many sources of information in one place that the salesperson might need. Includes items such as account data, competitor intelligence, and news about the industry, company and the economy.

sales puffery Exaggerated statements about the performance of products or services.

sales quota The minimum number of sales in units.

scope of change A critical element to consider about change; refers to the extent or degree to which the change affects an organization.

screens See *barriers*.

search engines The tools that individuals use to locate information on the Internet or on a specific website.

secondary call objectives Goals a salesperson hopes to achieve during a sales call that have somewhat less priority than the primary call objective.

seeding The seller sends the customer important and useful items or information prior to the meeting.

selective perception Occurs when we hear what we want to hear, not necessarily what the other person is saying.

selling See *personal selling*.

selling center A team that consists of all people in the selling organization who participate in a selling opportunity.

selling deeper Selling more to existing customers.

services End-user purchases such as Internet and telephone connections, employment agencies, consultants, and transportation.

sexual harassment Unwelcome sexual advances, requests for sexual favors, and other, similar verbal (such as jokes) and nonverbal (such as graffiti) behaviors.

simple cost–benefit analysis Simple listing of the costs and savings that a buyer can expect from an investment.

situational stress Short-term anxiety caused by a situational factor.

situation questions General data-gathering questions about background and current facts that are very broad in nature.

small talk Talk about current news, hobbies, and the like that usually breaks the ice for the actual presentation.

sneak attack See *ambush negotiating*.

social style matrix Method for classifying customers based on their preferred communication style. The two dimensions used to classify customers are assertiveness and responsiveness.

social zone That physical space around a person in which business transactions and other impersonal relationships are comfortable for the person. See also *public zone, intimate zone,* and *personal zone*.

soft savings The value of offset costs and productivity gains.

solo exchange Both the buyer and the seller pursue their own self-interests because they do not plan on doing business together again.

spam A term used for unwanted and unsolicited junk e-mail.

speaking–listening differential The difference between the 120-to-160-words-per-minute rate of speaking versus the 800-words-per-minute rate of listening.

spiffs (push money) Payments made by a producer to a reseller's salespeople to motivate the salespeople to sell the producer's products or services.

SPIN® Logical sequence of questions in which a prospect's needs are identified. The sequence is situation questions, problem questions, implication questions, and need payoff questions.

spotter See *bird dog*.

standard industrial classification (SIC) A uniform classification system for an industry. The SIC system is being replaced by the new North America industry classification system (NAICS).

standard memorized presentation Carefully prepared sales story that includes all the key selling points arranged in the most effective order; often called a *canned sales presentation*.

statutory laws Laws based on legislation passed by either state legislatures or Congress.

straight commission Pays a certain amount per sale; plan includes a base and a rate but not a salary.

straight-line routing Method of scheduling sales calls involving straight-line patterns from the home base in order to cover the sales territory.

straight rebuy Purchase decision process involving a customer with considerable knowledge gained from having purchased the product or service a number of times.

straight salary Compensation method that pays a fixed amount of money for working a specified amount of time.

strategic account manager (SAM) A company executive who coordinates all the salespeople who call on an account throughout the nation or the world. Also called *national account manager (NAM)*.

strategic partnership Long-term business relationship in which the buyer and seller have made significant investments to improve the profitability of both parties in the relationship. These relationships are characterized as win–win relationships.

strength of position Dimension of the sales call allocation grid that considers the seller's strength in landing sales at an account.

stress interview Any interview that subjects an applicant to significant stress; the purpose is to determine how the applicant handles stress.

submissive Selling style of salespeople who are often excellent socializers and like to spend a lot of time talking about nonbusiness activities. These people are usually reluctant to attempt to obtain commitment.

subordination Payment of large sums of money to officials to get them to do something that is illegal.

suggested retail price Price the manufacturer suggests the store charge for the product.

superior benefit method Type of compensation method of responding to an objection during a sales presentation that uses a high score on one attribute to compensate for a low score on another attribute.

supply chain management Set of programs undertaken to increase the efficiency of the distribution system that moves products from the producer's facilities to the end user.

supplier relationship management (SRM) The use of technology and statistics to identify important suppliers and opportunities for cost reduction, greater efficiency, and other benefits.

systems integrator Outside vendor who has been delegated the responsibility for purchasing; has the authority to buy products and services from others.

target position Negotiation objective that states what the team hopes to achieve by the time the session is completed.

task behaviors Actions taken by a manager to enable a subordinate to complete a task.

team selling Type of selling in which employees with varying areas of expertise within the firm work together to sell to the same account(s).

telemarketing Systematic and continuous program of communicating with customers and prospects via telephone and/or other person-to-person electronic media.

testimonial Statement, usually in the form of a letter, written by a satisfied customer about a product or service.

tests Personality or skills assessments used in assessing the match between a position's requirements and an applicant's personality or skills.

third-party-testimony method Method of responding to an objection during a sales presentation that uses a testimonial letter from a third party to corroborate a salesperson's assertions.

tickler file File or calendar used by salespeople to remind them when to call on specific accounts.

trade All members of the channel of distribution that resell the product between the manufacturer and the user.

trade discount Discount in which the price is quoted to a reseller in terms of a percentage off the suggested retail price.

trade fair The European term for *trade show*.

trade salespeople Salespeople who sell to firms that resell the products rather than using them within their own firms.

trade show Short exhibition of products by manufacturers and distributors.

trial close Questions the salesperson asks to take the pulse of the situation throughout a presentation.

trial order A small order placed by a buyer in order to test the product or the vendor. Not to be confused with *trial close*.

trust Firm belief or confidence in the honesty, integrity, and reliability of another person.

turnaround Amount of time taken to respond to a customer request or deliver a customer's order.

turnover (TO) Occurs when an account is given to another salesperson because the buyer refuses to deal with the current salesperson.

turnover How quickly a product sells; calculated by dividing net sales by average inventory.

24/7 service A phrase that highlights the fact that customers expect a selling firm to be available 24 hours a day, seven days a week.

two-way communication Interpersonal communication in which both parties act as senders and receivers. Salespeople send messages to customers and receive feedback from them; customers send messages to salespeople and receive responses.

tying agreement Agreement between a buyer and a seller in which the buyer is required to purchase one product to get another.

Uniform Commercial Code (UCC) Legal guide to commercial practice in the United States.

upgrading Convincing the customer to use a higher-quality product or a newer product.

users Members of a buying center that ultimately will use the product purchased.

value The total benefit that the seller's products and services provide to the buyer.

value analysis Problem-solving approach for reducing the cost of a product while providing the same level of performance. See *quantifying the solution*.

value proposition A written statement (usually one or two sentences) that clearly states how purchasing your product or service can help add shareholder value.

variable call patterns Occur when the salesperson must call on accounts in a nonsystematic method.

variable routing Method of scheduling sales calls used when customers are not visited on a cyclical or regular basis.

vendor A supplier.

vendor analysis A formal method used by organizational buyers to summarize the benefits and needs satisfied by a supplier.

vendor loyalty Develops when a buyer becomes committed to a specific supplier because of the supplier's superior performance.

verbal communication Communication involving the transmission of words in face-to-face communication, over the telephone, or through a written message.

versatility A characteristic, associated with the social style matrix, of people who increase the productivity of social relationships by adjusting to the needs of the other party.

videoconferencing Meetings in which people are not physically present in one location but are connected via voice and video; seems to be growing in usage.

virtual sales call See *webcast*.

visual presenters Similar to traditional overhead projectors in their ability to display transparencies. However, because they are essentially cameras, visual presenters are also capable of displaying any three-dimensional object without the use of a transparency (also called *document cameras*).

voice characteristics The rate of speech, loudness, pitch, quality, and articulation of a person's voice.

warranty Assurance by the seller that the goods will perform as represented.

webcast A videoconference in which the meeting is broadcast over the Internet.

willingness Salesperson's desire and commitment to accomplish an objective or task.

win–lose negotiating Negotiating philosophy in which the negotiator attempts to win all the important concessions and thus triumph over his or her opponent.

win–lose relationship Type of relationship characterized by one or a series of market exchanges wherein each party is concerned only with his or her own profits and not with the welfare of the other party.

win–win negotiating Negotiating philosophy in which the negotiator attempts to secure an agreement that completely satisfies both parties.

win–win not yet negotiating A negotiation session in which the buying team achieves its goals while the selling team does not. However, the sellers expect to achieve their goals in the near future, thanks to the results of that negotiation session.

win–win relationship Type of relationship in which firms make significant investments that can improve profitability for both partners because their partnership has given them some strategic advantage over their competitors.

word picture Story or scenario designed to help the buyer visualize a point.

zoning Method of scheduling calls that divides a territory into zones. Calls are made in a zone for a specified length of time and then made in another zone for the same amount of time.

COMPANY INDEX

NAME AND SUBJECT INDEX

ABC analysis, 396–397
account classification, 395–396
customer relationship management
    software, 399–400
grid analysis, 397–399
investing in accounts, 400–401
Responding to objections; *see also* Objections
acknowledge method, 294
compensation method, 291–293
direct denial, 289–290
indirect denial, 290–291
postpone method, 294–295
probing method, 288–289
referral method, 293
response preparation, 284–288
revisit method, 293–294
using the methods, 295–296
Response time, 137
Responsiveness, 154
Return on investment (ROI), 263, 265
Revenue quota, 425
Reverse auction, 109
Revisit method, 293–294
Rich, Anne K., 27
Rich, Michael K., 145
Richardson, Linda, EN8
Ridnour, Rick, 121, 127, 473, EN4
Rigdon, Edward E., 119
Righthand, Penny, EN1
Rinehart, Lloyd M., EN1
Ritter, Thomas, 55, EN2
Roberts, Julie, EN3
Robertson, Diana C., 84
Robertson, Kelley, 274
Rodrigo, Elaine M., EN1
Rogers, Jerry, 195
Rogers, Lewis C., EN10
Rogers, Martha, 246, EN1, EN8
Role ambiguity, 468
Role conflict, 468
Role overload, 469
Role stress, 468
Roman, Sergio, EN2
Rose, Gregory M., 166
Rose, Randall L., EN8
Rosenbloom, Bert, EN4
Rosenthal, Glenn, 197
Rosler, Rodney, 210
Ross, William T., 27, 84
Rossomme, Jeanne, EN3
Routine call patterns, 405
Routing, 405
Rozell, Elizabeth, 27, 473
Rudolph, Bettina, 387
Ruiz, Sergio, EN2
Rutigliano, Tony, EN8

Sabol, Barry, 56
Sager, Jeffrey K., 415
Salary, 426
Sale, 73
Sales allocation grid, 397–398
Sales calls
building credibility during call, 239–241
identifying prospect's needs; *see* Needs
    identification
importance of planning, 198, 213
impression management, 222–227
making an appointment, 209–212
obtaining precall information, 198–201
offering value, 234–238

selling to groups, 241–242
setting call objectives, 204–209
sources of precall information, 202–204
Sales-force intensive organizations, 6
Sales jobs, 13–16
Sales jobs continuum, 14–15
Sales portals, 202
Sales puffery, 74–76
Sales quota, 425
Salespeople
characteristics of successful, 16–20
communication and, 6–7
describing sales jobs, 13–14
ethical behavior, 61–65
examples of sales jobs, 15–16
rewards, 20–22
roles, 7–10
sales jobs continuum, 14–15
types, 11–13, 433–438
Sallis, James, 56
Salter, Chuck, EN1, EN2
Sanchez, Diane, 218, EN6
Sandlund, Chris, EN7
Sands, Jack, 438
Saren, Mike, 415
Satisfaction, 47
Sawers, Neil, 274
Schanck, John, EN9
Schaninger, Charles M., EN3
Schick, Elizabeth, 177
Schiffman, Stephan, EN6
Schlarcter, John L., 27
Schnebel, Eberhard, EN2
Schrage, Michael, 195, 213, EN5, EN7
Schultz, Don E., 27
Schultz, Roberta J., 443
Schurr, Paul, EN1, EN2
Schwepker, Charles H., Jr., 27, 28, 443, EN2,
    EN9
Scope of change, 377
Screens, 211
Search engines, 178
Secondary call objectives, 207
Seeding, 213
Selective perception, 238
Selling center, 202
Selling deeper, 175
Selnes, Fred, 56, EN2
Services, 88–89
Sexual harassment, 71
Shaars, Teo, 319
Shalley, Christina E., EN1
Sharma, Arun, 167, 387
Shaw, Doris, 169
Shaw, Eleanor, 387
Shaw, John, EN2
Shelton, Paula, 308
Shepherd, C. David, 127, EN4
Shervani, Tasaddug, 55
Shih, Chia-Mei, 473
Shoemaker, Mary E., 145, 167
Siguaw, Judy A., 119
Silver, Barry, 434
Silvera, Juan, 305
Simms, Jane, EN3
Simons, Tad, 274, EN1, EN4, EN7
Simple cost-benefit analysis, 263
Simpson, Penny M., 119
Singh, Jagdip, 56
Singh, Siddharta, 331
Sirdeshmuckh, Deepak, 56

Sirianni, Anita, EN6
Situation questions, 231
Situational stress, 468
Sivakumar, Kiva, 119
Skaates, Maria Anne, EN3
Skarmeas, Dionisis, 119
Small talk, 225
Smaros, Johanna, 443, EN9
Smeltzer, Larry R., EN3
Smith, Alan D., 473
Smith, Benson, EN8
Smith, Bob, 46
Smith, Jim, 177
Smith, Kirk, 119, EN4
Smyth, Josh, 176
Sneak attack, 344
Social style matrix
categories of social styles, 154–157
dimensions of social styles, 153–154
presentations, 157–159
versatility, 159–160
Social zone, 134
Sojka, Jane Z., 28, EN1
Solo exchange, 35
Solovic, Susan W., 91, EN3
Sooder, Karl, 236, 417, EN6
Spam, 179
Sparks, John R., 247
Speaking–listening differential, 126
Speece, Mark, 415, EN9
Sperry, Joe, EN9
Spiffs, 77
SPIN® technique, 230–233
Spiro, Rosann L., 246, 473
Spotters, 185
Sprague, David, EN3
Srinivason, Kannan, 273
Srivastava, Rajendra K., 55
Stack, Laura, 274
Stalh, Heinz K., 28
Standard industrial classification (SIC), 182
Standard memorized presentation, 148
Stanley, Jennifer, EN9
Statutory law, 72
Stein, Molly, EN1
Stevens, Charles D., 28
Stevens, Ruth P., 195, EN5
Stewart, Christopher, EN2
Stillman, David, EN4
Stinchfield, Chad R., 17
Stoddard, James E., 119
Stoeberl, Philipp A., 84
Straight commission, 427
Straight-line routing, 405
Straight rebuy, 97–98
Straight salary, 426–427
Strand, Linda, 177
Strategic account managers (SAMs), 434
Strategic partnerships, 37–38
Streit, Paula, EN9
Strelecky, John, 357
Stremersch, Stefan, 119, EN3
Strength of position, 398
Stress interview, 462
Stress management, 467–469
Strieter, Jeffrey, 221, 445
Strout, Erin, EN2, EN7
Strutton, David, 119
Stuart, Elenora, EN3
Stulz, Tasha, 169
Stump, Rodney L., 167